Introduction to Drama

Edited by
Paul J. Dolan
Grace M. Dolan

John Wiley & Sons, Inc.
New York   London   Sydney   Toronto

Copyright © 1974, by John Wiley & Sons, Inc.

All rights reserved.

No part of this book may be reproduced by any means, nor transmitted, nor translated into a machine language without the written permission of the publisher.

Library of Congress Cataloging in Publication Data:

Dolan, Paul J comp.
  Introduction to drama.

    1. Drama—Collections. I. Dolan, Grace M., joint comp. II. Title.
PN6112.D64   808'.2   73-18343
ISBN 0-471-21750-6

Printed in the United States of America

10 9 8 7 6 5 4 3 2 1

Credits and Acknowledgments

Copyrighted works, listed below, are printed by permission of the following.

Sophocles, *Oedipus Rex:* An English version by Dudley Fitts and Robert Fitzgerald, copyright 1949 by Harcourt Brace Jovanovich, Inc. and reprinted with their permission. *Antigone:* An English version by Dudley Fitts and Robert Fitzgerald, copyright 1939 by Harcourt Brace Jovanovich, Inc.; copyright 1967 by Dudley Fitts and Robert Fitzgerald. Reprinted by permission of the publisher. *Caution:* All rights, including professional, amateur, motion picture, recitation, lecturing, public reading, radio broadcasting, and television are strictly reserved. Inquiries on all rights should be addressed to Harcourt Brace Jovanovich, Inc. 757 Third Avenue, New York, N.Y. 10017.

Phaedra, by Jean Racine, from CLASSICAL FRENCH DRAMA, edited and translated by Wallace Fowlie. Copyright © 1962 by Bantam Books, Inc.

Miss Julie, by August Strindberg. Reprinted by permission of Collins-Knowlton-Wing, Inc. Copyright © 1955 by Elizabeth Sprigge.

Purgatory, by William Butler Yeats. Reprinted with permission of The Macmillan Company from COLLECTED PLAYS by William Butler Yeats. Copyright 1934, 1952 by The Macmillan Company.

The Dutchman, by LeRoi Jones. From DUTCHMAN AND THE SLAVE. Copyright © 1964 by LeRoi Jones. Reprinted by permission of The Sterling Lord Agency, Inc.

Benito Cereno, by Robert Lowell. Reprinted with the permission of Farrar, Straus & Giroux, Inc. from THE OLD GLORY by Robert Lowell, copyright © 1964, 1965, 1968, by Robert Lowell.

Tiger at the Gates, by Jean Giraudoux, translated by Christopher Fry. Copyright 1955 by Christopher Fry. Reprinted by permission of Oxford University Press, Inc.

The Misanthrope, Moliere, translated by Richard Wilbur. Copyright © 1954, 1955 by Richard Wilbur. Reprinted by permission of Harcourt Brace Jovanovich, Inc. *Caution:* professionals and amateurs are hereby warned that this translation, being fully protected under the copyright laws of the United States of America, the British Empire, including the Dominion of Canada, and all other countries, which are signatories to the Universal Copyright Convention and the International Copyright Union, is subject to royalty. All rights, including professional, amateur, motion picture, recitation, lecturing, public reading, radio broadcasting, and television are strictly reserved. Particular emphasis is laid on the question of readings, permission for which must be secured from the author's agent in writing. Inquiries on professional rights (except for amateur rights) should be addressed to Mr. Gilbert Parker, Curtis Brown Ltd., 60 East 56th Street, New York, N.Y. 10022. The amateur acting rights are controlled exclusively by the Dramatists Play Service, Inc., 440 Park Avenue South, New York, N.Y. 10016. No amateur performance of the play may be given without obtaining in advance the written permission of the Dramatists Play Service, Inc. and paying the requisite fee.

The Second Shepherds Play, from REPRESENTATIVE MEDIEVAL AND TUDOR PLAYS translated and edited by Henry W. Wells and Roger S. Loomis. Copyright 1942 Sheed & Ward, Inc., New York.

Henry IV, from the book NAKED MASKS: FIVE PLAYS by Luigi Pirandello, edited by Eric Bentley. Copyright 1922 by E. P. Dutton & Co., Inc. Renewal, 1950, in the names of Stefano, Fausto, & Lietto Pirandello. Published by E. P. Dutton & Co., Inc. in a paperback edition and used with their permission. Dramatic rights are controlled by Toby Cole, Agent, New York City.

An Enemy of the People, from the book GHOSTS: AN ENEMY OF THE PEOPLE: THE WARRIORS AT HELGELAND, by Henrik Ibsen, Tr. by R. Farquaharson Sharp. Everyman's Library edition. Published by E. P. Dutton & Co., Inc. and used with their permission. Dramatic rights are controlled by E. P. Dutton & Co., Inc.

St. Joan, by George Bernard Shaw. Copyright 1924, 1930, George Bernard Shaw. Copyright 1951, The Public Trustee as Executor of the Estate of George Bernard Shaw. Reprinted by permission of Dodd, Mead and Company, Inc. and the Society of Authors for the Estate of George Bernard Shaw.

Preface

Drama is what we try to make of life.

Our daily dramas of meeting and parting, comforting and confronting are improvisations in which our words and actions try to fix relationships and create patterns in which each actor can sustain a role. This urge to dramatize is so deeply rooted in our psyches, that the languages of stage and street are almost indistinguishable. *Climax, role, acting, dialogue, stage, hero, action,* the words of drama are the words of love and war, of psychology and education, in short, the words that help order our lives.

A play is a pattern of human relationships. It represents what people do with and to each other, seriously and comically, in joy and in pain. When the dramatist puts his first words on paper, he begins the process of starting a dialogue; we know that every day we attempt the same thing. There is a difference in drama, however. The dramatist begins a dialogue between characters; that dialogue grows to include other characters and ends when all that must be said has been said. The play itself, at the same time, is a dialogue with an audience in which, in the words and actions of the characters, the audience is made to see itself.

The problem with understanding drama as an art form is that, since it is the most common and most familiar art form, it is the most difficult to appreciate. We are familiar with so many forms of drama—from our own improvisations on meeting a stranger to the on-going television plays that happen in our living rooms—that we have difficulty in grasping the structure that the artist creates to make his drama out of our dramas. Psychodrama in group therapy, guerilla theater in the street, every movie, every serious television show, and every live and rerun broadcast of a significant event share the possibilities of dramatic art. We are concerned here with introducing students to the essentials of drama as an art. We do not mean to confuse art and life, or art and show business, but to sharpen the sense of difference.

Drama is the oldest of the major literary forms and it is still growing and changing. The image of growth and change is a valid one because drama has been, for more than 2000 years, a continuing form of human expression. In those two millennia there were long periods when no plays were written or performed, but the dramatic instinct was merely dormant and emerged to create again for a country and a time a stage on which people could see themselves. The Greeks gave us many things, but one of the most important was the art form that captured the nature, significance, and consequences of human actions for our understanding. This we call drama.

The Greeks did not invent drama. Instead, they discovered that it was possible to recreate in words and gestures the unique thing that is human action. This is why Aristotle was right when he said that drama is "the imitation of an action." He did not mean that in a play the actors mime some physical gesture. He meant that a play begins with a purpose, to get home, to get married, to become rich, famous, and happy; that it then shows the steps taken to realize this purpose and, finally, the consequences of the purpose and the deeds. Oedipus sets out to find the man responsible for the decay of his city. He questions everyone and carefully and systematically moves to the realization of his purpose. He does find the guilty man and then must accept the consequences of his action.

Human action is gestures with motives and consequences. "To get married and live happily ever after" or "to establish a meaningful relationship" are expressions of motive with which most of us are familiar. Drama shows us clearly what we learn confusedly in life. There is no easy way to realize our motives or achieve our goals and, as in the more bitter lesson of Oedipus, there is sometimes no worse tragedy than getting what we want. Drama gives us what we rarely get in life: the complete representation of an action. First, there is the creation in the mind of a state or a quality that does not now exist (a peaceful and prosperous city from which the polluter has been expelled); then steps are taken to bring that idea into reality; finally, there are the consequences for the actor and all those around him.

Plays are made of many things, but first come the words. The words are what we use to explain our motives to ourselves and our deeds to others. To the words may be added gestures, dance, spectacle, costume and music, and the "acting" that complete the "action" of the play. The gestures and the words are meant, of course, to involve the audience, because drama needs an audience to exist. Plays, in fact, cannot be read; only scripts can be read. Reading a play requires an imagination, so that the words come alive and reveal the action involved. You know you are reading a play and not just a script when you can visualize the expression on the face of the character who is not speaking. Words have consequences; they console and they cut. That is what they do in drama, and the recreation in the mind is the act of reading drama; we read the words and see their consequences.

Is that effort of imagination worth the trouble? It is for those who want to learn more about themselves and the people with whom they

Preface

must live. Drama separates from life a pattern of action and gives it back to us, as Aristotle said, "whole, complete and of a certain magnitude." The mirror, which Hamlet commanded the players to hold up to nature, not only reflects, it also refines. In understanding the play we understand ourselves as actors in the thousands of incomplete dramas that make up our lives.

Because we believe that drama is important to our lives, we have arranged this book thematically. To see how dramatists have dealt with the destructive power of love, with exile and alienation, with sudden and ritual violence, and with the demands of country and conscience is to see clearly that drama is a necessary creation of the human mind. To understand how laughter is the proper response to pretension and to realize that laughter is too important to be only a joking matter is to appreciate the role of drama in maintaining our sanity. The sections of the book have as their subjects human conduct. The plays, classic and contemporary, embody the conflicts within and among those who try to act. The conflicts are not between good guys and bad guys because there is no real drama in such a conflict. Instead, the plays deal with the attempt to realize an ideal and the fulfillment or the destruction that justly follows that attempt.

The book includes short and long plays, prose and verse dramas. Drama itself is too old and too new, too rich and too diverse to be captured in one volume. Our aim is expressed in our title: to introduce drama. Therefore, we have included different kinds of plays from as many periods and places as we could. We have grouped them in thematic sections to illustrate that all drama does, as Aristotle said it did, deal with significant human action.

Paul J. Dolan
Grace M. Dolan

Contents

One Parents, Lovers, and Other Enemies 1

Sophocles
Oedipus
Translated by Dudley Fitts and Robert Fitzgerald
5

Jean Racine
Phaedre
Translated by Wallace Fowlie
43

August Strindberg
Miss Julie
Translated by Elizabeth Sprigge
84

William Butler Yeats
Purgatory
114

Two Citizens and Strangers 121

William Shakespeare
Othello
125

LeRoi Jones
Dutchman
232

Robert Lowell
Benito Cereno
248

Three The Rewards of Virtue 285

Molière
The Misanthrope
Translated by Richard Wilbur
287

Anton Chekhov
The Cherry Orchard
Translated by Constance Garnett
333

Four The Play's the Thing: Spectacle,

Dance, and Ritual 377

Anonymous
The Second Shepherd's Play
Translated by Roger S. Loomis and Henry W. Wells
381

Luigi Pirandello
Henry IV
English version by Edward Storer
397

Five Country and Conscience 445

Sophocles
Antigone
Translated by Dudley Fitts and Robert Fitzgerald
447

Henrik Ibsen
An Enemy of the People
Translated by R. Farquharson Sharp
475

George Bernard Shaw
Saint Joan
551

Glossary
635

One

Parents, Lovers, and Other Enemies

The Book of Ecclesiastes says that a man's enemies are those of his own household. Any cop will tell you that homicide begins at home. The plays in this section deal with family, love, and violence and the timeless relationship among them.

The myth at the core of *Oedipus* is one of the central myths of our civilization. One need not accept the Freudian elaboration to understand the importance of the myth. It bears a striking resemblance to the story of Adam and Eve, and the Greek and Hebrew cultures are the sources of western civilization. Like Oedipus, Adam and Eve offend God the Father in seeking to escape from an immutable decree and to work out a destiny for themselves that exceeds His plan for their happiness. In both stories, self and destiny are somehow mysteriously in conflict. The moment of birth, the moment of creation, is, in these myths, the beginning of tragic possibilities. The tragic vision implicit in these stories is that evil, intentional or unintentional, begins within the family. Tragic grandeur comes, as Milton makes it come for Adam and Eve and Sophocles for Oedipus, when the self, the protagonist, recognizes that his struggle for identity involves him in the destruction of himself and others, and with this new knowledge, he accepts the consequences of his actions.

Aristotle rightly considered *Oedipus* as a perfect play. From the rich and complicated story of the abandoned child, the random murder, the solving of the riddle, and the reward of marriage, Sophocles fashioned a play in which the action of a few hours sums up a lifetime and will probably last forever. The play begins when Oedipus the King, and the symbolic father of his people, sets out to find the sinful man who is destroying Thebes. The play ends when he concludes his search. In the process, the audience watches his growing awareness of the complexity of his fate and the inevitable outcome of his innocent intentions. The audience always knows more than Oedipus does; at the end of the play, this knowledge has grown to the full symbolic implications of the literal sin for which Oedipus punishes himself.

Love is usually imagined as a creative and fulfilling force. But passionate love (*eros*) is closely related to death (*thanatos*), because when it is unleashed, love is a force that will have its object at any cost. The lover says that he will die for his beloved; that very exaggeration reveals the darker side of a consuming desire. To be willing to die, when not merely a conventional protestation, is uncomfortably close to being willing to kill. A person possessed by love is a person possessed, and if that passion is in any way misdirected, it must become tragic. Marriage is a social institution created to tame and domesticate the urges at the root of love. If, however,, marriage and family do not tame the passion, or if the object of passion changes, the power can only destroy those who are bound up in it. Racine's *Phaedre* explores the destructive power of love.

Great art depends on the ability of the artist to understand the limitations of his medium so thoroughly that they cease to be limitations and become the essential instrument in the realization of his vision. Racine, in *Phaedre*, is able to transform the rigid conventions of the French classical stage into a metaphor for his tragedy of incestuous passion. As its theater demanded, the play is stately and dignified and the form underscores the theme that a passion rigidly suppressed will flash out and destroy all those in its range. The form requires that the audience be aware that the actors are playing roles and delivering set speeches. The drama resides in the reality of the passion beneath the role. Phaedre, however, cannot sustain her role and when she ceases to act and follows her feelings, tragedy results. In adopting the *Hippolytus* of Euripides to the requirements of his stage and audience, Racine created the tragedy of a woman trapped in her feelings and her family role.

In *Miss Julie*, the story of a destructive love affair, Strindberg has ostensibly written a naturalistic drama of a well-born young lady who behaves foolishly with her father's valet. Early reactions to the play focused on its realistic sensuality, social implications, and reflections of a class struggle. Yet, because the mythic dimensions of the story are not submerged in the naturalistic form, the power of the play remains after the social conventions change.

The patterns of destruction in *Miss Julie* are personal, economic, and psychological. The most important man in Julie's life is the man who never appears on stage—her father. Her seduction of her father's valet leads to her suicide, but that final act was prepared long before the midsummer night in which the play is set. Julie tries to destroy something or someone by seducing Jean and succeeds in destroying herself. Father and lover determine her life; they are, in her madness, the enemies, and her passion, aimed at them, consumes her.

William Butler Yeats's stark tragedy, *Purgatory*, is a dramatic representation of the Biblical statement that the sins of the parents are visited on the children. This short play does not rely on a plot structure to embody its theme. *Purgatory*, the most modern play in the section, uses the oldest form of drama. The play is a ritual and the murder at the end is the ritual acting out of the tragic awareness of the Biblical proverb; the old man and the boy in the ditch, haunted by strange visions, are parent and child, old and young, generation after generation. The play is proverb and ritual, history, sociology, and psychology but, above all, it is drama. Words become lines and lines are accompanied by gestures and the play becomes a symbol for the tragic mystery of the existence of the past in the present, the old in the young, the other in the self.

Sophocles

Oedipus

translated by Dudley Fitts and Robert Fitzgerald

Persons represented

OEDIPUS	MESSENGER
A PRIEST	SHEPHERD OF LAÏOS
CREON	SECOND MESSENGER
TEIRESIAS	CHORUS OF THEBAN ELDERS
IOCASTE	

THE SCENE: *Before the palace of* OEDIPUS, *King of Thebes. A central door and two lateral doors open onto a platform which runs the length of the façade. On the platform, right and left, are altars; and three steps lead down into the "orchestra," or chorus-ground. At the beginning of the action these steps are crowded by suppliants who have brought branches and chaplets of olive leaves and who lie in various attitudes of despair.* OEDIPUS *enters.*

PROLOGUE

OEDIPUS: My children, generations of the living
In the line of Kadmos, nursed at his ancient hearth:
Why have you strewn yourselves before these altars
In supplication, with your boughs and garlands?
The breath of incense rises from the city
With a sound of prayer and lamentation.
                                        Children,
I would not have you speak through messengers,
And therefore I have come myself to hear you—
I, Oedipus, who bear the famous name.

(*To a* PRIEST)

You, there, since you are eldest in the company,
Speak for them all, tell me what preys upon you,

Whether you come in dread, ,or crave some blessing:
Tell me, and never doubt that I will help you
In every way I can; I should be heartless
Were I not moved to find you suppliant here.

PRIEST: Great Oedipus, O powerful King of Thebes!
You see how all the ages of our people
Cling to your altar steps: here are boys
Who can barely stand alone, and here are priests
By weight of age, as I am a priest of God,
And young men chosen from those yet unmarried;
As for the others, all that multitude,
They wait with olive chaplets in the squares,
At the two shrines of Pallas, and where Apollo
Speaks in the glowing embers.
       Your own eyes
Must tell you: Thebes is tossed on a murdering sea
And can not lift her head from the death surge.
A rust consumes the buds and fruits of the earth;
The herds are sick; children die unborn,
And labor is vain. The god of plague and pyre
Raids like detestable lightning through the city,
And all the house of Kadmos is laid waste,
All emptied, and all darkened: Death alone
Battens upon the misery of Thebes.
You are not one of the immortal gods, we know;
Yet we have come to you to make our prayer
As to the man surest in mortal ways
And wisest in the ways of God. You saved us
From the Sphinx, that flinty singer, and the tribute
We paid to her so long; yet you were never
Better informed than we, nor could we teach you:
It was some god breathed in you to set us free.
Therefore, O mighty King, we turn to you:
Find us our safety, find us a remedy,
Whether by counsel of the gods or men.
A king of wisdom tested in the past
Can act in a time of troubles, and act well.
Noblest of men, restore
Life to your city! Think how all men call you
Liberator for your triumph long ago;
Ah, when your years of kingship are remembered,
Let them not say *We rose, but later fell*—
Keep the State from going down in the storm!
Once, years ago, with happy augury,
You brought us fortune; be the same again!
No man questions your power to rule the land:
But rule over men, not over a dead city!

Ships are only hulls, citadels are nothing,
When no life moves in the empty passageways.
OEDIPUS: Poor children! You may be sure I know
All that you longed for in your coming here.
I know that you are deathly sick; and yet,
Sick as you are, not one is as sick as I.
Each of you suffers in himself alone
His anguish, not another's; but my spirit
Groans for the city, for myself, for you.
I was not sleeping, you are not waking me.
No, I have been in tears for a long while
And in my restless thought walked many ways.
In all my search, I found one helpful course,
And that I have taken: I have sent Creon,
Son of Menoikeus, brother of the Queen,
To Delphi, Apollo's place of revelation,
To learn there, if he can,
What act or pledge of mine may save the city.
I have counted the days, and now, this very day,
I am troubled, for he has overstayed his time.
What is he doing? He has been gone too long.
Yet whenever he comes back, I should do ill
To scant whatever duty God reveals.
PRIEST: It is a timely promise. At this instant
They tell me Creon is here.
OEDIPUS: O Lord Apollo!
May his news be fair as his face is radiant!
PRIEST: It could not be otherwise: he is crowned with bay,
The chaplet is thick with berries.
OEDIPUS: We shall soon know;
He is near enough to hear us now.
                        O Prince:

(Enter CREON)

Brother: son of Menoikeus:
What answer do you bring us from the god?
CREON: A strong one. I can tell you, great afflictions
Will turn out well, if they are taken well.
OEDIPUS: What was the oracle? These vague words
Leave me still hanging between hope and fear.
CREON: Is it your pleasure to hear me with all these
Gathered around us? I am prepared to speak,
But should we not go in?
OEDIPUS: Let them all hear it.
It is for them I suffer, more than for myself.
CREON: Then I will tell you what I heard at Delphi.
In plain words

> The god commands us to expel from the land of Thebes
> An old defilement we are sheltering.
> It is a deathly thing, beyond cure;
> We must not let it feed upon us longer.

OEDIPUS: What defilement? How shall we rid ourselves of it?

CREON: By exile or death, blood for blood. It was
> Murder that brought the plague-wind on the city.

OEDIPUS: Murder of whom? Surely the god has named him?

CREON: My lord: long ago Laïos was our king,
> Before you came to govern us.

OEDIPUS: I know;
> I learned of him from others; I never saw him.

CREON: He was murdered; and Apollo commands us now
> To take revenge upon whoever killed him.

OEDIPUS: Upon whom? Where are they? Where shall we find a clue
> To solve that crime, after so many years?

CREON: Here in this land, he said.
>   If we make enquiry,
> We may touch things that otherwise escape us.

OEDIPUS: Tell me: Was Laïos murdered in his house,
> Or in the field, or in some foreign country?

CREON: He said he planned to make a pilgrimage.
> He did not come home again.

OEDIPUS: And was there no one,
> No witness, no companion, to tell what happened?

CREON: They were all killed but one, and he got away
> So frightened that he could remember one thing only.

OEDIPUS: What was that one thing? One may be the key
> To everything, if we resolve to use it.

CREON: He said that a band of highwaymen attacked them,
> Outnumbered them, and overwhelmed the King.

OEDIPUS: Strange, that a highwayman should be so daring—
> Unless some faction here bribed him to do it.

CREON: We thought of that. But after Laïos' death
> New troubles arose and we had no avenger.

OEDIPUS: What troubles could prevent your hunting down the killers?

CREON: The riddling Sphinx's song
> Made us deaf to all mysteries but her own.

OEDIPUS: Then once more I must bring what is dark to light.
> It is most fitting that Apollo shows,
> As you do, this compunction for the dead.
> You shall see how I stand by you, as I should,
> To avenge the city and the city's god,
> And not as though it were for some distant friend,
> But for my own sake, to be rid of evil.
> Whoever killed King Laïos might—who knows?—
> Decide at any moment to kill me as well.

By avenging the murdered king I protect myself.
Come, then, my children: leave the altar steps,
Lift up your olive boughs!
                One of you go
And summon the people of Kadmos to gather here.
I will do all that I can; you may tell them that.

(Exit a PAGE*)*

So, with the help of God,
We shall be saved—or else indeed we are lost.
PRIEST: Let us rise, children. It was for this we came,
And now the King has promised it himself.
Phoibos has sent us an oracle; may he descend
Himself to save us and drive out the plague.

(Exeunt OEDIPUS *and* CREON *into the palace by the central door. The* PRIEST *and the* SUPPLIANTS *disperse R and L. After a short pause the* CHORUS *enters the orchestra.)*

PARODOS

CHORUS: What is God singing in his profound   (STROPHE 1)
   Delphia of gold and shadow?
What oracle for Thebes, the sunwhipped city?
Fear unjoints me, the roots of my heart tremble.
Now I remember, O Healer, your power, and wonder:
Will you send doom like a sudden cloud, or weave it
Like nightfall of the past?
Speak, speak to us, issue of holy sound:
Dearest to our expectancy: be tender!
Let me pray to Athenê, the immortal daughter of Zeus, (ANTISTROPHE 1)
And to Artemis her sister
Who keeps her famous throne in the market ring,
And to Apollo, bowman at the far butts of heaven—
O gods, descend! Like three streams leap against
The fires of our grief, the fires of darkness;
Be swift to bring us rest!
As in the old time from the brilliant house
Of air you stepped to save us, come again!
Now our afflictions have no end,   (STROPHE 2)
Now all our stricken host lies down
And no man fights off death with his mind;
The noble plowland bears no grain,
And groaning mothers can not bear—
See, how our lives like birds take wing,
Like sparks that fly when a fire soars,

To the shore of the god of evening.
The plague burns on, it is pitiless, (ANTISTROPHE 2)
Though pallid children laden with death
Lie unwept in the stony ways,
And old gray women by every path
Flock to the strand about the altars
There to strike their breasts and cry
Worship of Phoibos in wailing prayers:
Be kind, God's golden child!
There are no swords in this attack by fire, (STROPHE 3)
No shields, but we are ringed with cries.
Send the besieger plunging from our homes
Into the vast sea-room of the Atlantic
Or into the waves that foam eastward of Thrace—
For the day ravages what the night spares—
Destroy our enemy, lord of the thunder!
Let him be riven by lightning from heaven!
Phoibos Apollo, stretch the sun's bowstring, (ANTISTROPHE 3)
That golden cord, until it sing for us,
Flashing arrows in heaven!
                    Artemis, Huntress,
Race with flaring lights upon our mountains!
O scarlet god, O golden-banded brow,
O Theban Bacchos in a storm of Maenads,

(Enter OEDIPUS, *C.)*

Whirl upon Death, that all the Undying hate!
Come with blinding torches, come in joy!

Scene I

OEDIPUS: Is this your prayer? It may be answered. Come,
    Listen to me, act as the crisis demands,
    And you shall have relief from all these evils.
    Until now I was a stranger to this tale,
    As I had been a stranger to the crime.
    Could I track down the murderer without a clue?
    But now, friends,
    As one who became a citizen after the murder,
    I make this proclamation to all Thebans:
    If any man knows by whose hand Laïos, son of Labdakos,
    Met his death, I direct that man to tell me everything,
    No matter what he fears for having so long withheld it.
    Let it stand as promised that no further trouble
    Will come to him, but he may leave the land in safety.
    Moreover: If anyone knows the murderer to be foreign,

Let him not keep silent: he shall have his reward from me.
However, if he does conceal it; if any man
Fearing for his friend or for himself disobeys this edict,
Hear what I propose to do:
I solemnly forbid the people of this country,
Where power and throne are mine, ever to receive that man
Or speak to him, no matter who he is, or let him
Join in sacrifice, lustration, or in prayer.
I decree that he be driven from every house,
Being, as he is, corruption itself to us: the Delphic
Voice of Zeus has pronounced this revelation.
Thus I associate myself with the oracle
And take the side of the murdered king.
As for the criminal, I pray to God—
Whether it be a lurking thief, or one of a number—
I pray that that man's life be consumed in evil and wretchedness.
And as for me, this curse applies no less
If it should turn out that the culprit is my guest here,
Sharing my hearth.
                    You have heard the penalty.
I lay it no you now to attend to this
For my sake, for Apollo's, for the sick
Sterile city that heaven has abandoned.
Suppose the oracle had given you no command:
Should this defilement go uncleansed for ever?
You should have found the murderer: your king,
A noble king, had been destroyed!
                    Now I,
Having the power that he held before me,
Having his bed, begetting children there
Upon his wife, as he would have, had he lived—
Their son would have been my children's brother,
If Laïos had had luck in fatherhood!
(But surely ill luck rushed upon his reign)—
I say I take the son's part, just as though
I were his son, to press the fight for him
And see it won! I'll find the hand that brought
Death to Labdakos' and Polydoros' child,
Heir of Kadmos' and Agenor's line.
And as for those who fail me,
May the gods deny them the fruit of the earth,
Fruit of the womb, and may they rot utterly!
Let them be wretched as we are wretched, and worse!
For you, for loyal Thebans, and for all
Who find my actions right, I pray the favor
Of justice, and of all the immortal gods.

CHORAGOS: Since I am under oath, my lord, I swear

I did not do the murder, I can not name
The murderer. Might not the oracle
That has ordained the search tell where to find him?
OEDIPUS: An honest question. But no man in the world
Can make the gods do more than the gods will.
CHORAGOS: There is one last expedient—
OEDIPUS: Tell me what it is.
Though it seem slight, you must not hold it back.
CHORAGOS: A lord clairvoyant to the lord Apollo,
As we all know, is the skilled Teiresias.
One might learn much about this from him, Oedipus.
OEDIPUS: I am not wasting time:
Creon spoke of this, and I have sent for him—
Twice, in fact; it is strange that he is not here.
CHORAGOS: The other matter—that old report—seems useless.
OEDIPUS: Tell me. I am interested in all reports.
CHORAGOS: The King was said to have been killed by highwaymen.
OEDIPUS: I know. But we have no witnesses to that.
CHORAGOS: If the killer can feel a particle of dread,
Your curse will bring him out of hiding!
OEDIPUS: No.
The man who dared that act will fear no curse.

(*Enter the blind seer* TEIRESIAS, *led by a* PAGE)

CHORAGOS: But there is one man who may detect the criminal.
This is Teiresias, this is the holy prophet
In whom, alone of all men, truth was born.
OEDIPUS: Teiresias: seer: student of mysteries,
Of all that's taught and all that no man tells,
Secrets of Heaven and secrets of the earth:
Blind though you are, you know the city lies
Sick with plague; and from this plague, my lord,
We find that you alone can guard or save us.
Possibly you did not hear the messengers?
Apollo, when we sent to him,
Sent us back word that this great pestilence
Would lift, but only if we established clearly
The identity of those who murdered Laïos.
They must be killed or exiled.
Can you use
Birdflight or any art of divination
To purify yourself, and Thebes, and me
From this contagion? We are in your hands.
There is no fairer duty
Than that of helping others in distress.
TEIRESIAS: How dreadful knowledge of the truth can be

When there's no help in truth! I knew this well,
But made myself forget. I should not have come.
OEDIPUS: What is troubling you? Why are your eyes so cold?
TEIRESIAS: Let me go home. Bear your own fate, and I'll
Bear mine. It is better so: trust what I say.
OEDIPUS: What you say is ungracious and unhelpful
To your native country. Do not refuse to speak.
TEIRESIAS: When it comes to speech, your own is neither temperate
Nor opportune. I wish to be more prudent.
OEDIPUS: In God's name, we all beg you—
TEIRESIAS: You are all ignorant.
No; I will never tell you what I know.
Now it is my misery; then, it would be yours.
OEDIPUS: What! You do know something, and will not tell us?
You would betray us all and wreck the State?
TEIRESIAS: I do not intend to torture myself, or you.
Why persist in asking? You will not persuade me.
OEDIPUS: What a wicked old man you are! You'd try a stone's
Patience! Out with it! Have you no feeling at all?
TEIRESIAS: You call me unfeeling. If you could only see
The nature of your own feelings . . .
OEDIPUS: Why,
Who would not feel as I do? Who could endure
Your arrogance toward the city?
TEIRESIAS: What does it matter!
Whether I speak or not, it is bound to come.
OEDIPUS: Then, if "it" is bound to come, you are bound to tell me.
TEIRESIAS: No, I will not go on. Rage as you please.
OEDIPUS: Rage? Why not!
And I'll tell you what I think:
You planned it, you had it done, you all but
Killed him with your own hands: if you had eyes,
I'd say the crime was yours, and yours alone.
TEIRESIAS: So I charge you, then,
Abide by the proclamation you have made:
From this day forth
Never speak again to these men or to me;
You yourself are the pollution of this country.
OEDIPUS: You dare say that! Can you possibly think you have
Some way of going free, after such insolence?
TEIRESIAS: I have gone free. It is the truth sustains me.
OEDIPUS: Who taught you shamelessness? It was not your craft.
TEIRESIAS: You did. You made me speak. I did not want to.
OEDIPUS: Speak what? Let me hear it again more clearly.
TEIRESIAS: Was it not clear before? Are you tempting me?
OEDIPUS: I did not understand it. Say it again.
TEIRESIAS: I say that you are the murderer whom you seek.

OEDIPUS: Now twice you have spat out infamy. You'll pay for it!
TEIRESIAS: Would you care for more? Do you wish to be really angry?
OEDIPUS: Say what you will. Whatever you say is worthless,
TEIRESIAS: I say you live in hideous shame with those
   Most dear to you. You can not see the evil.
OEDIPUS: It seems you can go on mounting like this for ever.
TEIRESIAS: I can, if there is power in truth.
OEDIPUS: There is:
   But not for you, not for you,
   You sightless, witless, senseless, mad old man!
TEIRESIAS: You are the madman. There is no one here
   Who will not curse you soon, as you curse me.
OEDIPUS: You child of endless night! You can not hurt me
   Or any other man who sees the sun.
TEIRESIAS: True: it is not from me your fate will come.
   That lies within Apollo's competence,
   As it is his concern.
OEDIPUS: Tell me:
   Are you speaking for Creon, or for yourself?
TEIRESIAS: Creon is no threat. You weave your own doom.
OEDIPUS: Wealth, power, craft of statesmanship!
   Kingly position, everywhere admired!
   What savage envy is stored up against these,
   If Creon, whom I trusted, Creon my friend,
   For this great office which the city once
   Put in my hands unsought—if for this power
   Creon desires in secret to destroy me!
   He has bought this decrepit fortune-teller, this
   Collector of dirty pennies, this prophet fraud—
   Why, he is no more clairvoyant than I am!
                                    Tell us:
   Has your mystic mummery ever approached the truth?
   When that hellcat the Sphinx was performing here,
   What help were you to these people?
   Her magic was not for the first man who came along:
   It demanded a real exorcist. Your birds—
   What good were they? or the gods, for the matter of that?
   But I came by,
   Oedipus, the simple man, who knows nothing—
   I thought it out for myself, no birds helped me!
   And this is the man you think you can destroy,
   That you may be close to Creon when he's king!
   Well, you and your friend Creon, it seems to me,
   Will suffer most. If you were not an old man,
   You would have paid already for your plot.
CHORAGOS: We can not see that his words or yours
   Have been spoken except in anger, Oedipus,

Sophocles: *Oedipus*

    And of anger we have no need. How can God's will
    Be accomplished best? That is what most concerns us.
TEIRESIAS: You are a king. But where argument's concerned
    I am your man, as much a king as you.
    I am not your servant, but Apollo's.
    I have no need of Creon to speak for me.
    Listen to me. You mock my blindness, do you?
    But I say that you, with both your eyes, are blind:
    You can not see the wretchedness of your life,
    Nor in whose house you live, no, nor with whom.
    Who are your father and mother? Can you tell me?
    You do not even know the blind wrongs
    That you have done them, on earth and in the world below.
    But the double lash of your parents' curse will whip you
    Out of this land some day, with only night
    Upon your precious eyes.
    Your cries then—where will they not be heard?
    What fastness of Kithairon will not echo them?
    And that bridal-descant of yours—you'll know it then,
    The song they sang when you came here to Thebes
    And found your misguided berthing.
    All this, and more, that you can not guess at now,
    Will bring you to yourself among your children.
    Be angry, then. Curse Creon. Curse my words.
    I tell you, no man that walks upon the earth
    Shall be rooted out more horribly than you.
OEDIPUS: Am I to bear this from him?—Damnation
    Take you! Out of this place! Out of my sight!
TEIRESIAS: I would not have come at all if you had not asked me.
OEDIPUS: Could I have told that you'd talk nonsense, that
    You'd come here to make a fool of yourself, and of me?
TEIRESIAS: A fool? Your parents thought me sane enough.
OEDIPUS: My parents again!—Wait: who were my parents?
TEIRESIAS: This day will give you a father, and break your heart.
OEDIPUS: Your infantile riddles! Your damned abracadabra!
TEIRESIAS: You were a great man once at solving riddles.
OEDIPUS: Mock me with that if you like; you will find it true.
TEIRESIAS: It was true enough. It brought about your ruin.
OEDIPUS: But if it saved this town?
TEIRESIAS:

    (*To the* PAGE)

                        Boy, give me your hand.
OEDIPUS: Yes, boy; lead him away.
                      —While you are here
    We can do nothing. Go; leave us in peace.
TEIRESIAS: I will go when I have said what I have to say.

How can you hurt me? And I tell you again:
The man you have been looking for all this time,
The damned man, the murdered of Laïos,
That man is in Thebes. To your mind he is foreignborn,
But it will soon be shown that he is a Theban,
A revelation that will fail to please.
                              A blind man,
Who has his eyes now; a penniless man, who is rich now;
And he will go tapping the strange earth with his staff
To the children with whom he lives now he will be
Brother and father—the very same; to her
Who bore him, son and husband—the very same
Who came to his father's bed, wet with his father's blood.
Enough. Go think that over.
If later you find error in what I have said,
You may say that I have no skill in prophecy.

                    (*Exit* TEIRESIAS, *led by his* PAGE. OEDIPUS
                              goes into the palace.)

ODE I

CHORUS: The Delphic stone of prophecies   (STROPHE 1)
   Remembers ancient regicide
   And a still bloody hand.
   That killer's hour of flight has come.
   He must be stronger than riderless
   Coursers of untiring wind,
   For the son of Zeus armed with his father's thunder
   Leaps in lightning after him;
   And the Furies follow him, the sad Furies.
   Holy Parnassos' peak of snow   (ANTISTROPHE 1)
   Flashes and blinds that secret man,
   That all shall hunt him down:
   Though he may roam the forest shade
   Like a bull gone wild from pasture
   To rage through glooms of stone.
   Doom comes down on him; flight will not avail him;
   For the world's heart calls him desolate,
   And the immortal Furies follow, for ever follow.
   But now a wilder thing is heard   (STROPHE 2)
   From the old man skilled at hearing Fate in the wingbeat of a bird.
   Bewildered as a blown bird, my soul hovers and can not find
   Foothold in this debate, or any reason or rest of mind.
   But no man ever brought—none can bring

Proof of strife between Thebes' royal house,
Labdakos' line, and the son of Polybos;
And never until now has any man brought word
Of Laïos' dark death staining Oedipus the King.
Divine Zeus and Apollo hold (ANTISTROPHE 2)
Perfect intelligence alone of all tales ever told;
And well though this diviner works, he works in his own night;
No man can judge that rough unknown or trust in second sight,
For wisdom changes hands among the wise.
Shall I believe my great lord criminal
At a raging word that a blind old man let fall?
I saw him, when the carrion woman faced him of old,
Prove his heroic mind! These evil words are lies.

Scene II

CREON: Men of Thebes:
 I am told that heavy accusations
 Have been brought against me by King Oedipus.
 I am not the kind of man to bear this tamely.
 If in these present difficulties
 He holds me accountable for any harm to him
 Through anything I have said or done—why, then,
 I do not value life in this dishonor.
 It is not as though this rumor touched upon
 Some private indiscretion. The matter is grave.
 The fact is that I am being called disloyal
 To the State, to my fellow citizens, to my friends.
CHORAGOS: He may have spoken in anger, not from his mind.
CREON: But did you not hear him say I was the one
 Who seduced the old prophet into lying?
CHORAGOS: The thing was said; I do not know how seriously.
CREON: But you were watching him! Were his eyes steady?
 Did he look like a man in his right mind?
CHORAGOS: I do not know.
 I can not judge the behavior of great men.
 But here is the King himself.

 (*Enter* OEDIPUS)

OEDIPUS: So you dared come back
 Why? How brazen of you to come to my house,
 You murderer!
   Do you think I do not know
 That you plotted to kill me, plotted to steal my throne?
 Tell me, in God's name: am I a coward, a fool
 That you should dream you could accomplish this?

A fool who could not see your slippery game?
A coward, not to fight back when I saw it?
You are the fool, Creon, are you not? hoping
Without support or friends to get a throne?
Thrones may be won or bought: you could do neither.
CREON: Now listen to me. You have talked; let me talk, too.
You can not judge unless you know the facts.
OEDIPUS: You speak well: there is one fact; but I find it hard
To learn from the deadliest enemy I have.
CREON: That above all I must dispute with you.
OEDIPUS: That above all I will not hear you deny.
CREON: If you think there is anything good in being stubborn
Against all reason, then I say you are wrong.
OEDIPUS: If you think a man can sin against his own kind
And not be punished for it, I say you are mad.
CREON: I agree. But tell me: what have I done to you?
OEDIPUS: You advised me to send for that wizard, did you not?
CREON: I did. I should do it again.
OEDIPUS: Very well. Now tell me:
How long has it been since Laïos—
CREON: What of Laïos?
OEDIPUS: Since he vanished in that onset by the road?
CREON: It was long ago, a long time.
OEDIPUS: And this prophet,
Was he practicing here then?
CREON: He was; and with honor, as now
OEDIPUS: Did he speak of me at that time?
CREON: He never did;
At least, not when I was present.
OEDIPUS: But . . . the enquiry?
I suppose you held one?
CREON: We did, but we learned nothing.
OEDIPUS: Why did the prophet not speak against me then?
CREON: I do not know; and I am the kind of man
Who holds his tongue when he has no facts to go on.
OEDIPUS: There's one fact that you know, and you could tell it.
CREON: What fact is that? If I know it, you shall have it.
OEDIPUS: If he were not involved with you, he could not say
That it was I who murdered Laïos.
CREON: If he says that, you are the one that knows it!—
But now it is my turn to question you.
OEDIPUS: Put your questions. I am no murderer.
CREON: First, then: You married my sister?
OEDIPUS: I married your sister.
CREON: And you rule the kingdom equally with her?
OEDIPUS: Everything that she wants she has from me.

CREON: And I am the third, equal to both of you?
OEDIPUS: That is why I call you a bad friend.
CREON: No. Reason it out, as I have done.
   Think of this first: Would any sane man prefer
   Power, with all a king's anxieties,
   To that same power and the grace of sleep?
   Certainly not I.
   I have never longed for the king's power—only his rights.
   Would any wise man differ from me in this?
   As matters stand, I have my way in everything
   With your consent, and no responsibilities.
   If I were king, I should be a slave to policy.
   How could I desire a scepter more
   Than what is now mine—untroubled influence?
   No, I have not gone mad; I need no honors,
   Except those with the perquisites I have now.
   I am welcome everywhere; every man salutes me,
   And those who want your favor seek my ear,
   Since I know how to manage what they ask.
   Should I exchange this ease for that anxiety?
   Besides, no sober mind is treasonable.
   I hate anarchy
   And never would deal with any man who likes it.
   Test what I have said. Go to the priestess
   At Delphi, ask if I quoted her correctly.
   And as for this other thing: if I am found
   Guilty of treason with Teiresias,
   Then sentence me to death! You have my word
   It is a sentence I should cast my vote for—
   But not without evidence!
                            You do wrong
   When you take good men for bad, bad men for good.
   A true friend thrown aside—why, life itself
   Is not more precious!
                         In time you will know this well:
   For time, and time alone, will show the just man,
   Though scoundrels are discovered in a day.
CHORAGOS: This is well said, and a prudent man would ponder it.
   Judgments too quickly formed are dangerous.
OEDIPUS: But is he not quick in his duplicity?
   And shall I not be quick to parry him?
   Would you have me stand still, hold my peace, and let
   This man win everything, through my inaction?
CREON: And you want—what is it, then? To banish me?
OEDIPUS: No, not exile. It is your death I want,
   So that all the world may see what treason means.

CREON: You will persist, then? You will not believe me?
OEDIPUS: How can I believe you?
CREON: Then you are a fool.
OEDIPUS: To save myself?
CREON: In justice, think of me.
OEDIPUS: You are evil incarnate.
CREON: But suppose that you are wrong?
OEDIPUS: Still I must rule.
CREON: But not if you rule badly.
OEDIPUS: O city, city!
CREON: It is my city, too!
CHORAGOS: Now, my lords, be still. I see the Queen,
    Iocastê, coming from her palace chambers;
    And it is time she came, for the sake of you both.
    This dreadful quarrel can be resolved through her.

(*Enter* IOCASTE)

IOCASTE: Poor foolish men, what wicked din is this?
    With Thebes sick to death, is it not shameful
    That you should rake some private quarrel up?
    (*To* OEDIPUS)
    Come into the house.
                      —And you, Creon, go now:
    Let us have no more of this tumult over nothing.
CREON: Nothing? No, sister: what your husband plans for me
    Is one of two great evils: exile or death.
OEDIPUS: He is right.
                   Why, woman I have caught him squarely
    Plotting against my life.
CREON: No! Let me die
    Accurst if ever I have wished you harm!
IOCASTE: Ah, believe it, Oedipus!
    In the name of the gods, respect this oath of his
    For my sake, for the sake of these people here!

                                                     (STROPHE 1)
CHORAGOS: Open your mind to her, my lord. Be ruled by her, I beg you!
OEDIPUS: What would you have me do?
CHORAGOS: Respect Creon's word. He has never spoken like a fool,
    And now he has sworn an oath.
OEDIPUS: You know what you ask?
CHORAGOS: I do.
OEDIPUS: Speak on, then.
CHORAGOS: A friend so sworn should not be baited so,
    In blind malice, and without final proof.
OEDIPUS: You are aware, I hope, that what you say
    Means death for me, or exile at the least.

CHORAGOS: No, I swear by Helios, first in Heaven! (STROPHE 2)
    May I die friendless and accurst,
  The worst of deaths, if ever I meant that!
    It is the withering fields
      That hurt my sick heart:
    Must we bear all these ills,
      And now your bad blood as well?
OEDIPUS: Then let him go. And let me die, if I must,
  Or be driven by him in shame from the land of Thebes.
  It is your unhappiness, and not his talk,
  That touches me.
          As for him—
Wherever he goes, hatred will follow him.
CREON: Ugly in yielding, as you were ugly in rage!
  Natures like yours chiefly torment themselves.
OEDIPUS: Can you not go? Can you not leave me?
CREON: I can.
  You do not know me; but the city knows me,
  And in its eyes I am just, if not in yours.

(Exit CREON*)*

(ANTISTROPHE 1)
CHORAGOS: Lady Iocastê, did you not ask the King to go to his chambers?
IOCASTE: First tell me what has happened.
CHORAGOS: There was suspicion without evidence; yet it rankled
  As even false charges will.
IOCASTE: On both sides?
CHORAGOS: On both.
IOCASTE: But what was said?
CHORAGOS: Oh let it rest, let it be done with!
  Have we not suffered enough?
OEDIPUS: You see to what your decency has brought you:
  You have difficulties where my heart saw none.
CHORAGOS: Oedipus, it is not once only I have told you— (ANTISTROPHE 2)
    You must know I should count myself unwise
  To the point of madness, should I now foresake you—
    You, under whose hand,
      In the storm of another time,
    Our dear land sailed out free.
    But now stand fast at the helm!
IOCASTE: In God's name, Oedipus, inform your wife as well:
  Why are you so set in this hard anger?
OEDIPUS: I will tell you, for none of these men deserves
  My confidence as you do. It is Creon's work,
  His treachery, his plotting against me.
IOCASTE: Go on, if you can make this clear to me.

OEDIPUS: He charges me with the murder of Laïos.
IOCASTE: Has he some knowledge? Or does he speak from hearsay?
OEDIPUS: He would not commit himself to such a charge,
  But he has brought in that damnable soothsayer
  To tell his story.
IOCASTE: Set your mind at rest.
  If it is a question of soothsayers, I tell you
  That you will find no man whose craft gives knowledge
  Of the unknowable.
                  Here is my proof:
  An oracle was reported to Laïos once
  (I will not say from Phoibos himself, but from
  His appointed ministers, at any rate)
  That his doom would be death at the hands of his own son—
  His son, born of his flesh and of mine!
  Now, you remember the story: Laïos was killed
  By marauding strangers where three highways meet;
  But his child had not been three days in this world
  Before the King had pierced the baby's ankles
  And left him to die on a lonely mountainside.
  Thus, Apollo never caused that child
  To kill his father, and it was not Laïos' fate
  To die at the hands of his son, as he had feared.
  This is what prophets and prophecies are worth!
  Have no dread of them.
                  It is God himself
  Who can show us what he wills, in his own way.
OEDIPUS: How strange a shadowy memory crossed my mind,
  Just now while you were speaking; it chilled my heart
IOCASTE: What do you mean? What memory do you speak of?
OEDIPUS: If I understand you, Laïos was killed
  At a place where three roads meet.
IOCASTE: So it was said;
  We have no later story.
OEDIPUS: Where did it happen?
IOCASTE: Phokis, it is called: at a place where the Theban Way
  Divides into the roads toward Delphi and Daulia.
OEDIPUS: When?
IOCASTE: We had the news not long before you came
  And proved the right to your succession here.
OEDIPUS: Ah, what net has God been weaving for me?
IOCASTE: Oedipus! Why does this trouble you?
OEDIPUS: Do not ask me yet.
  First, tell me how Laïos looked, and tell me
  How old he was.
IOCASTE: He was tall, his hair just touched
  With white; his form was not unlike your own.

Sophocles: *Oedipus*

OEDIPUS: I think that I myself may be accurst
  By my own ignorant edict.
IOCASTE: You speak strangely.
  It makes me tremble to look at you, my King.
OEDIPUS: I am not sure that the blind man can not see.
  But I should know better if you were to tell me—
IOCASTE: Anything—though I dread to hear you ask it.
OEDIPUS: Was the King lightly escorted, or did he ride
  With a large company, as a ruler should?
IOCASTE: There were five men with him in all: one was a herald,
  And a single chariot, which he was driving.
OEDIPUS: Alas, that makes it plain enough!
                              But who—
Who told you how it happened?
IOCASTE: A household servant,
  The only one to escape.
OEDIPUS: And is he still
  A servant of ours?
IOCASTE: No; for when he came back at last
  And found you enthroned in the place of the dead king,
  He came to me, touched my hand with his, and begged
  That I would send him away to the frontier district
  Where only the shepherds go—
  As far away from the city as I could send him.
  I granted his prayer; for although the man was a slave,
  He had earned more than this favor at my hands.
OEDIPUS: Can he be called back quickly?
IOCASTE: Easily.
  But why?
OEDIPUS: I have taken too much upon myself
  Without enquiry; therefore I wish to consult him.
IOCASTE: Then he shall come.
                      But am I not one also
  To whom you might confide these fears of yours?
OEDIPUS: That is your right; it will not be denied you,
  Now least of all; for I have reached a pitch
  Of wild foreboding. Is there anyone
  To whom I should sooner speak?
  Polybos of Corinth is my father.
  My mother is a Dorian: Meropê.
  I grew up chief among the men of Corinth
  Until a strange thing happened—
  Not worth my passion, it may be, but strange.
  At a feast, a drunken man maundering in his cups
  Cries out that I am not my father's son!
  I contained myself that night, though I felt anger
  And a sinking heart. The next day I visited

My father and mother, and questioned them. They stormed,
Calling it all the slanderous rant of a fool;
And this relieved me. Yet the suspicion
Remained always aching in my mind;
I knew there was talk; I could not rest;
And finally, saying nothing to my parents,
I went to the shrine at Delphi.
The god dismissed my question without reply;
He spoke of other things.
      Some were clear,
Full of wretchedness, dreadful, unbearable:
As, that I should lie with my own mother, breed
Children from whom all men would turn their eyes;
And that I should be my father's murderer.
I heard all this, and fled. And from that day
Corinth to me was only in the stars
Descending in that quarter of the sky,
As I wandered farther and farther on my way
To a land where I should never see the evil
Sung by the oracle. And I come to this country
Where, so you say, King Laïos was killed.
I will tell you all that happened there, my lady.
There were three highways
Coming together at a place I passed;
And there a herald came toward me, and a chariot
Drawn by horses, with a man such as you describe
Seated in it. The groom leading the horses
Forced me off the road at his lord's command;
But as this charioteer lurched over towards me
I struck him in my rage. The old man saw me
And brought his double goad down upon my head
As I came abreast.
     He was paid back, and more!
Swinging my club in this right hand I knocked him
Out of his car, and he rolled on the ground.
            I killed him.
I killed them all.
Now if that stranger and Laïos were—kin,
Where is a man more miserable than I?
More hated by the gods? Citizen and alien alike
Must never shelter me or speak to me—
I must be shunned by all.
       And I myself
Pronounced this malediction upon myself!
Think of it: I have touched you with these hands,
These hands that killed your husband. What defilement!

Am I all evil, then? It must be so,
Since I must flee from Thebes, yet never again
See my own countrymen, my own country,
For fear of joining my mother in marriage
And killing Polybos, my father.
                              Ah,
If I were created so, born to this fate,
Who could deny the savagery of God?
O holy majesty of heavenly powers!
May I never see that day! Never!
Rather let me vanish from the race of men
Than know the abomination destined me!

CHORAGOS: We too, my lord, have felt dismay at this.
But there is hope: you have yet to hear the shepherd.

OEDIPUS: Indeed, I fear no other hope is left me.

IOCASTE: What do you hope from him when he comes?

OEDIPUS: This much:
If his account of the murder tallies with yours,
Then I am cleared.

IOCASTE: What was it that I said
Of such importance?

OEDIPUS: Why, "marauders," you said,
Killed the King, according to this man's story.
If he maintains that still, if there were several,
Clearly the guilt is not mine: I was alone.
But if he says one man, singlehanded, did it,
Then the evidence all points to me.

IOCASTE: You may be sure that he said there were several;
And can he call back that story now? He cán not.
The whole city heard it as plainly as I.
But suppose he alters some detail of it:
He can not ever show that Laïos' death
Fulfilled the oracle: for Apollo said
My child was doomed to kill him; and my child—
Poor baby!—it was my child that died first.
No. From now on, where oracles are concerned,
I would not waste a second thought on any.

OEDIPUS: You may be right.
                    But come: let someone go
For the shepherd at once. This matter must be settled.

IOCASTE: I will send for him.
I would not wish to cross you in anything,
And surely not in this.—Let us go in.

(Exeunt into the palace)

ODE II

CHORUS: Let me be reverent in the ways of right, (STROPHE 1)
   Lowly the paths I journey on;
   Let all my words and actions keep
   The laws of the pure universe
   From highest Heaven handed down.
   For Heaven is their bright nurse,
   Those generations of the realms of light;
   Ah, never of mortal kind were they begot,
   Nor are they slaves of memory, lost in sleep:
   Their Father is greater than Time, and ages not.
   The tyrant is a child of Pride (ANTISTROPHE 1)
   Who drinks from his great sickening cup
   Recklessness and vanity,
   Until from his high crest headlong
   He plummets to the dust of hope.
   That strong man is not strong.
   But let no fair ambition be denied;
   May God protect the wrestler for the State
   In government, in comely policy.
   Who will fear God, and on His ordinance wait.
   Haughtiness and the high hand of disdain (STROPHE 2)
   Tempt and outrage God's holy law;
   And any mortal who dares hold
   No immortal Power in awe
   Will be caught up in a net of pain:
   The price for which his levity is sold.
   Let each man take due earnings, then,
   And keeps his hands from holy things,
   And from blasphemy stand apart—
   Else the crackling blast of heaven
   Blows on his head, and on his desperate heart;
   Though fools will honor impious men,
   In their cities no tragic poet sings.
   Shall we lose faith in Delphi's obscurities, (ANTISTROPHE 2)
   We who have heard the world's core
   Discredited, and the sacred wood
   Of Zeus at Elis praised no more?
   The deeds and the strange prophecies
   Must make a pattern yet to be understood.
   Zeus, if needed you are lord of all,
   Throned in light over night and day,
   Mirror this in your endless mind:
   Our masters call the oracle
   Words on the wind, and the Delphic vision blind!

Their hearts no longer know Apollo,
And reverence for the gods has died away.

Scene III

(Enter IOCASTE*)*

IOCASTE: Princes of Thebes, it has occurred to me
  To visit the altars of the gods, bearing
  These branches as a suppliant, and this incense.
  Our King is not himself: his noble soul
  Is overwrought with fantasies of dread,
  Else he would consider
  The new prophecies in the light of the old.
  He will listen to any voice that speaks disaster,
  And my advice goes for nothing.
(She approaches the altar, R.)
                    To you, then, Apollo,
  Lycean lord, since you are nearest, I turn in prayer.
  Receive these offerings, and grant us deliverance
  From defilement. Our hearts are heavy with fear
  When we see our leader distracted, as helpless sailors
  Are terrified by the confusion of their helmsman.

(Enter MESSENGER*)*

MESSENGER: Friends, no doubt you can direct me:
Where shall I find the house of Oedipus,
  Or, better still, where is the King himself?
CHORAGOS: It is this very place, stranger; he is inside.
  This is his wife and mother of his children.
MESSENGER: I wish her happiness in a happy house,
  Blest in all the fulfillment of her marriage.
IOCASTE: I wish as much for you: your courtesy
  Deserves a like good fortune. But now, tell me:
  Why have you come? What have you to say to us?
MESSENGER: Good news, my lady, for your house and your husband.
IOCASTE: What news? Who sent you here?
MESSENGER: I am from Corinth.
  The news I bring ought to mean joy for you,
  Though it may be you will find some grief in it.
IOCASTE: What is it? How can it touch us in both ways?
MESSENGER: The word is that the people of the Isthmus
  Intend to call Oedipus to be their king.
IOCASTE: But old King Polybos—is he not reigning still?
MESSENGER: No. Death holds him in his sepulchre.

IOCASTE: What are you saying? Polybus is dead?
MESSENGER: If I am not telling the truth, may I die myself.
IOCASTE:
(*To a* MAIDSERVANT)
   Go in, go quickly; tell this to your master.
   O riddlers of God's will, where are you now!
   This was the man whom Oedipus, long ago,
   Feared so, fled so, in dread of destroying him—
   But it was another fate by which he died.

(*Enter* OEPIDUS, *C.*)

OEDIPUS: Dearest Iocastê, why have you sent for me?
IOCASTE: Listen to what this man says, and then tell me
   What has become of the solemn prophecies.
OEDIPUS: Who is this man? What is his news for me?
IOCASTE: He has come from Corinth to announce your father's death!
OEDIPUS: Is it true, stranger? Tell me in your own words.
MESSENGER: I can not say it more clearly: the King is dead.
OEDIPUS: Was it by treason? Or by an attack of illness?
MESSENGER: A little thing brings old men to their rest.
OEDIPUS: It was sickness, then?
MESSENGER: Yes, and his many years.
OEDIPUS: Ah!
   Why should a man respect the Pythian hearth, or
   Give heed to the birds that jangle above his head?
   They prophesied that I should kill Polybos,
   Kill my own father; but he is dead and buried,
   And I am here—I never touched him, never,
   Unless he died of grief for my departure,
   And thus, in a sense, through me. No. Polybos
   Has packed the oracles off with him underground.
   They are empty words.
IOCASTE: Had I not told you so?
OEDIPUS: You had; it was my faint heart that betrayed me.
IOCASTE: From now on never think of those things again.
OEDIPUS: And yet—must I not fear my mother's bed?
IOCASTE: Why should anyone in this world be afraid,
   Since Fate rules us and nothing can be foreseen?
   A man should live only for the present day.
   Have no more fear of sleeping with your mother:
   How many men, in dreams, have lain with their mothers!
   No reasonable man is troubled by such things.
OEDIPUS: That is true; only—
   If only my mother were not still alive!
   But she is alive. I can not help my dread.
IOCASTE: Yet this news of your father's death is wonderful.
OEDIPUS: Wonderful. But I fear the living woman.

Sophocles: *Oedipus*

MESSENGER: Tell me, who is this woman that you fear?
OEDIPUS: It is Meropê, man; the wife of King Polybos.
MESSENGER: Meropê? Why should you be afraid of her?
OEDIPUS: An oracle of the gods, a dreadful saying.
MESSENGER: Can you tell me about it or are you sworn to silence?
OEDIPUS: I can tell you, and I will.
  Apollo said through his prophet that I was the man
  Who should marry his own mother, shed his father's blood
  With his own hands. And so, for all these years
  I have kept clear of Corinth, and no harm has come—
  Though it would have been sweet to see my parents again.
MESSENGER: And is this the fear that drove you out of Corinth?
OEDIPUS: Would you have me kill my father?
MESSENGER: As for that
  You must be reassured by the news I gave you.
OEDIPUS: If you could reassure me, I would reward you.
MESSENGER: I had that in mind, I will confess: I thought
  I could count on you when you returned to Corinth.
OEDIPUS: No: I will never go near my parents again.
MESSENGER: Ah, son, you still do not know what you are doing—
OEDIPUS: What do you mean? In the name of God tell me!
MESSENGER: —If these are your reasons for not going home.
OEDIPUS: I tell you, I fear the oracle may come true.
MESSENGER: And guilt may come upon you through your parents?
OEDIPUS: That is the dread that is always in my heart.
MESSENGER: Can you not see that all your fears are groundless?
OEDIPUS: How can you say that? They are my parents, surely?
MESSENGER: Polybos was not your father.
OEDIPUS: Not my father?
MESSENGER: No more your father than the man speaking to you.
OEDIPUS: But you are nothing to me!
MESSENGER: Neither was he.
OEDIPUS: Then why did he call me son?
MESSENGER: I will tell you:
  Long ago he had you from my hands, as a gift.
OEDIPUS: Then how could he love me so, if I was not his?
MESSENGER: He had no children, and his heart turned to you.
OEDIPUS: What of you? Did you buy me? Did you find me by chance?
MESSENGER: I came upon you in the crooked pass of Kithairon.
OEDIPUS: And what were you doing there?
MESSENGER: Tending my flocks.
OEDIPUS: A wandering shepherd?
MESSENGER: But your savior son, that day.
OEDIPUS: From what did you save me?
MESSENGER: Your ankles should tell you that.
OEDIPUS: Ah, stranger, why do you speak of that childhood pain?
MESSENGER: I cut the bonds that tied your ankles together.

OEDIPUS: I have had the mark as long as I can remember.
MESSENGER: That was why you were given the name you bear.
OEDIPUS: God! Was it my father or my mother who did it? Tell me!
MESSENGER: I do not know. The man who gave you to me
   Can tell you better than I.
OEDIPUS: It was not you that found me, but another?
MESSENGER: It was another shepherd gave you to me.
OEDIPUS: Who was he? Can you tell me who he was?
MESSENGER: I think he was said to be one of Laïos' people.
OEDIPUS: You mean the Laïos who was king here years ago?
MESSENGER: Yes; King Laïos; and the man was one of his herdsmen.
OEDIPUS: Is he still alive? Can I see him?
MESSENGER: These men here
   Know best about such things.
OEDIPUS: Does anyone here
   Know this shepherd that he is talking about?
   Have you seen him in the fields, or in the town?
   If you have, tell me. It is time things were made plain.
CHORAGOS: I think the man he means is that same shepherd
   You have already asked to see. Iocastê perhaps
   Could tell you something.
OEDIPUS: Do you know anything
   About him, Lady? Is he the man we have summoned?
   Is that the man this shepherd means?
IOCASTE: Why think of him?
   Forget this herdsman. Forget it all.
   This talk is a waste of time.
OEDIPUS: How can you say that,
   When the clues to my true birth are in my hands?
IOCASTE: For God's love, let us have no more questioning!
   Is your life nothing to you?
   My own is pain enough for me to bear.
OEDIPUS: You need not worry. Suppose my mother a slave,
   And born of slaves: no baseness can touch you.
IOCASTE: Listen to me, I beg you: do not do this thing!
OEDIPUS: I will not listen; the truth must be made known.
IOCASTE: Everything that I say is for your own good!
OEDIPUS: My own good
   Snaps my patience, then; I want none of it.
IOCASTE: You are fatally wrong! May you never learn who you are!
OEDIPUS: Go, one of you, and bring the shepherd here.
   Let us leave this woman to brag of her royal name.
IOCASTE: Ah, miserable!
   That is the only word I have for you now.
   That is the only word I can ever have.

                              (*Exit into the palace*)

CHORAGOS: Why has she left us, Oedipus? Why has she gone

Sophocles: *Oedipus*

    In such a passion of sorrow? I fear this silence:
    Something dreadful may come of it.
OEDIPUS: Let it come!
    However base my birth, I must know about it.
    The Queen, like a woman, is perhaps ashamed
    To think of my low origin. But I
    Am a child of Luck; I can not be dishonored.
    Luck is my mother; the passing months, my brothers,
    Have seen me rich and poor.
                            If this is so,
    How could I wish that I were someone else?
    How could I not be glad to know my birth?

ODE III

CHORUS: If ever the coming time were known   (STROPHE)
    To my heart's pondering,
    Kithairon, now by Heaven I see the torches
    At the festival of the next full moon,
    And see the dance, and hear the choir sing
    A grace to your gentle shade:
    Mountain where Oedipus was found,
    O mountain guard of a noble race!
    May the god who heals us lend his aid,
    And let that glory come to pass
    For our king's cradling-ground.
Of the nymphs that flower beyond the years,   (ANTISTROPHE)
    Who bore you, royal child,
    To Pan of the hills or the timberline Apollo,
    Cold in delight where the upland clears,
    Or Hermês for whom Kyllenê's heights are piled?
    Or flushed as evening cloud,
    Great Dionysos, roamer of mountains,
    He—was it he who found you there,
    And caught you up in his own proud
    Arms from the sweet god-ravisher
    Who laughed by the Muses' fountains?

Scene IV

OEDIPUS: Sirs, though I do not know the man,
    I think I see him coming, this shepherd we want:
    He is old, like our friend here, and the men
    Bringing him seem to be servants of my house.
    But you can tell, if you have ever seen him.

(*Enter* SHEPHERD *escorted by servants*)

CHORAGOS: I know him,, he was Laïos' man. You can trust him.
OEDIPUS: Tell me first, you from Corinth: is this the shepherd
   We were discussing?
MESSENGER: This is the very man.
OEDIPUS:

(*To* SHEPHERD)

   Come here. No, look at me. You must answer
   Everything I ask.—You belonged to Laïos?
SHEPHERD: Yes: born his slave, brought up in his house.
OEDIPUS: Tell me: what kind of work did you do for him?
SHEPHERD: I was a shepherd of his, most of my life.
OEDIPUS: Where mainly did you go for pasturage?
SHEPHERD: Sometimes Kithairon, sometimes the hills near-by.
OEDIPUS: Do you remember ever seeing this man out there?
SHEPHERD: What would he be doing there? This man?
OEDIPUS: This man standing here. Have you ever seen him before?
SHEPHERD: No. At least, not to my recollection.
MESSENGER: And that is not strange, my lord. But I'll refresh
   His memory: he must remember when we two
   Spent three whole seasons together, March to September,
   On Kithairon or thereabouts. He had two flocks;
   I had one. Each autumn I'd drive mine home
   And he would go back with his to Laïos' sheepfold.—
   Is this not true, just as I have described it?
SHEPHERD: True, yes; but it was all so long ago.
MESSENGER: Well, then: do you remember, back in those days,
   That you gave me a baby boy to bring up as my own?
SHEPHERD: What if I did? What are you trying to say?
MESSENGER: King Oedipus was once that little child.
SHEPHERD: Damn you, hold your tongue!
OEDIPUS: No more of that!
   It is your tongue needs watching, not this man's.
SHEPHERD: My King, my Master, what is it I have done wrong?
OEDIPUS: You have not answered his question about the boy.
SHEPHERD: He does not know . . . He is only making trouble . . .
OEDIPUS: Come, speak plainly, or it will go hard with you.
SHEPHERD: In God's name, do not torture an old man!
OEDIPUS: Come here, one of you; bind his arms behind him.
SHEPHERD: Unhappy king! What more do you wish to learn?
OEDIPUS: Did you give this man the child he speaks of?
SHEPHERD: I did.
   And I would to God I had died that very day.
OEDIPUS: You will die now unless you speak the truth.
SHEPHERD: Yet if I speak the truth, I am worse than dead.
OEDIPUS: Very well; since you insist upon delaying—

SHEPHERD: No! I have told you already that I gave him the boy.
OEDIPUS: Where did you get him? From your house? From somewhere else?
SHEPHERD: Not from mine, no. A man gave him to me.
OEDIPUS: Is that man here? Do you know whose slave he was?
SHEPHERD: For God's love, my King, do not ask me any more!
OEDIPUS: You are a dead man if I have to ask you again.
SHEPHERD: Then . . . Then the child was from the palace of Laïos.
OEDIPUS: A slave child? or a child of his own line?
SHEPHERD: Ah, I am on the brink of dreadful speech!
OEDIPUS: And I of dreadful hearing. Yet I must hear.
SHEPHERD: If you must be told, then . . .
                                             They said it was Laïos' child;
But it is your wife who can tell you about that.
OEDIPUS: My wife!—Did she give it to you?
SHEPHERD: My lord, she did.
OEDIPUS: Do you know why?
SHEPHERD: I was told to get rid of it.
OEDIPUS: An unspeakable mother!
SHEPHERD: There had been prophecies . . .
OEDIPUS: Tell me.
SHEPHERD: It was said that the boy would kill his own father.
OEDIPUS: Then why did you give him over to this old man?
SHEPHERD: I pitied the baby, my King,
  And I thought that this man would take him far away
  To his own country.
                           He saved him—but for what a fate!
For if you are what this man says you are,
No man living is more wretched than Oedipus.
OEDIPUS: Ah God!
  It was true!
          All the prophecies!
                        —Now,
O Light, may I look on you for the last time!
I, Oedipus,
Oedipus, damned in his birth, in his marriage damned,
Damned in the blood he shed with his own hand!
                                (He rushes into the palace)

ODE IV

CHORUS: Alas for the seed of men.   (STROPHE 1)
  What measure shall I give these generations
  That breathe on the void and are void
  And exist and do not exist?
  Who bears more weight of joy

Than mass of sunlight shifting in images,
Or who shall make his thought stay on
That down time drifts away?
Your splendor is all fallen.
O naked brow of wrath and tears,
O change of Oedipus!
I who saw your days call no man blest—
Your great days like ghósts góne.

That mind was a strong bow. (ANTISTROPHE 1)
Deep, how deep you drew it then, hard archer,
At a dim fearful range,
And brought dear glory down!
You overcame the stranger—
The virgin with her hooking lion claws—
And though death sang, stood like a tower
To make pale Thebes take heart
Fortress against our sorrow!
True king, giver of laws,
Majestic Oedipus!
No prince in Thebes had ever such renown,
No prince won such grace of power.

And now of all men ever known (STROPHE 2)
Most pitiful is this man's story:
His fortunes are most changed, his state
Fallen to a low slave's
Ground under bitter fate.
O Oedipus, most royal one!
The great door that expelled you to the light
Gave at night—ah, gave night to your glory:
As to the father, to the fathering son.
All understood too late.
How could that queen whom Laïos won,
The garden that he harrowed at his height,
Be silent when that act was done?

But all eyes fail before time's eye, (ANTISTROPHE 2)
All actions come to justice there.
Though never willed, though far down the deep past,
Your bed, your dread sirings,
Are brought to book at last.
Child by Laïos doomed to die,
Then doomed to lose that fortunate little death,
Would God you never took breath in this air
That with my wailing lips I take to cry:
For I weep the world's outcast.
I was blind, and now I can tell why:
Asleep, for you had given ease of breath
To Thebes, while the false years went by.

EXODOS

(Enter, from the palace, SECOND MESSENGER*)*

SECOND MESSENGER: Elders of Thebes, most honored in this land,
What horrors are yours to see and hear, what weight
Of sorrow to be endured, if, true to your birth,
You venerate the line of Labdakos!
I think neither Istros nor Phasis, those great rivers,
Could purify this place of the corruption
It shelters now, or soon must bring to light—
Evil not done unconsciously, but willed.
The greatest griefs are those we cause ourselves.
CHORAGOS: Surely, friend, we have grief enough already;
What new sorrow do you mean?
SECOND MESSENGER: The Queen is dead.
CHORAGOS: Iocastê? Dead? But at whose hand?
SECOND MESSENGER: Her own.
The full horror of what happened you can not know,
For you did not see it; but I, who did, will tell you
As clearly as I can how she met her death.
When she had left us,
In passionate silence, passing through the court,
She ran to her apartment in the house
Her hair clutched by the fingers of both hands.
She closed the doors behind her; then, by that bed
Where long ago the fatal son was conceived—
That son who should bring about his father's death—
We heard her call upon Laïos, dead so many years,
And heard her wail for the double fruit of her marriage,
A husband by her husband, children by her child.
Exactly how she died I do not know:
For Oedipus burst in moaning and would not let us
Keep vigil to the end: it was by him
As he stormed about the room that our eyes were caught.
From one to another of us he went, begging a sword,
Cursing the wife who was not his wife, the mother
Whose womb had carried his own children and himself.
I do not know: it was none of us aided him,
But surely one of the gods was in control!
For with a dreadful cry
He hurled his weight, as though wrenched out of himself.
At the twin doors: the bolts gave, and he rushed in.
And there was saw her hanging, her body swaying
From the cruel cord she had noosed about her neck.
A great sob broke from him, heartbreaking to hear,
As he loosed the rope and lowered her to the ground.

I would blot out from my mind what happened next!
For the King ripped from her gown the golden brooches
That were her ornament, and raised them, and plunged them down
Straight into his own eyeballs, crying, "No more,
No more shall you look on the misery about me,
The horrors of my own doing! Too long you have known
The faces of those whom I should never have seen,
Too long been blind to those for whom I was searching!
From this hour, go in darkness!" And as he spoke,
He struck at his eyes—not once, but many times;
And the blood spattered his beard,
Bursting from his ruined sockets like red hail.
So from the unhappiness of two this evil has sprung,
A curse on the man and woman alike. The old
Happiness of the house of Labdakos
Was happiness enough: where is it today?
It is all wailing and ruin, disgrace, death—all
The misery of mankind that has a name—
And it is wholly and for ever theirs.

CHORAGOS: Is he in agony still? Is there no rest for him?
SECOND MESSENGER: He is calling for someone to lead him to the gates
So that all the children of Kadmos may look upon
His father's murderer, his mother's—no,
I can not say it!
                And then he will leave Thebes,
Self-exiled, in order that the curse
Which he himself pronounced may depart from the house.
He is weak, and there is none to lead him,
So terrible is his suffering.
                But you will see:
Look, the doors are opening; in a moment
You will see a thing that would crush a heart of stone.

(The central door is opened; OEDIPUS, *blinded, is led in)*

CHORAGOS: Dreadful indeed for men to see.
Never have my own eyes
Looked on a sight so full of fear.
Oedipus!
What madness came upon you, what daemon
Leaped on your life with heavier
Punishment than a mortal man can bear?
No: I can not even
Look at you, poor ruined one.
And I would speak, question, ponder,
If I were able. No.
You make me shudder.
OEDIPUS: God.   God.

Sophocles: *Oedipus*

   Is there a sorrow greater?
   Where shall I find harbor in this world?
   My voice is hurled far on a dark wind.
   What has God done to me?
CHORAGOS: Too terrible to think of, or to see.
OEDIPUS: O cloud of night, (STROPHE 1)
   Never to be turned away: night coming on,
   I can not tell how: night like a shroud!
   My fair winds brought me here.
                              O God. Again
   The pain of the spikes where I had sight,
   The flooding pain
   Of memory, never to be gouged out.
CHORAGOS: This is not strange.
   You suffer it all twice over, remorse in pain,
   Pain in remorse.
OEDIPUS: Ah dear friend (ANTISTROPHE 1)
   Are you faithful even yet, you alone?
   Are you still standing near me, will you stay here,
   Patient, to care for the blind?
                              The blind man!
   Yet even blind I know who it is attends me,
   By the voice's tone—
   Though my new darkness hide the comforter.
CHORAGOS: Oh fearful act!
   What god was it drove you to rake black
   Night across your eyes?
OEDIPUS: Apollo. Apollo. Dear (STROPHE 2)
   Children, the god was Apollo.
   He brought my sick, sick fate upon me.
   But the blinding hand was my own!
   How could I bear to see
   When all my sight was horror everywhere?
CHORAGOS: Everywhere; that is true.
OEDIPUS: And now what is left?
   Images? Love? A greeting even,
   Sweet to the senses? Is there anything?
   Ah, no, friends: lead me away.
   Lead me away from Thebes.
                              Lead the great wreck
   And hell of Oedipus, whom the gods hate.
CHORAGOS: Your fate is clear, you are not blind to that.
   Would God you had never found it out!
OEDIPUS: Death take the man who unbound (ANTISTROPHE 2)
   My feet on that hillside
   And delivered me from death to life! What life?
   If only I had died,

This weight of monstrous doom
Could not have dragged me and my darlings down.
CHORAGOS: I would have wished the same.
OEDIPUS: Oh never to have come here
With my father's blood upon me! Never
To have been the man they call his mother's husband!
Oh accurst! Oh child of evil,
To have entered that wretched bed—
                              the selfsame one!
More primal than sin itself, this fell to me.
CHORAGOS: I do not know how I can answer you.
You were better dead than alive and blind.
OEDIPUS: Do not counsel me any more. This punishment
That I have laid upon myself is just.
If I had eyes,
I do not know how I could bear the sight
Of my father, when I came to the House of Death,
Or my mother: for I have sinned against them both
So vilely that I could not make my peace
By strangling my own life.
                        Or do you think my children,
Born as they were born, would be sweet to my eyes?
Ah never, never! Nor this town with its high walls,
Nor the holy images of the gods.
                    For I,
Thrice miserable!—Oedipus, noblest of all the line
Of Kadmos, have condemned myself to enjoy
These things no more, by my own malediction
Expelling that man whom the gods declared
To be a defilement in the house of Laïos.
After exposing the rankness of my own guilt,
How could I look men frankly in the eyes?
No, I swear it,
If I could have stifled my hearing at its source,
I would have done it and made all this body
A tight cell of misery, blank to light and sound:
So I should have been safe in a dark agony
Beyond all recollection.
                      Ah Kithairon!
Why did you shelter me? When I was cast upon you,
Why did I not die? Then I should never
Have shown the world my execrable birth.
Ah Polybos! Corinth, city that I believed
The ancient seat of my ancestors: how fair
I seemed, your child! And all the while this evil
Was cancerous within me!
                      For I am sick

Sophocles: *Oedipus*

In my daily life, sick in my origin.
O three roads, dark ravine, woodland and way
Where three roads met: you, drinking my father's blood,
My own blood, spilled by my own hand can you remember
The unspeakable things I did there, and the things
I went on from there to do?
                          O marriage, marriage!
The act that engendered me, and again the act
Performed by the son in the same bed—
                                      Ah, the net
Of incest, mingling fathers, brothers, sons,
With brides, wives, mothers: the last evil
That can be known by men: no tongue can say
How evil!
          No. For the love of God, conceal me
Somewhere far from Thebes; or kill me; or hurl me
Into the sea, away from men's eyes for ever.
Come, lead me. You need not fear to touch me.
Of all men, I alone can bear this guilt.

(*Enter* CREON)

CHORAGOS: We are not the ones to decide; but Creon here
  May fitly judge of what you ask. He only
  Is left to protect the city in your place.
OEDIPUS: Alas, how can I speak to him? What right have I
  To beg his courtesy whom I have deeply wronged?
CREON: I have not come to mock you, Oedipus,
  Or to reproach you, either.

(*To* ATTENDANTS)

                              —You, standing there:
  If you have lost all respect for man's dignity,
  At least respect the flame of Lord Helios:
  Do not allow this pollution to show itself
  Openly here, an affront to the earth
  And Heaven's rain and the light of day. No, take him
  Into the house as quickly as you can.
  For it is proper
  That only the close kindred see his grief.
OEDIPUS: I pray you in God's name, since your courtesy
  Ignores my dark expectation, visiting
  With mercy this man of all men most execrable:
  Give me what I ask—for your good, not for mine.
CREON: And what is it that you would have me do?
OEDIPUS: Drive me out of this country as quickly as may be
  To a place where no human voice can ever greet me.

CREON: I should have done that before now—only,
  God's will had not been wholly revealed to me.
OEDIPUS: But his command is plain: the parricide
  Must be destroyed. I am that evil man.
CREON: That is the sense of it, yes; but as things are,
  We had best discover clearly what is to be done.
OEDIPUS: You would learn more about a man like me?
CREON: You are ready now to listen to the god.
OEDIPUS: I will listen. But it is to you
  That I must turn for help. I beg you, hear me.
  The woman in there—
  Give her whatever funeral you think proper:
  She is your sister.
    —But let me go, Creon!
  Let me purge my father's Thebes of the pollution
  Of my living here, and go out to the wild hills,
  To Kithairon, that has won such fame with me,
  The tomb my mother and father appointed for me,
  And let me die there, as they willed I should.
  And yet I know
  Death will not ever come to me through sickness
  Or in any natural way: I have been preserved
  For some unthinkable fate. But let that be.
  As for my sons, you need not care for them.
  They are men, they will find some way to live.
  But my poor daughters, who have shared my table,
  Who never before have been parted from their father—
  Take care of them, Creon; do this for me.
  And will you let me touch them with my hands
  A last time, and let us weep together?
  Be kind, my lord,
  Great prince, be kind!
    Could I but touch them,,
  They would be mine again, as when I had my eyes.

(*Enter* ANTIGONE *and* ISMENE, *attended*)

  Ah, God!
  Is it my dearest children I hear weeping?
  Has Creon pitied me and sent my daughters?
CREON: Yes, Oedipus: I knew that they were dear to you
  In the old days, and know you must love them still.
OEDIPUS: May God bless you for this—and be a friendlier
  Guardian to you than he has been to me!
  Children, where are you?
  Come quickly to my hands: they are your brother's—
  Hands that have brought your father's once clear eyes

To this way of seeing—
                    Ah dearest ones,
I had neither sight nor knowledge then, your father
By the woman who was the source of his own life!
And I weep for you—having no strength to see you—,
I weep for you when I think of the bitterness
That men will visit upon you all your lives.
What homes, what festivals can you attend
Without being forced to depart again in tears?
And when you come to marriageable age,
Where is the man, my daughters, who would dare
Risk the bane that lies on all my children?
Is there any evil wanting? Your father killed
His father; sowed the womb of her who bore him;
Engendered you at the fount of his own existence!
That is what they will say of you.
                              Then, whom
Can you ever marry? There are no bridegrooms for you,
And your lives must wither away in sterile dreaming.
O Creon, son of Menoikeus!
You are the only father my daughters have,
Since we, their parents, are both of us gone for ever.
They are your own blood: you will not let them
Fall into beggary and loneliness;
You will keep them from the miseries that are mine!
Take pity on them; see, they are only children,
Friendless except for you. Promise me this,
Great Prince, and give me your hand in token of it.
(CREON *clasps his right hand*)
Children:
I could say much, if you could understand me,
But as it is, I have only this prayer for you:
Live where you can, be as happy as you can—
Happier, please God, than God has made your father!
CREON: Enough. You have wept enough. Now go within.
OEDIPUS: I must; but it is hard.
CREON: Time eases all things.
OEDIPUS: But you must promise—
CREON: Say what you desire.
OEDIPUS: Send me from Thebes!
CREON: God grant that I may!
OEDIPUS: But since God hates me . . .
CREON: No, he will grant your wish.
OEDIPUS: You promise?
CREON: I can not speak beyond my knowledge.
OEDIPUS: Then lead me in.

CREON: Come now, and leave your children.
OEDIPUS: No! Do not take them from me!
CREON: Think no longer
  That you are in command here, but rather think
  How, when you were, you served your own destruction.

> (*Exeunt into the house all but the* CHORUS;
> *the* CHORAGOS *chants directly to the audience*)

CHORAGOS: Men of Thebes: look upon Oedipus.
  This is the king who solved the famous riddle
  And towered up, most powerful of men.
  No mortal eyes but looked on him with envy,
  Yet in the end ruin swept over him.
  Let every man in mankind's frailty
  Consider his last day; and let none
  Presume on his good fortune until he find
  Life, at his death, a memory without pain.

Jean Racine

Phaedra

a tragedy in five acts

translated by Wallace Fowlie

Characters

    THESEUS, *son of Aegeus, King of Athens*
    PHAEDRA, *wife of Theseus, daughter of Minos and Pasiphaë*
    HIPPOLYTUS, *son of Theseus and Antiope, Queen of the Amazons*
    ARICIA, *princess of the royal blood of Athens*
    THERAMENES, *tutor of Hippolytus*
    OENONE, *nurse and confidante of Phaedra*
    ISMENE, *confidante of Aricia*
    PANOPE, *lady-in-waiting to Phaedra*
    GUARDS

    OPENING SCENE: *Troezen, a city of the Peloponnesus.*

ACT I

Scene 1. *Hippolytus, Theramenes.*

HIPPOLYTUS: I have made up my mind, Theramenes.
I am leaving this place; I am leaving beautiful Troezen.
My idleness shames me
because of the deadly doubt filling my heart.
Separated from my father for more than six months,
I know nothing of his fate.
I do not even know the place where he hides.
THERAMENES: My lord, where will you go to look for him?
To placate your justified fear,
I have already crossed the two seas Corinth separates.

N.B. An index of proper names follows the translation.

I have asked about Theseus of the people on those shores
where the Acheron disappears into Hades.
I have visited Elis, and leaving Taenarus behind me,
I went as far as the sea into which Icarus fell.
With what new hope and in what happy land
do you expect to discover the trace of his passing?
And who can tell whether the King your father
wants the mystery of his absence to be known?
and whether, when with you we fear for his life,
that hero, at peace and concealing a new love,
is not waiting until his deceived mistress . . .

HIPPOLYTUS: Stop, Theramenes, and show respect for Theseus.
He has left all his youthful errors behind him
and is not detained now by any unworthy obstacle.
By her prayers Phaedra changed his fatal inconstancy
and for a long time has feared no rival.
I will be doing my duty if I look for him,
and I shall get away from Troezen which I no longer want to see.

THERAMENES: My lord, for how long have you feared the presence
of this peaceful town you loved as a boy,
and which I have seen you prefer
to the noise and pomp of Athens and the court?
What danger, or rather, what sorrow, sends you away?

HIPPOLYTUS: The time of happiness is over. Everything has changed
since the gods sent to these shores
the daughter of Minos and Pasiphaë.

THERAMENES: I understand. I know the cause of your suffering.
Phaedra makes you suffer and humiliates you.
She is a hostile stepmother who, when she saw you,
tried to send you into exile.
But her hatred, once fixed on you,
has disappeared or has diminished.
And what dangers can this dying woman,
who wants to die, make you endure?
Phaedra, struck down by a sickness she will not name,
tired of herself and the daylight around her,
cannot construct any plots against you.

HIPPOLYTUS: Her vain enmity is not what I fear.
Hippolytus is fleeing another enemy.
Let me confess it. I am fleeing Aricia,
the last fatal descendant of a house conspiring against us.

THERAMENES: Are you, also, my lord, persecuting her?
Never did the gentle sister of the Pallantides
participate in the plots of her treacherous brothers!
How can you hate her innocent charms?

HIPPOLYTUS: If I hated her, I would not flee her.

THERAMENES: My lord, may I try to explain your flight?

Is it possible you have ceased being proud Hippolytus,
the implacable enemy of the laws of love
and of the yoke which Theseus wore so often?
Does Venus, whom your pride scorned for so long a time,
want at last to justify Theseus?
And placing you in company with other mortals,
has she forced you to light incense on her altars?
Are you in love, my lord?

HIPPOLYTUS: You are bold to ask this question.
You who have known my heart since the beginning of my life,
can you ask me to disavow shamefully
the sentiments of so proud and scornful a heart?
My pride which amazes you was fed me
with my mother's milk and her Amazon pride.
When I reached an older age
I approved of all I learned about myself.
Serving me then with sincere zeal,
you told me the story of my father.
You know how my soul, attentive to your voice,
gloried in the tales of his noble exploits
when you portrayed him as an intrepid hero
consoling men for the absence of Hercules,
killing monsters and pursuing brigands:
Procrustus, Cercyon, Sirron, and Sinnis,
and scattering the bones of the giant of Epidaurus,
and saving Crete with the blood of the Minotaur.
But when you told me the less glorious deeds,
his promise of marriage offered in a hundred places—
Helen stolen from her parents in Sparta,
Salamis comforting the tears of Periboea,
and others whose names he has forgotten,
overconfident hearts whom his passion deceived,
Ariadne telling her story of injustice to the rocks,
Phaedra, brought to Athens for a legitimate cause—
as I listened embarrassed to those stories,
you remember how I urged you to shorten them,
happy if I could efface from memory
the unworthy half of so noble a life!
Can it be that now I, in my turn, am bound?
Can it be that now the gods have humiliated me?
I am more to be scorned in my cowardly sighs
because so many honors were the excuse for Theseus.
I have destroyed no monsters
and have therefore no right to weaken as he did.
Even if my pride could be softened,
should I have chosen Aricia for my conqueror?
Can't my bewildered senses remember any longer

the eternal obstacle which separates us?
My father disapproves of her, and a severe decree
forbids that her brothers should ever have nephews.
He fears an offspring from such a guilty line,
and wishes to bury their name with their sister.
He claims she is under his control until death,
and never will the marriage fire be lighted.
Can I espouse her rights against an angry father?
Shall I be the example of a presumptuous action,
and in this mad love, will my youth . . .
THERAMENES: My lord, once your fate is inscribed,
Heaven can take no account of your reasonings.
Theseus opened your eyes in wishing to close them,
and his hate, exciting a rebellious passion,
gives to his enemy a new grace.
But why be afraid of a chaste love?
If it is sweet to you, why not taste it?
Will you always be restrained by scruples?
Do you fear losing your way in following Hercules?
Think of the strong wills which Venus has overcome.
Where would you be, you who fight Venus,
If Antiope, opposing her laws,
had not desired Theseus with modest ardor?
Why pretend with these proud words?
Confess it and all will change. For several days now
you have seemed a proud and solitary figure, rarely
driving a chariot along the shore,
or, learned in that art invented by Neptune,
bending to a halter an untamed horse.
The forests resound less often now with our cries.
Your eyes have grown heavy with some inner torment.
There is no more doubt of it. You are in love and you are suffering.
You are perishing from a malady you conceal.
Has beautiful Aricia cast a spell over you?
HIPPOLYTUS: I am leaving, Theramenes, to search for my father.
THERAMENES: Will you not see Phaedra before going, my lord?
HIPPOLYTUS: It is my intention. You may inform her.
I will see her, for my duty demands this.
(OENONE *enters*.)
What new woe has upset her faithful Oenone?

Scene 2. *Hippolytus, Oenone, Theramenes.*

OENONE: Alas, my lord, what sorrow is equal to mine?
The Queen is approaching the end of her fate.
In vain I have been keeping watch over her day and night.
In my arms she is dying from a malady she hides from me.

An endless disorder reigns in her mind.
The suffering of her mind allows her no rest.
She wants to see the daylight, and her deep grief
insists that I send everyone away.
She is coming . . .

HIPPOLYTUS: I understand. I will leave her alone.
My presence would be displeasing to her.

Scene 3. Phaedra, Oenone.

PHAEDRA: Let us go no farther. Stay here, Oenone.
I cannot stand up. My strength has gone.
My eyes are dazzled by the daylight I see
and my trembling knees are giving way.
Alas! *(She sits down.)*

OENONE: Would that our tears might appease the gods!

PHAEDRA: These useless ornaments and these veils are heavy on me.
Some irksome hand, by weaving these knots,
has tied my hair tight over my head.
Everything pains and harms me, and conspires to harm me.

OENONE: Your wishes are destroyed as soon as they are expressed!
You yourself, condemning your unjust plans,
urged us just now to dress and prepare you.
You yourself, remembering your earlier strength,
wanted to appear and behold again the light of day.
But as soon as you see it, you turn to hide
as if you hate the very light you came to see.

PHAEDRA: O Sun, noble and shining author of a wretched family,
whose daughter my mother boasted of being,
and who perhaps now blushes at seeing my shame,
I am here to see you for the last time.

OENONE: Will you never renounce this cruel desire?
Am I to see you renouncing life
and making the funeral preparation of your death?

PHAEDRA: Why am I not sitting in the shadow of the forests?
When shall I follow with my eyes
through the dust of the roads, a chariot racing along the course?

OENONE: What did you say?

PHAEDRA: I am a fool. Where am I and what did I say?
To what extremes did my desires and my mind wander?
I have lost my mind. The gods have deprived me of it.
Oenone, shame is written over my face.
You can see too clearly my shameful grief,
and my eyes, in spite of myself, are filling with tears.

OENONE: If you must blush, let it be from that silence
which still embitters the violence of your woe.
Rebellious to our attention and deaf to our speech,

will you without feeling let your days end?
What madness limits them in the midst of their course?
What witchcraft or what poison has dried up their source?
Three times have shadows darkened the sky
since sleep entered your eyes.
And three times has day dispelled the blackness of night
since your body has languished without food.
By what terrifying plan are you being tempted?
What right have you to attack your own life?
You offend the gods who are authors of that life.
You fail your husband to whom you are joined in pledge.
And finally you fail your wretched children
whom you place under a rigorous yoke.
Remember that a single day will take their mother away
and give hope to the son of the foreign woman,
to that implacable enemy of your family,
the son who was carried in the womb of an Amazon,
Hippolytus . . .

PHAEDRA: Stop!
OENONE: My reproach moves you!
PHAEDRA: Wretched woman, what name did you utter?
OENONE: How justified is your anger!
I am glad to see you startled by that fatal name.
You must live and not allow a Scythian's son,
as he crushes your children under his hateful authority,
to command the noblest offspring of Greece and of the gods.
Do not delay. Each moment may be mortal.
Bring back now some of your impaired strength
while your life, on the point of being extinguished,
may still endure in its flame and be rekindled.
PHAEDRA: I have too far prolonged its guilty length.
OENONE: What kind of remorse torments you?
What crime has brought about such bewilderment?
Have your hands been soiled by innocent blood?
PHAEDRA: Thanks to heaven my hands are not criminal.
Would that my heart were as innocent as they are!
OENONE: What terrible project have you conceived
that your heart is so anguished by it?
PHAEDRA: I have said enough to you. Spare me the rest.
I wish to die in order not to make so cruel a confession.
OENONE: Die and maintain your inhuman silence.
But look for someone else to close your eyes.
Although you are left with so little inner light,
my soul will descend to the dead first.
Many easy ways lead there,
and my grief will choose the shortest.
Cruel mistress, when did my devotion ever betray you?
Remember that when you were born, my arms received you.

I left everything for you, my country and children.
Is this the reward for my faithfulness?
PHAEDRA: What can you hope for by thus forcing me?
If I break my silence, horror will seize you.
OENONE: What could you say that would be worse
than the horror of seeing you die before my eyes?
PHAEDRA: When you learn of my crime and the fate crushing me,
I shall not die any less, and I shall die more guilty.
OENONE: For the sake of the tears I have shed for you,
here, at your faltering legs which I embrace,
free my mind from this fatal doubt.
PHAEDRA: Since you must know it, stand up.
OENONE: Speak! I am listening.
PHAEDRA: What can I tell her? Where can I begin?
OENONE: Stop offending me by this vain terror.
PHAEDRA: The hatred of Venus and her fatal anger
caused a perverted love to grow in my mother.
OENONE: You must forget that. Hide that memory
in unbroken silence throughout all the future.
PHAEDRA: My sister Ariadne, wounded by a strange love,
died at the rock where she was left.
OENONE: Why are you saying this? What mortal torment
urges you today to speak against all your family?
PHAEDRA: It is the will of Venus that of all my family
I shall die the last and the most wretched.
OENONE: Are you in love?
PHAEDRA: I feel all the furies of love.
OENONE: For whom?
PHAEDRA: You are going to hear the extreme of all horrors.
I love . . . At his fatal name I shudder and tremble.
I love . . .
OENONE: What man?
PHAEDRA: You know the son of the Amazon woman,
the prince I persecuted for so long?
OENONE: Hippolytus? All gods of heaven!
PHAEDRA: It was you who named him.
OENONE: My blood is congealed in all my veins.
The despair of this crime! The accursed race!
The unhappy voyage! Why did you have to come
to the shore of this dangerous land?
PHAEDRA: My suffering comes from farther back. Scarcely was I bound
by the marriage law to the son of Aegeus,
my peace of mind and happiness seeming secure,
than Athens showed my proud enemy.
When I saw him I blushed and turned pale.
I grew troubled and anguished.
I was unable to see and unable to speak.
My body was either cold or on fire.

I recognized Venus and her fearful passion,
and the fatal torment of a family she persecutes.
I believed I could turn this aside by faithful prayers.
I built a temple in her name and adorned it.
Every hour I offered victims
and sought in their pierced flanks to recover my mind.
It was a powerless remedy for an incurable love.
Vainly I burned incense on the altars.
While my lips implored the name of the goddess,
I was worshipping Hippolytus. And seeing him constantly,
even at the foot of the altars where I made sacrifices,
I offered up everything to him I dared not name.
Wherever I went, I avoided him,
but I would see him in the features of his father.
At last I revolted against myself.
I stirred up my anger in order to persecute him.
In order to banish the enemy I idolized,
I pretended to show the meanness of an unjust stepmother.
I urged his exile and my endless cries
wrenched him away from the arms of his father.
Then I breathed, Oenone, and after his absence,
my days were less troubled and passed innocently.
Submissive to my husband, and hiding my torment,
I took care of the children of his unhappy marriage.
My fate made all this useless.
When Theseus himself brought me to Troezen,
I came upon the enemy I had sent away.
And the wound of love opened again.
It is no longer fire hidden in my veins.
It is Venus beating down on her prey with all her strength.
My crime now justly terrifies me.
I despise my life and my horrible love.
By dying I wanted to protect my honor,
and blot out from the day so black a flame.
I was unable to bear your tears and your questions.
So I have told you all, and I have no regret for this,
provided you will respect my death
and will not afflict me with unjust reproaches.
Do not try to recall
the remnants of a life which is ready to die.

Scene 4. Phaedra, Oenone, Panope.

PANOPE: I tried to conceal the sad news from you,
but I am forced to disclose it now.
Death has taken your invincible husband.

Only you are ignorant of this disaster.
PHAEDRA: Panope, what are you saying?
PANOPE: I say you are deceived,
and there is no point in asking heaven for Theseus' return.
From vessels now in the harbor,
Hippolytus, his son, has just learned of his death.
Athens is divided over the choice of a master.
Some give their vote to your son the prince,
and others, forgetful of the laws of the state,
dare give their votes to the son of the foreign woman.
It is even rumored that a bold plot
plans to place on the throne Aricia and the blood of the Pallantides.
I had to warn you of this peril.
Even Hippolytus is making plans to leave for Athens,
and it is feared that if he appears in this unforeseen turmoil,
the fickle part of the populace will rally around him.
OENONE: That's enough, Panope. The Queen has heard you
and will not neglect this important warning.

Scene 5. Phaedra. Oenone.

OENONE: My lady, I had given up urging you to live,
and already I had planned to follow you to the tomb.
I had no more desire to turn you away from it.
But this unexpected catastrophe forces other obligations on you.
Your position has changed and taken on a new meaning.
The King is dead, my lady, and you must take his place.
His death leaves you a son to whom you owe everything.
If you die, he will be a slave; if you live, he will be a king.
Who will be a support for him in this affliction?
There will be no one to dry his tears,
and his innocent cries, heard on high by the gods,
will work hardship on his mother and anger her ancestors.
You must live. You have nothing with which to reproach yourself.
Your love has become an ordinary love.
In his death Theseus has dissolved the complications
which made of your passion a fearful crime.
Hippolytus is less to be feared by you now.
You can see him without feeling guilty.
If he is convinced of your hate,
he may lead the revolt against you!
You must remove the error and bend his heart.
He is the king of this happy land. Troezen is his lot.
But he knows that the law gives to your son
the proud ramparts which Minerva has built.
Both of you have a natural enemy.

You should unite in order to oppose Aricia.
PHAEDRA: I agree and I yield to your advice.
I will live, if I can move back into life,
and if the love for my son at this moment of mourning,
can bring life to my weak spirit.

ACT II

Scene 1. Aricia, Ismene.

ARICIA: You say Hippolytus wants to see me here?
He is looking for me and wants to make his farewell?
Do you speak truthfully, Ismene? Or are you mistaken?
ISMENE: This is the first reaction to the death of Theseus.
You must be ready, my lady, to see from all sides
people flocking to you who were rejected by Theseus.
You are now the mistress of your fate
and you may soon see all of Greece at your feet.
ARICIA: Are you sure, Ismene, it is not an ill-founded rumor?
Am I through being a slave? Have I no more enemies?
ISMENE: No, my lady, the gods no longer oppose you.
Theseus has joined the shades of your brothers.
ARICIA: Is it known what accident ended his life?
ISMENE: Unbelievable stories are circulating about his death.
It is said he was the ravisher of a new mistress
and was drowned in the sea because of his infidelity.
It was even said—and this circulated widely—
that he descended into hell with Pirithous
where he saw the Cocytus and its dark banks,
and appeared as a living man before the spirits of the dead;
but that he could not get out from that wretched place
and cross back over those shores which are never crossed twice.
ARICIA: Am I to believe that a mortal, before his last hour,
can penetrate the deep dwelling of the dead?
What magic drew him to those fearful shores?
ISMENE: Theseus is dead, my lady, and you alone doubt this.
Athens is afraid. Troezen has learned of it
and has already recognized Hippolytus as its king.
Phaedra, in his palace, is trembling for her son
and asking advice of her worried friends.
ARICIA: Do you believe that Hippolytus, more humane toward me
than his father was, will lighten my slavery?
Do you think he will pity my affliction?
ISMENE: I do, my lady!
ARICIA: But do you know the coldness of Hippolytus?

What meager hope makes you think he will pity me
and respect in me alone a sex he scorns?
For some time he has been avoiding us
and seeking places where we are not.
ISMENE: I know what is said about his lack of feeling,
but I have seen this proud Hippolytus in your presence,
and as I watched him, the reports about his inhumanity
increased my curiosity.
His appearance did not correspond to these rumors.
As soon as you looked at him, he seemed upset.
His eyes, trying in vain to avoid looking,
full of yearning, could not leave you.
The name of lover offends his pride perhaps,
but he has the eyes of a lover, if he has not the language.
ARICIA: Dear Ismene, my heart listens avidly
to your words which doubtless have no basis.
You who know me, is it believable
that the sad plaything of a pitiless fate,
a heart like mine, fed on bitterness and tears,
could know love and its mad grief?
Descendant of a king and a noble family,
I alone escaped the fury of the war.
I lost, in the flower of their youth,
six brothers . . . They were the hope of a famous lineage!
The sword cut them down, and the wet earth
sorrowfully drank the blood of Erechtheus' nephews.
Since their death, you know of the severe law
which forbids the Greeks to pity me.
It is feared that the rash flame of the sister
will one day reanimate the ashes of her brothers.
But you also know how scornfully
I watched the worry of the suspicious conqueror.
You know my long opposition to love
and my gratitude to unjust Theseus
whose rigorous law happily supported my scorn.
My eyes at that time had not seen his son.
It is not that, shamefully bewitched by my eyes,
I love in him his beauty and his esteemed grace,
gifts by which nature has honored him,
which he himself repudiates or seems to ignore.
I love and esteem in him the noblest riches,
the virtues of his father, and not the weaknesses.
Let me confess it, I love the noble pride
which has never bent under the yoke of passion.
Vainly was Phaedra honored by the sighs of Theseus.
I am prouder than she, and I flee the easy glory
of winning an homage offered to a hundred others,

and entering a heart which has opened to so many.
What I want most and what excites me,
is to make an inflexible heart capitulate,
to convey suffering to an insensitive spirit,
to chain a captive stupefied by his irons,
vainly rebellious against a yoke he desires.
It was less difficult to disarm Hercules than Hippolytus.
He was conquered more often and defeated more quickly
and offered less glory to the one who tamed him.
But dear Ismene, see how imprudent I am!
All kinds of resistance will oppose me.
Humbly, in my anguish, you will perhaps hear me
lament over that same pride I admire today.
Might I have changed . . .

ISMENE: You will hear this from Hippolytus himself.
He is coming here.

Scene 2. *Hippolytus, Aricia, Ismene.*

HIPPOLYTUS: Before leaving,
I wanted to tell you what you may expect.
My father is dead. My legitimate fears
foretold the reasons of his prolonged absence.
Death alone, limiting my father's dazzling work,
was able to hide him from the universe.
At last the gods gave over to the murderous Fates
the friend, the companion, the successor of Hercules.
I suppose that your hate, refusing him his greatness,
hears with displeasure these names that are due him.
One hope softens my painful grief.
I am able to free you from a severe bondage.
I revoke the laws whose harshness I deplored.
You are free in body and heart.
Here in Troezen which is now my kingdom,
where once my ancestor Pittheus ruled,
and where immediately I was recognized as king,
I set you free. You are freer than I am.

ARICIA: Your excessive kindness is embarrassing.
By honoring my misfortune with so generous an interest,
you place me, my lord, more than you realize,
under those austere laws from which you are freeing me.

HIPPOLYTUS: Athens, uncertain over the choice of a successor,
speaks of you, names me, and does not forget the son of the Queen.

ARICIA: They speak of me?

HIPPOLYTUS: I am not deceived,
and know that an insolent law rejects me.

Greece reproaches me for my foreign mother.
But if as a rival I had only my brother,
I have true rights over him
and could save him from ill-founded laws.
A more legitimate obstacle arrests my boldness.
I yield to you, or rather I give to you the place
and the scepter which long ago your ancestors received
from the famous mortal conceived by the Earth;
the adoption put it into the hands of Aegeus.
Athens, enriched and protected by my father,
joyously recognized so noble a king,
and relegated your wretched brothers to oblivion.
Athens now recalls you to within its walls.
Long enough has it suffered from such a quarrel.
The blood of your family sinking into its furrows
has nourished the field from which it arose.
Troezen will obey me. The countryside of Crete
has offered a rich asylum to the son of Phaedra.
Attica belongs to you. I leave now, and for you I will assemble
all the votes divided among us.
ARICIA: I am amazed and upset by all I hear.
I fear, yes, I fear a dream is deceiving me.
Am I awake? Can I trust such a plan?
What god conceived it in your heart, my lord?
How rightfully you are praised everywhere!
The truth about you is greater than your fame.
But for me, you sacrifice your own interests.
Isn't it enough that you don't hate me,
and that for so long a time you forbade your heart a hatred . . . ?
HIPPOLYTUS: Hatred for you, my lady?
Despite the bad traits ascribed to my pride,
do people think some monster bore me in its womb?
What savage character, what hardened hate
would not be softened in your presence?
Could I resist the deceptive charm . . .
ARICIA: What are you saying, my lord?
HIPPOLYTUS: I have gone too far.
Reason, it is easy to see, has given me to Love.
Since I have begun the breaking of my silence,
my lady, let me continue. Let me tell you
of a secret my heart can no longer contain.
You see before you a pitiful prince,
the memorable example of presumptuous pride.
In proud revolt against love,
I long insulted the chains of its captives.
As I deplored the shipwrecks of weak mortals,
I thought I would always watch these storms from the shore.

But now, enslaved to the common law,
I am carried off far from myself by some fury!
One moment conquered my bold imprudence.
My soul which has been so proud is now dependent.
For six months, ashamed and desperate,
bearing everywhere the arrow which pierces my flesh,
I have tested myself in vain against you and against myself.
When you are here, I leave; when you are absent, I see you.
Your image follows me in the depths of the forest.
The light of day and the shadows of night
retrace before me your charms which I avoid.
The rebel Hippolytus has been caught by you.
As a result of my useless efforts,
I search for myself and cannot find myself.
I cannot remember the lessons of Neptune.
The woods resound only with my laments,
and my idle horses have forgotten my voice.
Perhaps the story of so wild a love
makes you, as you listen to it, blush at what you have caused.
These are mad words from a heart which bows before you,
and I am a strange captive for so beautiful a bond.
But the offering should be dearer to your eyes.
Remember that I am speaking in a foreign language
and do not reject these ill-expressed vows
which, without you, Hippolytus would never have said.

Scene 3. *Hippolytus, Aricia, Theramenes, Ismene.*

THERAMENES: My lord, the Queen is here. She follows me.
   She wishes to see you.
HIPPOLYTUS: To see me?
THERAMENES: I do not know her purpose.
   But she has asked to see you.
   Phaedra wishes to speak to you before you leave.
HIPPOLYTUS: Phaedra? What can I say to her? What can she want?
ARICIA: My lord, you cannot refuse to see her.
   Even if you are convinced she is your enemy,
   you owe some degree of pity to her tears.
HIPPOLYTUS: In the meantime you are leaving, and I don't know
   whether I have offended you,
   whether the heart I have placed in your hands . . .
ARICIA: You may depart, Prince, and carry out your noble plans.
   Make Athens tributary of my power.
   I accept the gifts you offer me.
   But, to me, the large glorious empire
   is not the most precious of all your gifts.

Jean Racine: *Phaedra*

Scene 4. Hippolytus, Theramenes.

HIPPOLYTUS: Is all in readiness? The Queen is coming.
 Leave and see that everything is swiftly prepared for the departure.
 Give the signal and the orders, and then come back
 to relieve me from this conversation I dread.

Scene 5. Phaedra, Hippolytus, Oenone.

PHAEDRA (*to* OENONE): There he is. All my blood mounts to my heart.
 When I see him, I forget what I must say.
OENONE: Remember your son. You are his only hope.
PHAEDRA: I am told that you are about to leave us,
 my lord. I am here to join my tears with yours.
 I have come to you to speak of my alarm over my son.
 He has no father now, and the day is not far off
 which will make him the witness of my own death.
 A thousand enemies are already attacking him in his childhood.
 You alone can take up his defense against them.
 But a secret remorse upsets my mind.
 I fear I have closed your ears to his cries.
 I tremble lest your just anger
 will persecute him because of his hated mother.
HIPPOLYTUS: I would not stoop so low, my lady.
PHAEDRA: I would not complain if you hated me.
 You have seen me bent upon bringing you harm.
 But you were not able to read the deep meaning of my heart.
 I took care to show you only my enmity.
 Wherever I lived in this land, I could not bear your presence.
 I had spoken against you publicly and secretly,
 and wanted to be separated from you by oceans.
 By specific law I even forbade
 your name being said in my presence.
 Yet if suffering is measured by the offense,
 if hate alone can call up hate in you,
 never was a woman more worthy of pity,
 and less worthy, my lord, of your enmity.
HIPPOLYTUS: A mother, jealous of the rights of her own children,
 rarely pardons the ways of a stepson.
 I know this, my lady. Constant suspicions
 are the commonest results of a second marriage.
 Another woman would have been equally jealous of me
 and I would have been perhaps more outraged by her.
PHAEDRA: I swear to you, my lord, that Heaven
 exempted me from this common law
 and that a very different matter rages within me.

HIPPOLYTUS: There is no reason to be upset any longer.
It is possible that your husband still lives.
Heaven may yet grant to our tears his return.
Neptune may protect him. My father's prayers
to his patron god may be efficacious.
PHAEDRA: It is not possible to cross the river of the dead twice.
If Theseus saw those dark banks,
no god can send him back to you.
The greedy Acheron will not release its prey.
But what am I saying? He is not dead since he breathes in you.
I believe I still see my husband standing before me.
I see him. I speak to him, and my heart . . . What madness,
my lord! In spite of myself, I am telling you of my passion.
HIPPOLYTUS: I can see the marvelous power of your love.
Dead as he is, you can still see Theseus,
Your soul is still enflamed by his love.
PHAEDRA: Yes, Prince, I suffer and burn for Theseus.
I love, not the man seen by hell,
the fickle worshiper of so many mistresses,
who will dishonor the god of the dead;
but the faithful man, proud, even a bit barbaric,
seductive, young, enflaming all the hearts he passes,
the man like our gods, or like you as I see you now.
He had your bearing, your eyes, your speech,
and the noble modesty which colors your countenance,
when he crossed the waters to Crete.
The daughters of Minos had reason to think of him.
What were you doing then? Why, without Hippolytus,
did he assemble the heroes of Greece?
You were still too young, but why weren't you
on the ships which brought him to our shore?
The monster of Crete would have perished at your hand
in spite of all the detours of his vast retreat.
To unravel the uncertain complexity,
my sister would have armed your hand with the fatal thread.
No! For I would have preceded her in this plan.
Love would have instantly inspired me with the right thought.
Prince, it is I, Phaedra, who would have served you
and taught you the detours of the labyrinth.
For your beauty I would have undertaken every risk.
A mere thread would not have asserted a woman's love for you.
I am the companion you needed in your peril.
I would have walked ahead of you.
Phaedra going down into the labyrinth at your side,
would have been lost or saved with you.
HIPPOLYTUS: What are these words? Have you forgotten
that Theseus is my father and your husband?

PHAEDRA: What makes you think I have forgotten him?
Is it possible I have lost all sense of honor?
HIPPOLYTUS: Forgive me, my lady. I blush when I confess
that I wrongfully accused an innocent speech.
My shame will not allow me to stay here
and I am leaving . . .
PHAEDRA: You have heard too much, cruel Hippolytus!
I have told enough for you to understand all.
So, know Phaedra and know all her fury!
I am in love. But do not think that in this love
I approve of myself and find myself innocent,
or that any cowardly complacence has fortified the poison
of the mad love which bewilders my reason.
I am the wretched victim of heavenly vengeance
and hate myself more than you detest me.
The gods are my witnesses; those gods who in my heart
kindled the fire fatal to all of my family.
Those are the gods who took a cruel pride
in depraving the heart of a weak woman.
You yourself can remember the past.
It was not enough to avoid you, cruel Hippolytus, I exiled you.
I tried to appear odious and inhuman.
In order better to resist you, I sought to provoke your hate.
What profit came from all these useless efforts?
Your hate grew as my love grew.
Your sorrow gave you more charm than ever.
In tears and passion I languished and lost strength.
You needed only your eyes to be convinced of this,
if for one moment your eyes would look at me.
What am I saying? This shameful confession which I have just spoken,
Trembling for a son I did not dare betray,
I came to beg you not to hate him.
Feeble projects of a heart too full with what it loves!
Alas! I would speak to you only about yourself.
Avenge yourself, punish me for this odious love.
Worthy son of a hero who begot you,
free the universe of a monster who irritates you!
The widow of Theseus dares to love Hippolytus!
Believe me, this monster should not escape you.
Here is my heart. This is where your dagger should strike.
Eager to expiate its offense,
it moves forward to encounter your weapon.
Strike me. If you think my heart unworthy of your thrusts,
if your hate refuses me so sweet a punishment,
if your hand would be spotted with too vile a blood,
lend me your sword since I haven't your arm.
Give it over.

OENONE: What are you doing, my lady?
  Someone is coming. We must avoid witnesses.
  Come with me. Let us leave this shameful scene.
                                           (*They leave.*)

Scene 6. Hippolytus, Theramenes.

THERAMENES: Is it Phaedra who is leaving? or who is being taken away?
  Why, my lord, all these signs of lamentation?
  You are without a sword, speechless, colorless.
HIPPOLYTUS: Let us leave, Theramenes. My surprise is extreme.
  I cannot look at myself without a feeling of horror.
  Phaedra . . . No! Let this horrible secret remain buried in deep oblivion.
THERAMENES: The ship is ready, if you wish to leave.
  But Athens, my lord, has already spoken.
  Its leaders have taken the votes of all the tribes.
  Your brother has won. Phaedra has the upper hand.
HIPPOLYTUS: Phaedra?
THERAMENES: A herald, entrusted with the wishes of Athens,
  is coming to place the control of the state in her hands.
  Her son is king, my lord.
HIPPOLYTUS: Oh! you gods who know her,
  is it her virtue you are rewarding?
THERAMENES: Yet meanwhile a new rumor says the King is alive.
  It is believed that Theseus has been seen in Epirus.
  But I who looked for him there, know better . . .
HIPPOLYTUS: No matter. We must listen carefully to every rumor.
  Let us track down the source of this last report.
  If it does not warrant putting off my departure,
  we will leave. Whatever the cost may be,
  we will put the scepter into the hands worthiest of bearing it.

ACT III

Scene 1. Phaedra, Oenone.

PHAEDRA: Take away all the honors that are being sent to me.
  Stop bothering me. I will see no one.
  My poor mind will not be deceived, do you hear?
  It is better to hide me. I have said too much.
  My passionate outburst became too visible.
  I said what never should have been heard.
  And how he listened to me! With endless tricks
  he eluded my speech like a man heartless.

Jean Racine: *Phaedra*

All he wanted was to get away as fast as possible.
The blush on his face increased my shame.
Why did you obstruct my plan for death?
When his sword was about to pierce my heart,
did he turn pale because of me? did he snatch it away from me?
It was enough that my hand touched it but once—
it has become something loathsome for him.
The wretched sword would now profane his hands.
OENONE: In your affliction, these complaints
feed a passion you should extinguish.
Wouldn't it be better for you, a worthy descendant of Minos,
to seek repose in some other way,
to rule in opposition to an ingrate who plans to flee,
and fix your attention on the governing of the state?
PHAEDRA: You want me to rule? to submit a state to my law,
when my weak mind cannot rule itself?
when I have given up the control of my own senses?
when I can barely breathe under my shameful yoke?
when I am dying!
OENONE: You must leave.
PHAEDRA: I cannot leave him.
OENONE: You dared banish him. Haven't you the courage to avoid him?
PHAEDRA: There is no time left.
He knows my insane passion.
I have moved beyond the fixed limits of modesty.
I have shown my shame to the eyes of my conqueror,
and hope, in spite of myself, has entered my heart.
You yourself, revived my weakened strength,
and my life which was expiring through my lips;
you gave me new hope by your deceptive advice
and made me see that I could love him.
OENONE: Innocent or guilty of your afflictions,
I was capable of any act in order to rescue you.
But if ever an offense distressed you,
could you forget the scorn of a proud man?
He looked at you with stubborn heartlessness
and left you almost prostrate at his feet.
His barbaric pride made him odious to me.
I wish you had seen him through my eyes at that moment.
PHAEDRA: Oenone, he may set aside this pride which is offensive to you.
Brought up in the forest, he has its savagery.
Hardened by those barbaric principles, Hippolytus
is hearing about love for the first time.
Perhaps astonishment explains his silence,
and perhaps we have complained too bitterly.
OENONE: Remember that a barbarian woman gave him birth.
PHAEDRA: She was a Scythian and barbarian, but she knew love.

OENONE: He was destined to hate all women.
PHAEDRA: Then I shall never have a rival.
   Your advice is unseasonal, Oenone.
   Serve my madness and not my reason.
   To love he opposes an inaccessible heart;
   to attack it let us find the most vulnerable spot.
   The attractiveness of an empire seemed to affect him.
   Athens appealed to him and this he did not conceal.
   His ships were already pointed in that direction
   and the sails abandoned to the wind.
   Seek out this ambitious youth in my name,
   Oenone, and tempt him with my sparkling crown.
   Let him put on his own brow the sacred diadem.
   All I wish is the honor of attaching it.
   I will yield to him the power I cannot keep.
   He will teach my son the art of command.
   Perhaps he will serve as a father to him.
   In his control I place both mother and son.
   Try every means to bend his will.
   Your words will be more heeded than mine.
   Urge him and weep in his presence.
   Do not fear begging him with your voice.
   I approve of whatever you do. You are my one hope.
   Go now. When you return, I will decide my fate.

Scene 2. Phaedra.

PHAEDRA: Relentless Venus, who knows the shame
   of my ancestors, am I sufficiently humiliated?
   You could not increase your cruelty.
   Your triumph is complete; every arrow has reached its mark.
   If you now seek a new glory,
   turn to an enemy more rebellious than I.
   Hippolytus avoids you, and defying your wrath
   he has never knelt before your altars.
   Your name seems to offend his proud ears.
   Goddess, avenge yourself! My cause is yours!
   Make him fall in love.
   Have you returned already,
   Oenone? He hates me and will not listen to you.

Scene 3. Phaedra, Oenone.

OENONE: You must stifle all thought of this impossible love.
   my lady. Bring back your past virtue.
   The King, who was believed dead, is about to appear before you.

Jean Racine: *Phaedra*

    Theseus has come. Theseus is in Troezen.
    The crowds are rushing to see him.
    By your order, I had gone out and was looking for Hippolytus,
    when a great wave of shouting . . .
PHAEDRA: My husband is alive, Oenone! Say no more.
    I have confessed a guilty love which will outrage him.
    He is alive. I wish to know nothing else.
OENONE: What are you saying?
PHAEDRA: I predicted this, but you would not listen.
    Your tears prevailed over my remorse.
    This morning, had I died, I would have been wept for honorably.
    I took your advice and now I will die dishonored.
OENONE: You will die?
PHAEDRA: This is my fatal day.
    My husband is going to appear and his son with him.
    I will see the witness to my adulterous love
    watch the way I dare greet his father.
    My heart will be heavy with the sighs he did not hear,
    and my eyes wet with tears spurned by him.
    He is sensitive to Theseus' honor; do you think
    he will conceal the love with which I am burning?
    Will he allow the betrayal of his father and his king?
    Will he be able to suppress the horror he feels toward me?
    But what if he does keep silent? I know my infidelity,
    Oenone, and I am not one of those bold women
    who enjoy tranquillity in crime
    and who show a countenance that never blushes.
    I know all my madness and can call it back to mind.
    Even now I can feel that these walls and ceilings
    are going to speak out, and, prepared to accuse me,
    they are waiting for my husband in order to disillusion him.
    Let me die. Let me be freed from such horror.
    Is dying so great a disaster?
    Death creates no fear for the unhappy.
    All I fear is the name I will leave after me.
    What a dire heritage for my wretched children!
    The blood of Jupiter will have to swell their courage.
    Yet despite the pride in such noble blood,
    a mother's crime is a heavy burden.
    I tremble lest one day words of too much truth
    will reproach them for having had a guilty mother.
    Oppressed by such a weight, I tremble
    lest neither one nor the other ever dare to raise his eyes.
OENONE: Have no doubt, my lady, I pity both of them.
    Never was fear more justified than yours.
    But why expose them to such insults?
    Why take up arms against yourself?
    The die is cast. It will be said that Phaedra, guilty,

fled the presence of her deceived husband.
Hippolytus is fortunate in that
your death will lend support to his words
And how will I answer your accuser?
In his presence I shall be easily silenced.
I will see him rejoice over his frightful triumph,
relating your share to any ear that will listen.
Rather than see this I would be devoured by a flame from heaven!
Do not deceive me now. Do you still love him?
What are your sentiments now for this bold prince?

PHAEDRA: He has become for me a terrible monster.

OENONE: Why grant him then a complete victory?
You fear him. Be the first to accuse him
of the crime he may impute to you today.
Who will contradict you? Everything is against him:
his sword is fortunately left with you,
your present sorrow, your past irritation,
your persistent warnings to his father,
and his exile already obtained by you.

PHAEDRA: Are you asking me to persecute and blacken an innocent man?

OENONE: My zeal needs only your silence.
I tremble as you do, and feel some of your remorse—
I would be swifter in facing a hundred deaths—
but I will lose you except for this unfortunate remedy;
there is nothing I would not do to save you.
I will speak. Theseus, angered by what I will tell him,
will limit his vengeance to exiling his son.
A father, when he punishes remains a father.
His anger will be appeased with some slight rebuke.
But even if innocent blood has to be shed,
your threatened honor has the right to demand anything.
It is too rich a treasure to be compromised.
Whatever law it dictates, you must submit to it.
Your honor is in peril and to save it
you must sacrifice everything, even virtue.
People are coming. I see Theseus.

PHAEDRA: And I see Hippolytus.
In his insolent eyes I see my defeat.
Do what you wish. I yield to you.
In my anxiety I can do nothing myself.

Scene 4. *Theseus, Hippolytus, Phaedra, Oenone, Theramenes.*

THESUS: Fortune is no longer against me,
my lady, and into your arms it puts . . .

PHAEDRA: Stop, Theseus,

and do not profane such pure joy.
I do not deserve your tender attentions.
You have been offended. Jealous fortune
has not spared your wife in your absence.
Unworthy of pleasing or embracing you,
I can now think only of hiding.

Scene 5. *Theseus, Hippolytus, Theramenes.*

THESEUS: My son, what is this strange welcome I have received?
HIPPOLYTUS: Phaedra alone can explain the mystery.
But if my ardent prayers are able to move you,
allow me, my lord, not to see her anymore.
Allow your disturbed son forever
to disappear from the city your wife inhabits.
THESEUS: You intend to leave me?
HIPPOLYTUS: I did not seek her out.
It was you who brought her to these shores.
You were pleased, my lord, when you left, to entrust
Aricia and the Queen to my care.
I was charged with the duty of watching over them.
But now no duty keeps me here.
My idle youth has practiced its skill
for long enough in the forests on insignificant enemies.
This is an unworthy leisure. Allow me to leave
and dip my javelins in more glorious blood.
You had not yet reached my present age,
when more than one tyrant, more than one savage monster
had felt the strength of your arm.
You had already persecuted violence
and made safe the banks of the two seas.
The free traveler had no fear of attack.
Hercules, hearing the skill of your exploits
was resting from his labors because of you.
And I, the unknown son of so famous a father,
am still unequal to the fame of my mother.
Let my courage at last be put to the test.
If some monster has escaped you,
allow me to place at your feet its honorable remains,
or allow the enduring memory of a noble death,
immortalizing a life so worthily cut short,
to prove to the universe that I was your son.
THESEUS: What is this? What horror in this house
causes everyone to flee from my presence?
If I am so little wanted and so feared,
why was I taken from my prison?

I had only one friend. His imprudent desire
was to abduct the wife of the tyrant of Epirus.
Against my will I served his passionate plan.
But angry fate blinded both of us.
The tyrant caught me unarmed and without defense.
I saw Pirithous, whom I wept for,
delivered by that barbarian to the cruel beasts
he fed on the blood of wretched men.
He locked me up in dark caverns,
deep in the earth and close to the empire of the dead.
At last, after six months, the gods took pity on me.
I was able to trick my guards
and I purged the world of a perfidious enemy.
He himself became food for his beasts.
And now when joyfully I draw near
to those I hold dearest in the world,
what do I find? When my soul, recovering,
wants to behold again these dear ones,
they welcome me in trembling and fear.
Everyone leaves, all refuse to embrace me.
As I feel the terror I inspire,
I wish I were still in the prisons of Epirus.
You must speak. Phaedra complains that I have been outraged.
Who has betrayed me? Why have I not been avenged?
Has Greece, which I have served so often,
given refuge to the criminal?
You don't answer? Is my own son
an accomplice of my enemies?
I must know. This doubt is too heavy to bear.
What is the crime and who is guilty?
Phaedra will have to explain why she is troubled.

Scene 6. *Hippolytus, Theramenes.*

HIPPOLYTUS: What was the meaning of Phaedra's speech?
    It chilled me. She is still a prey to her extreme fury.
    Does she intend to accuse herself and destroy herself?
    What will the King say? What deadly poison
    has love spread throughout the house!
    I am consumed by a love he will hate and blame.
    Today I am the same as he once knew me,
    though I am terrified by black forebodings.
    But innocence has nothing to fear.
    Let me find some way
    by which I may move my father to pity
    and tell him of my love, which he may oppose
    but which he is powerless to destroy.

ACT IV

Scene 1. Theseus, Oenone.

THESEUS: Ah! What are you telling me? What kind of a traitor
 prepared this outrage to his father's honor?
 How relentless this fate of mine!
 I don't know where I am or where I am going.
 Is this the reward for a father's care?
 Could any plan or thought be more loathsome?
 In order to succeed with this criminal love,
 he resorted to force.
 I know this sword which he used in his passion.
 I armed him with it, but for a nobler use.
 Couldn't he be restrained by the bonds of family?
 Why did Phaedra put off his punishment?
 Why did she protect him by her silence?
OENONE: My lord, she was protecting you, his father.
 Ashamed of the attempt of her passionate lover,
 ashamed of the criminal light in his eyes,
 Phaedra was dying. With her own hands
 she would have taken her life.
 I saw her raise her arm and I ran to save her.
 I saved her life for your love.
 And because I pitied both her dismay and your alarm,
 I have interpreted, in spite of myself, her tears to you.
THESEUS: The liar! He couldn't help turning pale,
 through fear, when he saw me. I saw him tremble.
 I was surprised by his lack of joy.
 He embraced me coldly and my love was chilled.
 But had he felt already in Athens
 this guilty love which devours him?
OENONE: My lord, remember how the Queen complained.
 This criminal love was the cause of her hate.
THESEUS: And so the passion began again in Troezen?
OENONE: I have told you everything that took place.
 But I have left the Queen too long with her grief.
 Allow me to leave you and go to her.

Scene 2. Theseus, Hippolytus.

THESEUS: There he is! By his noble bearing
 anyone else would be deceived as I was.
 How is it that on the countenance of an adulterer
 there shines the expression of virtue and innocence?
 Shouldn't we be able to recognize
 by certain signs the heart of a traitor?

HIPPOLYTUS: May I ask you what chagrin,
  my lord, has changed your noble face?
  Won't you trust me with your secret?
THESEUS: Liar! How do you dare come into my presence?
  Monster, whom Heaven has spared too long!
  You are the last of the bandits. I have slain all the others.
  After the passion of a horrible love
  bore you to your father's bed,
  you dare come before the man you wronged,
  you come into this place reeking with your infamy.
  You will not find, under a foreign sky,
  any land where my name is unknown.
  Leave now. Do not come here defying my hate
  and tempting an anger which I can scarcely restrain.
  I have my share of eternal opprobrium
  for having begotten so criminal a son,
  and must not allow your death, which would shame my memory,
  to desecrate the glory of my work.
  Go, I say. If you do not want a sudden punishment
  to add you to the rogues I have punished,
  see to it that the sun which lightens our world
  never beholds you again walking on these shores.
  Once more, go! Go forever
  and purge my land of your presence.
  Hear me, Neptune. If once my courage
  rid your banks of infamous cutthroats,
  remember that as a reward for my efforts,
  you promised to grant the first of my prayers.
  During the long cruel days in prison
  I did not call upon your immortal power.
  Greedy for the help I expect from you,
  I held back my prayers for a greater need.
  Today I beseech you. Avenge a wretched father.
  I give over this traitor to the fullness of your anger.
  Stifle with his own blood his licentious desires.
  Theseus will measure your generosity by your wrath.
HIPPOLYTUS: So Phaedra accuses Hippolytus of a criminal love!
  Such horror makes me speechless.
  So many attacks rain on me at once
  that I have no words to say and no voice with which to speak them . . .
THESEUS: Traitor, you imagined that in cowardly silence
  Phaedra would bury your brutish insolence.
  When you fled, you should not have left
  in her hands the sword which condemns you.
  Or rather you should have completed your attack,
  and taken from her both speech and life.
HIPPOLYTUS: I should tell the truth

of so black a lie that has overwrought you.
But I will not reveal a secret concerning you.
Please approve of the respect which forbids me to speak.
Do not increase the torments you already have.
Examine my life and remember who I am.
Small crimes always precede major crimes.
A man who has first transgressed the laws,
can violate then the most sacred rights.
Crime has its degrees as virtue has.
Never have you seen timid innocence
suddenly pass to extreme licence.
One day is not enough to make of a virtuous man
a perfidious murderer and an incestuous coward.
Conceived in the womb of a chaste heroine,
I have not betrayed the origin of her blood.
Pittheus, looked upon by all men as a sage,
was my teacher when I left my mother's care.
I do not wish to boast or speak of myself,
but I think I have shown hatred
for the crimes that are ascribed to me.
Hippolytus is known for this in all of Greece.
I have made virtue blunt.
The unbending rigor of my temperament is known.
Daylight is not purer than the depths of my heart.
And yet you say Hippolytus, intoxicated with profane love, has . . .
THESEUS: This is the very pride which condemns you.
I can see the odious principle of your coldness.
Phaedra alone bewitched your senses,
and for any other woman your heart
scorned an innocent love.
HIPPOLYTUS: No, father—I have concealed this too long—my heart
did not scorn an innocent love.
At your feet I will confess my real crime.
I am in love, but in defiance of your law.
Aricia has enslaved me to her law.
The daughter of Pallas has conquered your son.
I worship her. Rebellious to your command,
my heart breathes and yearns only for her.
THESEUS: You love Aricia? This is an obvious trick.
You acknowledge one crime in order to escape another.
HIPPOLYTUS: My lord, I have avoided her for six months,
and I still love her.
I came here in great fear to tell you.
Will nothing clear away your error?
What awesome oath is needed to reassure you?
By heaven and earth and all of nature . . .
THESEUS: Perjury is always the recourse of scoundrels.

Spare me any more of your words,
if they are the only pledge of your false virtue.
HIPPOLYTUS: It seems false and deceptive to you.
Phaedra in her heart does me better justice.
THESEUS: Your impudence arouses my anger.
HIPPOLYTUS: How long will you banish me and to what place?
THESEUS: If you were beyond the column of Alcides,
I would still think you too close.
HIPPOLYTUS: Charged with the terrible crime you suspect me of,
who will pity me when you send me away?
THESEUS: Seek out those friends whose fatal character
honors adultery and applauds incest,
traitors and ingrates without honor, without principle,
worthy of protecting a man like you.
HIPPOLYTUS: You keep speaking to me of incest and adultery.
I will hold my tongue. But Phaedra comes from a mother,
Phaedra is from a lineage—and my lord, you know this—
more filled with horrors than mine.
THESEUS: Now your rage has lost all restraint.
For the last time, leave my presence.
Leave now. Do not wait for an angry father
to expel you shamelessly from this land.

Scene 3. Theseus.

THESEUS: Hippolytus, you are rushing to your death.
Neptune, god of the sea, who is feared by other gods,
gave me his word and will carry it out.
An avenging god is at your heels. You will not escape him.
I loved you once, and in spite of your crime
my heart feels for you now.
But you forced me to condemn you.
Never has a father been more outraged.
Gods in heaven, see my grief!
Why did I ever beget so criminal a child?

Scene 4. Phaedra, Theseus.

PHAEDRA: My lord, I have come to you in terror and fear.
Your loud voice reached my ears.
I am afraid your threat was carried out too swiftly.
If there is still time, spare your son.
Don't turn against your family, I beg you.
Save me from the horror of hearing your blood cry out.
Do not plunge me into everlasting grief

for spilling your own son's blood.
THESEUS: Phaedra, I have spilled no blood.
Yet the ingrate has not escaped.
An immortal has charge of his death.
Neptune has promised me this. You will be avenged.
PHAEDRA: Neptune has promised? What angry prayers . . . ?
THESEUS: Are you afraid they will not be heeded?
Join yours with my just prayers.
Tell me his crimes in all their blackness.
Stir up my anger which has been too slow.
You do not yet know all of his crimes.
His fury lashed out at you,
and said your mouth is full of lies and deceit.
He insists that Aricia is the mistress of his heart,
and that he loves her.
PHAEDRA: What, my lord?
THESEUS: He said it to me.
But I saw through this obvious trick.
Let us hope for swift justice from Neptune.
I myself am going to his altars
to urge him to carry out his immortal promises.

Scene 5. *Phaedra, Oenone.*

PHAEDRA: What is this he said to me?
What fire flares up again in my heart?
What thunderbolt, O gods, what fatal news!
I came here to save my son.
I pulled myself away from terrified Oenone
and gave over to the remorse which has tormented me.
How far would this repentance have taken me?
I would have perhaps at last accused myself.
Perhaps, if my voice had not been cut off,
the terrible truth would have escaped from me.
Hippolytus feels nothing for me!
Aricia has his love and his faith!
When before my prayers the ruthless ingrate
armed himself with a haughty look and a proud countenance,
I believed that his heart, always closed to love,
was hostile equally to all women.
But one woman did affect his feelings.
One woman did find grace before his cruel eyes.
Perhaps he does have a heart easy to move.
I am the only one he could not bear.
Should I take on, then, the duty of defending him?

Scene 6. Phaedra, Oenone.

PHAEDRA: Dear Oenone, do you know what I have just learned?
OENONE: No, but I can't conceal that I am terrified for you.
   I tremble at the reason which made you come here.
   I fear some madness that will be fatal.
PHAEDRA: Who would have believed it, Oenone? I had a rival.
OENONE: What, my lady?
PHAEDRA: Hippolytus is in love, and I cannot doubt it.
   That wild enemy who could not be tamed,
   who was offended by respect and irritated by complaints,
   that tiger whom I never approached without fear,
   submissive and docile has recognized a conqueror.
   Aricia found the way to his heart.
OENONE: Aricia?
PHAEDRA: This suffering I had not yet felt!
   I had saved myself for this new torment.
   Whatever I suffered up until now: fears and passion,
   the fury of love and the horror of remorse,
   the unbearable pain of a cruel refusal—
   all that was but a weak foretaste of the torment I endure now.
   They are in love! By what spell were my eyes deceived?
   How did they meet? How long have they loved? Where did they meet?
   You knew this. Why did you let me be tricked?
   Couldn't you have told me about their furtive passion?
   Were they often seen speaking and looking for one another?
   Did they hide in the depths of the forest?
   Ah! It was permissible for them to see one another.
   Heaven approved the innocence of their sighs.
   Without remorse they could heed their instincts for love.
   Every day rose clear and serene for them.
   But I hid from the day and escaped from the light
   as if I were rejected by all nature.
   The only god I dared beseech was death.
   I waited for the moment of death,
   and fed on sorrow and tears.
   Yet when I was too closely watched in my suffering
   I did not dare give full vent to your tears.
   As I trembled, I felt that fatal pleasure,
   and with a serene face disguising my anguish,
   I had often to deprive myself of my own tears.
OENONE: But what will come of their vain love?
   They will not meet again.
PHAEDRA: Their love will continue always.
   At this very moment—oh! let me not think of it!—
   they are defying the fury of a jealous woman.
   Even despite the exile which will separate them,

they swear a thousand times not to leave one another.
I cannot bear their happiness which insults me,
Oenone. Take pity on my jealous rage.
Aricia must be killed. We must arouse the anger
of my husband against a hated family.
He must not stop with easy penalties.
The sister's crime exceeds her brothers'.
I will implore him in my jealous rage.
What am I doing? Have I lost control of my mind?
I am jealous! and Theseus is the man I am to implore!
My husband is living, and I still burn with passion.
And for whom? to whose heart are my prayers addressed?
Every word I say adds to my panic.
My crimes have become monstrous.
They include incest and imposture.
My hands of an assassin, so eager for revenge,
are about to plunge into innocenet blood.
And I continue to live. I am still seen
by the holy sun from which I am descended.
My ancestor is the father and the master of the gods.
The heavens, the entire universe is full of my ancestors.
Where can I hide? Let me turn to the darkness of Hades.
What am I saying? There my father holds the fatal urn.
The gods placed it in his severe hands.
In hell Minos judges the pale ghosts of men.
How his terrified spirit will tremble
when his daughter comes before him
and confesses these misdemeanors
and crimes which are unknown to hell!
Father, what will you say at such a horrible spectacle?
I can see the solemn urn drop from your hands.
I can see you looking for some new punishment
and becoming the executioner of your own family.
Forgive me. A cruel god laid waste to your family.
Behold his vengeance in the madness of your child.
Alas! my unhappy heart did not gather the fruit
of the terrible crime whose shame haunts me.
Pursued by woe until my last breath,
I relinquish in torment a painful life.
OENONE: My lady, you must repulse this ill-founded terror.
Consider differently an excusable error.
You are in love. Such a fate cannot be overcome.
You were impelled by some magical power of the gods.
Is this so unusual a prodigy for mankind?
Are you the only victim of love?
Weakness is innate in all of us.
You are mortal and you are involved in the fate of mortals.

You complain of a yoke imposed for all time.
Even the gods, inhabitants of Olympus,
who by scandal terrify criminals,
have sometimes suffered from illicit passion.

PHAEDRA: What are you saying? What advice do you dare offer me?
Are you bent on poisoning me to the very end,
wretched Oenone? This is how you ruined me.
You turned me back to the daylight I was fleeing.
Your entreaties made me forget my duty.
I was avoiding Hippolytus, and you forced me to look upon him.
What right did you have? Why did your imperious words,
as they accused him, blacken his life?
He may die because of this, and the sacrilegious vow
of a wrathful father is perhaps already carried out.
I will heed you no longer, for you are a monster.
Leave my presence.
I wish now to be alone with my tortured fate.
May the justice of heaven reward you,
and may your punishment forever terrify
all those who, like you, with loathsome means,
feed the weakness of unhappy rulers,
urge them to submit to the desires of their heart,
and dare open up the way to crime!
Detestable flatterers, they are the most pernicious gift
the anger of the gods can give to princess!

OENONE (*alone*): I gave up everything and did everything
in order to serve her.
I deserve the reward she has now given me.

ACT V

Scene 1. *Hippolytus, Aricia.*

ARICIA: Can you be silent in such extreme danger?
Can you permit your loving father to remain in error?
Cruel Hippolytus, if you scorn the power of my tears,
if, without pain, you consent to seeing me no more,
you will leave and we shall separate,
but at least safeguard your life.
Defend your honor from a shameful reproach,
and force your father to withdraw his vows.
There is still time. Why, through what caprice,
are you leaving the way open to your accuser?
Inform Theseus.

HIPPOLYTUS: I have said everything I could.

Should I have revealed the wrong of his wife?
In telling him the full details,
should I have covered his face with unworthy shame?
You alone saw through the hateful mystery.
I have only you and the gods with whom I can speak.
This is the measure of my love: I could not hide from you
what I wanted to hide from myself.
But remember the seal of secrecy under which I told you all.
You must forget, if you can, that I spoke to you.
Your lips that are so pure,
must never tell this horrible adventure.
I will trust the justice of the gods.
It is for their own good to justify me.
Phaedra one day will be punished for her crime,
and will not escape a deserving ignominy.
This is the one mark of respect I demand from you.
Everything else I permit my free anger.
Leave the slavery to which you have been reduced.
Dare to follow me, dare to come with me in my flight.
You must pull yourself away from this fatal, profaned place
where virtue breathes a poisoned air.
To conceal your abrupt departure,
profit from the confusion created by my disgrace.
I can assure you of the means for this flight.
Your only guards here are my men.
Powerful defenders will take our side.
Argos has asked us to come, and Sparta.
We will speak of our cause to our common friends
and prevent Phaedra, as she gathers what fortune we abandon,
from expelling both of us from the paternal throne
and promising her son my death and yours.
This is the right moment for us to seize.
What fear holds you back? You seem uncertain.
Your rights and your interest guide me in this plan.
I am burning with anticipation, and you seem coldly indifferent.
Are you afraid of following in the steps of an exile?
ARICIA: How precious, my lord, such an exile would be!
If I could join with your fate, how joyously
I would live far from the rest of mankind!
But we are not united in marriage.
Can I honorably escape this place with you?
I know that I can free myself
from your father without harming even the strictest honor.
It would not be an escape from my own family.
Escape is permitted if it is escape from a tyrant.
But you love me, my lord, and my honor . . .
HIPPOLYTUS: No, no! I have not forgotten your reputation.

A nobler plan brings me here before you.
Flee from your enemies and follow your husband.
Since it is the will of Heaven, we are free in our woes.
The pledge of our word depends on no one.
Marriage is not always surrounded by torches.
At the gates of Troezen, in the midst of tombs,
ancient sepulchers of the princes of my race,
is a sacred temple which does not allow perjury.
In that place men do not dare take false oaths.
The dishonest man would receive a swift punishment.
He would fear inevitable death.
The consequence of a lie would be too fearful.
There, if you believe my words, we will take
the solemn oath of eternal love.
Our witness will be the god we revere in that temple.
We will pray that he be a father for us.
I will call upon the names of the most sacred of the gods.
Chaste Diana, proud Juno,
all of the gods, witnesses of my affection,
will vouch for the sincerity of my holy promises.
ARICIA: The King is coming. You must leave, Hippolytus, at
this very moment.
I will stay briefly to conceal my departure.
Go. Leave me a faithful guide
who will direct my timid steps to you.

Scene 2. *Theseus, Aricia, Ismene.*

THESEUS: O gods, bring me light and show me
the truth I am searching for in this palace.
ARICIA: Make preparations, dear Ismene, and be ready for our flight.

Scene 3. *Theseus, Aricia.*

THESEUS: You change color, my lady, and seem embarrassed.
What was Hippolytus doing here?
ARICIA: My lord, he was saying a last farewell.
THESEUS: Your eyes subjugated his rebellious heart.
His first sighs were because of you.
ARICIA: My lord, I cannot hide the truth from you.
He did not inherit the unjust hate you feel.
He did not treat me as a criminal.
THESEUS: I know. He swore eternal love to you.
Do not put your trust in his inconstant heart.
He swore the same love to others that he swore to you.

ARICIA: Hippolytus, my lord?
THESEUS: You should have made him less fickle.
How could you stand sharing him with someone else?
ARICIA: And how can you allow such horrible words
to darken the days of so noble a life?
Have you so little knowledge of his heart?
Can't you discern the difference between crime and innocence?
Must you be the only one who cannot see
his virtue which shines forth for everyone else?
You have given him over to the malice of gossip.
You must repent of your homicidal prayers.
You should fear, my lord, that Heaven in its rigor
hates you enough to carry out your wishes.
In its wrath Heaven often receives our victims.
Its gifts are often the punishment for our crimes.
THESEUS: It will do you no good to cover up his sin.
Your love blinds you in favor of the ingrate.
I have put my faith in certain irreproachable witnesses.
I have seen the sincere tears of a woman.
ARICIA: Take care, my lord. Your invincible hands
have delivered mankind from countless monsters.
But all of them are not destroyed, and you allow
one of them to . . . Your son, my lord, has forbidden me to speak.
I know of the respect he will always have for you.
If I spoke now, I would grieve him.
Let me imitate his discreetness and leave your presence
so that I will not be forced to break my silence.

Scene 4. Theseus.

THESEUS: What is she trying to say? hWat is concealed
in the words which she only half uttered?
Are they bent on confusing me by some vain pretense?
Are they both agreed to torture me?
In spite of the severity of my judgment,
I can hear a plaintive cry in the depths of my heart.
A secret pity has taken hold of me and is affecting me.
I will question Oenone a second time.
I must learn more about the entire crime.
Guards, have Oenone come here alone.

Scene 5. Theseus, Panope.

PANOPE: My lord, I do not know what the Queen is planning,
but from her terrible state I fear the worst.

Her face shows a deathlike despair.
Already she has the pallor of death.
Oenone, whom she sent away in shame,
has already hurled herself into the sea.
We do not know how this madness came about,
but the waves have taken her from us forever.

THESEUS: What are you saying?

PANOPE: Her death did not quiet the Queen.
The anguish of her heart seemed to get worse.
From time to time, to diminish her secret grief,
she lifts up her children and covers them with tears,
and then suddenly, forgetting her maternal love,
she pushes them aside with horror.
She wanders about aimlessly.
Bewildered, she does not recognize us.
Three times she began to write, and changing her mind,
three times she tore up the letter.
I beg you see her, my lord, I beg you to help her.

THESEUS: So, Oenone is dead, and Phaedra wants to die.
Call back my son, let him come and defend himself!
I want him to speak. I am ready now to hear him.
Do not pour down your fatal blessings,
Neptune! I prefer now not to have my prayers heeded.
I have perhaps believed witnesses who were not trustworthy.
I raised my cruel hands to you too early.
Such vows I have taken would lead me to despair!

Scene 6. *Theseus, Theramenes.*

THESEUS: Is it you, Theramenes? What have you done with my son?
I gave him to you at an early age.
But what is the reason for your sadness and your tears?
What has happened to my son?

THERAMENES: Your solicitude comes too late.
Your affection is useless. Hippolytus is dead.

THESEUS: Ah!

THERAMENES: I have seen the most loving of mortals perish,
and I can say also, my lord, the least guilty.

THESEUS: My son is dead? When I am opening my arms to receive him,
did the impatient gods hasten his end?
How has he been taken from me? What thunderbolt fell?

THERAMENES: We had just left the gates of Troezen.
He was on his chariot. His grieving guards,
drawn up around him, were silent as he was.
Sadly he was taking the road to Mycenae.

His hand had loosened the reins on his horses.
These proud beasts which could be seen once
ardent and noble obeying his voice,
now with sad eyes and lowered heads,
seemed to respond to his grieving thought.
A terrible cry, coming from below the waves,
at that moment cut through the quiet of the scene.
From the bowels of the earth a formidable voice
wailed in answer to the fearful cry.
Our blood froze in our hearts.
The attentive horses reared in terror
while over the flat surface of the sea
a gigantic wave of foam rose up.
It came close, broke and spewed out in full sight,
in its waves of foam, a raging monster.
Its broad head was armed with dangerous horns.
Yellowish scales covered its body.
Was it an untamed bull or a bold dragon?
Its back was twisted in coils.
Its long shrieks shook the seacoast.
Heaven was horrified at seeing such a wild monster.
The earth was shocked and the air grew infected.
The wave, which had brought it, recoiled in terror.
Everyone fled—a man's courage would have been useless—
and sought shelter in the neighboring temple.
Only Hippolytus, as the worthy son of a hero,
stopped his horses, seized his spear,
and rushing at the monster, hurled his weapon with good aim
and tore a wide gash in the animal's side.
It leaped, and roaring with rage and pain,
fell at the feet of the horses,
rolled over, and opened a flaming mouth.
Fire, blood, and fumes covered them.
Fright overcame them, and this time deaf,
they heeded neither the reins nor their master's voice.
Vainly Hippolytus tried to control them.
They reddened their bridles with bloody foam.
Some say that in this great melee a god was seen
flogging their dust-covered sides.
Through fear they plunged from the rocks.
The axle creaked and broke. Courageous Hippolytus
saw his broken chariot split into fragments.
He himself fell, twisted into the harness.
Forgive my grief. This cruel picture
will be for me an eternal source of sorrow.
My lord, I saw your poor son

dragged by the horses his hand had fed.
He tried to call them, but his voice frightened them.
They kept running until all of his body was open wound.
The field resounded with our cries of grief.
They finally slowed their wild race,
and stopped, not far from those ancient tombs.
where lie the cold remains of his royal ancestors.
Anguished I rushed up and his guard followed me.
The trail of his noble blood led us.
The rocks were covered with it and the thorns
bore blood-stained bits of his hair.
I reached him and called to him. Then stretching out his hand,
he opened his eyes and closed them again.
"Heaven," he said, "is snatching from me an innocent life.
After my death, take care of poor Aricia.
Dear friend, if one day my father learns the truth,
and pities the fate of a falsely accused son,
tell him, if he wishes to appease my blood and my unquiet shade,
to treat his captive with gentleness,
to give back to her . . ." At those words the hero died
and left in my arms a disfigured body,
in which the anger of the gods triumphed,
and which his own father would not recognize.

THESEUS: Oh son! You were the hope I have lost!
Oh! relentless gods, you served me too well.
Nothing remains now but mortal grief.

THERAMENES: Modest Aricia came then.
My lord, she was fleeing your wrath
and accepting him as husband in the sight of the gods.
On drawing near, she saw the grass streaked with blood,
and then she saw (what an object for the eyes of a lover!)
Hippolytus stretched out, mangled and without color.
For some time she would not believe her affliction,
and not recognizing the hero she loved,
she kept calling for Hippolytus.
Finally she realized he was there before her,
and turning her face toward heaven,
cold, grieving, and almost lifeless,
she fell in a faint at the feet of her lover.
Ismene was close by. Ismene weeping
brought her back to life, or rather to tears.
And I, cursing my life,
came here to tell you that last wish of a hero,
and acquit myself of the painful duty
he asked of me as he died.
But I see his mortal enemy coming.

Jean Racine: *Phaedra*

Scene 7. *Theseus, Phaedra, Theramenes, Panope, Guards.*

THESEUS: My son is dead, Phaedra, and you are triumphant.
 I was right in my fears and suspicions
 when I excused him in my heart.
 But now he is dead. Take your victim.
 Gloat over his loss, whether just or unjust.
 I will not be undeceived, Phaedra.
 I believe him guilty since you have accused him.
 His death gives me enough reason for lament
 without my looking for some terrible enlightenment,
 which would not bring him back to life
 but would only increase my sorrow.
 Far from you and far from these shores,
 let me flee the image of my bleeding son.
 Obsessed with this memory of death,
 I will banish myself from the entire universe.
 Everything rises up against my injustice.
 The glory of my name increases my suffering.
 If I were less well known by men, I could hide more easily.
 I detest now the help which the gods have given me.
 I am going away in order to bewail their murderous favors,
 and I shall stop beseeching them with useless prayers.
 Whatever their power be, their fatal generosity
 cannot replace what they have taken from me.
PHAEDRA: No, Theseus, I must break my silence.
 I must give your son his innocence.
 He was not guilty.
THESEUS: Wretched father that I am!
 It was on your word I condemned him.
 Cruel Phaedra, how can you be forgiven?
PHAEDRA: I have but few moments left. You must hear me, Theseus.
 I was the impure, the incestuous one
 who hated to look at chaste respectful Hippolytus.
 Heaven put this fatal love in my heart.
 Wicked Oenone did all the rest.
 She feared that Hippolytus, learning of my madness,
 would tell of a passion which so horrified him.
 Profiting from my extreme weakness,
 she hastened to denounce him to you.
 She has punished herself, and escaping from my wrath,
 she sought in the sea an easy death.
 The sword would have already severed my life,
 if I had not allowed my suspected virtue to lament.
 I wanted to tell you of my remorse
 and descend by a slower path to the dead.

I have taken a poison which Medea brought to Athens,
It is coursing now through my veins.
It has already reached my heart
and has cast an unknown cold upon it.
There is a cloud over my eyes.
I can hardly see the sky and you whom my presence insults.
Death, stealing the light from my eyes
gives back to the day all of its purity.
PANOPE: She is dying, my lord!
THESEUS: Would that the memory
of so black a deed might die with her!
Now that I know my error,
I want to mingle my tears with the blood of my son.
I want to embrace what is left of his body
and expiate the madness of a vow I loathe.
I will give him the honors he deserves,
and to appease his troubled spirit,
I will, despite the plottings of her guilty family,
ask Aricia to be my daughter from today on.

Index of Proper Names

Acheron, river in Hell.
Aegeus, father of Theseus.
Alcides, columns of Hercules.
Amazon, one of a race of female warriors.
Antiope, mother of Hippolytus.
Argos, town in Greece.
Ariadne, daughter of Minos and sister of Phaedra.
Cercyon, fighter of Arcadia.
Cocytus, river in Hell.
Crete, island in the Mediterranean.
Diana, goddess of the forest and the hunt.
Elis, country of ancient Greece.
Epidaurus, city of ancient Greece.
Epirus, country of ancient Greece.
Erechtheus, king, ancestor of Aricia.
Hercules, Greek hero, celebrated for his strength.
Icarus, son of Daedalus, the architect who invented the labyrinth in Crete. Together they fled Crete on wings of feather and wax. Icarus flew too close to the sun, his wings melted, and he fell into the sea and drowned.
Juno, goddess of marriage.
Jupiter, god of the heavens. Minos descended from him.

Medea, wife of Jason, magician famous for her poisons.
Minerva, goddess of Athens.
Minos, father of Phaedra.
Minotaur, half-bull, half-man, offspring of Pasiphaë and a white bull. Was confined to labyrinth built by Daedalus. Theseus went to Crete to kill the Minotaur.
Mycenae, city of Greece.
Neptune, god of the sea.
Olympus, mountain in Thessaly, abode of the Olympian gods.
Pallantides, the sons of Pallas, brothers of Aricia. Theseus had them killed because he believed them a threat to his rule of Athens.
Pallas, father of Aricia, king of Athens.
Pasiphaë, mother of Phaedra.
Periboea, maiden who was to be sacrificed to the Minotaur and whom Theseus saved.
Pirithous, friend of Theseus.
Pittheus, maternal ancestor of Theseus.
Procrustus, brigand of Attica.
Salamis, city of Cyprus.
Scythia, ancient name of parts of Europe.
Sinnis, brigand of Corinth.
Sirron, brigand of Megarus.
Sparta, chief city of the Peloponnesus.
Taenarus, today Cape Matapan.
Venus, goddess of love.

August Strindberg
Miss Julie
a tragedy in one act
translated by Elizabeth Sprigge

Characters

> MISS JULIE, *aged 25*
> JEAN, *the valet, aged 30*
> KRISTIN, *the cook, aged 35*

SCENE: *The large kitchen of a Swedish manor house in a county district in the eighties.*
Midsummer eve.
The kitchen has three doors, two small ones into JEAN'S *and* KRISTIN'S *bedrooms, and a large, glass-fronted double one, opening on to a courtyard. This is the only way to the rest of the house.*
Through these glass doors can be seen part of a fountain with a cupid, lilac bushes in flower and the tops of some Lombardy poplars. On one wall are shelves edged with scalloped paper on which are kitchen utensils of copper, iron and tin.
To the left is the corner of a large tiled range and part of its chimney-hood, to the right the end of the servants' dinner table with chairs beside it.
The stove is decorated with birch boughs, the floor strewn with twigs of juniper. On the end of the table is a large Japanese spice jar full of lilac.
There are also an ice-box, a scullery table and a sink. Above the double door hangs a big old-fashioned bell; near it is a speaking-tube.
A fiddle can be heard from the dance in the barn near-by.
KRISTIN *is standing at the stove, frying something in a pan. She wears a light-coloured cotton dress and a big apron.*
JEAN *enters, wearing livery and carrying a pair of large riding-boots with spurs, which he puts in a conspicuous place.*

JEAN: Miss Julie's crazy again to-night, absolutely crazy.
KRISTIN: Oh, so you're back, are you?
JEAN: When I'd taken the Count to the station, I came back and dropped in at the Barn for a dance. And who did I see there but our young lady leading off with the game-keeper. But the moment she sets eyes on me, up she rushes and invites me to waltz with her. And how she waltzed— I've never seen anything like it! She's crazy.
KRISTIN: Always has been, but never so bad as this last fortnight since the engagement was broken off.
JEAN: Yes, that was a pretty business, to be sure. He's a decent enough chap, too, even if he isn't rich. Oh, but they're choosy! *(Sits down at the end of the table.)* In any case, it's a bit odd that our young—er— lady would rather stay at home with the yokels than go with her father to visit her relations.
KRISTIN: Perhaps she feels a bit awkward, after that bust-up with her fiancé.
JEAN: Maybe. That chap had some guts, though. Do you know the sort of thing that was going on, Kristin? I saw it with my own eyes, though I didn't let on I had.
KRISTIN: You saw them . . . ?
JEAN: Didn't I just! Came across the pair of them one evening in the stable-yard. Miss Julie was doing what she called "training" him. Know what that was? Making him jump over her riding-whip—the way you teach a dog. He did it twice and got a cut each time for his pains, but when it came to the third go, he snatched the whip out of her hand and broke it into smithereens. And then he cleared off.
KRISTIN: What goings on! I never did!
JEAN: Well, that's how it was with that little affair . . . Now, what have you got for me, Kristin? Something tasty?
KRISTIN *(serving from the pan to his plate)*: Well, it's just a little bit of kidney I cut off their joint.
JEAN *(smelling it)*: Fine! That's my special delice. *(Feels the plate.)* But you might have warmed the plate.
KRISTIN: When you choose to be finicky you're worse than the Count himself. *(Pulls his hair affectionately.)*
JEAN *(crossly)*: Stop pulling my hair. You know how sensitive I am.
KRISTIN: There, there! It's only love, you know.

(JEAN eats. KRISTIN brings a bottle of beer.)

JEAN: Beer on Midsummer Eve? No thanks! I've got something better than that. *(From a drawer in the table brings out a bottle of red wine with a yellow seal.*) Yellow seal, see! Now get me a glass. You use a glass with a stem of course when you're drinking it straight.

KRISTIN: (*giving him a wine-glass*): Lord help the woman who gets you for a husband, you old fusser! (*She puts the beer in the ice-box and sets a small saucepan on the stove.*)

JEAN: Nonsense! You'll be glad enough to get a fellow as smart as me. And I don't think it's done you any harm people calling me your fiancé. (*Tastes the wine.*) Good. Very good indeed. But not quite warmed enough. (*Warms the glass in his hand.*) We bought this in Dijon. Four francs the litre without the bottle, and duty on top of that. What are you cooking now? It stinks.

KRISTIN: Some bloody muck Miss Julie wants for Diana.

JEAN: You should be more refined in your speech, Kristin. But why should you spend a holiday cooking for that bitch? Is she sick or what?

KRISTIN: Yes, she's sick. She sneaked out with the pug at the lodge and got in the usual mess. And that, you know, Miss Julie won't have.

JEAN: Miss Julie's too high-and-mighty in some respects, and not enough in others, just like her mother before her. The Countess was more at home in the kitchen and cowsheds than anywhere else, but would she ever go driving with only one horse? She went round with her cuffs filthy, but she had to have the coronet on the cuff-links. Our young lady—to come back to her—hasn't any proper respect for herself or her position. I mean she isn't refined. In the Barn just now she dragged the gamekeeper away from Anna and made him dance with her—no waiting to be asked. We wouldn't do a thing like that. But that's what happens when the gentry try to behave like the common people—they become common . . . Still she's a fine girl. Smashing! What shoulders! And what—er—etcetera!

KRISTIN: Oh come off it! I know what Clara says, and she dresses her.

JEAN: Clara? Pooh, you're all jealous! But I've been out riding with her . . . and as for her dancing!

KRISTIN: Listen, Jean. You will dance with me, won't you, as soon as I'm through.

JEAN: Of course I will.

KRISTIN: Promise?

JEAN: Promise? When I say I'll do a thing I do it. Well, thanks for the supper. It was a real treat. (*Corks the bottle.*)

(JULIE *appears in the doorway, speaking to someone outside.*)

JULIE: I'll be back in a moment. Don't wait.

(JEAN *slips the bottle into the drawer and rises respectfully.*)
(JULIE *enters and joins* KRISTIN *at the stove.*)

August Strindberg: *Miss Julie* 87

Well, have you made it? (KRISTIN *signs that* JEAN *is near them.*)
JEAN (*gallantly*): Have you ladies got some secret?
JULIE (*flipping his face with her handkerchief*): You're very inquisitive.
JEAN: What a delicious smell! Violets.
JULIE (*coquettishly*): Impertinence! Are you an expert of scent too? I must say you know how to dance. Now don't look. Go away. (*The music of a schottische begins.*)
JEAN (*with impudent politeness*): Is it some witches' brew you're cooking on Midsummer Eve? Something to tell your stars by, so you can see your future?
JULIE (*sharply*): If you could see that you'd have good eyes. (*To* KRISTIN.) Put it in a bottle and cork it tight. Come and dance this schottische with me, Jean.
JEAN (*hesitating*): I don't want to be rude, but I've promised to dance this one with Kristin.
JULIE: Well, she can have another, can't you, Kristin? You'll lend me Jean, won't you?
KRISTIN (*bottling*): It's nothing to do with me. When you're so condescending, Miss, it's not his place to say no. Go on, Jean, and thank Miss Julie for the honour.
JEAN: Frankly speaking, Miss, and no offence meant, I wonder if it's wise for you to dance twice running with the same partner, specially as those people are so ready to jump to conclusions.
JULIE (*flaring up*): What did you say? What sort of conclusions? What do you mean?
JEAN (*meekly*): As you choose not to understand, Miss Julie, I'll have to speak more plainly. It looks bad to show a preference for one of your retainers when they're all hoping for the same unusual favour.
JULIE: Show a preference! The very idea! I'm surprised at you. I'm doing the people an honour by attending their ball when I'm mistress of the house, but if I'm really going to dance, I mean to have a partner who can lead and doesn't make me look ridiculous.
JEAN: If those are your orders, Miss, I'm at your service.
JULIE (*gently*): Don't take it as an order. To-night we're all just people enjoying party. There's no question of class. So now give me your arm. Don't worry, Kristin. I shan't steal your sweetheart.

(JEAN *gives* JULIE *his arm and leads her out.*)
(*Left alone,* KRISTIN *plays her scene in an unhurried, natural way, humming to the tune of the schottische, played on a distant violin. She clears* JEAN's *place, washes up and puts things away, then takes off her apron, brings out a small mirror from a drawer, props it against the jar of lilac, lights a candle, warms a small pair of tongs and curls her*

fringe. *She goes to the door and listens, then turning back to the table finds* MISS JULIE'S *forgotten handkerchief. She smells it, then meditatively smooths it out and folds it.*)
(*Enter* JEAN.)

JEAN: She really is crazy. What a way to dance! With people standing grinning at her too from behind the doors. What's got into her, Kristin?
KRISTIN: Oh, it's just her time coming on. She's always queer then. Are you going to dance with me now?
JEAN: Then you're not wild with me for cutting that one.
KRISTIN: You know I'm not—for a little thing like that. Besides, I know my place.
JEAN (*putting his arm round her waist*): You're a sensible girl, Kristin, and you'll make a very good wife . . .

(*Enter* JULIE, *unpleasantly surprised.*)

JULIE (*with forced gaiety*): You're a fine beau—running away from your partner.
JEAN: Not away, Miss Julie, but as you see back to the one I deserted.
JULIE (*changing her tone*): You really can dance, you know. But why are you wearing your livery on a holiday. Take it off at once.
JEAN: Then I must ask you to go away for a moment, Miss. My black coat's here. (*Indicates it hanging on the door to his room.*)
JULIE: Are you so shy of me—just over changing a coat? Go into your room then—or stay here and I'll turn my back.
JEAN: Excuse me then, Miss. (*He goes to his room and is partly visible as he changes his coat.*)
JULIE: Tell me, Kristin, is Jean your fiancé? You seem very intimate.
KRISTIN: My fiancé? Yes, if you like. We call it that.
JULIE: Call it?
KRISTIN: Well, you've had a fiancé yourself, Miss, and . . .
JULIE: But we really were engaged.
KRISTIN: All the same it didn't come to anything.

(JEAN *returns in his black coat.*)

JULIE: Très gentil, Monsieur Jean. Très gentil.
JEAN: Vous voulez plaisanter, Madame.
JULIE: Et vous voulez parler français. Where did you learn it?
JEAN: In Switzerland, when I was sommelier at one of the biggest hotels in Lucerne.
JULIE: You look quite the gentleman in that get-up. Charming.

(*Sits at the table.*)

JEAN: Oh, you're just flattering me!
JULIE: (*annoyed*): Flattering you?
JEAN: I'm too modest to believe you would pay real compliments to a man like me, so I must take it you are exaggerating—that this is what's known as flattery.
JULIE: Where on earth did you learn to make speeches like that? Perhaps you've been to the theatre a lot.
JEAN: That's right. And travelled a lot too.
JULIE: But you come from this neighborhood, don't you?
JEAN: Yes, my father was a labourer on the next estate—the District Attorney's place. I often used to see you, Miss Julie, when you were little, though you never noticed me.
JULIE: Did you really?
JEAN: Yes. One time specially I remember . . . But I can't tell you about that.
JULIE: Oh do! Why not? This is just the time.
JEAN: No, I really can't now. Another time perhaps.
JULIE: Another time means never. What harm in now?
JEAN: No harm, but I'd rather not. (*Points to* KRISTIN, *now fast asleep.*) Look at her.
JULIE: She'll make a charming wife, won't she? I wonder if she snores.
JEAN: No, she doesn't, but she talks in her sleep.
JULIE (*cynically*): How do you know she talks in her sleep?
JEAN (*brazenly*): I've heard her. (*Pause. They look at one another.*)
JULIE: Why don't you sit down?
JEAN: I can't take such a liberty in your presence.
JULIE: Supposing I order you to.
JEAN: I'll obey.
JULIE: Then sit down. No, wait a minute. Will you get me a drink first?
JEAN: I don't know what's in the ice-box. Only beer, I expect.
JULIE: There's no only about it. My taste is so simple I prefer it to wine.

(JEAN *take a bottle from the ice-box, fetches a glass and plate and serves the beer.*)

JEAN: At your service.
JULIE: Thank you. Won't you have some yourself?
JEAN: I'm not really a beer-drinker, but if it's an order . . .
JULIE: Order? I should have thought it was ordinary manners to keep your partner company.
JEAN: That's a good way of putting it. (*He opens another bottle and fetches a glass.*)
JULIE: Now drink my health. (*He hesitates.*) I believe the man really is shy!

(JEAN *kneels and raises his glass with mock ceremony.*)

JEAN: To the health of my lady!

JULIE: Bravo! Now kiss my shoe and everything will be perfect. (*He hesitates, then boldly takes hold of her foot and lightly kisses it.*) Splendid. You ought to have been an actor.

JEAN (*rising*): We can't go on like this, Miss Julie. Someone might come in and see us.

JULIE: Why would that matter?

JEAN: For the simple reason that they'd talk. And if you knew the way their tongues were wagging out there just now, you . . .

JULIE: What were they saying? Tell me, Sit down.

JEAN (*sitting*): No offence meant, Miss, but . . . well, their language wasn't nice, and they were hinting . . . oh, you know quite well what. You're not a child, and if a lady's seen drinking alone at night with a man—and a servant at that—then . . .

JULIE: Then what? Besides, we're not alone. Kristin's here.

JEAN: Yes, asleep.

JULIE: I'll wake her up. *Rises*. Kristin, are you asleep? (KRISTIN *mumbles in her sleep.*) Kristin! Goodness, how she sleeps!

KRISTIN (*in her sleep*): The Count's boots are cleaned—put the coffee on —yes, yes, at once . . . (*Mumbles incoherently.*)

JULIE (*tweaking her nose*): Wake up, can't you!

JEAN (*sharply*): Let her sleep.

JULIE: What?

JEAN: When you've been standing at the stove all day you're likely to be tired at night. And sleep should be respected.

JULIE (*changing her tone*): What a nice idea. It does you credit. Thank you for it. (*Holds out her hand to him*). Now come out and pick some lilac for me.

(*During the following* KRISTIN *goes sleepily in to her bedroom.*)

JEAN: Out with you, Miss Julie?

JULIE: Yes.

JEAN: It wouldn't do. It really wouldn't.

JULIE: I don't know what you mean. You can't possibly imagine that . . .

JEAN: I don't, but others do.

JULIE: What? That I'm in love with the valet?

JEAN: I'm not a conceited man, but such a thing's been known to happen, and to these rustics nothing's sacred.

JULIE: You, I take it, are an aristocrat.

JEAN: Yes, I am.

JULIE: And I am coming down in the world.

JEAN: Don't come down, Miss Julie. Take my advice. No one will believe you came down of your own accord. They'll all say you fell.
JULIE: I have a higher opinion of our people than you. Come and put it to the test. Come on. (*Gazes into his eyes.*)
JEAN: You're very strange, you know.
JULIE: Perhaps I am, but so are you. For that matter everything is strange. Life, human beings, everything, just scum drifting about on the water until it sinks—down and down. That reminds me of a dream I sometimes have, in which I'm on top of a pillar and can't see any way of getting down. When I look down I'm dizzy; I have to get down but I haven't the courage to jump. I can't stay there and I long to fall, but don't fall. There's no respite. There can't be any peace at all for me until I'm down, right down on the ground. And if I did get to the ground I'd want to be under the ground . . . Have you ever felt like that?
JEAN: No. In my dream I'm lying under a great tree in a dark wood. I want to get up, up to the top of it, and look out over the bright landscape where the sun is shining and rob that high nest of its golden eggs. And I climb and climb, but the trunk is so thick and smooth and it's so far to the first branch. But I know if I can once reach that first branch I'll go to the top just as if I'm on a ladder. I haven't reached it yet, but I shall get there, even if only in my dreams.
JULIE: Here I am chattering about dreams with you. Come on. Only into the park. (*She takes his arm and they go towards the door.*)
JEAN: We must sleep on nine midsummer flowers tonight; then our dreams will come true, Miss Julie. (*They turn at the door. He has a hand to his eye.*)
JULIE: Have you got something in your eye? Let me see.
JEAN: Oh, it's nothing. Just a speck of dust. It'll be gone in a minute.
JULIE: My sleeve must have rubbed against you. Sit down and let me see to it. (*Takes him by the arm and makes him sit down, bends his head back and tries to get the speck out with the corner of her handkerchief.*) Keep still now, quite still. (*Slaps his hand.*) Do as I tell you. Why, I believe you're trembling, big, strong man though you are! (*Feels his biceps.*) What muscles!
JEAN (*warning*): Miss Julie!
JULIE: Yes, Monsieur Jean?
JEAN: Attention. Je ne suis qu'un homme.
JULIE: Will you stay still! There now. It's out. Kiss my hand and say thank you.
JEAN (*rising*): Miss Julie, listen. Kristin's gone to bed now. Will you listen?
JULIE: Kiss my hand first.

JEAN: Very well, but you'll have only yourself to blame.
JULIE: For what?
JEAN: For what! Are you still a child at twenty-five? Don't you know it's dangerous to play with fire?
JULIE: Not for me. I'm insured.
JEAN (*bluntly*): No, you're not. And even if you are, there's still stuff here to kindle a flame.
JULIE: Meaning yourself?
JEAN: Yes. Not because I'm me, but because I'm a man and young and . . .
JULIE: And good-looking? What incredible conceit! A Don Juan perhaps? Or a Joseph? Good Lord, I do believe you are a Joseph!
JEAN: Do you?
JULIE: I'm rather afraid so.

(JEAN *goes boldly up and tries to put his arms round her and kiss her. She boxes his ears.*)

How dare you!
JEAN: Was that in earnest or a joke?
JULIE: In earnest.
JEAN: Then what went before was in earnest too. You take your games too seriously and that's dangerous. Anyhow I'm tired of playing now and beg leave to return to my work. The Count will want his boots first thing and it's past midnight now.
JULIE: Put those boots down.
JEAN: No. This is my work, which it's my duty to do. But I never undertook to be your playfellow and I never will be. I consider myself too good for that.
JULIE: You're proud.
JEAN: In some ways—not all.
JULIE: Have you ever been in love?
JEAN: We don't put it that way, but I've been gone on quite a few girls. And once I went sick because I couldn't have the one I wanted. Sick, I mean, like those princes in the Arabian Nights who couldn't eat or drink for love.
JULIE: Who was she? (*No answer.*) Who was she?
JEAN: You can't force me to tell you that.
JULIE: If I ask as an equal, ask as a—friend? Who was she?
JEAN: You.
JULIE (*sitting*): How absurd!
JEAN: Yes, ludicrous if you like. That's the story I wouldn't tell you before, see, but now I will . . . Do you know what the world looks like from below? No, you don't. No more than the hawks and falcons do whose backs one hardly ever sees because they're always soaring up

aloft. I lived in a labourer's hovel with seven other children and a pig, out in the grey fields where there isn't a single tree. But from the window I could see the wall around the Count's park with apple-trees above it. That was the Garden of Eden, guarded by many terrible angels with flaming swords. All the same I and the other boys managed to get to the tree of life. Does all this make you despise me?

JULIE: Goodness, all boys steal apples!

JEAN: You say that now, but all the same you do despise me. However, one time I went into the Garden of Eden with my mother to weed the onion beds. Close to the kitchen garden there was a Turkish pavilion hung all over with jasmine and honeysuckle. I hadn't any idea what it was used for, but I'd never seen such a beautiful building. People used to go in and then come out again, and one day the door was left open. I crept up and saw the walls covered with pictures of kings and emperors, and the windows had red curtains with fringes—you know now what the place was, don't you? I . . . (*Breaks off a piece of lilac and holds it for* JULIE *to smell. As he talks, she takes it from him.*) I had never been inside the manor, never seen anything but the church, and this was more beautiful. No matter where my thoughts went, they always came back—to that place. The longing went on growing in me to enjoy it fully, just once. Enfin, I sneaked in, gazed and admired. Then I heard someone coming. There was only one way out for the gentry, but for me there was another and I had no choice but to take it. (JULIE *drops the lilac on the table.*) Then I took to my heels, plunged through the raspberry canes, dashed across the strawberry beds and found myself on the rose terrace. There I saw a pink dress and a pair of white stockings—it was you. I crawled into a weed pile and lay there right under it among prickly thistles and damp rank earth. I watched you walking among the roses and said to myself: "If it's true that a thief can get to heaven and be with the angels, it's pretty strange that a labourer's child here on God's earth mayn't come in the park and play with the Count's daughter."

JULIE (*sentimentally*): Do you think all poor children feel the way you did?

JEAN (*taken aback, then rallying*): *All* poor children? . . . Yes, of course they do. Of course.

JULIE: It must be terrible to be poor.

JEAN (*with exaggerated distress*): Oh yes, Miss Julie, yes. A dog may lie on the Countess's sofa, a horse may have his nose stroked by a young lady, but a servant . . . (*change of tone*) well, yes, now and then you meet one with guts enough to rise in the world, but how often? Anyhow, do you know what I did? Jumped in the millstream with my clothes on, was pulled out and got a hiding. But the next Sunday, when

Father and all the rest went to Granny's, I managed to get left behind. Then I washed with soap and hot water, put my best clothes on and went to church so as to see you. I did see you and went home determined to die. But I wanted to die beautifully and peacefully, without any pain. Then I remembered it was dangerous to sleep under an elder bush. We had a big one in full bloom, so I stripped it and climbed into the oats-bin with the flowers. Have you ever noticed how smooth oats are? Soft to touch as human skin . . . Well, I closed the lid and shut my eyes, fell asleep, and when they woke me I was very ill. But I didn't die, as you see. What I meant by all that I don't know. There was no hope of winning you—you were simply a symbol of the hopelessness of ever getting out of the class I was born in.

JULIE: You put things very well, you know. Did you go to school?

JEAN: For a while. But I've read a lot of novels and been to the theatre. Besides, I've heard educated folk talking—that's what's taught me most.

JULIE: Do you stand round listening to what we're saying?

JEAN: Yes, of course. And I've heard quite a bit too! On the carriage box or rowing the boat. Once I heard you, Miss Julie, and one of your young lady friends . . .

JULIE: Oh! Whatever did you hear?

JEAN: Well, it wouldn't be nice to repeat it. And I must say I was pretty startled. I couldn't think where you had learnt such words. Perhaps, at bottom, there isn't as much difference between people as one's led to believe.

JULIE: How dare you! We don't behave as you do when we're engaged.

JEAN (*looking hard at her*): Are you sure? It's no use making out so innocent to me.

JULIE: The man I gave my love to was a rotter.

JEAN: That's what you always say—afterwards.

JULIE: Always?

JEAN: I think it must be always. I've heard the expression several times in similar circumstances.

JULIE: What circumstances?

JEAN: Like those in question. The last time . . .

JULIE (*rising*): Stop. I don't want to hear any more.

JEAN: Nor did *she*—curiously enough. May I go to bed now please?

JULIE (*gently*): Go to bed on Midsummer Eve?

JEAN: Yes. Dancing with that crowd doesn't really amuse me.

JULIE: Get the key of the boathouse and row me out on the lake. I want to see the sun rise.

JEAN: Would that be wise?

JULIE: You sound as though you're frightened for your reputation.

JEAN: Why not? I don't want to be made a fool of, nor to be sent packing without a character when I'm trying to better myself. Besides, I have Kristin to consider.

JULIE: So now it's Kristin.

JEAN: Yes, but it's you I'm thinking about too. Take my advice and go to bed.

JULIE: Am I to take orders from you?

JEAN: Just this once, for your own sake. Please. It's very late and sleepiness goes to one's head and makes one rash. Go to bed. What's more, if my ears don't deceive me, I hear people coming this way. They'll be looking for me, and if they find us here, you're done for.

(*The* CHORUS *approaches, singing. During the following dialogue the song is heard in snatches, and in full when the peasants enter.*)

>   Out of the wood two women came,
>   Tridiri-ralla, tridiri-ra.
>   The feet of one were bare and cold,
>   Tridiri-ralla-la.
>
>   The other talked of bags of gold,
>   Tridiri-ralla, tridiri-ra.
>   But neither had a sou to her name,
>   Tridiri-ralla-la.
>
>   The bridal wreath I give to you,
>   Tridiri-ralla, tridiri-ra.
>   But to another I'll be true,
>   Tridiri-ralla-la.

JULIE: I know our people and I love them, just as they do me. Let them come. You'll see.

JEAN: No, Miss Julie, they don't love you. They take your food, then spit at it. You must believe me. Listen to them, just listen to what they're singing . . . No, don't listen.

JULIE (*listening*): What are they singing?

JEAN: They're mocking—you and me.

JULIE: Oh no! How horrible! What cowards!

JEAN: A pack like that's always cowardly. But against such odds there's nothing we can do but run away.

JULIE: Run away? Where to? We can't get out and we can't go into Kristin's room.

JEAN: Into mine then. Necessity knows no rules. And you can trust me. I really am your true and devoted friend.

JULIE: But supposing . . . supposing they were to look for you in there?

JEAN: I'll bolt the door, and if they try to break in I'll shoot. Come on. (*Pleading.*) Please come.

JULIE (*tensely*): Do you promise . . . ?
JEAN: I swear!

> (JULIE *goes quickly into his room and he excitedly follows her.*)
> (*Led by the fiddler, the peasants enter in festive attire with flowers in their hats. They put a barrel of beer and a keg of spirits, garlanded with leaves, on the table, fetch glasses and begin to carouse. The scene becomes a ballet. They form a ring and dance and sing and mime:* "Out of the wood two women came." *Finally they go out, still singing.*)
> (JULIE *comes in alone. She looks at the havoc in the kitchen, wrings her hands, then takes out her powder puff and powders her face.*)
> (JEAN *enters in high spirits.*)

JEAN: Now you see! And you heard, didn't you? Do you still think it's possible for us to stay here?
JULIE: No, I don't. But what can we do?
JEAN: Run away. Far away. Take a journey.
JULIE: Journey? But where to?
JEAN: Switzerland. The Italian lakes. Ever been there?
JULIE: No. Is it nice?
JEAN: Ah! Eternal summer, oranges, evergreens . . . ah!
JULIE: But what would we do there?
JEAN: I'll start a hotel. First-class accommodation and first-class customers.
JULIE: Hotel?
JEAN: There's life for you. New faces all the time, new languages—no time for nerves or worries, no need to look for something to do—work rolling up of its own accord. Bells ringing night and day, trains whistling, buses coming and going, and all the time gold pieces rolling on to the counter. There's life for you!
JULIE: For *you*. And I?
JEAN: Mistress of the house, ornament of the firm. With your looks, and your style . . . oh, it's bound to be a success! Terrific! You'll sit like a queen in the office and set your slaves in motion by pressing an electric button. The guests will file past your throne and nervously lay their treasure on your table. You've no idea the way people tremble when they get their bills. I'll salt the bills and you'll sugar them with your sweetest smiles. Ah, let's get away from here! (*Produces a time-table.*) At once, by the next train. We shall be at Malmö at six-thirty, Hamburg eight-forty next morning, Frankfurt-Basle the following day, and Como by the St. Gothard pass in—let's see—three days. Three days!
JULIE: That's all very well. But Jean, you must give me courage. Tell me you love me. Come and take me in your arms.
JEAN (*reluctantly*): I'd like to, but I daren't. Not again in this house. I

love you—that goes without saying. You can't doubt that, Miss Julie, can you?

JULIE (*shyly, very feminine*): Miss? Call me Julie. There aren't any barriers between us now. Call me Julie.

JEAN (*uneasily*): I can't. As long as we're in this house, there *are* barriers between us. There's the past and there's the Count. I've never been so servile to anyone as I am to him. I've only got to see his gloves on a chair to feel small. I've only to hear his bell and I shy like a horse. Even now, when I look at his boots, standing there so proud and stiff, I feel my back beginning to bend. (*Kicks the boots.*) It's those old, narrow-minded notions drummed into us as children . . . but they can soon be forgotten. You've only got to get to another country, a republic, and people will bend themselves double before my porter's livery. Yes, double they'll bend themselves, but I shan't. I wasn't born to bend. I've got guts, I've got character, and once I reach that first branch, you'll watch me climb. Today I'm valet, next year I'll be proprietor, in ten years I'll have made a fortune, and then I'll go to Roumania, get myself decorated and I may, I only say *may*, mind you, end up as a Count.

JULIE (*sadly*): That would be very nice.

JEAN: You see in Roumania one can buy a title, and then you'll be a Countess after all. My Countess.

JULIE: What do I care about all that? I'm putting those things behind me. Tell me you love me, because if you don't . . . if you don't, what am I?

JEAN: I'll tell you a thousand times over—later. But not here. No sentimentality now or everything will be lost. We must consider this thing calmly like reasonable people. (*Takes a cigar, cuts and lights it.*) You sit down there and I'll sit here and we'll talk as if nothing has happened.

JULIE: My God, have you no feelings at all?

JEAN: Nobody has more. But I know how to control them.

JULIE: A short time ago you were kissing my shoe. And now . . .

JEAN (*harshly*): Yes, that was then. Now we have something else to think about.

JULIE: Don't speak to me so brutally.

JEAN: I'm not. Just sensibly. One folly's been committed, don't let's have more. The Count will be back at any moment and we've got to settle our future before that. Now, what do you think of my plans? Do you approve?

JULIE: It seems a very good idea—but just one thing. Such a big undertaking would need a lot of capital. Have you got any?

JEAN (*chewing his cigar*): I certainly have. I've got my professional skill, my wide experience and my knowledge of foreign languages. That's capital worth having, it seems to me.

JULIE: But it won't buy even one railway ticket.

JEAN: Quite true. That's why I need a backer to advance some ready cash.

JULIE: How could you get that at a moment's notice?

JEAN: You must get it, if you want to be my partner.

JULIE: I can't. I haven't any money of my own. (*Pause.*)

JEAN: Then the whole thing's off.

JULIE: And . . . ?

JEAN: We go on as we are.

JULIE: Do you think I'm going to stay under this roof as your mistress? With everyone pointing at me. Do you think I can face my father after this? No. Take me away from here, away from this shame, this humiliation. Oh my God, what have I done? My God, my God! (*Weeps.*)

JEAN: So that's the tune now, is it? What have you done? Same as many before you.

JULIE (*hysterically*): And now you despise me. I'm falling, I'm falling.

JEAN: Fall as far as me and I'll lift you up again.

JULIE: Why was I so terribly attracted to you? The weak to the strong, the falling to the rising? Or was it love? Is that love? Do you know what love is?

JEAN: Do I? You bet I do. Do you think I never had a girl before?

JULIE: The things you say, the things you think!

JEAN: That's what life's taught me, and that's what I am. It's no good getting hysterical or giving yourself airs. We're both in the same boat now. Here, my dear girl, let me give you a glass of something special. (*Opens the drawer, takes out the bottle of wine and fills two used glasses.*)

JULIE: Where did you get that wine?

JEAN: From the cellar.

JULIE: My father's burgundy.

JEAN: Why not, for his son-in-law?

JULIE: And I drink beer.

JEAN: That only shows your taste's not so good as mine.

JULIE: Thief!

JEAN: Are you going to tell on me?

JULIE: Oh God! The accomplice of a petty thief! Was I blind drunk? Have I dreamt this whole night? Midsummer Eve, the night for innocent merrymaking.

JEAN: Innocent, eh?

JULIE: Is anyone on earth as wretched as I am now?

JEAN: Why should *you* be? After such a conquest. What about Kristin in there? Don't you think she has any feelings?

JULIE: I did think so, but I don't any longer. No. A menial is a menial . . .

JEAN: And a whore is a whore.

JULIE (*falling to her knees, her hands clasped.*): O God in heaven, put an end to my miserable life! Lift me out of this filth in which I'm sinking. Save me! Save me!

JEAN: I must admit I'm sorry for you. When I was in the onion bed and saw you up there among the roses, I . . . yes, I'll tell you now . . . I had the same dirty thoughts as all boys.

JULIE: You, who wanted to die because of me?

JEAN: In the oats-bin? That was just talk.

JULIE: Lies, you mean.

JEAN (*getting sleepy*): More or less. I think I read a story in some paper about a chimney-sweep who shut himself up in a chest full of lilac because he'd been summonsed for not supporting some brat . . .

JULIE: So this is what you're like.

JEAN: I had to think up something. It's always the fancy stuff that catches the women.

JULIE: Beast!

JEAN: Merde!

JULIE: Now you have seen the falcon's back.

JEAN: Not exactly its *back*.

JULIE: I was to be the first branch.

JEAN: But the branch was rotten.

JULIE: I was to be a hotel sign.

JEAN: And I the hotel.

JULIE: Sit at your counter, attract your clients and cook their accounts.

JEAN: I'd have done that myself.

JULIE: That any human being can be so steeped in filth!

JEAN: Clean it up then.

JULIE: Menial! Lackey! Stand up when I speak to you.

JEAN: Menial's whore, lackey's harlot, shut your mouth and get out of here! Are you the one to lecture me for being coarse? nobody of my kind would ever be as coarse as you were tonight. Do you think any servant girl would throw herself at a man that way? Have you ever seen a girl of my class asking for it like that? I haven't. Only animals and prostitutes.

JULIE (*broken*): Go on. Hit me, trample on me—it's all I deserve. I'm rotten. But help me If there's any way out at all, help me.

JEAN (*more gently*): I'm not denying myself a share in the honour of seducing you, but do you think anybody in my place would have dared look in your direction if you yourself hadn't asked for it? I'm still amazed . . .

JULIE: And proud.

JEAN: Why not? Though I must admit the victory was too easy to make me lose my head.

JULIE: Go on hitting me.

JEAN (*rising*): No. On the contrary I apologise for what I've said. I don't hit a person who's down—least of all a woman. I can't deny there's a certain satisfaction in finding that what dazzled one below was just moonshine, that that falcon's back is grey after all, that there's powder on the lovely cheek, that polished nails can have black tips, that the handkerchief is dirty although it smells of scent. On the other hand it hurts to find that what I was struggling to reach wasn't high and isn't real. It hurts to see you fallen so low you're far lower than your own cook. Hurts like when you see the last flowers of summer lashed to pieces by rain and turned to mud.

JULIE: You're talking as if you're already my superior.

JEAN: I am. I might make you a Countess, but you could never make me a Count, you know.

JULIE: But I am the child of a Count, and you could never be that.

JEAN: True, but I might be the father of Counts if . . .

JULIE: You're a thief. I'm not.

JEAN: There are worse things than being a thief—much lower. Besides, when I'm in a place I regard myself as a member of the family to some extent, as one of the children. You don't call it stealing when children pinch a berry from overladen bushes. (*His passion is roused again.*) Miss Julie, you're a glorious woman, far too good for a man like me. You were carried away by some kind of madness, and now you're trying to cover up your mistake by persuading yourself you're in love with me. You're not, although you may find me physically attractive, which means your love's no better than mine. But I wouldn't be satisfied with being nothing but an animal for you, and I could never make you love me.

JULIE: Are you sure?

JEAN: You think there's a chance? Of my loving you, yes, of course. You're beautiful, refined, (*takes her hand*) educated, and you can be nice when you want to be. The fire you kindle in a man isn't likely to go out. (*Puts his arm round her.*) You're like mulled wine, full of spices, and your kisses . . . (*He tries to pull her to him, but she breaks away.*)

JULIE: Let go of me! You won't win me that way.

JEAN: Not that way, how then? Not by kisses and fine speeches, not by planning the future and saving you from shame? How then?

JULIE: How? How? I don't know. There isn't any way. I loathe you—loathe you as I loathe rats, but I can't escape from you.

JEAN: Escape with me.

JULIE (*pulling herself together*): Escape? Yes, we must escape. But I'm so tired. Give me a glass of wine. (*He pours it out. She looks at her watch.*) First we must talk. We still have a little time. (*Empties the glass and holds it out for more.*)

JEAN: Don't drink like that. You'll get tipsy.

JULIE: What's that matter?

JEAN: What's it matter? It's vulgar to get drunk. Well, what have you got to say?

JULIE: We've got to run away, but we must talk first—or rather, I must, for so far you've done all the talking. You've told me about your life, now I want to tell you about mine, so that we really know each other before we begin this journey together.

JEAN: Wait. Excuse my saying so, but don't you think you may be sorry afterwards if you give away your secrets to me?

JULIE: Aren't you my friend?

JEAN: On the whole. But don't rely on me.

JULIE: You can't mean that. But anyway everyone knows my secrets. Listen. My mother wasn't well-born; she came of quite humble people, and was brought up with all those new ideas of sex-equality and women's rights and so on. She thought marriage was quite wrong. So when my father proposed to her, she said she would never become his *wife* . . . but in the end she did. I came into the world, as far as I can make out, against my mother's will, and I was left to run wild, but I had to do all the things a boy does—to prove women are as good as men. I had to wear boys' clothes; I was taught to handle horses—and I wasn't allowed in the dairy. She made me groom and harness and go out hunting; I even had to try to plough. All the men on the estate were given the women's jobs, and the women the men's, until the whole place went to rack and ruin and we were the laughing-stock of the neighbourhood. At last my father seems to have come to his senses and rebelled. He changed everything and ran the place his own way. My mother got ill—I don't know what was the matter with her, but she used to have strange attacks and hide herself in the attic or the garden. Sometimes she stayed out all night. Then came the great fire which you have heard people talking about. The house and the stables and the barns—the whole place burnt to the ground. In very suspicious circumstances. Because the accident happened the very day the insurance had to be renewed, and my father had sent the new premium, but through some carelessness of the messenger it arrived too late. (*Refills her glass and drinks.*)

JEAN: Don't drink any more.
JULIE: Oh, what does it matter? We were destitute and had to sleep in the carriages. My father didn't know how to get money to rebuild, and then my mother suggested he should borrow from an old friend of hers, a local brick manufacturer. My father got the loan and, to his surprise, without having to pay interest. So the place was rebuilt. (*Drinks.*) Do you know who set fire to it?
JEAN: Your lady mother.
JULIE: Do you know who the brick manufacturer was?
JEAN: Your mother's lover?
JULIE: Do you know whose the money was?
JEAN: Wait . . . no, I don't know that.
JULIE: It was my mother's.
JEAN: In other words the Count's, unless there was a settlement.
JULIE: There wasn't any settlement. My mother had a little money of her own which she didn't want my father to control, so she invested it with her—friend.
JEAN: Who grabbed it.
JULIE: Exactly. He appropriated it. My father came to know all this. He couldn't bring an action, couldn't pay his wife's lover, nor prove it was his wife's money. That was my mother's revenge because he made himself master in his own house. He nearly shot himself then—at least there's a rumour he tried and didn't bring it off. So he went on living, and my mother had to pay dearly for what she'd done. Imagine what those five years were like for me. My natural sympathies were with my father, yet I took my mother's side, because I didn't know the facts. I'd learnt from her to hate and distrust men—you know how she loathed the whole male sex. And I swore to her I'd never become the slave of any man.
JEAN: And so you got engaged to that attorney.
JULIE: So that he should be my slave.
JEAN: But he wouldn't be.
JULIE: Oh yes, he wanted to be, but he didn't have the chance. I got bored with him.
JEAN: Is that what I saw—in the stable-yard?
JULIE: What did you see?
JEAN: What I saw was him breaking off the engagement.
JULIE: That's a lie. It was I who broke it off. Did he say it was him? The cad.
JEAN: He's not a cad. Do you hate men, Miss Julie?
JULIE: Yes . . . most of the time. But when that weakness comes, oh . . . the shame!
JEAN: Then do you hate me?

JULIE: Beyond words. I'd gladly have you killed like an animal.
JEAN: Quick as you'd shoot a mad dog, eh?
JULIE: Yes.
JEAN: But there's nothing here to shoot with—and there isn't a dog. So what do we do now?
JULIE: Go abroad.
JEAN: To make each other miserable for the rest of our lives?
JULIE: No, to enjoy ourselves for a day or two, for a week, for as long as enjoyment lasts, and then—to die . . .
JEAN: Die? How silly! I think it would be far better to start a hotel.
JULIE (*without listening*): . . . die on the shores of Lake Como, where the sun always shines and at Christmas time there are green trees and glowing oranges.
JEAN: Lake Como's a rainy hole and I didn't see any oranges outside the shops. But it's a good place for tourists. Plenty of villas to be rented by—er—honeymoon couples. Profitable business that. Know why? Because they all sign a lease for six months and all leave after three weeks.
JULIE (*naïvely*): After three weeks? Why?
JEAN: They quarrel, of course. But the rent has to be paid just the same. And then it's let again. So it goes on and on, for there's plenty of love although it doesn't last long.
JULIE: You don't want to die with me?
JEAN: I don't want to die at all. For one thing I like living and for another I consider suicide's a sin against the Creator who gave us life.
JULIE: You believe in God—*you?*
JEAN: Yes, of course. And I go to church every Sunday. Look here, I'm tired of all this. I'm going to bed.
JULIE: Indeed! And do you think I'm going to leave things like this? Don't you know what you owe the woman you've ruined?
JEAN (*taking out his purse and throwing a silver coin on the table*): There you are. I don't want to be an anybody's debt.
JULIE (*pretending not to notice the insult*): Don't you know what the law is?
JEAN: There's no law unfortunately that punishes a woman for seducing a man.
JULIE: But can you see anything for it but to go abroad, get married and then divorce?
JEAN: What if I refuse this mésalliance?
JULIE: Mésalliance?
JEAN: Yes, for me. I'm better bred than you, see! Nobody in my family committed arson.
JULIE: How do you know?

JEAN: Well, you can't prove otherwise, because we haven't any family records outside the Registrar's office. But I've seen your family tree in that book on the drawing-room table. Do you know who the founder of your family was? A miller who let his wife sleep with the King one night during the Danish war. I haven't any ancestors like that. I haven't any ancestors at all, but I might become one.

JULIE: This is what I get for confiding in someone so low, for sacrificing my family honour . . .

JEAN: Dishonour! Well, I told you so. One shouldn't drink, because then one talks. And one shouldn't talk.

JULIE: Oh, how ashamed I am, how bitterly ashamed! If at least you loved me!

JEAN: Look here—for the last time—what do you want? Am I to burst into tears? Am I to jump over your riding whip? Shall I kiss you and carry you off to Lake Como for three weeks, after which . . . What am I to do? What do you want? This is getting unbearable, but that's what comes of playing around with women. Miss Julie, I can see how miserable you are; I know you're going through hell, but I don't understand you. We don't have scenes like this; we don't go in for hating each other. We make love for fun in our spare time, but we haven't all day and all night for it like you. I think you must be ill. I'm sure you're ill.

JULIE: Then you must be kind to me. You sound almost human now.

JEAN: Well, be human yourself. You spit at me, then won't let me wipe it off—on you.

JULIE: Help me, help me! Tell me what to do, where to go.

JEAN: Jesus, as if I knew!

JULIE: I've been mad, raving mad, but there must be a way out.

JEAN: Stay here and keep quiet. Nobody knows anything.

JULIE: I can't. People do know. Kristin knows.

JEAN: They don't know and they wouldn't believe such a thing.

JULIE (*hesitating*): But—it might happen again.

JEAN: That's true.

JULIE: And there might be—consequences.

JEAN (*in panic*): Consequences! Fool that I am I never thought of that. Yes, there's nothing for it but to go. At once. I can't come with you. That would be a complete giveaway. You must go alone—abroad—anywhere.

JULIE: Alone? Where to? I can't.

JEAN: You must. And before the Count gets back. If you stay, we know what will happen. Once you've sinned you feel you might as well go on, as the harm's done. Then you get more and more reckless and in the end you're found out. No. You must go abroad. Then write to the Count and tell him everything, except that it was me. He'll never guess that—and I don't think he'll want to.

JULIE: I'll go if you come with me.

JEAN: Are you crazy, woman? "Miss Julie elopes with valet." Next day it would be in the headlines, and the Count would never live it down.

JULIE: I can't go. I can't stay. I'm so tired, so completely worn out. Give me orders. Set me going. I can't think any more, can't act . . .

JEAN: You see what weaklings you are. Why do you give yourselves airs and turn up your noses as if you're the lords of creation? Very well, I'll give you your orders. Go upstairs and dress. Get money for the journey and come down here again.

JULIE (*softly*): Come up with me.

JEAN: To your room? Now you've gone crazy again. (*Hesitates a moment.*) No! Go along at once. (*Takes her hand and pulls her to the door.*)

JULIE (*as she goes*): Speak kindly to me, Jean.

JEAN: Orders always sound unkind. Now you know. Now you know.

(*Left alone,* JEAN *sighs with relief, sits down at the table, takes out a note-book and pencil and adds up figures, now and then aloud. Dawn begins to break.* KRISTIN *enters dressed for church, carrying his white dickey and tie.*)

KRISTIN: Lord Jesus, look at the state the place is in! What have you been up to? (*Turns out the lamp.*)

JEAN: Oh, Miss Julie invited the crowd in. Did you sleep through it? Didn't you hear anything?

KRISTIN: I slept like a log.

JEAN: And dressed for church already.

KRISTIN: Yes, you promised to come to Communion with me today.

JEAN: Why, so I did. And you've got my bib and tucker, I see. Come on then. (*Sits.* KRISTIN *begins to put his things on. Pause. Sleepily.*) What's the lesson today?

KRISTIN: It's about the beheading of John the Baptist, I think.

JEAN: That's sure to be horribly long. Hi, you're choking me! Oh Lord, I'm so sleepy, so sleepy!

KRISTIN: Yes, what have you been doing up all night? You look absolutely green.

JEAN: Just sitting here talking with Miss Julie.

KRISTIN: She doesn't know what's proper, that one. (*Pause.*)

JEAN: I say, Kristin.

KRISTIN: What?

JEAN: It's queer really, isn't it, when you come to think of it? Her.

KRISTIN: What's queer?

JEAN: The whole thing. *(Pause.)*
KRISTIN *(looking at the half-filled glasses on the table)*: Have you been drinking together too?
JEAN: Yes.
KRISTIN: More shame you. Look me straight in the face.
JEAN: Yes.
KRISTIN: Is it possible? Is it possible?
JEAN *(after a moment)*: Yes, it is.
KRISTIN: Oh! This I would never have believed. How low!
JEAN: You're not jealous of her, surely?
KRISTIN: No, I'm not. If it had been Clara or Sophie I'd have scratched your eyes out. But not of her. I don't know why; that's how it is though. But it's disgusting.
JEAN: You're angry with her then.
KRISTIN: No. With you. It was wicked of you, very, very wicked. Poor girl. And, mark my words, I won't stay here any longer now—in a place where one can't respect one's employers.
JEAN: Why should one respect them?
KRISTIN: You should know since you're so smart. But you don't want to stay in the service of people who aren't respectable, do you? I wouldn't demean myself.
JEAN: But it's rather a comfort to find out they're no better than us.
KRISTIN: I don't think so. If they're no better there's nothing for us to live up to. Oh and think of the Count! Think of him. He's been through so much already. No, I won't stay in the place any longer. A fellow like you too! If it had been that attorney now or somebody of her own class . . .
JEAN: Why, what's wrong with . . .
KRISTIN: Oh, you're all right in your own way, but when all's said and done there is a difference between one class and another. No, this is something I'll never be able to stomach. That our young lady who was so proud and so down on men you'd never believe she'd let one come near her should go and give herself to one like you. She who wanted to have poor Diana shot for running after the lodge-keeper's pug. No, I must say . . . ! Well, I won't stay here any longer. On the twenty-fourth of October I quit.
JEAN: And then?
KRISTIN: Well, since you mention it, it's about time you began to look around, if we're ever going to get married.
JEAN: But what am I to look for? I shan't get a place like this when I'm married.
KRISTIN: I know you won't. But you might get a job as porter or caretakes in some public institution. Government rations are small but sure, and there's a pension for the widow and children.

JEAN: That's all very fine, but it's not in my line to start thinking at once about dying for my wife and children. I must say I had rather bigger ideas.
KRISTIN: You and your ideas! You've got obligations too, and you'd better start thinking about them.
JEAN: Don't *you* start pestering me about obligations. I've had enough of that. (*Listens to a sound upstairs.*) Anyway we've plenty of time to work things out. Go and get ready now and we'll be off to church.
KRISTIN: Who's that walking about upstairs?
JEAN: Don't know—unless it's Clara.
KRISTIN (*going*): You don't think the Count could have come back without our hearing him?
JEAN (*scared*): The Count? No, he can't have. He'd have rung for me.
KRISTIN: God help us! I've never known such goings on.

(*Exit.*)

(*The sun has now risen and is shining on the treetops. The light gradually changes until it slants in through the windows.* JEAN *goes to the door and beckons.* JULIE *enters in travelling clothes, carrying a small bird-cage covered with a cloth which she puts on a chair.*)

JULIE: I'm ready.
JEAN: Hush! Kristin's up.
JULIE (*in a very nervous state*): Does she suspect anything?
JEAN: Not a thing. But, my God, what a sight you are!
JULIE: Sight? What do you mean?
JEAN: You're white as a corpse and—pardon me—your face is dirty.
JULIE: Let me wash then. (*Goes to the sink and washes her face and hands.*) There. Give me a towel. Oh! The sun is rising!
JEAN: And that breaks the spell.
JULIE: Yes. The spell of Midsummer Eve . . . But listen, Jean. Come with me. I've got the money.
JEAN (*sceptically*): Enough?
JULIE: Enough to start with. Come with me. I can't travel alone today. It's Midsummer Day, remember. I'd be packed into a suffocating train among crowds of people who'd all stare at me. And it would stop at every station while I yearned for wings. No, I can't do that, I simply can't. There will be memories too; memories of Midsummer Days when I was little. The leafy church—birch and lilac—the gaily spread dinner table, relatives, friends—evening in the park—dancing and music and flowers and fun. Oh, however far you run away—there'll always be memories in the baggage car—and remorse and guilt.
JEAN: I will come with you, but quickly now then, before it's too late. At once.
JULIE: Put on your things. (*Picks up the cage.*)

JEAN: No luggage mind. That would give us away.
JULIE: No, only what we can take with us in the carriage.
JEAN (*fetching his hat*): What on earth have you got there? What is it?
JULIE: Only my greenfinch. I don't want to leave it behind.
JEAN: Well, I'll be damned! We're to take a bird-cage along, are we? You're crazy. Put that cage down.
JULIE: It's the only thing I'm taking from my home. The only living creature who cares for me since Diana went off like that. Don't be cruel. Let me take it.
JEAN: Put that cage down, I tell you—and don't talk so loud. Kristin will hear.
JULIE: No, I won't leave it in strange hands. I'd rather you killed it.
JEAN: Give the little beast here then and I'll wring it's neck.
JULIE: But don't hurt it, don't . . . no, I can't.
JEAN: Give it here. I *can*.
JULIE (*taking the bird out of the cage and kissing it.*): Dear little Serena, must you die and leave your mistress?
JEAN: Please don't make a scene. It's *your* life and future we're worrying about. Come on, quick now!

(*He snatches the bird from her, puts it on a board and picks up a chopper.* JULIE *turns away.*)

You should have learnt how to kill chickens instead of target-shooting. Then you wouldn't faint at a drop of blood.
JULIE (*screaming*): Kill me too! Kill me! You who can butcher an innocent creature without a quiver. Oh, how I hate you, how I loathe you! There is blood between us now. I curse the hour I first saw you. I curse the hour I was conceived in my mother's womb.
JEAN: What's the use of cursing. Let's go.
JULIE (*going to the chopping-block as if drawn against her will.*): No, I won't go yet. I can't . . . I must look. Listen! There's a carriage. (*Listens without taking her eyes off the board and chopper.*) You don't think I can bear the sight of blood. You think I'm so weak. Oh, how I should like to see your blood and your brains on a chopping-block! I'd like to see the whole of your sex swimming like that in a sea of blood. I think I could drink out of your skull, bathe my feet in your broken breast and eat your heart roasted whole. You think I'm weak. You think I love you, that my womb yearned for your seed and I want to carry your offspring under my heart and nourish it with my blood. You think I want to bear your child and take your name. By the way, what is your name? I've never heard your surname. I don't suppose you've got one. I should be "Mrs. Hovel" or "Madam Dunghill." You dog wearing my collar, you lackey with my crest on your buttons! I share you with my cook; I'm my own servant's rival! Oh! Oh! Oh! . . . You think I'm a

coward and will run away. No, now I'm going to stay—and let the storm break. My father will come back . . . find his desk broken open . . . his money gone. Then he'll ring that bell—twice for the valet—and then he'll send for the police . . . and I shall tell everything. Everything. Oh how wonderful to make an end of it all—a real end! He has a stroke and dies and that's the end of all of us. Just peace and quietness . . . eternal rest. The coat of arms broken on the coffin and the Count's line extinct . . . But the valet's line goes on in an orphanage, wins laurels in the gutter and ends in jail.

JEAN: There speaks the noble blood! Bravo, Miss Julie. But now, don't let the cat out of the bag.

(KRISTIN *enters dressed for church, carrying a prayer-book.* JULIE *rushes to her and flings herself into her arms for protection.*)

JULIE: Help me, Kristin! Protect me from this man!

KRISTIN (*unmoved and cold.*): What goings-on for a feast day morning! (*Sees the board.*) And what a filthy mess. What's it all about? Why are you screaming and carrying on so?

JULIE: Kristin, you're a woman and my friend. Beware of that scoundrel!

JEAN (*embarrassed*): While you ladies are talking things over, I'll go and shave. (*Slips into his room.*)

JULIE: You must understand. You must listen to me.

KRISTIN: I certainly don't understand such loose ways. Where are you off to in those travelling clothes? And he had his hat on, didn't he, eh?

JULIE: Listen, Kristin. Listen, I'll tell you everything.

KRISTIN: I don't want to know anything.

JULIE: You must listen.

KRISTIN: What to? Your nonsense with Jean? I don't care a rap about that; it's nothing to do with me. But if you're thinking of getting him to run off with you, we'll soon put a stop to that.

JULIE (*very nervously*): Please try to be calm, Kristin, and listen. I can't stay here, nor can Jean—so we must go abroad.

KRISTIN: Hm, hm!

JULIE (*brightening*): But you see, I've had an idea. Supposing we all three go—abroad—to Switzerland and start a hotel together . . . I've got some money, you see . . . and Jean and I could run the whole thing —and I thought you would take charge of the kitchen. Wouldn't that be splendid? Say yes, do. If you come with us everything will be fine. Oh do say yes! (*Puts her arms round* KRISTIN.)

KRISTIN (*coolly thinking*): Hm, hm.

JULIE (*presto tempo*): You've never travelled, Kristin. You should go abroad and see the world. You've no idea how nice it is travelling by train—new faces all the time and new countries. On our way through Hamburg we'll go to the zoo—you'll love that—and we'll go to the theatre and the opera too . . . and when we get to Munich there'll be the museums, dear, and pictures by Rubens and Raphael—the great painters, you know . . . You've heard of Munich, haven't you? Where King Ludwig lived—you know, the king who went mad. . . . We'll see his castles—some of his castles are still just like in fairy-tales . . . and from there it's not far to Switzerland—and the Alps. Think of the Alps, Kristin dear, covered with snow in the middle of summer . . . and there are oranges there and trees that are green the whole year round . . .

(JEAN *is seen in the door of his room, sharpening his razor on a strop which he holds with his teeth and his left hand. He listens to the talk with satisfaction and now and then nods approval.* JULIE *continues, tempo prestissimo.*)

And then we'll get a hotel . . . and I'll sit at the desk, while Jean receives the guests and goes out marketing and writes letters . . . There's life for you! Trains whistling, buses driving up, bells ringing upstairs and downstairs . . . and I shall make out the bills—I shall cook them too . . . you've no idea how nervous travellers are when it comes to paying their bills. And you—you'll sit like a queen in the kitchen . . . of course there won't be any standing at the stove for you. You'll always have to be nicely dressed and ready to be seen, and with your looks—no, I'm not flattering you—one find day you'll catch yourself a husband . . . some rich Englishman, I shouldn't wonder—they're the ones who are easy (*slowing down*) to catch . . . and then we'll get rich and build ourselves a villa on Lake Como . . . of course it rains there a little now and then—but (*dully*) the sun must shine there too sometimes—even though it seems gloomy—and if not—then we can come home again—come back (*pause*) here—or somewhere else . . .

KRISTIN: Look here, Miss Julie, do you believe all that yourself?

JULIE (*exhausted*): Do I believe it?

KRISTIN: Yes.

JULIE (*wearily*): I don't know. I don't believe anything any more. (*Sinks down on the bench; her head in her arms on the table.*) Nothing. Nothing at all.

KRISTIN (*turning to* JEAN): So you meant to beat it, did you?

JEAN (*disconcerted, putting the razor on the table*): Beat it? What are you talking about? You've heard Miss Julie's plan, and though she's tired now with being up all night, it's a perfectly sound plan.

KRISTIN: Oh, is it? If you thought I'd work for that . . .

JEAN (*interrupting*): Kindly use decent language in front of your mistress. Do you hear?

KRISTIN: Mistress?

JEAN: Yes.

KRISTIN: Well, well, just listen to that!

JEAN: Yes, it would be a good thing if you did listen and talked less. Miss Julie is your mistress and what's made you lose your respect for her now ought to make you feel the same about yourself.

KRISTIN: I've always had enough self-respect——

JEAN: To despise other people.

KRISTIN: —not to go below my own station. Has the Count's cook ever gone with the groom or the swineherd? Tell me that.

JEAN: No, you were lucky enough to have a high-class chap for your beau.

KRISTIN: High-class all right—selling the oats out of the Count's stable.

JEAN: You're a fine one to talk—taking a commission on the groceries and bribes from the butcher.

KRISTIN: What the devil . . . ?

JEAN: And now you can't feel any respect for your employers. You, you!

KRISTIN: Are you coming to church with me? I should think you need a good sermon after your fine deeds.

JEAN: No, I'm not going to church today. You can go alone and confess your own sins.

KRISTIN: Yes, I'll do that and bring back enough forgiveness to cover yours too. The Saviour suffered and died on the cross for all our sins, and if we go to Him with faith and a penitent heart, He takes all our sins upon Himself.

JEAN: Even grocery thefts?

JULIE: Do you believe that, Kristin?

KRISTIN: That is my living faith, as sure as I stand here. The faith I learnt as a child and have kept ever since, Miss Julie. "But where sin abounded, grace did much more abound."

JULIE: Oh, if I had your faith! Oh, if . . .

KRISTIN: But you see you can't have it without God's special grace, and it's not given to all to have that.

JULIE: Who is it given to then?

KRISTIN: That's the great secret of the workings of grace, Miss Julie. God is no respecter of persons, and with Him the last shall be first . . .

JULIE: Then I suppose He does respect the last.

KRISTIN (*continuing*): . . . and it is easier for a camel to go through the eye of a needle than for a rich man to enter into the kingdom of God. That's how it is, Miss Julie. Now I'm going—alone, and on my way I shall tell the groom not to let any of the horses out, in case anyone should want to leave before the Count gets back. Goodbye.

(*Exit.*)

JEAN: What a devil! And all on account of a greenfinch.

JULIE (*wearily*): Never mind the greenfinch. Do you see any way out of this, any end to it?

JEAN (*pondering*): No.

JULIE: If you were in my place, what would you do?
JEAN: In your place? Wait a bit. If I was a woman—a lady of rank who had—fallen. I don't know. Yes, I do know now.
JULIE (*picking up the razor and making a gesture*): This?
JEAN: Yes. But *I* wouldn't do it, you know. There's a difference between us.
JULIE: Because you're a man and I'm a woman? What is the difference?
JEAN: The usual difference—between man and woman.
JULIE (*holding the razor*): I'd like to. But I can't. My father couldn't either, that time he wanted to.
JEAN: No, he didn't want to. He had to be revenged first.
JULIE: And now my mother is revenged again, through me.
JEAN: Didn't you ever love your father, Miss Julie?
JULIE: Deeply, but I must have hated him too—unconsciously. And he let me be brought up to despise my own sex, to be half woman, half man. Whose fault is what's happened? My father's, my mother's or my own? My own? I haven't anything that I didn't get from my father, one emotion that didn't come from my mother, and as for this last idea—about all people being equal—I got that from him, my fiancé—that's why I call him a cad. How can it be my fault? Push the responsibility on to Jesus, like Kristin does? No, I'm too proud and—thanks to my father's teaching—too intelligent. As for all that about a rich person not being able to get into heaven, it's just a lie, but Kristin, who has money in the savings-bank, will certainly not get in. Whose fault is it? What does it matter whose fault it is? In any case I must take the blame and bear the consequences.
JEAN: Yes, but . . . (*There are two sharp rings on the bell.* JULIE *jumps to her feet.* JEAN *changes into his livery.*) The Count is back. Supposing Kristin . . . (*Goes to the speaking-tube, presses it and listens.*)
JULIE: Has he been to his desk yet?
JEAN: This is Jean, sir. (*Listens.*) Yes, sir. very good sir. (*Listens.*) At once, sir? (*Listens.*) Very good, sir. In half an hour.
JULIE (*in panic*): What did he say? My God, what did he say?
JEAN: He ordered his boots and his coffee in half an hour.
JULIE: Then there's half an hour . . . Oh, I'm so tired! I can't do anything. Can't be sorry, can't run away, can't stay, can't live—can't die. Help me. Order me, and I'll obey like a dog. Do me this last service—save my honour, save his name. You know what I ought to do, but haven't the strength to do. Use your strength and order me to do it.
JEAN: I don't know why—I can't now—I don't understand . . . It's just as if this coat made me—I can't give you orders—and now that the Count has spoken to me—I can't quite explain, but . . . well, that devil of a lackey is bending my back again. I believe if the Count came down now and ordered me to cut my throat, I'd do it on the spot.

JULIE: Then pretend you're him and I'm you. You did some fine acting before, when you knelt to me and played the aristocrat. Or . . . Have you ever seen a hypnotist at the theatre? (*He nods.*) He says to the person "Take the broom," and he takes it. He says "Sweep," and he sweeps . . .

JEAN: But the person has to be asleep.

JULIE (*as if in a trance*): I am asleep already . . . the whole room has turned to smoke—and you look like a stove—a stove like a man in black with a tall hat—your eyes are glowing like coals when the fire is low—and your face is a white patch like ashes. (*The sunlight has now reached the floor and lights up* JEAN.) How nice and warm it is! (*She holds out her hands as though warming them at a fire.*) And so light— and so peaceful.

JEAN (*putting the razor in her hand*): Here is the broom. Go now while it's light—out to the barn—and . . . (*Whispers in her ear.*)

JULIE (*waking*): Thank you. I am going now—to rest. But just tell me that even the first can receive the gift of grace.

JEAN: The first? No, I can't tell you that. But wait . . . Miss Julie, I've got it! You aren't one of the first any longer. You're one of the last.

JULIE: That's true. I'm one of the very last. I *am* the last. Oh! . . . But now I can't go. Tell me again to go.

JEAN: No, I can't now either. I can't.

JULIE: And the first shall be last.

JEAN: Don't think, don't think. You're taking my strength away too and making me a coward. What's that? I thought I saw the bell move . . . To be so frightened of a bell! Yes, but it's not just a bell. There's somebody behind it—a hand moving it—and something else moving the hand—and if you stop your ears—if you stop your ears—yes, then it rings louder than ever. Rings and rings until you answer—and then it's too late. Then the police come and . . . and . . . (*The bell rings twice loudly.* JEAN *flinches, then straightens himself up.*) It's horrible. But there's no other way to end it . . . Go!

(JULIE *walks firmly out through the door.*)

CURTAIN

William Butler Yeats

Purgatory

Persons in the play

A Boy
An Old Man

SCENE: *A ruined house and a bare tree in the background.*

BOY: Half-door, hall door,
   Hither and thither day and night,
   Hill or hollow, shouldering this pack,
   Hearing you talk.
OLD MAN: Study that house.
   I think about its jokes and stories;
   I try to remember what the butler
   Sáid to a drunken gamekeeper
   In mid-October, but I cannot.
   If I cannot, none living can.
   Where are the jokes and stories of a house,
   Its threshold gone to patch a pig-sty?
BOY: So you have come this path before?
OLD MAN: The moonlight falls upon the path,
   The shadow of a cloud upon the house,
   And that's symbolical; study that tree.
   What is it like?
BOY: A silly old man.
OLD MAN: It's like—no matter what it's like.
   I saw it a year ago stripped bare as now,
   So I chose a better trade.
   I saw it fifty years ago
   Before the thunderbolt had riven it.
   Green leaves, ripe leaves, leaves thick as butter,
   Fat, greasy life. Stand there and look,
   Because there is somebody in that house,
   (*The* BOY *puts down pack and stands in the doorway.*)
BOY: There's nobody here.
OLD MAN: There's somebody there.
BOY: The floor is gone, the windows gone,

And where there should be roof there's sky,
And here's a bit of an egg-shell thrown
Out of a jackdaw's nest.
OLD MAN: But there are some
That do not care what's gone, what's left:
The souls in Purgatory that come back
To habitations and familiar spots.
BOY: Your wits are out again.
OLD MAN: Re-live
Their transgressions, and that not once
But many times; they know at last
The consequence of those transgressions
Whether upon others or upon themselves;
Upon others, others may bring help,
For when the consequence is at an end
The dream must end; if upon themselves,
There is no help but in themselves
And in mercy of God.
BOY: I have had enough!
Talk to the jackdaws, if talk you must.
OLD MAN: Stop! Sit there upon that stone.
That is the house where I was born.
BOY: The big old house that was burnt down?
OLD MAN: My Mother that was your grand-dam owned it,
This scenery and this countryside,
Kennel and stable, horse and hound—
She had a horse at the Curragh, and there met
My father, a groom in a training stable,
Looked at him and married him.
Her mother never spoke to her again,
And she did right.
BOY: What's right and wrong?
My grand-dad got the girl and the money.
OLD MAN: Looked at him and married him,
And he squandered everything she had.
She never knew the worst, because
She died in giving birth to me,
But now she knows it all, being dead.
Great people lived and died in this house;
Magistrates, colonels, members of Parliament,
Captains and Governors, and long ago
Men that had fought at Aughrim and the Boyne.
Some that had gone on Government work
To London or to India came home to die,
Or came from London every spring
To look at the may-blossom in the park.
They had loved the trees that he had cut down

>   To pay what he had lost at cards
>   Or spent on horses, drink and women;
>   Had loved the house, had loved all
>   The intricate passages of the house,
>   But he killed the house; to kill a house
>   Where great men grew up, married, died,
>   I here declare a capital offence.
> BOY: My God, but you had luck! Grand clothes,
>   And may be a grand horse to ride.
> OLD MAN: That he might keep me upon his level
>   He never sent me to school, but some
>   Half-loved me for my half of her:
>   A gamekeeper's wife taught me to read,
>   A Catholic curate taught me Latin.
>   There were old books and books made fine
>   By eighteenth-century French binding, books
>   Modern and ancient, books by the ton.
> BOY: What education have you given me?
> OLD MAN: I gave the education that befits
>   A bastard that a peddler got
>   Upon a tinker's daughter in a ditch.
>   When I had come to sixteen years old
>   My father burned down the house when drunk.
> BOY: But that is my age, sixteen years old,
>   At the Puck Fair.
> OLD MAN: And everything was burnt;
>   Books, library, all were burnt.
> BOY: Is what I have heard upon the road the truth,
>   That you killed him in the burning house?
> OLD MAN: There's nobody here but our two selves?
> BOY: Nobody, Father.
> OLD MAN: I stuck him with a knife,
>   That knife that cuts my dinner now,
>   And after that I left him in the fire.
>   They dragged him out, somebody saw
>   The knife-wound but could not be certain
>   Because the body was all black and charred.
>   Then some that were his drunken friends
>   Swore they would put me upon trial,
>   Spoke of quarrels, a threat I had made.
>   The gamekeeper gave me some old clothes,
>   I ran away, worked here and there
>   Till I became a pedlar on the roads,
>   No good trade, but good enough
>   Because I am my father's son,
>   Because of what I did or may do.
>   Listen to the hoof-beats! Listen, listen!
> BOY: I cannot hear a sound.

William Butler Yeats: *Purgatory*

OLD MAN: Beat! Beat!
    This night is the anniversary
    Of my mother's wedding night,
    Or of the night wherein I was begotten.
    My father is riding from the public-house,
    A whiskey-bottle under his arm.

    (*A window is lit showing a young girl.*)

    Look at the window; she stands there
    Listening, the servants are all in bed,
    She is alone, he has stayed late
    Bragging and drinking in the public-house.
BOY: There's nothing but an empty gap in the wall.
    You have made it up. No, you are mad!
    You are getting madder every day.
OLD MAN: It's louder now because he rides
    Upon a gravelled avenue
    All grass to-day. The hoof-beat stops,
    He has gone to the other side of the house,
    Gone to the stable, put the horse up.
    She has gone down to open the door.
    This night she is no better than her man
    And does not mind that he is half drunk,
    She is mad about him. They mount the stairs,
    She brings him into her own chamber.
    And that is the marriage-chamber now.
    The window is dimly lit again.

    Do not let him touch you! It is not true
    That drunken men cannot beget,
    And if he touch he must beget
    And you must bear his murderer.
    Deaf! Both deaf! If I should throw
    A stick or a stone they would not hear;
    And that's a proof my wits are out.
    But there's a problem: she must live
    Through everything in exact detail,
    Driven to it by remorse, and yet
    Can she renew the sexual act
    And find no pleasure in it, and if not,
    If pleasure and remorse must both be there,
    Which is the greater?
                        I lack schooling.
    Go fetch Tertullian; he and I
    Will ravel all that problem out
    While those two lie upon the mattress
    Begetting me.
               Come back! Come back!

And so you thought to slip away,
My bag of money between your fingers,
And that I could not talk and see!
You have been rummaging in the pack.

(*The light in the window has faded out.*)

BOY: You never gave me my right share.
OLD MAN: And had I given it, young as you are,
You would have spent it upon drink.
BOY: What if I did? I had a right
To get it and spend it as I choose.
OLD MAN: Give me that bag and no more words.
BOY: I will not.
OLD MAN: I will break your fingers.
(*They struggle for the bag. In the struggle it drops, scattering the money. The* OLD MAN *staggers but does not fall. They stand looking at each other. The window is lit up. A man is seen pouring whiskey into a glass.*)
BOY: What if I killed you?
Because you were young and he was old.
Now I am young and you are old.
OLD MAN (*staring at window*): Better-looking, those sixteen years—
BOY: What are you muttering?
OLD MAN: Younger—and yet
She should have known he was not her kind.
BOY: What are you saying? Out with it (OLD MAN *points to window*).
My God! The window is lit up
And somebody stands there, although
The floorboards are all burnt away.
OLD MAN: The window is lit up because my father
Has come to find a glass for his whiskey.
He leans there like some tired beast.
BOY: A dead, living, murdered man!
OLD MAN: 'Then the bride-sleep fell upon Adam':
Where did I read those words?
And yet
There's nothing leaning in the window
But the impression upon my mother's mind;
Being dead she is alone in her remorse.
BOY: A body that was a bundle of old bones
Before I was born. Horrible! Horrible!

(*He covers his eyes.*)

OLD MAN: That beast there would know nothing, being nothing,
If I should kill a man under the window
He would not even turn his head.

(*He stabs the* BOY.)

My father and my son on the same jack-knife!
That finishes—there—there—there—

(*He stabs again and again. The window grows dark.*)

'Hush-a-bye baby, thy father's a knight,
Thy mother a lady, lovely and bright.
No, that is something that I read in a book,
And if I sing it must be to my mother,
And I lack rhyme.

(*The stage has grown dark except where the tree stands in white light.*)

               Study that tree.
It stands there like a purified soul,
All cold, sweet, glistening light.
Dear mother, the window is dark again,
But you are in the light because
I finished all that consequence.
I killed that lad because had he grown up
He would have struck a woman's fancy,
Begot, and passed pollution on.
I am a wretched foul old man
And therefore harmless. When I have stuck
This old jack-knife into a sod
And pulled it out all bright again,
And picked up all the money that he dropped,
I'll to a distant place, and there
Tell my old jokes among new men.

(*He cleans the knife and begins to pick up money.*)

Hoof-beats! Dear God,
How quickly it returns—beat—beat—!

Her mind cannot hold up that dream.
Twice a murderer and all for nothing,
And she must animate that dead night
Not once but many times!
               O God,
Release my mother's soul from its dream!
Mankind can do no more. Appease
The misery of the living and the remorse of the dead.

THE END

Two
Citizens and Strangers

A play occurs in three places simultaneously. It is performed by actors on a stage; it exists in the minds of the audience watching it; and, it is set somewhere in this or another world. Setting is not a matter of props and backdrops. The alley, the house, the ship, the barren heath, each is the imagined stage for the human action in which the players are engaged. Setting, realistic or abstract, routine or exotic, is part of the symbolic structure of the play and helps to shape the experience of the play in the mind of the audience. Participation in a play by an audience requires a breakdown of any sharp separation between the audience, the character, and the specific corner of the world that character inhabits.

One task of the dramatist, then, is to create a world in which his characters belong. Yet a constant question of almost every person at one time or another is, "Where do I belong?" Therefore a drama may deal with the question of citizenship in the profoundest sense. Characters, in a particular setting, may discover to what degree they do or do not belong in their world. The audience, temporary inhabitants of that world, comes in turn to some knowledge of its citizenship in the larger world beyond the theatre.

Each play in this section raises many questions of human conduct. *Othello*, for example, is a remarkable study of the insecurity and self-deception that is called jealousy. *Benito Cereno* explores the paradox of slavery: the person who keeps slaves becomes the slave of his slaves. The demands of being the master create their own bondage. *Dutchman* is a play of violent language and violent action in which Clay is forced to respond to a strange woman who represents, in part, his most private thoughts about himself. In some sense, Lula is a witch or spirit who haunts men like Clay.

As varied as they are, however, each of these plays raises in a special way for the protagonist the question, "Do I really belong here?" Each play makes specific use of its setting to emphasize the exile, the alienation, the isolation of its central character. The setting and the action merge into a powerful symbol of the human question of full participation in some community of which the person is, nominally, a citizen.

Because Shakespeare is not limited by realism in his settings, he is able to transform them into immediate symbols. When, for example, in *The Winter's Tale*, the scene shifts to the "seacoast" of landlocked Bohemia, the setting is appropriate. For Shakespeare and his audience, Bohemia represented a strange place where exotic and "bohemian" things could happen. The immediacy of that shared understanding of the symbol transcends the error in geography. So, too, in *Othello*, the setting is part of the complex symbolism of a play that raises many disturbing questions of a man's "place" in his society.

Othello is a mercenary employed by a city-state to defend its interests. But he is also a very strong and foolish man. He breaks out of his role of servant of the state and creates a personal bond that ties him in a way very different from that of the status accorded him as a successful general, a servant of the state. Othello can be made insanely jealous because he is so unsure of himself when not in command in battle. Iago sees his vulnerability and uses it to destroy him. Othello's last long speech is a strange combination of apology and self-justification. In the end, bereft of any meaning for his life, he reminds his listeners that he was a loyal citizen of his adopted country. His ruin comes partly because he saw himself in some way as a servant of the state who had overreached himself in claiming a personal reward.

The subway, an impersonal means of movement within a large city, is a symbol for the herding together of people who have nothing in common except the need to get away from one place to another. Part of the power of *Dutchman* derives from the contrast between the impersonal public setting and the intense personal confrontation that takes place. Clay's sense of himself, his race, and his manhood is challenged by Lula in a setting that stands for the lonely crowd of modern, urban civilization. The disposal of his body is the appropriate end to the assembly-line movement of people that the subway represents.

In Robert Lowell's *Benito Cereno*, the citizens of three nations come into conflict aboard a ship. Isolated from his native country, each character acts as the representative of the legal and moral values of his nation. The question is one of sovereignty, not in the sense of national policy, but in the relationship of one human being to another and who will, should, or must, according to what code of values, have sovereignty over the other.

Benito Cereno is one of three plays Lowell collected under the title *The Old Glory*. He adapted these plays from stories by Hawthorne and Melville, which were rooted in American history. Like Shakespeare and Racine, Lowell saw new dramatic possibilities in old stories and took double advantage of his sources. He transformed Melville's novella into a verse drama and, at the same time, turned the nineteenth-century allegory of the stain of slavery on the American mind into a twentieth-century vision of the nature of slavery for slave and master alike.

The settings, words, and actions of these plays are very different. Yet each starts with the recognition that citizenship in a race, in a country, and in humanity are not always easily maintained and that the struggle to unite them may be tragic.

William Shakespeare

Othello
the tragedy of the moor of Venice

The Names of the Actors

DUKE OF VENICE
BRABANTIO, *a Senator, father to Desdemona*
SENATORS
GRATIANO, *brother to Brabantio* ⎱ *two noble*
LODOVICO, *kinsman to Brabantio* ⎰ *Venetians*
OTHELLO, *the Moor, in the service of Venice*
CASSIO, *his honourable Lieutenant*
IAGO, *his Ancient, a villain*
RODERIGO, *a gull'd Venetian gentleman*
MONTANO, *former Governor of Cyprus*
CLOWN, *servant to Othello*
DESDEMONA, *daughter to Brabantio and wife to Othello*
EMILIA, *wife to Iago*
BIANCA, *a courtesan, in love with Cassio*
SAILOR, MESSENGER, HERALD, OFFICERS, GENTLEMEN, MUSICIANS, ATTENDANTS

SCENE: *Venice; Cyprus*

ACT ONE

Scene I. Venice. A street.

(*Enter* RODERIGO *and* IAGO.)

RODERIGO: Tush, never tell me! I take it much unkindly
That thou, Iago, who hast had my purse
As if the strings were thine, shouldst know of this.
IAGO: 'Sblood, but you will not hear me!
If ever I did dream of such a matter, 5
Abhor me.
RODERIGO: Thou told'st me thou didst hold him in thy hate
IAGO: Despise me if I do not. Three great ones of the city,
In personal suit to make me his lieutenant,
Off-capp'd to him; and, by the faith of man, 10
I know my price, I am worth no worse a place.
But he, as loving his own pride and purposes,
Evades them with a bombast circumstance,
Horribly stuff'd with epithets of war;
And, in conclusion. 15
Nonsuits my mediators; for, "Certes," says he,
"I have already chose my officer."
And what was he?
Forsooth, a great arithmetician,
One Michael Cassio, a Florentine 20
(A fellow almost damn'd in a fair wife),
That never set a squadron in the field,
Nor the division of a battle knows

I.i. This scene takes place at night. It opens in the midst of an excited conversation between Iago and his dupe, the Venetian gallant Roderigo, who is upbraiding him for concealing some matter of great importance. What this is we learn at the end of the scene [K].   3 *this* the marriage of Othello and Desdemona.   4 *'Sblood* by God's blood.   6 *Abhor* shrink in horror from.   7 *him* Othello.   9 *In personal suit* requesting in person.   10 *Off-capp'd* stood with hat in hand, a sign of respect and subservience.   11 *price* value, worth. *worse a place* lower a position.   13 *bombast circumstance* bombastic circumlocution. "Bombast" is literally a kind of cotton padding.   14 *epithets* technical terms.   16 *Nonsuits my mediators* denies the pleas of those who had interceded for me. *Certes* certainly.   19 *arithmetician* Iago has the veteran's contempt for the scientific soldier who knows more of mathematics than of actual warfare [K].   20 *Florentine* Since the Florentines were great merchants, he may also allude to Cassio's bookkeeping accomplishments, to which he refers in line 31 [K].   21 *A fellow . . . wife* A puzzling line which has been much disputed. An Italian proverb holds that a man with a fair wife is damned. Perhaps he means that Cassio is about to marry. Perhaps Shakespeare at the time he wrote the line meant to follow Cinthio, in whose account Cassio is married. [K] refers to the original notes of George Lyman Kittredge, which were retained in Professor Ribner's Revision.

> More than a spinster; unless the bookish theoric,
> Wherein the toged consuls can propose
> As masterly as he. Mere prattle, without practice,
> Is all his soldiership. But he, sir, had th' election;
> And I (of whom his eyes had seen the proof
> At Rhodes, at Cyprus, and on other grounds
> Christian and heathen) must be belee'd and calm'd
> By debitor and creditor, this counter-caster.
> He (in good time!) must his lieutenant be,
> And I (God bless the mark!) his Moorship's ancient.
>
> RODERIGO: By heaven, I rather would have been his hangman.
> IAGO: Why, there's no remedy; 'tis the curse of service.
> Preferment goes by letter and affection,
> And not by old gradation, where each second
> Stood heir to th' first. Now, sir, be judge yourself,
> Whether I in any just term am affin'd
> To love the Moor.
> RODERIGO: I would not follow him then.
> IAGO: O, sir, content you.
> I follow him to serve my turn upon him.
> We cannot all be masters, nor all masters
> Cannot be truly follow'd. You shall mark
> Many a duteous and knee-crooking knave
> That, doting on his own obsequious bondage,
> Wears out his time, much like his master's ass,
> For naught but provender; and when he's old, cashier'd.
> Whip me such honest knaves! Others there are
> Who, trimm'd in forms and visages of duty,

23 *division of a battle* how an army should be drawn up [K].   24 *unless . . . theoric* except in pedantic theory [K].   25 *toged consuls* the Venetian senators wearing the toga, a traditional robe of peace. *propose* speak.   27 *had th' election* was chosen.   30 *must be belee'd and calm'd* must "have the wind taken out of my sails," as we say. A boat is "belee'd" when another runs between her and the wind so that she is "to the leeward." Thus she is more or less "becalmed" and loses headway. The nautical metaphor is appropriate for a Venetian officer [K].   31 *debitor and creditor* bookkeeper. *counter-caster* one who makes petty computations by means of counters—tokens, pieces of metal or uncurrent coin used in "casting" accounts or making change [K].   33 *bless the mark* avert the evil omen (a common expression). *ancient* ensign, literally a standard-bearer.   35 *service* military service.   36-7 *Preferment . . . old gradation* promotion depends upon influence (letter) and favouritism (affection) rather than upon the old way of promotion from grade to grade according to seniority.   39-40 *Whether . . . To love the Moor* whether I stand in any such relation to the Moor as justly binds me to love him [K]. *term* manner. *affin'd* related.   44 *truly* loyally.   45 *knee-crooking* flattering, subservient. *knave* fellow.   46 *doting on* loving beyond reason.   47 *time* lifetime.   48 *cashier'd* dismissed from service.   49 *Whip me* let them be whipped (for all I care). *honest* honourable. *knaves* fellows.   50 *trimm'd* dressed, ornamented. *forms and visages* manners and outward appearances. *duty* loyalty.

Keep yet their hearts attending on themselves;
And, throwing but shows of service on their lords,
Do well thrive by them, and when they have lin'd their coats,
Do themselves homage. These fellows have some soul;
And such a one do I profess myself. For sir, 55
It is as sure as you are Roderigo,
Were I the Moor, I would not be Iago.
In following him, I follow but myself;
Heaven is my judge, not I for love and duty,
But seeming so, for my peculiar end; 60
For when my outward action doth demonstrate
The native act and figure of my heart
In compliment extern, 'tis not long after
But I will wear my heart upon my sleeve
For daws to peck at. I am not what I am. 65
RODERIGO: What a full fortune does the thick-lips owe
  If he can carry't thus!
IAGO: Call up her father,
  Rouse him.—Make after him, poison his delight,
  Proclaim him in the streets. Incense her kinsmen,
  And though he in a fertile climate dwell, 70
  Plague him with flies; though that his joy be joy,
  Yet throw such changes of vexation on't
  As it may lose some colour.
RODERIGO: Here is her father's house. I'll call aloud.
IAGO: Do, with like timorous accent and dire yell 75
  As when, by night and negligence, the fire
  Is spied in populous cities.
RODERIGO: What, ho, Brabantio! Signior Brabantio, ho!
IAGO: Awake! What, ho, Brabantio! Thieves! thieves! thieves!
  Look to your house, your daughter, and your bags! 80
  Thieves! thieves!
  (Enter BRABANTIO *above, at a window.)*
BRABANTIO: What is the reason of this terrible summons?
  What is the matter there?

---

52 *throwing* bestowing.   *shows* appearances.   53 *lin'd their coats* enriched themselves.
54 *Do themselves homage* abandon their masters and serve only themselves [K].
57 *Were I . . . be Iago* This amounts to an assertion that Iago is always himself—always devoted to his own interests [K]. Each man is what he is, and were he someone else (the Moor) he would not be what he now is (Iago).   60 *peculiar* special, personal.
62 *native act and figure* true actions and feelings.   63 *compliment extern* outward appearance and behaviour [K].   65 *daws* jackdaws, proverbially stupid birds (F1; Q1: "doues").   66 *full fortune* good luck.   *owe* possess.   67 *carry't thus* get away with what he has done.   68 *after him* Othello.   70 *in a fertile climate dwell* is enjoying abundant good fortune [K].   71 *flies* petty annoyances.   72 *changes of vexation* vexatious disturbances.   73 *As* so that   *it* his joy   *lose some colour* be tarnished
75 *like timorous accent* such terrifying voice.   80 *bags* money bags.

RODERIGO: Signior, is all your family within?
IAGO: Are your doors, lock'd?
BRABANTIO: Why, wherefore ask you this?
IAGO: Zounds, sir, y'are robb'd! For shame put on your gown!
Your heart is burst; you have lost half your soul.
Even now, now, very now, an old black ram
Is tupping your white ewe. Arise, arise!
Awake the snorting citizens with the bell,
Or else the devil will make a grandsire of you.
Arise, I say!
BRABANTIO: What, have you lost your wits?
RODERIGO: Most reverend signior, do you know my voice?
BRABANTIO: Not I. What are you?
RODERIGO: My name is Roderigo.
BRABANTIO: The worser welcome!
I have charg'd thee not to haunt about my doors.
In honest plainness thou hast heard me say
My daughter is not for thee; and now, in madness,
Being full of supper and distemp'ring draughts,
Upon malicious bravery dost thou come
To start my quiet.
RODERIGO: Sir, sir, sir—
BRABANTIO: But thou must needs be sure
My spirit and my place have in them power
To make this bitter to thee.
RODERIGO: Patience, good sir.
BRABANTIO: What tell'st thou me of robbing? This is Venice;
My house is not a grange.
RODERIGO: Most grave Brabantio,
In simple and pure soul I come to you.
IAGO: Zounds, sir, you are one of those that will not serve God
if the devil bid you. Because we come to do you service,
and you think we are ruffians, you'll have your daughter
cover'd with a Barbary horse; you'll have your nephews
neigh to you; you'll have coursers for cousins, and
gennets for germans.

---

86 *Zounds* by God's wounds. *For shame . . . gown* Iago means that it is shameful for Brabantio to be sleeping when he ought to be up and dressed attending to his affairs [K]. *gown* dressing gown. 89 *tupping* covering. 90 *snorting* snoring. *bell* tocsin, general alarm bell. 91 *the devil* traditionally represented as black. 99 *distemp'ring draughts* intoxicating drinks. 100 *Upon malicious bravery* on account of a malicious wish to defy me—to brave my wrath [K]. 101 *start* startle, disturb. *quiet* sleep. 103 *place* position (as senator). 106 *grange* lonely farmhouse. 107 *simple* honest, sincere. 108-9 *you are one . . . bid you* You are one of those men that will not take the best advice in the world if it comes from a person that you do not like [K]. 111 *nephews* grandsons. 113 *gennets for germans* horses (of a Spanish breed) for kinsmen.

BRABANTIO: What profane wretch are thou?
IAGO: I am one, sir, that come to tell you your daughter and   115
    the Moor are now making the beast with two backs.
BRABANTIO: Thou art a villain.
IAGO: You are a senator.
BRABANTIO: This thou shalt answer. I know thee, Roderigo.
RODERIGO: Sir, I will answer anything. But I beseech you,
    If't be your pleasure and most wise consent   120
    (As partly I find it is) that your fair daughter,
    At this odd-even and dull watch o' th' night,
    Transported, with no worse nor better guard
    But with a knave of common hire, a gondolier,
    To the gross clasps of a lascivious Moor—   125
    If this be known to you, and your allowance,
    We then have done you bold and saucy wrongs;
    But if you know not this, my manners tell me
    We have your wrong rebuke. Do not believe
    That, from the sense of all civility,   130
    I thus would play and trifle with your reverence.
    Your daughter, if you have not given her leave,
    I say again, hath made a gross revolt,
    Tying her duty, beauty, wit, and fortunes
    In an extravagant and wheeling stranger   135
    Of here and everywhere. Straight satisfy yourself.
    If she be in her chamber, or your house,
    Let loose on me the justice of the state
    For thus deluding you.
BRABANTIO: Strike on the tinder, ho!
    Give me a taper! Call up all my people!   140
    This accident is not unlike my dream.
    Belief of it oppresses me already.
    Light, I say! light!   (*Exit above.*)
IAGO: Farewell, for I must leave you.
    It seems not meet, nor wholesome to my place,

---

114 *profane* foul-mouthed [K].   118 *answer* be called to account for.   122 *odd-even* about midnight, when one hardly knows whether it is night or morning [K].   *dull watch* sleepy time of night.   126 *your allowance* approved by you.   127 *saucy* insolent.   128 *manners* knowledge of proper behaviour—of the way gentlemen should treat each other [K].   130 *from . . . civility* contrary to proper and decent behaviour.   131 *your reverence* the respect to which you are entitled.   133 *gross* indecent.   135 *extravagant* wandering.   *wheeling* having no fixed abode [K].   *stranger* alien.   136 *Straight* immediately.   *satisfy* inform.   140 *taper* candle.   141 *accident* event.   *dream* To be taken literally rather than in the sense of "what I thought might happen"; for Brabantio has had no suspicion of Desdemona's love for Othello. We are to suppose he had had a bad dream, which he now thinks was prophetic [K].   144 *meet*

>   To be produc'd (as, if I stay, I shall) 145
>   Against the Moor. For I do know the state,
>   However this may gall him with some check,
>   Cannot with safety cast him; for he's embark'd
>   With such loud reason to the Cyprus wars,
>   Which even now stand in act, that for their souls 150
>   Another of his fathom they have none
>   To lead their business; in which regard,
>   Though I do hate him as I do hell pains,
>   Yet, for necessity of present life,
>   I must show out a flag and sign of love, 155
>   Which is indeed but sign. That you shall surely find him,
>   Lead to the Sagittary the raised search;
>   And there will I be with him. So farewell. *(Exit.)*

(Enter, below, BRABANTIO, *in his nightgown, and* SERVANTS *with torches.)*

> BRABANTIO: It is too true an evil. Gone she is;
>   And what's to come of my despised time 160
>   Is naught but bitterness. Now, Roderigo,
>   Where didst thou see her?—O unhappy girl!—
>   With the Moor, say'st thou?—Who would be a father?—
>   How didst thou know 'twas she?—O, she deceives me
>   Past thought!—What said she to you?—Get moe tapers! 165
>   Raise all my kindred!—Are they married, think you?
> RODERIGO: Truly I think they are.
> BRABANTIO: O heaven! How got she out? O treason of the blood!
>   Fathers, from hence trust not your daughters' minds
>   By what you see them act. Is there not charms 170
>   By which the property of youth and maidhood
>   May be abus'd? Have you not read, Roderigo,
>   Of some such thing?
> RODERIGO: Yes, sir, I have indeed.
> BRABANTIO: Call up my brother.—O, would you had had her!—
>   Some one way, some another.—Do you know 175
>   Where we may apprehend her and the Moor?

---

proper. *wholesome* healthy. *to my place* for my position (as Othello's ensign). [145] *produc'd* made a witness. [147] *gall* annoy. *check* reprimand. [148] *cast* dismiss. [149] *loud* urgent. [150] *stand in act* are in progress. [151] *fathom* capacity, ability. [154] *life* livelihod. [156] *That* so that. [157] *Sagittary* probably the name of an inn with an archer or centaur with drawn bow on its signboard. [160] *what's... time* the remainder of my life. [165] *moe* more. [168] *treason of the blood* treachery of my own child. [170] *charms* magic spells. [171] *property* special quality. [172] *abus'd* deceived, deluded, led astray. Belief in love charms (philters) was prevalent in Shakespeare's time. See Kittredge, WITCHCRAFT IN OLD AND NEW ENGLAND, Chapter IV

RODERIGO: I think I can discover him, if you please
To get good guard and go along with me.
BRABANTIO: Pray you lead on. At every house I'll call;
I may command at most.—Get weapons, ho! 180
And raise some special officers of night.—
On, good Roderigo. I'll deserve your pains. *(Exeunt.)*

[K].   177 *discover* uncover.   180 *I may command at most* at most of the houses. Brabantio is a person of such high rank and such extensive family connections that he can summon the retainers of almost any house to his aid [K].   181 *raise . . . night* call to my assistance some of the officers whose special duty it is to guard the city by night [K].   182 *deserve your pains* show myself grateful for the exertion you make in my behalf.

Scene II. Venice. Another street.

(Enter OTHELLO, IAGO, *and* ATTENDANTS *with torches.)*

IAGO: Though in the trade of war I have slain men,
Yet do I hold it very stuff o' th' conscience
To do no contriv'd murder. I lack iniquity
Sometimes to do me service. Nine or ten times
I had thought t' have yerk'd him here under the ribs. 5
OTHELLO: 'Tis better as it is.
IAGO: Nay, but he prated,
And spoke such scurvy and provoking terms
Against your honour
That with the little godliness I have
I did full hard forbear him. But I pray you, sir, 10
Are you fast married? Be assur'd of this,
That the magnifico is much belov'd,
And hath in his effect a voice potential—
As double as the Duke's. He will divorce you,
Or put upon you what restraint and grievance 15
The law, with all his might to enforce it on,
Will give him cable.

I.II   2 *very . . . conscience* a matter of strict conscientious scruple; something that conscience imperatively requires [K].   3 *contriv'd* deliberate.   5 *yerk'd* jabbed.   *him* Roderigo, whose conversation Iago is now reporting to Othello.   7 *scurvy* insulting.   10 *did full . . . him* with difficulty kept my hands off him.   12 *magnifico* Venetian lord, Brabantio.   13 *in his . . . potential* a powerful voice when it comes to executing his wishes.   14 *double as the Duke's* The Doge (Duke of Venice) was commonly, though erroneously, believed by the Elizabethans to have two votes. Hence Iago says, hyperbolically, that Brabantio's voice (or vote) is as much a double vote as the Duke's itself [K].   16 *enforce it on* force it (the law) to be executed with utmost rigour.   17 *cable* scope (another nautical metaphor).

William Shakespeare: *Othello*

OTHELLO: Let him do his spite.
My services which I have done the signiory
Shall outtongue his complaints. 'Tis yet to know—
Which, when I know that boasting is an honour,   20
I shall promulgate—I fetch my life and being
From men of royal siege; and my demerits
May speak unbonneted to as proud a fortune
As this that I have reach'd. For know, Iago,
But that I love the gentle Desdemona,   25
I would not my unhoused free condition
Put into circumscription and confine
For the sea's worth.

(Enter CASSIO, *and* OFFICERS *with torches.)*

                      But look what lights come yond.
IAGO: Those are the raised father and his friends.
   You were best go in.
OTHELLO: Not I. I must be found.   30
My parts, my title, and my perfect soul
Shall manifest me rightly. Is it they?
IAGO: By Janus, I think no.
OTHELLO: The servants of the Duke? and my lieutenant?
   The goodness of the night upon you, friends!   35
   What is the news?
CASSIO: The Duke does greet you, General;
And he requires your haste-post-haste appearance
Even on the instant.
OTHELLO: What's the matter, think you?
CASSIO: Something from Cyprus, as I may divine.
   It is a business of some heat. The galleys   40
   Have sent a dozen sequent messengers

---

17 *do his spite* do the utmost that his enmity can accomplish [K].   18 *signiory* governing body of Venice.   19 *outtongue* speak louder than.   20-1 *Which, when . . . promulgate* The inference is that Othello does not intend to disclose his royal descent until he finds that honour demands that he make it public [K].   22 *siege* literally seat, hence rank, *demerits* deserts.   23 *May speak . . . fortune* entitle me to meet unabashed even so great an honour as an alliance with Brabantio's family—I say it with all due modesty [K].   *unbonneted* courteously, hat in hand—not arrogantly, as with his hat on his head [K]. It is more likely, from the context of the term, that it means the opposite: that Othello may speak without removing his hat, thus on equal terms. The term has been much disputed.   26 *unhoused* unconfined, unmarried.   28 *sea's worth* The sea was regarded as a treasure-house because of the sunken ships on its bottom.   29 *raised* roused to action—not roused from sleep [K].   31-2 *My parts . . . me rightly* my past deeds (which have all been honourable), my title as general-in-chief (which vouches for my honour), and finally, my unblemished conscience will surely do me justice—justify me [K].   33 *Janus* a two-faced god.   41 *sequent* one after another.

This very night at one another's heels;
And many of the consuls, rais'd and met,
Are at the Duke's already. You have been hotly call'd for;
When, being not at your lodging to be found, 45
The Senate hath sent about three several quests
To search you out.
OTHELLO: 'Tis well I am found by you.
I will but spend a word here in the house,
And go with you. *(Exit.)*
CASSIO: Ancient, what makes he here?
IAGO: Faith, he to-night hath boarded a land carack. 50
If it prove lawful prize, he's made for ever.
CASSIO: I do not understand.
IAGO: He's married.
CASSIO: To who?

(Enter OTHELLO.)

IAGO: Marry, to—Come, Captain, will you go?
OTHELLO: Have with you.
CASSIO: Here comes another troop to seek for you.

(Enter BRABANTIO, RODERIGO, and OFFICERS with torches and weapons.)

IAGO: It is Brabantio. General, be advis'd. 55
He comes to bad intent.
OTHELLO: Holla! stand there!
RODERIGO: Signior, it is the Moor.
BRABANTIO: Down with him, thief!

(They draw on both sides.)

IAGO: You, Roderigo! Come, sir, I am for you.
OTHELLO: Keep up your bright swords, for the dew will rust them.
Good signior, you shall more command with years 60
Than with your weapons.
BRABANTIO: O thou foul thief, where hast thou stow'd my daughter?
Damn'd as thou art, thou hast enchanted her!
For I'll refer me to all things of sense,
If she in chains of magic were not bound, 65

---

50 *carack* merchant vessel.   52 *To who* Cassio either does not know of the elopement or does not choose to disclose his knowledge to Iago. Cassio had often been a messenger in the course of Othello's wooing (III.iii.941–100, 111–12), but nothing in the play indicates that he was now aware of the marriage [K].   55 *advis'd* cautious.   58 *You, Roderigo . . . you* Probably Iago wishes to protect Roderigo so that he can continue to supply him with money. His singling out a weak opponent is not to be taken as a sign of cowardice in Iago.   59 *bright swords* A trace of the soldier's contempt for armed civilians [K]. Othello speaks with the calm self-assurance of the professional soldier.   62 *stow'd* bestowed, hidden.   64 *refer me . . . sense* appeal

Whether a maid so tender, fair, and happy,
So opposite to marriage that she shunn'd
The wealthy curled darlings of our nation,
Would ever have (t' incur a general mock)
Run from her guardage to the sooty bosom 70
Of such a thing as thou—to fear, not to delight.
Judge me the world if 'tis not gross in sense
That thou hast practis'd on her with foul charms,
Abus'd her delicate youth with drugs or minerals
That weaken motion. I'll have't disputed on. 75
'Tis probable, and palpable to thinking.
I therefore apprehend and do attach thee
For an abuser of the world, a practiser
Of arts inhibited and out of warrant.
Lay hold upon him. If he do resist, 80
Subdue him at his peril.
OTHELLO: Hold your hands,
Both you of my inclining and the rest.
Were it my cue to fight, I should have known it
Without a prompter. Where will you that I go
To answer this your charge?
BRABANTIO: To prison, till fit time 85
Of law and course of direct session
Call thee to answer.
OTHELLO: What if I do obey?
How may the Duke be therewith satisfied,
Whose messengers are here about my side
Upon some present business of the state 90
To bring me to him?
OFFICER: 'Tis true, most worthy signior.
The Duke's in council, and your noble self
I am sure is sent for.

for judgment to all creatures that have their senses [K].   67 *opposite to marriage* This indicates merely that Desdemona had never favoured any of the Venetian gallants who had wooed her, not that she was more averse to marriage than other girls her age [K].   69 *general mock* universal ridicule.   70 *her guardage* my guardianship. 72 *Judge me the world* let the whole world judge for me [K].   *gross in sense* obvious (large) to ordinary perception.   73 *practis'd* acted with evil intent, imposed. 74 *Abus'd . . . youth* deluded her, young and delicate as she is, and therefore easily influenced by magic [K].   75 *That weaken motion* that dull the perceptive faculties. The point is that unless her mind and perceptions had been disordered she would have seen Othello as he was—ugly, and not attractive [K].   *motion* normal reaction. *disputed on* debated (by experts).   79 *inhibited* prohibited. *out of warrant* illegal. 82 *of my inclining* who are ready to take sides with me [K].   85-6 *fit time . . . law* the time legally appointed in the court calendar for a regular session of the court. Brabantio means that Othello shall be confined until the next court sits [K]. 90 *present* immediate, urgent.

BRABANTIO: How? The Duke in council?
In this time of the night? Bring him away!
Mine's not an idle cause. The Duke himself, 95
Or any of my brothers of the state,
Cannot but feel this wrong as 'twere their own;
For if such actions may have passage free,
Bondslaves and pagans shall our statesmen be.

(Exeunt.)

Scene III. Venice. A council chamber.

(Enter DUKE *and* SENATORS, *set at a table, with lights and* ATTENDANTS.*)*

DUKE: There is no composition in these news
That gives them credit.
1. SENATOR: Indeed they are disproportion'd.
My letters say a hundred and seven galleys.
DUKE: And mine a hundred forty.
2. SENATOR: And mine two hundred.
But though they jump not on a just account 5
(As in these cases where the aim reports
'Tis oft with difference), yet do they all confirm
A Turkish fleet, and bearing up to Cyprus.
DUKE: Nay, it is possible enough to judgment.
I do not so secure me in the error 10
But the main article I do approve
In fearful sense.
SAILOR *(within)*: What, ho! what, ho! what, ho!
(Enter Sailor.*)*
OFFICER: A messenger from the galleys.
DUKE: Now, what's the business?
SAILOR: The Turkish preparation makes for Rhodes.
So was I bid report here to the state 15
By Signior Angelo.

---

99 *Bondslaves . . . be* slaves and pagans will be at liberty to marry our daughters and their descendants will rule the Venetian state. Brabantio meets the difficulty raised by Othello with respect to the Duke's mandate by insisting that the case may be heard at once by the Duke and Senators, since they are already in session [K].

I.iii. 1 *composition* consistency.   2 *credit* credibility.   *disproportion'd* inconsistent. 5 *jump not* disagree.   *just account* accurate number.   6-7 *As in . . . difference* as in cases like this, where reports are made on the basis of guesswork, there is often a discrepancy [K].   10-12 *I do not so . . . sense* I do not allow the inconsistency in numbers to make me feel so free from anxiety as to prevent me from crediting the main point of the dispatches—and that too, in a way that makes me anxious [K].   11 *article* item.   *approve* believe.

DUKE: How say you by this change?
1. SENATOR: This cannot be
  By no assay of reason. 'Tis a pageant
  To keep us in false gaze. When we consider
  Th' importancy of Cyprus to the Turk,   20
  And let ourselves again but understand
  That, as it more concerns the Turk than Rhodes,
  So may he with more facile question bear it,
  For that it stands not in such warlike brace,
  But altogether lacks th' abilities   25
  That Rhodes is dress'd in—if we make thought of this,
  We must not think the Turk is so unskilful
  To leave that latest which concerns him first,
  Neglecting an attempt of ease and gain
  To wake and wage a danger profitless.   30
DUKE: Nay, in all confidence he's not for Rhodes.
OFFICER: Here is more news.

(Enter a MESSENGER.)

MESSENGER: The Ottomites, reverend and gracious,
  Steering with due course toward the isle of Rhodes,
  Have there injointed them with an after fleet.   35
1. SENATOR: Ay, so I thought. How many, as you guess?
MESSENGER: Of thirty sail; and now they do restem
  Their backward course, bearing with frank appearance
  Their purposes toward Cyprus. Signior Montano,
  Your trusty and most valiant servitor,   40
  With his free duty recommends you thus,
  And prays you to believe him.
DUKE: 'Tis certain then for Cyprus.
  Marcus Luccicos, is not he in town?
1. SENATOR: He's now in Florence.   45
DUKE: Write from us to him; post-post-haste dispatch.

---

18 *assay of reason* test which reason can apply.   *pageant* mere spectacle or show. 19 *false gaze* looking in the wrong direction.   23 *may* can.   *more facile question* To "question" is to "contest."   *bear it* capture it.   *in such warlike brace* so well prepared to withstand an attack. The figure is of a person who is "braced" (in a posture of defence) to meet a blow or an assault [K].   25 *abilities* means of defence.   26 *dress'd in* equipped with.   27 *unskilful* undiscriminating, lacking in judgment [K]. 29 *attempt* undertaking.   30 *wake* stir up.   *wage* risk.   35 *injointed them* joined themselves.   *after* second.   37-8 *restem . . . course* steer their course back again [K]. 38 *frank appearance* no attempt at concealment.   41 *free duty* expressions of unqualified respect.   *recommends* informs, reports to.   44 *Marcus Luccicos* A strange name, which may or may not be misprinted. Doubtless some foreigner in the service of the Venetian state [K].

(*Enter* BRABANTIO, OTHELLO, CASSIO, IAGO, RODERIGO, *and* OFFICERS)

1. SENATOR: Here comes Brabantio and the valiant Moor.
DUKE: Valiant Othello, we must straight employ you
  Against the general enemy Ottoman.
  (*To* BRABANTIO) I did not see you. Welcome, gentle signior. 50
  We lack'd your counsel and your help to-night.
BRABANTIO: So did I yours. Good your Grace, pardon me.
  Neither my place, nor aught I heard of business,
  Hath rais'd me from my bed; nor doth the general care
  Take hold on me; for my particular grief 55
  Is of so floodgate and o'erbearing nature
  That it engluts and swallows other sorrows,
  And it is still itself.
DUKE: Why, what's the matter?
BRABANTIO: My daughter! O, my daughter!
ALL: Dead?
BRABANTIO: Ay, to me!
  She is abus'd, stol'n from me, and corrupted 60
  By spells and medicines bought of mountebanks;
  For nature so prepost'rously to err,
  Being not deficient, blind, or lame of sense,
  Sans witchcraft could not.
DUKE: Whoe'er he be that in this foul proceeding 65
  Hath thus beguil'd your daughter of herself,
  And you of her, the bloody book of law
  You shall yourself read in the bitter letter
  After your own sense; yea, though our proper son
  Stood in your action. 70

---

48 *straight* at once.   49 *general enemy* the enemy of all Christendom [K].   55 *particular* personal.   56 *floodgate* like a sluice-gate, which when opened allowed the water (his tears) to pour through.   *o'erbearing* overwhelming.   57 *engluts* swallows.   58 *And . . . itself* it remains distinct and unchanged after it has swallowed up all other sorrows [K].   60 *abus'd* deluded.   61 *bought of mountebanks* Brabantio's belief that Othello has used love charms has become so definite that he actually adds a detail with regard to the persons from whom Othello procured them. Mountebanks (strolling quacks) were well known to deal in such wares [K].   62 *prepost'rously* absurdly.   *err* go wrong, become abnormal.   63 *deficient* feeble-minded.   *lame of sense* crippled in mental power.   64 *Sans* without.   66 *beguil'd . . . herself* cheated your daughter of herself; by means of charms caused her to be something other than she normally is.   67 *bloody book of law* The punishment for witchcraft was death, practically everywhere in the world [K].   69 *After your own sense* according to whatever interpretation you may choose to put upon it—i.e. upon the letter of the law. The passage is not to be taken with strict literalness. The Duke means that Brabantio shall have the satisfaction of seeing the law executed with all the rigour that he could possibly wish [K].   69 *proper* own.   70 *Stood* were the defendent.   *action* lawsuit.

BRABANTIO: Humbly I thank your Grace.
Here is the man—this Moor, whom now, it seems,
Your special mandate, for the state affairs,
Hath hither brought.
ALL: We are very sorry for't.
DUKE (*to* OTHELLO): What, in your own part, can you say to this?
BRABANTIO: Nothing, but this is so. 75
OTHELLO: Most potent, grave, and reverend signiors,
My very noble, and approv'd good masters,
That I have ta'en away this old man's daughter,
It is most true; true I have married her.
The very head and front of my offending 80
Hath this extent, no more. Rude am I in my speech,
And little bless'd with the soft phrase of peace;
For since these arms of mine had seven years' pith
Till now some nine moons wasted, they have us'd
Their dearest action in the tented field; 85
And little of this great world can I speak
More than pertains to feats of broil and battle;
And therefore little shall I grace my cause
In speaking for myself. Yet, by your gracious patience,
I will a round unvarnish'd tale deliver 90
Of my whole course of love—what drugs, what charms,
What conjuration, and what mighty magic
(For such proceeding am I charg'd withal)
I won his daughter.
BRABANTIO: A maiden never bold;
Of spirit so still and quiet that her motion 95
Blush'd at herself; and she—in spite of nature,
Of years, of country, credit, everything—
To fall in love with what she fear'd to look on!
It is a judgment maim'd and most imperfect
That will confess perfection so could err 100
Against all rules of nature, and must be driven
To find out practices of cunning hell
Why this should be. I therefore vouch again
That with some mixtures pow'rful o'er the blood,

---

80 *head and front* entire substance. 81 *Rude* unpolished, unpractised in the art of the orator [K]. 82 *soft phrase of peace* mild and insinuating eloquence that befits an advocate or politician [K]. 83 *pith* strength. 84 *moons wasted* months ago. 85 *dearest* most intense. 88 *grace my cause* make my case attractive (by eloquent language). 90 *round* plain. 95-6 *her motion . . . herself* any strong emotion made her blush at herself as if it were an indecorum [K]. *motion* emotion. 97 *credit* reputation. 100 *confess* believe. 101 *driven* obliged, forced. 102 *find out* discover. *practices* evil devices, machinations. 103 *vouch* assert. 104 *blood* passions.

    Or with some dram, conjur'd to this effect, 105
    He wrought upon her.
DUKE: To vouch this is no proof,
    Without more certain and more overt test
    Than these thin habits and poor likelihoods
    Of modern seeming do prefer against him.
1. SENATOR: But, Othello, speak. 110
    Did you by indirect and forced courses
    Subdue and poison this young maid's affections?
    Or came it by request, and such fair question
    As soul to soul affordeth?
OTHELLO: I do beseech you,
    Send for the lady to the Sagittary 115
    And let her speak of me before her father.
    If you do find me foul in her report,
    The trust, the office, I do hold of you
    Not only take away, but let your sentence
    Even fall upon my life.
DUKE: Fetch Desdemona hither. 120
OTHELLO: Ancient, conduct them; you best know the place.
             (*Exeunt* IAGO *and two or three* ATTENDANTS)
    And till she come, as truly as to heaven
    I do confess the vices of my blood,
    So justly to your grave ears I'll present
    How I did thrive in this fair lady's love, 125
    And she in mine.
DUKE: Say it, Othello.
OTHELLO: Her father lov'd me, oft invited me;
    Still question'd me the story of my life
    From year to year—the battles, sieges, fortunes 130
    That I have pass'd.
    I ran it through, even from my boyish days
    To th' very moment that he bade me tell it.
    Wherein I spake of most disastrous chances,
    Of moving accidents by flood and field; 135
    Of hairbreadth scapes i' th' imminent deadly breach;
    Of being taken by the insolent foe
    And sold to slavery; of my redemption thence
    And portance in my travel's history;

---

105 *conjur'd* made effective by means of spells.   107 *overt test* tangible evidence.   108 *thin habits* flimsy coverings (habits) of slight evidence.   *poor likelihoods* mere conjectures.   109 *modern* commonplace.   111 *indirect* underhanded.   *forced courses* violent means.   113-14 *such fair . . . affordeth* such fair words as a lover uses when he speaks heart-to-heart with his ladylove [K].   117 *foul* guilty.   123 *vices of my blood* faults of my nature [K].   129 *Still* continually.   135 *moving accidents* affecting or stirring events—such adventures as would thrill the hearer [K].   136 *th' imminent deadly breach* the breach (in the wall of a city or fortress) which threatened death [K].   139 *portance* bearing, conduct.

Wherein of antres vast and deserts idle, 140
Rough quarries, rocks, and hills whose heads touch heaven,
It was my hint to speak—such was the process;
And of the Cannibals that each other eat,
The Anthropophagi, and men whose heads
Do grow beneath their shoulders. This to hear 145
Would Desdemona seriously incline;
But still the house affairs would draw her thence;
Which ever as she could with haste dispatch,
She'ld come again, and with a greedy ear
Devour up my discourse. Which I observing, 150
Took once a pliant hour, and found good means
To draw from her a prayer of earnest heart
That I would all my pilgrimage dilate,
Whereof by parcels she had something heard,
But not intentively. I did consent, 155
And often did beguile her of her tears
When I did speak of some distressful stroke
That my youth suffer'd. My story being done,
She gave me for my pains a world of sighs.
She swore, in faith, 'twas strange, 'twas passing strange; 160
'Twas pitiful, 'twas wondrous pitiful.
She wish'd she had not heard it; yet she wish'd
That heaven had made her such a man. She thank'd me;
And bade me, if I had a friend that lov'd her,
I should but teach him how to tell my story, 165
And that would woo her. Upon this hint I spake.
She lov'd me for the dangers I had pass'd,
And I lov'd her that she did pity them.
This only is the witchcraft I have us'd.
Here comes the lady. Let her witness it. 170

(*Enter* DESDEMONA, IAGO, ATTENDANTS)

DUKE: I think this tale would win my daughter too.
  Good Brabantio,

---

140 *antres* caves. *idle* empty, desolate. 142 *hint* occasion. 144 *Anthropophagi* man-eaters. Shakespeare here is drawing upon the travel literature widely popular in his day. 144-5 *heads . . . shoulders* Such headless men are specifically mentioned in Pliny's NATURAL HISTORY and in Sir Walter Raleigh's DISCOVERY OF GUIANA. 147 *still* ever and anon. 151 *pliant hour* a time when I could influence Desdemona and get her to ask, as a favour, what I was myself eager to do [K]. 153 *dilate* narrate fully (not extend). 154 *parcels* small portions. 155 *intentively* in such a way that she could give her full attention to it [K]. 160 *passing* surpassingly. 163 *That heaven . . . a man* There are two interpretations in the field: (a) "that heaven had created such a man for her" (to be her husband); (b) "that she had been born a man like me, so that she might have had such adventures and done such deeds." One cannot hesitate long in preferring the second [K].

    Take up this mangled matter at the best.
    Men do their broken weapons rather use
    Than their bare hands.
BRABANTIO: I pray you hear her speak.   175
    If she confess that she was half the wooer,
    Destruction on my head if my bad blame
    Light on the man! Come hither, gentle mistress.
    Do you perceive in all this noble company
    Where most you owe obedience?
DESDEMONA: My noble father,   180
    I do perceive here a divided duty.
    To you I am bound for life and education;
    My life and education both do learn me
    How to respect you: you are the lord of duty;
    I am hitherto your daughter. But here's my husband;   185
    And so much duty as my mother show'd
    To you, preferring you before her father,
    So much I challenge that I may profess
    Due to the Moor my lord.
BRABANTIO: God b' wi' ye! I have done.
    Please it your Grace, on to the state affairs.   190
    I had rather to adopt a child than get it.
    Come hither, Moor.
    I here do give thee that with all my heart
    Which, but thou hast already, with all my heart
    I would keep from thee. For your sake, jewel,   195
    I am glad at soul I have no other child;
    For thy escape would teach me tyranny,
    To hang clogs on them. I have done, my lord.
DUKE: Let me speak like yourself and lay a sentence
    Which, as a grise or step, may help these lovers   200
    Into your favour.
    When remedies are past, the griefs are ended
    By seeing the worst, which late on hopes depended.

---

173 *Take up . . . best* make the best of this confused and confusing business [K].   177 *bad* since in that case I should do wrong to blame him [K].   182 *education* bringing up.   183 *learn* teach.   184 *How to respect you* in what light to regard you.   187 *preferring . . . father* advancing you to a higher position than her father with respect to duty [K].   188 *challenge . . . profess* claim the right to affirm.   191 *get* beget. Brabantio thinks that an adopted child would be quite as likely to be dutiful, and that, if it were not, the father's sorrow would be less than in the case of a child of his own [K].   195 *For your sake* on your account.   198 *clogs* shackles.   199 *like yourself* as you would speak if you were not angry [K].   *lay a sentence* state a principle or maxim.   200 *grise* step.   202-3 *When remedies . . . depended* one now knows the worst, whereas a little while ago one's idea of what the worst might be depended on one's fears [K].   *hopes* expectations, fears.

William Shakespeare: *Othello*

    To mourn a mischief that is past and gone
    Is the next way to draw new mischief on.   205
    What cannot be preserv'd when fortune takes,
    Patience her injury a mock'ry makes.
    The robb'd that smiles steals something from the thief;
    He robs himself that spends a bootless grief.
BRABANTIO: So let the Turk of Cyprus us beguile: 210
    We lose it not, so long as we can smile.
    He bears the sentence well that nothing bears
    But the free comfort which from thence he hears;
    But he bears both the sentence and the sorrow
    That to pay grief must of poor patience borrow.   215
    These sentences, to sugar, or to gall,
    Being strong on both sides, are equivocal.
    But words are words. I never yet did hear
    That the bruis'd heart was pieced through the ear.
    Beseech you, now to the affairs of state.   220
DUKE: The Turk with a most mighty preparation makes for Cyprus. Othello, the fortitude of the place is best known to you; and though we have there a substitute of most allowed sufficiency, yet opinion, a sovereign mistress of effects, throws a more safer voice on you. You must therefore be content to slubber the gloss of   225 your new fortunes with this more stubborn and boist'rous expedition.
OTHELLO: The tyrant custom, most grave senators,
    Hath made the flinty and steel couch of war   230
    My thrice-driven bed of down. I do agnize
    A natural and prompt alacrity
    I find in hardness; and do undertake
    These present wars against the Ottomites.
    Most humbly, therefore, bending to your state,   235

---

204 *mischief* misfortune.   205 *next* nearest.   206-7 *What cannot . . . makes* when Fortune takes away something that we cannot keep, we make a mockery of her injury by bearing it calmly. Fortune was conceived more personally by the Elizabethans than by us. She is here regarded as malicious; and her malice is thwarted when the victim refuses to give her the satisfaction of seeing that he is distressed [K]   209 *spends a bootless grief* indulges in unavailing sorrow [K].   216-17 *These sentences . . . equivocal* maxims such as these are ambiguous, since they have a strong tendency in two directions —to sweeten misfortune and to embitter it [K].   219 *pieced* cured, made of one piece after being broken.   222 *fortitude* strength.   224 *allowed sufficiency* proven ability. 224-5 *opinion . . . on you* public opinion, which is important in determining policy, considers you safer to have in the position.   226 *slubber* smear, tarnish. 227 *boist'rous* rough.   231 *thrice-driven* thrice sorted and winnowed in order that only the softest feathers might be used [K].   231-3 *agnize . . . hardness* I recognize in my own nature an instinctive and spontaneous stimulus that I find in hardship [K]. 234 *These* MALONE; F1, Q1: "This."   235 *state* authority.

    I crave fit disposition for my wife;
    Due reference of place, and exhibition,
    With such accommodation and besort
    As levels with her breeding.
DUKE: If you please,
    Be't at her father's.
BRABANTIO: I'll not have it so.   240
OTHELLO: Nor I.
DESDEMONA: Nor I. I would not there reside,
    To put my father in impatient thoughts
    By being in his eye. Most gracious Duke,
    To my unfolding lend your prosperous ear,
    And let me find a charter in your voice,   245
    T' assist my simpleness.
DUKE: What would you, Desdemona?
DESDEMONA: That I did love the Moor to live with him,
    My downright violence, and storm of fortunes,
    May trumpet to the world. My heart's subdu'd   250
    Even to the very quality of my lord.
    I saw Othello's visage in his mind,
    And to his honours and his valiant parts
    Did I my soul and fortunes consecrate.
    So that, dear lords, if I be left behind,   255
    A moth of peace, and he go to the war,
    The rights for which I love him are bereft me,
    And I a heavy interim shall support
    By his dear absence. Let me go with him.
OTHELLO: Let her have your voices.   260
    Vouch with me heaven, I therefore beg it not
    To please the palate of my appetite,
    Nor to comply with heat—the young affects

---

237 *Due reference of place* a suitable residence.   *exhibition* monetary allowance.   238 *besort* company, attendants.   239 *levels with* is appropriate to.   *breeding* birth, social position.   244 *unfolding* disclosure.   *prosperous ear* favourable hearing.   245 *charter in your voice* authority (or encouragement) in your assent [K].   246 *simpleness* lack of skill in pleading.   249 *downright* plain and obvious.   *violence* violent action. *storm of fortunes* Desdemona has, as it were, "taken her fortunes (her lot in life) by storm," instead of submitting passively to whatever arrangements for her marriage her father might make [K].   250 *trumpet* proclaim loudly.   250-1 *heart's subdu'd . . . my lord* heart is brought into harmony with the very profession of my husband. I have fallen in love with his profession as well as himself [K].   253 *valiant parts* heroic deeds (in battle).   256 *moth* parasitic idler.   257 *bereft* taken from.   258-9 *And I . . . absence* and besides, I shall have to endure a sad interval of loneliness because of the absence of him who is so dear to me. Thus Desdemona drops her exalted tone and expresses the simple and natural feelings of a wife who misses her husband [K].   260 *voices* votes of approval.   263 *comply with heat* satisfy sexual desire.

    In me defunct—and proper satisfaction;
    But to be free and bounteous to her mind. 265
    And heaven defend your good souls that you think
    I will your serious and great business scant
    For she is with me. No, when light-wing'd toys
    Of feather'd Cupid seel with wanton dullness
    My speculative and offc'd instruments, 270
    That my disports corrupt and taint my business,
    Let housewives make a skillet of my helm,
    And all indign and base adversities
    Make head against my estimation!
DUKE: Be it as you shall privately determine, 275
    Either for her stay or going. Th' affair cries haste,
    And speed must answer it. You must hence to-night.
DESDEMONA: To-night, my lord?
DUKE: This night.
OTHELLO: With all my heart.
DUKE: At nine i' th' morning here we'll meet again.
    Othello, leave some officer behind, 280
    And he shall our commission bring to you;
    With such things else of quality and respect
    As doth import you.
OTHELLO: So please your Grace, my ancient.
    A man he is of honesty and trust.
    To his conveyance I assign my wife, 285
    With what else needful your good Grace shall think
    To be sent after me.
DUKE: Let it be so.
    Good night to every one. (*To* BRABANTIO) And, noble signior,
    If virtue no delighted beauty lack,
    Your son-in-law is far more fair than black. 290
1. SENATOR: Adieu, brave Moor. Use Desdemona well.

---

264 *me* UPTON; F¹, Q¹: "my."   264 *defunct* Othello means, not that passion is dead in him, but simply that the ungovernable force of youthful passion is held in check by the self-control of mature years [K]. Yet Shakespeare is anxious to stress that the relation between Desdemona and Othello is one in which sexual passion is not important. *proper satisfaction* my own self-gratification [K].   265 *mind* wishes.   268 *For* because. *light-wing'd* frivolous.   *toys* trifles.   269 *seel* sew up.   270 *speculative . . . instruments* my organs of sight (the eyes of my mind), which have their imperative duties to perform [K]. The metaphor is from the practice of "seeling," sewing up the eyes of a hawk with silk in the process of taming it. *offic'd* provided with duties.   271 *disports* recreations.   *taint* impair.   273-4 *all indign . . . estimation* let all manner of disgraceful calamities gather in a troop to attack my reputation [K].   282 *of quality and respect* pertaining to the honour that is to be yours and to your high position [K].   283 *import* concern.   285 *conveyance* escort.   298 *delighted* endowed with delight (an adjective).

BRABANTIO: Look to her, Moor, if thou hast eyes to see.
  She has deceiv'd her father, and may thee.
                    (*Exeunt* DUKE, SENATORS, OFFICERS, &c.)
OTHELLO: My life upon her faith!—Honest Iago,
  My Desdemona must I leave to thee.   295
  I prithee let thy wife attend on her,
  And bring them after in the best advantage.
  Come, Desdemona. I have but an hour
  Of love, of wordly matters and direction,
  To spend with thee. We must obey the time.   300
                    (*Exeunt* MOOR *and* DESDEMONA.)
RODERIGO: Iago.
IAGO: What say'st thou, noble heart?
RODERIGO: What will I do, think'st thou?
IAGO: Why, go to bed and sleep.
RODERIGO: I will incontinently drown myself.   305
IAGO: If thou dost, I shall never love thee after. Why, thou silly gentleman!
RODERIGO: It is silliness to live when to live is torment; and then have we a prescription to die when death is our physician.
IAGO: O villainous! I have look'd upon the world for four times 310
  seven years; and since I could distinguish betwixt a benefit and
  an injury, I never found man that knew how to love himself. Ere
  I would say I would drown myself for the love of a guinea hen,
  I would change my humanity with a baboon.   315
RODERIGO: What should I do? I confess it is my shame to be so fond, but it is not in my virtue to amend it.
IAGO: Virtue? a fig! 'Tis in ourselves that we are thus or thus. Our
  bodies are our gardens, to the which our wills are gardeners; so
  that if we will plant nettles or sow lettuce, set hyssop and weed up 320
  thyme, supply it with one gender of herbs or distract it with many
  —either to have it sterile with idleness or manured with industry
  —why, the power and corrigible authority of this lies in our wills.
  If the balance of our lives had not one scale of reason to poise 325
  another of sensuality, the blood and baseness of our natures
  would conduct us to most prepost'rous conclusions. But we have

297 *in the best advantage* as soon as you have a favourable opportunity [K]   316 *fond* foolishly in love.   321 *hyssop* an herb of the mint family.   *thyme* another aromatic herb.   *gender* kind, species.   322 *distract it with* divide it among.   323 *idleness* lack of cultivation.   324 *corrigible authority* corrective authority; ability to regulate the matter [K].   325-6 *If the balance . . . sensuality* Life is conceived of as a scale with reason weighing down one side and sensuality the other.   326-7 *blood and baseness* base passions.   328 *conclusions* results.   328-9 *we have reason . . . lusts* Iago conceives of reason as the purely human ability to govern the passions by control of will; its source is in the mind of man and not, as the more orthodox believed, in a power above man.   *motions* impulses.   *unbitted* unbridled, uncontrolled.

reason to cool our raging motions, our carnal stings, our unbitted lusts; whereof I take this that you call love to be a sect or scion. 330
RODERIGO: It cannot be.
IAGO: It is merely a lust of the blood and a permission of the will. Come, be a man! Drown thyself? Drown cats and blind puppies! I have profess'd me thy friend, and I confess me knit to thy 335 deserving with cables of perdurable toughness. I could never better stead thee than now. Put money in thy purse. Follow these wars; defeat thy favour with an usurp'd beard. I say, put money in thy purse. It cannot be that Desdemona should long continue 340 her love to the Moor—put money in thy purse—nor he his to her. It was a violent commencement, and thou shalt see an answerable sequestration. Put but money in thy purse. These Moors are changeable in their wills. Fill thy purse with money. The food 345 that to him now is as luscious as locusts shall be to him shortly as bitter as coloquintida. She must change for youth. When she is sated with his body, she will find the error of her choice. She must have change, she must. Therefore put money in thy purse. If thou wilt needs damn thyself, do it a more delicate way than drowning. 350 Make all the money thou canst. If sanctimony and a frail vow betwixt an erring barbarian and a supersubtle Venetian be not too hard for my wits and all the tribe of hell, thou shalt enjoy her. Therefore make money. A pox of drowning thyself! It is clean out 355 of the way. Seek thou rather to be hang'd in compassing thy joy than to be drown'd and go without her.
RODERIGO: Wilt thou be fast to my hopes, if I depend on the issue?
IAGO: Thou art sure of me. Go, make money. I have told thee often, 360 and I retell thee again and again, I hate the Moor. My cause is hearted; thine hath no less reason. Let us be conjunctive in our revenge against him. If thou canst cuckold him, thou dost thyself

---

330-1 *sect or scion* literally, a cutting or graft from a tree.   336 *knit to thy deserving* bound to thee for favours received [K].   *perdurable* very durable   337 *stead* be of service to.   338-9 *defeat . . . usurp'd beard* spoil thy pretty face by growing a beard to which it has no right [K].   *favour* face.   343 *answerable sequestration* corresponding—and equally abrupt—estrangement [K].   345 *wills* desires.   346 *locusts* probably St. John's bread, the fruit of the locust tree; it is not likely that Iago is referring to the insect.   347 *coloquintida* bitter apple or colocynth, a bitter fruit from which a medicinal purge was made.   349 *She must have change, she must* Q¹; not in F¹; omitted by some editors as a probable memorial improvisation of "She must change for youth" (line 347) which Q¹, in turn omits.   352 *sanctimony* the religious obligation of the marriage bond [K].   353 *erring* wandering.   *supersubtle* Iago does not mean that Desdemona is more subtle than other Venetians, but that subtlety is a regular Venetian trait [K].   356-7 *Seek thou . . . hang'd* if you wish to destroy yourself, take the risk of being hanged for seducing the General's wife [K].   *compassing* achieving.   359 *fast* true.   362 *hearted* deeply fixed in my heart.   363 *conjunctive* united.

a pleasure, me a sport. There are many events in the womb of
time, which will be delivered. Traverse! go! provide thy money! 365
We will have more of this to-morrow. Adieu.
RODERIGO: Where shall we meet i' th' morning?
IAGO: At my lodging.
RODERIGO: I'll be with thee betimes. 370
IAGO: Go to, farewell.—Do you hear, Roderigo?
RODERIGO: What say you?
IAGO: No more of drowning, do you hear?
RODERIGO: I am chang'd. I'll go sell all my land. *(Exit.)*
IAGO: Thus do I ever make my fool my purse; 375
For I mine own gain'd knowledge should profane
If I would time expend with such a snipe
But for my sport and profit. I hate the Moor;
And it is thought abroad that 'twixt my sheets
'Has done my office. I know not if't be true; 380
Yet I, for mere suspicion in that kind,
Will do as if for surety. He holds me well;
The better shall my purpose work on him.
Cassio's a proper man. Let me see now:
To get his place, and to plume up my will 385
In double knavery—How, how? Let's see.
After some time, to abuse Othello's ear
That he is too familiar with his wife.
He hath a person and a smooth dispose
To be suspected—fram'd to make women false. 390
The Moor is of a free and open nature
That thinks men honest that but seem to be so;
And will as tenderly be led by th' nose
As asses are.
I have 't! It is engend'red! Hell and night 395
Must bring this monstrous birth to the world's light.
(Exit.)

366 *Traverse* forward march.   370 *betimes* early.   371-4 *Go to . . . land* These lines represent a conflatation of the Q¹ and F¹ texts about which there has been considerable disagreement among editors. Kittredge's arrangement is followed here.   377 *snipe* silly fellow (an extremely contemptuous term).   378-96 *I hate . . . world's light* This is the soliloquy which Coleridge described as the "motive-hunting of motiveless malignity." Iago, however, lists several motives, including most prominently his fears about Emilia. 379 *it is thought abroad* rumours are current.   381 *kind* regard.   382 *do as if for surety* act as though I were certain of it. *well* in high regard.   384 *proper* handsome. 385 *plume up* gratify—literally, deck with plumes (as a cap) [K].   387 *abuse* deceive. 389-90 *a smooth . . . be suspected* a pleasant and affable disposition and manner, such as would make one easily suspect him in such a case. This prepares us for the elegant and somewhat flourishing manners of Cassio [K].   391 *free* frank.   393 *tenderly* easily, with little resistance.   395-6 *Hell and night . . . light* This is, in effect, an invocation to the powers of evil to assist his plot [K].

William Shakespeare: *Othello*

ACT TWO

Scene I. A seaport in Cyprus. An open place.

(*Enter* MONTANO *and two* GENTLEMEN.)

MONTANO: What from the cape can you discern at sea?
1. GENTLEMAN: Nothing at all. It is a high-wrought flood.
   I cannot 'twixt the heaven and the main
   Descry a sail.
MONTANO: Methinks the wind hath spoke aloud at land; 5
   A fuller blast ne'er shook our battlements.
   If it hath ruffian'd so upon the sea,
   What ribs of oak, when mountains melt on them,
   Can hold the mortise? What shall we hear of this?
2. GENTLEMAN: A segregation of the Turkish fleet. 10
   For do but stand upon the foaming shore,
   The chidden billow seems to pelt the clouds;
   The wind-shak'd surge, with high and monstrous main,
   Seems to cast water on the burning Bear
   And quench the Guards of th' ever-fixed pole. 15
   I never did like molestation view
   On the enchafed flood.
MONTANO: If that the Turkish fleet
   Be not enshelter'd and embay'd, they are drown'd.
   It is impossible they bear it out.

(*Enter a third* GENTLEMAN.)

3. GENTLEMAN: News, lads! Our wars are done. 20
   The desperate tempest hath so bang'd the Turks
   That their designment halts. A noble ship of Venice
   Hath seen a grievous wrack and sufferance
   On most part of their fleet.

II.i   1 *the cape* from which the Gentleman has just returned to bring his report to Montano, who is in charge of affairs in Cyprus [K].   2*high-wrought flood* high and angry sea.   3 *main* sea.   7 *ruffian'd* raged.   9 *hold the mortise* hold together.   10 *segregation* dispersal.   12 *chidden* beaten (by the wind). Thus F1; Q1; "chiding" is preferred by some editors.   13 *main* great body of waters (Q1, F1; KNIGHT, K: "mane"). Knight's emendation, followed by Kittredge, would see in the line a metaphoric allusion to the white horses of the sea. But the image of the horses throwing water on the bear is somewhat ludicrous and un-Shakespearean. Since the F1, Q1 reading makes perfect sense, there is no need to emend.   15 *the Guards* two stars in the constellation of the Little Bear. The hyperbole in this description of a storm follows an ancient literary convention [K]. *ever fixed pole* North star.   16 *like molestation* similar disturbance.   17 *enchafed flood* enraged ocean.   18 *embay'd* protected in a bay.   19 *bear it out* weather the storm.   22 *designment* plan, designs.   *halts* limps, is checked.   23 *wrack* wreck.   *sufferance* disaster.

MONTANO: How? Is this true?
3. GENTLEMAN: The ship is here put in,   25
  A Veronesa; Michael Cassio,
  Lieutenant to the warlike Moor Othello,
  Is come on shore; the Moor himself at sea,
  And is in full commission here for Cyprus.
MONTANO: I am glad on't. 'Tis a worthy governor.   30
3. GENTLEMAN: But this same Cassio, though he speak of comfort
  Touching the Turkish loss, yet he looks sadly
  And prays the Moor be safe, for they were parted
  With foul and violent tempest.
MONTANO: Pray heaven he be;
  For I have serv'd him, and the man commands   35
  Like a full soldier. Let's to the seaside, ho!
  As well to see the vessel that's come in
  As to throw out our eyes for brave Othello,
  Even till we make the main and th' aerial blue
  An indistinct regard.
3. GENTLEMAN: Come, let's do so;   40
  For every minute is expectancy
  Of more arrivance.

  (Enter CASSIO.*)*

CASSIO: Thanks you, the valiant of this warlike isle,
  That so approve the Moor! O, let the heavens
  Give him defence against the elements,   45
  For I have lost him on a dangerous sea!
MONTANO: Is he well shipp'd?
CASSIO: His bark is stoutly timber'd, and his pilot
  Of very expert and approv'd allowance.
  Therefore my hopes (not surfeited to death)   50
  Stand in bold cure.
                    (Within) "A sail, a sail, a sail!"
  (Enter a MESSENGER.*)*
CASSIO: What noise?
MESSENGER: The town is empty; on the brow o' th' sea
  Stand ranks of people, and they cry "A sail!"
CASSIO: My hopes do shape him for the Governor.   55

26 *Veronesa* Why Shakespeare should have Cassio, a Florentine from Venice, land in a ship of Verona, has puzzled editors. Perhaps it was a specific type of ship.   36 *full perfect*   39-40 *till we make . . . regard* so far out to sea that the blue water and the blue sky are no longer distinguishable from each other [K].   49 *approv'd allowance* demonstrated ability.   50-1 *my hopes . . . bold cure* Hope is surfeited to death when it has lasted so long that it changes to despair. Cassio says that his hopes have not yet been indulged long enough to reach this fatal stage; and that, though they are somewhat sick (mingled with anxiety), they are in confident expectation of being cured (becoming a certainty, being fulfilled).   55 *shape . . . Governor* wishfully imagine it to be the Governor's ship.

(A shot.)
2. GENTLEMAN: They do discharge their shot of courtesy.
  Our friends at least.
CASSIO: I pray you, sir, go forth
  And give us truth who 'tis that is arriv'd.
2. GENTLEMAN: I shall.   *(Exit.)*
MONTANO: But, good Lieutenant, is your general wiv'd?
CASSIO: Most fortunately. He hath achiev'd a maid
  That paragons description and wild fame;
  One that excels the quirks of blazoning pens,
  And in th' essential vesture of creation
  Does tire the ingener.

(Enter SECOND GENTLEMAN.*)*
            How now? Who has put in?
2. GENTLEMAN: 'Tis one Iago, ancient to the General.
CASSIO: Has had most favourable and happy speed.
  Tempests themselves, high seas, and howling winds,
  The gutter'd rocks and congregated sands,
  Traitors ensteep'd to clog the guiltless keel,
  As having sense of beauty, do omit
  Their mortal natures, letting go safely by
  The divine Desdemona.
MONTANO: What is she?
CASSIO: She that I spake of, our great captain's captain,
  Left in the conduct of the bold Iago,
  Whose footing here anticipates our thoughts
  A se'nnight's speed. Great Jove, Othello guard,
  And swell his sail with thine own pow'rful breath,
  That he may bless this bay with his tall ship,
  Make love's quick pants in Desdemona's arms,
  Give renew'd fire to our extincted spirits,
  And bring all Cyprus comfort!

(Enter DESDEMONA, IAGO, EMILIA, *and* RODERIGO, *with* ATTENDANTS.*)*
            O, behold!

---

61 *achiev'd* won.   62 *paragons* surpasses.   *wild fame* rumour in her wildest mood, when most given to exaggeration [K].   63 *excels . . . pens* is superior to any flourishes that those who write in praise of her can make in their description [K].   64 *essential vesture of creation* real excellence with which God has created her.   65 *tire the ingener* wear out the most skilful contriver of compliments (K; F1: "tyre the Ingeniuer"; Q1: "bear all excellency").   70 *ensteep'd* sunk in the sea.   71-2 *omit . . . natures* give up for the time being their deadly natures [K].   75 *conduct* escort.   76-7 *Whose footing . . . speed* whose arrival is a week earlier than we expected.   81 *extincted* despondent.

> The riches of the ship is come on shore!
> Ye men of Cyprus, let her have your knees.
> Hail to thee, lady! and the grace of heaven, 85
> Before, behind thee, and on every hand,
> Enwheel thee round!

DESDEMONA: I thank you, valiant Cassio.
> What tidings can you tell me of my lord?

CASSIO: He is not yet arriv'd; nor know I aught
> But that he's well and will be shortly here. 90

DESDEMONA: O, but I fear! How lost you company?

CASSIO: The great contention of the sea and skies
> Parted our fellowship.

(Within) "A sail, a sail!"

(A shot.)
> But hark. A sail!

2. GENTLEMAN: They give their greeting to the citadel. 95
> This likewise is a friend.

CASSIO: See for the news.

(Exit GENTLEMAN.*)*

> Good ancient, you are welcome.
> *(To* EMILIA*)*
> Welcome, mistress.—
> Let it not gall your patience, good Iago,
> That I extend my manners. 'Tis my breeding
> That gives me this bold show of courtesy. 100
> *(Kisses her.)*

IAGO: Sir, would she you so much of her lips
> As of her tongue she oft bestows on me,
> You would have enough.

DESDEMONA: Alas, she has no speech!

IAGO: In faith, too much.
> I find it still when I have list to sleep. 105
> Marry, before your ladyship, I grant,
> She puts her tongue a little in her heart
> And chides with thinking.

EMILIA: You have little cause to say so.

---

87 *enwheel* encircle.   93 *parted our fellowship* separated our ships.   95 *give their greeting* by firing a shot.   98 *gall* irritate.   99 *extend my manners* give evidence of my courtesy.   100 *bold show of courtesy* For Cassio to greet Emilia with a kiss was in accordance with Elizabethan custom. Cassio speaks in a vein of persiflage. He has no fear that his action will gall Iago's patience, nor is there anything "bold" about it [K].   103 *Alas, she has no speech* Spoken in smiling protest. The whole of the dialogue that follows should be spoken lightly. Iago's satire passes for mere badinage; though in fact, despite his jesting air, it expresses, with a sincerity little suspected by his hearers, his real opinion of human nature [K].   105 *still* always.   *list* desire.   107-8 *puts her tongue ... thinking* holds her tongue while she chides mentally.

William Shakespeare: *Othello*

IAGO: Come on, come on! You are pictures out of doors,
    Bells in your parlours, wildcats in your kitchens,
    Saints in your injuries, devils being offended,
    Players in your housewifery, and housewives in your beds.
DESDEMONA: O, fie upon thee, slanderer!
IAGO: Nay, it is true, or else I am a Turk.
    You rise to play, and go to bed to work.
EMILIA: You shall not write my praise.
IAGO: No, let me not.
DESDEMONA: What wouldst thou write of me, if thou shouldst praise me?
IAGO: O gentle lady, do not put me to't.
    For I am nothing if not critical.
DESDEMONA: Come on, assay.—There's one gone to the harbour?
IAGO: Ay, madam.
DESDEMONA: I am not merry; but I do beguile
    The thing I am by seeming otherwise.
    Come, how wouldst thou praise me?
IAGO: I am about it; but indeed my invention
    Comes from my pate as birdlime does from frieze—
    It plucks out brains and all. But my Muse labours,
    And thus she is deliver'd:
        If she be fair and wise, fairness and wit—
    The one's for use, the other useth it.
DESDEMONA: Well prais'd! How if she be black and witty?
IAGO: If she be black, and thereto have a wit,
    She'll find a white that shall her blackness fit.
DESDEMONA: Worse and worse!
EMILIA: How if fair and foolish?
IAGO: She never yet was foolish that was fair,
    For even her folly help'd her to an heir.
DESDEMONA: These are old fond paradoxes to make fools laugh i' th'

---

110 *pictures* as pretty as pictures—with a suggestion that they owe their beauty to painting [K].   111 *Bells* with voices as sweet as bells.   112 *Saints in your injuries* when you injure anybody in speech or act, you do it with a saintly air [K].   113 *Players* triflers.   *housewives* hussies.   114 *O, fie ... slanderer* Iago's freedom of speech would not have offended the most fastidious lady of Shakespeare's time, if he spoke in jest. The way in which Desdemona smiles at his satire, and even encourages him to continue, proves that nobody takes his talk seriously [K].   117 *You shall ... praise* when I want a complimentary copy of verses written I won't employ you [K].   120 *critical* censorious.   121 *assay* make the attempt.   123-4 *beguile ... otherwise* disguise my true feelings—perhaps out of anxiety for Othello—by seeming to be what I am not (merry).   127 *birdlime* a sticky substance spread on bushes to catch small birds.   *frieze* coarse woolen cloth.   129 *is deliver'd* gives birth.   132 *black* dark-haired or -complexioned.   134 *She'll find a white* even if she is not beautiful—for only blondes were admired by the Elizabethans—yet she'll use her wits to find a fair lover.   138 *folly* (a) foolishness (b) unchastity.   139 *fond* foolish.

alehouse. What miserable praise hast thou for her that's foul and   140
foolish?
IAGO: There's none so foul, and foolish thereunto,
   But does foul pranks which fair and wise ones do.
DESDEMONA: O heavy ignorance! Thou praisest the worst best. But
what praise couldst thou bestow on a deserving woman indeed—   145
one that, in the authority of her merit, did justly put on the
vouch of very malice itself?
IAGO: She that was ever fair, and never proud;
   Had tongue at will, and yet was never loud;
   Never lack'd gold, and yet went never gay;   150
   Fled from her wish, and yet said "Now I may";
   She that, being ang'red, her revenge being nigh,
   Bade her wrong stay, and her displeasure fly;
   She that in wisdom never was so frail
   To change the cod's head for the salmon's tail;   155
   She that could think, and ne'er disclose her mind;
   See suitors following, and not look behind:
   She was a wight (if ever such wight were)—
DESDEMONA: To do what?
IAGO: To suckle fools and chronicle small beer.   160
DESDEMONA: O most lame and impotent conclusion! Do not learn of
him, Emilia, though he be thy husband. How say you, Cassio? Is
he not a most profane and liberal counsellor?
CASSIO: He speaks home, madam. You may relish him more in the
soldier than in the scholar.   165
IAGO (aside): He takes her by the palm. Ay, well said, whisper! With
as little a web as this will I ensnare as great a fly as Cassio. Ay,
smile upon her, do! I will gyve thee in thine own courtship.
You say true; 'tis so, indeed! If such tricks as these strip you out
of your lieutenantry, it had been better you had not kiss'd your   170

141 *foul* ugly.   142 *thereunto* in addition.   144 *heavy* stupid.   145 *deserving woman* really praiseworthy woman. There is a wit combat between Desdemona and Iago: his game is to describe all women in uncomplimentary terms; hers is to propose as a subject for his verses a woman whom he cannot help praising [K].   146-7 *in the authority . . . itself* by virtue of her admitted merit did rightly prompt even the most malicious to testify in her favour [K].   149 *tongue at will* ability to express her feelings easily.   150 *gay* gorgeously dressed.   154 *Fled from . . . I may* refrained from doing something that she wished to do, though she knew that it was in her power to do it [K].   152 *ang'red* offended.   *nigh* ready at hand.   153 *Bade . . . stay* chose to endure her injury.   155 *To change . . . tail* to exchange the best part of a cheap fish for the worst part of an expensive one—to prefer ostentatious worthlessness to homely excellence [K].   158 *wight* person.   160 *chronicle small beer* keep the petty household accounts. Iago wins the game by saying that all this paragon is good for is to act as nurse and housekeeper [K].   163 *liberal* licentious.   164 *speaks home* speaks directly and to the point.   168 *gyve* ensnare (literally, with fetters)   169 *courtship* courtly manners.

three fingers so oft—which now again you are most apt to play
the sir in. Very good! well kiss'd! an excellent curtsy! 'Tis so,
indeed. Yet again your fingers to your lips? Would they were
clyster pipes for your sake! *(Trumpet within.)* The Moor! I know
his trumpet.   175
CASSIO: 'Tis truly so.
DESDEMONA: Let's meet him and receive him.
CASSIO: Lo, where he comes!

(Enter OTHELLO *and* ATTENDANTS*)*

OTHELLO: O my fair warrior!
DESDEMONA: My dear Othello!   180
OTHELLO: It gives me wonder great as my content
 To see you here before me. O my soul's joy!
 If after every tempest come such calms,
 May the winds blow till they have waken'd death!
 And let the labouring bark climb hills of seas   185
 Olympus-high, and duck again as low
 As hell's from heaven! If it were now to die,
 'Twere now to be most happy; for I fear
 My soul hath her content so absolute
 That not another comfort like to this   190
 Succeeds in unknown fate.
DESDEMONA: The heavens forbid
 But that our loves and comforts should increase
 Even as our days do grow!
OTHELLO: Amen to that, sweet powers!
 I cannot speak enough of this content;
 It stops me here; it is too much of joy.   195
 And this, and this, the greatest discords be
 (They kiss.)
 That e'er our hearts shall make!
IAGO *(aside)*: O, you are well tun'd now!
 But I'll set down the pegs that make this music,
 As honest as I am.
OTHELLO: Come, let us to the castle.
 News, friends! Our wars are done; the Turks are drown'd.   200
 How does my old acquaintance of this isle?—

---

¹⁷² *now* at this very moment.   ¹⁷²⁻³ *apt . . . the sir* ready to act as a courtly gentleman.   ¹⁷⁵ *clyster pipes* medical syringes, used primarily for enemas.   ¹⁸⁰ *O my fair warrior* This greeting recalls Desdemona's desire to share her husband's warlike life [K].   ¹⁸¹ *content* happiness.   ¹⁸⁹ *absolute* perfect and complete.   ¹⁹⁵ *here* in his heart.   ¹⁹⁸ *set down the pegs* The strings of some musical instruments were kept taut by means of pegs. To loosen the pegs puts the instrument out of tune [K]. Iago will turn their harmony into discord.

Honey, you shall be well desir'd in Cyprus;
I have found great love amongst them. O my sweet,
I prattle out of fashion, and I dote
In mine own comforts. I prithee, good Iago, 205
Go to the bay and disembark my coffers.
Bring thou the master to the citadel.
He is a good one, and his worthiness
Does challenge much respect.—Come, Desdemona,
Once more well met at Cyprus. 210

(*Exeunt all but* IAGO *and* RODERIGO.)

IAGO (*to an* ATTENDANT, *who goes out*): Do thou meet me presently at the harbour. (*To* RODERIGO) Come hither. If thou be'st valiant (as they say base men being in love have then a nobility in their natures more than is native to them), list me. The Lieutenant to-night watches on the court of guard. First, I must tell thee 215 this: Desdemona is directly in love with him.

RODERIGO: With him? Why, 'tis not possible.

IAGO: Lay thy finger thus, and let thy soul be instructed. Mark me with what violence she first lov'd the Moor, but for bragging and 220 telling her fantastical lies; and will she love him still for prating? Let not thy discreet heart think it. Her eye must be fed; and what delight shall she have to look on the devil? When the blood is made dull with the act of sport, there should be, again to inflame 225 it and to give satiety a fresh appetite, loveliness in favour, sympathy in years, manners, and beauties; all which the Moor is defective in. Now for want of these requir'd conveniences, her delicate tenderness will find itself abus'd, begin to heave the gorge, disrelish and abhor the Moor. Very nature will instruct her 230 in it and compel her to some second choice. Now sir, this granted (as it is a most pregnant and unforc'd position), who stands so eminent in the degree of this fortune as Cassio does? A knave very voluble; no further conscionable than in putting on the mere 235 form of civil and humane seeming for the better compassing of his salt and most hidden loose affection? Why, none! why, none! A slipper and subtle knave; a finder-out of occasions; that has an eye can stamp and counterfeit advantages, though true advantage 240

---

202 *well desir'd* warmly welcomed.   204 *out of fashion* unbecomingly.   205 *comforts* happiness.   206 *coffers* luggage.   207 *master* captain of the ship.   209 *challenge* claim, deserve.   211 *presently* at once.   215 *list* listen to.   216 *court of guard* headquarters of the guard.   219 *thus* on the lips.   222 *still* forever.   *prating* speaking foolishly.   226 *favour* features.   227*sympathy* agreement, correspondence.   229 *requir'd conveniences* requisite points of fitness [K].   *tenderness* fastidiousness.   230 *abus'd* deceived.   *heave the gorge* suffer nausea.   233 *most pregnant . . . position* obvious and logical proposition.   234 *stands so eminent . . . fortune* stands so high on the steps that lead to this good fortune [K].   235 *voluble* fickle, easily changing.   *conscionable* conscientious.   237 *compassing* attaining.   *salt* licentious.   238 *loose* lustful.   239 *slipper* slippery.   *occasions* opportunities.

never present itself; a devilish knave! Besides, the knave is handsome, young, and hath all those requisites in him that folly and green minds look after. A pestilent complete knave! and the woman hath found him already.

RODERIGO: I cannot believe that in her. She's full of most blessed condition.

IAGO: Blessed fig's-end! The wine she drinks is made of grapes. If she had been blessed, she would never have lov'd the Moor. Blessed pudding! Didst thou not see her paddle with the palm of his hand? Didst not mark that?

RODERIGO: Yes, that I did; but that was but courtesy.

IAGO: Lechery, by this hand! an index and obscure prologue to the history of lust and foul thoughts. They met so near with their lips that their breaths embrac'd together. Villainous thoughts, Roderigo! When these mutualities so marshal the way, hard at hand comes the master and main exercise, th' incorporate conclusion. Pish! But, sir, be you rul'd by me. I have brought you from Venice. Watch you to-night; for the command, I'll lay't upon you. Cassio knows you not. I'll not be far from you. Do you find some occasion to anger Cassio, either by speaking too loud, or tainting his discipline, or from what other course you please which the time shall more favourably minister.

RODERIGO: Well.

IAGO: Sir, he is rash and very sudden in choler, and haply with his truncheon may strike at you. Provoke him that he may; for even out of that will I cause these of Cyprus to mutiny; whose qualification shall come into no true taste again but by the displanting of Cassio. So shall you have a shorter journey to your desires by the means I shall then have to prefer them; and the impediment most profitably removed without the which there were no expectation of our prosperity.

RODERIGO: I will do this if you can bring it to any opportunity.

IAGO: I warrant thee. Meet me by-and-by at the citadel. I must fetch his necessaries ashore. Farewell. *(Exit.)*

---

243 *green* inexperienced.   245 *found him* discovered what he is.   246-7 *blessed condition* heavenly qualities.   248 *The wine . . . grapes* she is a human being, not an angel, and so has the natural traits of mankind [K].   250 *pudding* sausage (a contemptuous expression).   *paddle* play suggestively.   256 *mutualities* reciprocal familiarities.   257 *marshal* lead.   *hard at hand* soon afterward.   258 *incorporate* united (by the joining of bodies).   263 *tainting* insulting.   265 *minister* provide.   267 *rash* hasty.   *choler* anger.   *haply* perhaps.   268 *truncheon* baton of office.   270-1 *whose qualification . . . Cassio* and they will never be fully appeased unless Cassio is dismissed [K]. *qualification* appeasement, pacification.   273 *prefer* forward.   276 *you* F1; Q1, K: "I." The tenour of the passage indicates Roderigo's dependence upon Iago and thus supports the F1 reading.   277 *warrant thee* assure thee (that there will be an opportunity). 278 *his necessaries* Othello's luggage.

RODERIGO: Adieu.
IAGO: That Cassio loves her, I do well believe it; 280
That she loves him, 'tis apt and of great credit.
The Moor (howbeit that I endure him not)
Is of a constant, loving, noble nature,
And I dare think he'll prove to Desdemona
A most dear husband. Now I do love her too; 285
Not out of absolute lust (though peradventure
I stand accountant for as great a sin)
But partly led to diet my revenge,
For that I do suspect the lusty Moor
Hath leap'd into my seat; the thought whereof 290
Doth, like a poisonous mineral, gnaw my inwards;
And nothing can or shall content my soul
Till I am even'd with him, wife for wife;
Or failing so, yet that I put the Moor
At least into a jealousy so strong 295
That judgment cannot cure. Which thing to do,
If this poor trash of Venice, whom I trash
For his quick hunting, stand the putting on,
I'll have our Michael Cassio on the hip,
Abuse him to the Moor in the rank garb 300
(For I fear Cassio with my nightcap too),
Make the Moor thank me, love me, and reward me
For making him egregiously an ass
And practising upon his peace and quiet
Even to madness. 'Tis here, but yet confus'd. 305
Knavery's plain face is never seen till us'd.   (*Exit.*)

281 *apt* likely.   *of great credit* very credible.   288 *led to diet* led on by the wish to feed—to glut or satisfy [K].   290 *leap'd into my seat* The metaphor is from horsemanship.   294 *yet that* until.   297 *whom I trash* whom I hold in check. To "trash" a hound in hunting is to hang clogs on his collar to prevent him from outrunning the pack. (STEEVENS; F1: "trace"; Q1: "crush"). While Steevens' emendation has been generally accepted, some editors would read "leash," which has essentially the same meaning.   298 *For his quick hunting* to prevent him from running (hunting) too fast.   *stand the putting on* be steadfast (do not fail me) when I incite him to action (put him on).   229 *on the hip* in my power. The term is from wrestling.   300 *Abuse* slander.   *in the rank garb* in the coarse fashion—by bringing the vilest kind of accusation against him [K].   304 *practising upon* plotting (*successfully*) against [K].   305 *yet confus'd* confused as yet. Iago's plots develop as he takes advantage of one opportunity after another. He adapts them to the moment. He sees the main points of what he wishes to accomplish, but has not yet thought out the precise ways to fit them together [K].   306 *Knavery's . . . us'd* no knave sees his plan clearly in all its details until he puts it into practice [K].

William Shakespeare: *Othello*

Scene II. Cyprus. A street.

(*Enter* OTHELLO'S HERALD, *reading a proclamation; people following.*)

HERALD: It is Othello's pleasure, our noble and valiant general, that, upon certain tidings now arriv'd, importing the mere perdition of the Turkish fleet, every man put himself into triumph; some to dance, some to make bonfires, each man to what sport and revels his addiction leads him. For, besides these beneficial news, it is the celebration of his nuptial. So much was his pleasure should be proclaimed. All offices are open, and there is full liberty of feasting from this present hour of five still the bell have told eleven. Heaven bless the isle of Cyprus and our noble general Othello! (*Exeunt.*)

Scene III. Cyprus. A hall in the Castle.

(*Enter* OTHELLO, DESDEMONA, CASSIO, *and* ATTENDANTS.)

OTHELLO: Good Michael, look you to the guard to-night.
Let's teach ourselves that honourable stop,
Not to outsport discretion.
CASSIO: Iago hath direction what to do;
But notwithstanding, with my personal eye
Will I look to't.
OTHELLO: Iago is most honest.
Michael, good night. To-morrow with your earliest
Let me have speech with you.—Come, my dear love.
The purchase made, the fruits are to ensue;
That profit's yet to come 'tween me and you.—
Good night.
(*Exeunt* OTHELLO *and* DESDEMONA *with* ATTENDANTS.)
(*Enter* IAGO.)
CASSIO: Welcome, Iago. We must to the watch.
IAGO: Not this hour, Lieutenant; 'tis not yet ten o' th' clock. Our general cast us thus early for the love of his Desdemona; who let us not therefore blame. He hath not yet made wanton the night with her, and she is sport for Jove.
CASSIO: She's a most exquisite lady.
IAGO: And I'll warrant her, full of game.

II.II. ² *upon* because of.   ³ *mere perdition* utter destruction.   ⁴ *triumph* joyous celebration.   ⁵ *addiction* inclination.   ⁸ *offices* rooms where servants performed their duties, served food and drink.   *open* for food and drink.   ¹⁰ *told* counted.
II.III. ³ *outsport discretion* celebrate to excess.   ¹⁰ *profit's yet . . . and you* The marriage has not yet been consummated.   ¹⁴ *cast us* dismissed us.   ¹⁹ *game* love play.

CASSIO: Indeed, she's a most fresh and delicate creature. 20
IAGO: What an eye she has! Methinks it sounds a parley to provocation.
CASSIO: An inviting eye; and yet methinks right modest.
IAGO: And when she speaks, is it not an alarum to love?
CASSIO: She is indeed perfection. 25
IAGO: Well, happiness to their sheets! Come, Lieutenant, I have a stoup of wine, and here without are a brace of Cyprus gallants that would fain have a measure to the health of black Othello.
CASSIO: Not to-night, good Iago. I have very poor and unhappy 30
brains for drinking. I could well wish courtesy would invent some other custom of entertainment.
IAGO: O, they are our friends. But one cup! I'll drink for you.
CASSIO: I have drunk but one cup to-night, and that was craftily qualified too; and behold what innovation it makes here. I am 35
unfortunate in the infirmity and dare not task my weakness with any more.
IAGO: What, man! 'Tis a night of revels. The gallants desire it.
CASSIO: Where are they?
IAGO: Here at the door. I pray you call them in. 40
CASSIO: I'll do't, but it dislikes me. (*Exit.*)
IAGO: If I can fasten but one cup upon him
With that which he hath drunk to-night already,
He'll be as full of quarrel and offence
As my young mistress' dog. Now my sick fool Roderigo, 45
Whom love hath turn'd almost the wrong side out,
To Desdemona hath to-night carous'd
Potations pottle-deep; and he's to watch.
Three lads of Cyprus—noble swelling spirits,
That hold their honours in a wary distance, 50
The very elements of this warlike isle—
Have I to-night fluster'd with flowing cups,
And they watch too. Now, 'mongst this flock of drunkards

21-2 *parley to provocation* literally, a call to battle, i.e. a summons to the arms of love. 24 *alarum* summons. The military metaphor is continued. 27 *stoup* large cup, holding two quarts. *brace* pair. 28 *fain have a measure* gladly drink a toast. 34-5 *craftily qualified* diluted on the sly. *innovation* disturbance. 36 *here* with a gesture indicating his head or face. 37 *task my weakness* burden (task) my poor powers of resistance (with more than they can support). 41 *dislikes* displeases. 44 *offence* readiness to take offence. 48 *pottle-deep* as deep as the bottom of the pottle. A "pottle" (literally, "little pot") was a big goblet. Every one of Roderigo's healths has emptied his glass. This was a point of manners in old times [K]. 49 *swelling* arrogant. 50 *That hold . . . wary distance* who are scrupulously sensitive to even the remotest infringement on their personal honour [K]. 51 *very elements* characteristic types—the individuals being warlike as the island itself is warlike. 53 *watch* are awake (when normally one should be in bed).

Am I to put our Cassio in some action
That may offend the isle.

(Enter CASSIO, MONTANO, *and* GENTLEMEN; SERVANT *with wine.)*

                              But here they come.
If consequence do but approve my dream,
My boat sails freely, both with wind and stream.
CASSIO: Fore God, they have given me a rouse already.
MONTANO: Good faith, a little one; not past a pint, as I am a soldier.
IAGO: Some wine, ho!
   (Sings)
      And let me the canakin clink, clink;
      And let me the canakin clink.
        A soldier's a man;
        O, man's life's but a span,
      Why then, let a soldier drink.
Some wine, boys!
CASSIO: Fore God, an excellent song!
IAGO: I learn'd it in England, where indeed they are most potent in potting. Your Dane, your German, and your swag-bellied Hollander—Drink, ho!—are nothing to your English.
CASSIO: Is your Englishman so expert in his drinking?
IAGO: Why, he drinks you with facility your Dane dead drunk; he sweats not to overthrow your Almain; he gives your Hollander a vomit ere the next pottle can be fill'd.
CASSIO: To the health of our General!
MONTANO: I am for it, Lieutenant, and I'll do you justice.
IAGO: O sweet England!
   (Sings)
      King Stephen was and a worthy peer;
        His breeches cost him but a crown;
      He held 'em sixpence all too dear,
        With that he call'd the tailor lown.
      He was a wight of high renown,
        And thou art but of low degree.
      'Tis pride that pulls the country down;
        Then take thine auld cloak about thee.
Some wine, ho!

---

56 *If consequence . . . dream* if what follows only proves my expectation true [K]. 58 *rouse* bumper full of drink. 62 *canakin* small can. 70 *potent in potting* strong drinkers. 70-1 *Your Dane . . . Hollander* The Danes, the Germans, and the Dutch were proverbially hard drinkers [K]. 75 *sweats not* need not exert himself. *Almain* German. 75-6 *gives . . . vomit* drinks enough to make a Dutchman throw up. 80-3 *King Stephen . . . lown* A stanza of an old song entitled "Bell My Wife," familiar to everybody in the audience [K]. *lown* rascal. 86 *'Tis pride . . . down* it is extravagance in dress that causes hard times in our country [K]. 87 *Then take . . . thee* This is the substance of Bell's advice to her husband in the interest of economy [K].

CASSIO: Fore God, this is a more exquisite song than the other.
IAGO: Will you hear't again? 90
CASSIO: No, for I hold him to be unworthy of his place that does those things. Well, God's above all; and there be souls must be saved, and there be souls must not be saved.
IAGO: It's true, good Lieutenant.
CASSIO: For mine own part—no offence to the General, nor any 95 man of quality—I hope to be saved.
IAGO: And so do I too, Lieutenant.
CASSIO: Ay, but, by your leave, not before me. The lieutenant is to be saved before the ancient. Let's have no more of this; let's to our affairs. God forgive us our sins! Gentlemen, let's look to our 100 business. Do not think, gentlemen, I am drunk. This is my ancient. This is my right hand, and this is my left. I am not drunk now. I can stand well enough, and speak well enough.
ALL: Excellent well! 105
CASSIO: Why, very well then. You must not think then that I am drunk. *(Exit.)*
MONTANO: To th' platform, masters. Come, let's set the watch.
IAGO: You see this fellow that is gone before.
    He is a soldier to fit to stand by Caesar 110
    And give direction; and do but see his vice.
    'Tis to his virtue a just equinox,
    The one as long as th' other. 'Tis pity of him.
    I fear the trust Othello puts him in,
    On some odd time of his infirmity, 115
    Will shake this island.
MONTANO: But is he often thus?
IAGO: 'Tis evermore the prologue to his sleep.
    He'll watch the horologe a double set
    If drink rock not his cradle.
MONTANO: It were well
    The General were put in mind of it. 120
    Perhaps he sees it not, or his good nature
    Prizes the virtue that appears in Cassio
    And looks not on his evils. Is not this true?

(Enter RODERIGO.*)*
IAGO *(aside to him)*: How now, Roderigo?

---

[91] *place* position.   [92-3] *there be souls . . . not be saved* Cassio applies the doctrine of preordination to the question of propriety in the matter of drinking [K].   [96] *quality* rank.   [108] *platform* the esplanade or paved court where the guard is mustered; the court of guard [K].   *set the watch* mount the guard.   [110] *stand by* act as right-hand man to.   [112] *just equinox* exact equivalent; it counterbalances his virtue just as night and day are equal at the equinox.   [115] *On some . . . infirmity* at some time or other when this weakness of his has overcome him [K].   [119] *watch . . . double set* stay awake for twenty-four hours.   [118] *If drink . . . cradle* if drink has not put him to sleep. The point is that Cassio cannot sleep without drinking first, according to Iago.   [122] *virtue* general excellence.

I pray you after the Lieutenant, go!

(*Exit* RODERIGO)

MONTANO: And 'tis great pity that the noble Moor
Should hazard such a place as his own second
With one of an ingraft infirmity.
It were an honest action to say
So to the Moor.
IAGO: Not I, for this fair island!
I do love Cassio well and would do much
To cure him of this evil.
(*Within*) "Help! help!"
But hark! What noise?
(*Enter* CASSIO, *driving in* RODERIGO.)
CASSIO: Zounds, you rogue! you rascal!
MONTANO: What's the matter, Lieutenant?
CASSIO: A knave teach me my duty?
I'll beat the knave into a twiggen bottle.
RODERIGO: Beat me?
CASSIO: Dost thou prate, rogue?

(*Strikes him.*)

MONTANO: Nay, good Lieutenant!
(*Stays him.*)
I pray you, sir, hold your hand.
CASSIO: Let me go, sir,
Or I'll knock you o'er the mazzard.
MONTANO: Come, come, you're drunk!

CASSIO: Drunk?
IAGO (*aside to* RODERIGO): Away, I say! Go out and cry a mutiny!
(*They fight.*)

(*Exit* RODERIGO.)

Nay, good Lieutenant. God's will, gentlemen!
Help, ho!—Lieutenant—sir—Montano—sir—
Help, masters!—Here's a goodly watch indeed!
(*A bell rung.*)
Who's that which rings the bell? Diablo, ho!
The town will rise. God's will, Lieutenant, hold!
You will be sham'd for ever.
(*Enter* OTHELLO *and* GENTLEMEN *with weapons.*)
OTHELLO: What is the matter here?
MONTANO: Zounds, I bleed still. I am hurt to the death. He dies!
(*Thrusts at* CASSIO.)

---

[127] *second* second in command. [128] *ingraft* ingrafted, inveterate. [135] *twiggen* covered with woven twigs of wicker work. [138] *mazzard* head. [140] *mutiny* riot. [144] *the bell* the alarum bell, which is rung because Roderigo has cried "a mutiny" [K]. [147] *He dies* F1; not in Q1, K. *Thrusts at Cassio.* The stage direction is needed to indicate that Montano is speaking in anger.

OTHELLO: Hold for your lives!
IAGO: Hold, hold! Lieutenant—sir—Montano—gentlemen!
   Have you forgot all sense of place and duty?
   Hold! The General speaks to you. Hold, hold, for shame!
OTHELLO: Why, how now, ho? From whence ariseth this?
   Are we turn'd Turks, and to ourselves do that
   Which heaven hath forbid the Ottomites?
   For Christian shame put by this barbarous brawl!
   He that stirs next to carve for his own rage
   Holds his soul light; he dies upon his motion.
   Silence that dreadful bell! It frights the isle
   From her propriety. What's the matter, masters?
   Honest Iago, that looks dead with grieving,
   Speak. Who began this? On thy love, I charge thee.
IAGO: I do not know. Friends all but now, even now,
   In quarter, and in terms like bride and groom
   Devesting them for bed; and then, but now
   (As if some planet had unwitted men)
   Swords out, and tilting one at other's breast
   In opposition bloody. I cannot speak
   Any beginning to this peevish odds,
   And would in action glorious I had lost
   Those legs that brought me to a part of it!
OTHELLO: How comes it, Michael, you are thus forgot?
CASSIO: I pray you pardon me. I cannot speak.
OTHELLO: Worthy Montano, you were wont be civil;
   The gravity and stillness of your youth
   The world hath noted, and your name is great
   In mouths of wisest censure. What's the matter
   That you unlace your reputation thus
   And spend your rich opinion for the name
   Of a night-brawler? Give me answer to't.
MONTANO: Worthy Othello, I am hurt to danger.
   Your officer, Iago, can inform you,

---

[169] *in action glorious* on the battlefield.   [171] *are thus forgot* have so forgotten yourself.   [156] *carve for his own rage* indulge his own rage in sword-play [K].   [159] *From her propriety* out of herself, out of her senses.   [163] *In quarter* in friendship, observing each his proper station.   [164] *Devesting* undressing.   [165] *planet . . . men* It was commonly believed that the influence of certain planets, most notably the moon, could drive men to madness.   [166] *tilting* thrusting.   [168] *peevish odds* childish quarrel. [169] *in action glorious* on the battlefield.   [171] *are thus forgot* have so forgotten *your*self.   [174] *stillness* sober behaviour.   [175-6] *your name . . . censure* you have an excellent reputation among men of wise judgment.   [177] *unlace* disorder, disgrace.   [178] *spend* squander.   *rich opinion* valuable reputation.   *for* in exchange for.

While I spare speech, which something now offends me,
Of all that I do know; nor know I aught
By me that's said or done amiss this night,
Unless self-charity be sometimes a vice,
And to defend ourselves it be a sin
When violence assails us.
OTHELLO: Now, by heaven,
My blood begins my safer guides to rule,
And passion, having my best judgment collied,
Assays to lead the way. If I once stir
Or do but lift this arm, the best of you
Shall sink in my rebuke. Give me to know
How this foul rout began, who set it on;
And he that is approv'd in this offence,
Though he had twinn'd with me, both at a birth,
Shall lose me. What! in a town of war,
Yet wild, the people's hearts brimful of fear,
To manage private and domestic quarrel?
In night, and on the court and guard of safety?
'Tis monstrous. Iago, who began 't?
MONTANO: If partially affin'd, or leagu'd in office,
Thou dost deliver more or less than truth,
Thou art no soldier.
IAGO: Touch me not so near.
I had rather have this tongue cut from my mouth
Than it should do offence to Michael Cassio.
Yet I persuade myself, to speak the truth
Shall nothing wrong him. Thus it is, General.
Montano and myself being in speech,
There comes a fellow crying out for help,
And Cassio following him with determin'd sword
To execute upon him. Sir, this gentleman
Steps in to Cassio and entreats his pause.
Myself the crying fellow did pursue,
Lest by his clamour (as it so fell out)
The town might fall in fright. He, swift of foot,
Outran my purpose; and I return'd the rather

---

182 *something* somewhat.   *offends* hurts: Montano means that he cannot speak without pain on account of his wound [K].   185 *self-charity* concern for one's self, self-defence.   183 *blood* anger.   *safer guides* saner judgment.   189 *collied* darkened (literally, blackened with coal).   190 *Assays* attempts.   194 *approv'd in* found guilty of.   198 *manage* carry on, engage in.   199 *on the court . . . safety* in the headquarters of the guard.   201 *affin'd* bound. *leagu'd in office* prejudiced because he is your fellow officer.   211 *execute* carry out his purpose.   212 *entreats his pause* pleads with him to stop.   214-15 *Lest by his clamour . . . fright* This is Iago's only misrepresentation of any consequence [K].   216 *the rather* all the sooner.

For that I heard the clink and fall of swords,
And Cassio high in oath; which till to-night
I ne'er might say before. When I came back
(For this was brief) I found them close together 220
At blow and thrust, even as again they were
When you yourself did part them.
More of this matter cannot I report;
But men are men; the best sometimes forget.
Though Cassio did some little wrong to him, 225
As men in rage strike those that wish them best,
Yet surely Cassio I believe receiv'd
From him that fled some strange indignity,
Which patience could not pass.
OTHELLO: I know, Iago,
Thy honesty and love doth mince this matter, 230
Making it light to Cassio. Cassio, I love thee;
But never more be officer of mine.

(Enter DESDEMONA, *attended.)*

Look if my gentle love be not rais'd up!
I'll make thee an example.
DESDEMONA: What's the matter?
OTHELLO: All's well now, sweeting; come away to bed. 235
 (To MONTANO*)* Sir, for your hurts, myself will be your surgeon.
Lead him off.
 (MONTANO *is led off.*)
Iago, look with care about the town
And silence those whom this vile brawl distracted.
Come, Desdemona. 'Tis the soldiers' life 240
To have their balmy slumbers wak'd with strife.
               (Exeunt all but IAGO *and* CASSIO.*)*
IAGO: What, are you hurt, Lieutenant?
CASSIO: Ay, past all surgery.
IAGO: Marry, God forbid!
CASSIO: Reputation, reputation, reputation! O, I have lost my repu- 245
   tation! I have lost the immortal part of myself, and what remains
   is bestial. My reputation, Iago, my reputation!
IAGO: As I am an honest man, I thought you had receiv'd some bodily
   wound. There is more sense in that than in reputation. Repu- 250
   tation is an idle and most false imposition; oft got without merit

---

217 *For that* because.   218 *high in oath* swearing loudly.   219 *might* could   225 *him* Montano.   228 *indignity* insult.   229 *patience* self-control. *pass* endure.   230 *mince* play down.   235 *sweeting* sweetheart.   240 *'Tis the soldiers' life* this is the kind of life you must expect if you wish to share my life as a soldier [K].   250 *sense* feeling.   251 *imposition* that which is placed upon a man by others.

and lost without deserving. You have lost no reputation at all unless you repute yourself such a loser. What, man! there are ways to recover the General again. You are but now cast in his mood— a punishment more in policy than in malice, even so as one would beat his offenceless dog to affright an imperious lion. Sue to him again, and he's yours.

CASSIO: I will rather use to be despis'd than to deceive so good a commander with so slight, so drunken, and so indiscreet an officer. Drunk? and speak parrot? and squabble? swagger? swear? and discourse fustian with one's own shadow? O thou invisible spirit of wine, if thou hast no name to be known by, let us call thee devil!

IAGO: What was he that you follow'd with your sword? What had he done to you?

CASSIO: I know not.

IAGO: Is't possible?

CASSIO: I remember a mass of things, but nothing distinctly; a quarrel, but nothing wherefore. O God, that men should put an enemy in their mouths to steal away their brains! that we should with joy, pleasance, revel, and applause transform ourselves into beasts!

IAGO: Why, but you are now well enough. How came you thus recovered?

CASSIO: It hath pleas'd the devil drunkenness to give place to the devil wrath. One unperfectness shows me another, to make me frankly despise myself.

IAGO: Come, you are too severe a moraler. As the time, the place, and the condition of this country stands, I could heartily wish this had not so befall'n; but since it is as it is, mend it for your own good.

CASSIO: I will ask him for my place again: he shall tell me I am a drunkard! Had I as many mouths as Hydra, such an answer would stop them all. To be now a sensible man, by-and-by a fool, and presently a beast! O strange! Every inordinate cup is unblest, and the ingredience is a devil.

---

254 *recover* win back.   255 *cast* dismissed. *in his mood* as a result of his anger.   256 *more in policy than in malice* inflicted rather because he thinks it good policy to punish you (for the maintenance of discipline) than because he feels any ill will toward you [K].   257-8 *beat his . . . imperious lion* punish an insignificant person to warn an important one against doing wrong (an old proverb).   258 *Sue* appeal.   260 *slight* worthless (F¹; Q¹; "light"). Some editors prefer the Q¹ reading as meaning "irresponsible."   261 *speak parrot* talk nonsense, without knowing what one is saying.   262 *fustian* nonsense. The word originally was the name of a coarse kind of cloth, like corduroy.   277 *unperfectness* imperfection, weakness.   278 *frankly* without reserve.   284 *Hydra* the many-headed serpent of Greek mythology, destroyed by Hercules; when one head was cut off, two new ones sprang out to replace it.   287 *inordinate* beyond moderation. *ingredience* contents.

IAGO: Come, come, good wine is a good familiar creature if it be
well us'd. Exclaim no more against it. And, good Lieutenant, I
think you think I love you. 290
CASSIO: I have well approv'd it, sir. I drunk?
IAGO: You or any man living may be drunk at a time, man. I'll tell
you what you shall do. Our General's wife is now the General. I
may say so in this respect, for that he hath devoted and given up
himself to the contemplation, mark, and denotement of her parts 295
and graces. Confess yourself freely to her. Importune her help to
put you in your place again. She is of so free, so kind, so apt, so
blessed a disposition she holds it a vice in her goodness not to do
more than she is requested. This broken joint between you and 300
her husband entreat her to splinter; and my fortunes against any
lay worth naming, this crack of your love shall grow stronger
than 'twas before.
CASSIO: You advise me well.
IAGO: I protest, in the sincerity of love and honest kindness. 305
CASSIO: I think it freely; and betimes in the morning will I beseech
the virtuous Desdemona to undertake for me. I am desperate of
my fortunes if they check me here.
IAGO: You are in the right. Good night, Lieutenant. I must to the
watch. *(Exit.)* 310
CASSIO: Good night, honest Iago.
IAGO: And what's he then that says I play the villain,
When this advice is free I give and honest,
Probal to thinking, and indeed the course
To win the Moor again? For 'tis most easy 315
Th' inclining Desdemona to subdue
In any honest suit. She's fram'd as fruitful
As the free elements. And then for her
To win the Moor — were't to renounce his baptism —
All seals and symbols of redeemed sin — 320
His soul is so enfetter'd to her love
That she may make, unmake, do what she list,
Even as her appetite shall play the god

---

296 *parts* accomplishment.   *graces* charms.   298 *free* bounteous.   *apt* ready (to do kindness).   300 *joint* relationship.   301 *splinter* bind with splints.   302 *lay* wager, stake.   303 *crack . . . before* It was an old notion that a broken bone mended would be stronger than it was before the break.   306 *betimes* early.   308 *desperate* hopeless.   *check me* fail me.   314 *Probal to thinking* such as would be approved by good judgment [K].   316 *inclining* inclining by nature to do what is asked of her [K].   *subdue* persuade.   317 *fruitful* generous.   320 *All seals . . . redeemed sin* Baptism is the seal (or confirmation) of a man's redemption from sin; and, being a rite of purification, is also a symbol of restoration to innocence. "Seals and symbols" is in a kind of apposition with "baptism":—"to renounce his baptism—yes, and whatever other seals and symbols of redemption there are in Christianity" [K].   323 *her appetite* his sexual desire for her.   *play the god* rule absolutely.

With his weak function. How am I then a villain
To counsel Cassio to this parallel course,
Directly to his good? Divinity of hell!
When devils will the blackest sins put on,
They do suggest at first with heavenly shows,
As I do now. For whiles this honest fool
Plies Desdemona to repair his fortunes,
And she for him pleads strongly to the Moor,
I'll pour this pestilence into his ear —
That she repeals him for her body's lust;
Any by how much she strives to do him good,
She shall undo her credit with the Moor.
So will I turn her virtue into pitch,
And out of her own goodness make the net
That shall enmesh them all.

(*Enter* RODERIGO.)

How now, Roderigo?
RODERIGO: I do follow here in the chase, not like a hound that hunts, but one that fills up the cry. My money is almost spent; I have been tonight exceedingly well cudgell'd; and I think the issue will be — I shall have so much experience for my pains; and so, with no money at all, and a little more wit, return again to Venice.
IAGO: How poor are they that have not patience!
What wound did ever heal but by degrees?
Thou know'st we work by wit, and not by witchcraft;
And wit depends on dilatory time.
Does't not go well? Cassio hath beaten thee,
And thou by that small hurt hast cashier'd Cassio.
Though other things grow fair against the sun.
Yet fruits that blossom first will first be ripe.

---

324 *weak function* human powers of mind and body, specifically his sexual power which, since Othello is old, Iago regards as inadequate to satisfy Desdemona.   325 *parallel* leading to the same end, Othello's destruction.   326 *Directly to* in complete accord with.   *Divinity of hell* the kind of theological reasoning (divinity) which a devil might use.   327 *put on* instigate.   328 *suggest* tempt. *heavenly shows* mere appearances of holiness.   330 *Plies* urges.   333 *repeals* is trying to procure his recall.   335 *undo her credit* destroy her reputation.   336 *pitch* (a) blackness (b) that which has the power to ensnare, as pitch was sometimes used because of its viscous quality.   340 *fills up the cry* merely makes up one of the pack.   344 *wit* intelligence.   347 *wit* clever planning.   350 *cashier'd Cassio* procured Cassio's dismissal. Iago plays on words contemptuously [K].   351-2 *Though other things . . . be ripe* even though our other plans (your attaining of Desdemona) are developing favourably, the more immediate steps (the dismissal of Cassio) must be accomplished before we can attain the ultimate goal; first things must come first.

Content thyself awhile. By th' mass, 'tis morning!
Pleasure and action make the hours seem short.
Retire thee; go where thou art billeted. 355
Away, I say! Thou shalt know more hereafter. (*Exit* RODERIGO.)
Nay, get thee gone!
               Two things are to be done:
My wife must move for Cassio to her mistress;
I'll set her on;
Myself the while to draw the Moor apart 360
And bring him jump when he may Cassino find
Soliciting his wife. Ay, that's the way!
Dull not device by coldness and delay. (*Exit.*)

ACT THREE

Scene I. Cyprus. Before the Castle.

(*Enter* CASSIO, *with* MUSICIANS.)

CASSIO: Masters, play here, I will content your pains:
  Something that's brief; and bid "Good morrow, General."
They play.
(*Enter the Clown.*)
CLOWN: Why, masters, have your instruments been at Naples,
  that they speak i' th' nose thus?
MUSICIANS: How, sir, how? 5
CLOWN: Are these, I pray, call'd wind instruments?
MUSICIANS: Ay, marry, are they, sir.
CLOWN: O, thereby hangs a tail.
MUSICIANS: Whereby hangs a tale, sir?
CLOWN: Marry, sir, by many a wind instrument that I know. 10
  But, masters, here's money for you; and the General so

---

355 *billeted* quartered. The "billet" is the "little bill" or document designating the person at whose house a soldier is to lodge [K].   358 *move* plead.   361 *jump* exactly at the right time.   363 *device* strategy.   *coldness* lack of energy, sluggishness.
III.i. 1 *play here* Such a greeting of music to the newly married was a courteous custom. The dramatic purpose of the episode is to make an interval in the main action before the reappearance of Iago [K].   *content your pains* reward you for your trouble.
3-4 *Naples . . . nose thus* This obviously bawdy reference has never been satisfactorily explained. Naples was known as the center of venereal disease. The clown seems to be criticizing the music as sounding like the speech of sufferers from this malady.   8 *tail* slang for penis.   10 *wind instrument* buttocks, capable of producing wind.

likes your music that he desires you, of all loves, to
make no more noise with it.
MUSICIANS: Well, sir, we will not.
CLOWN: If you have any music that may not be heard, to't again. 15
But, as they say, to hear music the General does not
greatly care.
MUSICIANS: We have none such, sir.
CLOWN: Then put up your pipes in your bag, for I'll away.
Go, vanish into air, away!   (*Exeunt* MUSICIANS.) 20
CASSIO: Dost thou hear, my honest friend?
CLOWN: No, I hear not your honest friend. I hear you.
CASSIO: Prithee keep up thy quillets. There's a poor piece of
gold for thee. If the gentlewoman that attends the Gen-
eral's wife be stirring, tell her there's one Cassio entreats 25
her a little favour of speech. Wilt thou do this?
CLOWN: She is stirring, sir. If she will stir hither, I shall seem to
notify unto her.   (*Exit* CLOWN.)
CASSIO: Do, good my friend.
(*Enter* IAGO.)
                        In happy time, Iago.
IAGO: You have not been abed then? 30
CASSIO: Why, no. The day had broke
Before we parted. I have made bold, Iago.
To send in to your wife. My suit to her
Is that she will to virtuous Desdemona
Procure me some access.
IAGO: I'll send her to you presently; 35
And I'll devise a mean to draw the Moor
Out of the way, that your converse and business
May be more free.   (*Exit* IAGO.)
CASSIO: I humbly thank you for't.
                        I never knew
A Florentine more kind and honest. 40

(*Enter* EMILIA.)

EMILIA: Good morrow, good Lieutenant. I am sorry
For your displeasure; but all will sure be well.
The General and his wife are talking of it,
And she speaks for you stoutly. The Moor replies
That he you hurt is of great fame in Cyprus 45

---

12 *of all loves* for the sake of any affection you may feel for him [K].   15 *to't* go to it.
23 *keep up* keep to yourself.   *quillets* quips, puns.   27 *seem* to arrange to.   29 *In happy time* well met.   36 *mean* means.   37 *converse* conversation.   40 *A Florentine* even a Florentine, as Cassio himself is; Iago, of course, is a Venetian.   42 *displeasure* being out of favour.

And great affinity, and that in wholesome wisdom
He might not but refuse you. But he protests he loves you,
And needs no other suitor but his likings
To take the safest occasion by the front
To bring you in again.
CASSIO: Yet I beseech you, 50
If you think fit, or that it may be done,
Give me advantage of some brief discourse
With Desdemona alone.
EMILIA: Pray you come in.
I will bestow you where you shall have time
To speak your bosom freely.
CASSIO: I am much bound to you. 55

(*Exeunt.*)

Scene II. *Cyprus. A room in the Castle.*

(*Enter* OTHELLO, IAGO, *and* GENTLEMEN.)

OTHELLO: These letters give, Iago, to the pilot
And by him do my duties to the state.
That done, I will be walking on the works.
Repair there to me.
IAGO: Well, my good lord, I'll do't.
OTHELLO: This fortification, gentlemen, shall we see't? 5
GENTLEMEN: We'll wait upon your lordship.

(*Exeunt.*)

Scene III. *Cyprus. The garden of the Castle.*

(*Enter* DESDEMONA, CASSIO, *and* EMILIA.)

DESDEMONA: Be thou assur'd, good Cassio, I will do
All my abilities in thy behalf.

⁴⁶ *affinity* family connections.   *in wholesome wisdom* out of a prudent regard for good policy [K].   ⁴⁸ *likings* affections.   ⁴⁹ *occasion* opportunity.   *front* forehead; forelock. Occasion (like Time and Fortune) was described and figured as bald except for one long lock on the forehead. Shakespeare remembered the proverb as he had read it in the so-called DISTICHA CATONIS, ii, 26—a primary schoolbook in his time [K]. The proverb occurs very often in Elizabethan literature.   ⁵⁴ *bestow* place.

III.II The purpose of this scene is to explain the absence of Othello during Cassio's interview with Desdemona. Iago meant "to draw the Moor out of the way" (III.I.36-7); but apparently luck had played into his hand and no "device" was necessary. Certain gentlemen of Cyprus had called upon Othello, with whom he thought it necessary to inspect some part of the fortifications ("the works") [K].   ² *do my duties* pay my respects.   ⁴ *Repair* come.

III.III. The short scene that precedes has given Emilia time to conduct Cassio to her

EMILIA: Good madam, do. I warrant it grieves my husband
    As if the cause were his.
DESDEMONA: O, that's an honest fellow. Do not doubt, Cassio,
    But I will have my lord and you again
    As friendly as you were.
CASSIO: Bounteous madam,
    Whatever shall become of Michael Cassio,
    He's never anything but your true servant.
DESDEMONA: I know't; I thank you. You do love my lord;
    You have known him long; and be you well assur'd
    He shall in strangeness stand no farther off
    Than in a politic distance.
CASSIO: Ay, but, lady,
    That policy may either last so long,
    Or feed upon such nice and waterish diet,
    Or breed itself so out of circumstance,
    That, I being absent, and my place supplied,
    My general will forget my love and service.
DESDEMONA: Do not doubt that. Before Emilia here
    I give thee warrant of thy place. Assure thee,
    If I do vow a friendship, I'll perform it
    To the last article. My lord shall never rest;
    I'll watch him tame and talk him out of patience;
    His bed shall seem a school, his board a shrift;
    I'll intermingle everything he does
    With Cassio's suit. Therefore be merry, Cassio,
    For thy solicitor shall rather die
    Than give thy cause away.

(*Enter* OTHELLO *and* IAGO.)

EMILIA: Madam, here comes my lord.
CASSIO: Madam, I'll take my leave.
DESDEMONA: Why, stay, and hear me speak.
CASSIO: Madam, not now. I am very ill at ease
    Unfit for mine own purposes.

mistress. Scene III opens in the midst of the conversation. Cassio has already made his petition to Desdemona [K]. This "temptation" scene is the pivotal scene of the play, in which Othello is forced to choose between Iago and Desdemona. At the beginning he is the self-sufficient master of his passions; at the end he is an inhuman monster, ravaged by jealousy, completely in the power of Iago.   12-13 *He shall . . . politic distance* his estrangement will assuredly last no longer than policy requires [K].   15 *feed upon . . . diet* be kept alive by such trivial and insignificant considerations [K].   16 *breed . . . circumstance* perpetuate itself by new circumstances which may occur.   17 *place supplied* position occupied (by another).   19 *doubt* fear.   20 *warrant* promise.   23 *watch him tame* tame him by keeping him awake. An allusion to the method of taming falcons [K].   24 *shrift* confessional.   26 *merry* cheerful.   28 *give thy cause away* abandon it.

DESDEMONA: Well, do your discretion.

(*Exit* CASSIO.)

IAGO: Ha! I like not that.
OTHELLO: What dost thou say?
IAGO: Nothing, my lord; or if — I know not what.
OTHELLO: Was not that Cassio parted from my wife?
IAGO: Cassio, my lord? No, sure, I cannot think it.
   That he would steal away so guilty-like,
   Seeing you coming.
OTHELLO: I do believe 'twas he.
DESDEMONA: How now, my lord?
   I have been talking with a suitor here,
   A man that languishes in your displeasure.
OTHELLO: Who is't you mean?
DESDEMONA: Why, your lieutenant, Cassio. Good my lord,
   If I have any grace or power to move you,
   His present reconciliation take;
   For if he be not one that truly loves you,
   That errs in ignorance, and not in cunning,
   I have no judgment in an honest face.
   I prithee call him back,
OTHELLO: Went he hence now?
DESDEMONA: Yes, faith; so humbled
   That he hath left part of his grief with me
   To suffer with him. Good love, call him back.
OTHELLO: Not now, sweet Desdemona; some other time.
DESDEMONA: But shall't be shortly?
OTHELLO: The sooner, sweet, for you.
DESDEMONA: Shall't be to-night at supper?
OTHELLO: No, not to-night.
DESDEMONA: To-morrow dinner then?
OTHELLO: I shall not dine at home.
   I meet the captains at the citadel.
DESDEMONA: Why then, to-morrow night, or Tuesday morn,
   Or Tuesday noon or night, or Wednesday morn.
   I prithee name the time, but let it not
   Exceed three days. I' faith, he's penitent;

---

35 *I like not that* Iago takes instant advantage of Cassio's hurried departure. He utilizes every chance occurrence [K]. With this line the temptation of Othello begins.   46 *grace* favour in your eyes.   47 *reconciliation* repentence with the hope of reconciliation. *take* accept.   49 *in cunning* knowingly, on purpose.   55 *some other time* Othello has no suspicions as yet; nor is he either displeased or impatient. He is simply very busy, and not quite ready to receive Cassio [K]. Although Iago's subtle insinuations had begun at line 34, Othello is not abnormally jealous, and it will take much more provocation before he begins to fall.   58 *dinner* the noonday meal.

And yet his trespass, in our common reason
(Save that, they say, the wars must make examples 65
Out of their best) is not almost a fault
T' incur a private check. When shall he come?
Tell me, Othello. I wonder in my soul
What you could ask me that I should deny
Or stand so mamm'ring on. What? Michael Cassio 70
That came-a-wooing with you, and so many a time,
When I have spoke of you dispraisingly,
Hath ta'en your part — to have so much to do
To bring him in? Trust me, I could do much —
OTHELLO: Prithee no more. Let him come when he will! 75
I will deny thee nothing.
DESDEMONA: Why, this is not a boon.
'Tis as I should entreat you wear your gloves,
Or feed on nourishing dishes, or keep you warm,
Or sue to you to do a peculiar profit
To your own person. Nay, when I have a suit 80
Wherein I mean to touch your love indeed,
It shall be full of poise and difficult weight,
And fearful to be granted.
OTHELLO: I will deny thee nothing!
Whereon I do beseech thee grant me this,
To leave me but a little to myself. 85
DESDEMONA: Shall I deny you? No. Farewell, my lord.
OTHELLO: Farewell, my Desdemona. I'll come to thee straight.
DESDEMONA: Emilia, come. — Be as your fancies teach you.
Whate'er you be, I am obedient.

(*Exeunt* DESDEMONA *and* EMILIA.)

OTHELLO: Excellent wretch! Perdition catch my soul 90
But I do love thee! and when I love thee not,
Chaos is come again.
IAGO: My noble lord —
OTHELLO: What dost thou say, Iago?

---

⁶⁴ *in our common reason* if judged as we ordinarily regard such things [K].   ⁶⁵⁻⁶ *the wars . . . their best* military discipline demands that the best man be sometimes punished as examples to the others.   ⁶⁷ *private check* personal rebuke.   ⁷⁰ *mamm'ring* hesitating.   ⁷⁹ *peculiar* personal.   ⁸¹ *touch* test.   ⁸² *poise* weight.   ⁸⁷ *straight* soon.   ⁸⁸ *fancies* inclinations.   *teach* guide.   ⁹¹⁻² *and when I love . . . come again* I shall love thee as long as the universe lasts. This speech is sometimes strangely misunderstood, as if Othello meant that, if anything should cause him to cease to love her, the result would be chaos. But Othello is in no questioning mood; he is not contemplating the possibility of ceasing to love Desdemona, but emphasizing its impossibility. By-and-by, when the catastrophe comes, we are at liberty to remember his words and, if we like, to perceive that they were, if taken in a sense not meant by him, a prophecy of coming ruin. This tragic irony was doubtless intentional on Shakespeare's part [K].

IAGO: Did Michael Cassio, when you woo'd my lady,
    Know of your love? 95
OTHELLO: He did, from first to last. Why dost thou ask?
IAGO: But for a satisfaction of my thought;
    No further harm.
OTHELLO: Why of thy thought, Iago?
IAGO: I did not think he had been acquainted with her.
OTHELLO: O, yes, and went between us very oft. 100
IAGO: Indeed?
OTHELLO: Indeed? Ay, indeed! Discern'st thou aught in that?
    Is he not honest?
IAGO: Honest, my lord?
OTHELLO: Honest? Ay, honest.
IAGO: My lord, for aught I know.
OTHELLO: What dost thou think?
IAGO: Think, my lord?
OTHELLO: Think, my lord? 105
    By heaven, he echoes me,
    As if there were some monster in his thought
    Too hideous to be shown. Thou dost mean something.
    I heard thee say even now, thou lik'st not that,
    When Cassio left my wife. What didst not like? 110
    And when I told thee he was of my counsel
    In my whole course of wooing, thou cried'st "Indeed?"
    And didst contract and purse thy brow together,
    As if thou then hadst shut up in thy brain
    Some horrible conceit. If thou dost love me, 115
    Show me thy thought.
IAGO: My lord, you know I love you.
OTHELLO: I think thou dost;
    And, for I know thou'rt full of love and honesty
    And weigh'st thy words before thou giv'st them breath,
    Therefore these stops of thine fright me the more; 120
    For such things in a false disloyal knave
    Are tricks of custom; but in a man that's just
    They are close dilations, working from the heart
    That passion cannot rule.

[96] *Why dost thou ask* Iago has succeeded in arousing Othello's curiosity and thus to lead him into discussion.   [103] *honest* honourable.   [107-8] *As if . . . to be shown* Iago has now fully aroused Othello into active consideration of the possibility of some evil unknown to him. He now reviews all of the stages of Iago's assault and demands further elucidation.   [123-4] *They are close dilations . . . cannot rule* they are secret emotions, forcing their way from the speaker's very heart, which cannot control its agitation. The man's heart is stirred by some horrible thought which he wishes to conceal, but, though he controls his tongue, he cannot prevent the emotions of his heart from interrupting speech [K].

William Shakespeare: *Othello*

IAGO: For Michael Cassio,
   I dare be sworn I think that he is honest.
OTHELLO: I think so too.
IAGO: Men should be what they seem;
   Or those that be not, what they might seem none!
OTHELLO: Certain, men should be what they seem.
IAGO: Why then, I think Cassio's an honest man.
OTHELLO: Nay, yet there's more in this.
   I prithee speak to me, as to thy thinkings,
   As thou dost ruminate, and give thy worst of thoughts
   The worst of words.
IAGO: Good my lord, pardon me.
   Though I am bound to every act of duty,
   I am not bound to that all slaves are free to.
   Utter my thoughts? Why, say they are vile and false,
   As where's that palace whereinto foul things
   Sometimes intrude not? Who has a breast so pure
   But some uncleanly apprehensions
   Keep leets and law days, and in session sit
   With meditations lawful?
OTHELLO: Thou dost conspire against thy friend, Iago.
   If thou but think'st him wrong'd, and mak'st his ear
   A stranger to thy thoughts.
IAGO: I do beseech you —
   Though I perchance am vicious in my guess
   (As I confess it is my nature's plague
   To spy into abuse, and oft my jealousy
   Shapes faults that are not), that your wisdom yet
   From one that so imperfectly conceits
   Would take no notice, nor build yourself a trouble

---

127 *would they might seem none* would they might not seem to be men at all (but monsters, as they really are) [K]. Iago is suggesting that Cassio's is only a seeming virtue and vehemently lamenting that this should be so.   131-2 *speak to me . . . dost ruminate* tell me thy thoughts exactly as thou dost think them [K].   135 *bound to . . . free to* obliged to do even what slaves are not obliged to do, utter my thoughts.   137-8 *As where's . . . intrude not* just as foul things sometimes intrude into the most splendid palace, so vile and false thoughts come now and then, unbidden, into the purest breast. Iago contrives to assert his well-known "honesty" even in the act of admitting that he entertains suspicions which may be "vile and false" [K].   139 *apprehensions* thoughts.   140 *leets* court sessions.   145 *vicious in my guess* mistaken (literally, faulty) in what I suspect [K].   147 *jealousy* tendency to scrutinize closely and carefully.   149 *so imperfectly conceits* has such vague, unformed ideas on the subject [K].

Out of his scattering and unsure observance.
It were not for your quiet nor your good,
Nor for my manhood, honesty, or wisdom,
To let you know my thoughts.
OTHELLO: What dost thou mean?
IAGO: Good name in man and woman, dear my lord, 155
Is the immediate jewel of their souls.
Who steals my purse steals trash; 'tis something, nothing;
'Twas mine, 'tis his, and has been slave to thousands;
But he that filches from me my good name
Robs me of that which not enriches him 160
And makes me poor indeed.
OTHELLO: By heaven, I'll know thy thoughts!
IAGO: You cannot, if my heart were in your hand;
Nor shall not whilst 'tis in my custody.
OTHELLO: Ha!
IAGO: O, beware, my lord, of jealousy! 165
It is the green-ey'd monster, which doth mock
The meat it feeds on. That cuckold lives in bliss
Who, certain of his fate, loves not his wronger;
But O, what damned minutes tells he o'er
Who dotes, yet doubts—suspects, yet strongly loves! 170
OTHELLO: O misery!
IAGO: Poor and content is rich, and rich enough;
But riches finelss is as poor as winter
To him that ever fears he shall be poor.
Good heaven, the souls of all my tribe defend 175
From jealousy!
OTHELLO: Why, why is this?
Think'st thou I'ld make a life of jealousy,
To follow still the changes of the moon
With fresh suspicions? No! To be once in doubt
Is once to be resolv'd. Exchange me for a goat 180
When I shall turn the business of my soul

---

151 *scattering* random. *observance* observation.   156 *immediate jewel of* treasure closest to.   162 *By heaven . . . thoughts* Iago's little homily on reputation has served to raise Othello's curiosity and fear to a fever pitch.   165 *O, beware . . . of jealousy* Here, for the first time, Iago insinuates that Desdemona may be unfaithful. Hitherto all his efforts have been directed to rousing suspicion of Cassio [K]   166-7 *mock . . . feeds on* Jealousy is conceived of not as something arising from within man, but as a lurking monster from without, which seizes upon man (his meat) and plays with him as a cat plays with a mouse.   168 *his wronger* the wife who is betraying him.   170 *strongly* Q1; Some editors read "fondly," an emendation of F1 "soundly."   173 *fineless* boundless.   178 *still* ever, always.   180 *to be resolv'd* to have doubt cleared up.

>   To such exsufflicate and blown surmises,
>   Matching thy inference. 'Tis not to make me jealous
>   To say my wife is fair, feeds well, loves company,
>   Is free of speech, sings, plays, and dances well. 185
>   Where virtue is, these are more virtuous.
>   Nor from mine own weak merits will I draw
>   The smallest fear or doubt of her revolt,
>   For she had eyes, and chose me. No Iago;
>   I'll see before I doubt; when I doubt, prove; 190
>   And on the proof there is no more but this —
>   Away at once with love or jealousy!
> IAGO: I am glad of it; for now I shall have reason
>   To show the love and duty that I bear you
>   With franker spirit. Therefore, as I am bound, 195
>   Receive it from me. I speak not yet of proof.
>   Look to your wife; observe her well with Cassio;
>   Wear your eye thus, not jealous nor secure.
>   I would not have your free and noble nature,
>   Out of self-bounty, be abus'd. Look to't. 200
>   I know our country disposition well:
>   In Venice they do let heaven see the pranks
>   They dare not show their husbands; their best conscience
>   Is not to leave't undone, but keep't unknown. 205
> OTHELLO: Dost thou say so?
> IAGO: She did deceive her father, marrying you;
>   And when she seem'd to shake and fear your looks,
>   She lov'd them most.
> OTHELLO: And so she did.
> IAGO: Why, go to then!
>   She that, so young, could give out such a seeming 210
>   To seel her father's eyes up close as oak —
>   He though 'twas witchcraft—but I am much to blame.
>   I humbly do beseech you of your pardon

182 *exsufflicate* insubstantial, blown up with air.   *blown* (a) blown up (b) flyblown, odious.   183 *Matching thy inference* in accordance with your description of the suspicions of a jealous man [K].   186 *Where virtue . . . more virtuous*, when a woman is virtuous, these things merely add to her excellence.   187 *weak merits* unattractive physical features.   188 *revolt* unfaithfulness.   190 *prove* put the matter to a test.   195 *franker* more open.   198 *jealous* suspicious   *secure* blindly confident.   199 *free* open and generous.   200 *self-bounty* innate goodness.   *abus'd* deceived, tricked.   201 *I know . . . well* An insidious suggestion, as coming from one who is known to be uncommonly observant (cf. lines 259–60) and is regarded by all as "honest" [K]. Iago plays on the fact that Othello is an alien in Venice, unfamiliar with its customs.   202-3 *In Venice . . . their husbands* Historically, Venice was, in fact, famous for its courtesans.   206-8 *She did deceive . . . most* Here and in his next speech Iago recalls to Othello's mind Brabantio's ominous words (I.III.292–3) [K].

For too much loving you.
OTHELLO: I am bound to thee for ever.
IAGO: I see this hath a little dash'd your spirits.
OTHELLO: Not a jot, not a jot.
IAGO: I' faith, I fear it has,   215
   I hope you will consider what is spoke
   Comes from my love. But I do see y'are mov'd.
   I am to pray you not to strain my speech
   To grosser issues nor to larger reach
   Than to suspicion.   220
OTHELLO: I will not.
IAGO: Should you do so, my lord,
   My speech should fall into such vile success
   As my thoughts aim not at. Cassio's my worthy friend —
   My lord, I see y'are mov'd.
OTHELLO: No, not much mov'd.
   I do not think but Desdemona's honest.   225
IAGO: Long live she so! and long live you to think so!
OTHELLO: And yet, how nature erring from itself —
IAGO: Ay, there's the point! as (to be bold with you)
   Not to affect many proposed matches
   Of her own clime, complexion, and degree,   230
   Whereto we see in all things nature tends —
   Foh! one may smell in such a will most rank,
   Foul disproportion, thoughts unnatural —
   But pardon me — I do not in position
   Distinctly speak of her; though I may fear   235
   Her will, recoiling to her better judgment,
   May fall to match you with her country forms,
   And happily repent.

[219] *grosser issues* greater consequences.   [222] *fall into such vile success* have such an odious result.   [225] *honest* chaste.   [229] *affect* care for. Othello, in reflecting that nature may prove false to itself, is thinking of the possibility that Desdemona has sinned with Cassio. Iago instantly gives the remark a sinister twist. Desdemona's nature, he argues, has already "erred from itself," for it was abnormal for a woman like her to reject all the suitors of her own race and age and fall in love with a man like Othello. His argument is based on the general principle that "like will to like" [K].   [230] *clime* country. *complexion* (a) colour (b) temperament (literally, the peculiar combination of humours in the body).   *degree* social rank.   [232] *will* carnal desire.   [233] *disproportion* abnormality.   [234-5] *I do not . . . of her* I do not mean to lay down a proposition that applies to her in particular. Iago suggests, insidiously, that Desdemona may possibly be an exception to the general rule [K].   [236] *recoiling* reverting.   [237] *fall to match you* chance to compare you. *her country forms* the physical appearances, forms of beauty, of her own country, Venice.   [238] *And happily* and so, perhaps. The argument is that, if Desdemona's love for Othello was a mere caprice of passion, her nature may recover its balance, and she may come to dislike him [K].

OTHELLO: Farewell, farewell!
    If more thou dost perceive, let me know more.
    Set on the wife to observe. Leave me, Iago. 240
IAGO: My lord, I take my leave.
    (Going.)
OTHELLO: Why did I marry? This honest creature doubtless
    Sees and knows more, much more, than he unfolds.
IAGO *(returns)*: My lord, I would I might entreat your Honour
    To scan this thing no further. Leave it to time. 245
    Though it be fit that Cassio have his place.,
    For sure he fills it up with great ability,
    Yet, if you please to hold him off awhile,
    You shall by that perceive him and his means.
    Note if your lady strain his entertainment 250
    With any strong or vehement importunity.
    Much will be seen in that. In the mean time
    Let me be thought too busy in my fears
    (As worthy cause I have to fear I am)
    And hold her free, I do beseech your Honour. 255
OTHELLO: Fear not my government.
IAGO: I once more take my leave.
OTHELLO: This fellow's of exceeding honesty,
    And knows all qualities, with a learned spirit
    Of human dealings. If I do prove her haggard, 260
    Though that her jesses were my dear heartstrings,
    I'd whistle her off and let her down the wind
    To prey at fortune. Haply, for I am black
    And have not those soft parts of conversation
    That chamberers have, or for I am declin'd 265
    Into the vale of years (yet that's not much),
    She's gone. I am abus'd, and my relief
    Must be to loathe her. O curse of marriage,

---

245 *scan* examine closely. 249 *his means* the means he uses to procure reinstatement [K]. 250 *strain* press, urge. *his entertainment* that he be entertained, received back into favour. 253 *too busy* too much of a busybody. 255 *hold her free* consider her innocent. 256 *government* self-control. 259 *qualities* human natures. 259-60 *learned spirit . . . dealings* mind experienced in the way in which people act in their dealings with each other [K]. 260 *haggard* wild, improperly trained, unfaithful. A "haggard" was a wild female hawk. 261 *jesses* straps, usually of leather, by which a falcon's legs were attached to the leash. *heartstrings* certain tendons or nerves which, according to old notions of anatomy, were attached to the heart and supported it in place. 262 *whistle her off* the falconer's signal of dismissal or rejection [K]. 262-3 *let her down . . . prey at fortune* let her fly away, whithersoever chance may carry her; let her shift for herself and take such prey as fortune may afford [K]. 263 *Haply, for* perhaps because. 265 *chamberers* wanton gallants. *for* because. *declin'd . . . years* past the meridian of life [K]. 267 *abus'd* deceived.

That we can call these delicate creatures ours,
And not their appetites! I had rather be a toad   270
And live upon the vapour of a dungeon
Than keep a corner in the thing I love
For others' uses. Let 'tis the plague of great ones;
Prerogativ'd are they less than the base.
'Tis destiny unshunnable, like death.   275
Even then this forked plague is fated to us
When we do quicken. Desdemona comes.

(*Enter* DESDEMONA *and* EMILIA.)

If she be false, O, then heaven mocks itself!
I'll not believe't.
DESDEMONA: How now, my dear Othello?
Your dinner, and the generous islanders   280
By you invited, do attend your presence.
OTHELLO: I am to blame.
DESDEMONA: Why do you speak so faintly?
Are you not well?
OTHELLO: I have a pain upon my forehead, here.
DESDEMONA: Faith, that's with watching; 'twill away again. 285
Let me but bind it hard, within this hour
It will be well.
OTHELLO: Your napkin is too little.
(*He puts the handkerchief from him, and she drops it.*)
Let it alone. Come, I'll go in with you.
DESDEMONA: I am very sorry that you are not well.
            (*Exeunt* OTHELLO *and* DESDEMONA.)
EMILIA: I am glad I have found this napkin.   290
This was her first remembrance from the Moor.
My wayward husband hath a hundred times
Woo'd me to steal it; but she so loves the token
(For he conjur'd her she should ever keep it)
That she reserves it evermore about her   295

---

274 *Prerogativ'd* exempt by privilege (from this curse of unfaithfulness in marriage) [K]. The implication is that greatness in rank provides no exemption from cuckoldry, but it is difficult to determine precisely Othello's meaning here.   *base* lowly (in social position).   276 *forked plague* plague of horns. The husband of an unfaithful wife was said to have horns grow upon his forehead. [K]   277 *quicken* are born.   278-9 *If she be false . . . believe't* The sight of Desdemona immediately brings Othello back from the condition to which Iago has reduced him. Othello's fall is not an easy one, and with this appearance of Desdemona, the struggle for his soul is resumed.   280 *generous* noble.   282 *to blame* at fault (for keeping them waiting).   284 *upon my forehead* An allusion to the sprouting horns of the cuckold. Desdemona does not understand.   285 *watching* loss of sleep.   287 *napkin* handkerchief.   291 *remembrance* keepsake.   292 *wayward* capricious.   294 *conjur'd her* made her swear.   296 *work* embroidery.   *ta'en out* copied.

To kiss and talk to. I'll have the work ta'en out
And give't Iago.
What he will do with it heaven knows, not I;
I nothing but to please his fantasy.

(*Enter* IAGO.)

IAGO: How now? What do you here alone?
EMILIA: Do not you chide; I have a thing for you.
IAGO: A thing for me? It is a common thing—
EMILIA: Ha?
IAGO: To have a foolish wife.
EMILIA: O, is that all? What will you give me now
For that same handkerchief?
IAGO: What handkerchief?
EMILIA: What handkerchief?
Why, that the Moor first gave to Desdemona;
That which so often you did bid me steal.
IAGO: Hast stol'n it from her?
EMILIA: No, faith; she let it drop by negligence,
And to th' advantage, I, being here, took't up.
Look, here it is.
IAGO: A good wench! Give it me.
EMILIA: What will you do with't, that you have been so earnest
To have me filch it?
IAGO: Why, what's that to you?
(*Snatches it.*)
EMILIA: If it be not for some purpose of import,
Give't me again. Poor lady, she'll run mad
When she shall lack it.
Go, leave me.   (*Exit* EMILIA.)
I will in Cassio's lodging lose this napkin
And let him find it. Trifles light as air
Are to the jealous confirmations strong
As proofs of holy writ. This may do something.
The Moor already changes with my poison
Dangerous conceits are in their natures poisons
Which at the first are scarce found to distaste,
But with a little act upon the blood
Burn like the mines of sulphur.

---

299 *fantasy* whim.   301 *thing* slang for sex organ.   302 *common* open to all. Iago is calling his wife a whore.   304 *To have . . . wife* Emilia's "Ha" of understanding causes Iago to change the tenour of his remark.   312 *to th' advantage* opportunely.   316 *import* importance.   318 *lack* miss.   319 *Be not you acknown on't* don't acknowledge that you know anything about it.   325 *changes with* is affected by.   326 *conceits* conceptions, imaginings.   327 *distaste* taste bad.   328 *with a little . . . blood* after a little action upon the blood.

(*Enter* OTHELLO)
                          I did say so.
Look where he comes! Not poppy nor mandragora,   330
Nor all the drowsy syrups of the world,
Shall ever medicine thee to that sweet sleep
Which thou ow'dst yesterday.
OTHELLO: Ha! ha! false to me?
IAGO: Why, how now, General? No more of that!
OTHELLO: Avaunt! be gone! Thou hast set me on the rack.   335
  I swear 'tis better to be much abus'd
  Than but to know't a little.
IAGO: How now, my lord?
OTHELLO: What sense had I of her stol'n hours of lust?
  I saw't not, thought it not, it harm'd not me.
  I slept the next night well, fed well, was free and merry; 340
  I found not Cassio's kisses on her lips.
  He that is robb'd, not wanting what is stol'n,
  Let him not know't, and he's not robb'd at all.
IAGO: I am sorry to hear this.
OTHELLO: I had been happy if the general camp,   345
  Pioners and all, had tasted her sweet body,
  So I had nothing known. O, now for ever
  Farewell the tranquil mind! farewell content!
  Farewell the plumed troop, and the big wars
  That make ambition virtue! O, farewell!   350
  Farewell the neighing steed and the shrill trump,
  The spirit-stirring drum, th' ear-piercing fife,
  The royal banner, and all quality,
  Pride, pomp, and circumstance of glorious war!
  And O ye mortal engines whose rude throats   355
  Th' immortal Jove's dread calmours counterfeit,
  Farewell! Othello's occupation's gone!

329 *mines of sulphur* the sulphur mines on the Æolian islands between Sicily and Italy which, according to Pliny's NATURAL HISTORY (XXXV, 15, 50, 174) caused those islands to be perpetually aflame.   330 *poppy* opium. *mandragora* mandrake; used in sleeping potions.   331 *drowsy syrups* sleeping potions.   333 *ow'dst* didst possess. *Ha! ha! false to me* Othello speaks to himself, not noticing the presence of Iago [K]. In the speeches which follow Othello reveals an ever-increasing mental confusion; his reason is collapsing.   336 *'tis better . . . abus'd* it is better to be the unknowing victim of deception   338 *sense* feeling. By this time Othello has come to accept Iago's slander of Desdemona without question.   340 *fed well* F1; Q1, K omit, thus making the line more metrical, but Alexandrines are common in Shakespeare.   342 *wanting* missing.
346 *Pioners* sappers, diggers of trenches, soldiers of the lowest rank.   347 *So* if only.
350 *make ambition virtue* ambition, which is usually reprehensible, is made justifiable and even meritorious by the splendour of warfare.   353 *quality* military rank.   354 *circumstance* splendour, pageantry.   357 *Othello's occupation's gone* He can no longer be a soldier because, as a cuckold, his honour has been forfeited.

IAGO: Is't possible, my lord?
OTHELLO: Villain, be sure thou prove my love a whore!
  Be sure of it; give me the ocular proof; 360
  Or, by the worth of mine eternal soul,
  Thou hadst been better have been born a dog
  Than answer my wak'd wrath!
IAGO: Is't come to this?
OTHELLO: Make me to see't; or at the least so prove it
  That the probation bear no hinge nor loop 365
  To hang a doubt on—or woe upon thy life!
IAGO: My noble lord—
OTHELLO: If thou dost slander her and torture me,
  Never pray more; abandon all remorse;
  On horror's head horrors accumulate; 370
  Do deeds to make heaven weep, all earth amaz'd;
  For nothing canst thou to damnation add
  Greater than that.
IAGO: O grace! O heaven forgive me!
  Are you a man? Have you a soul or sense?—
  God b' wi' you! take mine office. O wretched fool, 375
  That liv'st to make thine honesty a vice!
  O monstrous world! Take note, take note, O world,
  To be direct and honest is not safe.
  I thank you for this profit; and from hence
  I'll love no friend, sith love breeds such offence. 380
OTHELLO: Nay, stay. Thou shouldst be honest.
IAGO: I should be wise; for honesty's a fool
  And loses that it works for.
OTHELLO: By the world,
  I think my wife be honest, and think she is not;
  I think that thou art just, and think thou art not. 385
  I'll have some proof. Her name, that was as fresh
  As Dian's visage, is now begrim'd and black
  As mine own face. If there be cords, or knives,
  Poison, or fire, or suffocating streams,
  I'll not endure it. Would I were satisfied! 390
IAGO: I see, sir, you are eaten up with passion.

---

358 *Is't possible* that you should be so beside yourself [K].   361 *mine* F1; Q1, K: "man's."   363 *answer* be exposed to, meet.   365 *probation* proof.   369 *remorse* compassion or humane feeling—not remorse of conscience [K].   371 *all earth amaz'd* to make all mankind paralyzed with horror [K].   376 *vice* fault.   379 *profit* lesson. *hence* this time forth.   380 *sith love . . . offence* since I find that love for a friend does me such injury, by making my friend distrust me [K].   381 *shouldst be* ought to be, probably are.   383 *that it works for* trust.   384 *honest* chaste.   385 *just* honest, upright.   386 *fresh* stainless.   387 *Dian's visage* the white face of Diana, goddess of the moon (hence white) and of chastity.

    I do repent me that I put it to you.
    You would be satisfied?
OTHELLO: Would? Nay, I will.
IAGO: And may. But how? how satisfied, my lord?
    Would you, the supervisor, grossly gape on?   395
    Behold her topp'd?
OTHELLO: Death and damnation! O!
IAGO: It were a tedious difficulty, I think,
    To bring them to that prospect. Damn them then,
    If ever mortal eyes do see them bolster
    More than their own! What then? How then?   400
    What shall I say? Where's satisfaction?
    It is impossible you should see this,
    Were they as prime as goats, as hot as monkeys,
    As salt as wolves in pride, and fools as gross
    As ignorance made drunk. But yet, I say,   405
    If imputation and strong circumstances
    Which lead directly to the door of truth
    Will give you satisfaction, you may have't.
OTHELLO: Give me a living reason she's disloyal.
IAGO: I do not like the office.   410
    But sith I am enter'd in this cause so far,
    Prick'd to't by foolish honesty and love,
    I will go on. I lay with Cassio lately,
    And being troubled with a raging tooth,
    I could not sleep.   415
    There are a kind of men so loose of soul
    That in their sleeps will mutter their affairs.
    One of this kind is Cassio.
    In sleep I heard him say, "Sweet Desdemona,
    Let us be wary, let us hide our loves!"   420
    And then, sir, would he gripe and wring my hand,
    Cry "O sweet creature!" and then kiss me hard,
    As if he pluck'd up kisses by the roots
    That grew upon my lips; then laid his leg
    Over my thigh, and sigh'd, and kiss'd, and then   425
    Cried "Cursed fate that gave thee to the Moor!"
OTHELLO: O monstrous! monstrous!

---

392 *put* suggested this doubt.   395 *supervisor* eyewitness. Iago now becomes more brutal and direct, goading Othello to madness with visual details.   395 *gape* stare open-mouthed.   398 *bring them to that prospect* cause them to present such a view.   399 *bolster* go to bed together.   403 *prime* lecherous.   *goats* traditional symbols of lechery.   *monkeys* also proverbially lustful animals.   404 *salt* lustful.   *pride* heat.   409 *living* based on experience rather than conjecture.   411 *sith* since.   412 *Pric'd* urged, spurred on.   413 *lay* slept.   421 *gripe* grip.   428 *But this . . . conclusion* although what he said and did was in a dream, it nevertheless pointed definitely to something that he had actually experienced before [K].

IAGO: Nay, this was but his dream.
OTHELLO: But this denoted a foregone conclusion.
    'Tis a shrewd doubt, though it be but a dream.
IAGO: And this may help to thicken other proofs 430
    That do demonstrate thinly.
OTHELLO: I'll tear her all to pieces!
IAGO: Nay, but be wise. Yet we see nothing done;
    She may be honest yet. Tell me but this—
    Have you not sometimes seen a handkerchief
    Spotted with strawberries in your wife's hand? 435
OTHELLO: I gave her such a one; 'twas my first gift.
IAGO: I know not that; but such a handkerchief
    (I am sure it was your wife's) did I to-day
    See Cassio wipe his beard with.
OTHELLO: If't be that—
IAGO: If it be that, or any that was hers, 440
    It speaks against her, with the other proofs.
OTHELLO: O, that the slave had forty thousand lives!
    One is too poor, too weak for my revenge.
    Now do I see 'tis true. Look here, Iago:
    All my fond love thus do I blow to heaven. 445
    'Tis gone.
    Arise, black vengeance, from the hollow hell!
    Yield up, O love, thy crown and hearted throne
    To tyrannous hate! Swell, bosom, with thy fraught,
    For 'tis of aspics' tongues!
IAGO: Yet be content. 450
OTHELLO: O, blood, blood, blood!
IAGO: Patience, I say. Your mind perhaps may change.
OTHELLO: Never, Iago. Like to the Pontic sea.
    Whose icy current and compulsive course
    Ne'er feels retiring ebb, but keeps due on 455
    To the Propontic and the Hellespont;

429 *shrewd doubt* painfully suspicious thing. Q1, followed by some editors, gives this line to Iago; F1 is followed here.   430 *thicken* add to.   442 *the slave* Cassio.   445 *fond* foolish.   447 *the hollow hell* Vengeance is conceived as dwelling in the nethermost abyss—the infernal regions [K] (F1; Q1: "thy hollow cell").   448 *hearted throne* throne in my heart.   449 *fraught* freight, burden.   450 *aspics'* asps   452 *Your mind . . . change* Iago makes this insidious suggestion in order to win from Othello some definite expression of his purpose of vengeance. By suggesting that the Moor's mind may change he takes the best means for confirming Othello's resolution. His success is shown by the fact that he receives before the end of the scene distinct orders to put Cassio out of the way [K]   453 *Pontic sea* Black Sea.   454 *compulsive* all-compelling, irresistible.   455 *feels* Q2; F1: "keepes"; omitted in Q1.   456 *Propontic* Sea of Marmora. *Hellespont* the Bosporus. In Philemon Holland's translation of Pliny's NATURAL HISTORY (1601), Shakespeare may have read that "The sea Pontus euermore floweth and runneth out into Propontis, but the sea neuer retireth backe again within Pontus."

Even so my bloody thoughts with violent pace,
Shall ne'er look back, ne'er ebb to humble love,
Till that a capable and wide revenge
Swallow them up. (*He kneels.*) Now, by yond marble heaven, 460
In the due reverence of a sacred vow
I here engage my words.
IAGO: Do not rise yet.
  (IAGO *kneels.*)
Witness, you ever-burning lights above,
You elements that clip us round about,
Witness that here Iago doth give up   465
The execution of his wit, hands, heart
To wrong'd Othello's service! Let him command,
And to obey shall be in me remorse,
What bloody business ever.

  (*They rise.*)

OTHELLO: I greet thy love,
  Not with vain thanks but with acceptance bounteous,   470
  And will upon the instant put thee to't.
  Within these three days let me hear thee say
  That Cassio's not alive.
IAGO: My friend is dead; 'tis done at your request.
  But let her live.
OTHELLO: Damn her, lewd minx! O, damn her!   475
  Come, go with me apart. I will withdraw
  To furnish me with some swift means of death
  For the fair devil. Now art thou my lieutenant.
IAGO: I am your own for ever.   (*Exeunt.*)

Scene IV. *Cyprus. Before the Castle.*

(*Enter* DESDEMONA, EMILIA, *and* CLOWN.)

DESDEMONA: Do you know, sirrah, where Lieutenant Cassio lies?
CLOWN: I dare not say he lies anywhere.

---

459 *capable* capacious, all-embracing.   460 *marble* The adjective "marble" was an established epithet for the sky when Shakespeare wrote [K]. Precisely what it meant is not clear.   462 *engage* pledge.   464 *clip* embrace.   466 *execution of his wit* all that his intellect can do [K].   468 *to obey . . . remorse* however bloody the work that Othello enjoins, I shall regard its performance not as cruelty but as pity. This may be taken merely as strong hyperbole, or as indicating that Iago will regard the work as done out of compassion for Othello's wrongs [K].   469 *greet* meet.   471 *to't* to the test.   479 *I am your own for ever.* In this solemn ritual of kneeling and swearing Othello and Iago are, in effect, symbolically joined. It is the seal of Othello's acceptance of evil and total commitment to it.

DESDEMONA: Why, man?
CLOWN: He's a soldier; and for one to say a soldier lies is stabbing.
DESDEMONA: Go to. Where lodges he?
CLOWN: To tell you where he lodges is to tell you where I lie.
DESDEMONA: Can anything be made of this?
CLOWN: I know not where he lodges; and for me to devise a lodging, and say he lies here or he lies there, were to lie in mine own throat.
DESDEMONA: Can you inquire him out, and be edified by report?
CLOWN: I will catechize the world for him; that is, make questions and by them answer.
DESDEMONA: Seek him, bid him come hither. Tell him I have mov'd my lord on his behalf and hope all will be well.
CLOWN: To do this is within the compass of man's wit, and therefore I'll attempt the doing of it. *(Exit.)*
DESDEMONA: Where should I lose that handkerchief, Emilia?
EMILIA: I know not, madam.
DESDEMONA: Believe me, I had rather have lost my purse
Full of crusadoes; and but my noble Moor
Is true of mind, and made of no such baseness
As jealous creatures are, it were enough
To put him to ill thinking.
EMILIA: Is he not jealous?
DESDEMONA: Who? he? I think the sun where he was born
Drew all such humours from him.

(Enter OTHELLO.*)*

EMILIA: Look where he comes.
DESDEMONA: I will not leave him now till Cassio
Be call'd to him.—How is't with you, my lord?
OTHELLO: Well, my good lady. *(Aside)* O, hardness to dissemble!—
How do you, Desdemona?
DESDEMONA: Well, my good lord.
OTHELLO: Give me your hand. This hand is moist, my lady.
DESDEMONA: It yet hath felt no age nor known no sorrow.
OTHELLO: This argues fruitfulness and liberal heart.
Hot, hot, and moist. This hand of yours requires

III.iv. m ¹ *lies* lodges. The clown takes the word in its other sense.   9-10 *lie in mine own throat* tell a deep, deliberate lie—as contrasted with a casual misrepresentation or "white lie" [K].   11 *edified* instructed.   14 *mov'd* spoken to.   16 *compass* range.   21 *crusadoes* Portuguese gold coins bearing the stamp of a cross. *but* but that.   24 *Is he not jealous* Emilia's general attitude is that all men are jealous and that their difficulties must be put up with. This may in part explain why she does not reveal the theft of the handkerchief. She must put up with her "wayward" husband in spite of any misgivings about what he has asked her to do.   26 *humours* whims.   31 *hand is moist* A hot moist palm was taken as an indication of a lustful temperament, just as a dry palm indicated sexual debility.   33 *liberal* free (with the affections), wanton.

A sequester from liberty, fasting and prayer, 35
Much castigation, exercise devout;
For here's a young and sweating devil here
That commonly rebels. 'Tis a good hand,
A frank one.
DESDEMONA: You may, indeed, say so;
For 'twas that hand that gave away my heart. 40
OTHELLO: A liberal hand! The hearts of old gave hands;
But our new heraldry is hands, not hearts.
DESDEMONA: I cannot speak of this. Come now, your promise!
OTHELLO: What promise, chuck?
DESDEMONA: I have sent to bid Cassio come speak with you. 45
OTHELLO: I have a salt and sorry rheum offends me.
Lend me thy handkerchief.
DESDEMONA: Here, my lord.
OTHELLO: That which I gave you.
DESDEMONA: I have it not about me.
OTHELLO: Not?
DESDEMONA: No indeed, my lord.
OTHELLO: That is a fault.
That handkerchief 50
Did an Egyptian to my mother give.
She was a charmer, and could almost read
The thoughts of people. She told her, while she kept it,
'Twould make her amiable and subdue my father
Entirely to her love; but if she lost it 55
Or made a gift of it, my father's eye
Should hold her loathly, and his spirits should hunt
After new fancies. She, dying, gave it me,
And bid me, when my fate would have me wive,
To give it her. I did so; and take heed on't; 60
Make it a darling like your precious eye.
To lose't or give't away were such perdition
As nothing else could match.

---

35 *sequester* retirement.   36 *castigation* austere self-discipline.   37 *devil* the spirit of sensual desire [K].   38 *rebels* against virtuous self-control [K].   39 *frank* Several meanings are possible: (a) candid, outspoken, which reveals its owner's nature (b) generous. Desdemona takes it in the second sense.   41 *hearts* . . . hands love (hearts) in former times (old days) prescribed marriage (hands).   42 *new heraldry* . . . *hearts* our new-fashioned symbolism (heraldry) prescribes the joining of hands (marriage) without love (not hearts).   44 *chuck* chick (a term of affection).   46 *rheum* cold in the head. *offends* troubles.   51 an *Egyptian* an Egyptian sorceress; a gypsy. The gypsies were thought to be of Egyptian origin [K].   54 *amiable* desirable, lovable (much stronger than in our modern sense).   58 *fancies* loves.   62 *perdition* irrevocable loss (like the soul's damnation).

DESDEMONA: Is't possible?
OTHELLO: 'Tis true. There's magic in the web of it.
   A sibyl that had numb'red in the world
   The sun to course two hundred compasses,
   In her prophetic fury sew'd the work;
   The worms were hallowed that did breed the silk;
   And it was dy'd in mummy which the skilful
   Conserv'd of maiden's hearts.
DESDEMONA: I' faith? Is't true?
OTHELLO: Most veritable. Therefore look to't well.
DESDEMONA: Then would to God that I had never seen't!
OTHELLO: Ha! Wherefore?
DESDEMONA: Why do you speak so startingly and rash?
OTHELLO: Is't lost? Is't gone? Speak, is it out o' th' way?
DESDEMONA: Heaven bless us!
OTHELLO: Say you?
DESDEMONA: It is not lost. But what an if it were?
OTHELLO: How?
DESDEMONA: I say it is not lost.
OTHELLO: Fetch't, let me see't!
DESDEMONA: Why, so I can, sir; but I will not now.
   This is a trick to put me from my suit.
   Pray you let Cassio be receiv'd again.
OTHELLO: Fetch me the handkerchief! My mind misgives.
DESDEMONA: Come, come!
   You'll never meet a more sufficient man.
OTHELLO: The handkerchief!
DESDEMONA: I pray talk me of Cassio.
OTHELLO: The handkerchief!
DESDEMONA: A man that all his time
   Hath founded his good fortunes on your love,
   Shar'd dangers with you—
OTHELLO: The handkerchief!
DESDEMONA: In sooth, you are to blame.
OTHELLO: Away! *(Exit.)*
EMILIA: Is not this man jealous?
DESDEMONA: I ne'er saw this before.
   Sure there's some wonder in this handkerchief.

---

64 *web* weave. 66 *compasses* yearly circuits. 67 *work* embroidered pattern. 69 *mummy* liquid supposedly derived from embalmed human flesh, reputed to have great medicinal and magical properties. 70 *Conserv'd* prepared as a drug. *of* out of. 78 *It is not lost* Desdemona is startled (though not frightened), and she is unwilling to admit even to herself that the handkerchief is "lost": it is, she thinks, merely mislaid [K]. 86 *sufficient* able. 92 *to blame* blameworthy—for speaking so roughly to me. 95 *this* this trait—such violence on Othello's part [K].

    I am most unhappy in the loss of it.
EMILIA: 'Tis not a year or two shows us a man.
    They are all but stomachs, and we all but food;
    They eat us hungerly, and when they are full,   100
    They belch us.

    (*Enter* IAGO *and* CASSIO.)

            Look you—Cassio and my husband!
IAGO: There is no other way; 'tis she must do't.
    And lo the happiness! Go and importune her.
DESDEMONA: How now, good Cassio? What's the news with you?
CASSIO: Madam, my former suit. I do beseech you   105
    That by your virtuous means I may again
    Exist, and be a member of his love
    Whom I with all the office of my heart
    Entirely honour. I would not be delay'd.
    If my offence be of such mortal kind   110
    That neither service past, nor persent sorrows,
    Nor purpos'd merit in futurity,
    Can ransom me into his love again,
    But to know so must be my benefit.
    So shall I clothe me in a forc'd content,   115
    And shut myself up in some other course,
    To fortune's alms.
DESDEMONA: Alas, thrice-gentle Cassio!
    My advocation is not now in tune.
    My lord is not my lord; nor should I know him,
    Were he in favour as in humor alter'd.   120
    So help me every spirit sanctified
    As I have spoken for you all my best
    And stood within the blank of his displeasure
    For my free speech! You must awhile be patient.
    What I can do I will; and more I will   125
    Than for myself I dare. Let that suffice you.
IAGO: Is my lord angry?

---

98 *'Tis not . . . a man* it does not take as much as a year or two for a man to reveal his true nature: he reveals it much sooner.   99 *stomachs* sexual appetites   106 *virtuous means* powerful ability to help.   107 *be a member of* have a share in.   108 *office* devoted service.   112 *purpos'd merit in futurity* esteem (merit) I am determined to deserve in the future.   114 *But to know . . . benefit* I must regard it as a favour merely to know the worst. Anything is better than this uncertainty [K].   115 *clothe me . . . content* force myself to accept my situation.   116 *shut myself . . . course* confine myself to some humbler course of life [K].   117 *To fortune's alms* receiving from fortune whatever she can dole out to me.   118 *advocation* intercession, pleading.   *in tune* well-received (like harmony).   120 *favour* features.   *humour* disposition.   123 *within the blank of* in the range of.

EMILIA: He went hence but now,
And certainly in strange unquietness.
IAGO: Can he be angry? I have seen the cannon
When it hath blown his ranks into the air
And, like the devil, from his very arm
Puff'd his own brother—and can he be angry?
Something of moment then. I will go meet him.
There's matter in't indeed if he be angry.
DESDEMONA: I prithee do so. *(Exit* IAGO.*)*
                              Something sure of state,
Either from Venice or some unhatch'd practice
Made demonstrable here in Cyprus to him,
Hath puddled his clear spirit; and in such cases
Men's natures wrangle with inferior things,
Though great ones are their object. 'Tis even so.
For let our finger ache, and it endues
Our other, healthful, members even to that sense
Of pain. Nay, we must think men are not gods,
Nor of them look for such observancy
As fits the bridal. Beshrew me much, Emilia,
I was (unhandsome warrior as I am!)
Arraigning his unkindness with my soul;
But now I find I had suborn'd the witness,
And he's indicted falsely.
EMILIA: Pray heaven it be state matters, as you think,
And no conception nor no jealous toy
Concerning you.
DESDEMONA: Alas the day! I never gave him cause.
EMILIA: But jealous souls will not be answer'd so.
They are not ever jealous for the cause,
But jealous for they are jealous. 'Tis a monster
Begot upon itself, born on itself.
DESDEMONA: Heaven keep that monster from Othello's mind!
EMILIA: Lady, amen.

---

135 *Something sure of state* certainly some government business.   136 *unhatch'd practice* plot not yet matured [K].   137 *Made demonstrable* revealed.   138 *puddled* made muddy, disturbed. *clear spirit* usual serenity of mind.   140 *object* target, real concern.   141 *endues* brings into accord.   144 *observancy* attention, devotion.   145 *fits* the bridal is appropriate at the time of the wedding.   146 *unhandsome* improper, unfair.   147 *Arraigning . . . soul* accusing him of unkindness at my soul's tribunal. The legal figure is carried out in what follows [K].   148 *suborn'd the witness* induced him to swear falsely. The "witness" is Othello's harshness, which, she says, she had induced to give false evidence against him—had wilfully misinterpreted [K]. It should be noted that Desdemona always takes upon herself the blame for Othello's shortcomings.   151 *conception* idea, notion.   *jealous toy* suspicious fancy.

DESDEMONA: I will go seek him. Cassio, walk here about.   160
   If I do find him fit, I'll move your suit
   And seek to effect it to my uttermost.
CASSIO: I humbly thank your ladyship.
                          (*Exeunt* DESDEMONA *and* EMILIA.)
   (*Enter* BIANCA.)
BIANCA: Save you, friend Cassio!
CASSIO: What make you from home?
   How is it with you, my most fair Bianca?   165
   I' faith, sweet love, I was coming to your house.
BIANCA: And I was going to your lodging, Cassio.
   What, keep a week away? seven days and nights?
   Eightscore eight hours? and lovers' absent hours,
   More tedious than the dial eightscore times?   170
   O weary reck'ning!
CASSIO: Pardon me, Bianca.
   I have this while with leaden thoughts been press'd;
   But I shall in a more continuate time
   Strike off this score of absence. Sweet Bianca,

   (*Gives her* DESDEMONA'S *handkerchief.*)

   Take me this work out.
BIANCA: O Cassio, whence came this?   175
   This is some token from a newer friend.
   To the felt absence now I feel a cause.
   Is't come to this? Well, well.
CASSIO: Go to, woman!
   Throw your vile guesses in the devil's teeth,
   From whence you have them. You are jealous now   180
   That this is from some mistress, some remembrance.
   No, by my faith, Bianca.
BIANCA: Why, whose is it?
CASSIO: I know not, sweet. I found it in my chamber.
   I like the work well. Ere it be demanded,
   As like enough it will, I would have it copied.   185
   Take it and do't, and leave me for this time.
BIANCA: Leave you? Wherefore?
CASSIO: I do attend here on the General
   And think it no addition, nor my wish,

---

161 *I'll move your suit* This shows how far Desdemona is from suspecting that Cassio is involved, even when she has begun to entertain the idea that Othello may be jealous [K].   170 *the dial* the whole round of the clock's hand [K].   173 *continuate* uninterrupted.   174 *Strike off this score* pay off this debt. A "score" was a reckoning at a tavern.   175 *Take me this work out* copy this embroidered pattern for me.   176 *friend* sweetheart.   188 *attend here on* wait here for.   189 *addition* credit to me.   190 *woman'd* accompanied by a woman. Bianca's profession would be obvious enough from her dress and manner [K].

William Shakespeare: *Othello*

    To have him see me woman'd.
BIANCA: Why, I pray you?
CASSIO: Not that I love you not.
BIANCA: But that you do not love me!
    I pray you bring me on the way a little,
    And say if I shall see you soon at night.
CASSIO: 'Tis but a little way that I can bring you,
    For I attend here; but I'll see you soon.
BIANCA: 'Tis very good. I must be circumstanc'd.   *(Exeunt.)*

ACT FOUR

Scene I. Cyprus. Before the Castle.

(Enter OTHELLO *and* IAGO.*)*

IAGO: Will you think so?
OTHELLO: Think so, Iago?
IAGO: What,
    To kiss in private?
OTHELLO: An unauthoriz'd kiss.
IAGO: Or to be naked with her friend in bed
    An hour, or more, not meaning any harm?
OTHELLO: Naked in bed, Iago, and not mean harm?
    It is hypocrisy against the devil.
    They that mean virtuously, and yet do so,
    The devil their virtue tempts, and they tempt heaven.
IAGO: So they do nothing, 'tis a venial slip.
    But if I give my wife a handkerchief—
OTHELLO: What then?
IAGO: Why, then 'tis hers, my lord; and being hers,
    She may, I think, bestow't on any man.
OTHELLO: She is protectress of her honour too.
    May she give that?
IAGO: Her honour is an essence that's not seen;
    They have it very oft that have it not.
    But for the handkerchief—

---

192 *bring . . . way* escort me.   194 *bring* accompany.   195 *attend* wait.   196 *circumstanc'd* satisfied with the necessities of the moment.   IV.I 1 *Will you think so* Shakespeare telescopes time, indicating that Iago has worked further upon Othello since we last saw them, so that Othello is now reduced to complete credulity. 2 *unauthoriz'd* unwarrantable.   6 *hypocrisy against the devil* Hypocrisy against God is to act with an appearance of virtue but with evil intent. Hypocrisy against the devil, then, would be to act with an appearance of evil but without "meaning any harm" [K].   9 *So* provided that.   *venial* excusable.   17 *They have . . . have it not* persons who are not honourable are often reputed to be honourable, and persons who are not so reputed are often really honourable. Compare what Iago says of reputation (II.III) [K].

OTHELLO: By heaven, I would most gladly have forgot it!
Thou said'st (O, it comes o'er my memory   20
As doth the raven o'er the infected house,
Boding to all!) he had my handkerchief.
IAGO: Ay, what of that?
OTHELLO: That's not so good now.
IAGO: What
If I had said I had seen him do you wrong?
Or heard him say—as knaves be such abroad   25
Who having, by their own importunate suit,
Or voluntary dotage of some mistress,
Convinced or supplied them, cannot choose
But they must blab—
OTHELLO: Hath he said anything?
IAGO: He hath, my lord; but be you well assur'd, 30
No more than he'll unswear.
OTHELLO: What hath he said?
IAGO: Faith, that he did—I know not what he did.
OTHELLO: What? what?
IAGO: Lie—
OTHELLO: With her?
IAGO: With her, on her; what you will
OTHELLO: Lie with her? lie on her?—We say lie on her when they 35
belie her.—Lie with her! Zounds, that's fulsome.—Handkerchief
—confessions—handkerchief!—To confess, and be hang'd for his
labour—first to be hang'd, and then to confess! I tremble at it.
Nature would not invest herself in such shadowing passion with- 40
out some instruction. It is not words that shakes me thus.—Pish!
Noses, ears, and lips? Is't possible?—Confess?—handkerchief—
O devil!
(Falls in a trance.)
IAGO: Work on,
My medicine, work! Thus credulous fools are caught,   45
And many worthy and chaste dames even thus,
All guiltless, meet reproach.—What, ho! my lord!

21 *raven . . . house* Ravens were believed to hover over houses infected with the plague. They were traditional harbingers of death.   22 *Boding* ominous.   25 *as . . . abroad* as there are such knaves at large.   28 *Convinced* overcome their reluctance (by importunate suit).   *supplied* satisfied (the voluntary dotage of the mistress). 28-9 *cannot choose . . . blab* are forced by inner necessity to blab (about their conquests).   31 *unswear* deny on oath.   35-43 *Lie with . . . O devil* Shakespeare shifts into disjoined prose to indicate the final collapse of Othello into incoherent madness. 37-8 *confess, and be hanged* An old proverb. In practice the Elizabethan criminal was given a chance to confess before his hanging.   39-41 *Nature . . . instruction* my natural faculties would not thus suddenly be overshadowed unless it were as a sign to teach me that what I have heard is true [K].

My lord, I say! Othello!

(*Enter* CASSIO.)

How now, Cassio?
CASSIO: What's the matter?
IAGO: My lord is fall'n into an epilepsy.
This is his second fit; he had one yesterday.
CASSIO: Rub him about the temples.
IAGO: No, forbear.
The lethargy must have his quiet course.
If not, he foams at mouth, and by-and-by
Breaks out to savage madness. Look, he stirs.
Do you withdraw a little while.
He will recover straight. When he is gone,
I would on great occasion speak with you. (*Exit* CASSIO.)
How is it, General? Have you not hurt your head?
OTHELLO: Dost thou mock me?
IAGO: I mock you? No, by heaven.
Would you would bear your fortune like a man!
OTHELLO: A horned man's a monster and a beast.
IAGO: There's many a beast then in a populous city,
And many a civil monster.
OTHELLO: Did he confess it?
IAGO: Good sir, be a man.
Think every bearded fellow that's but yok'd
May draw with you. There's millions now alive
That nightly lie in those unproper beds
Which they dare swear peculiar. Your case is better.
O, 'tis the spite of hell, the fiend's arch-mock,
To lip a wanton in a secure couch,
And to suppose her chaste! No, let me know;
And knowing what I am, I know what she shall be.
OTHELLO: O, thou art wise! 'Tis certain.
IAGO: Stand you awhile apart;
Confine yourself but in a patient list.

---

52 *forbear* let him alone.   53 *lethargy* unconsciousness.   54 *by-and-by* immediately.
57 *straight* in a moment.   58 *on great occasion* about important business.   60 *mock me* Any reference to his head makes Othello think of the horns of a cuckold—"a horned man" [K].   64 civil among the citizens.   67 *draw with you* (a) be in the same situation (b) pull the cart as the ox, a horned beast, does.   68 *unproper* not exclusively their own.   69 *peculiar* reserved for themselves. *better* because you know the truth [K].   71 *lip* kiss. *secure* unsuspecting.   73 *And knowing . . . shall be* knowing my own essential nature as a man, I know also what woman must be. In this is an indication of Iago's view of mankind as naturally debased, cuckoldry the natural fate of the married man as treachery is the natural characteristic of woman.   74 *O thou, . . . certain* Othello has come to see humanity through the eyes of Iago.   75 *in a patient list* within the bounds of patience.

Whilst you were here, o'erwhelmed with your grief
(A passion most unsuiting such a man),
Cassio came hither. I shifted him away
And laid good 'scuse upon your ecstasy;
Bade him anon return, and here speak with me; 80
The which he promis'd. Do but encave yourself
And mark the fleers, the gibes, and notable scorns
That dwell in every region of his face;
For I will make him tell the tale anew—
Where, how, how oft, how long ago, and when 85
He hath, and is again to cope your wife.
I say, but mark his gesture. Marry, patience!
Or I shall say you are all in all in spleen,
And nothing of a man.

OTHELLO: Dost thou hear, Iago?
I will be found most cunning in my patience; 90
But (dost thou hear?) most bloody.

IAGO: That's not amiss;
But yet keep time in all. Will you withdraw?

(OTHELLO *retires*.)

Now will I question Cassio of Bianca,
A housewife that by selling her desires
Buys herself bread and clothes. It is a creature 95
That dotes on Cassio, as 'tis the strumpet's plague
To beguile many and be beguil'd by one.
He, when he hears of her, cannot refrain
From the excess of laughter. Here he comes.

(*Enter* CASSIO)

As he shall smile, Othello shall go mad; 100
And his unbookish jealousy must construe
Poor Cassio's smiles, gestures, and light behaviour
Quite in the wrong. How do you now, Lieutenant?

CASSIO: The worser that you give me the addition
Whose want even kills me. 105

IAGO: Ply Desdemona well, and you are sure on't.
Now, if this suit lay in Bianca's power,
How quickly should you speed!

CASSIO: Alas! poor caitiff!

77 *unsuiting* Q¹; F¹: "resulting"; CAPELL, K: "unfitting." There is little justification for the emendation which merely provides a synonym for the Q¹ reading.   79 *ecstasy* fit of unconsciousness.   81 *encave* conceal.   82 *fleers* sneers.   86 *cope* encounter, close with.   87 *gesture* bearing, demeanour.   88 *in spleen* governed by impulses. Excited, irrational behaviour was traditionally attributed to the action of the spleen.   92 *keep time* maintain control, act reasonably. The figure is from music.   94 *housewife* hussy.   101 *unbookish* ignorant.   102 *light* licentious.   104 *give . . . addition* call me lieutenant.   107 *power* Q¹; F¹: "dowre" (dower) has much to recommend it, as Iago seems to be thinking in terms of Cassio's marriage to Bianca.

OTHELLO: Look how he laughs already!
IAGO: I never knew a woman love man so.
CASSIO: Alas, poor rogue! I think, i' faith, she loves me.
OTHELLO: Now he denies it faintly, and laughs it out.
IAGO: Do you hear, Cassio?
OTHELLO: Now he importunes him
  To tell it o'er. Go to! Well said, well said!
IAGO: She gives it out that you shall marry her.
  Do you intend it?
CASSIO: Ha, ha, ha!
OTHELLO: Do you triumph, Roman? Do you triumph?
CASSIO: I marry her? What, a customer? Prithee bear some charity
  to my wit; do not think it so unwholesome. Ha, ha, ha!
OTHELLO: So, so, so, so! Laugh that wins!
IAGO: Faith, the cry goes that you shall marry her.
CASSIO: Prithee say true.
IAGO: I am a very villain else.
OTHELLO: Have you scor'd me? Well.
CASSIO: This is the monkey's own giving out. She is persuaded I will
  marry her out of her own love and flattery, not out of my promise.
OTHELLO: Iago beckons me. Now he begins the story.
CASSIO: She was here even now; she haunts me in every place. I was
  t'other day talking on the sea bank with certain Venetians, and
  thither comes the bauble, and, by this hand, she falls me thus
  about my neck—
OTHELLO: Crying "O dear Cassio!" as it were. His gesture imports it.
CASSIO: So hangs, and lolls, and weeps upon me; so hales and pulls
  me! Ha, ha, ha!
OTHELLO: Now he tells how she pluck'd him to my chamber. O, I
  see that nose of yours, but not that dog I shall throw't to.
CASSIO: Well, I must leave her company.

(Enter BIANCA.*)*

IAGO: Before me! Look where she comes.
CASSIO: 'Tis such another fitchew! marry, a perfum'd one. What do
  you mean by this haunting of me?

---

108 *speed* succeed.   *caitiff* wretch.   112 *faintly* half-heartedly, not really meaning it.   118 *Roman* proud fellow. The word is suggested by "triumph" from a natural association of ideas [K].   119 *customer* harlot.   119-20 *bear some . . . wit* have some belief in my intellect [K].   120 *unwholesome* diseased.   122 *Laugh that wins* let him laugh that wins (a common proverb).   123 *cry* rumour.   126 *scor'd me* There seem to be three possible meanings: (a) "marked me (with infamy)"—as with lashes from a whip (b) "scored me up," posted my name—as a cuckold (c) "added up my score," settled my account, summed me up. The third seems to be the best [K].   127 *giving out* report.   128 *flattery* self-deception.   133 *bauble* plaything, bit of frippery.   137 *hales* tugs at.   144 *fitchew* polecat, traditionally regarded as a lustful animal.   146 *dam* mother.

BIANCA: Let the devil and his dam haunt you! What did you mean by that same handkerchief you gave me even now? I was a fine fool to take it. I must take out the whole work? I likely piece of work that you should find it in your chamber and know not who left it there! This is some minx's token, and I must take out the 150 work? There! give it your hobby-horse. Wheresoever you had it, I'll take out no work on't.

CASSIO: How now, my sweet Bianca? How now? how now?

OTHELLO: By heaven, that should be my handkerchief! 155

BIANCA: And you'll come to supper to-night, you may; an you will not, come when you are next prepar'd for. *(Exit.)*

IAGO: After her, after her!

CASSIO: Faith, I must; she'll rail i' th' street else.

IA7*: Will you sup there? 160

IAGO: Yes, I intend so.

IAGO: Well, I may chance to see you; for I would very fain speak with you.

CASSIO: Prithee come. Will you?

IAGO: Go to! say no more. 165

OTHELLO *(comes forward)*: How shall I murder him, Iago? *(Exit* CASSIO.*)*

IAGO: Did you perceive how he laugh'd at his vice?

OTHELLO: O Iago!

IAGO: And did you see the handkerchief?

OTHELLO: Was that mine? 170

IAGO: Yours, by this hand! And to see how he prizes the foolish woman your wife! She gave it him, and he hath giv'n it his whore.

OTHELLO: I would have him nine years a-killing!—A fine woman! a fair woman! a sweet woman! 175

IAGO: Nay, you must forget that.

OTHELLO: Ay, let her rot, and perish, and be damn'd to-night; for she shall not live. No, my heart is turn'd to stone. I strike it, and it hurts my hand. O, the world hath not a sweeter creature! She 180 might lie by an emperor's side and command him tasks.

IAGO: Nay, that's not your way.

OTHELLO: Hang her! I do but say what she is. So delicate with her needle! an admirable musician! O, she will sing the savageness 185 out of a bear! Of so high and plenteous wit and invention!

IAGO: She's the worse for all this.

OTHELLO: O, a thousand thousand times! And then, of so gentle a condition!

IAGO: Ay, too gentle. 190

OTHELLO: Nay, that's certain. But yet the pity of it, Iago! O Iago, the pity of it, Iago!

---

148 *take out* copy.   152 *hobby-horse* whore (easily mounted).   155 *should be* must be.   156 *An* if.   171 *prizes* values.   182 *your way* your usual manner of thinking and talking about her.   188-9 *gentle a condition* high-born social status.   190 *gentle* yielding, to men.

IAGO: If you are so fond over her iniquity, give her patent to offend; for if it touch not you, it comes near nobody.
OTHELLO: I will chop her into messes! Cuckold me!
IAGO: O, 'tis foul in her.
OTHELLO: With mine officer!
IAGO: That's fouler.
OTHELLO: Get me some poison, Iago, this night. I'll not expostulate with her, lest her body and beauty unprovide my mind again. This night, Iago!
IAGO: Do it not with poison. Strangle her in her bed, even the bed she hath contaminated.
OTHELLO: Good, good! The justice of it pleases. Very good!
IAGO: And for Cassio, let me be his undertaker. You shall hear more by midnight.
OTHELLO: Excellent good!

(A trumpet.)
                        What trumpet is that same?
IAGO: Something from Venice, sure.

(Enter LODOVICO, DESDEMONA, and ATTENDANTS.)

                        'Tis Lodovico,
Come from the Duke; and see, your wife is with him.
LODOVICO: God save you, worthy General!
OTHELLO: With all my heart, sir.
LODOVICO: The Duke and Senators of Venice greet you.

(Gives him a letter.)

OTHELLO: I kiss the instrument of their pleasures.
(Opens the letter and reads.)
DESDEMONA: And what's the news, good cousin Lodovico?
IAGO: I am very glad to see you, signior. Welcome to Cyprus.
LODOVICO: I thank you. How does Lieutenant Cassio?
IAGO: Lives, sir.
DESDEMONA: Cousin, there's fall'n between him and my lord An unkind breach; but you shall make all well.
OTHELLO: Are you sure of that?
DESDEMONA: My lord?
OTHELLO *(reads)*: "This fail you not to do, as you will—"
LODOVICO: He did not call; he's busy in the paper. Is there division 'twixt thy lord and Cassio?

---

193 *fond* foolish.   193 *patent* license.   194 *comes near* concerns, harms.   195 *messes* small bits of food.   199 *expostulate* reason, argue.   200 *unprovide my mind* impair my resolution to act.   205 *be his undertaker* undertake to dispose of him. Some modern readers need to be warned that "undertaker" in the sense of "funeral undertaker" (contractor for funerals) is a sense unknown to Shakespeare's generation [K].   211 *kiss* welcome, greet.   *instrument* the letter.   *pleasures* desires.   216 *shall* shall surely.

DESDEMONA: A most unhappy one. I would do much
 T'atone them, for the love I bear to Cassio.
OTHELLO: Fire and brimstone!
DESDEMONA: My lord?
OTHELLO: Are you wise?
DESDEMONA: What, is he angry?
LODOVICO: May be the letter mov'd him; 225
 For, as I think, they do command him home,
 Deputing Cassio in his government.
DESDEMONA: By my troth, I am glad on't.
OTHELLO: Indeed?
DESDEMONA: My lord?
OTHELLO: I am glad to see you mad.
DESDEMONA: Why, sweet Othello!
OTHELLO: Devil! 230
 (Strikes her.)
DESDEMONA: I have not deserv'd this.
LODOVICO: My lord, this would not be believ'd in Venice,
 Though I should swear I saw't. 'Tis very much.
 Make her amends; she weeps.
OTHELLO: O devil, devil!
 If that the earth could teem with woman's tears, 235
 Each drop she falls would prove a crocodile.
 Out of my sight!
DESDEMONA: I will not stay to offend you.

 (Going.)

LODOVICO: Truly, an obedient lady.
 I do beseech your lordship call her back. 240
OTHELLO: Mistress!
DESDEMONA: My lord?
OTHELLO: What would you with her, sir?
LODOVICO: Who? I, my lord?
OTHELLO: Ay! You did wish that I would make her turn.
 Sir, she can turn, and turn, and yet go on,
 And turn again; and she can weep, sir, weep; 245
 And she's obedient; as you say, obedient,

[223] *atone* reconcile   [224] *Are you wise* Desdemona's continued expression of interest in Cassio seems to Othello like madness on her part, since he supposes that, being guilty, she must know that he suspects her and that her words will confirm his suspicion [K].   [227] *government* position as governor.   [229] *I am . . . mad* This line has long puzzled commentators and, in fact, defies rational explanation.   [235] *teem* become pregnant.   [236] *falls* lets fall.   *crocodile* false tear. The crocodile, according to ancient accounts, wept for his victim before devouring him.   [243] *turn come back.*   [244] *can turn . . . go on* is skilful in advancing toward her evil purposes by devious ways [K]. "Turn" in this sense means "change."   [246] *obedient* complaisant, yielding to whatever men ask of her.

Very obedient.—Proceed you in your tears.—
Concerning this, sir (O well-painted passion!),
I am commanded home.—Get you away;
I'll send for you anon.—Sir, I obey the mandate   250
And will return to Venice.—Hence, avaunt!
                                            (*Exit* DESDEMONA.)
Cassio shall have my place. And, sir, to-night
I do entreat that we may sup together.
You are welcome, sir, to Cyprus.—Goats and monkeys!
                                                        (*Exit.*)
LODOVICO: Is this the noble Moor whom our full Senate   255
   Call all in all sufficient? Is this the nature
   Whom passion could not shake? whose solid virtue
   The shot of accident nor dart of chance
   Could neither graze nor pierce?
IAGO: He is much chang'd.
LODOVICO: Are his wits safe? Is he not light of brain?   260
IAGO: He's that he is. I may not breathe my censure.
   What he might be—if what he might he is not—
   I would to heaven he were!
LODOVICO: What, strike his wife?
IAGO: Faith, that was not so well; yet would I knew
   That stroke would prove the worst!
LODOVICO: Is it his use?   265
   Or did the letters work upon his blood
   And new-create this fault?
IAGO: Alas, alas!
   It is not honesty in me to speak
   What I have seen and known. You shall observe him,
   And his own courses will denote him so   270
   That I may save my speech. Do but go after
   And mark how he continues.
LODOVICO: I am sorry that I am deceiv'd in him.   (*Exeunt.*)

Scene II. Cyprus. A room in the Castle.

(*Enter* OTHELLO *and* EMILIA.)

OTHELLO: You have seen nothing then?
EMILIA: Nor ever heard, nor ever did suspect.
OTHELLO: Yes, you have seen Cassio and she together.

---

248 *this* the letter.   254 *Goats and monkeys* Both of these animals were types of lasciviousness [K]   256 *all sufficient* the master of all situations.   257 *solid virtue* firm stability of character [K].   259 *graze* by the shot.   *pierce* by the dart.   260 *safe* sound.   261 *that* that which.   *breathe* speak.   *censure* judgment.   265 *use* custom.   266 *work upon his blood* arouse his emotions.   267 *new-create* cause to be committed for the first time.   270 *courses* behaviour.

EMILIA: But then I saw no harm, and then I head
    Each syllable that breath made up between them. 5
OTHELLO: What, did they never whisper?
EMILIA: Never, my lord.
OTHELLO: Nor send you out o' th' way?
EMILIA: Never.
OTHELLO: To fetch her fan, her gloves, her mask, nor nothing?
EMILIA: Never, my lord. 10
OTHELLO: That's strange.
EMILIA: I durst, my lord, to wager she is honest,
    Lay down my soul at stake. If you think other,
    Remove your thought; it doth abuse your bosom.
    If any wretch have put this in your head, 15
    Let heaven requit it with the serpent's curse!
    For if she be not honest, chaste, and true,
    There's no man happy; the purest of their wives
    Is foul as slander.
OTHELLO: Bid her come hither. Go.   (*Exit* EMILIA.)
    She says enough; yet she's a simple bawd 20
    That cannot say as much. This is a subtle whore,
    A closet lock and key of villainous secrets;
    And yet she'll kneel and pray; I have seen her do't.
    (*Enter* DESDEMONA *and* EMILIA.)
DESDEMONA: My lord, what is your will?
OTHELLO: Pray, chuck, come hither.
DESDEMONA: What is your pleasure?
OTHELLO: Let me see your eyes. 25
    Look in my face.
DESDEMONA: What horrible fancy's this?
OTHELLO (*to* EMILIA): Some of your function, mistress.
    Leave procreants alone and shut the door;
    Cough or cry hem if anybody come.
    Your mystery, your mystery! Nay, dispatch!   (*Exit* EMILIA.) 30
DESDEMONA: Upon my knees what doth your speech import?
    I understand a fury in your words.
    But not the words.
OTHELLO: Why, what art thou?

IV.II. [3] *she* Common Elizabethan grammar [K].   [9] *mask* worn often by Elizabethan ladies in public places.   [14] *abuse* deceive.   [16] *serpent's curse* the curse pronounced upon the serpent in the Garden of Eden (GENESIS, III, 14).   [18] *happy* fortunate.   [20] *bawd* brothel manager. Othello assumes that if Desdemona is guilty Emilia must be her accomplice.   [22] *closet lock and key* safekeeper of the storeroom (closet). Usually "closet" in Shakespeare refers to any small room, but here it seems to have more specific application.   [27] *your function* as bawd. Othello pretends that Desdemona is a whore, Emilia her bawd, and he a client in their brothel.   [30] *mystery* trade. *dispatch* make haste.

William Shakespeare: *Othello*

DESDEMONA: Your wife, my lord; your true
  And loyal wife.
OTHELLO: Come, swear it, damn thyself;
  Lest, being like one of heaven, the devils themselves
  Should fear to seize thee. Therefore be double-damn'd —
  Swear thou art honest.
DESDEMONA: Heaven doth truly know it.
OTHELLO: Heaven truly knows that thou art false as hell.

DESDEMONA: To whom, my lord? With whom? How am I false?
OTHELLO: O, Desdemona! away! away! away!
DESDEMONA: Alas the heavy day! Why do you weep?
  Am I the motive of these tears, my lord?
  If haply you my father do suspect
  An instrument of this your calling back,
  Lay not your blame on me. If you have lost him,
  Why, I have lost him too.
OTHELLO: Had it pleas'd heaven
  To try me with affliction, had they rain'd
  All kinds of sores and shames on my bare head,
  Steep'd me in poverty to the very lips,
  Given to captivity me and my utmost hopes,
  I should have found in some place of my soul
  A drop of patience. But, alas, to make me
  A fixed figure for the time of scorn
  To point his slow unmoving finger at!
  Yet could I bear that too; well, very well.
  But there where I have garner'd up my heart,
  Where either I must live or bear no life,
  The fountain from the which my current runs
  Or else dries up — to be discarded thence,
  Or keep it as a cistern for foul toads
  To knot and gender in — turn thy complexion there,
  Patience, thou young and rose-lipp'd cherubin!
  Ay, there look grim as hell!

42 *heavy* sorrowful.   43 *motive* moving cause.   44 *haply* perhaps.   47-8 *Had it pleas'd . . . affliction* Othello sees his supposed misfortunes as analogous to those of the suffering Job.   48 *they* the heavens.   53 *patience* ability to bear misfortunes with hope of ultimate good. The use of the word in this theological sense supports the Job analogy.   54 *time of scorn* scornful world.   55 *slow unmoving* The finger of the scornful world is slowly raised to the position of pointing; and then, after it has directed itself at its object, it becomes "unmoving"—never ceasing to point at the poor wretch who is set up as a "fixed figure" for contempt [K]. (Q1; F1: "slow, and mouing").   57 *garner'd up* stored the harvest of.   59 *fountain* spring, well-head.   61 *it* the fountain.   62 *knot and gender* be joined and mate with one another.   62-3 *turn thy . . . cherubin* at that point—when required to endure that—let the rosy cherub Patience change to grim and savage wrath [K].   64 *there* THEOBALD; F1, Q1: "here."

DESDEMONA: I hope my noble lord esteems me honest. 65
OTHELLO: O, ay! as summer flies are in the shambles,
 That quicken even with blowing. O thou weed,
 Who art so lovely fair, and smell'st so sweet,
 That the sense aches at thee, would thou hadst ne'er
 been born!
DESDEMONA: Alas, what ignorant sin have I committed? 70
OTHELLO: Was this fair paper, this most goodly book,
 Made to write "whore" upon? What committed?
 Committed? O thou public commoner!
 I should make very forges of my cheeks
 That would to cinders burn up modesty, 75
 Did I but speak thy deeds. What committed?
 Heaven stops the nose at it, and the moon winks;
 The bawdy wind, that kisses all it meets,
 Is hush'd within the hollow mine of earth
 And will not hear it. What committed? 80
 Impudent strumpet!
DESDEMONA: By heaven, you do me wrong!
OTHELLO: Are not you a strumpet?
DESDEMONA: No, as I am a Christian!
 If to preserve this vessel for my lord
 From any other foul unlawful touch
 Be not to be a strumpet, I am none. 85
OTHELLO: What, not a whore?
DESDEMONA: No, as I shall be sav'd!
OTHELLO: Is't possible?
DESDEMONA: O, heaven forgive us!

OTHELLO: I cry you mercy then.
 I took you for that cunning whore of Venice
 That married with Othello. — You, mistress, 90
 That have the office opposite to Saint Peter
 And keep the gate of hell!
 (*Enter* EMILIA.)
 You, you, ay, you!

66 *summer flies* An image of horrible promiscuity [K]. *shambles* slaughterhouse. 67 *quicken . . . blowing* come to life like maggots in flyblown meat [K]. 70 *ignorant* unknown to me. 73 *commoner* prostitute. 74 *make very forges of* burn up (with blushing). 77 *moon* symbol of chastity. *winks* closes her eyes so as not to see. 79 *mine* cave. The winds were supposed to issue from the interior of the earth. So, when it was calm, they had retired to their subterranean home [K]. 83 *this vessel* myself. A Biblical figure. See for example, I PETER, III, 7; ROMANS, IX, 22 [K]. 88 *I cry you mercy* I beg your pardon. Othello returns to the "horrible fancy" with which he had begun the interview. In summoning Emilia he pretends to take her for a bawd [K]. 92 *keep the gate of hell* cf. PROVERBS, VII, 27: "Her [the harlot's] house is the way to hell, going down to the chambers of death" [K].

We have done our course. There's money for your pains.
I pray you turn the key, and keep our counsel.
                                                      (Exit.)
EMILIA: Alas, what does this gentleman conceive?
   How do you, madam? How do you, my good lady?
DESDEMONA: Faith, half asleep.
EMILIA: Good madam, what's the mater with my lord?
DESDEMONA: With who?
EMILIA: Why, with my lord, madam.
DESDEMONA: Who is thy lord?
EMILIA: He that is yours, sweet lady.
DESDEMONA: I have none. Do not talk to me, Emilia.
   I cannot weep; nor answer have I none
   But what should go by water. Prithee to-night
   Lay on my bed my wedding sheets, remember;
   And call thy husband hither.
EMILIA: Here's a change indeed!
                                                      (Exit.)
DESDEMONA: 'Tis meet I shoul be us'd so, very meet.
   How have I been behav'd, that he might stick
   The small'st opinion on my least misuse?

(*Enter* IAGO *and* EMILIA.)
IAGO: What is your pleasure, madam? How is't with you?
DESDEMONA: I cannot tell. Those that do teach young babes
   Do it with gentle means and easy tasks.
   He might have chid me so; for, in good faith,
   I am a child to chiding.
IAGO: What is the matter, lady?
EMILIA: Alas, Iago, my lord hath so bewhor'd her,
   Thrown such despite and heavy terms upon her
   As true hearts cannot bear.
DESDEMONA: Am I that name, Iago?
IAGO: What name, fair lady?
DESDEMONA: Such as she says my lord did say I was.
EMILIA: He call'd her whore. A beggar in his drink
   Could not have laid such terms upon his callet.

---

93 *done our course* completed our business.   94 *turn the key* to open the door. *keep our counsel* keep our interview a secret [K].   95 *conceive* imagine.   97 *half asleep* Desdemona is stunned by Othello's violent language and tired out by the intensity of her emotions [K]. She finds it difficult to believe that she has not been dreaming.   104 *go by water* be expressed in tears.   107 *meet* proper, fitting.   108-9 *might stick . . . least misuse* attach the slightest censure (opinion) to my smallest fault (misuse).   113 *chid* scolded.   114 *a child to chiding* like a child when I am scolded.   115 *bewhor'd her* treated her like a whore. To satisfy logical probability, we must assume that Emilia has been listening at the door.   116 *despite* abuse, contempt.   121 *callet* trull, vagabond harlot.

IAGO: Why did he so?
DESDEMONA: I do not know. I am sure I am none such.
IAGO: Do not weep, do not weep. Alas the day!
EMILIA: Hath she forsook so many noble matches, 125
    Her father and her country, all her friends,
    To be call'd whore? Would it not make one weep?
DESDEMONA: It is my wretched fortune.
IAGO: Beshrew him for't!
    How comes this trick upon him?
DESDEMONA: Nay, heaven doth know.
EMILIA: I will be hang'd if some eternal villain, 130
    Some busy and insinuating rogue,
    Some cogging, cozening slave, to get some office,
    Have not devis'd this slander. I'll be hang'd else.
IAGO: Fie, there is no such man! It is impossible.
DESDEMONA: If any such there be, heaven pardon him! 135
EMILIA: A halter pardon him! and hell gnaw his bones!
    Why should he call her whore? Who keeps her company?
    What place? what time? what form? what likelihood?
    The Moor's abus'd by some most villainous knave,
    Some base notorious knave, some scurvy fellow. 140
    O heaven, that such companions thou'dst unfold,
    And put in every honest hand a whip
    To last the rascals naked through the world
    Even from the East to th' West!
IAGO: Speak within door.
EMILIA: O, fie upon them! Some such squire he was 145
    That turn'd your wit the seamy side without
    And made you to suspect me with the Moor.
IAGO: You are a fool. Go to.
DESDEMONA: O good Iago,
    What shall I do to win my lord again?
    Good friend, go to him; for, by this light of heaven, 150
    I know not how I lost him. Here I kneel.

128 *Beshrew* curse.   129 *trick* freak behaviour.   130 *eternal* everlasting, unmitigated. 131 *busy* prying.   132 *cogging, cozening* Both words mean "cheating."   *to get some office* Emilia has no suspicion that her description fits Iago. Her horrified surprise when his guilt is revealed (v.ii.140ff.) leaves no room for doubt that until that moment she had not suspected his villainy [K]. There are nevertheless inconsistencies in Emilia's behaviour which no amount of logical analysis will explain.   134 *no such* none so bad.   136 *halter* hangman's noose.   138 *form* evidence.   139 *abus'd* deceived. 140 *notorious* notable.   *scurvy* vile.   141 *companions* knaves.   *unfold* reveal, expose. 144 *within door* not so loudly.   145 *squire* used contemptuously.   146 *seamy side without* wrong side out.   147 *suspect . . . Moor* Iago has apparently made Emilia aware of his suspicions of her. It is ironical that Iago should have given his wife the opportunity for denial whereas the more noble Othello should have been incapable of such action.

If e'er my will did trespass 'gainst his love,
Either in discourse of thought or actual deed,
Or that mine eyes, mine ears, or any sense
Delighted them in any other form,   155
Or that I do not yet, and ever did,
And ever will (though he do shake me off
To beggarly divorcement) love him dearly,
Comfort forswear me! Unkindness may do much;
And his unkindness may defeat my life.   160
But never taint my love. I cannot say "whore."
It doth abhor me now I speak the word;
To do the act that might th' addition earn
Not the world's mass of vanity could make me.
IAGO: I pray you be content. 'Tis but his humour.   165
  The business of the state does him offence,
  And he does chide with you.
DESDEMONA: If 'twere no other —
IAGO: 'Tis but so, I warrant.

(Trumpets within.)

  Hark how these instruments summon you to supper.
  The messengers of Venice stay the meat.   170
  Go in, and weep not. All things shall be well.
                          (Exeunt DESDEMONA *and* EMILIA.*)*
(Enter RODERIGO.*)*
  How now, Roderigo?
RODERIGO: I do not find that thou deal'st justly with me.
IAGO: What in the contrary?
RODERIGO: Every day thou daff'st me with some device, Iago, and 175
  rather, as it seems to me now, keep'st from me all conveniency
  than suppliest me with the least advantage of hope. I will indeed
  no longer endure it; nor am I yet persuaded to put up in peace
  what already I have foolishly suffer'd.   180
IAGO: Will you hear me, Roderigo?
RODERIGO: Faith, I have heard too much; for your words and performance are no kin together.

---

¹⁵³ *discourse of thought* process of thought (with no notion of speech).   ¹⁵⁹ *Comfort forswear me* may all that sustains life and makes it happy forsake me as if by a solemn vow [K].   ¹⁶⁰ *defeat* destroy.   ¹⁶¹ *never taint my love* In the unshakable love of Desdemona for Othello in spite of what tortures she may suffer at his hands, some critics have seen an analogy to Christ's love for mankind.   ¹⁶² *abhor* disgust.   ¹⁶³ *addition* title (of whore).   ¹⁶⁴ *world's mass of vanity* this whole world with all its vain delights [K].   ¹⁶⁵ *humour* mood.   ¹⁷⁰ *messengers of Venice* Lodovico and his associates.   *stay the meat* are waiting for supper.   ¹⁷⁵ *daff'st me* put me off.   *device* trick.   ¹⁷⁶ *conveniency* opportunity (to court Desdemona).   ¹⁷⁷⁻⁸ *advantage of hope* advantage that may further my hopes [K].   ¹⁷⁹ *put up in peace* endure without resentment [K].   ¹⁸⁰ *suffer'd* permitted to occur.

IAGO: You charge me most unjustly.
RODERIGO: With naught but truth. I have wasted myself out of means. The jewels you have had from me to deliver to Desdemona would half have corrupted a votarist. You have told me she hath receiv'd them, and return'd me expectations and comforts of sudden respect and acquintance; but I find none.
IAGO: Well, go to; very well.
RODERIGO: Very well! go to! I cannot go to, man; nor 'tis not very well. Nay, I think it is scurvy, and begin to find myself fopp'd in it.
IAGO: Very well.
RODERIGO: I tell you 'tis not very well. I will make myself known to Desdemona. If she will return me my jewels, I will give over my suit and repent my unlawful solicitation. If not, assure yourself I will seek satisfaction of you.
IAGO: You have said now.
RODERIGO: Ay, and said nothing but what I protest intendment of doing.
IAGO: Why, now I see there's mettle in thee; and even from this instant do build on thee a better opinion than ever before. Give me thy hand, Roderigo. Thou hast taken against me a most just exception; but yet I protest Ihave dealt most directly in thy affair.
RODERIGO: It hath not appear'd.
IAGO: I grant indeed it hath not appear'd; and your suspicion it not without wit and judgment. But, Roderigo, if thou hast that in thee indeed which I have greater reason to believe now than ever (I mean purpose, courage, and valour), this night show it. If thou the next night following enjoy not Desdemona, take me from this world with treachery and devise engines for my life.
RODERIGO: Well, what is it? Is it within reason and compass?
IAGO: Sir, there is especial commission come from Venice to depute Cassio in Othello's place.
RODERIGO: Is that true? Why, then Othello and Desdemona return again to Venice.

187 *votarist* nun.   189 *comforts* comforting reports.   *sudden* immediate.   *respect* consideration (on Desdemona's part).   189-90 *acquaintance* meeting (with her) (F1, Q2; Q1: "acquittance"—release from debt).   191 *go to* enough; say no more. Iago speaks as if Roderigo's complaints were the last straw [K].   194 *fopp'd* made a fool of.   196 *make myself known* Roderigo means simply that he will have a personal explanation with Desdemona. So far Iago has managed to prevent an interview (cf. line 189–90). There is certainly no reference to Roderigo's being disguised [K].   198 *give over* abandon.   199 *seek satisfaction* demand repayment (or challenge to a duel).   200 *You have said now* Iago pretends to be admiring Roderigo's spirit. A modern equivalent might be "Now you're talking."   201 *protest* proclaim.   *intendment* intention.   203 *mettle* spirit and courage.   206 *just exception* fair objection or criticism.   207 *directly* fairly, straightforwardly.   216 *engines for* plots against.   217 *within reason and compass*—within the reasonable limits of accomplishment [K].

IAGO: O, no. He goes into Mauritania and takes away with him the fair Desdemona, unless his abode be linger'd here by some accident; wherein none can be so determinate as the removing of Cassio. 225
RODERIGO: How do you mean removing of him?
IAGO: Why, by making him uncapable of Othello's place—knocking out his brains.
RODERIGO: And that you would have me to do?
IAGO: Ay, if you dare do yourself a profit and a right. He sups 230 to-night with a harlotry, and thither will I go to him. He knows not yet of his honourable fortune. If you will watch his going thence, which I will fashion to fall out between twelve and one, you may take him at your pleasure. I will be near to second your attempt, and he shall fall between us. Come, stand not amaz'd at 235 it, but go along with me. I will show you such a necessity in his death that you shall think yourself bound to put it on him. It is now high supper time, and the night grows to waste. About it! 240
RODERIGO: I will hear further reason for this.
IAGO: And you shall be satisfied.

(Exeunt.)

Scene III. Cyprus. Another room in the Castle.

(Enter OTHELLO, LODOVICO, DESDEMONA, EMILIA, *and* ATTENDANTS.*)*

LODOVICO. I do beseech you sir, trouble yourself no further.
OTHELLO: O, pardon me; 'twill do me good to walk.
LODOVICO: Madam, good night. I humbly thank your ladyship.
DESDEMONA: Your Honour is most welcome.
OTHELLO: Will you walk sir?
O, Desdemona — 5
DESDEMONA: My lord?
OTHELLO: Get you to bed on th' instant. I will be return'd forthwith. Dispatch your attendant there. Look 't be done.
DESDEMONA: I will, my lord.

(Exeunt OTHELLO, LODOVICO, *and* ATTENDANTS.*)*

EMILIA: How goes it now? He looks gentler than he did. 10
DESDEMONA: He says he will return incontinent.

---

222 *Mauritania* the supposed home of the Moors in Northwest Africa. The name is Roman. 223 *abode* stay. *linger'd* lengthened. 224 *wherein none . . . determinate* and no occurrence can be so decisive in lengthening his stay [K]. 227 *uncapable of* unable to succeed to. *place* position (as governor). 231 *harlotry* harlot. 236 *amaz'd* in a maze, dumbfounded [K]. 239-40 *grows to waste* is passing. 242 *satisfied* have satisfactory reasons. IV.III. 1 *trouble . . . further* Othello is offering to escort Lodovico to his lodgings [K]. 8 *Dispatch* dismiss. 11 *incontinent* immediately.

      He hath commanded me to go to bed,
      And bid me to dismiss you.
EMILIA: Dismiss me?
DESDEMONA: It was his bidding. Therefore, good Emilia,
      Give me my nightly wearing, and adieu.   15
      We must not now displease him.
EMILIA: I would you had never seen him!
DESDEMONA: So would not I. My love doth so approve him
      That even his stubbornness, his checks, his frowns
      (Prithee unpin me) have grace and favour in them.   20
EMILIA: I have laid those sheets you bade me on the bed.
DESDEMONA: All's one. Good faith, how foolish are our minds!
      If I do die before thee, prithee shroud me
      In one of those same sheets.
EMILIA: Come, come! you talk.
DESDEMONA: My mother had a maid call'd Barbary.   25
      She was in love; and he she lov'd prov'd mad
      And did forsake her. She had a song of "Willow."
      An old thing 'twas; but it express'd her fortune,
      And she died singing it. That song to-night
      Will not go from my mind. I have much to do   30
      But to go hang my head all at one side
      And sing it like poor Barbary. Prithee dispatch.
EMILIA: Shall I go fetch your nightgown?
DESDEMONA: No, unpin me here.
      This Lodovico is a proper man.
EMILIA: A very handsome man.   35
DESDEMONA: He speaks well.
EMILIA: I know a lady in Venice would have walk'd barefoot to
      Palestine for a touch of his nether lip.
DESDEMONA: (*sings*):
      The poor soul sat sighing by a sycamore tree,
      Sing all a green willow: 40
      Her hand on her bosom, her head on her knee,
      Sing willow, willow, willow.
      The fresh streams ran by her and murmur'd her moans;
      Sing Willow, willow, willow;

---

19 *stubbornness* roughness.   *checks* rebukes.   20 *grace and favour* something about them that I find pleasing [K].   22 *All's one* it is no matter.   24 *talk* talk foolishly.   26 *mad* wild and wayward—not, insane [K].   30-1 *I have much . . . But to* I have all I can do to keep myself from.   34 *proper* handsome. Desdemona talks idly of Lodovico to keep her mind from her troubles. There is no reason to suppose that the line has been misassigned and should be given to Emilia.   39 *The poor soul* The song is a popular ballad well known to Shakespeare's audience. It appears in various versions. In those we know the forsaken lover is a man, but Shakespeare has adapted the song to fit his play. The willow was a traditional symbol of unrequited love.   47 *these* probably some jewels.

Her salt tears fell from her, and soft'ned the stones. 45
 Sing willow —
 Lay by these.
  willow, willow;
 Prithee hie thee; he'll come anon.
 Sing all a green willow must be my garland.
 Let nobody blame him; his scorn I approve — 50
 Nay, that's not next. Hark! who is't that knocks?
EMILIA: It is the wind.
DESDEMONIA: I call'd my love false love; but what said he then?
 Sing willow, willow, willow:
 If I court moe women, you'll couch with moe men. 55
 So, get thee gone; good night. Mine eyes do itch.
 Doth that bode weeping?
EMILIA: 'Tis neither here nor there.
DESDEMONA: I have heard it said so. O, these men, these men!
 Dost thou in conscience think — tell me, Emilia —
 That there be women do abuse their husbands 60
 In such gross kind?
EMILIA: There be some such, no question.

EMILIA: Why, would not you?
DESDEMONA: No, by this heavenly light!
EMILIA: Nor I neither by this heavenly light. I might do't as well
 i' th' dark. 65
DESDEMONA: Wouldst thou do such a deed for all the world?
EMILIA: The world's a huge thing. It is a great price for a small
 vice.
DESDEMONA: Good troth, I think thou wouldst not.
EMILIA: By my troth, I think I should; and undo't when I had done 70
 it. Marry, I would not do such a thing for a joint-ring, nor for
 measures of lawn, nor for gowns, petticoats, nor caps, nor any
 petty exhibition; but, for all the whole world — 'Ud's pity!
 who would not make her husband a cuckold to make him a
 monarch? I should venture purgatory for't. 75
DESDEMONA: Beshrew me if I would do such a wrong
 For the whole world.
EMILIA: Why, the wrong is but a wrong i' th' world; and having the
 world for your labor, 'tis a wrong in your own world, and you 80
 might quickly make it right.

55 *moe* more (not a contraction of "more" but an independent formation from the same root [K]).   57 *neither here nor there* means nothing.   59 *in conscience* with real conviction.   60 *abuse* deceive.   61 *gross kind* obscene manner.   70 *undo't* make it right again.   71 *joint-ring* a ring made of separable halves, commonly used as a love token.   72 *lawn* fine linen.   73 *exhibition* offer of a gift.   74 *'Ud's pity* by God's pity (an oath).   77 *Beshrew* curse.   81 *make it right* by your decree as ruler of the world.

DESDEMONA: I do not think there is any such woman.
EMILIA: Yes, a dozen; and as many to th' vantage as would store
   the world they play'd for.
   But I do think it is their husbands' faults
   If wives do fall. Say that they slack their duties   85
   And pour our treasures into foreign laps;
   Or else break out in peevish jealousies,
   Throwing restraint upon us; or say they strike us,
   Or scant our former having in despite —
   Why, we have galls; and though we have some grace,   90
   Yet have we some revenge. Let husbands know
   Their wives have sense like them. They see, and smell,
   And have their palates both for sweet and sour,
   As husbands have. What is it that they do
   When they change us for others? Is it sport?   95
   I think it is. And doth affection breed it?
   I think it doth. Is't frailty that thus errs?
   It is so too. And have not we affections,
   Desires for sport, and frailty, as men have?
   Then let them use us well; else let them know,   100
   The ills we do, their ills instruct us so.
DESDEMONA: Good night, good night. Heaven me such uses send,
   Not to pick bad from bad, but by bad mend!

(Exeunt.)

ACT FIVE

Scene I. Cyprus. A street.

(Enter IAGO *and* RODERIGO.*)*

IAGO: Here, stand behind this bulk; straight will he come.
   Wear thy good rapier bare, and put it home.
   Quick, quick! Fear nothing; I'll be at thy elbow.
   It makes us, or it mars us — think on that,

---

[83] *to th' vantage* to boot, in addition.   *store* populate.   [84] *But I do think* Emilia drops her jesting and speaks with some feeling. She does not, however, defend unfaithful wives on moral grounds, but merely asserts that faithless or abusive husbands have no just ground of complaint if their wives avenge themselves by infidelity [K].   [87] *peevish* childish.   [88] *Throwing* inflicting.   [89] *scant . . . despite* reduce our allowance to spite us.   [90] *galls* capacity for resentment.   *grace* virtue.   [91] *revenge* vindictiveness.   [92] *sense* feelings.   [96] *affection* desire for pleasure [K].   [99] *frailty* weakness of the flesh.   [102] *uses* ways, practices.   [103] *Not to pick . . . bad mend* that I may not let ill treatment teach me to return evil for evil but may use it as discipline for my own improvement [K].
V.I [1] *bulk* some structure—perhaps a "stall" or small shop [K]   *straight* straightway.

William Shakespeare: *Othello*

    And fix most firm thy resolution. 5
RODERIGO: Be near at hand. I may miscarry in't.
IAGO: Here, at thy hand. Be hold, and take thy stand.

(Stands aside.)

RODERIGO: I have no great devotion to the deed,
    'Tis but a man gone. Forth my sword! He dies! 10
    And yet he hath given be satisfying reasons.
IAGO: I have rubb'd this young quat almost to the sense,
    And grows angry. Now whether he kill Cassio,
    Or Cassio him, or each do kill the other,
    Every way makes my game. Live Roderigo,
    He calls me to a restitution large 15
    Of gold and jewels that I bobb'd from him
    As gifts to Desdemona.
    It must not be. If Cassio do remain,
    He hath a daily beauty in his life
    That makes me ugly; and besides, the Moor 20
    May unfold me to him; there stand I in much peril.
    No, he must die. But so! I hear him coming.

(Enter CASSIO.*)*

RODERIGO: I know his gait. 'Tis he. Villain, thou diest!

(Makes a pass at CASSIO.*)*

CASSIO: That thrust had been mine enemy indeed
    But that my coat is better than thou know'st. 25
    I will make proof of thine.

(Draws, and wounds RODERIGO.*)*

RODERIGO: O, I am slain!

    (IAGO *rushes from his post, wounds* CASSIO *in the leg, and exit.*)
CASSIO: I am maim'd for ever. Help, ho! Murder! murder!

(Falls.)
(Enter OTHELLO.*)*

OTHELLO: The voice of Cassio. Iago keeps his word.
RODERIGO: O, villain that I am!
OTHELLO: It is even so.
CASSIO: O, help, ho! light! a surgeon! 30
OTHELLO: 'Tis he. O brave Iago, honest and just,
    That hast such noble sense of thy friend's wrong!

---

6 *miscarry* fail; go wrong. Roderigo is nervous, not timid [K].   11 *quat* contemptible youngster—literally, pimple [K].   *to the sense* so that he feels it. The pimple has been rubbed to the quick.   14 *makes my game* helps me win the game [K] (Q1; F1: "gaine"). This reading has been much disputed. *Live Roderigo* if Roderigo lives (the subjunctive).   16 *bobb'd* cheated.   21 *unfold* expose.   25 *coat is better* Cassio wears a shirt of mail under his coat [K].   32 *sense of* feeling for.

Thou teachest me. Minion, your dear lies dead,
And your unblest fate hies. Strumpet, I come.
Forth of my heart those charms, thine eyes, are blotted. 35
Thy bed, lust-strain'd, shall with lust's blood be spotted.

(Exit.)

(Enter LODOVICO *and* GRATIANO.*)*
CASSIO: What, ho? No watch? No passage? Murder! murder!
GRATIANO: 'Tis some mischance. The cry is very direful.
CASSIO: O, help! 40
LODOVICO: Hark!
RODERIGO: O wretched villain!
LODOVICO: Two or three groan. It is a heavy night.
  These may be counterfeits. Let's think't unsafe
  To come in to the cry without more help.
RODERIGO: Nobody come? Then shall I bleed to death. 45
LODOVICO: Hark!
(Enter IAGO, *with a light.)*
GRATIANO: Here's one comes in his shirt, with light and weapons.
IAGO: Who's there? Whose noise is this that cries on murder?
LODOVICO: We do not know.
IAGO: Did not you hear a cry?
CASSIO: Here, here! For heaven's sake, help me!
IAGO: What's the matter? 50
GRATIANO: This is Othello's ancient, as I take it.
LODOVICO: The same indeed, a very valiant fellow.
IAGO: What are you here that cry so grievously?
CASSIO: Iago? O, I am spoil'd, undone by villains!
  Give me some help. 55
IAGO: O me, Lieutenant! What villains have done this?
CASSIO: I think that one of them is hereabout
  And cannot make away.
IAGO: O treacherous villains!
  What are you there? Come in, and give some help.
  (To LODOVICO *and* GRATIANO.*)*
RODERIGO: O, help me here! 60
CASSIO: That's one of them.
IAGO: O murd'rous slave! O villain!
  (Stabs RODERIGO.*)*
RODERIGO: O damn'd Iago! O inhuman dog!
IAGO: Kill men i' th' dark? Where be these bloody thieves?
  How silent is this town! Ho! murder! murder!
  What may you be? Are you of good or evil? 65

---

33 *Minion* darling, Desdemona (used with contempt).   34 *hies* quickly approaches.
35 *Forth of* from forth.   37 *passage* passers-by.   42 *heavy* thick and cloudy.   44 *cries on* cries out, shouts.   54 *spoil'd* crippled.

LODOVICO: As you shall prove us, praise us.
IAGO: Signior Lodovico?
LODOVICO: He, sir.
IAGO: I cry you mercy. Here's Cassio hurt by villains.
GRATIANO: Cassio?
IAGO: How is it, brother?
CASSIO: My leg is cut in two.
IAGO: Marry, heaven forbid!
   Light, gentlemen. I'll bind it with my shirt.
   (*Enter* BIANCA.)
BIANCA: What is the matter, ho? Who is't that cried?
IAGO: Who is't that cried?
BIANCA: O my dear Cassio! my sweet Cassio!
   O Cassio, Cassio, Cassio!
IAGO: O notable strumpet! — Cassio, may you suspect
   Who they should be that thus have mangled you?
CASSIO: No.
GRATIANO: I am sorry to find you thus. I have been to seek you.
IAGO: Lend me a garter. So. O for a chair.
   To bear him easily hence!
BIANCA: Alas, he faints! O Cassio, Cassio, Cassio!
IAGO: Gentlemen all, I do suspect this trash
   To be a party in this injury. —
   Patience awhile, good Cassio. — Come, come!
   Lend me a light. Know we this face or no?
   Alas, my friend and my dear countryman
   Roderigo? No. Yes, sure. O heaven! Roderigo.
GRATIANO: What, of Venice?
IAGO: Even he, sir. Did you know him?
GRATIANO: Know him? Ay.
IAGO: Signior Gratiano? I cry you gentle pardon.
   These bloody accidents must excuse my manners
   That so neglected you.
GRATIANO: I am glad to see you.
IAGO: How do you, Cassio?—O, a chair, a chair?
GRATIANO: Roderigo?
IAGO: He, he, 'tis he! (*A chair brought in.*) O, that's well said!
   the chair.
   Some good man bear him carefully from hence.
   I'll fetch the General's surgeon. (*To* BIANCA) For you, mistress.
   Save you your labour.—He that lies slain here, Cassio,
   Was my dear friend. What malice was between you?

---

66 *As you ... praise us* value (literally, appraise) us as you find us out to be.   82 *chair* kind of litter.   85 *trash* worthless creature, Bianca.   94 *accidents* sudden happenings.   95 *neglected* failed to recognize.   98 *well said* well done.   101 *Save you your labour* don't trouble yourself. Bianca is attempting to care for Cassio [K].

CASSIO: None in the world; nor do I know the man.
IAGO (*to* BIANCA): What, look you pale?—O, bear him out o' th'air.

(CASSIO *and* RODERIGO *are borne off.*)

Stay you, good gentlemen.—Look you pale, mistress?— 105
Do you perceive the gastness of her eye?—
Nay, an you stare, we shall hear more anon.
Behold her well; I pray you look upon her.
Do you see, gentlemen? Nay, guiltiness will speak,
Though tongues were out of use. 110

(*Enter* EMILIA.)

EMILIA: 'Las, what's the matter? What's the matter, husband?
IAGO: Cassio hath here been set on in the dark
   By Roderigo, and fellows that are scap'd.
   He's almost slain, and Roderigo dead.
EMILIA: Alas, good gentleman! alas, good Cassio! 115
IAGO: This is the fruit of whoring. Prithee, Emilia,
   Go know of Cassio where he supp'd to-night.
   (*To* BIANCA) What, do you shake at that?
BIANCA: He supp'd at my house; but I therefore shake not.
IAGO: O, did he so? I charge you go with me. 120
EMILIA: Fie, fie upon thee, strumpet!
BIANCA: I am no strumpet, but of life as honest
   As you that thus abuse me.
EMILIA: As I? Foh! fie upon thee!
IAGO: Kind gentlemen, let's go see poor Cassio dress'd.
   (*To* BIANCA) Come, mistress, you must tell's another tale.— 125
   Emilia, run you to the citadel
   And tell my lord and lady what hath happ'd.—
   Will you go on afore? [*Aside*] This is the night
   That either makes me or fordoes me quite.   (*Exeunt.*)

Scene II. *Cyprus. A bedchamber in the Castle.*

(DESDEMONA *in her bed. Enter* OTHELLO *with a light.*)

OTHELLO: It is the cause, it is the cause, my soul.

---

[103] *nor do I know the man* We have already seen that Cassio was not acquainted with Roderigo (II.i.261; II.iii.265-7) [K].   [117] *know of* learn from.   [119] *shake* with fear.   [122] *honest* chaste.   [124] *dress'd* have his wounds dressed.   [129] *fordoes* ruins.

   V.II. [1] *It is the cause* Othello has subdued his fury. He is resolved to kill Desdemona as an act of justice. He will not think of his own wrongs but solely of her offence [K]. Othello's taking upon himself the power to execute justice is the supreme point of his tragic madness; in the guise of the impartial judge he executes the most horrible of crimes.   [2] *it* her supposed unchastity.

William Shakespeare: *Othello*

Let me not name it to you, you chaste stars!
It is the cause. Yet I'll not shed her blood,
Nor scar that whiter skin of her than snow,
And smooth as monumental alablaster. 5
Yet she must die, else she'll betray more men.
Put out the light, and then put out the light.
If I quench thee, thou flaming minister,
I can again thy former light restore,
Should I repent me; but once put out thy light, 10
Thou cunning'st pattern of excelling nature,
I know not where is that Promethean heat
That can thy light relume. When I have pluck'd the rose,
I cannot give it vital growth again;
It needs must wither. I'll smell it on the tree. 15

(He kisses her).

O balmy breath, that dost almost persuade
Justice to break her sword! One more, one more!
Be thus when thou art dead, and I will kill thee,
And love thee after. One more, and this the last!
So sweet was ne'er so fatal. I must weep, 20
But they are cruel tears. This sorrow's heavenly;
It strikes where it doth love. She wakes.
DESDEMONA: Who's there? Othello?
OTHELLO: Ay, Desdemona.
DESDEMONA: Will you come to bed, my lord?
OTHELLO: Have you pray'd to-night, Desdemona?
DESDEMONA: Ay, my lord. 25
OTHELLO: If you bethink yourself of any crime
Unreconcil'd as yet to heaven and grace,

---

5 *alablaster* alabaster, a white translucent stone.   7 *Put out . . . the light* extinguish the light he holds and then extinguish the light of her life.   8 *flaming minister* the torch in his hand.   10 *thy* Desdemona's.   11 *cunning'st* most perfectly created. *pattern . . . nature* reflection of the perfection and excellence of all creation.   12 *Promethean heat* Prometheus stole fire from heaven to animate a clay image that he had made [K]. Only the fire of heaven can rekindle life.   13 *relume* light again (F1; Q1: "returne").   17 *Justice* This makes it clear that Othello is thinking of justice—as opposed to revenge—in line 1 [K]. The sword and the scale were traditional emblems of justice.   21 *cruel tears* not tears of mercy [K].   *This sorrow's heavenly* my sorrow is like that which God feels when he punishes the guilty; he loves the sinner, yet punishes the sin. Cf. HEBREWS, XII, 6: "Whom the Lord loveth he chasteneth." Here again we see that Othello regards himself as the agent of divine justice. He strives to maintain this attitude of mind throughout the scene, but in vain [K].

    Solicit for it straight.
DESDEMONA: Alack, my lord, what may you mean by that?
OTHELLO: Well, do it, and be brief; I will walk by.   30
    I would not kill thy unprepared spirit.
    No, heaven forfend! I would not kill thy soul.
DESDEMONA: Talk you of killing?
OTHELLO: Ay, I do.
DESDEMONA: Then heaven
    Have mercy on me!
OTHELLO: Amen, with all my heart!
DESDEMONA: If you say so, I hope you will not kill me.   35
OTHELLO: Humh!
DESDEMONA: And yet I fear you; for you are fatal then
    When your eyes roll so. Why I should fear I know not,
    Since guiltiness I know not; but yet I feel I fear.
OTHELLO: Think on thy sins.
DESDEMONA: They are loves I bear to you.   40
OTHELLO: Ay, and for that thou diest.
DESDEMONA: That death's unnatural that kills for loving.
    Alas, why gnaw you so your nether lip?
    Some bloody passion shakes your very frame.
    These are portents; but yet I hope, I hope,   45
    They do not point on me.
OTHELLO: Peace and be still!
DESDEMONA: I will so. What's the matter?
OTHELLO: That handkerchief which I so lov'd and gave thee
    Thou gav'st to Cassio.
DESDEMONA: No, by my life and soul!
    Send for the man and ask him.
OTHELLO: Sweet soul, take heed,   50
    Take heed of perjury; thou art on thy deathbed.
DESDEMONA: Ay, but not yet to die.
OTHELLO: Yes, presently.
    Therefore confess thee freely of thy sin;
    For to deny each article with oath
    Cannot remove nor choke the strong conception   55
    That I do groan withal. Thou art to die.

---

[28] *Solicit* pray. *straight* at one. [30] *walk by* step aside. [32] *forfend* forbid. [40] *They are loves . . . you* I am conscious of no sin, unless it be the sin of loving you too much. An allusion to the idea that to idolize a mortal is a sin against God [K]. [41] *that* love; but Othello means her love for other men. [47] *the matter* the real issue disturbing you. [50] *Sweet soul, take heed* Othello masters his rising anger and becomes once more, for a moment, the compassionate and inexorable judge [K]. [52] *presently* immediately. [54] *article* item (in the list of sins of which he is accusing her). [55] *conception* belief, conviction. [56] *groan withal* groan with thinking of.

DESDEMONA: Then Lord have mercy on me!
OTHELLO: I say amen.
DESDEMONA: And have you mercy too! I never did
  Offend you in my life; never lov'd Cassio
  But with such general warranty of heaven 60
  As I might love. I never gave him token.
OTHELLO: By heaven, I saw my handkerchief in's hand!
  O perjur'd woman! thou dost stone my heart,
  And mak'st me call what I intend to do
  A murder, which I thought a sacrifice. 65
  I saw the handkerchief.
DESDEMONA: He found it then.
  I never gave it him. Send for him hither.
  Let him confess a truth.
OTHELLO: He hath confess'd.
DESDEMONA: What, my lord?
OTHELLO: That he hath us'd thee.
DESDEMONA: How? unlawfully?
OTHELLO: Ay. 70
DESDEMONA: He will not say so.
OTHELLO: No, his mouth is stopp'd.
  Honest Iago hath ta'en order for't.
DESDEMONA: O, my fear interprets. What, is he dead?
OTHELLO: Had all his hairs been lives, my great revenge
  Had stomach for them all. 75
DESDEMONA: Alas, he is betray'd, and I undone!
OTHELLO: Out, strumpet! Weep'st thou for him to my face?
DESDEMONA: O, banish me, my lord, but kill me not!
OTHELLO: Down, strumpet!
DESDEMONA: Kill me to-morrow; let me live to-night! 80
OTHELLO: Nay, an you strive—
DESDEMONA: But half an hour!
OTHELLO: Being done, there is no pause.
DESDEMONA: But while I say one prayer!

---

60 *with such . . . heaven* with that love for one's fellow men which heaven warrants us in feeling [K].   63 *stone* harden. Othello does not wish to kill her in anger, but he is afraid that her supposed perjury is driving him to this.   65 *sacrifice* to offended justice.   72 *ta'en order* arranged.   75 *stomach* appetite, capacity.   76 *Alas . . . undone* Desdemona means that Cassio has been the victim of some plot, and that she is lost because his death makes it impossible for him to testify to her innocence. To Othello, however, her words appear to be a confession of guilt. He takes her to mean that Cassio's intrigue with her has been disclosed. Her terrified appeals for mercy only add to his misunderstanding [K].   82 *Being done . . . pause* once the deed of execution has begun, there is no stopping.

OTHELLO: It is too late.

(He smothers her.)
(EMILIA at the door.)

EMILIA *(calls within)*: My lord, my lord! What, ho! my lord, my lord!
OTHELLO: What noise is this? Not dead? not yet quite dead?   85
   I that am cruel am yet merciful;
   I would not have thee linger in thy pain.
   So, so.
EMILIA *(within)*: What, ho! my lord, my lord!
OTHELLO: Who's there?
EMILIA *(within)*: O, good my lord, I would speak a word with you!   90
OTHELLO: Yes, 'tis Emilia.—By-and-by.—She's dead.—
   'Tis like she comes to speak of Cassio's death.
   The noise was here. Ha! no more moving?
   Still as the grave.—Shall she come in? Were't good?—
   I think she stirs again. No.—What's the best?   95
   If she come in, she'll sure speak to my wife.
   My wife! my wife! what wife? I have no wife.
   O, insupportable! O heavy hour!
   Methinks it should be now a huge eclipse
   Of sun and moon, and that th' affrighted globe   100
   Should yawn at alteration.
EMILIA: [*within*] I do beseech you
   That I may speak with you, O good my lord!
OTHELLO: I had forgot thee. O come in, Emilia.
   Soft, by-and-by.—Let me the curtains draw.—
   Where art thou?

(Opens the door.)
(Enter EMILIA.)

                        What's the matter with thee now?   105
EMILIA: O my good lord, yonder's foul murder done!
OTHELLO: What? now?
EMILIA: But now, my lord.
OTHELLO: It is the very error of the moon.
   She comes more nearer earth than she was wont   110
   And makes men mad.

---

84 *My lord, my lord* The effect of this sudden outcry of Emilia, who is coming with important news, is precisely like that of the knocking at the gate in MACBETH [K].   88 *So, so* With these words Othello presses the pillow down more firmly on Desdemona's head [K].   92 *like* likely that.   93 *The noise* of a movement on Desdemona's part [K].   99 *it should . . . eclipse.* Such heavenly phenomena were usually seen as reflections of horror and disorder on earth.   100 *affrighted globe* terrified earth.   101 *yawn* open wide, in an earthquake.   *at alteration* at the dreadful change in the order of nature that such an eclipse portends [K].   111 *makes men mad* Lunacy, as the word implies, was thought to be due to the malign influence of the moon [K].

EMILIA: Cassio, my lord, hath kill'd a young Venetian
  Call'd Roderigo.
OTHELLO: Roderigo kill'd?
  And Cassio kill'd?
EMILIA: No, Cassio is not kill'd.
OTHELLO: Not Cassio kill'd? Then murder's out of tune, 115
  And sweet revenge grows harsh.
DESDEMONA: O, falsely, falsely murder'd!
EMILIA: O Lord! what cry is that?
OTHELLO: That? What?
EMILIA: Out and alas! that was my lady's voice.
  Help! help, ho! help! O lady, speak again! 120
  Sweet Desdemona! O sweet mistress, speak!
DESDEMONA: A guiltless death I die.
EMILIA: O, who hath done this deed?
DESDEMONA: Nobody—I myself. Farewell.
  Commend me to my kind lord. O, farewell! 125

(She dies.)

OTHELLO: Why, how should she be murd'red?
EMILIA: Alas, who knows?
OTHELLO: You heard her say herself, it was not I.
EMILIA: She said so. I must needs report a truth.
OTHELLO: She's like a liar gone to burning hell!
  'Twas I that kill'd her.
EMILIA: O, the more angel she, 130
  And you the blacker devil!
OTHELLO: She turn'd to folly, and she was a whore.
EMILIA: Thou dost belie her, and thou art a devil.
OTHELLO: She was false as water.
EMILIA: Thou art rash as fire to say
  That she was false. O she was heavenly true! 135
OTHELLO: Cassio did top her. Ask thy husband else.
  O, I were damn'd beneath all depth in hell
  But that I did proceed upon just grounds
  To this extremity. Thy husband knew it all.
EMILIA: My husband? 140

---

119 *Out* Originally a rallying cry; then, often, a cry for help or an interjection of distress [K]   124 *Nobody* With her dying breath Desdemona takes upon herself the guilt for Othello's sin.   125 *Commend me* give my love.   132 *folly* unchastity.   133 *belie* slander.   134 *false as water* A proverbial comparison. Water takes every shape, having none of its own [K].   139 *extremity* final punishment.   140 *My husband* Emilia's astonishment, which comes out in her helpless repetition of the word, proves that she had not suspected Iago. Her denunciation of "some eternal villain" (IV.II.130ff.) was purely impersonal [K]

OTHELLO: Thy husband.
EMILIA: That she was false to wedlock?
OTHELLO: Ay, with Cassio. Nay, had she been true,
　If heaven would make me such another world
　Of one entire and perfect chrysolite, 145
　I'ld not have sold her for it.
EMILIA: My husband?
OTHELLO:　　　　　　Ay, 'twas he that told me first.
　An honest man he is, and hates the slime
　That sticks on filthy deeds.
EMILIA:　　　　　　My husband?
OTHELLO: What needs this iterance, woman? I say, thy husband. 150
EMILIA: O mistress, villainy hath made mocks with love!
　My husband say that she was false?
OTHELLO:　　　　　　He, woman.
　I say, thy husband. Dost understand the word?
　My friend, thy husband; honest, honest Iago.
EMILIA: If he say so, may his pernicious soul 155
　Rot half a grain a day! he lies to th' heart.
　She was too fond of her most filthy bargain.
OTHELLO: Ha!
EMILIA: Do thy worst.
　This deed of thine is no more worthy heaven 160
　Than thou wast worthy her.
OTHELLO:　　　　　　Peace, you were best.
EMILIA: Thou hast not half the power to do me harm
　As I have to be hurt. O gull! O dolt!
　As ignorant as dirt! thou has done a deed—
　I care not for thy sword; I'll make thee known, 165
　Though I lost twenty lives. Help! help! O, help!
　The Moor hath kill'd my mistress! Murder! murder!

(*Enter* MONTANO, GRATIANO, IAGO, *and others.*)

MONTANO: What is the matter? How now, General?
EMILIA: O, are you come, Iago? You have done well,
　That men must lay their murders on your neck. 170
GRATIANO: What is the matter?
EMILIA: Disprove this villain, if thou be'st a man.
　He says thou told'st him that his wife was false.

---

145 *chrysolite* topaz, a semiprecious stone.　　150 *iterance* repetition.　　151 *villainy hath . . . with love* some villain has bemocked your wife's love for you—by false evidence that she is unfaithful. Emilia cannot yet believe that this villain is Iago. See lines 172ff. [K].　　161 *you were best* it would be best for you.　　163 *to be hurt* to endure the utmost harm that you can do me [K].　　*gull* dupe.　　*dolt* stupid creature.　　165 *thy sword* Othello lays his hand on his sword. We are not to suppose that he actually draws it [K].

I know thou didst not; thou'rt not such a villain.
Speak, for my heart is full.
IAGO: I told him what I thought, and told no more
Than what he found himself was apt and true.
EMILIA: But did you ever tell him she was false?
IAGO: I did.
EMILIA: You told a lie, an odious damned lie!
Upon my soul, a lie! a wicked lie!
She false with Cassio? Did you say with Cassio?
IAGO: With Cassio, mistress. Go to, charm your tongue.
EMILIA: I will not charm my tongue; I am bound to speak:
My mistress here lies murdered in her bed—
ALL: O heavens forfend!
EMILIA: And your reports have set the murder on.
OTHELLO: Nay, stare not, masters. It is true indeed.
GRATIANO: 'Tis a strange truth.
MONTANO: O monstrous act!
EMILIA: Villainy, villainy, villainy!
I think upon't, I think! I smell't! O villainy!
I thought so then. I'll kill myself for grief.
O villainy, villainy!
IAGO: What, are you mad? I charge you get you home.
EMILIA: Good gentlemen, let me have leave to speak.
'Tis proper I obey him, but not now.
Perchance, Iago, I will ne'er go home.
OTHELLO: O! O! O!

(Falls on the bed.)

EMILIA: Nay, lay thee down and roar!
For thou hast kill'd the sweetest innocent
That e'er did lift up eye.
OTHELLO: O, she was foul!
(Rises.)
I scarce did know you, uncle. There lies your niece,
Whose breath, indeed, these hands have newly stopp'd.
I know this act shows horrible and grim.

---

177 *apt* plausible, likely.   183 *charm* silence (as though it were spellbound). 184 *bound* in duty bound.   192 *I thought so then* An obvious reference to Emilia's outburst in IV.ii.130ff. What she means is not that she thought that Iago was to blame, but merely that she had suspected "some villainy" as the cause of Othello's suspicion [K].   197 *Perchance . . . go home* "I will" should not be understood as "I shall." Emilia means that, if what she suspects is true, she may refuse to live with Iago as his wife. But her words are ominous [K].   201 *you, uncle* Gratiano, Brabantio's brother.   203 *shows* appears.

GRATIANO: Poor Desdemona! I am glad thy father's dead.
　Thy match was mortal to him, and pure grief
　Shore his old threat atwain. Did he live now,
　This sight would make him do a desperate turn;
　Yea, curse his better angel from his side,
　And fall to reprobance.
OTHELLO: 'Tis pitiful; but yet Iago knows
　That she with Cassio hath the act of shame
　A thousand times committed. Cassio confess'd it;
　And she did gratify his amorous works
　With that recognizance and pledge of love
　Which I first gave her. I saw it in his hand.
　It was a handkerchief, an antique token
　My father gave my mother.
EMILIA: O God! O heavenly pow'rs!
IAGO: Zounds, hold your peace!
EMILIA: 　　　　　　　　'Twill out, 'twill out! I peace?
　No, I will speak as liberal as the North.
　Let heaven and men and devils, let them all,
　All, all, cry shame against me, yet I'll speak.
IAGO: Be wise, and get you home.
EMILIA: 　　　　　　　I will not.

(IAGO *draws and threatens* EMILIA.)

GRATIANO: 　　　　　　　　Fie!
　Your sword upon a woman?
EMILIA: O thou dull Moor, that handkerchief thou speak'st of
　I found by fortune, and did give my husband;
　For often with a solemn earnestness
　(More than indeed belong'd to such a trifle)
　He begg'd of me to steal't.
IAGO: 　　　　　　　Villainous whore!
EMILIA: She give it Cassio? No, alas, I found it,
　And I did give't my husband.
IAGO: 　　　　　　　Filth, thou liest!
EMILIA: By heaven, I do not, I do not, gentlemen.
　O murd'rous coxcomb! what should such a fool
　Do with so good a wife?

---

206 *thread* of his life, cut by the Fate, Atrapos, with her shears.　207 *a desperate turn* some desperate act.　209 *reprobance* damnation of his soul (by driving away his "better angel") (F1; Q1: "reprobation" which has the same meaning and is preferred by some editors).　213 *gratify* reward.　214 *recognizance* token (literally, a legal term for a recorded obligation).　220 *liberal as the North* freely as the north wind blows.　233 *coxcomb* fool.　234 *stones* thunderbolts. Has heaven no spare bolt to smite down this villain? Is it keeping all its stones in store to discharge in thunderstorms? [K].

OTHELLO: Are there no stones in heaven
But what serves for the thunder? Precious villain!
(*The* MOOR *runs at* IAGO, *but is disarmed by* MONTANO.
IAGO *kills his wife.*)
GRATIANO: The woman falls. Sure he hath kill'd his wife.
EMILIA: Ay, ay. O, lay me by my mistress' side. (*Exit* IAGO.)
GRATIANO: He's gone, but his wife's kill'd.
MONTANO: 'Tis notorious villain. Take you this weapon,
Which I have here recover'd from the Moor.
Come, guard the door without. Let him not pass,
But kill him rather. I'll after that same villain,
For 'tis a damned slave.
(*Exeunt* MONTANO *and* GRATIANO *with others.*
Manent OTHELLO *and* EMILIA.)
OTHELLO: I am not valiant neither;
But every puny whipster gets my sword.
But why should honour outlive honesty?
Let it go all.
EMILIA: What did thy song bode, lady?
Hark, canst thou hear me? I will play the swan,
And die in music. [*Sings*] "Willow, willow, willow."
Moor, she was chaste; she lov'd thee, cruel Moor.
So come my soul to bliss as I speak true.
So speaking as I think, I die, I die.
(*She dies.*)
OTHELLO: I have another weapon in this chamber:
It is a sword of Spain, the ice-brook's temper.
O, here it is.—Uncle, I must come forth.
GRATIANO (*within*): If thou attempt it, it will cost thee dear.
Thou hast no weapon, and perforce must suffer.
OTHELLO: Look in upon me then and speak with me,
Or, naked as I am, I will assault thee.
(*Enter* GRATIANO.)
GRATIANO: What is the matter?
OTHELLO: Behold, I have a weapon.
A better never did itself sustain

239 *notorious* notable.   240 *recover'd* secured.   243 *I am not valiant neither* so my valour is gone—as well as my good conscience. I am a coward, it seems, as well as a murderer. [K].   244 *whipster* whippersnapper [K]. The exact meaning of the term is uncertain, although it is clear that it is contemptuous.   245 *honour outlive honesty* reputation, the external signs of honour, outlive true honourable behaviour.   247-8 *swan . . . music* The swan was reputed to sing just one song in its lifetime, and that one immediately before death.   253 *sword of Spain* Toledo and Bilbao in Spain were famous for the excellence of their swords.   *ice-brook's temper* tempered in ice-cold water, as the finest swords were treated.   256 *suffer* suffer reath.   258 *naked* unarmed.

Upon a soldier's thigh. I have seen the day
That with this little arm and this good sword
I have made my way through more impediments
Than twenty times your stop. But O vain boast! 265
Who can control his fate? 'Tis not so now.
Be not afraid, though you do see me weapon'd.
Here is my journey's end, here is my butt,
And very seamark of my utmost sail.
Do you go back dismay'd? 'Tis a lost fear. 270
Man but a rush against Othello's breast,
And he retires. Where should Othello go?
Now, how dost thou look now? O ill-starr'd wench!
Pale as thy smock! When we shall meet at compt,
This look of thine will hurl my soul from heaven,
And fiends will snatch at it. Cold, cold, my girl? 275
Even like thy chastity.—O cursed slave!
Whip me, ye devils,
From the possession of this heavenly sight!
Blow me about in winds! roast me in sulphur!
Wash me in steep-down gulfs of liquid fire! 280
O Desdemona, Desdemona! dead!
O! O! O!

(*Enter* LODOVICO, MONTANO, IAGO *as prisoner, and* OFFICE;
CASSIO *in a chair.*)

LODOVICO: Where is this rash and most unfortunate man?
OTHELLO: That's he that was Othello. Here I am.
LODOVICO: Where is that viper? Bring the villain forth. 285
OTHELLO: I look down towards his feet—but that's a fable.
    If that thou be'st a devil, I cannot kill thee.

(*Wounds* IAGO.)

LODOVICO: Wrench his sword from him,
    (OTHELLO *is disarmed.*)
IAGO: I bleed, sir, but not kill'd.
OTHELLO: I am not sorry neither. I'd have thee live;

---

264 *your stop* what you can stop.   267 *butt* in archery, hence the farthest limit of the arrow's flight.   268 *seamark* a beacon, or any other object by which a mariner checks his course.   *utmost sail* the farthest I can sail.   269 *lost fear* wasted fear—you have no reason to fear me [K].   270 *Man* wield or point.   *rush* bulrush, reed—the slightest possible weapon to be used as a spear.   273 *at compt* at the last judgment, when all accounts must be settled.   274 *look of thine . . . heaven* Othello now sees damnation as just punishment for his crime.   279-80 *Blow me . . . liquid fire* traditional pains of hell which appear often in medieval and Renaissance literature.   286 *I look . . . his feet* to see if they are cloven, like the feet of Satan [K].

For in my sense, 'tis happiness to die.
LODOVICO: O thou Othello that wert once so good,
  Fall'n in the practice of a damned slave,
  What shall be said to thee?
OTHELLO: Why, anything:
  An honourable murderer, if you will;
  For naught did I in hate, but all in honour.
LODOVICO: This wretch hath part confess'd his villainy.
  Did you and he consent in Cassio's death?
OTHELLO: Ay.
CASSIO: Dear General, I never gave you cause.
OTHELLO: I do believe it, and I ask your pardon.
  Will you, I pray, demand that demi-devil
  Why he hath thus ensnar'd my soul and body?
IAGO: Demand me nothing. What you know, you know.
  From this time forth I never will speak word.
LODOVICO: What, not to pray?
GRATIANO: Torments will ope your lips.
OTHELLO: Well, thou dost best.
LODOVICO: Sir, you shall understand what hath befall'n.
  Which, as I think, you know not. Here is a letter
  Found in the pocket of the slain Roderigo;
  And here another. The one of them imports
  The death of Cassio to be undertook
  By Roderigo.
OTHELLO: O villain
CASSIO: Most heathenish and most gross!
LODOVICO: Now here's another discontented paper
  Found in his pocket too; and this, it seems,
  Roderigo meant t' have sent this damned villain;
  But that, belike, Iago in the nick
  Came in and satisfied him.
OTHELLO: O thou pernicious caitiff!—
  How came you, Cassio, by that handkerchief
  That was my wife's?
CASSIO: I found it in my chamber;
  And he himself confess'd but even now
  That there he dropp'd it for a special purpose
  Which wrought to his desire.

---

290 *sense* opinion.   292 *in the practice* through the machinations.   297 *consent in* agree upon.   301 *demi-devil* not a devil (line 287), but a creature who is half-devil—human in shape, but a fiend in his nature[K].   305 *ope your lips* force you to confess. We may be sure that no torture will subdue Iago's resolution]K[.   306 *thou dost best* for thy crime is unspeakable [K].   313 *gross* flagrant, monstrous.   314 *discontented paper* letter expressing dissatisfaction.   317 *belike* probably.   *nick* nick of time (Q¹; F¹, K: "interim"). The F¹ word is a sophistication which, in fact, renders the line unmetrical.   318 *Came in* interposed. *caitiff* wretch.   323 *wrought to his desire* worked out in accordance with his wishes [K].

OTHELLO: O fool! fool! fool!
CASSIO: There is besides in Roderigo's letter,
   How he upbraids Iago that he made him 325
   Brave me upon the watch; whereon it came
   That I was cast; and even but now he spake,
   After long seeming dead—Iago hurt him,
   Iago set him on.
LODOVICO: You must forsake this room and go with us. 330
   Your power and your command is taken off,
   And Cassio rules in Cyprus. For this slave,
   If there be any cunning cruelty
   That can torment him much and hold him long,
   It shall be his. You shall close prisoner rest 335
   Till that the nature of your fault be known
   To the Venetian state. Come, bring away.
OTHELLO: Soft you! a word or two before you go.
   I have done the state some service, and they know't—
   No more of that. I pray you, in your letters, 340
   When you shall these unlucky deeds relate,
   Speak of me as I am. Nothing extenuate,
   Nor set down aught in malice. Then must you speak
   Of one that lov'd not wisely, but too well;
   Of one not easily jealous, but, being wrought, 345
   Perplex'd in the extreme; of one whose hand
   (Like the base Indian) threw a pearl away
   Richer than all his tribe; of one whose subdu'd eyes,
   Albeit unused to the melting mood,
   Drop tears as fast as the Arabian trees 350
   Their med'cinable gum. Set you down this;
   And say besides that in Aleppo once,

326 *Brave* insult. *whereon it came* because of which it happened. 327 *cast* dismissed. 328 *hurt* wounded. 333 *cunning cruelty* Shakespeare is true to Continental custom. According to Roman law torture was inflicted to extort confession. Such was also the rule in Scotland—not, however, in England, though the English often adopted the foreign custom in this regard [K]. 335 *rest* remain. 338 *Soft you* wait a moment. 342 *extenuate* diminish, tone down (not "excuse"). 345 *not easily jealous* not naturally prone to suspicion. Othello refers to his general temperament—not especially to the present case. Shakespeare certainly means us to believe him. His words accord with Iago's testimony (I.III.391-2) [K]. *wrought* worked upon. 347 *Indian* Q1; F1: "Iudean" [Judean]. This reading has been much disputed. Kittredge, who preferred Q1, pointed out that "the supposed ignorance of savages with regard to the value of precious stones had become proverbial." Those who prefer F1 hold that the reference is to Judas Iscariot the betrayer of Christ (thus supporting the Christ-symbolism of Desdemona) or to Herod who, in a fit of jealousy, rejected Miriamne. 348 *subdu'd* overcome by emotion. 349 *melting mood* weeping. 352 *Aleppo* city in Turkey where Venetians were allowed special trading privileges but where it was death for a Christian to strike a Turk. Othello thus risked his life for Venice.

Where a malignant and a turban'd Turk
Beat a Venetian and traduc'd the state
I took by th' throat the circumcised dog   355
And smote him—thus.

(He stabs himself.)

LODOVICO: O bloody period!
GRATIANO: All that's spoke is marr'd.
OTHELLO: I kiss'd thee ere I kill'd thee. No way but this—
Killing myself, to die upon a kiss.

(He falls upon the bed and dies.)

CASSIO: This did I fear, but thought he had no weapon;   360
For he was great of heart,
LODOVICO: O Spartan dog,
More fell than anguish, hunger, or the sea!
Look on the tragic loading of this bed.
This is thy work. The object poisons sight;
Let it be hid. Gratiano, keep the house,   365
And seize upon the fortunes of the Moor,
For they succeed on you. To you, Lord Governor.
Remains the censure of this hellish villain.
The time, the place, the torture—O, enforce it!
Myself will straight aboard, and to the state   370
This heavy act with heavy heart relate.   *(Exeunt omnes.)*

---

354 *traduc'd* insulted.   356 *thus* A stage direction indicating that at this point Othello stabs himself.   357 *period* conclusion.   *All that's . . . marr'd* Othello's fine speech has been spoiled by this bloody peroration.   361 *Spartan dog* The allusion seems to be both to the ferocity of the hounds of Sparta and to the traditional stony calmness of the Spartans themselves [K].   362 *fell* fierce, cruel. *anguish* physical pain.   363 *loading* F1; Q1: "lodging" is supported by some editors. 365 *Let it be hid* At this, no doubt, a curtain is drawn, shutting the bed from sight of the audience [K].   367 *succeed on* descend on.   *you* Gratiano, since he is Desdemona's uncle and Othello has no heirs.   368 *censure* judgement.   370 *straight* straightway.   371 *heavy* sorrowful.

LeRoi Jones

Dutchman

People in the play

CLAY, *a 20-year-old Negro*
LULA, *a 30-year-old white woman*
YOUNG NEGRO
CONDUCTOR
RIDERS OF COACH (*white and black*)

SCENE: *In the flying underbelly of the city. Steaming hot, and summer on top, outside. Underground. The subway heaped in modern myth.*

SCENE I

(Opening scene is a man sitting in a subway seat, holding a magazine, but looking vacantly just above its wilting pages. Occasionally he looks blankly toward the window on his right. Dim lights and darkness whistling by against the glass. (Or paste the lights, as admitted props, right on the subway windows. Have them move, even dim and flicker. But give the sense of speed. Also stations, whether the train is stopped or the glitter and activity of these stations merely flashes by the windows.)

The man is sitting alone. That is, only his seat is visible. Though the rest of the car is outfitted as a complete subway car. But only his seat is shown. There might be, for a time, as the play begins, a loud scream of the actual train. And it can recur wherever, throughout the play, or continue on a lower key once the diaglogue starts.

The train slows after a time, pulling to a brief stop at one of the stations. The man looks idly up, until he sees a woman's face staring at him through the window, which, when it realizes that the man has noticed it, begins very premeditatedly to smile. The man smiles too, for a moment, without a trace of self-consciousness. Almost an instinctive though undesirable response. Then a kind of awkwardness sets in, or embarrassment, and the man makes to look away, is further embarrassed, so he brings back his eyes to where the face was, but by now the train is moving again, and the face would seem to be left behind by the way the man turns his head to look back through the other windows at the slowly fading platform. He smiles then, more comfortably confident, hoping perhaps that his memory of this brief encounter will be pleasant. And then he is idle again.

Train roars. Lights flash outside the windows.

LULA enters from the rear of the car in bright, skimpy summer clothes and sandals. She carries a net bag full of paper books, fruit, and other anonymous articles. She is wearing sunglasses, which she pushes up on her forehead from time to time. LULA is a tall, slender, beautiful woman with long red hair hanging straight down her back, wearing only loud lipstick in somebody's good taste. She is eating an apple, very daintily. Coming down the car towards CLAY.

She stops beside CLAY's seat, and hangs languidly from the strap, still managing to eat the apple. It is apparent that she is going to sit in the seat next to CLAY, and that she is only waiting for him to notice her before she sits.

CLAY sits as before, looking just beyond his magazine, now and again pulling the magazine slowly back and forth in front of his face in a hopeless effort to fan himself. Then he sees the woman hanging there beside him, and he looks up into her face, smiling quizzically.)

LULA: Hello.
CLAY: Uh, hi're you?
LULA: I'm going to sit down—OK?
CLAY: Sure.
LULA (*swings down onto the seat, pushing her legs straight out as if she is very weary*): Oooof! Too much weight.
CLAY: Ha, doesn't look like much to me. (*Leaning back against the window, a little surprised and maybe stiff.*)
LULA: It's so anyway. (*And she moves her toes in the sandals, then pulls her right leg up on the left knee better to inspect the bottoms of the sandals and the back of her heel. She appears for a second not to notice that* CLAY *is sitting next to her, or that she has spoken to him just a second before.* CLAY *looks at the magazine, then out the black window. As he does this, she turns very quickly toward him.*) Weren't you staring at me through the window?
CLAY (*wheeling around and very much stiffened*): What?
LULA: Weren't you staring at through the window? At the last stop?
CLAY: Staring at you? What do you mean?
LULA: Don't you know what "staring" means?
CLAY: I saw you through the window—if that's what it means. I don't know if I was staring. Seems to me you were staring through the window at me.
LULA: I was. But only after I'd turned around and saw you staring through that window down in the vicinity of my ass and legs.

CLAY: Really?

LULA: Really. I guess you were just taking those idle potshots. Nothing else to do. Run your mind over people's flesh.

CLAY: Oh, boy. Wow, now I admit I was looking in your direction. But the rest of that weight is yours.

LULA: I suppose.

CLAY: Staring through train windows is weird business. Much weirder than staring very sedately at abstract asses.

LULA: That's why I came looking through the window—so you'd have more than that to go on. I even smiled at you.

CLAY: That's right.

LULA: I even got into this train, going some other way than mine. Walked down the aisle . . . searching you out.

CLAY: Really? That's pretty funny.

LULA: That's pretty funny—God, you're dull.

CLAY: Well, I'm sorry, lady, but I really wasn't prepared for party talk.

LULA: No, you're not. What are you prepared for? *(Wrapping the apple core in a kleenex and dropping it on the floor.)*

CLAY *(takes her conversation as pure sex talk. He turns to confront her squarely with this idea)*: I'm prepared for anything. How about you?

LULA *(laughing loudly and cutting it off abruptly)*: What do you think you're doing?

CLAY: What?

LULA: You think I want to pick you up, get you to take me somewhere and screw me, huh?

CLAY: Is that the way I look?

LULA: You look like you been trying to grow a beard. That's exactly what you look like. You look like you live in New Jersey with your parents and are trying to grow a beard. That's what. You look like you've been reading Chinese poetry and drinking lukewarm sugarless tea. *(Laughs, uncrossing and recrossing her legs.)* You look like death eating a soda cracker.

CLAY *(cocking his head from one side to the oher, embarrassed and trying to make some comeback, but also intrigued by what the woman is saying . . . even the sharp city coarseness of her voice, which is still a kind of gentle sidewalk throb)*: Really? I look like all that?

LULA: Not all of it. *(She feints a seriousness to cover an actual somber tone.)* I lie a lot. [*Smiling.*] It helps me control the world.

CLAY *(relieved and laughing louder than the humor)*: Yeh, I bet.

LULA: But it's true, most of it, right? Jersey? Your bumpy neck?

CLAY: How'd you know all that? Huh? Really, I mean about Jersey . . . and even the beard. I met you before? You know Warren Enright?

LULA: You tried to make it with your sister when you were ten. (CLAY *leans hard against the back of the seat, his eyes opening now still trying*

to look amused.) But I succeeded a few weeks ago. (*She starts to laugh again.*)
CLAY: What're you talking about? Warren tell you that? You're a friend of Georgia's?
LULA: I told you I lie. I don't know your sister. I don't know Warren Enright.
CLAY: You mean you're just picking these things out of the air?
LULA: Is Warren Enright a tall, skinny, black black boy with a phoney English accent?
CLAY: I figured you knew him.
LULA: But I don't. I just figured you would know somebody like that. (*Laughs.*)
CLAY: Yeah, yeah.
LULA: You're probably on your way to his house now.
CLAY: That's right.
LULA (*putting her hand on* CLAY's *closest knee, drawing it from the knee up to the thigh's hinge, then removing it, watching his face very closely, and continuing to laugh, perhaps more gently than before*): Dull, dull, dull. I bet you think I'm exciting.
CLAY: You're OK.
LULA: Am I exciting you now?
CLAY: Right. That's not what's supposed to happen?
LULA: How do I know? (*She returns her hand, without moving it, then takes it away and plunges it in her bag to draw out an apple.*) You want this?
CLAY: Sure.
LULA (*she gets one out of the bag for herself*): Eating apples together is always the first step. Or walking up uninhabited Seventh Avenue in the Twenties on weekends. (*Bites and giggles, glancing at* CLAY *and speaking in loose sing-song.*) Can get you involved . . . boy! Get us involved. Umhuh. (*Mock seriousness.*) Would you like to get involved with me, Mister Man?
CLAY (*trying to be as flippant as* LULA, *whacking happily at the apple*): Sure, Why not? A beautiful woman like you. Huh, I'd be a fool not to.
LULA: And I bet you're sure you know what you're talking about. (*Taking him a little roughly by the wrist, so he cannot eat the apple, then shaking the wrist.*) I bet you're sure of almost everything anybody ever asked you about—right? (*Shakes his wrist harder.*) Right?
CLAY: Yeh, right . . . wow, you're pretty strong, you know? Whatta you, a lady wrestler or something?
LULA: What's wrong with lady wrestlers? And don't answer because you never knew any. Huh. (*Cynically.*) That's for sure. They don't have any lady wrestlers in that part of Jersey. That's for sure.
CLAY: Hey, you still haven't told me how you know so much about me.

LULA: I told you I didn't know anything about *you* . . . you're a well-known type.
CLAY: Really?
LULA: Or at least I know the type very well. And your skinny English friend too.
CLAY: Anonymously?
LULA (*settles back in seat singlemindedly finishing her apple, and humming snatches of rhythm and blues song*): What?
CLAY: Without knowing us specifically?
LULA: Oh, boy. (*Looking quickly at* CLAY). What a face. You know you could be a handsome man.
CLAY: I can't argue with you.
LULA (*vague, off-center response*): What?
CLAY (*raising his voice, thinking the train noise has drowned part of his sentence*): I can't argue with you.
LULA: My hair is turning gray. A gray hair for each year and type I've come through.
CLAY: Why do you want to sound so old?
LULA: But it's always gentle when it starts. (*Attention drifting.*) Hugged against tenements, day or night.
CLAY: What?
LULA (*refocussing*): Hey, why don't you take me to that party you're going to?
CLAY: You must be a friend of Warren's to know about the party.
LULA: Wouldn't you like to take me to the party? (*Imitates clinging vine.*) Oh, come on, ask me to your party.
CLAY: Of course, I'll ask you to come with me to the party. And I'll bet you're a friend of Warren's.
LULA: Why not be a friend of Warren's? Why not? (*Taking his arm.*) Have you asked me yet?
CLAY: How can I ask you when I don't know your name?
LULA: Are you talking to my name?
CLAY: What is it, a secret?
LULA: I'm Lena the Hyena.
CLAY: The famous woman poet?
LULA: Poetess! The same!
CLAY: Well, you know so much about me . . . what's my name?
LULA: Morris the Hyena.
CLAY: The famous woman poet?
LULA: The same. (*Laughing and going into her bag.*) You want another apple?
CLAY: Can't make it, lady. I only have to keep one doctor away a day.
LULA: I bet your name is . . . something like . . . uh, Gerald or Walter. Huh?

CLAY: God, no.
LULA: Lloyd, Norman? One of those hopeless colored names creeping out of New Jersey. Leonard? Gag . . .
CLAY: Like Warren?
LULA: Definitely. Just exactly like Warren. Or Everett.
CLAY: Gag . . .
LULA: Well, for sure, it's not Willie.
CLAY: It's Clay.
LULA: Clay? Really? Clay what?
CLAY: Take your pick. Jackson, Johnson, or Williams.
LULA: Oh, really? Good for you. But it's got to be Williams. You're too pretentious to be a Jackson or Johnson.
CLAY: Thassright.
LULA: But Clay's OK.
CLAY: So's Lena.
LULA: It's Lula.
CLAY: Oh?
LULA: Lula the hyena.
CLAY: Very good.
LULA (*starts laughing again*): Now you say to me,"Lula, Lula, why don't you go to this party with me tonight?" It's your turn, and let those be your lines.
CLAY: Lula, why don't you go to this party with me tonight? Huh?
LULA: Say my name twice before you ask, and no huh's.
CLAY: Lula, Lula, why don't you go to this party with me tonight?
LULA: I'd like to go, Clay, but how can you ask me to go when you barely know me?
CLAY: That is strange, isn't it?
LULA: What kind of reaction is that? You're supposed to say "Aw, come on, we'll get to know each other better at the party."
CLAY: That's pretty corny.
LULA: What are you into anyway? (*Looking at him half-sullenly but still amused.*) What thing are you playing at, Mister? Mister Clay Williams? (*Grabs his thigh, up near the crotch.*) What are *you* thinking about?
CLAY: Watch it now, you're gonna excite me for real.
LULA (*taking her hand away, and throwing her apple core through the window*): I bet. (*She slumps in the seat and is heavily silent.*)
CLAY: I thought you knew everything about me? What happened? (LULA *look at him, then looks slowly away, then over where the other aisle would be. Noise of the train. She reaches in her bag and pulls out one of the paper books. She puts it on her leg and thumbs the pages listlessly.* CLAY *cocks his head to see the title of the book. Noise of the train.* LULA *flips pages and her eyes drift. Both remain silent.*) Are you going to the party with me, Lula?

LULA (*bored and not even looking*): I don't even know you.

CLAY: You said you know my type.

LULA (*strangely irritated*): Don't get smart with me, Buster. I know you like the palm of my hand.

CLAY: The one you eat the apples with?

LULA: Yeh. And the one I open doors late Saturday evening with. That's my door. Up at the top of the stairs. Five flights. Above a lot of Italians, and lying Americans. And scrape carrots with. Also . . . (*Looks at him.*) the same hand I unbutton my dress with, or let my skirt fall down. Same hand. Lover.

CLAY: Are you angry about something? Did I say something wrong?

LULA: Everything you say is wrong. (*Mock smile.*) That's what makes you so attractive. Ha. In that funnybook jacket with all the buttons. (*More animate, taking hold of his jacket.*) What've you got that jacket and tie on in all this heat for? And why're you wearing a jacket and tie like that? Did your people ever burn witches or start revolutions over the price of tea? Boy, those narrow shoulder clothes come from a tradition you ought to feel oppressed by. A three-button suit. What right do you have to be wearing a three-button suit and striped tie? Your grandfather was a slave, he didn't go to Harvard.

CLAY: My grandfather was a night watchman.

LULA: And you went to a colored college where everybody thought they were Averell Harriman.

CLAY: All except me.

LULA: And who did you think you were? Who do you think you are now?

CLAY (*laughs as if to make light of the whole trend of the conversation*): Well, in college I thought I was Baudelaire. But I've slowed down since.

LULA: I bet you never once thought you were a black nigger. (*Mock serious, then she howls with laughter.* CLAY *is stunned but after initial reaction, he quickly tries to appreciate the humor.* LULA *almost shrieks.*) A black Baudelaire.

CLAY: That's right.

LULA: Boy, are you corny. I take back what I said before. Everything you say is not wrong. It's perfect. You should be on television.

CLAY: You act like you're on television already.

LULA: That's because I'm an actress.

CLAY: I thought so.

LULA: Well, you're wrong. I'm no actress. I told you I always lie. I'm nothing, honey, and don't you ever forget it. (*Lighter.*) Although my mother was a Communist. The only person in my family ever to amount to anything.

CLAY: My mother was a Republican.

LULA: And your father voted for the man rather than the party.
CLAY: Right!
LULA: Yea for him. Yea, yea for him.
CLAY: Yea!
LULA: And yea for America where he is free to vote for the mediocrity of his choice! Yea!
CLAY: Yea!
LULA: And yea for both your parents who, even though they differ about so crucial a matter as the body politics, still forged a union of love and sacrifice that was destined to flower at the birth of the noble Clay— what's your middle name?
CLAY: Clay.
LULA: A union of love and sacrifice that was destined to flower at the birth of the noble Clay Clay Williams. Yea! And most of all yea yea for you, Clay Clay. The Black Baudelaire! Yes! *(And with knifelike cynicism.)* My Christ. My Christ.
CLAY: Thank you, ma'm.
LULA: May the people accept you as a ghost of the future. And love you, that you might not kill them when you can.
CLAY: What?
LULA: You're a murderer, Clay, and you know it. *(Her voice darkening with significance.)* You know goddam well what I mean.
CLAY: I do?
LULA: So we'll pretend the air is light and full of perfume.
CLAY *(sniffing at her blouse)*: It is.
LULA: And we'll pretend the people cannot see you. That is, the citizens. And that you are free of your own history. And I am free of my history. We'll pretend that we are both anonymous beauties smashing along through the city's entrails. *(She yells as loud as she can.)* GROOVE!

Blackout

SCENE II

(Scene is the same as before, though now there are other seats visible in the car. And throughout the scene other people get on the subway. There are maybe one or two seated in the car as the scene opens, though neither CLAY nor LULA notices them. CLAY's tie is open. LULA is hugging his arm.)

CLAY: The party!
LULA: I know it'll be something good. You can come in with me, looking

casual and significant. I'll be strange, haughty and silent, and walk with long slow strides.

CLAY: Right.

LULA: When you get drunk, pat me once, very lovingly, on the flanks, and I'll look at you cryptically, licking my lips.

CLAY: It sounds like something we can do.

LULA: You'll go around talking to young men about your mind, and to old men about your plans. If you meet a very close friend who is also with someone like me, we can stand together, sipping our drinks and exchanging codes of lust. The atmosphere will be slithering in love and half-love and very open moral decision.

CLAY: Great. Great.

LULA: And everyone will pretend they don't know your name, and then ... (*She pauses heavily.*) later, when they have to, they'll claim a friendship that denies your sterling character.

CLAY (*kissing her neck and fingers*): And then what?

LUDA: Then? Well then we'll go down the street, late night, eating apples and winding very deliberately toward my house.

CLAY: Deliberately?

LULA: I mean, we'll look in all the shop windows, and make fun of the queers. Maybe we'll meet a Jewish Buddhist and flatten his conceits over some very pretentious coffee.

CLAY: In honor of whose God?

LULA: Mine.

CLAY: Who is . . . ?

LULA: Me . . . and you?

CLAY: A corporate godhead.

LULA: Exactly. Exactly. (*Notices one of the other people entering.*)

CLAY: Go on with the chronicle. Then what happens to us?

LULA (*a mild depression, but she still makes her description triumphant and increasingly direct*): To my house, of course.

CLAY: Of course.

LULA: And up the narrow steps of the tenement.

CLAY: You live in a tenement?

LULA: Wouldn't live anywhere else. Reminds me specifically of my novel form of insanity.

CLAY: Up the tenement stairs.

LULA: And with my apple-eating hand I push open the door, and lead you, my tender big-eyed prey, into my—God, what can I call it—into my hovel.

CLAY: The what happens?

LULA: After the dancing and games, after the long drinks and long walks, the real fun begins.

CLAY: Ah, the real fun. (*Embarrassed, in spite of himself.*) Which is . . . ?
LULA (*laughs at him*): Real fun in the dark house. Hah! Real fun in the dark house, high up above the street and the ignorant cowboys. I lead you in, holding your wet hand gently in my hand. . . .
CLAY: Which is not wet?
LULA: Which is dry as ashes.
CLAY: And cold?
LULA: Don't think you'll get out of your responsibility that way. It's not cold at all. You Fascist! Into my dark living room. Where we'll sit and talk endlessly, endlessly.
CLAY: About what?
LULA: About what? About your manhood, what do you think? What do you think we've been talking about all this time?
CLAY: Well, I didn't know it was that. That's for sure. Every other thing in the world but that. (*Notices another person entering, looks quickly, almost involuntarily up and down the car, seeing the other people in the car.*) Hey, I didn't even notice when those people got on.
LULA: Yeh, I know.
CLAY: Man, this subway is slow.
LULA: Yeh, I know.
CLAY: Well, go on. We were talking about my manhood.
LULA: We still are. All the time.
CLAY: We were in your living room.
LULA: My dark living room. Talking endlessly.
CLAY: About my manhood.
LULA: I'll make you a map of it. Just as soon as we get to my house.
CLAY: Well, that's great.
LULA: One of the things we do while we talk. And screw.
CLAY (*trying to make his smile broader and less shaky*): We finally got there.
LULA: And you'll call my rooms black as a grave. You'll say, "This place is like Juliet's tomb."
CLAY (*laughs*): I might.
LULA: I know. You've probably said it before.
CLAY: And is that all? The whole grand tour?
LULA: Not all. You'll say to me very close to my face, many, many times, you'll say, even whisper, that you love me.
CLAY: Maybe I will.
LULA: And you'll be lying.
CLAY: I wouldn't lie about something like that.
LULA: Hah. It's the only kind of thing you will lie about. Especially if you think it'll keep me alive.
CLAY: Keep you alive? I don't understand.

LULA (*bursting out laughing, but too shrilly*): Don't understand? Well, don't look at me. It's the path I take, that's all. Where both feet take me when I set them down. One in front of the other.

CLAY: Morbid. Morbid. You sure you're not an actress? All that self-aggrandizement.

LULA: Well, I told you I wasn't an actress . . . but I also told you I lie all the time. Draw your own conclusions.

CLAY: I will. And is this all of our life together you've described? There's no more?

LULA: I've told you all I know. Or almost all.

CLAY: There're no funny parts?

LULA: I thought it was all funny.

CLAY: But you mean peculiar, not hah, hah.

LULA: You don't know what I mean.

CLAY: Well, tell me the almost part then. You said almost all. What else? I want the whole story.

LULA (*searching aimlessly through her bag. She begins to talk breathlessly, with a light and silly tone*): All stories are whole stories. All of 'em. Our whole story . . . nothing but change. How could things go on like that forever? Huh? (*Slaps him on the shoulder, begins finding things in her bag, taking them out and throwing them over her shoulder into the aisle.*) Except, I do go on as I do. Apples and long walks with deathless, intelligent lovers. But you mix it up. Look out the window, all the time. Turning pages. Change change change. Till, shit, I don't know you. Wouldn't, for that matter. You're too serious. I bet you're even too serious to be psychoanalyzed. Like all those Jewish poets from Yonkers, who leave their mothers looking for other mothers, or others' mothers, on whose baggy tits they lay their fumbling heads. Their poems are always funny, and all about sex.

CLAY: They sound great. Like movies.

LULA: But you change. (*Blankly.*) And things work on you till you hate them.

(*More people come into the train. They come closer to the couple, some of them not sitting, but swinging drearily on the straps, staring at the two with uncertain interest.*)

CLAY: Wow. All these people, so suddenly. They must all come from the same place.

LULA: Right. That they do.

CLAY: Oh? You know about them, too?

LULA: Oh, yeh. About them more than I know about you. Do they frighten you?

CLAY: Frighten me? Why should they frighten me?

LULA: Cause you're an escaped nigger.

CLAY: Yeh?
LULA: Cause you crawled through the wire, and made tracks to my side.
CLAY: Wire?
LULA: Don't they have wire around plantations?
CLAY: You must be Jewish. All you can think about is wire. Plantations didn't have any wire. Plantations were big, open, whitewashed places like heaven, and everybody on 'em was grooved to be there. Just strumming and hummin' all day.
LULA: Yes, yes.
CLAY: And that's how the blues was born.
LULA: Yes, yes. And that's how the blues was born. (*Begins to make up a song that becomes quickly hysterical. As she sings she rises from her seat still throwing things out of her bag into the aisle, beginning a rhythmical shudder and twist-like wiggle, which she continues up and down the aisle, bumping into many of the standing people and tripping over the feet of those sitting. Each time she runs into a person, she lets out a very vicious piece of profanity, wiggling and stepping all the time.*) And that's how the blues was born. Yes. Yes. Son of a bitch, get out of the way. Yes. Quack. Yes. Yea. And that's how the blues was born. Ten little niggers sitting on a limb, but none of them ever looked like him. (*Points to* CLAY, *returns toward the seat, with her hands extended for him to rise and dance with her.*) And that's how blues was born. Yes. Come on, Clay. Let's do the Nasty. Rub bellies. Rub bellies.
CLAY (*waves his hands to refuse. He is embarrassed, but determined to get a kick out of the proceedings*) : Hey, what was in those apples? Mirror, mirror on the wall, who's the fairest one of all? Snow White, baby and don't you forget it.
LULA (*grabbing for his hands, which he draws away*): Come on, Clay. Let's rub bellies on the train. The Nasty. The Nasty. Do the gritty grind, like our ol' rag-head mammy. Grind till you lose your mind. Shake it, shake it, shake it, shake it! OOOOweeee! Come on, Clay. Let's do the choo choo train shuffle, the navel scratcher.
CLAY: Hey, you coming on like the lady who smoked up her grass skirt.
LULA (*becoming annoyed that he will not dance, and becoming more animated as if to embarrass him still further*): Come on, Clay . . . let's do the thing. Uhh! Uhh! Clay! Clay! You middle-class black bastard. Forget your social-working mother for a few seconds and let's knock stomachs. Clay, you liver-lipped white man. You would-be Christian. You ain't no nigger, you're just a dirty white man. Get up, Clay. Dance with me, Clay.
CLAY: Lula! Sit down, now. Be cool.
LULA (*mocking him, in wild dance*): "Be cool. Be cool." That's all you

know . . . shaking that wildroot creme oil on your knotty head, jackets buttoning up to your chin, so full of white man's words. Christ. God. Get up and scream at these people. A dada man. Like scream meaningless shit in these hopeless faces. (*She screams at people in train, still dancing.*) Red trains cough Jewish underwear for keeps! Expanding smells of silence. Gravy snot whistling like sea birds. Clay. Clay, you got to break out. Don't sit there dying the way they want you to die. Get up.

CLAY: Oh, sit down. (*He moves to restrain her.*) Sit down, goddamn it.

LULA (*twisting out of his reach*): Screw yourself, Uncle Tom. Thomas Wooly-Head. (*Begins to dance a kind of jig, mocking* CLAY *with loud forced humor.*) There is Uncle Tom . . . I mean, Uncle Thomas Wooly-Head. With old white matted mane. He hobbles on his wooden cane. Old Tom. Old Tom. Let the white man hump his ol' mama, and he jes' shuffle off in the woods and hide his gentle gray head. Ol' Thomas Wooly-Head.

(*Some of the other riders are laughing now. A drunk gets up and joins* LULA *in her dance, singing as best he can, her "song."* CLAY *gets up out of his seat, and visibly scans the faces of the other riders.*)

CLAY: Lula! Lula! (*She is dancing and turning, still shouting as loud as she can. The drunk too is shouting, and waving his hands wildly.*) Lula . . . you dumb bitch. Why don't you stop it? (*He rushes half stumbling from his seat, and grabs one of her flailing arms.*)

LULA: Let me go! You black son-of-a-bitch. (*She struggles against him.*) Let me go! Help!

(CLAY *is dragging her towards her seat, and the drunk seeks to interfere. He grabs* CLAY *around the shoulders and begins wrestling with him.* CLAY *clubs the drunk to the floor without releasing* LULA, *who is still screaming.* CLAY *finally gets her to the seat and throws her into it.*)

CLAY: Now, you shut the hell up. (*Grabbing her shoulders.*) Just shut up. You don't know what you're talking about. You don't know anything. So just keep your stupid mouth closed.

LULA: You're afraid of white people. And your father was. Uncle Tom Big Lip!

CLAY (*slaps her has hard as he can, across the mouth.* LULA's *head bangs against the back of the seat. When she raises it again,* CLAY *slaps her again*): Now, you shut up and let me talk. (*He turns toward the other riders, some of whom are sitting on the edge of their seats. The drunk is on one knee, rubbing his head, and singing softly the same song. He shuts up, too, when he sees* CLAY *watching him. The others go back to newspapers, or stare out the windows.*) Shit, you don't have any sense, Lula, nor feelings either. I could murder you now. Such a tiny ugly throat. I could squeeze it flat, and watch you turn blue, on a humble.

For dull kicks. And all these weak-faced ofays squatting around here, staring over their papers at me. Murder them too. Even if they expected it. That man there . . . (*Points to a well-dressed man.*) I could rip that *Times* right out of his hand, as skinny, and middle-classed as I am, I could rip that paper out his hand and just as easily rip out his throat. It takes no great effort. For what? To kill you soft idiots? You don't understand anything but luxury.

LULA: You fool!

CLAY (*pushing her against the seat*): I'm not telling you again Tallulah Bankhead! Luxury. In your face and your fingers. You telling me what I ought to do. (*Sudden scream frightening the whole coach.*) Well, don't! Don't you tell me anything! If I'm a middle-class fake white man . . . let me be. And let me be in the way I want. (*Through his teeth.*) I'll rip your lousy breasts off! Let me be who I feel like being. Uncle Tom. Thomas. Whoever. It's none of your business. You don't know anything except what's there for you to see. An act. Lies. Device. Not the pure heart, the pumping black heart. You don't ever know that. And I sit here, in this buttoned-up suit to keep myself from cutting all your throats. I mean wantonly. You great liberated whore! You fuck some black man, and right away you're an expert on black people. What a lotta shit that is. The only thing you know is that you come if he bangs you hard enough. And that's all. The belly rub? You wanted to do the belly rub? Shit, you don't even know how. You don't know how. That ol' dipty-dip shit you do, rolling your ass like an elephant. That's not my kind of belly rub. Belly rub is not Queens. Belly rub is dark places, with big hats and overcoats held up with one arm. Belly rub hates you. Old baldheaded four-eyed ofays popping their fingers . . . and don't know yet what they're doing. They say, "I love Bessie Smith." And don't even understand that Bessie Smith is saying, "Kiss my ass, kiss my black unruly ass." Before love, suffering, desire, anything you can explain, she's saying, and very plainly, "Kiss my black ass." And if you don't know that, it's you that's doing the kissing.

Charlie Parker? Charlie Parker. All the hip white boys scream for Bird. And Bird saying, "Up your ass, feebleminded ofay! Up your ass." And they sit there talking about the tortured genius of Charlie Parker. Bird would've played not a note of music if he just walked up to East Sixty-seventh Street and killed the first ten white people he saw. Not a note! And I'm the great would-be poet. Yes. That's right! Poet. Some kind of bastard literature . . . all it needs is a simple knife thrust. Just let me bleed you, you loud whore, and one poem vanished. A whole people of neurotics, struggling to keep from being sane. And the only thing that would cure neurosis would be your murder. Simple as that. I mean, if I murdered you, then other white people would begin to understand me. You understand? No. I guess not. If Bessie Smith had killed some white people, she wouldn't have needed that music. She could have talked very straight and plain about the world. No metaphors. No grunts. No wiggles in the dark of her soul. Just straight two and two are four. Money. Power. Luxury. Like that. All of them. Crazy niggers turning their backs on sanity. When all it needs is that simple act. Murder. Just murder! Would make us all sane. (*Suddenly weary.*) Ahhh. Shit But who needs it? I'd rather be a fool. Insane. Safe with my words, and no deaths, and clean, hard thoughts, urging me to new conquests. My people's madness. Hah! That's a laugh. My people. They don't need me to claim them. They got legs and arms of their own. Personal insanities. Mirrors. They don't need all these words. They don't need any defense. But listen, though, one more thing. And you tell this to your father, who's probably the kind of man who needs to know at once. So he can plan ahead. Tell him not to preach so much rationalism and cold logic to these niggers. Let them alone. Let them sing curses at you in code and see your filth as simple lack of style. Don't make the mistake through some irresponsible surge of Christian charity, of talking too much about the advantages of Western rationalism, or the great intellectual legacy of the white man, or maybe they'll begin to listen. And then, maybe one day, you'll find they actually do understand exactly what you are talking about, all these fantasy people. All these blues people. And on that day, as sure as shit, when you really believe you can "accept" them into your fold, as half-white trusties late of the subject peoples, with no more blues, except the very old ones, and not a watermelon in sight, the great missionary heart will have triumphed, and all of those ex-coons will be stand-up Western men, with eyes for clean, hard, useful lives, sober, pious and sane, and they'll murder you. They'll murder you, and have very rational explanations. Very much like your own. They'll cut your throats, and drag you out to the edge of your cities so the flesh can fall away from your bones in sanitary isolation.

LULA (*her voice takes on a different, more businesslike quality*): I've heard enough.

CLAY (*reaching for his books*): I bet you have. I guess I better collect my stuff and get off this train. Looks like we won't be acting out that little pageant you outlined before.

LULA: No. We won't. You're right about that, at least. (*She turns to look quickly around the rest of the car.*) All right!
(*The others respond.*)

CLAY (*bending across the girl to retrieve his belongings*): Sorry, baby, I don't think we could make it.

(As he is bending over her, the girl brings up a small knife and plunges it into CLAY's *chest. Twice. He slumps across her knees, his mouth working stupidly.)*

LULA: Sorry is right. *(Turning to the others in the car who have already gotten up from their seats.)* Sorry is the rightest thing you've said. Get this man off me! Hurry now! *(The others come and drag* CLAY's *body down the aisle.)* Throw his body off between the cars—and the rest of you get off at the next stop.

(LULA *busies herself straightening her things. Getting everything in order, she takes out a notebook and makes quick scribbling notes. Drops notebook into her bag. The train apparently stops and the others get off, leaving her alone in the coach.*

Very soon a young Negro of about 20 comes in to the coach with a couple of books under his arm. He sits a few seats in back of LULA. *She starts to move out of the car, sees the young man, changes her mind, and sits somewhat nearer to him. When she is seated she turns and gives him a long slow look. She smiles. He becomes aware of her staring and looks up from his book. He drops the book to his lap as they continue to stare at one another. She turns away, satisfied that he is intrigued, takes an apple from her bag. She bites into it, smiling, as the lights and sound slowly fade.)*

Curtain

Robert Lowell
Benito Cereno

Characters

    CAPTAIN AMASA DELANO
    JOHN PERKINS
    DON BENITO CERENO
    BABU
    ATUFAL
    FRANCESCO
    AMERICAN SAILORS
    SPANISH SAILORS
    NEGRO SLAVES

    THE SCENE: *About the year 1800, an American sealing vessel, the* President Adams, *at anchor in an island harbor off the coast of Trinidad. The stage is part of the ship's deck. Everything is unnaturally clean, bare and ship-shape. To one side, a polished, coal-black cannon. The American captain,* AMASA DELANO *from Duxbury, Massachusetts, sits in a cane chair. He is a strong, comfortable looking man in his early thirties who wears a spotless blue coat and white trousers. Incongruously, he has on a straw hat and smokes a corncob pipe. Beside him stands* JOHN PERKINS, *his bosun, a very stiff green young man, a relative of* DELANO'S. THREE SAILORS, *one carrying an American flag, enter.* EVERYONE *stands at attention and salutes with machinelike exactitude. Then the* THREE SAILORS *march off-stage.* DELANO *and* PERKINS *are alone.*)

DELANO: There goes the most beautiful woman in South America.
PERKINS: We never see any women, Sir;
    just this smothering, overcast Equator,
    a seal or two,
    the flat dull sea,
    and a sky like a gray wasp's nest.
DELANO: I wasn't talking about women,
    I was calling your attention to the American flag.
PERKINS: Yes, Sir! I wish we were home in Duxbury.

DELANO: We are home. America is wherever her flag flies.
My own deck is the only place in the world
where I feel at home.
PERKINS: That's too much for me, Captain Delano.
I mean I wish I were at home with my wife;
these world cruises are only for bachelors.
DELANO: Your wife will keep. You should smoke, Perkins.
Smoking turns men into philosophers
and swabs away their worries.
I can see my wife and children or not see them
in each puff of blue smoke.
PERKINS: You are always tempting me, Sir!
I try to keep fit,
I want to return to my wife as fit as I left her.
DELANO: You're much too nervous, Perkins.
Travel will shake you up. You should let
a little foreign dirt rub off on you.
I've taught myself to speak Spanish like a Spaniard.
At each South American port, they mistake me for a
Castilian Don.
PERKINS: Aren't you lowering yourself a little, Captain?
Excuse me, Sir, I have been wanting to ask you a question
Don't you think our President, Mr. Jefferson, is lowering himself
by being so close to the French?
I'd feel a lot safer in this unprotected place
if we'd elected Mr. Adams instead of Mr. Jefferson.
DELANO: The better man ran second!
Come to think of it, he rather let us down
by losing the election just after we had named this ship
the *President Adams*. Adams is a nervous dry fellow.
When you're travelled as much as I have,
you'll learn that that sort doesn't export, Perkins.
Adams didn't get a vote outside New England!
PERKINS: He carried every New England state;
that was better than winning the election.
I'm afraid I'm a dry fellow, too, Sir.
DELANO: Not when I've educated you!
When I am through with you, Perkins,
you'll be as worldly as the Prince Regent of England,
only you'll be a first class American officer.
I'm all for Jefferson, he has the popular touch.
Of course he's read too many books,
but I've always said an idea or two won't sink our Republic.

I'll tell you this, Perkins,
Mr. Jefferson is a gentleman and an American.
PERKINS: They say he has two illegitimate Negro children.
DELANO: The more the better! That's the quickest way
to raise the blacks to our level.
I'm surprised you swallow such Federalist bilge, Perkins!
I told you Mr. Jefferson is a gentleman and an American;
when a man's in office, Sir, we all pull behind him!
PERKINS: Thank God our Revolution ended where the French one began.
DELANO: Oh the French! They're like the rest of the Latins,
they're hardly white people,
they start with a paper republic
and end with a toy soldier, like Bonaparte.
PERKINS: Yes, Sir. I see a strange sail making for the harbor.
They don't know how to sail her.
DELANO: Hand me my telescope.
PERKINS: Aye, aye, Sir!
DELANO: *(with telescope)*:
I see an ocean undulating in long scoops of swells;
it's set like the beheaded French Queen's high wig;
the sleek surface is like waved lead,
cooled and pressed in the smelter's mould.
I see flights of hurried gray fowl,
patches of fluffy fog.
They skim low and fitfully above the decks,
like swallows sabering flies before a storm.
This gray boat foreshadows something wrong.
PERKINS: It does, Sir!
They don't know how to sail her!
DELANO: I see a sulphurous haze above her cabin,
the new sun hangs like a silver dollar to her stern;
low creeping clouds blow on from them to us.
PERKINS: What else, Sir?
DELANO: The yards are woolly
the ship is furred with fog.
On the cracked and rotten head-boards,
the tarnished, gilded letters say, the *San Domingo*.
A rat's nest messing up the deck,
black faces in white sheets are fussing with the ropes.
I think it's a cargo of Dominican monks.
PERKINS: Dominican monks, Sir! God help us,
I thought they were outlawed in the new world.
DELANO: No, it's nothing. I see they're only slaves.

The boat's transporting slaves.
PERKINS: Do you believe in slavery, Captain Delano?
DELANO: In a civilized country, Perkins,
  everyone disbelieves in slavery,
  everyone disbelieves in slavery and wants slaves.
  We have the perfect uneasy answer;
  in the North, we don't have them and want them;
  Mr. Jefferson has them and fears them.
PERKINS: Is that how you answer, Sir,
  when a little foreign dirt has rubbed off on you?
DELANO: Don't ask me such intense questions.
  You should take up smoking, Perkins.
  There was a beautiful, dumb English actress—
  I saw her myself once in London.
  They wanted her to look profound,
  so she read Plato and the Bible and Benjamin Franklin,
  and thought about them every minute.
  She still looked like a moron
  Then they told her to think about nothing.
  She thought about nothing, and looked like Socrates.
  That's smoking, Perkins, you think about nothing and look deep.
PERKINS: I don't believe in slavery, Sir.
DELANO: You don't believe in slavery or Spaniards
  or smoking or long cruises or monks or Mr. Jefferson!
  You are a Puritan, all faith and fire.
PERKINS: Yes, Sir.
DELANO: God save America from Americans!

(Take up the telescope)

  I see octogonal network bagging out
  from her heavy top like decayed beehives.
  The battered forecastle looks like a raped Versailles.
  On the stern-piece, I see the fading arms of Spain.
  There's a masked satyr, or something
  with its foot on a big white goddess.
  She has quite a figure.
PERKINS: They oughtn't to be allowed on the ocean!
DELANO: Who oughtn't? Goddesses?
PERKINS: I mean Spaniards, who cannot handle a ship,
  and mess up its hull with immoral statues.
DELANO: You're out of step. You're much too dry.
  Bring me my three-cornered hat.
  Order some men to clear a whaleboat.

I am going to bring water and fresh fish to the *San Domingo*.
These people have had some misfortune, Perkins!
PERKINS: Aye, aye, Sir.
DELANO: Spaniards? The name gets you down,
you think their sultry faces and language
make them Zulus.
You take the name *Delano*—
I've always thought it had some saving
Italian or Spanish virtue in it.
PERKINS: Yes, Sir.
DELANO: A Spaniard isn't a negro under the skin,
particularly a Spaniard from Spain—
these South American ones mix too much with the Indians.
Once you get inside a Spaniard,
he talks about as well as your wife in Duxbury.
PERKINS (*shouting*): A boat for the captain! A whaleboat for
Captain Delano!

(*A bosun's whistle is heard, the lights dim. When they come up, we are on the deck of San Domingo, the same set, identical except for litter and disorder.* THREE AMERICAN SAILORS *climb on board. They are followed by* PERKINS *and* DELANO, *now wearing a three-cornered hat. Once on board, the* AMERICAN SAILORS *salute* DELANO *and stand stiffly at attention like toys.* NEGROES *from the* San Domingo *drift silently and furtively forward)*

DELANO: I see at wen of barnacles hanging to the waterline of this ship.
It sticks out like the belly of a pregnant woman.
Have a look at our dory Bosun.
PERKINS: Aye, aye, Sir!

(*By now, about twenty blacks and two Spanish sailors have drifted in. They look like some gaudy, shabby, unnautical charade, ,and pay no attention to the Americans, until an unseen figure in the rigging calls out a single sharp warning in an unknown tongue. Then they all rush forward, shouting, waving their arms and making inarticulate cries like birds. Three shrill warnings come from the rigging. Dead silence. The men from the* SAN DOMINGO *press back in a dense semicircle. One by one, individuals come forward, make showy bows to* DELANO, *and speak)*

FIRST NEGRO: Scurvy, Master Yankee!
SECOND NEGRO: Yellow fever, Master Yankee!
THIRD NEGRO: Two men knocked overboard rounding Cape Horn,,
Master Yankee!
FOURTH NEGRO: Nothing to eat, Master Yankee!
NEGRO WOMAN: Nothing to drink, Master Yankee!

SECOND NEGRO WOMAN: Our mouths are dead wood, Master Yankee!
DELANO: You see, Perkins,
these people have had some misfortune.

(General hubbub, muttering, shouts, gestures, ritual and dumbshow of distress. The rigging, hitherto dark, lightens, as the sun comes out of a cloud, and shows THREE OLD NEGROES, *identical down to their shabby patches. They perch on cat's-heads; their heads are grizzled like dying willow tops; each is picking bits of unstranded rope for oakum. It is they who have been giving the warnings that control the people below. Everyone,* DELANO *along with the rest, looks up.* DELANO *turns aside and speaks to* PERKINS)

It is like a Turkish bazaar.
PERKINS: They are like gypsies showing themselves for money
at a county fair, Sir.
DELANO: This is enchanting after the blank gray roll of the ocean!
Go tell the Spanish captain I am waiting for him.

(PERKINS *goes off. Sharp warnings from the* OAKUM-PICKERS. *A big black spread of canvas is pulled creakingly and ceremoniously aside.* SIX FIGURES *stand huddled on a platform about four feet from the deck. They look like weak old invalids in bathrobes and nightcaps until they strip to the waist and turn out to be huge, shining young negroes. Saying nothing, they set to work cleaning piles of rusted hatchets. From time to time, they turn and clash their hatchets together with a rhythmic shout.* PERKINS *returns)*

PERKINS: Their captain's name is Don Benito Cereno,
he sends you his compliments, Sir.
He looks more like a Mexican planter than a seaman.
He's put his fortune on his back:
he doesn't look as if he had washed since they left port.
DELANO: Did you tell him I was waiting for him?
A captain should be welcomed by his fellow-captain.
I can't understand this discourtesy.
PERKINS: He's coming, but there's something wrong with him.
(BENITO CERENO, *led by his negro servant,* BABU, *enters.* BENITO, *looking sick and dazed, is wearing a sombrero and is dressed with a singular but shabby richness. Head bent to one side, he leans in a stately coma against the rail, and stares unseeingly at* DELANO. BABU, *all in scarlet, and small and quick, keeps whispering, pointing and pulling at* BENITO's *sleeve.* DELANO *walks over to them)*
DELANO: Your hand, Sir. I am Amasa Delano,
captain of the *President Adams,*

a sealing ship from the United States.
This is your lucky day,
the sun is out of hiding for the first time in two weeks,
and here I am aboard your ship
like the Good Samaritan with fresh food and water.
BENITO: The Good Samaritan? Yes, yes,
we mustn't use the Scriptures lightly.
Welcome, Captain. It is the end of the day.
DELANO: The end? It's only morning.
I loaded and lowered a whaleboat
as soon as I saw how awkwardly your ship was making for the harbor.
BENITO: Your whaleboat's welcome, Capain.
I am afraid I am still stunned by the storm.
DELANO: Buck up. Each day is a new beginning.
Assign some sailors to help me dole out my provisions.
BENITO: I have no sailors.
BABU (*in a quick sing-song*): Scurvy, fellow fever,
ten men knocked off on the Horn,
doldrums, nothing to eat, nothing to drink!
By feeding us, you are feeding the King of Spain.
DELANO: Sir, your slave has a pretty way of talking.
What do you need?

(DELANO *waits for* BENITO *to speak. When nothing more is said, he shifts awkwardly from foot to foot, then turns to his* SAILORS)

Stand to, men!
(*The* AMERICAN SAILORS, *who have been lounging and gaping, stand in a row, as if a button had been pressed*)
Lay our fish and water by the cabin!
(*The* SAILORS *arrange the watercans and baskets of fish by the cabin. A sharp whistle comes from the* OAKUM-PICKERS. *Almost instantly, the provisions disappear*)
Captain Cereno, you are surely going to taste my water!
BENITO: A captain is a servant, almost a slave, Sir.
DELANO: No, a captain's a captain.
I am sending for more provisions.
Stand to!

(*The* AMERICAN SAILORS *stand to*)

Row back to the ship. When you get there,
take on five hogsheads of fresh water,
and fifty pounds of soft bread.
(FIRST SAILOR *salutes and goes down the ladder*)
Bring all our remaining pumpkins!

(SECOND and THIRD SAILORS *salute and go down the ladder*)
My bosun and I will stay on board,
until our boat returns.
I imagine you can use us.
BENITO: Are you going to stay here alone?
Won't your ship be lost without you?
Won't you be lost without your ship?
BABU: Listen to Master!
He is the incarnation of courtesy, Yankee Captain.
Your ship doesn't need you as much we do.
DELANO: Oh, I've trained my crew.
I can sail my ship in my sleep.
(Leaning over the railing and calling)
Men, bring me a box of lump sugar,
and six bottles of my best cider.
(Turning to BENITO)
Cider isn't my favorite drink, Don Benito,
but it's a New England specialty;
I'm ordering six bottles for your table.

(BABU *whispers and gestures to* DON BENITO, *who is exhausted and silent*)

BABU: *Une bouteille du vin* (to NEGROES)
My master wishes to give you a bottle
of the oldest wine in Seville.

(He whistles. A negro woman rushes into the cabin and returns with a dusty beribboned bottle, which she holds like a baby)
(BABU *ties a rope around the bottle*)

BABU: I am sending this bottle of wine to your cabin.
When you drink it, you will remember us.
Do you see these ribbons? The crown of Spain is tied to one.
Forgive me for tying a rope around the King of Spain's neck.
(Lowers the wine on the rope to the whaleboat)
DELANO *(shouting to his* SAILORS*)*: Pick up your oars!
SAILORS: Aye, aye, Sir!
DELANO: We're New England Federalists;
we can drink the King of Spain's health.

(BENITO *stumbles off-stage on* BABU's *arm*)

PERKINS: Captain Cereno hasn't travelled as much as you have;
I don't think he knew what you meant by the New England Federalists.
DELANO *(leaning comfortably on the rail; half to himself and half to* PERKINS*)*: The wind is dead. We drift away.

We will be left alone all day,
here in this absentee empire.
Thank God, I know my Spanish!
PERKINS: You'll have to watch them, Sir.
Brown men in charge of black men—
it doesn't add up to much!
This Babu, I don't trust him!
Why doesn't he talk with a Southern accent,
Like Mr. Jefferson? They're out of hand, Sir!
DELANO: Nothing relaxes order more than misery.
They need severe superior officers.
They haven't one.
Now, if this Benito were a man of energy . . .
a Yankee . . .
PERKINS: How can a Spaniard sail?
DELANO: Some can. There was Vasco da Gama and Columbus . . .
No, I guess they were Italians. Some can,
but this captain is tubercular.
PERKINS: Spaniards and Negroes have no business on a ship.
DELANO: Why is this captain so indifferent to me?
If only I could stomach his foreign reserve!
This absolute dictator of his ship
only gives orders through his slaves!
He is like some Jesuit-haunted Hapsburg king
about to leave the world and hope the world will end.
PERKINS: He said he was lost in the storm.
DELANO: Perhaps it's only policy,
a captain's icy dignity
obliterating all democracy—
PERKINS: He's like someone walking in his sleep.
DELANO: Ah, slumbering dominion!
He is so self-conscious in his imbecility . . .
No, he's sick. He sees his men no more than me.
This ship is like a crowded immigration boat;
needs severe superior officers,
the friendly arm of a strong mate.
Perhaps, I ought to take it over by force.
No, they're sick, they've been through the plague.
I'll go and speak and comfort my fellow captain.
I think you can help me, Captain. I'm feeling useless.
My own thoughts oppress me, there's so much to do.
I wonder if you would tell me the whole sad story of your voyage.
Talk to me as captain to captain.

We have sailed the same waters.
Please tell me your story.
BENITO: A story? A story! That's out of place.
When I was a child, I used to beg for stories back in Lima.
Now my tongue's tied and my heart is bleeding.

(Stops talking, as if his breath were gone. He stares for a few moments, then looks up at the rigging, as if he were counting the ropes one by one. DELANO *turns abruptly to* PERKINS*)*

DELANO: Go through the ship, Perkins,
and see if you can find me a Spaniard who can talk.
BENITO: You must be patient, Captain Delano:
if we only see with our eyes,
sometimes we cannot see at all.
DELANO: I stand corrected, Captain;
tell me about your voyage.
BENITO: It's now a hundred and ninety days . . .
This ship, well manned, well officered, with several cabin passengers,
carrying a cargo of Paraguay tea and Spanish cutlery.
That parcel of Negro slaves, less than four score now,
was once three hundred souls.
Ten sailors and three officers fell from the mainyard off the Horn;
part of our rigging fell overboard with them,
as they were beating down the icy sail.
We threw away all our cargo,
Broke our waterpipes,
Lashed them on deck
this was the chief cause of our suffering.
DELANO: I must interrupt you, Captain.
How did you happen to have three officers on the mainyard?
I never heard of such a disposal,
it goes against all seamanship.
BABU: Our officers never spared themselves;
if there was any danger, they rushed in
to save us without thinking.
DELANO: I can't understand such an oversight.
BABU: There was no oversight. My master had a hundred eyes.
He had an eye for everything.
Sometimes the world falls on a man.
The sea wouldn't let Master act like a master,
yet he saved himself and many lives.
He is still a rich man, and he saved the ship.
BENITO: Oh my God, I wish the world had fallen on me,

and the terrible cold sea had drowned me;
   that would have been better than living through what I've
   lived through!
BABU: He is a good man, but his mind is off;
   he's thinking about the fever when the wind stopped—
   poor, poor Master!
   Be patient, Yankee Captain, these fits are short,
   Master will be the master once again.
BENITO: The scurvy was raging through us.
   We were on the Pacific. We were invalids
   and couldn't man our mangled spars.
   A hurricane blew us northeast through the fog.
   Then the wind died.
   We lay in irons fourteen days in unknown waters,
   our black tongues stuck through our mouths,
   but we couldn't mend our broken waterpipes.
BABU: Always those waterpipes,
   he dreams about them like a pile of snakes!
BENITO: Yellow fever followed the scurvy,
   the long heat thickened in the calm,
   my Spaniards turned black and died like slaves,
   The blacks died too. I am my only officer left.
BABU: Poor, poor Master! He had a hundred eyes,
   he lived our lives for us.
   He is still a rich man.
BENITO: In the smart winds beating us northward,
   our torn sails dropped like sinkers in the sea;
   each day we dropped more bodies.
   Almost without a crew, canvas, water, or a wind,
   we were bounced about by the opposing waves
   through cross-currents and the weedy calms,
   and dropped our dead.
   Often we doubled and redoubled on our track
   like children lost in jungle. The thick fog
   hid the Continent and our only port from us.
BABU: We were poor kidnapped jungle creatures.
   We only lived on what he could give us.
   He had a hundred eyes, he was the master.
BENITO: These Negroes saved me, Captain.
   Through the long calamity,
   they were as gentle as their owner, Don Aranda, promised.
   Don Aranda took away their chains before he died.
BABU: Don Aranda saved our lives, but we couldn't save his.

Even in Africa I was a slave.
He took away my chains.
BENITO: I gave them the freedom of my ship.
I did not think they were crates or cargo or cannibals.
But it was Babu—under God, I swear I owe my life to Babu!
He calmed his ignorant, wild brothers,
never left me, saved the *San Domingo*.
BABU: Poor, poor Master. He is still a rich man.
Don't speak of Babu. Babu is the dirt under your feet.
He did his best.
DELANO: You are a good fellow, Babu.
You are the salt of the earth. I envy you, Don Benito;
he is no slave, Sir, but your friend.
BENITO: Yes, he is salt in my wounds.
I can never repay him, I mean.
Excuse me, Captain, my strength is gone.
I have done too much talking. I want to rest.
(BABU *leads* BENITO *to a shabby straw chair at the side.* BENITO *sits.* BABU *fans him with his sombrero*)
PERKINS: He's a fine gentleman, but no seaman.
A cabin boy would have known better
than to send his three officers on the mainyard.
DELANO (*paying no attention*):
A terrible story. I would have been unhinged myself.

(*Looking over toward* BABU *and* BENITO)

There's a true servant. They do things better
in the South and in South America—
trust in return for trust!
The beauty of that relationship is unknown
in New England. We're too much alone
in Massachusetts, Perkins.
How do our captains and our merchants live,
each a republic to himself.
Even Sam Adams had no friends and only loved the mob.
PERKINS: Sir, you are forgetting that
New England seamanship brought them their slaves.
DELANO: Oh, just our Southern slaves;
we had nothing to do with these fellows.
PERKINS: The ocean would be a different place
if every Spaniard served an apprenticeship on an American ship
before he got his captain's papers.
DELANO: This captain's a gentleman, not a sailor.

His little yellow hands
　　　got their command before they held a rope—
　　　in by the cabin-window, not the hawse-hole!
　　　Do you want to know why
　　　they drifted hog-tied in those easy calms—
　　　inexperience, sickness, impotence and aristocracy!
PERKINS: Here comes Robinson Crusoe and his good man Friday.
DELANO: We don't beat a man when he's down.

　　　(BENITO *advances uncertainly on* BABU'S *arm*)

　　　I am glad to see you on your feet again,
　　　That's the only place for a Captain, sir!
　　　I have the cure for you, I have decided
　　　to bring you medicine and a sufficient supply of water.
　　　A first class deck officer, a man from Salem,
　　　shall be stationed on your quarter deck,
　　　a temporary present from my owners.
　　　We shall refit your ship and clear this mess.
BENITO: You will have to clear away the dead.
BABU: This excitement is bad for him, Yankee Master.
　　　He's lived with death. He lives on death still;
　　　this sudden joy will kill him. You've heard
　　　how thirsty men die from overdrinking!
　　　His heart is with his friend, our owner, Don Aranda.
BENITO: I am the only owner.

　　　(He looks confused and shaken)
　　　(BABU *scurries off and brings up the straw chair.* BENITO *sits*)

DELANO: Your friend is dead? He died of fever?
BENITO: He died very slowly and in torture.
　　　He was the finest man in Lima.
　　　We were brought up together,
　　　I am lost here.
DELANO: Pardon me, Sir. You are young at sea.
　　　My experience tells me what your trouble is:
　　　this is the first body you have buried in the ocean.
　　　I had a friend like yours, a warm honest fellow,
　　　who would look you in the eye—
　　　we had to throw him to the sharks.
　　　Since then I've brought embalming gear on board.
　　　Each man of mine shall have a Christian grave on land.
　　　You wouldn't shake so, if Don Aranda were on board,

I mean, if you'd preserved the body.
BENITO: If he were on board this ship?
If I had preserved his body?
BABU: Be patient, Master!
We still have the figurehead.
DELANO: You have the figurehead?
BABU: You see that thing wrapped up in black cloth?
It's a figurehead Don Aranda bought us in Spain.
It was hurt in the storm. It's very precious.
Master takes comfort in it,
he is going to give it to Don Aranda's widow.
It's time for the pardon ceremony, Master.

(Sound of clashing hatchets)

DELANO: I am all for these hatchet-cleaners.
They are saving cargo. They make
an awful lot of pomp and racket though
about a few old, rusty knives.
BENITO: They think steel is worth its weight in gold.

(A slow solemn march is sounded on the gongs and other instruments. A gigantic coal-black NEGRO comes up the steps. He wears a spiked iron collar to which a chain is attached that goes twice around his arms and ends padlocked to a broad band of iron. The NEGRO comes clanking forward and stands dumbly and like a dignitary in front of BENITO. Two small black boys bring BENITO a frail rattan cane and a silver ball, which they support on a velvet cushion. BENITO springs up, holds the ball, and raises the cane rigidly above the head of the negro in chains. For a moment, he shows no trace of sickness. The assembled blacks sing, "Evviva, Benito!" three times)

BABU *(at one side with the Americans, but keeping an eye on BENITO)*:
You are watching the humiliation of King Atufal,
once a ruler in Africa. He ruled as much land there as your President.
Poor Babu was a slave even in Africa,
a black man's slave, and now a white man's.
BENITO *(in a loud, firm voice)*: Former King Atufal, I call on you to kneel!
Say, "My sins are black as night,
I ask the King of Spain's pardon
through his servant, Don Benito."
(Pause. ATUFAL doesn't move)
NEGROES: Yours sins are black as night, King Atufal!
Your sins are black as night, ,King Atufal!
DELANO: What has King Atufal done?

BABU: I will tell you later, Yankee Captain.
BENITO: Ask pardon, former King Atufal.
  If you will kneel,
  I will strike away your chains.
  (ATUFAL *slowly raises his chained arms and lets them drop*)
  Ask pardon!
WOMAN SLAVE: Ask pardon King Atufal.
BENITO: Go!

(*Sound of instruments. The* BLACK BOYS *take* BENITO's *ball and cane. The straw chair is brought up.* BENITO *sits.* FRANCESCO *then leads him off-stage*)

BABU: Francesco!
  I will be with you in a moment, Master.
  You mustn't be afraid,
  Francesco will serve you like a second Babu.
BENITO: Everyone serves me alike here,
  but no one can serve me as you have.
BABU: I will be with you in a moment.
  The Yankee master is at sea on our ship.
  He wants me to explain our customs.

(BENITO *is carried off-stage*)

  You would think Master's afraid of dying,
  if Babu leaves him!
DELANO: I can imagine your tenderness during his sickness.
  You were part of him,
  you were almost a wife.
BABU: You say such beautiful things,
  the United States must be a paradise for people like Babu.
DELANO: I don't know.
  We have our faults. We have many states,
  some of them could stand improvement.
BABU: The United States must be heaven.
DELANO: I suppose we have fewer faults than other countries.
  What did King Atufal do?
BABU: He used the Spanish flag for toilet paper.
DELANO: That's treason.
  Did Atufal know what he was doing?
  Perhaps the flag was left somewhere it shouldn't have been.
  Things aren't very strict here.
BABU: I never thought of that.
  I will go and tell Master.

DELANO: Oh, no, you mustn't do that!
 I never interfere with another man's ship.
 Don Benito is your lord and dictator.
 How long has this business with King Atufal been going on?
BABU: Ever since the yellow fever,
 and twice a day.
DELANO: He did a terrible thing, but he looks like a royal fellow.
 You shouldn't call him a king, though,
 it puts ideas into his head.
BABU: Atufal had gold wedges in his ears in Africa;
 now he wears a padlock and Master bears the key.
DELANO: I see you have a feeling for symbols of power.
 You had better be going now,
 Don Benito will be nervous about you.

(BABU *goes off*)

 That was a terrible thing to do with a flag;
 everything is untidy and unravelled here—
 this sort of thing would never happen on the *President Adams*.
PERKINS: Your ship is as shipshape as our country, Sir.
DELANO: I wish people wouldn't take me as representative of our country:
 America's one thing, I am another;
 we shouldn't have to bear one another's burdens.
PERKINS: You are a true American for all your talk, Sir;
 I can't believe you were mistaken for a Castilian Don.
DELANO: No one would take me for Don Benito.
PERKINS: I wonder if he isn't an imposter, some traveling actor from
 a circus?
DELANO: No, Cereno is a great name in Peru, like Winthrop or
 Adams with us.
 I recognize the family features in our captain.

(*An* OLD SPANISH SAILOR, *grizzled and dirty, is seen crawling on all fours with an armful of knots toward the Americans. He points to where* BENITO *and* BABU *have disappeared and whistles. He holds up the knots as though he were in chains, then throws them out loosely on the deck in front of him. A* GROUP OF NEGROES *forms a circle around him, holding hands and singing childishly. Then, laughing, they carry the* SPANIARD *off-stage on their shoulders*)

 These blacks are too familiar!
 We are never alone!
 (*Sound of gongs. Full minute's pause, as if time were passing.* DELANO *leans on the railing. The sun grows brighter*)
 This ship is strange.

These people are too spontaneous—all noise and show, no character!
Real life is a simple monotonous thing.
I wonder about that story about the calms; it doesn't stick.
Don Benito hesitated himself in telling it.
No one could run a ship so stupidly,
and place three officers on one yard.
(BENITO *and* BABU *return*)
A captain has unpleasant duties;
I am sorry for you, Don Benito.
BENITO: You find my ship unenviable, Sir?
DELANO: I was talking about punishing Atufal;
he acted like an animal!
BENITO: Oh, yes, I was forgetting . . .
He was a King,
How long have you lain in at this island, Sir?
DELANO: Oh, a week today.
BENITO: What was your last port, Sir?
DELANO: Canton.
BENITO: You traded seal-skins and American muskets
for Chinese tea and silks, perhaps?
DELANO: We took in some silks.
BENITO: A little gold and silver too?
DELANO: Just a little silver. We are only merchants.
We take in a dollar here and there. We have no Peru,
or a Pizarro who can sweat gold out of the natives.
BENITO: You'll find things have changed
a little in Peru since Pizarro, Captain.

(*Starts to move away.* BABU *whispers to him, and he comes back abruptly, as if he had forgotten something important*)

How many men have you on board, Sir?
DELANO: Some twenty-five, Sir. Each man is at his post.
BENITO: They're all on board, Sir now?
DELANO: They're all on board. Each man is working.
BENITO: They'll be on board tonight, Sir?
DELANO: Tonight? Why do you ask, Don Benito?
BENITO: Will they all be on board tonight, Captain?
DELANO: They'll be on board for all I know.
(PERKINS *makes a sign to* DELANO)
Well, no to tell the truth, today's our Independence Day.
A gang is going ashore to see the village.
A little diversion improves their efficiency,
a little regulated corruption.

BENITO: You North Americans take no chances. Generally, I suppose,
   even your merchant ships go more or less armed?
DELANO: A rack of muskets, sealing spears and cutlasses.
   Oh, and a six-pounder or two; we are a sealing ship,
   but with us each merchant is a privateer—
   only in case of oppression, of course.
   You've heard about how we shoot pirates.
BABU: Boom, boom, come Master.

(BENITO *walks away on* BABU'S *arm and sits down, almost off-stage in his straw chair. They whisper. Meanwhile, a* SPANISH SAILOR *climbs the rigging furtively, spread-eagles his arms and shows a lace shirt under his shabby jacket. He points to* BENITO *and* BABU *and winks. At a cry from* ONE OF THE OAKUM PICKERS, THREE NEGROES *help the* SPANIARD *down with servile, ceremonious attentions*)

PERKINS: Did you see that sailor's lace shirt, Sir?
   He must have robbed one of the cabin passengers.
   I hear that people strip the dead
   in these religious countries.
DELANO: No, you don't understand the Spaniards.
   In these old Latin countries,
   each man's a beggar or a noble, often both;
   they have no middle class. With them it's customary
   to sew a mess of gold and pearls on rags—
   that's how an aristocracy that's going to the dogs
   keeps up its nerve.
DELANO: It's odd though,
   that Spanish sailor seemed to want to tell me something.
   He ought to dress himself properly and speak his mind.
   That's what we do. That's why we're strong:
   everybody trusts us. Nothing gets done
   when every man's a noble. I wonder why
   the captain asked me all those questions?
PERKINS: He was passing the time of day Sir;
   It's a Latin idleness.
DELANO: It's strange. Did you notice how Benito stopped rambling?
   He was conventional . . . consecutive for the first time since we met him.
   Something's wrong. Perhaps, they've men below the decks,
   a sleeping volcano of Spanish infantry. The Malays do it,
   play sick and cut your throat.
   A drifting boat, a dozen doped beggars on deck,
   two hundred sweating murderers packed below like sardines—
   that's rot! Anyone can see these people are really sick,

sicker than usual. Our countries are at peace.
I wonder why he asked me all those questions?
PERKINS: Just idle curiosity. I hear
the gentlemen of Lima sit at coffee-tables from sun to sun
and gossip. They don't even have women to look at;
they're all locked up with their aunts.
DELANO: Their sun is going down. These old empires go.
They are much too familiar with their blacks.
I envy them though, they have no character,
they feel no need to stand alone.
We stand alone too much,
that's why no one can touch us for sailing a ship;
When a country loses heart, it's easier to live.
Ah, Babu! I suppose Don Benito's indisposed again!
Tell him I want to talk to his people;
there's nothing like a well man to help the sick.
BABU: Master is taking his siesta, Yankee Master.
His siesta is sacred, I am afraid to disturb it.
Instead, let me show you our little entertainment.
DELANO: Let's have your entertainment;
if you know a man's pleasure
you know his measure.
BABU: We are a childish people. Our pleasures are childish.
No one helped us, we know nothing
about your important amusements,
such as killing seals and pirates.
DELANO: I'm game. Let's have your entertainment.

(BABU *signals. The gong sounds ten times and the canvas is pulled from the circular structure. Enclosed in a triangular compartment, an* OLD SPANISH SAILOR *is dipping naked white dolls in a tar-pot*)

BABU: This little amusement keeps him alive, Yankee Master.
He is especially fond of cleaning the dolls
after he has dirtied them.

(*The* OLD SPANISH SAILOR *laughs hysterically, and then smears his whole face with tar*)

OLD SPANISH SAILOR: My soul is white!
BABU: The yellow fever destroyed his mind.
DELANO: Let's move on. This man's brain,
as well as his face, is defiled with pitch!
BABU: He says his soul is white.

(*The structure is pushed around and another triangular compartment appears. A* NEGRO BOY *is playing chess against a splendid Spanish doll*

with a crown on its head. He stops and holds two empty wine bottles to his ears)
This boy is deaf.
The yellow fever destroyed his mind.
DELANO: Why is he holding those bottles to his ears?
BABU: He is trying to be a rabbit,
or listening to the ocean, his mother—
who knows?
DELANO: If he's deaf, how can he hear the ocean?
Anyway, he can't hear me.
I pass, let's move on.

(The structure is pushed around to a third compartment. A SPANISH SAILOR *is holding a big armful of rope)*

What are you knotting there, my man?
SPANISH SAILOR: The knot.
DELANO: So I see, but what's it for?
SPANISH SAILOR: For someone to untie. Catch!
(Throws the knot to DELANO*)*
BABU *(snatching the knot from* DELANO*)*:
It's dirty, it will dirty your uniform.
DELANO: Let's move on. Your entertainment
is rather lacking in invention, Babu.
BABU: We have to do what we can
We are just beginners at acting.
This next one will be better.

(The structure is pushed around and shows a beautiful NEGRO WOMAN. *She is dressed and posed as the Virgin Mary. A Christmas crèche is arranged around her. A* VERY WHITE SPANIARD *dressed as Saint Joseph stands behind her. She holds a Christ-child, the same crowned doll, only black, the* NEGRO BOY *was playing chess against)*

She is the Virgin Mary. That man is not the father.
DELANO: I see. I suppose her son is the King of Spain.
BABU: The Spaniards taught us everything,
there's nothing we can learn from you, Yankee Master.
When they took away our country, they gave us a better world.
Things do not happen in that world as they do here.
DELANO: That's a very beautiful,
though unusual Virgin Mary.
BABU: Yes, the Bible says, "I am black not white."
When Don Aranda was dying,
we wanted to give him the Queen of Heaven

because he took away our chains.
PERKINS: The Spaniards must have taught them everything;
they're all mixed up, they don't even know their religion.
DELANO: No, no! The Catholic Church doesn't just teach,
it knows how to take from its converts.
BABU: Do you want to shake hands with the Queen of Heaven,
Yankee Master?
DELANO: No, I'm not used to royalty.
Tell her I believe in freedom of religion,
if people don't take liberties.
Let's move on.
BABU *(kneeling to the Virgin Mary)*:
I present something Your Majesty has never seen,
a white man who doesn't believe in taking liberties,
Your Majesty.

(The structure is pushed around and shows ATUFAL *in chains but with a crown on his head)*

BABU: This is the life we believe in.
THE NEGROES ALL TOGETHER: Ask pardon, King Atufal!
Kiss the Spanish flag!
DELANO: Please don't ask me to shake hands with King Atufal!

(The canvas is put back on the structure)

BABU: You look tired and serious, Yankee Master.
We have to have what fun we can.
We never would have lived through the deadly calms
without a little amusement.
(Bows and goes off)
(The NEGROES *gradually drift away.* DELANO *sighs with relief)*
DELANO: Well, that wasn't much!
I suppose Shakespeare started that way.
PERKINS: Who cares?
I see a speck on the blue sea, Sir,
our whaleboat is coming.
DELANO: A speck? My eyes are speckled.
I seem to have been dreaming. What's solid?
(Touches the ornate railing; a piece falls onto the deck)
This ship is nothing, Perkins!
I dreamed someone was trying to kill me!
How could he? Jack-of-the-beach,
they used to call me on the Duxbury shore.
Carrying a duck-satchel in my hand, I used to paddle
along the waterfront from a hulk to school.

    I didn't learn much there. I was always shooting duck
    or gathering huckleberries along the marsh with Cousin Nat!
    I like nothing better than breaking myself on the surf.
    I used to track the seagulls down the five-mile stretch of beach for eggs.
    How can I be killed now at the ends of the earth
    by this insane Spaniard?
    Who could want to murder Amasa Delano?
    My conscience is clean. God is good.
    What am I doing on board this nigger-pirate ship?
PERKINS: You're not talking like a skipper, Sir.
    Our boat's a larger spot now.
DELANO: I am childish.
    I am doddering and drooling into my second childhood.
    God help me, nothing's solid!
PERKINS: Don Benito, Sir. Touch him,
    he's as solid as his ship.
DELANO: Don Benito? He's a walking ghost!

(BENITO *comes up to* DELANO. BABU *is a few steps behind him*)
BENITO: I am the ghost of myself, Captain.
    Excuse me, I heard you talking about dreams and childhood.
    I was a child, too, once, I have dreams about it.
DELANO (*starting*): I'm sorry.
    This jumping's just a nervous habit.
    I thought you were part of my dreams.
BENITO: I was taking my siesta,
    I dreamed I was a boy back in Lima.
    I was with my brothers and sisters,
    and we were dressed for the festival of Corpus Christi
    like people at our Bourbon court.
    We were simple children, but something went wrong;
    little black men came on us with beetle backs.
    They had caterpillar heads and munched away on our fine clothes.
    They made us lick their horned and varnished insect legs.
    Our faces turned brown from their spit,
    we looked like bugs, but nothing could save our lives!
DELANO: Ha, ha, Captain. We are like two dreams meeting head-on.
    My whaleboat's coming,
    we'll both feel better over a bottle of cider.

(BABU *blows a bosun's whistle. The gongs are sounded with descending notes. The* NEGROES *assemble in ranks*)
BABU: It's twelve noon, Master Yankee.
    Master wants his midday shave.
ALL THE NEGROES: Master wants his shave! Master wants his shave!

BENITO: Ah, yes, the razor! I have been talking too much.
You can see how badly I need a razor.
I must leave you, Captain.
BABU: No, Don Amasa wants to talk.
Come to the cabin, Don Amasa.
Don Amasa will talk, Master will listen.
Babu will lather and strop.
DELANO: I want to talk to you about navigation.
I am new to these waters.
BENITO: Doubtless, doubtless, Captain Delano.
PERKINS: I think I'll take my siesta, Sir.

(He walks off)

(BENITO, BABU, and DELANO walk toward the back of the stage. A scrim curtain lifts, showing a light deck cabin that forms a sort of attic. The floor is matted, partitions that still leave splintered traces have been knocked out. To one side, a small table screwed to the floor; on it, a dirty missal; above it, a small crucifix, rusty crossed muskets on one side, rusty crossed cutlasses on the other. BENITO sits down in a broken throne-like and gilded chair. BABU begins to lather. A magnificent array of razors, bottles and other shaving equipment lies on a table beside him. Behind him, a hammock with a pole in it and a dirty pillow)

DELANO: So this is where you took your siesta.
BENITO: Yes, Captain, I rest here when my fate will let me.
DELANO: This seems like a sort of dormitory, sitting-room,
sail-loft, chapel, armory, and private bedroom all together.
BENITO: Yes, Captain: events have not been favorable
to much order in my personal arrangements.

(BABU moves back and opens a locker. A lot of flags, torn shirts and socks tumble out. He takes one of the flags, shakes it with a flourish, and ties it around BENITO's neck)

BABU: Master needs more protection.
I do everything I can to save his clothes.
DELANO: The Castle and the Lion of Spain.
Why, Don Benito, this is the flag of Spain you're using!
It's well it's only I and not the King of Spain who sees this!
All's one, though, I guess, in this carnival world.
I see you like gay colors as much as Babu.
BABU *(giggling)*: The bright colors draw the yellow fever
from Master's mind.

(Raises the razor)
(BENITO begins to shake)

Now, Master now, Master!
BENITO: You are talking while you hold the razor.
BABU: You mustn't shake so, Master.
Look, Don Amasa, Master always shakes when I shave him,
though he is braver than a lion and stronger than a castle.
Master knows Babu has never yet drawn blood.
I may, though, sometimes, if he shakes so much.
Now, Master!
Come, Don Amasa, talk to Master about the gales and calms,
he'll answer and forget to shake.
DELANO: Those calms, the more I think of them the more I wonder.
You say you were two months sailing here;
I made that stretch in less than a week.
We never met with any calms.
If I'd not heard your story from your lips,
and seen your ruined ship,
I would have said something was missing,
I would have said this was a mystery ship.
BENITO: For some men the whole world is a mystery;
they cannot believe their senses.

(BENITO *shakes, the razor gets out of hand and cuts his cheek*)

Santa Maria!
BABU: Poor, poor Master, see, you shook so;
this is Babu's first blood.
Please answer Don Amasa, while I wipe
this ugly blood from the razor and strop it again.
BENITO: The sea was like the final calm of the world
On, on it went. It sat on us and drank our strength,
crosscurrents eased us out to sea,
the yellow fever changed our blood to poison.
BABU: You stood by us. Some of us stood by you!
BENITO: Yes, my Spanish crew was weak and surly, but the blacks,
the blacks were angels. Babu has kept me in this world.
I wonder what he is keeping me for?
You belong to me. I belong to you forever.
BABU: Ah, Master, spare yourself.
Forever is a very long time;
nothing's forever.

(With great expertness, delicacy and gentleness, BABU *massages* BENITO'S *cheeks, shakes out the flag, pours lotion from five bottles on* BENITO'S *hair, cleans the shaving materials, and stands off admiring his work)*

Master looks just like a statue.
He's like a figurehead. Don Amasa!
(DELANO *looks, then starts to walk out leaving* BENITO *and* BABU. *The curtain drops upon them.* DELANO *rejoins* PERKINS, *lounging at the rail*)

PERKINS: Our boat is coming.
DELANO (*gaily*): I know!
I don't know how I'll explain this pomp
and squalor to my own comfortable family of a crew.
Even shaving here is like a High Mass.
There's something in a Negro, something
that makes him fit to have around your person.
His comb and brush are castanets.
What tact Babu had!
What noiseless, gliding briskness!
PERKINS: Our boat's about along side, Sir.
DELANO: What's more, the Negro has a sense of humor.
I don't mean their boorish giggling and teeth-showing,
I mean his easy cheerfulness in every glance and gesture.
You should have been Babu toss that Spanish flag like a juggler,
and change it to a shaving napkin!
PERKINS: The boat's here, Sir.
DELANO: We need inferiors, Perkins,
more manners, more docility, no one has an inferior mind in America.
PERKINS: Here is your crew, Sir.

(BABU *runs out from the cabin. His cheek is bleeding*)

DELANO: Why, Babu, what has happened?
BABU: Master will never get better from his sickness.
His bad nerves and evil fever made him use me so.
I gave him one small scratch by accident,
the only time I've nicked him, Don Amasa.
He cut me with his razor. Do you think I will die?
I'd rather die than bleed to death!
DELANO: It's just a pinprick, Babu. You'll live.
BABU: I must attend my master.

(*Runs back into cabin*)

DELANO: Just a pinprick, but I wouldn't have thought
Don Benito had the stuff to swing a razor.
Up north we use our fists instead of knives.
I hope Benito's not dodging around some old grindstone
in the hold, and sharpening a knife for me.
Here, Perkins, help our men up the ladder.

(Two immaculate AMERICAN SAILORS *appear carrying great casks of water. Two more follow carrying net baskets of wilted pumpkins. The* NEGROES *begin to crowd forward, shouting, "We want Yankee food, we want Yankee drink!"* DELANO *grandiosely holds up a pumpkin; an* OLD NEGRO *rushes forward, snatches at the pumpkin, and knocks* DELANO *off-balance into* PERKIN'S *arms.* DELANO *gets up and knocks the* NEGRO *down with his fist. All is tense and quiet. The* SIX HATCHET-CLEANERS *lift their hatchets above their heads)*

DELANO *(furious)*: Americans, stand by me! Stand by your captain!
(Like lightning, the AMERICANS *unsling their muskets, fix bayonets, and kneel with their guns pointing at the* NEGROES*)*
Don Benito, Sir call your men to order!

BABU: We're starving, Yankee Master. We mean no harm;
we've never been so scared.

DELANO: You try my patience, Babu.
I am talking to Captain Cereno;
call your men to order, Sir.

BENITO: Make them laugh, Babu. The Americans aren't going to shoot.

*(*BABU *airily waves a hand. The* NEGROES *smile.* DELANO *turns to* BENITO*)*

You mustn't blame them too much; they're sick and hungry.
We have kept them cooped up for ages.

DELANO *(as the* NEGROES *relax)*: Form them in lines, Perkins!
Each man shall have his share.
That's how we run things in the States—
to each man equally, no matter what his claims.

NEGROES *(standing back, bleating like sheep)*:
Feed me, Master Yankee! Feed me, Master Yankee!

DELANO: You are much too close.
Here, Perkins, take the provisions aft.
You'll save lives by giving each as little as you can,
Be sure to keep a tally.

*(*FRANCESCO, *a majestic, yellow-colored mulatto, comes up to* DELANO*)*

FRANCESCO: My master requests your presence at dinner, Don Amasa.

DELANO: Tell him I have indigestion.
Tell him to keep better order on his ship.
It's always the man of good will that gets hurt;
my fist still aches from hitting that old darky.

FRANCESCO: My master has his own methods of discipline
that are suitable for our unfortunate circumstances.
Will you come to dinner, Don Amasa?

DELANO: I'll come. When in Rome, do as the Romans.

Excuse my quick temper, Sir.
It's better to blow up than to smoulder.
(*The scrim curtain is raised. In the cabin, a long table loaded with silver has been laid out. The locker has been closed and the Spanish flag hangs on the wall.* DON BENITO *is seated,* BABU *stands behind him. As soon as* DELANO *sits down,* FRANCESCO *begins serving with great dignity and agility*)

FRANCESCO: A finger bowl, Don Amasa.
(*After each statement, he moves about the table*)
A napkin, Don Amasa.
A glass of American water, Don Amasa.
A slice of American pumpkin, Don Amasa.
A goblet of American cider, Don Amasa.

(DELANO *drinks a great deal of cider,* BENITO *hardly touches his*)

DELANO: This is very courtly for a sick ship, Don Benito.
The Spanish Empire will never go down, if she keeps her chin up.
BENITO: I'm afraid I shan't live long enough to enjoy your prophecy.
DELANO: I propose a toast to the Spanish Empire
on which the sun never sets;
may you find her still standing, when you land, Sir!
BENITO: Our Empire has lasted three hundred years,
I suppose she will last another month.
I wish I could say the same for myself. My sun is setting,
I hear the voices of the dead in this calm.
DELANO: You hear the wind lifting;
it's bringing our two vessels together.
We are going to take you into port, Don Benito.
BENITO: You are either too late or too early with your good works.
Our yellow fever may break out again.
You aren't going to put your men in danger, Don Amasa?
DELANO: My boys are all healthy, sir.
BENITO: Health isn't God, I wouldn't trust it.
FRANCESCO: May I fill your glass, Don Amasa?
BABU: New wine in new bottles,
that's the American spirit, Yankee Master.
They say all men are created equal in North America.
DELANO: We prefer merit to birth, boy.

(BABU *motions imperiously for* FRANCESCO *to leave. As he goes, bowing to the* CAPTAINS, FOUR NEGROES *play the* Marseillaise)

Why are they playing the *Marseillaise?*
BABU: His uncle is supposed to have been in the French Convention,

and voted for the death of the French King.
DELANO: This polite and royal fellow is no anarchist!
BABU: Francesco is very *ancien regime,*
    he is even frightened of the Americans.
    He doesn't like the way you treated King George.
    Babu is more liberal.
DELANO: A royal fellow,
    this usher of yours, Don Benito!
    He is as yellow as a goldenrod.
    He is a king, a king of kind hearts.
    What a pleasant voice he has!
BENITO (*glumly*): Francesco is a good man.
DELANO: As long as you've known him,
    he's been a worthy fellow, hasn't he?
    Tell me, I am particularly curious to know.
BENITO: Francesco is a good man.
DELANO: I'm glad to hear it, I am glad to hear it!
    You refute the saying of a planter friend of mine.
    He said, "When a mulatto has a regular European face,
    look out for him, he is a devil."
BENITO: I've heard your planter's remark applied
    to intermixtures of Spaniards and Indians;
    I know nothing about mulattoes.
DELANO: No, no, my friend's refuted;
    if we're so proud of our white blood,
    surely a little added to the blacks improves their breed.
    I congratulate you on your servants, Sir.
BABU: We've heard that Jefferson, the King of your Republic,
    would like to free his slaves.
DELANO: Jefferson has read too many books, boy,
    but you can trust him. He's a gentleman and an American!
    He's not lifting a finger to free his slaves.
BABU: We hear you have a new capital modelled on Paris,
    and that your President is going to set up
    a guillotine on the Capitol steps.
DELANO: Oh, Paris! I told you you could trust Mr. Jefferson, boy,
    he stands for law and order like your mulatto.
    Have you been to Paris, Don Benito?
BENITO: I'm afraid I'm just a provincial Spaniard, Captain.
DELANO: Let me tell you about Paris.
    You know what French women are like—
    nine parts sex and one part logic.
    Well, one of them in Paris heard

that my ship was the *President Adams*. She said,
"You are descended from Adam, Captain,
you must know everything,
tell me how Adam and Eve learned to sleep together."
Do you know what I said?

BENITO: No, Captain.

DELANO: I said, "I guess Eve was a Frenchwoman,
the first Frenchwoman."
Do you know what she answered?

BENITO: No, Captain Delano.

DELANO: She said, "I was trying to provoke a philosophical discussion, Sir."
A philosophical discussion, ha, ha!
You look serious, Sir. You know, something troubles me.

BENITO: Something troubles you, Captain Delano?

DELANO: I still can't understand those calms,
but let that go. The scurvy,
why did it kill off three Spaniards in every four,
and only half the blacks?
Negroes are human, but surely you couldn't have favored them
before your own flesh and blood!

BENITO: This is like the Inquisition, Captain Delano.
I have done the best I could.

(BABU *dabs* BENITO's *forehead with cider*)

BABU: Poor, poor Master; since Don Aranda died,
he trusts no one except Babu.

DELANO: Your Babu is an uncommonly intelligent fellow;
you are right to trust him, Sir.
Sometimes I think we overdo our talk of freedom.
If you looked into our hearts, we all want slaves.

BENITO: Disease is a mysterious thing;
it takes one man, and leaves his friend.
Only the unfortunate can understand misfortune.

DELANO: I must return to my bosun;
he's pretty green to be left alone here.
Before I go I want to propose a last toast to you!
A good master deserves good servants!
(*He gets up. As he walks back to* PERKINS, *the scrim curtain falls, concealing* BENITO *and* BABU)
That captain must have jaundice,
I wish he kept better order.
I don't like hitting menials.

PERKINS: I've done some looking around, Sir. I've used my eyes.
DELANO: That's what they're for, I guess. You have to watch your step,
    this hulk, this rotten piece of finery,
    will fall apart. This old world needs new blood
    and Yankee gunnery to hold it up.
    You shouldn't mess around, though, it's their ship;
    you're breaking all the laws of the sea.
PERKINS: Do you see that man-shaped thing in canvas?
DELANO: I see it.
PERKINS: Behind the cloth, there's a real skeleton,
    a man dressed up like Don Benito.
DELANO: They're Catholics, and worship bones.
PERKINS: There's writing on its coat. It says,
    "I am Don Aranda," and, "Follow your leader."
DELANO: Follow your leader?
PERKINS: I saw two blacks unfurling a flag,
    a black skull and crossbones on white silk.
DELANO: That's piracy. We've been ordered
    to sink any ship that flies that flag.
    Perhaps they were playing.
PERKINS: I saw King Atufal throw away his chains,
    He called for food, the Spaniards served him two pieces of pumpkin,
    and a whole bottle of your cider.
DELANO: Don Benito has the only key to Atufal's padlock.
    My cider was for the captain's table.
PERKINS: Atufal pointed to the cabin where you were dining,
    and drew a finger across his throat.
DELANO: Who could want to kill Amasa Delano?
PERKINS: I warned our men to be ready for an emergency.
DELANO: You're a mind reader,
    I couldn't have said better myself;
    but we're at peace with Spain.
PERKINS: I told them to return with loaded muskets
    and fixed bayonets.
DELANO: Here comes Benito. Watch how I'll humor him
    and sound him out.

(BABU *brings out* BENITO's *chair.* BENITO *sits in it*)

It's good to have you back on deck, Captain.
Feel the breeze! It holds and will increase.
My ship is moving nearer. Soon we will be together.
We have seen you through your troubles.
BENITO: Remember, I warned you about the yellow fever.

I am surprised you haven't felt afraid.
DELANO: Oh, that will blow away.
Everything is going to go better and better;
the wind's increasing, soon you'll have no cares.
After the long voyage, the anchor drops into the harbor.
It's a great weight lifted from the captain's heart.
We are getting to be friends, Don Benito.
My ship's in sight, the *President Adams!*
How the wind braces a man up!
I have a small invitation to issue to you.
BENITO: An invitation?
DELANO: I want you to take a cup of coffee
with me on my quarter deck tonight.
The Sultan of Turkey never tasted such coffee
as my old steward makes. What do you say, Don Benito?
BENITO: I cannot leave my ship.
DELANO: Come, come, you need a change of climate.
The sky is suddenly blue, Sir,
my coffee will make a man of you.
BENITO: I cannot leave my ship.
Even now, I don't think you understand my position here.
DELANO: I want to speak to you alone.
BENITO: I am alone, as much as I ever am.
DELANO: In America, we don't talk about money
in front of servants and children.
BENITO: Babu is not my servant.
You spoke of money—since the yellow fever,
he has had a better head for figures than I have.
DELANO: You embarrass me, Captain,
but since circumstances are rather special here,
I will proceed.
BENITO: Babu takes an interest in all our expenses.
DELANO: Yes, I am going to talk to you about your expenses.
I am responsible to my owners for all
the sails, ropes, food and carpentry I give you.
You will need a complete rerigging, almost a new ship, in fact,
You shall have our services at cost.
BENITO: I know, you are a merchant.
I suppose I ought to pay you for our lives.
DELANO: I envy you, Captain. You are the only owner
of the *San Domingo*, since Don Aranda died.
I am just an employee. Our owners would sack me,
if I followed my better instincts.

BENITO: You can give your figures to Babu, Captain.
DELANO: You are very offhand about money, Sir;
 I don't think you realize the damage that has been done to your ship.
 Ah, you smile. I'm glad you're loosening up.
 Look, the water gurgles merrily, the wind is high,
 a mild light is shining. I sometimes think
 such a tropical light as this must have shone
 on the tents of Abraham and Isaac.
 It seems as if Providence were watching over us.
PERKINS: There are things that need explaining here, Sir.
DELANO: Yes, Captain, Perkins saw some of your men
 unfurling an unlawful flag,
 a black skull and crossbones.
BENITO: You know my only flag is the Lion and Castle of Spain.
DELANO: No, Perkins says he saw a skull and crossbones.
 That's piracy. I trust Perkins.
 You've heard about how my government blew
 the bowels out of the pirates at Tripoli?
BENITO: Perhaps my Negroes . . .
DELANO: My government doesn't intend
 to let you play at piracy!
BENITO: Perhaps my Negroes were playing.
 When you take away their chains . . .
DELANO: I'll see that you are all put back in chains,
 if you start playing pirates!
PERKINS: There's something else he can explain, Sir.
DELANO: Yes, Perkins saw Atufal throw off his chains
 and order dinner.
BABU: Master has the key, Yankee Master.
BENITO: I have the key.
 You can't imagine how my position exhausts me, Captain.
DELANO: I can imagine. Atufal's chains are fakes.
 You and he are in cahoots, Sir!
PERKINS: They don't intend to pay for our sails and service.
 They think America is Santa Claus.
DELANO: The United States are death on pirates and debtors.
PERKINS: There's one more thing for him to explain, Sir.
DELANO: Do you see that man-shaped thing covered with black
 cloth, Don Benito?
BENITO: I always see it.
DELANO: Take away the cloth. I order you to take away the cloth!
BENITO: I cannot. Oh, Santa Maria, have mercy!
DELANO: Of course, you can't. It's no Virgin Mary.

You have done something terrible to your friend, Don Aranda.
Take away the cloth, Perkins!

(*As* PERKINS *moves forward,* ATUFAL *suddenly stands chainless and with folded arms, blocking his way*)

BABU (*dancing up and down and beside himself*):
Let them see it! Let them see it!
I can't stand any more of their insolence;
the Americans treat us like their slaves!
(BABU *and* PERKINS *meet at the man-shaped object and start pulling away the cloth.* BENITO *rushes between them, and throws them back and sprawling on the deck.* BABU *and* PERKINS *rise, and stand hunched like wrestlers, about to close in on* BENITO, *who draws his sword with a great gesture. It is only a hilt. He runs at* BABU *and knocks him down.* ATUFAL *throws off his chains and signals to the* HATCHET-CLEANERS. *They stand behind* BENITO *with raised hatchets. The* NEGROES *shout ironically, "Evviva Benito!"*)
You too, Yankee Captain!
If you shoot, we'll kill you.
DELANO: If a single American life is lost,
I will send this ship to the bottom,
and all Peru after it.
Do you hear me, Don Benito?
BENITO: Don't you understand? I am as powerless as you are!
BABU: He is as powerless as you are.
BENITO: Don't you understand? He has been holding a knife at my back.
I have been talking all day to save your life.
BABU (*holding a whip*):
Do you see this whip? When Don Aranda was out of temper,
he used to snap pieces of flesh off us with it.
Now I hold the whip.
When I snap it, Don Benito jumps!

(*Snaps the whip.* DON BENITO *flinches*)

DELANO (*beginning to understand*): It's easy to terrorize the defenseless.
BABU: That's what we thought when Don Aranda held the whip.
DELANO: You'll find I am made of tougher stuff than your Spaniards.
ATUFAL: We want to kill you.
NEGROE: We want to kill you, Yankee Captain.
DELANO: Who could want to kill Amasa Delano?
BABU: Of course. We want to keep you alive.
We want you to sail us back to Africa.
Has anyone told you how much you are worth, Captain?

DELANO: I have another course in mind.
BABU: Yes, there's another course if you don't like Africa, there's
  another course.
  King Atufal, show the Yankee captain
  the crew that took the other course!

(Three dead SPANISH SAILORS *are brought on stage)*

ATUFAL: Look at Don Aranda?
BABU: Yes, you are hot-tempered and discourteous, Captain.
  I am going to introduce you to Don Aranda.
  You have a new command, Captain. You must meet your new owner.

(The black cloth is taken from the man-shaped object and shows a chalk-white skeleton dressed like DON BENITO*)*

  Don Amasa, Don Aranda!
  You can see that Don Aranda was a white man like you,
  because his bones are white.
NEGROES: He is a white because his bones are white!
  He is a white because his bones are white!
ATUFAL *(pointing to the ribbon on the skeleton's chest)*:
  Do you see that ribbon?
  It says, "Follow the leader."
  We wrote it in his blood.
BABU: He was a white man
  even though his blood was red as ours.
NEGROES: He is white because his bones are white!
BABU: Don Aranda is our figurehead,
  we are going to chain him to the bow of our ship
  to scare off devils.
ATUFAL: This is the day of Jubilee,
  I am raising the flag of freedom!
NEGROES: Freedom! Freedom! Freedom!

(The black skull and crossbones is raised on two poles. The NEGROES *form two lines, leading up to the flag, and leave an aisle. Each man is armed with some sort of weapon)*

BABU: Spread out the Spanish flag!
  (The Lion and Castle of Spain is spread out on the deck in front of the skull and crossbones)
  The Spanish flag is the road to freedom.
  Don Benito mustn't hurt his white feet on the splinters.
  (Kneeling in front of BENITO*)*
  Your foot, Master!

(BENITO *holds out his foot.* BABU *takes off* BENITO'S *shoes*)
Give Don Benito back his sword!
(*The sword-hilt is fastened back in* BENITO'S *scabbard*)
Load him with chains!
(*Two heavy chains are draped on* BENITO'S *neck. The cane and ball are handed to him*)
Former Captain Benito Cereno, kneel!
Ask pardon of man!

BENITO (*kneeling*): I ask pardon for having been born a Spaniard.
I ask pardon for having enslaved my fellow man.

BABU: Strike off the oppressor's chain!

(*One of* BENITO'S *chains is knocked off, then handed to* ATUFAL, *who dashes it to the deck*)

Former Captain Benito Cereno,
you must kiss the flag of freedom.
(*Points to* DON ARANDA)
Kiss the mouth of the skull!
(BENITO *walks barefoot over the Spanish flag and kisses the mouth of* DON ARANDA)

NEGROES: *Evviva Benito! Evviva Benito!*

(*Sounds are heard from* PERKINS, *whose head has been covered with the sack*)

ATUFAL: The bosun wants to kiss the mouth of freedom.

BABU: March over the Spanish flag, Bosun.

(PERKINS *starts forward*)

DELANO: You are dishonoring your nation, Perkins!
Don't you stand for anything?

PERKINS: I only have one life, Sir.

(*Walks over the Spanish flag and kisses the mouth of the skull*)

NEGROES: *Evviva* Bosun! *Evviva* Bosun!

DELANO: You are no longer an American, Perkins!

BABU: He was free to choose freedom, Captain.

ATUFAL: Captain Delano wants to kiss the mouth of freedom.

BABU: He is jealous of the bosun.

ATUFAL: In the United States, all men are created equal.

BABU: Don't you want to kiss the mouth of freedom, Captain?

DELANO (*lifting his pocket and pointing the pistol*):
Do you see what I have in my hand?

BABU: A pistol.

DELANO: I am unable to miss at this distance.

BABU: You must take your time, Yankee Master.

You must take your time.
DELANO: I am unable to miss.
BABU: You can stand there like a block of wood
as long as you want to, Yankee Master.
You will drop asleep, then we will tie you up,
and make you sail us back to Africa.

(General laughter. Suddenly, there's a roar of gunfire. Several NEGROES, *mostly women, fall.* AMERICAN SEAMAN *in spotless blue and white throw themselves in a lying position on deck.* MORE *kneel above them, then* MORE *stand above these. All have muskets and fixed bayonets. The First Row fires. More* NEGROES *fall. They start to retreat. The Second Row fires. More* NEGROES *fall. They retreat further. The Third Row fires. The Three* AMERICAN LINES *march forward, but all the* NEGROES *are either dead or in retreat.* DON BENITO *has been wounded. He staggers over to* DELANO *and shakes his hand)*

BENITO: You have saved my life.
I thank you for my life.
DELANO: A man can only do what he can,
We have saved American lives.
PERKINS *(pointing to* ATUFAL's *body)*: We have killed King Atufal,
we have killed their ringleader.

(BABU *jumps up. He is unwounded*)

BABU: I was the King. Babu, not Atufal
was the king, who planned, dared and carried out
the seizure of this ship, the *San Domingo*.
Untouched by blood myself, I had all
the most dangerous and useless Spaniards killed.
I freed my people from their Egyptian bondage.
The heartless Spaniards slaved for me like slaves.
(BABU *steps back, and quickly picks up a crown from the litter*)
This is my crown.
(Puts crown on his head. He snatches BENITO's *rattan cane)*
This is my rod.
(Picks up silver ball)
This is the earth.
(Holds the ball out with one hand and raises the cane)
This is the arm of the angry God.
(Smashes the ball)
PERKINS: Let him surrender. Let him surrender.
We want to save someone.
BENITO: My God how little these people understand!

BABU *(holding a white handkerchief and raising both his hands)*:
   Yankee Master understand me. The future is with us.
DELANO *(raising his pistol)*: This is your future.

   (BABU *falls and lies still.* DELANO *pauses, then slowly empties the five remaining barrels of his pistol into the body. Lights dim.)*

Curtain

Three
The Rewards of Virtue

Comedy embodies the impulse of the human psyche toward wholeness, balance, and sanity. A comedy asks its audience to consider itself honestly as a social unit, on the assumption that people can come to terms with each other in some sort of equilibrium. The situation comedy of television, in which disaster threatens and peace is restored in $24\frac{1}{2}$ minutes every week, is the least common denominator of comic form.

In tragedy, the protagonist is forced to confront the world and to test the validity of its laws. The limits are exceeded and the protagonist is both destroyed and exulted in cracking the bonds of ordinary experience. Comedy, on the other hand, is based on limits. It deals with reward and punishment in a human, temporal, and fixed world. The "business" of comedy, the gestures, pratfalls, sight gags, double takes, timing, all reflect the limited human emphasis. In tragedy the confrontation is something that the social fabric cannot hold. In comedy the emphasis is on the social fabric itself, and the gestures represent the accommodations, successful or otherwise, of individuals to their community.

Any play or poem that had a happy ending was once called a comedy, and "boy meets girl and finds fortune" is still the basic comic plot. But in the hands of the great comic dramatists the emphasis shifted from a simple happy ending to the more realistic and more profoundly human sense that the ending of a comedy is a setting of the characters in their appropriate places. Reward and punishment are part of the controlling pattern of appropriate arrangements, but, witness Chekhov, this is not a simple idea of reward and punishment. In the relationship of each to each and each to the world of the play, the characters get what they deserve. Comedy obviously comes close to tragedy here. The difference is that in tragedy, one or more of the characters absorbs all the reward and punishment while the other actors watch and then, at the end, they try to pick up the pieces that are left. At the end of a comedy, each character has been assigned a place by the logic of events and steps into that role as the curtain descends. At the end of tragedy, we say, "How awesome." At the end of comedy, we say, "How appropriate."

The audience at a tragedy, like the chorus in *The Women of Troy*, sits and watches individuals struggle against the order of the world. The audience at a comedy watches individuals struggle with other individuals. That is why hypocrisy, greed, pretension, ego, and self-importance are the natural subjects of comedy. Comic characters want more than their share of the goods and pleasures of their world. They do not challenge the validity of their world order; they misinterpret their place in that order. Comedy begins in assertion and ends in balance.

The movement of a comedy, then, is from excess to proportion, from angles to roundness, from part to whole, from individual gain to common good. The good characters are, in the end, fully integrated with their society (the happy ending) and the bad characters have reformed or been banished. This does not mean, however, that good comedy is facile or that in the comic vision the individual must adapt. Instead, the virtues and limits of all parties are recognized with no compromise. Love and marriage are part of comedy because they are based on acceptance with full knowledge. Comedy requires that its players and its audience experience the limits of being human and reconcile themselves to those limits.

The comedies in this section have been grouped under the heading *The Rewards Of Virtue* for more than the obviously ironic meanings. The plays deal with virtues and vices in individuals and societies and the complex relationships among them. Part of the nature of comedy is that it deals with real conduct in contrast with professed ideals and with real consequences rather than expected rewards. *The Misanthrope* raises serious questions about goodness and self-justification. Molière plays brilliantly with the dilemma of the individual who declares the corruption of others and is then unable to know if he has become corrupt. At the end of *The Cherry Orchard*, it has become clear that not all virtues can be rewarded and in this world some virtues get more rewards.

Comedy never glosses over the faults of the world. It starts with the same premise as tragedy: the human is a divided animal, part beast, part angel. Mankind is, as Pope said, "darkly wise and rudely great." In tragedy, this division rends the hero. In comedy, the division is accepted and the search is for some connection for the divided self in a divided world.

Moliere

The Misanthrope

Translated by Richard Wilbur

Characters

ALCESTE, *in love with Célimène*
PHILINTE, *Alceste's friend*
ORONTE, *in love with Célimène*
CELIMENE, *Alceste's beloved*
ELIANTE, *Célimène's cousin*
ARSINOE, *a friend of Célimène's*

ACASTE \
CLITANDRE / *marquesses*
BASQUE, *Célimène's servant*
A GUARD *of the Marshalsea*
DUBOIS, *Alceste's valet*

The scene throughout is in CELIMENE'S *house at Paris.*

ACT ONE

Scene One. Philinte, Alceste.

PHILINTE: Now, what's got into you?
ALCESTE (*seated*): Kindly leave me alone.
PHILINTE: Come, come. what is it? This lugubrious tone . . .
ALCESTE: Leave me, I said; you spoil my solitude.
PHILINTE: Oh, listen to me, now, and don't be rude.
ALCESTE: I choose to be rude, Sir, and to be hard of hearing.
PHILINTE: These ugly moods of yours are not endearing;
   Friends though we are, I really must insist . . .
ALCESTE (*abruptly rising*):
   Friends? Friends, you say? Well, cross me off your list.
   I've been your friend till now, as you well know;
   But after what I saw a moment ago
   I tell you flatly that our ways must part.
   I wish no place in a dishonest heart.
PHILINTE: Why, what have I done, Alceste? Is this quite just?
ALCESTE: My God, you ought to die of self-disgust.
   I call your conduct inexcusable, Sir,
   And every man of honor will concur.
   I see you almost hug a man to death,

Exclaim for joy until you're out of breath,
And supplement these loving demonstrations
With endless offers, vows, and protestations;
Then when I ask you "Who was that?", I find
That you can barely bring his name to mind!
Once the man's back is turned, you cease to love him,
And speak with absolute indifference of him!
By God, I say it's base and scandalous
To falsify the heart's affections thus;
If I caught myself behaving in such a way,
I'd hang myself for shame, without delay.

PHILINTE: It hardly seems a hanging matter to me;
I hope that you will take it graciously
If I extend myself a slight reprieve,
And live a little longer, by your leave.

ALCESTE: How dare you joke about a crime so grave?

PHILINTE: What crime? How else are people to behave?

ALCESTE: I'd have them be sincere, and never part
With any word that isn't from the heart.
With any word that isn't from the heart.

PHILINTE: When someone greets us with a show of pleasure,
It's but polite to give him equal measure,
Return his love the best that we know how,
And trade him offer for offer, vow for vow.

ALCESTE: No, no, this formula you'd have me follow,
However fashionable, is false and hollow,
And I despise the frenzied operations
Of all these barterers of protestations,
These lavishers of meaningless embraces,
These utterers of obliging commonplaces,
Who court and flatter everyone on earth
And praise the fool no less than the man of worth.
Should you rejoice that someone fondles you,
Offers his love and service, swears to be true,
And fills your ears with praises of your name,
When to the first damned fop he'll say the same?
No, no: no self-respecting heart would dream
Of prizing so promiscuous an esteem;
However high the praise, there's nothing worse
Than sharing honors with the universe.
Esteem is founded on comparison:
To honor all men is to honor none.
Since you embrace this indiscriminate vice,
Your friendship comes at far too cheap a price;
I spurn the easy tribute of a heart
Which will not set the worthy man apart:
I choose, Sir, to be chosen; and in fine,

> The friend of mankind is no friend of mine.
>
> PHILINTE: But in polite society, custom decrees
> That we show certain outward courtesies. . . .
>
> ALCESTE: Ah, no! we should condemn with all our force
> Such false and artificial intercourse.
> Let men behave like men; let them display
> Their inmost hearts in everything they say;
> Let the heart speak, and let our sentiments
> Not mask themselves in silly compliments.
>
> PHILINTE: In certain cases it would be uncouth
> And most absurd to speak the naked truth;
> With all respect for your exalted notions,
> It's often best to veil one's true emotions.
> Wouldn't the social fabric come undone
> If we were wholly frank with everyone?
> Suppose you met with someone you couldn't bear;
> Would you inform him of it then and there?
>
> ALCESTE: Yes.
>
> PHILINTE: Then you'd tell old Emilie it's pathetic
> The way she daubs her features with cosmetic
> And plays the gay coquette at sixty-four?
>
> ALCESTE: I would.
>
> PHILINTE: And you'd call Dorilas a bore,
> And tell him every ear at court is lame
> From hearing him brag about his noble name?
>
> ALCESTE: Precisely.
>
> PHILINTE: Ah, you're joking.
>
> ALCESTE: *Au contraire:*
> In this regard there's none I'd choose to spare.
> All are corrupt; there's nothing to be seen
> In court or town but aggravates my spleen.
> I fall into deep gloom and melancholy
> When I survey the scene of human folly,
> Finding on every hand base flattery,
> Injustice, fraud, self-interest, treachery. . . .
> Ah, it's too much; mankind has grown so base,
> I mean to break with the whole human race.
>
> PHILINTE: This philosophic rage is a bit extreme;
> You've no idea how comical you seem;
> Indeed, we're like those brothers in the play
> Called *School for Husbands*,[1] one of whom was prey . . .
>
> ALCESTE: Enough, now! None of your stupid similes.
>
> PHILINTE: Then let's have no more tirades, if you please.
> The world won't change, whatever you say or do;
> And since plain speaking means so much to you,

---

[1] A play by Molière.

I'll tell you plainly that by being frank
You've earned the reputation of a crank,
And that you're thought ridiculous when you rage
And rant against the manners of the age.
ALCESTE: So much the better; just what I wish to hear.
No news could be more grateful to my ear.
All men are so detestable in my eyes,
I should be sorry if they thought me wise.
PHILINTE: Your hatred's very sweeping, is it not?
ALCESTE: Quite right: I hate the whole degraded lot.
PHILINTE: Must all poor human creatures be embraced,
Without distinction, by your vast distaste?
Even in these bad times, there are surely a few . . .
ALCESTE: No, I include all men in one dim view:
Some men I hate for being rogues; the others
I hate because they treat the rogues like brothers,
And, lacking a virtuous scorn for what is vile,
Receive the villain with a complaisant smile.
Notice how tolerant people choose to be
Toward that bold rascal who's at law with me.
His social polish can't conceal his nature;
One sees at once that he's a treacherous creature;
No one could possibly be taken in
By those soft speeches and that sugary grin.
The whole world knows the shady means by which
The low-brow's grown so powerful and rich,
And risen to a rank so bright and high
That virtue can but blush, and merit sigh.
Whenever his name comes up in conversation,
None will defend his wretched reputation;
Call him knave, liar, scoundrel, and all the rest,
Each head will nod, and no one will protest.
And yet his smirk is seen in every house,
He's greeted everywhere with smiles and bows,
And when there's any honor that can be got
By pulling strings, he'll get it, like as not.
My God! It chills my heart to see the ways
Men come to terms with evil nowadays;
Sometimes, I swear, I'm moved to flee and find
Some desert land unfouled by humankind.
PHILINTE: Come, let's forget the follies of the times
And pardon mankind for its petty crimes;
Let's have an end of rantings and of railings,
And show some leniency toward human failings.
This world requires a pliant rectitude;
Too stern a virtue makes one stiff and rude;
Good sense views all extremes with detestation,

And bids us to be noble in moderation.
The rigid virtues of the ancient days
Are not for us; they jar with all our ways
And ask of us too lofty a perfection.
Wise men accept their times without objection,
And there's no greater folly, if you ask me,
Than trying to reform society.
Like you, I see each day a hundred and one
Unhandsome deeds that might be better done,
But still, for all the faults that meet my view,
I'm never known to storm and rave like you.
I take men as they are, or let them be,
And teach my soul to bear their frailty;
And whether in court or town, whatever the scene,
My phlegm's as philosophic as your spleen.[2]
ALCESTE: This phlegm which you so eloquently commend,
Does nothing ever rile it up, my friend?
Suppose some man you trust should treacherously
Conspire to rob you of your property,
And do his best to wreck your reputation?
Wouldn't you feel a certain indignation?
PHILINTE: Why, no. These faults of which you so complain
Are part of human nature, I maintain,
And it's no more a matter for disgust
That men are knavish, selfish and unjust,
Than that the vulture dines upon the dead,
And wolves are furious, and apes ill-bred.
ALCESTE: Shall I see myself betrayed, robbed, torn to bits,
And not . . . Oh, let's be still and rest our wits.
Enough of reasoning, now. I've had my fill.
PHILINTE: Indeed, you would do well, Sir, to be still.
Rage less at your opponent, and give some thought
To how you'll win this lawsuit that he's brought.
ALCESTE: I assure you I'll do nothing of the sort.
PHILINTE: Then who will plead your case before the court?
ALCESTE: Reason and right and justice will plead for me.
PHILINTE: Oh, Lord. What judges do you plan to see?[3]
ALCESTE: Why, none. The justice of my cause is clear.
PHILINTE: Of course, man; but there's politics to fear. . . .
ALCESTE: No, I refuse to lift a hand. That's flat.
I'm either right, or wrong.
PHILINTE: Don't count on that.
ALCESTE: No, I'll do nothing.

---

[2] A reference to opposing "humours" in the old physiology. A preponderance of phlegm produced an apathetic temperament; a preponderance of bile a splenetic temperament.
[3] It was customary to try to influence judges before a trial.

PHILINTE: Your enemy's influence
Is great you know . . .
ALCESTE: That makes no difference.
PHILINTE: It will; you'll see.
ALCESTE: Must honor bow to guile?
If so, I shall be proud to lose the trial.
PHILINTE: Oh, really . . .
ALCESTE: I'll discover by this case
Whether or not men are sufficiently base
And impudent and villainous and perverse
To do me wrong before the universe.
PHILINTE: What a man!
ALCESTE: Oh, I could wish, whatever the cost,
Just for the beauty of it, that my trial were lost.
PHILINTE: If people heard you talking so, Alceste,
They'd split their sides. Your name would be a jest.
ALCESTE: So much the worse for jesters.
PHILINTE: May I enquire
Whether this rectitude you so admire,
And these hard virtues you're enamored of
Are qualities of the lady whom you love?
It much surprises me that you, who seem
To view mankind with furious disesteem,
Have yet found something to enchant your eyes
Amidst a species which you so despise.
And what is more amazing, I'm afraid,
Is the most curious choice your heart has made.
The honest Eliante is fond of you,
Arsinoé, the prude, admires you too;
And yet your spirit's been perversely led
To choose the flighty Célimène instead,
Whose brittle malice and coquettish ways
So typify the manners of our days.
How is it that the traits you most abhor
Are bearable in this lady you adore?
Are you so blind with love that you can't find them?
Or do you contrive, in her case, not to mind them?
ALCESTE: My love for that young widow's not the kind
That can't perceive defects; no, I'm not blind.
I see her faults, despite my ardent love,
And all I see I fervently reprove.
And yet I'm weak; for all her falsity,
That woman knows the art of pleasing me,
And though I never cease complaining of her,
I swear I cannot manage not to love her.
Her charm outweighs her faults; I can but aim
To cleanse her spirit in my love's pure flame.
PHILINTE: That's no small task; I wish you all success.

Molière: *The Misanthrope*

    You think then that she loves you?
ALCESTE: Heavens, yes!
    I wouldn't love her did she not love me.
PHILINTE: Well, if her taste for you is plain to see,
    Why do these rivals cause you such despair?
ALCESTE: True love, Sir, is possessive, and cannot bear
    To share with all the world. I'm here today
    To tell her she must send that mob away.
PHILINTE: If I were you, and had your choice to make,
    Eliante, her cousin, would be the one I'd take;
    That honest heart, which cares for you alone,
    Would harmonize far better with your own.
ALCESTE: True, true: each day my reason tells me so;
    But reason doesn't rule in love, you know.
PHILINTE: I fear some bitter sorrow is in store;
    This love . . .

Scene Two. *Oronte, Alceste, Philinte.*

ORONTE (*to* ALCESTE): The servants told me at the door
    That Eliante and Célimène were out,
    But when I heard, dear Sir, that you were about,
    I came to say, without exaggeration,
    That I hold you in the vastest admiration,
    And that it's always been my dearest desire
    To be the friend of one I so admire.
    I hope to see my love of merit requited,
    And you and I in friendship's bond united.
    I'm sure you won't refuse—if I may be frank—
    A friend of my devotedness—and rank.

(*During this speech of* ORONTE'S, ALCESTE *is abstracted, and seems unaware that he is being spoken to. He only breaks off his reverie when* ORONTE *says*)

    It was for you, if you please, that my words were intended.
ALCESTE: For me, Sir?
ORONTE: Yes, for you. You're not offended?
ALCESTE: By no means. But this much surprises me. . . .
    The honor comes most unexpectedly. . . .
ORONTE: My high regard should not astonish you;
    The whole world feels the same. It is your due.
ALCESTE: Sir . . .
ORONTE: Why, in all the State there isn't one
    Can match your merits; they shine, Sir, like the sun.
ALCESTE: Sir . . .
ORONTE: You are higher in my estimation
    Then all that's most illustrious in the nation.

ALCESTE: Sir . . .
ORONTE: If I lie, may heaven strike me dead!
  To show you that I mean what I have said,
  Permit me, Sir, to embrace you most sincerely,
  And swear that I will prize our friendship dearly.
  Give me your hand. And now, Sir, if you choose,
  We'll make our vows.
ALCESTE: Sir . . .
ORONTE: What! You refuse?
ALCESTE: Sir, it's a very great honor you extend:
  But friendship is a sacred thing, my friend;
  It would be profanation to bestow
  The name of friend on one you hardly know.
  All parts are better played when well-rehearsed;
  Let's put off friendship, and get acquainted first.
  We may discover it would be unwise
  To try to make our natures harmonize.
ORONTE: By heaven! You're sagacious to the core;
  This speech has made me admire you even more.
  Let time, then, bring us closer day by day;
  Meanwhile, I shall be yours in every way.
  If, for example, there should be anything
  You wish at court, I'll mention it to the King.
  I have his ear, of course; it's quite well known
  That I am much in favor with the throne.
  In short, I am your servant. And now, dear friend,
  Since you have such fine judgment, I intend
  To please you, if I can, with a small sonnet
  I wrote not long ago. Please comment on it,
  And tell me whether I ought to publish it.
ALCESTE: You must excuse me, Sir; I'm hardly fit
  To judge such matters.
ORONTE: Why not?
ALCESTE: I am, I fear,
  Inclined to be unfashionably sincere.
ORONTE: Just what I ask; I'd take no satisfaction
  In anything but your sincere reaction.
  I beg you not to dream of being kind.
ALCESTE: Since you desire it, Sir, I'll speak my mind.
ORONTE: *Sonnet. It's a sonnet. . . . Hope . . . The poem's addressed
  To a lady who wakened hopes within my breast.
  Hope . . . this is not the pompous sort of thing,
  Just modest little verses, with a tender ring.*
ALCESTE: Well, we shall see.
ORONTE: *Hope . . . I'm anxious to hear
  Whether the style seems properly smooth and clear,
  And whether the choice of words is good or bad.*

ALCESTE: We'll see, we'll see.
ORONTE: Perhaps I ought to add
 That it took me only a quarter-hour to write it.
ALCESTE: The time's irrelevant, Sir: kindly recite it.
ORONTE (*reading*): Hope comforts us awhile, t'is true,
 Lulling our cares with careless laughter,
 And yet such joy is full of rue,
 My Phyllis, if nothing follows after.
PHILINTE: I'm charmed by this already; the style's delightful.
ALCESTE (*sotto voce to* PHILINTE): How can you say that?
 Why, the thing is frightful.
ORONTE: Your fair face smiled on me awhile,
 But was it kindness so to enchant me?
 'Twould have been fairer not to smile,
 If hope was all you meant to grant me.
PHILINTE: What a clever thought! How handsomely you phrase it!
ALCESTE (*sotto voce to* PHILINTE): You know the thing is trash.
 How dare you praise it?
ORONTE: If it's to be my passion's fate
 Thus everlastingly to wait,
 Then death will come to set me free:
 For death is fairer than the fair;
 Phyllis, to hope is to despair
 When one must hope eternally.
PHILINTE: The close is exquisite—full of feeling and grace.
ALCESTE (*sotto voce, aside*): Oh, blast the close;
 you'd better close your face
 Before you send your lying soul to hell.
PHILINTE: I can't remember a poem I've liked so well.
ALCESTE (*sotto voce, aside*): Good Lord!
ORONTE (*to* PHILINTE): I fear you're flattering me a bit.
PHILINTE: Oh, no!
ALCESTE (*sotto voce, aside*): What else d'you call it, you hypocrite?
ORONTE (*to* ALCESTE): But you, Sir, keep your promise now: don't shrink
 From telling me sincerely what you think.
ALCESTE: Sir, these are delicate matters; we all desire
 To be told that we've the true poetic fire.
 But once, to one whose name I shall not mention,
 I said, regarding some verse of his invention,
 That gentlemen should rigorously control
 That itch to write which often afflicts the soul;
 That one should curb the heady inclination
 To publicize one's little avocation;
 And that in showing off one's works of art
 One often plays a very clownish part.
ORONTE: Are you suggesting in a devious way
 That I ought not . . .

ALCESTE: Oh, that I do not say.
   Further, I told him that no fault is worse
   Than that of writing frigid, lifeless verse,
   And that the merest whisper of such a shame
   Suffices to destroy a man's good name.
ORONTE: D'you mean to say my sonnet's dull and trite?
ALCESTE: I don't say that. But I went on to cite
   Numerous cases of once-respected men
   Who came to grief by taking up the pen.
ORONTE: And am I like them? Do I write so poorly?
ALCESTE: I don't say that. But I told this person, "Surely
   You're under no necessity to compose;
   Why you should wish to publish, heaven knows.
   There's no excuse for printing tedious rot
   Unless one writes for bread, as you do not.
   Resist temptation, then, I beg of you;
   Conceal your pastimes from the public view;
   And don't give up, on any provocation,
   Your present high and courtly reputation,
   To purchase at a greedy printer's shop
   The name of silly author and scribbling fop."
   These were the points I tried to make him see.
ORONTE: I sense that they are also aimed at me;
   But now—about my sonnet—I'd like to be told . . .
ALCESTE: Frankly, that sonnet should be pigeonholed.
   You've chosen the worst models to imitate.
   The style's unnatural. Let me illustrate:

> Followed by, *'Twould have been fairer not to smile!*
> For example, *Your fair face smiled on me awhile,*
> Or this: *such joy is full of rue;*
> Or this: *For death is fairer than the fair;*
> Or, *Phyllis, to hope is to despair*
>   *When one must hope eternally!*

This artificial style, that's all the fashion,
Has neither taste nor honesty, nor passion;
It's nothing but a sort of wordy play,
And nature never spoke in such a way.
What, in this shallow age, is not debased?
Our fathers, though less refined, had better taste;
I'd barter all that men admire today
For one old love-song I shall try to say:

> If the King had given me for my own
> Paris, his citadel,
> And I for that must leave alone
> Her whom I love so well,
> I'd say then to the Crown,
> Take back your glittering town;

Molière: *The Misanthrope*

> My darling is more fair, I swear,
> My darling is more fair.

The rhyme's not rich, the style is rough and old,
But don't you see that it's the purest gold
Beside the tinsel nonsense now preferred,
And that there's passion in its every word?

> If the King had given me for my own
> Paris, his citadel,
> And I for that must leave alone
> Her whom I love so well,
> I'd say then to the Crown,
> Take back your glittering town;
> My darling is more fair, I swear,
> My darling is more fair.

There speaks a loving heart. (*To* PHILINTE) You're laughing, eh?
Laugh on, my precious wit. Whatever you say,
I hold that song's worth all the bibelots
That people hail today with ah's and oh's.

ORONTE: And I maintain my sonnet's very good.
ALCESTE: It's not at all surprising that you should.
  You have your reasons; permit me to have mine
  For thinking that you cannot write a line.
ORONTE: Others have praised my sonnet to the skies.
ALCESTE: I lack their art of telling lies.
ORONTE: You seem to think you've got no end of wit.
ALCESTE: To praise your verse, I'd need still more of it.
ORONTE: I'm not in need of your approval, Sir.
ALCESTE: That's good; you couldn't have it if you were.
ORONTE: Come now, I'll lend you the subject of my sonnet;
  I'd like to see you try to improve upon it.
ALCESTE: I might, by chance, write something just as shoddy;
  But then I wouldn't show it to everybody.
ORONTE: You're most opinionated and conceited.
ALCESTE: Go find your flatterers, and be better treated.
ORONTE: Look here, my little fellow, pray watch your tone.
ALCESTE: My great big fellow, you'd better watch your own.
PHILINTE (*stepping between them*): Oh, please, please, gentlemen!
  This will never do.
ORONTE: The fault is mine, and I leave the field to you.
  I am your servant, Sir, in every way.
ALCESTE: And I, Sir, am your most abject valet.

Scene Three. Philinte, Alceste.

PHILINTE: Well, as you see, sincerity in excess
  Can get you into a very pretty mess;

Oronte was hungry for appreciation. . . .
ALCESTE: Don't speak to me.
PHILINTE: What?
ALCESTE: No more conversation.
PHILINTE: Really, now . . .
ALCESTE: Leave me alone.
PHILINTE: If I . . .
ALCESTE: Out of my sight!
PHILINTE: But what . . .
ALCESTE: I won't listen.
PHILINTE: But . . .
ALCESTE: Silence!
PHILINTE: Now, is it polite . . .
ALCESTE: By heaven, I've had enough. Don't follow me.
PHILINTE: Ah, you're just joking. I'll keep you company.

ACT TWO

Scene One. Alceste, Celimene.

ALCESTE: Shall I speak plainly, Madam? I confess
  Your conduct gives me infinite distress,
  And my resentment's grown too hot to smother.
  Soon, I foresee, we'll break with one another.
  If I said otherwise, I should deceive you;
  Sooner or later, I shall be forced to leave you,
  And if I swore that we shall never part,
  I should misread the omens of my heart.
CELIMENE: You kindly saw me home, it would appear,
  So as to pour invectives in my ear.
ALCESTE: I've no desire to quarrel. But I deplore
  Your inability to shut the door
  On all these suitors who beset you so.
  There's what annoys me, if you care to know.
CELIMENE: It is my fault that all these men pursue me?
  Am I to blame if they're attracted to me?
  And when they gently beg an audience,
  Ought I to take a stick and drive them hence?
ALCESTE: Madam, there's no necessity for a stick;
  A less responsive heart would do the trick.
  Of your attractiveness I don't complain;
  But those your charms attract, you then detain
  By a most melting and receptive manner,
  And so enlist their hearts beneath your banner.
  It's the agreeable hopes which you excite
  That keep these lovers round you day and night;

Were they less liberally smiled upon,
   That sighing troop would very soon be gone.
   But tell me, Madam, why it is that lately
   This man Clitandre interests you so greatly?
   Because of what high merits do you deem
   Him worthy of the honor of your esteem?
   Is it that your admiring glances linger
   On the splendidly long nail of his little finger?
   Or do you share the general deep respect
   For the blond wig he chooses to affect?
   Are you in love with his embroidered hose?
   Do you adore his ribbons and his bows?
   Or is it that this paragon bewitches
   Your tasteful eye with his vast German breeches?
   Perhaps his giggle, or his falsetto voice,
   Makes him the latest gallant of your choice?[4]
CELIMENE: You're much mistaken to resent him so.
   Why I put up with him you surely know:
   My lawsuit's very shortly to be tried,
   And I must have his influence on my side.
ALCESTE: Then lose your lawsuit, Madam, or let it drop;
   Don't torture me by humoring such a fop.
CELIMENE: You're jealous of the whole world, Sir.
ALCESTE: That's true,
   Since the whole world is well-received by you.
CELIMENE: That my good nature is so unconfined
   Should serve to pacify your jealous mind;
   Were I to smile on one, and scorn the rest,
   Then you might have some cause to be distressed.
ALCESTE: Well, if I mustn't be jealous, tell me, then,
   Just how I'm better treated than other men.
CELIMENE: You know you have my love. Will that not do?
ALCESTE: What proof have I that what you say is true?
CELIMENE: I would expect, Sir, that my having said it
   Might give the statement a sufficient credit.
ALCESTE: But how can I be sure that you don't tell
   The selfsame thing to other men as well?
CELIMENE: What a gallant speech! How flattering to me!
   What a sweet creature you make me out to be!
   Well then, to save you from the pangs of doubt,
   All that I've said I hereby cancel out;
   Now, none but yourself shall make a monkey of you:
   Are you content?
ALCESTE: Why, why am I doomed to love you?
   I swear that I shall bless the blissful hour
   When this poor heart's no longer in your power!

---

[4] Molière frequently ridicules the fashionable fops of the day.

> I make no secret of it: I've done my best
> To exorcise this passion from my breast;
> But thus far all in vain; it will not go;
> It's for my sins that I must love you so.

CELIMENE: Your love for me is matchless, Sir; that's clear.
ALCESTE: Indeed, in all the world it has no peer;
> Words can't describe the nature of my passion,
> And no man ever loved in such a fashion.

CELIMENE: Yes, it's a brand-new fashion, I agree:
> You show your love by castigating me,
> And all your speeches are enraged and rude.
> I've never been so furiously wooed.

ALCESTE: Yet you could calm that fury, if you chose.
> Come, shall we bring our quarrels to a close?
> Let's speak with open hearts, then, and begin . . .

Scene Two. Celimene, Alceste, Basque.

CELIMENE: What is it?
BASQUE: Acaste is here.
CELIMENE: Well, send him in.

Scene Three. Celimene, Alceste.

ALCESTE: What! Shall we never be alone at all?
> You're always ready to receive a call,
> And you can't bear, for ten ticks of the clock,
> Not to keep open house for all who knock.

CELIMENE: I couldn't refuse him: he'd be most put out.
ALCESTE: Surely that's not worth worrying about.
CELIMENE: Acaste would never forgive me if he guessed
> That I consider him a dreadful pest.

ALCESTE: If he's a pest, why bother with him then?
CELIMENE: Heavens! One can't antagonize such men;
> Why, they're the chartered gossips of the court,
> And have a say in things of every sort.
> One must receive them, and be full of charm;
> They're no great help, but they can do you harm,
> And though your influence be ever so great,
> They're hardly the best people to alienate.

ALCESTE: I see, dear lady, that you could make a case
> For putting up with the whole human race;
> These friendships that you calculate so nicely . . .

Scene Four. Alceste, Celimene, Basque.

BASQUE: Madam, Clitandre is here as well.

Molière: *The Misanthrope*

ALCESTE: Precisely.
CELIMENE: Where are you going?
ALCESTE: Elsewhere.
CELIMENE: Stay.
ALCESTE: No, no.
CELIMENE: Stay, Sir.
ALCESTE: I can't.
CELIMENE: I wish it.
ALCESTE: No, I must go.
    I beg you, Madam, not to press the matter;
    You know I have no taste for idle chatter.
CELIMENE: Stay: I command you.
ALCESTE: No, I cannot stay.
CELIMENE: Very well; you have my leave to go away.

Scene Five. Eliante, Philinte, Acaste, Clitandre, Alceste, Celimene, Basque.

ELIANTE (*to* CELIMENE): The Marquesses have kindly come to call.
    Were they announced?
CELIMENE: Yes, Basque, bring chairs for all.

    (BASQUE *provides the chairs, and exits*)
    (*To* ALCESTE)

    You haven't gone?
ALCESTE: No; and I shan't depart
    Till you decide who's foremost in your heart.
CELIMENE: Oh, hush.
ALCESTE: It's time to choose; take them, or me.
CELIMENE: You're mad.
ALCESTE: I'm not, as you shall shortly see.
CELIMENE: Oh?
ALCESTE: You'll decide.
CELIMENE: You're joking now, dear friend.
ALCESTE: No, no; you'll choose; my patience is at an end.
CLITANDRE: Madam, I come from court, where poor Cléonte
    Behaved like a perfect fool, as is his wont.
    Has he no friend to counsel him, I wonder,
    And teach him less unerringly to blunder?
CELIMENE: It's true, the man's a most accomplished dunce;
    His gauche behavior strikes the eye at once;
    And every time one sees him, on my word,
    His manner's grown a trifle more absurd.
ACASTE: Speaking of dunces, I've just now conversed
    With old Damon, who's one of the very worst;
    I stood a lifetime in the broiling sun
    Before his dreary monologue was done.

CELIMENE: Oh, he's a wondrous talker, and has the power
  To tell you nothing hour after hour:
  If, by mistake, he ever came to the point,
  The shock would put his jawbone out of joint.
ELIANTE (*to* PHILINTE): The conversation takes its usual turn,
  And all our dear friends' ears will shortly burn.
CLITANDRE: Timante's a character, Madam.
CELIMENE: Isn't he though?
  A man of mystery from top to toe,
  Who moves about in a romantic mist
  On secret missions which do not exist.
  His talk is full of eyebrows and grimaces;
  How tired one gets of his momentous faces;
  He's always whispering something confidential
  Which turns out to be quite inconsequential;
  Nothing's too slight for him to mystify;
  He even whispers when he says "good-by."
ACASTE: Tell us about Géralde.
CELIMENE: That tiresome ass.
  He mixes only with the titled class,
  And fawns on dukes and princes, and is bored
  With anyone who's not at least a lord.
  The man's obsessed with rank, and his discourses
  Are all of hounds and carriages and horses;
  He uses Christian names with all the great,
  And the word Milord, with him, is out of date.
CLITANDRE: He's very taken with Bélise, I hear.
CELIMENE: She is the dreariest company, poor dear.
  Whenever she comes to call, I grope about
  To find some topic which will draw her out,
  But, owing to her dry and faint replies,
  The conversation wilts, and droops, and dies.
  In vain one hopes to animate her face
  By mentioning the ultimate commonplace;
  But sun or shower, even hail or frost
  Are matters she can instantly exhaust.
  Meanwhile her visit, painful though it is,
  Drags on and on through mute eternities,
  And though you ask the time, and yawn, and yawn,
  She sits there like a stone and won't be gone.
ACASTE: Now for Adraste.
CELIMENE: Oh, that conceited elf
  Has a gigantic passion for himself;
  He rails against the court, and cannot bear it
  That none will recognize his hidden merit;
  All honors given to others give offense
  To his imaginary excellence.

CLITANDRE: What about young Cléon? His house, they say,
  Is full of the best society, night and day.
CELIMENE: His cook has made him popular, not he:
  It's Cléon's table that people come to see.
ELIANTE: He gives a splendid dinner, you must admit.
CELIMENE: But must he serve himself along with it?
  For my taste, he's a most insipid dish
  Whose presence sours the wine and spoils the fish.
PHILINTE: Damis, his uncle, is admired no end.
  What's your opinion, Madam?
CELIMENE: Why, he's my friend.
PHILINTE: He seems a decent fellow, and rather clever.
CELIMENE: He works too hard at cleverness, however.
  I hate to see him sweat and struggle so
  To fill his conversation with bon mots.
  Since he's decided to become a wit
  His taste's so pure that nothing pleases it;
  He scolds at all the latest books and plays,
  Thinking that wit must never stoop to praise,
  That finding fault's a sign of intellect,
  That all appreciation is abject,
  And that by damning everything in sight
  One shows oneself in a distinguished light.
  He's scornful even of our conversations:
  Their trivial nature sorely tries his patience;
  He folds his arms, and stands above the battle,
  And listens sadly to our childish prattle.
ACASTE: Wonderful, Madam! You've hit him off precisely.
CLITANDRE: No one can sketch a character so nicely.
ALCESTE: How bravely, Sirs, you cut and thrust at all.
  These absent fools, till one by one they fall:
  But let one come in sight, and you'll at once
  Embrace the man you lately called a dunce,
  Telling him in a tone sincere and fervent
  How proud you are to be his humble servant.
CLITANDRE: Why pick on us? Madame's been speaking, Sir,
  And you should quarrel, if you must, with her.
ALCESTE: No, no, by God, the fault is yours, because
  You lead her on with laughter and applause,
  And make her think that she's the more delightful
  The more her talk is scandalous and spiteful.
  Oh, she would stoop to malice far, far less
  If no such claque approved her cleverness.
  It's flatterers like you whose foolish praise
  Nourishes all the vices of these days.
PHILINTE: But why protest when someone ridicules
  Those you'd condemn, yourself, as knaves or fools?

CELIMENE: Why, Sir? Because he loves to make a fuss.
   You don't expect him to agree with us,
   When there's an opportunity to express
   His heaven-sent spirit of contrariness?
   What other people think, he can't abide;
   Whatever they say, he's on the other side;
   He lives in deadly terror of agreeing;
   'Twould make him seem an ordinary being.
   Indeed, he's so in love with contradiction,
   He'll turn against his most profound conviction
   And with a furious eloquence deplore it,
   If only someone else is speaking for it.
ALCESTE: Go on, dear lady, mock me as you please;
   You have your audience in ecstasies.
PHILINTE: But what she says is true: you have a way
   Of bridling at whatever people say;
   Whether they praise or blame, your angry spirit
   Is equally unsatisfied to hear it.
ALCESTE: Men, Sir, are always wrong, and that's the reason
   That righteous anger's never out of season;
   All that I hear in all their conversation
   Is flattering praise or reckless condemnation.
CELIMENE: But . . .
ALCESTE: No, no, Madam, I am forced to state
   That you have pleasures which I deprecate,
   And that these others, here, are much to blame
   For nourishing the faults which are your shame.
CLITANDRE: I shan't defend myself, Sir; but I vow
   I'd thought this lady faultless until now.
ACASTE: I see her charms and graces, which are many;
   But as for faults, I've never noticed any.
ALCESTE: I see them, Sir; and rather than ignore them,
   I strenuously criticize her for them.
   The more one loves, the more one should object
   To every blemish, every least defect.
   Were I this lady, I would soon get rid
   Of lovers who approved of all I did,
   And by their slack indulgence and applause
   Endorsed my follies and excused my flaws.
CELIMENE: If all hearts beat according to your measure,
   The dawn of love would be the end of pleasure;
   And love would find its perfect consummation
   In ecstasies of rage and reprobation.
ELIANTE: Love, as a rule, affects men otherwise,
   And lovers rarely love to criticize.
   They see their lady as a charming blur,

Molière: *The Misanthrope*

And find all things commendable in her.
If she has any blemish, fault, or shame,
They will redeem it by a pleasing name.
The pale-faced lady's lily-white, perforce;
The swarthy one's a sweet brunette, of course;
The spindly lady has a slender grace;
The fat one has a most majestic pace;
The plain one, with her dress in disarray,
They classify as *beauté négligée;*
The hulking one's a goddess in their eyes,
The dwarf, a concentrate of Paradise;
The haughty lady has a noble mind;
The mean one's witty, and the dull one's kind;
The chatterbox has liveliness and verve,
The mute one has a virtuous reserve.
So lovers manage, in their passion's cause,
To love their ladies even for their flaws.[5]

ALCESTE: But I still say . . .
CELIMENE: I think it would be nice.
To stroll around the gallery once or twice.
What! You're not going, Sirs?
CLITANDRE AND ACASTE: No, Madam, no.
ALCESTE: You seem to be in terror lest they go.
Do what you will, Sirs; leave, or linger on,
But I shan't go till after you are gone.
ACASTE: I'm free to linger, unless I should perceive
Madame is tired, and wishes me to leave.
CLITANDRE: And as for me, I needn't go today
Until the hour of the King's *coucher.*
CELIMENE (*to* ALCESTE): You're joking, surely?
ALCESTE: Not in the least; we'll see
Whether you'd rather part with them, or me.

Scene Six. Alceste, Celimene, Eliante, Acaste, Philinte, Clitandre, Basque.

BASQUE (*to* ALCESTE): Sir, there's a fellow here who bids me state
That he must see you, and that it can't wait.
ALCESTE: Tell him that I have no such pressing affairs.
BASQUE: It's a long tailcoat that this fellow wears,
With gold all over.

---

[5] A paraphrase of a passage from Lucretius, *De Rerum Natura,* Book IV. Molière is said to have translated Lucretius' poem as a student.

CELIMENE *(to* ALCESTE*)*: You'd best go down and see.
Or—have him enter.

Scene Seven. *Alceste, Celimene, Eliante, Acaste, Philinte, Clitandre, a Guard of the Marshalsea.*

ALCESTE *(confronting the* GUARD*)*: Well, what do want with me?
Come in, Sir.
GUARD: I've a word, Sir, for your ear.
ALCESTE: Speak it aloud, Sir; I shall strive to hear.
GUARD: The Marshals have instructed me to say
You must report to them without delay.
ALCESTE: Who? Me, Sir?
GUARD: Yes, Sir; you.
ALCESTE: But what do they want?
PHILINTE *(to* ALCESTE*)*: To scotch your silly quarrel with Oronte.
CELIMENE *(to* PHILINTE*)*: What quarrel?
PHILINTE: Oronte and he have fallen out
Over some verse he spoke his mind about;
The Marshals wish to arbitrate the matter.[6]
ALCESTE: Never shall I equivocate or flatter!
PHILINTE: You'd best obey their summons; come, let's go.
ALCESTE: How can they mend our quarrel, I'd like to know?
Am I to make a cowardly retraction,
And praise those jingles to his satisfaction?
I'll not recant; I've judged that sonnet rightly.
It's bad.
PHILINTE: But you might say so more politely. . . .
ALCESTE: I'll not back down; his verses make me sick.
PHILINTE: If only you could be more politic!
But come, let's go.
ALCESTE: I'll go, but I won't unsay
A single word.
PHILINTE: Well, let's be on our way.
ALCESTE: Till I am ordered by my lord the King
To praise that poem, I shall say the thing
Is scandalous, by God, and that the poet
Ought to be hanged for having the nerve to show it.
(To CLITANDRE *and* ACASTE, *who are laughing)*
By heaven Sirs, I really didn't know
That I was being humorous.
CELIMENE: Go, Sir, go;
Settle your business.
ALCESTE: I shall, and when I'm through,
I shall return to settle things with you.

[6] The Marshals were charged with preventing duels, which, though against the law, were frequent.

Molière: *The Misanthrope*

ACT THREE

Scene One. Clitandre, Acaste.

CLITANDRE: Dear Marquess, how contented you appear;
　All things delight you, nothing mars your cheer.
　Can you, in perfect honesty, declare
　That you've a right to be so debonair?
ACASTE: By Jove, when I survey myself, I find
　No cause whatever for distress of mind.
　I'm young and rich; I can in modesty
　Lay claim to an exalted pedigree;
　And owing to my name and my condition
　I shall not want for honors and position.
　Then as to courage, that most precious trait,
　I seem to have it, as was proved of late
　Upon the field of honor, where my bearing,
　They say, was very cool and rather daring.
　I've wit, of course; and taste in such perfection
　That I can judge without the least reflection,
　And at the theater, which is my delight,
　Can make or break a play on opening night,
　And lead the crowd in hisses or bravos,
　And generally be known as one who knows.
　I'm clever, handsome, gracefully polite;
　My waist is small, my teeth are strong and white;
　As for my dress, the world's astonished eyes
　Assure me that I bear away the prize.
　I find myself in favor everywhere,
　Honored by men, and worshiped by the fair;
　And since these things are so, it seems to me
　I'm justified in my complacency.
CLITANDRE: Well, if so many ladies hold you dear,
　Why do you press a hopeless courtship here?
ACASTE: Hopeless, you say? I'm not the sort of fool
　That likes his ladies difficult and cool.
　Men who are awkward, shy, and peasantish
　May pine for heartless beauties, if they wish,
　Grovel before them, bear their cruelties,
　Woo them with tears and sighs and bended knees,
　And hope by dogged faithfulness to gain
　What their poor merits never could obtain.
　For men like me, however, it makes no sense
　To love on trust, and foot the whole expense.
　Whatever any lady's merits be,
　I think, thank God, that I'm as choice as she;
　That if my heart is kind enough to burn

       For her, she owes me something in return;
       And that in any proper love affair
       The partners must invest an equal share.
CLITANDRE: You think, then, that our hostess favors you?
ACASTE: I've reason to believe that that is true.
CLITANDRE: How did you come to such a mad conclusion?
       You're blind, dear fellow. This is sheer delusion.
ACASTE: All right, then: I'm deluded and I'm blind.
CLITANDRE: Whatever put the notion in your mind?
ACASTE: Delusion.
CLITANDRE: What persuades you that you're right?
ACASTE: I'm blind.
CLITANDRE: But have you any proofs to cite?
ACASTE: I tell you I'm deluded.
CLITANDRE: Have you, then,
       Received some secret pledge from Célimène?
ACASTE: Oh, no: she scorns me.
CLITANDRE: Tell me the truth, I beg.
ACASTE: She just can't bear me.
CLITANDRE: Ah, don't pull my leg.
       Tell me what hope she's given you, I pray.
ACASTE: I'm hopeless, and it's you who win the day.
       She hates me thoroughly, and I'm so vexed
       I mean to hang myself on Tuesday next.
CLITANDRE: Dear Marquess, let us have an armistice
       And make a treaty. What do you say to this?
       If ever one of us can plainly prove
       That Célimène encourages his love,
       The other must abandon hope, and yield,
       And leave him in possession of the field.
ACASTE: Now, there's a bargain that appeals to me;
       With all my heart, dear Marquess, I agree.
       But hush.

Scene Two. *Celimene, Acaste, Clitandre.*

CELIMENE: Still here?
CLITANDRE: T'was love that stayed our feet.
CELIMENE: I think I heard a carriage in the street.
       Whose is it? D'you know?

Scene Three. *Celimene, Acaste, Clitandre, Basque.*

BASQUE: Arsinoé is here,
       Madame.

Molière: *The Misanthrope*

CELIMENE: Arsinoé, you say? Oh, dear.
BASQUE: Eliante is entertaining her below.
CELIMENE: What brings the creature here, I'd like to know?
ACASTE: They say she's dreadfully prudish, but in fact
   I think her piety . . .
CELIMENE: It's all an act.
   At heart she's wordly, and her poor success
   In snaring men explains her prudishness.
   It breaks her heart to see the beaux and gallants
   Engrossed by other women's charms and talents,
   And so she's always in a jealous rage
   Against the faulty standards of the age.
   She lets the world believe that she's a prude.
   To justify her loveless solitude,
   And strives to put a brand of moral shame
   On all the graces that she cannot claim.
   But still she'd love a lover; and Alceste
   Appears to be the one she'd love the best.
   His visits here are poison to her pride;
   She seems to think I've lured him from her side;
   And everywhere, at court or in the town,
   The spiteful, envious woman runs me down.
   In short, she's just as stupid as can be,
   Vicious and arrogant in the last degree,
   And . . .

Scene Four. Arsinoe, Celimene, Clitandre, Acaste.

CELIMENE: Ah! What happy chance has brought you here?
   I've thought about you ever so much, my dear.
ARSINOE: I've come to tell you something you should know.
CELIMENE: How good of you to think of doing so!
                        (CLITANDRE *and* ACASTE *go out, laughing*)

Scene Five. Arsinoe, Celimene.

ARSINOE: It's just as well those gentlemen didn't tarry.
CELIMENE: Shall we sit down?
ARSINOE: That won't be necessary.
   Madam, the flame of friendship ought to burn
   Brightest in matters of the most concern,
   And as there's nothing which concerns us more
   Than honor, I have hastened to your door
   To bring you, as your friend, some information
   About the status of your reputation.

I visited, last night, some virtuous folk,
And, quite by chance, it was of you they spoke;
There was, I fear, no tendency to praise
Your light behavior and your dashing ways.
The quantity of gentlemen you see
And your by now notorious coquetry
Were both so vehemently criticized
By everyone, that I was much surprised.
Of course, I needn't tell you where I stood;
I came to your defense as best I could,
Assured them you were harmless, and declared
Your soul was absolutely unimpaired.
But there are some things, you must realize,
One can't excuse, however hard one tries,
And I was forced at last into conceding
That your behavior, Madam, is misleading,
That it makes a bad impression, giving rise
To ugly gossip and obscene surmise,
And that if you were more *overtly* good,
You wouldn't be so much misunderstood.
Not that I think you've been unchaste—no! no!
The saints preserve me from a thought so low!
But mere good conscience never did suffice:
One must avoid the outward show of vice.
Madam, you're too intelligent, I'm sure,
To think my motives anything but pure
In offering you this counsel—which I do
Out of a zealous interest in you.
CELIMENE: Madam, I haven't taken you amiss;
I'm very much obliged to you for this;
And I'll at once discharge the obligation
By telling you about *your* reputation.
You've been so friendly as to let me know
What certain people say of me, and so
I mean to follow your benign example
By offering you a somewhat similar sample.
The other day, I went to an affair
And found some most distinguished people there
Discussing piety, both false and true.
The conversation soon came round to you.
Alas! Your prudery and bustling zeal
Appeared to have a very slight appeal.
Your affectation of a grave demeanor,
Your endless talk of virtue and of honor,
The aptitude of your suspicious mind
For finding sin where there is none to find.
Your towering self-esteem, that pitying face

With which you contemplate the human race,
Your sermonizings and your sharp aspersions
On people's pure and innocent diversions
All these were mentioned, Madam, and, in fact,
Were roundly and concertedly attacked.
"What good," they said, "are all these outward shows,
When everything belies her pious pose?
She prays incessantly; but then, they say,
She beats her maids and cheats them of their pay;
She shows her zeal in every holy place,
But still she's vain enough to paint her face;
She holds that naked statues are immoral,
But with a naked *man* she'd have no quarrel."
Of course, I said to everybody there
That they were being viciously unfair;
But still they were disposed to criticize you,
And all agreed that someone should advise you
To leave the morals of the world alone,
And worry rather more about your own.
They felt that one's self-knowledge should be great
Before one thinks of setting others straight;
That one should learn the art of living well
Before one threatens other men with hell,
And that the Church is best equipped, no doubt,
To guide our souls and root our vices out.
Madam, you're too intelligent, I'm sure,
To think my motives anything but pure
In offering you this counsel—which I do
Out of a zealous interest in you.
ARSINOE: I dared not hope for gratitude, but I
Did not expect so acid a reply;
I judge, since you've been so extremely tart,
That my good counsel pierced you to the heart.
CELIMENE: Far from it, Madam. Indeed, it seems to me
We ought to trade advice more frequently.
One's vision of oneself is so defective
That it would be an excellent corrective.
If you are willing, Madam, let's arrange
Shortly to have another frank exchange
In which we'll tell each other, *entre nous*,
What you've heard tell of me, and I of you.
ARSINOE: Oh, people never censure you, my dear;
It's me they criticize. Or so I hear.
CELIMENE: Madam, I think we either blame or praise
According to our taste and length of days.
There is a time of life for coquetry,
And there's a season, too, for prudery.

When all one's charms are gone, it is, I'm sure,
Good strategy to be devout and pure:
It makes one seem a little less forsaken.
Some day, perhaps, I'll take the road you've taken:
Time brings all things. But I have time aplenty,
And see no cause to be a prude at twenty.
ARSINOE: You give your age in such a gloating tone
That one would think I was an ancient crone;
We're not so far apart, in sober truth,
That you can mock me with a boast of youth!
Madam, you baffle me. I wish I knew
What moves you to provoke me as you do.
CELIMENE: For my part, Madam, I should like to know
Why you abuse me everywhere you go.
Is it my fault, dear lady, that your hand
Is not, alas, in very great demand?
If men admire me, if they pay me court
And daily make me offers of the sort
You'd dearly love to have them make to you,
How can I help it? What would you have me do?
If what you want is lovers, please feel free
To take as many as you can from me.
ARSINOE: Oh, come. D'you think the world is losing sleep
Over that flock of lovers which you keep,
Or that we find it difficult to guess
What price you pay for their devotedness?
Surely you don't expect us to suppose
Mere merit could attract so many beaux?
It's not your virtue that they're dazzled by;
Nor is it virtuous love for which they sigh.
You're fooling no one, Madam; the world's not blind;
There's many a lady heaven has designed
To call men's noblest, tenderest feelings out,
Who has no lovers dogging her about;
From which it's plain that lovers nowadays
Must be acquired in bold and shameless ways,
And only pay one court for such reward
As modesty and virtue can't afford.
Then don't be quite so puffed up, if you please,
About your tawdry little victories;
Try, if you can, to be a shade less vain,
And treat the world with somewhat less disdain.
If one were envious of your amours,
One soon could have a following like yours;
Lovers are no great trouble to collect
If one prefers them to one's self-respect.
CELIMENE: Collect them then, my dear; I'd love to see

You demonstrate that charming theory;
Who knows, you might . . .
ARSINOE: Now, Madam, that will do;
It's time to end this trying interview.
My coach is late in coming to your door,
Or I'd have taken leave of you before.
CELIMENE: Oh, please don't feel that you must rush away;
I'd be delighted, Madam, if you'd stay.
However, lest my conversation bore you,
Let me provide some better company for you;
This gentleman, who comes most apropos,
Will please you more than I could do, I know.

Scene Six. *Alceste, Celimene, Arsinoe.*

CELIMENE: Alceste, I have a little note to write
Which simply must go out before tonight;
Please entertain *Madame*; I'm sure that she
Will overlok my incivility.

Scene Seven. *Alceste, Arsinoe.*

ARSINOE: Well, Sir, our hostess graciously contrives
For us to chat until my coach arrives;
And I shall be forever in her debt
For granting me this little tête-à-tête.
We women very rightly give our hearts
To men of noble character and parts,
And your especial merits, dear Alceste,
Have roused the deepest sympathy in my breast.
Oh, how I wish they had sufficient sense
At court, to recognize your excellence!
They wrong you greatly, Sir. How it must hurt you
Never to be rewarded for your virtue!
ALCESTE: Why, Madam, what cause have I to feel aggrieved?
What great and brilliant thing have I achieved?
What service have I rendered to the King
That I should look to him for anything?
ARSINOE: Not everyone who's honored by the State
Has dones great services. A man must wait
Till time and fortune offer him the chance.
Your merit, Sir, is obvious at a glance,
And . . .
ALCESTE: Ah, forget my merit; I'm not neglected.
The court, I think, can hardly be expected

    To mine men's souls for merit, and unearth
    Our hidden virtues and our secret worth.
ARSINOE: *Some* virtues, though, are far too bright to hide;
    Yours are acknowledged, Sir, on every side.
    Indeed, I've heard you warmly praised of late
    By persons of considerable weight.
ALCESTE: This fawning age has praise for everyone,
    And all distinctions, Madam, are undone.
    All things have equal honor nowadays,
    And no one should be gratified by praise.
    To be admired, one only need exist,
    And every lackey's on the honors list.
ARSINOE: I only wish, Sir, that you had your eye
    On some position at court, however high;
    You'd only have to hint at such a notion
    For me to set the proper wheels in motion;
    I've certain friendships I'd be glad to use
    To get you any office you might choose.
ALCESTE: Madam, I fear that any such ambition
    Is wholly foreign to my disposition.
    The soul God gave me isn't of the sort
    That prospers in the weather of a court.
    It's all too obvious that I don't possess
    The virtues necessary for success.
    My one great talent is for speaking plain;
    I've never learned to flatter or to feign;
    And anyone so stupidly sincere
    Had best not seek a courtier's career.
    Outside the court, I know, one must dispense
    With honors, privilege, and influence;
    But still one gains the right, foregoing these,
    Not to be tortured by the wish to please.
    One needn't live in dread of snubs and slights,
    Nor praise the verse that every idiot writes,
    Nor humor silly Marquesses, nor bestow
    Politic sighs on Madam So-and-So.
ARSINOE: Forget the court, then; let the matter rest.
    But I've another cause to be distressed
    About your present situation, Sir.
    It's to your love affair that I refer.
    She whom you love, and who pretends to love you,
    Is, I regret to say, unworthy of you.
ALCESTE: Why, Madam! Can you seriously intend
    To make so grave a charge against your friend?
ARSINOE: Alas, I must. I've stood aside too long
    And let that lady do you grievous wrong;
    But now my debt to conscience shall be paid:

I tell you that your love has been betrayed.
ALCESTE: I thank you, Madam; you're extremely kind.
  Such words are soothing to a lover's mind.
ARSINOE: Yes, though she *is* my friend, I say again
  You're very much too good for Célimène.
  She's wantonly misled you from the start.
ALCESTE: You may be right; who knows another's heart?
  But ask yourself if it's the part of charity
  To shake my soul with doubts of her sincerity.
ARSINOE: Well, if you'd rather be a dupe than doubt her,
  That's your affair. I'll say no more about her.
ALCESTE: Madam, you know that doubt and vague suspicion
  Are painful to a man in my position;
  It's most unkind to worry me this way
  Unless you've some real proof of what you say.
ARSINOE: Sir, say no more: all doubt shall be removed,
  And all that I've been saying shall be proved.
  You've only to escort me home, and there
  We'll look into the heart of this affair.
  I've ocular evidence which will persuade you
  Beyond a doubt, that Célimène's betrayed you.
  Then, if you're saddened by that revelation,
  Perhaps I can provide some consolation.

ACT FOUR

Scene One. Eliante, Philinte.

PHILINTE: Madam, he acted like a stubborn child;
  I thought they never would be reconciled;
  In vain we reasoned, threatened, and appealed;
  He stood his ground and simply would not yield.
  The Marshals, I feel sure, have never heard
  An argument so splendidly absurd.
  "No, gentlemen," said he, "I'll not retract.
  His verse is bad: extremely bad, in fact.
  Surely it does the man no harm to know it.
  Does it disgrace him, not to be a poet?
  A gentleman may be respected still,
  Whether he writes a sonnet well or ill.
  That I dislike his verse should not offend him;
  In all that touches honor, I commend him;
  He's noble, brave, and virtuous—but I fear
  He can't in truth be called a sonneteer.
  I'll gladly praise his wardrobe; I'll endorse

His dancing, or the way he sits a horse;
But, gentlemen, I cannot praise his rhyme.
In fact, it ought to be a capital crime
For anyone so sadly unendowed
To write a sonnet, and read the thing aloud."
At length he fell into a gentler mood
And, striking a concessive attitude,
He paid Oronte the following courtesies:
"Sir, I regret that I'm so hard to please,
And I'm profoundly sorry that your lyric
Failed to provoke me to a panegyric."
After these curious words, the two embraced,
And then the hearing was adjourned—in haste.

ELIANTE: His conduct has been very singular lately;
  Still, I confess that I respect him greatly.
  The honesty in which he takes such pride
  Has—to my mind—its noble, heroic side.
  In this false age, such candor seems outrageous;
  But I could wish that it were more contagious.

PHILINTE: What most intrigues me in our friend Alceste
  Is the grand passion that rages in his breast.
  The sullen humors he's compounded of
  Should not, I think, dispose his heart to love;
  But since they do, it puzzles me still more
  That he should choose your cousin to adore.

ELIANTE: It does, indeed, belie the theory
  That love is born of gentle sympathy,
  And that the tender passion must be based
  On sweet accords of temper and of taste.

PHILLINTE: Does she return his love, do you suppose?

ELIANTE: Ah, that's a difficult question, Sir. Who knows?
  How can we judge the truth of her devotion?
  Her heart's a stranger to its own emotion.
  Sometimes it thinks it loves, when no love's there;
  At other times it loves quite unaware.

PHILINTE: I rather think Alceste is in for more
  Distress and sorrow than he's bargained for;
  Were he of my mind, Madam, his affection
  Would turn in quite a different direction,
  And we would see him more responsive to
  The kind regard which he receives from you.

ELIANTE: Sir, I believe in frankness, and I'm inclined,
  In matters of the heart, to speak my mind.
  I don't oppose his love for her; indeed,
  I hope with all my heart that he'll succeed,
  And were it in my power, I'd rejoice
  In giving him the lady of his choice.
  But if, as happens frequently enough

> In love affairs, he meets with a rebuff—
> If Célimène should grant some rival's suit—
> I'd gladly play the role of substitute;
> Nor would his tender speeches please me less
> Because they'd once been made without success.

PHILINTE: Well, Madam, as for me, I don't oppose
> Your hopes in this affair; and heaven knows
> That in my conversations with the man
> I plead your cause as often as I can.
> But if those two should marry, and so remove
> All chance that he will offer you his love,
> Then I'll declare my own, and hope to see
> Your gracious favor pass from him to me.
> In short, should you be cheated of Alceste,
> I'd be most happy to be second best.

ELIANTE: Philinte, you're teasing.

PHILINTE: Ah, Madam, never fear;
> No words of mine were ever so sincere,
> And I shall live in fretful expectation
> Till I can make a fuller declaration.

Scene Two. Alceste, Eliante, Philinte.

ALCESTE: Avenge me, Madam! I must have satisfaction,
> Or this great wrong will drive me to distraction!

ELIANTE: Why, what's the matter? What's upset you so?

ALCESTE: Madam, I've had a mortal, mortal blow.
> If Chaos repossessed the universe,
> I swear I'd not be shaken any worse.
> I'm ruined. . . . I can say no more. . . . My soul . . .

ELIANTE: Do try, Sir, to regain your self-control.

ALCESTE: Just heaven! Why were so much beauty and grace
> Bestowed on one so vicious and so base?

ELIANTE: Once more, Sir, tell us. . . .

ALCESTE: My world has gone to wrack;
> I'm—I'm betrayed; she's stabbed me in the back:
> Yes, Célimène (who would have thought it of her?)
> Is false to me, and has another lover.

ELIANTE: Are you quite certain? Can you prove these things?

PHILINTE: Lovers are prey to wild imaginings
> And jealous fancies. No doubt there's some mistake. . . .

ALCESTE: Mind your own business, Sir, for heaven's sake.

(*To* ELIANTE)

> Madam, I have the proof that you demand
> Here in my pocket, penned by her own hand.
> Yes, all the shameful evidence one could want

Lies in this letter written to Oronte—
Oronte! whom I felt sure she couldn't love,
And hardly bothered to be jealous of.
PHILINTE: Still, in a letter, appearances may deceive;
This may not be so bad as you believe.
ALCESTE: Once more I beg you, Sir, to let me be;
Tend to your own affairs; leave mine to me.
ELIANTE: Compose yourself; this anguish that you feel . . .
ALCESTE: Is something, Madam, you alone can heal.
My outraged heart, beside itself with grief,
Appeals to you for comfort and relief.
Avenge me on your cousin, whose unjust
And faithless nature has deceived my trust;
Avenge a crime your pure soul must detest.
ELIANTE: But how, Sir?
ALCESTE: Madam, this heart within my breast
Is yours; pray take it; redeem my heart from her,
And so avenge me on my torturer.
Let her be punished by the fond emotion,
The ardent love, the bottomless devotion,
The faithful worship which this heart of mine
Will offer up to yours as to a shrine.
ELIANTE: You have my sympathy, Sir, in all you suffer;
Nor do I scorn the noble heart you offer;
But I suspect you'll soon be mollified,
And this desire for vengeance will subside.
When some beloved hand has done us wrong
We thirst for retribution—but not for long;
However dark the deed that she's committed,
A lovely culprit's very soon acquitted.
Nothing's so stormy as an injured lover.
And yet no storm so quickly passes over.
ALCESTE: No, Madam, no—this is no lovers' spat;
I'll not forgive her; it's gone too far for that;
My mind's made up; I'll kill myself before
I waste my hopes upon her any more.
Ah, here she is. My wrath intensifies.
I shall confront her with her tricks and lies,
And crush her utterly, and bring you then
A heart no longer slave to Célimène.

Scene Three. Celimene, Alceste.

ALCESTE (*aside*): Sweet heaven, help me to control my passion.
CELIMENE (*aside to* ALCESTE):
Oh, Lord. Why stand there staring in that fashion?

Molière: *The Misanthrope*

And what d'you mean by those dramatic sighs,
And that malignant glitter in your eyes?
ALCESTE: I mean that sins which cause the blood to freeze
Look innocent beside your treacheries;
That nothing Hell's or Heaven's wrath could do
Ever produced so bad a thing as you.
CELIMENE: Your compliments were always sweet and pretty.
ALCESTE: Madam, it's not the moment to be witty.
No, blush and hang your head; you've ample reason,
Since I've the fullest evidence of your treason.
Ah, this is what my sad heart prophesied;
Now all my anxious fears are verified;
My dark suspicion and my gloomy doubt
Divined the truth, and now the truth is out.
For all your trickery, I was not deceived;
It was my bitter stars that I believed.
But don't imagine that you'll go scot-free;
You shan't misuse me with impunity.
I know that love's irrational and blind;
I know the heart's not subject to the mind,
And can't be reasoned into beating faster;
I know each soul is free to choose its master;
Therefore had you but spoken from the heart,
Rejecting my attentions from the start,
I'd have no grievance, or at any rate
I could complain of nothing but my fate.
Ah, but so falsely to encourage me—
That was a treason and a treachery
For which you cannot suffer too severely,
And you shall pay for that behavior dearly.
Yes, now I have no pity, not a shred;
My temper's out of hand; I've lost my head;
Shocked by the knowledge of your double-dealings,
My reason can't restrain my savage feelings;
A righteous wrath deprives me of my senses,
And I won't answer for the consequences.
CELIMENE: What does this outburst mean? Will you please explain?
Have you, by any chance, gone quite insane?
ALCESTE: Yes, yes, I went insane the day I fell
A victim to your black and fatal spell,
Thinking to meet with some sincerity
Among the treacherous charms that beckoned me.
CELIMENE: Pooh. Of what treachery can you complain?
ALCESTE: How sly you are, how cleverly you feign!
But you'll not victimize me any more.
Look: here's a document you've seen before.
This evidence, which I acquired today,

Leaves you, I think, without a thing to say.
CELIMENE: Is this what sent you into such a fit?
ALCESTE: You should be blushing at the sight of it.
CELIMENE: Ought I to blush? I truly don't see why.
ALCESTE: Ah, now you're being bold as well as sly;
  Since there's no signature, perhaps you'll claim . . .
CELIMENE: I wrote it, whether or not it bears my name.
ALCESTE: And you can view with equanimity
  This proof of your disloyalty to me!
CELIMENE: Oh, don't be so outrageous and extreme.
ALCESTE: You take this matter lightly, it would seem.
  Was it no wrong to me, no shame to you,
  That you should send Oronte this billet-doux?
CELIMENE: Oronte! Who said it was for him?
ALCESTE: Why, those
  Who brought me this example of your prose.
  But what's the difference? If you wrote the letter
  To someone else, it pleases me no better.
  My grievance and your guilt remain the same.
CELIMENE: But need you rage, and need I blush for shame,
  If this was written to a *woman* friend?
ALCESTE: Ah! Most ingenious. I'm impressed no end;
  And after that incredible evasion
  Your guilt is clear. I need no more persuasion.
  How dare you try so clumsy a deception?
  D'you think I'm wholly wanting in perception?
  Come, come, let's see how brazenly you'll try
  To bolster up so palpable a lie:
  Kindly construe this ardent closing section
  As nothing more than sisterly affection!
  Here, let me read it. Tell me, if you dare to,
  That this is for a woman . . .
CELIMENE: I don't care to.
  What right have you to badger and berate me,
  And so highhandedly interrogate me?
ALCESTE: Now, don't be angry; all I ask of you
  Is that you justify a phrase or two . . .
CELIMENE: No, I shall not. I utterly refuse,
  And you may take those phrases as you choose.
ALCESTE: Just show me how this letter could be meant
  For a woman's eyes, and I shall be content.
CELIMENE: No, no, it's for Oronte; you're perfectly right.
  I welcome his attentions with delight,
  I prize his character and his intellect,
  And everything is just as you suspect.
  Come, do your worst now; give your rage free rein;
  But kindly cease to bicker and complain.

Molière: *The Misanthrope*

ALCESTE *(aside):* Good God! Could anything be more inhuman?
  Was ever a heart so mangled by a woman?
  When I complain of how she has betrayed me,
  She bridles, and commences to upbraid me!
  She tries my tortured patience to the limit;
  She won't deny her guilt; she glories in it!
  And yet my heart's too faint and cowardly
  To break these chains of passion, and be free,
  To scorn her as it should, and rise above
  This unrewarded, mad, and bitter love.
  [*To* CELIMENE]
  Ah, traitress, in how confident a fashion
  You take advantage of my helpless passion,
  And use my weakness for your faithless charms
  To make me once again throw down my arms!
  But do at least deny this black transgression;
  Take back that mocking and perverse confession;
  Defend this letter and your innocence,
  And I, poor fool, will aid in your defense.
  Pretend, pretend, that you are just and true,
  And I shall make myself believe in you.
CELIMENE: Oh, stop it. Don't be such a jealous dunce,
  Or I shall leave off loving you at once.
  Just why should I *pretend*? What could impel me
  To stoop so low as that? And kindly tell me
  Why, if I loved another, I shouldn't merely
  Inform you of it, simply and sincerely!
  I've told you where you stand, and that admission
  Should altogether clear me of suspicion;
  After so generous a guarantee,
  What right have you to harbor doubts of me?
  Since women are (from natural reticence)
  Reluctant to declare their sentiments,
  And since the honor of our sex requires
  That we conceal our amorous desires,
  Ought any man for whom such laws are broken
  To question what the oracle has spoken?
  Should he not rather feel an obligation
  To trust that most obliging declaration?
  Enough, now. Your suspicions quite disgust me;
  Why should I love a man who doesn't trust me?
  I cannot understand why I continue,
  Fool that I am, to take an interest in you.
  I ought to choose a man less prone to doubt,
  And give you something to be vexed about.
ALCESTE: Ah, what a poor enchanted fool I am;
  These gentle words, no doubt, were all a sham;

But destiny requires me to entrust
My happiness to you, and so I must.
I'll love you to the bitter end, and see
How false and treacherous you dare to be.
CELIMENE: No, you don't really love me as you ought.
ALCESTE: I love you more than can be said or thought;
Indeed, I wish you were in such distress
That I might show my deep devotedness.
Yes, I could wish that you were wretchedly poor,
Unloved, uncherished, utterly obscure;
That fate had set you down upon the earth
Without possessions, rank, or gentle birth;
Then, by the offer of my heart, I might
Repair the great injustice of your plight;
I'd raise you from the dust, and proudly prove
The purity and vastness of my love.
CELIMENE: This is a strange benevolence indeed!
God grant that I may never be in need....
Ah, here's Monsieur Dubois, in quaint disguise.

Scene Four. Celimene, Alceste, Dubois.

ALCESTE: Well, why this costume? Why those frightened eyes?
What ails you?
DUBOIS: Well, Sir, things are most mysterious.
ALCESTE: What do you mean?
DUBOIS: I fear they're very serious.
ALCESTE: What?
DUBOIS: Shall I speak more loudly?
ALCESTE: Yes; speak out.
DUBOIS: Isn't there someone here, Sir?
ALCESTE: Speak, you lout!
Stop wasting time.
DUBOIS: Sir, we must slip away.
ALCESTE: How's that?
DUBOIS: We must decamp without delay.
ALCESTE: Explain yourself.
DUBOIS: I tell you we must fly.
ALCESTE: What for?
DUBOIS: We mustn't pause to say good-by.
ALCESTE: Now what d'you mean by all of this, you clown?
DUBOIS: I mean, Sir, that we've got to leave this town.
ALCESTE: I'll tear you limb from limb and joint from joint
If you don't come more quickly to the point.
DUBOIS: Well, Sir, today a man in a black suit,
Who wore a black and ugly scowl to boot,

Molière: *The Misanthrope*

Left us a document scrawled in such a hand
As even Satan couldn't understand.
It bears upon your lawsuit, I don't doubt;
But all hell's devils couldn't make it out.
ALCESTE: Well, well, go on. What then? I fail to see
How this event obliges us to flee.
DUBOIS: Well, Sir: an hour later hardly more,
A gentleman who's often called before
Came looking for you in an anxious way.
Not finding you, he asked me to convey
(Knowing I could be trusted with the same)
The following message. . . . Now, what *was* his name?
ALCESTE: Forget his name, you idiot. What did he say?
DUBOIS: Well, it was one of your friends, Sir, anyway.
He warned you to begone, and he suggested
That if you stay, you may well be arrested.
ALCESTE: What? Nothing more specific? Think, man, think!
DUBOIS: No, Sir. He had me bring him pen and ink,
And dashed you off a letter which, I'm sure,
Will render things distinctly less obscure.
ALCESTE: Well—let me have it!
CELIMENE: What *is* this all about?
ALCESTE: God knows; but I have hopes of finding out.
How long am I to wait, you blitherer?
DUBOIS (*after a protracted search for the letter*):
I must have left it on your table, Sir.
ALCESTE: I ought to . . .
CELIMENE: No, no, keep your self-control;
Go find out what's behind his rigmarole.
ALCESTE: It seems that fate, no matter what I do,
Has sworn that I may not converse with you;
But, Madam, pray permit your faithful lover
To try once more before the day is over.

ACT FIVE

Scene One. Alceste, Philinte.

ALCESTE: No, it's too much. My mind's made up, I tell you.
PHILINTE: Why should this blow, however hard, compel you . . .
ALCESTE: No, no, don't waste your breath in argument;
Nothing you say will alter my intent
This age is vile, and I've made up my mind
To have no further commerce with mankind.
Did not truth, honor, decency, and the laws

Oppose my enemy and approve my cause?
My claims were justified in all men's sight;
I put my trust in equity and right;
Yet, to my horror and the world's disgrace,
Justice is mocked, and I have lost my case!
A scoundrel whose dishonesty is notorious
Emerges from another lie victorious!
Honor and right condone his brazen fraud,
While rectitude and decency applaud!
Before his smirking face, the truth stands charmed,
And virtue conquered, and the law disarmed!
His crime is sanctioned by a court decree!
And not content with what he's done to me,
The dog now seeks to ruin me by stating
That I composed a book now circulating,
A book so wholly criminal and vicious
That even to speak its title is seditious!
Meanwhile Oronte, my rival, lends his credit
To the same libelous tale, and helps to spread it!
Oronte! a man of honor and of rank,
With whom I've been entirely fair and frank;
Who sought me out and forced me, willy-nilly,
To judge some verse I found extremely silly;
And who, because I properly refused
To flatter him, or see the truth abused,
Abets my enemy in a rotten slander!
There's the reward of honesty and candor!
The man will hate me to the end of time
For failing to commend his wretched rhyme!
And not this man alone, but all humanity
Do what they do from interest and vanity;
They prate of honor, truth, and righteousness,
But lie, betray, and swindle nonetheless.
Come then: man's villainy is too much to bear;
Let's leave this jungle and this jackal's lair.
Yes! treacherous and savage race of men,
You shall not look upon my face again.
PHILINTE: Oh, don't rush into exile prematurely;
   Things aren't as dreadful as you make them, surely.
   It's rather obvious, since you're still at large,
   That people don't believe your enemy's charge.
   Indeed, his tale's so patently untrue
   That it may do more harm to him than you.
ALCESTE: Nothing could do that scoundrel any harm:
   His frank corruption is his greatest charm,
   And, far from hurting him, a further shame
   Would only serve to magnify his name.

Molière: *The Misanthrope*

PHILINTE: In any case, his bald prevarication
   Has done no injury to your reputation,
   And you may feel secure in that regard.
   As for your lawsuit, it should not be hard
   To have the case reopened, and contest
   This judgment . . .
ALCESTE: No, no, let the verdict rest.
   Whatever cruel penalty it may bring,
   I wouldn't have it changed for anything.
   It shows the times' injustice with such clarity
   That I shall pass it down to our posterity
   As a great proof and signal demonstration
   Of the black wickedness of this generation.
   It may cost twenty thousand francs; but I
   Shall pay their twenty thousand, and gain thereby
   The right to storm and rage at human evil,
   And send the race of mankind to the devil.
PHILINTE: Listen to me. . . .
ALCESTE: Why? What can you possibly say?
   Don't argue, Sir; your labor's thrown away.
   Do you propose to offer lame excuses
   For men's behavior and the times' abuses?
PHILINTE: No, all you say I'll readily concede:
   This is a low, conniving age indeed;
   Nothing but trickery prospers nowadays,
   And people ought to mend their shabby ways.
   Yes, man's a beastly creature; but must we then
   Abandon the society of men?
   Here in the world, each human frailty
   Provides occasion for philosophy,
   And that is virtue's noblest exercise;
   If honesty shone forth from all men's eyes,
   If every heart were frank and kind and just,
   What could our virtues do but gather dust
   (Since their employment is to help us bear
   The villainies of men without despair)?
   A heart well-armed with virtue can endure. . . .
ALCESTE: Sir, you're a matchless reasoner, to be sure;
   Your words are fine and full of cogency;
   But don't waste time and eloquence on me.
   My reason bids me go, for my own good.
   My tongue won't lie and flatter as it should;
   God knows what frankness it might next commit,
   And what I'd suffer on account of it.
   Pray let me wait for Célimène's return
   In peace and quiet. I shall shortly learn,
   By her response to what I have in view,

Whether her love for me is feigned or true.
PHILINTE: Till then, let's visit Eliante upstairs.
ALCESTE: No, I am too weighed down with somber cares.
Go to her, do; and leave me with my gloom
Here in the darkened corner of this room.
PHILINTE: Why, that's no sort of company, my friend;
I'll see if Eliante will not descend.

Scene Two. Celimene, Oronte, Alceste.

ORONTE: Yes, Madam, if you wish me to remain
Your true and ardent lover, you must deign
To give me some more positive assurance.
All this suspense is quite beyond endurance.
If your heart shares the sweet desires of mine,
Show me as much by some convincing sign;
And here's the sign I urgently suggest:
That you no longer tolerate Alceste,
But sacrifice him to my love, and sever
All your relations with the man forever.
CELIMENE: Why do you suddenly dislike him so?
You praised him to the skies not long ago.
ORONTE: Madam, that's not the point. I'm here to find
Which way your tender feelings are inclined.
Choose, if you please, between Alceste and me,
And I shall stay or go accordingly.
ALCESTE (*emerging from the corner*):
Yes, Madam, choose; this gentleman's demand
Is wholly just, and I support his stand.
I too am true and ardent; I too am here
To ask you that you make your feelings clear.
No more delays, now; no equivocation;
The time has come to make your declaration.
ORONTE: Sir, I've no wish in any way to be
An obstacle to your felicity.
ALCESTE: Sir, I've no wish to share her heart with you;
That may sound jealous, but at least it's true.
ORONTE: If, weighing us, she leans in your direction . . .
ALCESTE: If she regards you with the least affection . . .
ORONTE: I swear I'll yield her to you there and then.
ALCESTE: I swear I'll never see her face again.
ORONTE: Now, Madam, tell us what we've come to hear.
ALCESTE: Madam, speak openly and have no fear.
ORONTE: Just say which one is to remain your lover.
ALCESTE: Just name one name, and it will all be over.
ORONTE: What! Is it possible that you're undecided?

ALCESTE: What! Can your feelings possibly be divided?
CELIMENE: Enough: this inquisition's gone too far:
  How utterly unreasonable you are!
  Not that I couldn't make the choice with ease;
  My heart has no conflicting sympathies;
  I know full well which one of you I favor,
  And you'd not see me hesitate or waver.
  But how can you expect me to reveal
  So cruelly and bluntly what I feel?
  I think it altogether too unpleasant
  To choose between two men when both are present;
  One's heart has means more subtle and more kind
  Of letting its affections be divined,
  Nor need one be uncharitably plain
  To let a lover know he loves in vain.
ORONTE: No, no, speak plainly; I for one can stand it.
  I beg you to be frank.
ALCESTE: And I demand it.
  The simple truth is what I wish to know,
  And there's no need for softening the blow.
  You've made an art of pleasing everyone,
  But now your days of coquetry are done:
  You have no choice now, Madam, but to choose,
  For I'll know what to think if you refuse;
  I'll take your silence for a clear admission
  That I'm entitled to my worst suspicion.
ORONTE: I thank you for this ultimatum, Sir,
  And I may say I heartily concur.
CELIMENE: Really, this foolishness is very wearing:
  Must you be so unjust and overbearing?
  Haven't I told you why I must demur?
  Ah, here's Eliante; I'll put the case to her.

Scene Three. *Eliante, Philinte, Celimene, Oronte, Alceste.*

CELIMENE: Cousin, I'm being persecuted here
  By these two persons, who, it would appear,
  Will not be satisfied till I confess
  Which one I love the more, and which the less,
  And tell the latter to his face that he
  Is henceforth banished from my company.
  Tell me, has ever such a thing been done?
ELIANTE: You'd best not turn to me; I'm not the one
  To back you in a matter of this kind:
  I'm all for those who frankly speak their mind.
ORONTE: Madam, you'll search in vain for a defender.

ALCESTE: You're beaten, Madam, and may as well surrender.
ORONTE: Speak, speak, you must; and end this awful strain.
ALCESTE: Or don't, and your position will be plain.
ORONTE: A single word will close this painful scene.
ALCESTE: But if you're silent, I'll know what you mean.

Scene Four. Arsinoe, Celimene, Eliante, Alceste, Philinte, Acaste, Clitandre, Oronte.

ACASTE (*to* CELIMENE): Madam, with all due deference, we two
   Have come to pick a little bone with you.
CLITANDRE (*to* ORONTE *and* ALCESTE):
   I'm glad you're present, Sirs; as you'll soon learn,
   Our business here is also your concern.
ARSINOE (*to* CELIMENE): Madam, I visit you so soon again
   Only because of these two gentlemen,
   Who came to me indignant and aggrieved
   About a crime too base to be believed.
   Knowing your virtue, having such confidence in it,
   I couldn't think you guilty for a minute,
   In spite of all their telling evidence;
   And, rising above our little difference,
   I've hastened here in friendship's name to see
   You clear yourself of this great calumny.
ACASTE: Yes, Madam, let us see with what composure
   You'll manage to respond to this disclosure.
   You lately sent Clitandre this tender note.
CLITANDRE: And this one, for Acaste, you also wrote.
ACASTE (*to* ORONTE *and* ALCESTE):
   You'll recognize this writing, Sirs, I think;
   The lady is so free with pen and ink
   That you must know it all too well, I fear.
   But listen: this is something you should hear.
   "How absurd you are to condemn my lightheartedness in society, and to accuse me of being happiest in the company of others. Nothing could be more unjust; and if you do not come to me instantly and beg pardon for saying such a thing, I shall never forgive you as long as I live. Our big bumbling friend the Viscount . . ."
   What a shame that he's not here.
   "Our big bumbling friend the Viscount, whose name stands first in your complaint, is hardly a man to my taste; and ever since the day I watched him spend three-quarters of an hour spitting into a well, so as to make circles in the water, I have been unable to think highly of him. As for the little Marquess . . ."
   In all modesty, gentlemen, that is I.
   "As for the little Marquess, who sat squeezing my hand for such a long while yesterday, I find him in all respects the most trifling creature

alive; and the only things of value about him are his cape and his sword. As for the man with the green ribbons..."

(*To* ALCESTE)

It's your turn now, Sir.

"As for the man with the green ribbons, he amuses me now and then with his bluntness and his bearish ill-humor; but there are many times indeed when I think him the greatest bore in the world. And as for the sonneteer..."

(*To* ORONTE)

Here's your helping.

"And as for the sonneteer, who has taken it into his head to be witty, and insists on being an author in the teeth of opinion, I simply cannot be bothered to listen to him, and his prose wearies me quite as much as suppose; that I long for your company, more than I dare to say, at all his poetry. Be assured that I am not always so well-entertained as you these entertainments to which people drag me; and that the presence of those one loves is the true and perfect seasoning to all one's pleasures."

CLITANDRE: And now for me.

"Clitandre whom you mention, and who so pesters me with his saccharine speeches, is the last man on earth for whom I could feel any affection. He is quite mad to suppose that I love him, and so are you, to doubt that you are loved. Do come to your senses; exchange your suppositions for his; and visit me as often as possible, to help me bear the annoyance of his unwelcome attentions."

It's a sweet character that these letters show,
And what to call it, Madam, you well know.
Enough. We're off to make the world acquainted
With this sublime self-portrait that you've painted.

ACASTE: Madam, I'll make you no farewell oration;
No, you're not worthy of my indignation.
Far choicer hearts than yours, as you'll discover,
Would like this little Marquess for a lover.

Scene Five. Celimene, Eliante, Arsinoe, Alceste, Oronte, Philinte.

ORONTE: So! After all those loving letters you wrote,
You turn on me like this, and cut my throat!
And your dissembling, faithless heart, I find,
Has pledged itself by turns to all mankind!
How blind I've been! But now I clearly see;
I thank you, Madam, for enlightening me.
My heart is mine once more, and I'm content;
The loss of it shall be your punishment.

(*To* ALCESTE)

Sir, she is yours; I'll seek no more to stand
  Between your wishes and this lady's hand.

Scene Six. *Celimene, Eliante, Arsinoe, Alceste, Phiilinte.*

ARSINOE (*To* CELIMENE): Madam, I'm forced to speak. I'm far too stirred
  To keep my counsel, after what I've heard.
  I'm shocked and staggered by your want of morals.
  It's not my way to mix in others' quarrels;
  But really, when this fine and noble spirit,
  This man of honor and surpassing merit,
  Laid down the offering of his heart before you,
  How *could* you . . .
ALCESTE: Madam, permit me, I implore you,
  To represent myself in this debate.
  Don't bother, please, to be my advocate.
  My heart, in any case, could not afford
  To give your services their due reward;
  And if I chose, for consolation's sake,
  Some other lady, t'would not be you I'd take.
ARSINOE: What makes you think you could, Sir? And how dare you
  Imply that I've been trying to ensnare you?
  If you can for a moment entertain
  Such flattering fancies, you're extremely vain.
  I'm not so interested as you suppose
  In Célimène's discarded gigolos.
  Get rid of that absurd illusion, do.
  Women like me are not for such as you.
  Stay with this creature, to whom you're so attached;
  I've never seen two people better matched.

Scene Seven. *Celimene, Eliante, Alceste, Philinte.*

ALCESTE (*to* CELIMENE): Well, I've been still throughout this exposé,
  Till everyone but me has said his say.
  Come, have I shown sufficient self-restraint?
  And may I now . . .
CELIMENE: Yes, make your just complaint.
  Reproach me freely, call me what you will;
  You've every right to say I've used you ill.
  I've wronged you, I confess it; and in my shame
  I'll make no effort to escape the blame.
  The anger of those others I could despise;

My guilt toward you I sadly recognize.
Your wrath is wholly justified, I fear;
I know how culpable I must appear,
I know all things bespeak my treachery,
And that, in short, you've grounds for hating me.
Do so; I give you leave.
ALCESTE: Ah, traitress—how,
How should I cease to love you, even now?
Though mind and will were passionately bent
On hating you, my heart would not consent.
[*To* ELIANTE *and* PHILINTE]
Be witness to my madness, both of you;
See what infatuation drives one to;
But wait; my folly's only just begun,
And I shall prove to you before I'm done
How strange the human heart is, and how far
From rational we sorry creatures are.
[*To* CELIMENE]
Woman, I'm willing to forget your shame,
And clothe your treacheries in a sweeter name;
I'll call them youthful errors, instead of crimes,
And lay the blame on these corrupting times.
My one condition is that you agree
To share my chosen fate, and fly with me
To that wild, trackless, solitary place
In which I shall forget the human race.
Only by such a course can you atone
For those atrocious letters; by that alone
Can you remove my present horror of you,
And make it possible for me to love you.
CELIMENE: What! *I* renounce the world at my young age,
And die of boredom in some hermitage?
ALCESTE: Ah, if you really loved me as you ought,
You wouldn't give the world a moment's thought;
Must you have me, and all the world beside?
CELIMENE: Alas, at twenty one is terrified
Of solitude. I fear I lack the force
And depth of soul to take so stern a course.
But if my hand in marriage will content you,
Why, there's a plan which I might well consent to,
And . . .
ALCESTE: No, I detest you now. I could excuse
Everything else, but since you thus refuse
To love me wholly, as a wife should do,
And see the world in me, as I in you,
Go! I reject your hand and disenthrall

My heart from your enchantments, once for all.

Scene Eight. Eliante, Alceste, Philinte.

ALCESTE (*to* ELIANTE): Madam, your virtuous beauty has no peer;
   Of all this world, you only are sincere;
   I've long esteemed you highly, as you know;
   Permit me ever to esteem you so,
   And if I do not now request your hand,
   Forgive me, Madam, and try to understand.
   I feel unworthy of it; I sense that fate
   Does not intend me for the married state,
   That I should do you wrong by offering you
   My shattered heart's unhappy residue,
   And that in short . . .
ELIANTE: Your argument's well taken:
   Nor need you fear that I shall feel forsaken.
   Were I to offer him this hand of mine,
   Your friend Philinte, I think, would not decline.
PHILINTE: Ah, Madam, that's my heart's most cherished goal,
   For which I'd gladly give my life and soul.
ALCESTE (*to* ELIANTE *and* PHILINTE):
   May you be true to all you now profess,
   And so deserve unending happiness.
   Meanwhile, betrayed and wronged in everything,
   I'll flee this bitter world where vice is king,
   And seek some spot unpeopled and apart
   Where I'll be free to have an honest heart.
PHILINTE: Come, Madam, let's do everything we can
   To change the mind of this unhappy man.

Anton Chekhov
The Cherry Orchard
Translated by Constance Garnett

Characters

> MADAME RANEVSKY (LYUBOV ANDREYEVNA), *the owner of the Cherry Orchard*
> ANYA, *her daughter, aged 17*
> VARYA, *her adopted daughter, aged 24*
> GAEV (LEONID ANDREYEVITCH), *brother of Madame Ranevsky*
> LOPAHIN (YERMOLAY ALEXEYEVITCH), *a merchant*
> TROFIMOV (PYOTR SERGEYEVITCH), *a student*
> SEMYONOV-PISHTCHIK, *a landowner*
> CHARLOTTA IVANOVNA, *a governess*
> EPIHODOV (SEMYON PANTALEYEVITCH), *a clerk*
> DUNYASHA, *a maid*
> FIRS, *an old valet, aged 87*
> YASHA, *a young valet*
> A WAYFARER
> THE STATION MASTER
> A POST-OFFICE CLERK
> VISITORS, SERVANTS

> *The action takes place on the estate of* MADAME RANEVSKY.

ACT 1

(A room, which has always been called the nursery. One of the doors leads into ANYA's room. Dawn, sun rises during the scene. May, the cherry trees in flower, but it is cold in the garden with the frost of early morning. Windows closed.)

> *Enter* DUNYASHA *with a candle and* LOPAHIN *with a book in his hand.*

LOPAHIN: The train's late! Two hours, at least. (*Yawns and stretches.*) I'm
DUNYASHA: Nearly two o'clock. (*Puts out the candle.*) It's daylight already.
LOPAHIN: The train's late! Two hours, at least. (*Yawns and stretches.*) I'm

a pretty one; what a fool I've been. Came here on purpose to meet them at the station and dropped asleep. . . . Dozed off as I sat in the chair. It's annoying. . . . You might have waked me.

DUNYASHA: I thought you had gone. (*Listens.*) There, I do believe they're coming!

LOPAHIN (*listens*): No, what with the luggage and one thing and another. (*A pause.*) Lyubov Andreyevna has been abroad five years; I don't know know what she is like now. . . . She's a splendid woman. A good natured, kind-hearted woman. I remember when I was a lad of fifteen, my poor father—he used to keep a little shop here in the village in those days—gave me a punch in the face with his fist and made my nose bleed. We were in the yard here, I forget what we'd come about—he had had a drop. Lyubov Andreyevna—I can see her now—she was a slim young girl then—took me to wash my face, and then brought me into this very room, into the nursery. "Don't cry, little peasant," says she, "it will be well in time for your wedding day." . . . [*A pause.*] Little peasant. . . . My father was a peasant, it's true, but here am I in a white waistcoat and brown shoes, like a pig in a bun shop. Yes, I'm a rich man, but for all my money, come to think, a peasant I was, and a peasant I am. (*Turns over the pages of the book.*) I've been reading this book and I can't make head or tail of it. I fell asleep over it.

(*A pause.*)

DUNYASHA: The dogs have been awake all night, they feel that the mistress is coming.

LOPAHIN: Why, what's the matter with you, Dunyasha?

DUNYASHA: My hands are all of a tremble. I feel as though I should faint.

LOPAHIN: You're a spoilt soft creature, Dunyasha. And dressed like a lady too, and your hair done up. That's not the thing. One must know one's place.

(*Enter* EPIHODOV *with a nosegay; he wears a pea-jacket and highly polished creaking top-boots; he drops the nosegay as he comes in.*)

EPIHODOV (*picking up the nosegay*): Here! the gardener's sent this, says you're to put it in the dining-room (*Gives* DUNYASHA *the nosegay.*)

LOPAHIN: And bring me some kvass.

DUNYASHA: I will. (*Goes out.*)

EPIHODOV: It's chilly this morning, three degrees of frost, though the cherries are all in flower. I can't say much for our climate. (*Sighs.*) I can't. Our climate is not often propitious to the occasion. Yermolay Alexeyevitch, permit me to call your attention to the fact that I purchased myself a pair of boots the day before yesterday, and they creak, I venture to assure you, so that there's no tolerating them. What ought I to grease them with?

LOPAHIN: Oh, shut up! Don't bother me.

EPIHODOV: Every day some misfortune befalls me. I don't complain, I'm used to it, and I wear a smiling face.

(DUNYASHA *comes in, hands* LOPAHIN *the kvass.*)

EPIHODOV: I am going. (*Stumbles against a chair, which falls over.*) There! (*As though triumphant.*) There you see now, excuse the expression, an accident likt that among others. . . . It's positively remarkable. (*Goes out.*)

DUNYASHA: Do you know, Yermolay Alexeyevitch, I must confess, Epihodov has made me a proposal.

LOPAHIN: Ah!

DUNYASHA: I'm sure I don't know. . . . He's a harmless fellow, but sometimes when he begins talking, there's no making anything of it. It's all very fine and expressive, only there's no understanding it. I've a sort of liking for him too. He loves me to distraction. He's an unfortunate man; every day there's something. They tease him about it—two and twenty misfortunes they call him.

LOPAHIN (*listening*): There! I do believe they're coming.

DUNYASHA: They are coming! What's the matter with me? . . . I'm cold all over.

LOPAHIN: They really are coming. Let's go and meet them. Will she know me? It's five years since I saw her.

DUNYASHA (*in a flutter*): I shall drop this very minute. . . . Ah, I shall drop.

(*There is a sound of two carriages driving up to the house.* LOPAHIN *and* DUNYASHA *go out quickly. The stage is left empty. A noise is heard in the adjoining rooms.* FIRS, *who has driven to meet* MADAME RANEVSKY, *crosses the stage hurriedly leaning on a stick. He is wearing old-fashioned livery and a high hat. He says something to himself, but not a word can be distinguished. The noise behind the scenes goes on increasing. A voice:* "Come, let's go in here." *Enter* LYUBOV ANDREYEVNA, ANYA, *and* CHARLOTTA IVANOVNA *with a pet dog on a chain, all in traveling dresses.* VARYA *in an out-door coat with a kerchief over her head,* GAEV, SEMYONOV-PISHTCHIK, LOPAHIN, DUNYASHA *with bag and parasol, servants with other articles. All walk across the room.*)

ANYA: Let's come in here. Do you remember what room this is, mamma?

LYUBOV (*joyfully, through her tears*): The nursery!

VARYA: How cold it is, my hands are numb. (*To* LYUBOV ANDREYEVNA.) Your rooms, the white room and the lavender one, are just the same as ever, mamma.

LYUBOV: My nursery, dear delightful room. . . . I used to sleep here when I was little. . . . (*Cries*). And here I am, like a little child. . . . (*Kisses her brother and* VARYA, *and then her brother again.*) Varya's just the same as ever, like a nun. And I knew Dunyasha. (*Kisses* DUNYASHA.)

GAEV: The train was two hours late. What do you think of that? Is that the way to do things?

CHARLOTTA (*to* PISHTCHIK): My dog eats nuts, too.

PISHTCHIK (*wonderingly*): Fancy that!

(*They all go out except* ANYA *and* DUNYASHA.)

DUNYASHA: We've been expecting you so long. (*Takes* ANYA's *hat and coat*).

ANYA: I haven't slept for four nights on the journey. I feel dreadfully cold.

DUNYASHA: You set out in Lent, there was snow and frost, and now? My darling (*Laughs and kisses her.*) I *have* missed you, my precious, my joy. I must tell you . . . I can't put it off a minute. . . .

ANYA (*wearily*): What now?

DUNYASHA: Epihodov, the clerk, made me a proposal just after Easter.

ANYA: It's always the same thing with you. . . . (*Straightening her hair.*) I've lost all my hairpins. (*She is staggering from exhaustion.*)

DUNYASHA: I don't know what to think, really. He does love me, he does love me so!

ANYA (*looking toward her door, tenderly*): My own room, my windows just as though I had never gone away. I'm home! Tomorrow morning I shall get up and run into the garden. . . . Oh, if I could get to sleep! I haven't slept all the journey, I was so anxious and worried.

DUNYASHA: Pyotr Sergeyevitch came the day before yesterday.

ANYA (*joyfully*): Petya!

DUNYASHA: He's asleep in the bath house, he has settled in there. I'm afraid of being in their way, says he. (*Glancing at her watch.*) I was to have waked him, but Varvara Mihalovna told me not to. Don't you wake him, says she.

(*Enter* VARYA *with a bunch of keys at her waist.*)

VARYA: Dunyasha, coffee and make haste . . . Mamma's asking for coffee.

DUNYASHA: This very minute. (*Goes out.*)

VARYA: Well, thank God, you've come. You're home again. (*Petting her.*) My little darling has come back(My precious beauty has come back again!

ANYA: I have had a time of it!

VARYA: I can fancy.

ANYA: We set off in Holy Week—it was so cold then, and all the way Charlotta would talk and show off her tricks. What did you want to burden me with Charlotta for?

VARYA: You couldn't have traveled all alone, darling. At seventeen!
ANYA: We got to Paris at last, it was cold there—snow. I speak French shockingly. Mamma lives on the fifth floor, I went up to her and there were a lot of French people, ladies, an old priest with a book. The place smelt of tobacco and so comfortless. I felt sorry, oh! so sorry for mamma all at once, I put my arms round her neck, and hugged her and wouldn't let her go. Mamma was as kind as she could be, and she cried. . . .
VARYA (*through her tears*): Don't speak of it, don't speak of it!
ANYA: She had sold her villa at Mentone, she had nothing left, nothing. I hadn't a farthing left either, we only just had enough to get here. And mamma doesn't understand! When we had dinner at the stations, she always ordered the most expensive things and gave the waiters a whole ruble. Charlotta's just the same. Yasha too must have the same as we do; it's simply awful. You know Yasha is mamma's valet now, we brought him here with us.
VARYA: Yes, I've seen the young rascal.
ANYA: Well, tell me—have you paid the arrears on the mortgage?
VARYA: How could we get the money?
ANYA: Oh, dear! Oh, dear!
VARYA: In August the place will be sold.
ANYA: My goodness!
LOPAHIN (*peeps in at the door and moos like a cow*): Moo! (*Disappears.*)
VARYA (*weeping*): There, that's what I could do to him. (*Shakes her fist.*)
ANYA (*embracing* VARYA, *softly*): Varya, has he made you an offer? (VARYA *shakes her head.*) Why, but he loves you, Why is it you don't come to an understanding? What are you waitng for?
VARYA: I believe that there never will be anything between us. He has a lot to do, he has no time for me . . . and takes no notice of me. Bless the man, it makes me miserable to see him. . . . Everyone's talking of our being married, everyone's congratulating me, and all the while there's really nothing in it; it's all like a dream. (*In another tone.*) You have a new brooch like a bee.
ANYA (*mournfully*): Mamma bought it. (*Goes into her own room and talks in a light-hearted childish tone.*) And you know, in Paris I went up in a balloon!
VARYA: My darling's home again! My pretty is home again!
(DUNYASHA *returns with the coffee-pot and is making the coffee*).
VARYA (*standing at the door*): All day long, darling, as I go about looking after the house, I keep dreaming all the time. If only we could marry you to a rich man, then I should feel more at rest. Then I would go off by myself on a pilgrimmage to Kiev, to Moscow . . . and so I would spend my life going from one holy place to another. . . . I would go on and on. . . . What bliss!

ANYA: The birds are singing in the garden. What time is it?
VARYA: It must be nearly three. It's time you were asleep, darling. (*Going into* ANYA's *room.*) What bliss!

(YASHA *enters with a rug and a traveling bag.*)

YASHA (*crosses the stage, mincingly*): May one come in here, pray?
DUNYASHA: I shouldn't have known you, Yasha. How you have changed abroad.
YASHA: H'm! . . . And who are you?
DUNYASHA: When you went away, I was that high. (*Shows distance from floor.*) Dunyasha, Fyodor's daughter. . . . You don't remember me!
YASHA: H'm! . . . You're a peach! (*Looks round and embraces her: she shrieks and drops a saucer.* YASHA *goes out hastily.*)
VARYA (*in the doorway, in a tone of vexation*): What now?
DUNYASHA (*through her tears*): I have broken a saucer.
VARYA: Well, that brings good luck.
ANYA (*coming out of her room*): We ought to prepare mamma: Petya is here.
VARYA: I told them not to wake him.
ANYA (*dreamily*): It's six years since father died. Then only a month later little brother Grisha was drowned in the river, such a pretty boy he was, only seven. It was more than mamma could bear, so she went away, went away without looking back. (*Shuddering.*) . . . How well I understand her, if only she knew! (*A pause.*) And Petya Trofimov was Grisha's tutor, he may remind her.

(*Enter* FIRS; *he is wearing a pea-jacket and a white waistcoat.*)

FIRS (*goes up to the coffee-pot, anxiously*): The mistress will be served here. (*Puts on white gloves.*) Is the coffee ready? (*Sternly to* DUNYASHA.) Girl! Where's the cream?
DUNYASHA: Ah, mercy on us! (*Goes out quickly.*)
FIRS (*fussing round the coffee-pot*): Ech! you good-for-nothing! (*Muttering to himself.*) Come back from Paris. And the old master used to go to Paris too . . . horses all the way. (*Laughs.*)
VARYA: What is it, Firs?
FIRS: What is your pleasure? (*Gleefully.*) My lady has come home! I have lived to see her again! Now I can die.

(*Weeps with joy. Enter* LYUBOV ANDREYEVNA, GAEV *and* SEMYONOV-PISHTCHIK; *the latter is in a short-waisted full coat of fine cloth, and full trousers.* GAEV, *as he comes in, makes a gesture with his arms and his whole body, as though he were playing billiards.*)

LYUBOV: How does it go? Let me remember. Cannon off the red!

GAEV: That's it—in off the white! Why, once, sister, we used to sleep together in this very room, and now I'm fifty-one, strange as it seems.
LOPAHIN: Yes, time flies.
GAEV: What do you say?
LOPAHIN: Time, I say, flies.
GAEV: What a smell of patchouli!
ANYA: I'm going to bed. Good night, mamma. (*Kisses her mother.*)
LYUBOV: My precious darling. (*Kisses her hands.*) Are you glad to be home? I can't believe it.
ANYA: Good night, uncle.
GAEV (*kissing her face and hands*): God bless you! How like you are to your mother! (*To his sister.*) At her age you were just the same, Lyuba. (ANYA *shakes hands with* LOPAHIN *and* PISHTCHIK, *then goes out, shutting the door after her.*)
LYUBOV: She's quite worn out.
PISHTCHIK: Aye, it's a long journey, to be sure.
VARYA (*to* LOPAHIN *and* PISHTCHIK): Well, gentlemen? It's three o'clock and time to say good-by.
LYUBOV (*laughs*): You're just the same as ever, Varya. (*Draws her to her and kisses her.*) I'll just drink my coffee and then we will all go and rest. (FIRS *puts a cushion under her feet.*) Thanks, friend. I am so fond of coffee, I drink it day and night. Thanks, dear old man. (*Kisses* FIRS.)
VARYA: I'll just see whether all the things have been brought in. (*Goes out.*)
LYUBOV: Can it really be me sitting here? (*Laughs.*) I want to dance about and clap my hands. (*Covers her face with her hands.*) And I could drop asleep in a moment! God knows I love my country, I love it tenderly; I couldn't look out of the window in the train, I kept crying so. (*Through her tears*). But I must drink my coffee, though. Thank you, Firs, thanks, dear old man. I'm so glad to find you still alive.
FIRS: The day before yesterday.
GAEV: He's rather deaf.
LOPAHIN: I have to set off for Harkov directly, at five o'clock. . . . It is annoying! I wanted to have a look at you, and a little talk. . . . You are just as splendid as ever.
PISHTCHIK (*breathing heavily*): Handsomer, indeed. . . . Dressed in Parisian style . . . completely bowled me over.
LOPAHIN: Your brother, Leonid Andreyevitch here, is always saying that I'm a low-born knave, that I'm a money-grubber, but I don't care one straw for that. Let him talk. Only I do want you to believe in me as you used to. I do want your wonderful tender eyes to look at me as they used to in the old days. Merciful God! My father was a serf of your father and of your grandfather, but you—you—did so much for me

once, that I've forgotten all that; I love you as though you were my kin . . . more than my kin.

LYUBOV: I can't sit still, I simply can't. . . . (*Jumps up and walks about in violent agitation.*) This happiness is too much for me. . . . You may laugh at me, I know I'm silly. . . . My own bookcase. (*Kisses the bookcase.*) My little table.

GAEV: Nurse died while you were away.

LYUBOV (*sits down and drinks coffee*): Yes, the Kingdom of Heaven be hers! You wrote me of her death.

GAEV: And Anastasy is dead. Squinting Petruchka has left me and is in service now with the police captain in the town. (*Takes a box of caramels out of his pocket and sucks one.*)

PISHTCHIK: My daughter, Dashenka, wishes to be remembered to you.

LOPAHIN: I want to tell you something very pleasant and cheering. (*Glancing at his watch.*) I'm going directly . . . there's no time to say much . . . well, I can say it in a couple of words. I needn't tell you your cherry orchard is to be sold to pay your debts; the 22nd of August is the date fixed for the sale; but don't you worry, dearest lady, you may sleep in peace, there is a way of saving it. . . . That is what I propose. I beg your attention(Your estate is not twenty miles from the town, the railway runs close by it, and if the cherry orchard and the land along the river bank were cut up into building plots and then let on lease for summer villas, you would make an income of at least 25,000 rubles a year out of it.

GAEV: That's all rot, if you'll excuse me.

LYUBOV: I don't quite understand you, Yermolay Alexeyevitch.

LOPAHIN: You will get a rent of at least twenty-five rubles a year for a three-acre plot from summer visitors, and if you say the word now, I'll bet you what you like there won't be one square foot of ground vacant by the autumn, all the plots will be taken up. I congratulate you; in fact, you are saved. It's a perfect situation with that deep river. Only, of course, it must be cleared—all the old buildings, for example, must be removed, this house too, which is really good for nothing, and the old cherry orchard must be cut down.

LYUBOV: Cut down? My dear fellow, forgive me, but you don't know what you are talking about. If there is one thing interesting—remarkable indeed—in the whole province, it's just our cherry orchard.

LOPAHIN: The only thing remarkable about the orchard is that it's a very large one. There's a crop of cherries every alternate year, and then there's nothing to be done with them, no one buys them.

GAEV: This orchard is mentioned in the *Encyclopædia*.

LOPAHIN (*glancing at his watch*): If we don't decide on something and don't take some steps, on the 22nd of August the cherry orchard and the whole estate too will be sold by auction. Make up your minds! There is no other way of saving it, I'll take my oath on that. No, No!

FIRS: In old days, forty or fifty years ago, they used to dry the cherries, soak them, pickle them, make jam too, and they used—

GAEV: Be quiet, Firs.

FIRS: And they used to send the preserved cherries to Moscow and to Markov by the wagon-load. That brought the money in! And the preserved cherries in those days were soft and juicy, sweet and fragrant.... They knew the way to do them then....

LYUBOV: And where is the recipe now?

FIRS: It's forgotten. Nobody remembers it.

PISHTCHIK (*to* LYUBOV ANDREYEVNA): What's it like in Paris? Did you eat frogs there?

LYUBOV: Oh, I ate crocodiles.

PISHTCHIK: Fancy that now!

LOPAHIN: There used to be only the gentlefolks and the peasants in the country, but now there are these summer visitors. All the towns, even the small ones, are surrounded, nowadays, by these summer villas. And one may say for sure, that in another twenty years there'll be many more of these people and that they'll be everywhere. At present the summer visitor only drinks tea in his veranda, but maybe he'll take to working his bit of land too, and then your cherry orchard would become happy, rich and prosperous....

GAEV (*indignant*): What rot!

[*Enter* VARYA *and* YASHA.]

VARYA: There are two telegrams for you, mamma. (*Takes out keys and opens a old-fashioned bookcase with a loud crack.*) Here they are.

LYUBOV: From Paris. (*Tears the telegrams, without reading them.*) I have done with Paris.

GAEV: Do you know, Lyuba, how old that bookcase is? Last week I pulled out the bottom drawer and there I found the date branded on it. The bookcase was made just a hundred years ago. What do you say to that? We might have celebrated its jubilee. Though it's an inanimate object, still it is a *book*case.

PISHTCHIK (*amazed*): A hundred years! Fancy that now.

GAEV: Yes.... It is a thing.... (*Feeling the bookcase.*) Dear, honored, bookcase! Hail to thee who for more than a hundred years hast served the pure ideals of good and justice; thy silent call to fruitful labor has never flagged in those hundred years, maintaining [*in tears*] in the generations of man, courage and faith in a brighter future and fostering in us ideals of good and social consciousness.

(*A pause.*)

LOPAHIN: Yes . . .

LYUBOV: You are just the same as ever, Leonid.

GAEV (*a little embarrassed*): Cannon off the right into the pocket!

LOPAHIN (*looking at his watch*): Well, it's time I was off.

YASHA (*handing* LYUBOV ANDREYEVNA *medicine*): Perhaps you will take your pills now.

PISHTCHIK: You shouldn't take medicines, my dear madam . . . they do no harm and no good. Give them here . . . honored lady. (*Takes the pillbox, pours the pills into the hollow of his hand, blows on them, puts them in his mouth and drinks off some kvass.*) There!

LYUBOV (*in alarm*): Why, you must be out of your mind!

PISHTCHIK: I have taken all the pills.

LOPAHIN: What a glutton!

(*All laugh.*)

FIRS: His honor stayed with us in Easter week, ate a gallon and a half of cucumbers. . . . (*Mutters.*)

LYUBOV: What is he saying?

VARYA: He has taken to muttering like that for the last three years. We are used to it.

YASHA: His declining years!

(CHARLOTTA IVANOVNA, *a very thin, lanky figure in a white dress with a lorgnette in her belt, walks across the stage.*)

LOPAHIN: I beg your pardon, Charlotta Ivanovna, I have not had time to greet you. (*Tries to kiss her hand.*)

CHARLOTTA (*pulling away her hand*): If I let you kiss my hand, you'll be wanting to kiss my elbow, and then my shoulder.

LOPAHIN: I've no luck today! (*All laugh.*) Charlotta Ivanovna, show us some tricks!

LYUBOV: Charlotta, do show us some tricks!

CHARLOTTA: I don't want to. I'm sleepy. (*Goes out.*)

LOPAHIN: In three weeks' time we shall meet again. (*Kisses* LYUBOV ANDREYEVNA'S *hand.*) Good-by till then—I must go. (*To* GAEV.) Good-by. (*Kisses* PISHTCHIK.) Good-by. (*Gives his hand to* VARYA, *then to* FIRS *and* YASHA.) I don't want to go. (*To* LYUBOV ANDREYEVNA.) If you think over my plan for the villas and make up your mind, then let me know; I will lend you 50,000 rubles. Think of it seriously.

VARYA (*angrily*): Well, do go, for goodness' sake.

LOPAHIN: I'm going, I'm going. (*Goes out.*)

GAEV: Low-born knave! I beg pardon, though . . . Varya is going to marry him, he's Varya's fiancé.

VARYA: Don't talk nonsense, uncle.

LYUBOV: Well, Varya, I shall be delighted. He's a good man.

PISHTCHIK: He is, one must acknowledge, a most worthy man. And my Dashenka . . . says too that . . . she says . . . various things. (*Snores, but at once wakes up.*) But all the same, honored lady, could you oblige me . . . with a loan of 240 rubles . . . to pay the interest on my mortgage tomorrow?

VARYA (*dismayed*): No, no.

LYUBOV: I really haven't any money.

PISHTCHIK: It will turn up. (*Laughs.*) I never lose hope. I thought everything was over, I was a ruined man, and lo and behold—the railway passed through my land and . . . they paid me for it. And something else will turn up again, if not today, then tomorrow . . . Dashenka'll win two hundred thousand . . . she's got a lottery ticket.

LYUBOV: Well, we've finished our coffee, we can go to bed.

FIRS (*brushes* GAEV, *reprovingly*): You have got on the wrong trousers again! What am I to do with you?

VARYA (*softly*): Anya's asleep. (*Softly opens the window.*) Now the sun's risen, it's not a bit cold. Look, mamma, what exquisite trees! My goodness! And the air! The starlings are singing!

GAEV (*opens another window*): The orchard is all white. You've not forgotten it, Lyuba? That long avenue that runs straight, straight as an arrow, how it shines on a moonlight night. You remember? You've not forgotten?

LYUBOV (*looking out of the window into the garden*): Oh, my childhood, my innocence! It was in this nursery I used to sleep, from here I looked out into the orchard, happiness waked with me every morning and in those days the orchard was just the same, nothing has changed. (*Laughs with delight.*) All, all white! Oh, my orchard! After the dark gloomy autumn, and the cold winter; you are young again and full of happiness, the heavenly angels have never left you. . . . If I could cast off the burden that weighs on my heart, if I could forget the past!

GAEV: H'm! and the orchard will be sold to pay our debts; it seems strange. . . .

LYUBOV: See, our mother walking . . . all in white, down the avenue (*Laughs with delight.*) It is she!

GAEV: Where?

VARYA: Oh, don't, mamma!

LYUBOV: There is no one. It was my fancy. On the right there, by the path to the arbor, there is a white tree bending like a woman. . . .

(*Enter* TROFIMOV *wearing a shabby student's uniform and spectacles.*)

LYUBOV: What a ravishing orchard! White masses of blossom, blue sky. . . .

TROFIMOV: Lyubov Andreyevna! (*She looks round at him.*) I will just pay my respects to you and then leave you at once. (*Kisses her hand warmly.*)

I was told to wait until morning, but I hadn't the patience to wait any longer....

(LYUBOV ANDREYEVNA *looks at him in perplexity.*)

VARYA (*through her tears*): This is Petya Trofimov.

TROFIMOV: Petya Trofimov, who was your Grisha's tutor.... Can I have changed so much?

(LYUBOV ANDREYEVNA *embraces him and weeps quietly.*)

GAEV (*in confusion*): There, there, Lyuba.

VARYA (*crying*): I told you, Petya, to wait till tomorrow.

LYUBOV: My Grisha... my boy... Grisha... my son!

VARYA: We can't help it, mamma, it is God's will.

TROFIMOV (*softly through his tears*): There... there.

LYUBOV (*weeping quietly*): My boy was lost... drowned. Why, Oh, why, dear Petya? (*More quietly.*) Anya is asleep in there, and I'm talking loudly... making this noise.... But, Petya? Why have you grown so ugly? Why do you look so old?

TROFIMOV: A peasant-woman in the train called me a mangy-looking gentleman.

LYUBOV: You were quite a boy then, a pretty little student, and now your hair's thin—and spectacles. Are you really a student still? (*Goes toward the door.*)

TROFIMOV: I seem likely to be a perpetual student.

LYUBOV (*kisses her brother, then* VARYA): Well, go to bed.... You are older too, Leonid.

PISHTCHIK (*follows her*): I suppose it's time we were asleep.... Ugh! my gout. I'm staying the night! Lyubov Andreyevna, my dear soul, if you could... tomorrow morning... 240 rubles.

GAEV: That's always his story.

PISHTCHIK: 240 rubles... to pay the interest on my mortgage.

LYUBOV: My dear man, I have no money.

PISHTCHIK: I'll pay it back, my dear... a trifling sum.

LYUBOV: Oh, well, Leonid will give it you.... You give him the money, Leonid.

GAEV: Me give it him! Let him wait till he gets it!

LYUBOV: It can't be helped, give it him. He needs it. He'll pay it back.

(LYUBOV ANDREYEVNA, TROFIMOV, PISHTCHIK *and* FIRS *go out.* GAEV, VARYA *and* YASHA *remain.*)

GAEV: Sister hasn't got out of the habit of flinging away her money. (*To* YASHA.) Get away, my good fellow, you smell of the hen-house.

YASHA (*with a grin*): And you, Leonid Andreyevitch, are just the same as ever.

GAEV: What's that? (*To* VARYA.) What did he say?

VARYA (*to* YASHA): Your mother has come from the village; she has been sitting in the servants' room since yesterday, waiting to see you.

YASHA: Oh, bother her!

VARYA: For shame!

YASHA: What's the hurry? She might just as well have come tomorrow. (*Goes out.*)

VARYA: Mamma's just the same as ever, she hasn't changed a bit. If she had her own way, she'd give away everything.

GAEV: Yes. (*A pause.*) If a great many remedies are suggested for some disease, it means that the disease is incurable. I keep thinking and racking my brains; I have many schemes, a great many, and that really means none. If we could only come in for a legacy from somebody, or marry our Anya to a very rich man, or we might go to Yaroslavl and try our luck with our old aunt, the Countess. She's very, very rich, you know.

VARYA (*weeps*): If God would help us.

GAEV: Don't blubber. Aunt's very rich, but she doesn't like us. First, sister married a lawyer instead of a nobleman....

(ANYA *appears in the doorway.*)

GAEV: And then her conduct, one can't call it virtuous. She is good, and kind, and nice, and I love her, but, however one allows for extenuating circumstances, there's no denying that she's an immoral woman. One feels it in her slightest gesture.

VARYA (*in a whisper*): Anya's in the doorway.

GAEV: What do you say? (*A pause.*) It's queer, there seems to be something wrong with my right eye. I don't see as well as I did. And on Thursday when I was in the distict Court ...

(*Enter* ANYA.)

VARYA: Why aren't you asleep, Anya?

ANYA: I can't get to sleep.

GAEV: My pet. (*Kisses* ANYA's *face and hands.*) My child. (*Weeps.*) You are not my niece, you are my angel, you are everything to me. Believe me, believe....

ANYA: I believe you, uncle. Everyone loves you and respects you ... but, uncle dear, you must be silent ... simply be silent. What were you saying just now about my mother, about your own sister? What made you say that?

GAEV: Yes, yes.... (*Puts his hand over his face.*) Really, that was awful! My God, save me! And today I made a speech to the bookcase ... so stupid! And only when I had finished, I saw how stupid it was.

VARYA: It's true, uncle, you ought to keep quiet. Don't talk, that's all.

ANYA: If you could keep from talking, it would make things easier for you, too.

GAEV: I won't speak. (*Kisses* ANYA's *and* VARYA's *hands*.) I'll be silent. Only this is about business. On Thursday I was in the district Court; well, there was a large party of us there and we began talking of one thing and another, and this and that, and do you know, I believe that it will be possible to raise a loan on an I.O.U. to pay the arrears on the mortgage.

VARYA: If the Lord would help us!

GAEV: I'm going on Tuesday; I'll talk of it again. (*To* VARYA.) Don't blubber. (*To* ANYA.) Your mamma will talk to Lopahin; of course, he won't refuse her. And as soon as you're rested you shall go to Yaroslavl to the Countess, your great-aunt. So we shall all set to work in three directions at once, and the business is done. We shall pay off arrears. I'm convinced of it. (*Puts a caramel in his mouth.*) I swear on my honor, I swear by anything you like, the estate shan't be sold. (*Excitedly.*) By my own happiness, I swear it! Here's my hand on it, call me the basest, vilest of men, if I let it come to an auction! Upon my soul I swear it!

ANYA (*her equanimity has returned, she is quite happy*): How good you are, uncle, and how clever! (*Embraces her uncle.*) I'm at peace now! Quite at peace! I'm happy!

(*Enter* FIRS.)

FIRS (*reproachfully*): Leonid Andreyevitch, have you no fear of God? When are you going to bed?

GAEV: Directly, directly. You can go, Firs. I'll . . . yes, I will undress myself. Come children, by-by. We'll go into details tomorrow, but now go to bed. (*Kisses* ANYA *and* VARYA.) I'm a man of the eighties. They run down that period, but still I can say I have had to suffer not a little for my convictions in my life, it's not for nothing that the peasant loves me. One must know the peasant! One must know how. . . .

ANYA: At it again, uncle!

VARYA: Uncle dear, you'd better be quiet!

FIRS (*angrily*): Leonid Andreyevitch!

GAEV: I'm coming. I'm coming. Go to bed. Potted the shot—there's a shot for you! A beauty! (*Goes out,* FIRS *hobbling after him.*)

ANYA: My mind's at rest now. I don't want to go to Yaroslavl, I don't like my great-aunt, but still my mind's at rest. Thanks to uncle. (*Sits down.*)

VARYA: We must go to bed. I'm going. Something unpleasant happened while you were away. In the old servants' quarters there are only the old servants, as you know—Efimyushka, Polya and Yevstigney—and Karp too. They began letting stray people in to spend the night—I said

Anton Chekhov: *The Cherry Orchard*

nothing. But all at once I heard they had been spreading a report that I gave them nothing but pease pudding to eat. Out of stinginess, you know. . . . And it was all Yevstigney's doing. . . . Very well, I said to myself. . . . If that's how it is, I thought, watit a bit. I sent for Yevstigney. . . . (*Yawns.*) He comes. . . . "How's this, Yevstigney," I said, "you could be such a fool as to? . . . " (*Looking at* ANYA.) Anitchka! (*A pause.*) She's asleep. (*Puts her arm around* ANYA.) Come to bed . . . come along! (*Leads her.*) My darling has fallen asleep! Come . . .

(*They go. Far away beyond the orchard a shepherd plays on a pipe.* TROFIMOV *crosses the stage and, seeing* VARYA *and* ANYA, *stand still.*)

VARYA: Sh! asleep, asleep. Come, my own.
ANYA (*softly, half asleep*): I'm so tired. Still those bells. Uncle . . . dear . . . mamma and uncle. . . .
VARYA: Come, my own, come along.

(*They go into* ANYA's *room.*)

TROFIMOV (*tenderly*): My sunshine! My spring.

Curtain

ACT 2

(The open country. An old shrine, long abandoned and fallen out of the perpendicular; near it a well, large stones that have apparently once been tombstones, and an old garden seat. The road to GAEV's house is seen. On one side rise dark poplars; and there the cherry orchard begins. In the distance a row of telegraph poles and far, far away on the horizon there is faintly outlined a great town, only visible in very fine clear weather. It is near sunset. CHARLOTTA, YASHA *and* DUNYASHA are sitting on the seat. EPIHODOV is standing near, playing something mournful on a guitar. All sit plunged in thought. CHARLOTTA wears an old forage cap; she has taken a gun from her shoulder and is tightening the buckle on the strap.)

CHARLOTTA (*musingly*): I haven't a real passport of my own, and I don't know how old I am, and I always feel that I'm a young thing. When I was a little girl, my father and mother used to travel about to fairs and give performances—very good ones. And I used to dance *salto mortale* and all sorts of things. And when papa and mamma died, a German lady took me and had me educated. And so I grew up and became a governess. But where I came from, and who I am, I don't know. . . . Who my parents were, very likely they weren't married. . . . I don't know. (*Takes a cucumber out of her pocket and eats.*) I know nothing at all. (*A pause.*) One wants to talk and has no one to talk to. . . . I have nobody.

EPIHODOV (*plays on the guitar and sings*): "What care I for the noisy world! What care I for friends or foes!" How agreeable it is to play on the mandolin!

DUNYASHA: That's a guitar, not a mandolin. (*Looks in a hand-mirror and powders herself.*)

EPIHODOV: To a man mad with love, it's a mandolin. (*Sings.*) "Were her heart but aglow with love's mutual flame."

(YASHA *joins in.*)

CHARLOTTA: How shockingly these people sing! Foo! Like jackals!

DUNYASHA (*to* YASHA): What happiness, though, to visit foreign lands.

YASHA: Ah, yes! I rather agree with you there. (*Yawns, then lights a cigar.*)

EPIHODOV: That's comprehensible. In foreign lands everything has long since reached full complexion.

YASHA: That's so, of course.

EPIHODOV: I'm a cultivated man, I read remarkable books of all sorts, but I can never make out the tendency I am myself precisely inclined for, whether to live or to shoot myself, speaking precisely, but nevertheless I always carry a revolver. Here it is. . . . (*Shows revolver.*)

CHARLOTTA: I've had enough, and now I'm going. (*Puts on the gun.*) Epihodov, you're a very clever fellow, and a very terrible one too, all the women must be wild about you. Br-r-r! (*Goes.*) These clever fellows are all so stupid; there's not a creature for me to speak to. . . . Always alone, alone, nobody belonging to me . . . and who I am, and why I'm on earth, I don't know. (*Walks away slowly.*)

EPIHODOV: Speaking precisely, not touching upon other subjects, I'm bound to admit about myself, that destiny behaves mercilessly to me, as a storm to a little boat. If, let us suppose, I am mistaken, then why did I wake up this morning, to quote an example, and look round, and there on my chest was a spider of fearful magnitude . . . like this. (*Shows with both hands.*) And then I take up a jug of kvass, to quench my thirst, and in it there is something in the highest degree unseemly of the nature of a cockroach. (*A pause.*) Have you read Buckle? (*A pause.*) I am desirous of troubling you, Dunyasha, with a couple of words.

DUNYASHA: Well, speak.

EPIHODOV: I should be desirous to speak with you alone. (*Sighs.*)

DUNYASHA (*embarrassed*): Well—only bring me my mantle first. It's by the cupboard. It's rather damp here.

EPIHODOV: Certainly. I will fetch it. Now I know what I must do with my revolver. (*Takes guitar and goes off playing on it.*)

Anton Chekhov: *The Cherry Orchard*

YASHA: Two and twenty misfortunes! Between ourselves, he's a fool. (*Yawns.*)
DUNYASHA: God grant he doesn't shoot himself! (*A pause.*) I am so nervous, I'm always in a flutter. I was a little girl when I was taken into our lady's house, and now I have quite grown out of peasant ways, and my hands are white, as white as a lady's. I'm such a delicate, sensitive creature, I'm afraid of everything. I'm so frightened. And if you deceive me, Yasha, I don't know what will become of my nerves.
YASHA (*kisses her*): You're a peach! Of course a girl must never forget herself; what I dislike more than anything is a girl being flighty in her behavior.
DUNYASHA: I'm passionately in love with you, Yasha; you are a man of culture—you can give your opinion about anything.

(*A pause.*)

YASHA (*yawns*): Yes, that's so. My opinion is this: if a girl loves anyone, that means that she has no principles. (*A pause.*) It's pleasant smoking a cigar in the open air. (*Listens.*) Someone's coming this way . . . it's the gentlefolk. (DUNYASHA *embraces him impulsively.*) Go home, as though you had been to the river to bathe; go by that path, or else they'll meet you and suppose I have made an appointment with you here. That I can't endure.
DUNYASHA (*coughing softly*): The cigar has made my head ache. . . .
(*Goes off.* YASHA *remains sitting near the shrine. Enter* LYUBOV ANDREYEVNA, GAEV *and* LOPAHIN.)
LOPAHIN: You must make up your mind once for all—there's no time to lose. It's quite a simple question, you know. Will you consent to letting the land for building or not? One word in answer: Yes or no? Only one word!
LYUBOV: Who is smoking such horrible cigars here? (*Sits down.*)
GAEV: Now the railway line has been brought near, it's made things very convenient. (*Sits down.*) Here we have been over and lunched in town. Cannon off the white! I should like to go home and have a game.
LOPAHIN: Only one word! (*Beseechingly.*) Give me an answer!
GAEV (*yawning*): What do you say?
LYUBOV (*looks in her purse*): I had quite a lot of money here yesterday, and there's scarcely any left today. My poor Varya feeds us all on milk soup for the sake of economy; the old folks in the kitchen get nothing but pease pudding, while I waste my money in a senseless way. (*Drops purse, scattering gold pieces.*) There, they have all fallen out! (*Annoyed.*)
YASHA: Allow me. I'll soon pick them up. (*Collects the coins.*)
LYUBOV: Pray, do, Yasha. And what did I go off to the town to lunch for? Your restaurant's a wretched place with its music and tablecloth

smelling of soap. . . . Why drink so much, Leonid? And eat so much? And talk so much? Today you talked a great deal again in the restaurant, and all so inappropriately. About the era of the seventies, about the decadents. And to whom? Talking to waiters about decadents!
LOPAHIN: Yes.
GAEV (*waving his hand*): I'm incorrigible; that's evident. (*Irritably to* YASHA.) Why is it you keep fidgeting about in front of us!
YASHA (*laughs*): I can't help laughing when I hear your voice.
GAEV (*to his sister*): Either I or he. . . .
LYUBOV: Get along! Go away, Yasha.
YASHA (*gives* LYUBOV ANDREYNA *her purse*): Directly. (*Hardly able to suppress his laughter.*) This minute. . . . (*Goes off.*)
LOPAHIN: Deriganov, the millionaire, means to buy your estate. They say he is coming to the sale himself.
LYUBOV: Where did you hear that?
LOPAHIN: That's what they say in town.
GAEV: Our aunt in Yaroslavl has promised to send help; but when, and how much she will send, we don't know.
LOPAHIN: How much will she send? A hundred thousand? Two hundred?
LYUBOV: Oh, well! . . . Ten or fifteen thousand, and we must be thankful to get that.
LOPAHIN: Forgive me, but such reckless people as you are—such queer, unbusinesslike people—I never met in my life. One tells you in plain Russian your estate is going to be sold, and you seem not to understand it.
LYUBOV: What are we to do? Tell us what to do.
LOPAHIN: I do tell you every day. Every day I say the same thing. You absolutely must let the cherry orchard and the land on building leases; and do it at once, as quick as may be—the auction's close upon us! Do understand! Once make up your mind to build villas, and you can raise as much money as you like, and then you are saved.
LYUBOV: Villas and summer visitors—forgive me saying so—it's so vulgar.
GAEV: There I perfectly agree with you.
LOPAHIN: I shall sob, or scream, or fall into a fit. I can't stand it! You drive me mad! (*To* GAEV.) You're an old woman!
GAEV: What do you say?
LOPAHIN: An old woman! (*Gets up to go.*)
LYUBOV (*in dismay*): No, don't go! Do stay, my dear friend! Perhaps we shall think of something.
LOPAHIN: What is there to think of?
LYUBOV: Don't go, I entreat you! With you here it's more cheerful, anyway. (*A pause.*) I keep expecting something, as though the house were going to fall about our ears.
GAEV (*in profound dejection*): Potted the white! It fails—a kiss.

Anton Chekhov: *The Cherry Orchard*

LYUBOV: We have been great sinners. . . .

LOPAHIN: You have no sins to repent of.

GAEV (*puts a caramel in his mouth*): They say I've eaten up my property in caramels. (*Laughs.*)

LYUBOV: Oh, my sins! I've always thrown my money away recklessly like a lunatic. I married a man who made nothing but debts. My husband died of champagne—he drank dreadfully. To my misery I loved another man, and immeditely—it was my first punishment—the blow fell upon me, here in the river . . . my boy was drowned and I went abroad—went away forever, never to return, not to see that river again . . . I shut my eyes and fled, distracted, and *he* after me . . . pitilessly, brutally. I bought a villa at Mentone, for *he* fell ill there, and for three years I had no rest day or night. His illness wore me out, my soul was dried up. And last year, when my villa was sold to pay my debts, I went to Paris and there he robbed me of everything and abandoned me for another woman; and I tried to poison myself. . . . So stupid, so shameful! . . . And suddenly I felt a yearning for Russia, for my country, for my little girl. . . . (*Dries her tears.*) Lord, Lord, be merciful! Forgive my sins! Do not chastise me more! (*Takes a telegram out of her pocket.*) I got this today from Paris. He implores forgiveness, entreats me to return. (*Tears up the telegram.*) I fancy there is music somewhere. (*Listens.*)

GAEV: That's our famous Jewish orchestra. You remember, four violins, a flute and a double bass.

LYUBOV: That still in existence? We ought to send for them one evening, and give a dance.

LOPAHIN (*listens*): I can't hear. . . . (*Hums softly.*) "For money the Germans will turn a Russian into a Frenchman." (*Laughs.*) I did see such a piece at the theater yesterday! It was funny!

LYUBOV: And most likely there was nothing funny in it. You shouldn't look at plays, you should look at yourselves a little oftener. How gray your lives are! How much nonsense you talk.

LOPAHIN: That's true. One may say honestly, we live a fool's life. (*Pause.*) My father was a peasant, an idiot; he knew nothing and taught me nothing, only beat me when he was drunk, and always with his stick. In reality I am just such another blockhead and idiot. I've learnt nothing properly. I write a wretched hand. I write so that I feel ashamed before folks, like a pig.

LYUBOV: You ought to get married, my dear fellow.

LOPAHIN: Yes . . . that's true.

LYUBOV: You should marry our Varya, she's a good girl.

LOPAHIN: Yes.

LYUBOV: She's a good-natured girl, she's busy all day long, and what's more, she loves you. And you have liked her for ever so long.

LOPAHIN: Well? I'm not against it.... She's a good girl.

(*Pause.*)

GAEV: I've been offered a place in the bank: 6000 rubles a year. Did you know?

LYUBOV: You would never do for that! You must stay as you are.

(*Enter* FIRS *with overcoat.*)

FIRS: Put it on, sir, it's damp.

GAEV (*putting it on*): You bother me, old fellow.

FIRS: You can't go on like this. You went away in the morning without leaving word. (*Looks him over.*)

LYUBOV: You look older, Firs!

FIRS: What is your pleasure?

LOPAHIN: You look older, she said.

FIRS: I've had a long life. They were arranging my wedding before your papa was born.... (*Laughs.*) I was the head footman before the emancipation came. I wouldn't consent to be set free then; I stayed on with the old master.... (*A pause.*) I remember what rejoicings they made and didn't know themselves what they were rejoicing over.

LOPAHIN: Those were fine old times. There was flogging anyway.

FIRS (*not hearing*): To be sure! The peasants knew their place, and the masters knew theirs; but now they're all at sixes and sevens, there's no making it out.

GAEV: Hold your tongue, Firs. I must go to town tomorrow. I have been promised an introduction to a general, who might let us have a loan.

LOPAHIN: You won't bring that off. And you won't pay your arrears, you may rest assured of that.

LYUBOV: That's all his nonsense. There is no such general.

(*Enter* TROFIMOV, ANYA *and* VARYA.)

GAEV: Here come our girls.

ANYA: There's mamma on the seat.

LYUBOV (*tenderly*): Come here, come along. My darlings! (*Embraces* ANYA *and* VARYA.) If you only knew how I love you both. Sit beside me, there, like that. (*All sit down.*)

LOPAHIN: Our perpetual student is always with the young ladies.

TROFIMOV: That's not your business.

LOPAHIN: He'll soon be fifty, and he's still a student.

TROFIMOV: Drop your idiotic jokes.

LOPAHIN: Why are you so cross, you queer fish?

TROFIMOV: Oh, don't persist!

LOPAHIN (*laughs*): Allow me to ask you what's your idea of me?

TROFIMOV: I'll tell you my idea of you. Yermolay Alexeyevitch; you are a rich man, you'll soon be a millionaire. Well, just as in the economy of nature a wild beast is of use, who devours everything that comes in his way, so you too have your use.

(All laugh.)

VARYA: Better tell us something about the planets, Petya.
LYUBOV: No, let us go on with the conversation we had yesterday.
TROFIMOV: What was it about?
GAEV: About pride.
TROFIMOV: We had a long conversation yesterday, but we came to no conclusion. In pride, in your sense of it, there is something mystical. Perhaps you are right from your point of view; but if one looks at it simply, without subtlety, what sort of pride can there be, what sense is there in it, if man in his physiological formation is very imperfect, if in the immense majority of cases he is coarse, dull-witted, profoundly unhappy? One must give up glorification of self. One should work, and nothing else.
GAEV: One must die in any case.
TROFIMOV: Who knows? And what does it mean—dying? Perhaps man has a hundred senses, and only the five we know are lost at death, while the other ninety-five remain alive.
LYUBOV: How clever you are, Petya!
LOPAHIN *(ironically)*: Fearfully clever!
TROFIMOV: Humanity progresses, perfecting its powers. Everything that is beyond its ken now will one day become familiar and comprehensible; only we must work, we must with all our powers aid the seeker after truth. Here among us in Russia the workers are few in number as yet. The vast majority of the intellectual people I know, seek nothing, do nothing, are not fit as yet for work of any kind. They call themselves intellectual, but they treat their servants as inferiors, behave to the peasants as though they were animals, learn little, read nothing seriously, do practically nothing, only talk about science and know very little about art. They are all serious people, they all have severe faces, they all talk of weighty matters and air their theories, and yet the vast majority of us—ninety-nine per cent—live like savages, at the least thing fly to blows and abuse, eat piggishly, sleep in filth and stuffiness, bugs everywhere, stench and damp and moral impurity. And it's clear all our fine talk is only to divert our attention and other people's. Show me where to find the *crèches* there's so much talk about, and the reading-rooms? They only exist in novels: in real life there are none of them. There is nothing but filth and vulgarity and Asiatic apathy. I fear and dislike very serious faces. I'm afraid of serious conversation. We should do better to be silent.

LOPAHIN: You know, I get up at five o'clock in the morning, and I work from morning to night; and I've money, my own and other people's, always passing through my hands, ad I see what people are made of all round me. One has only to begin to do anything to see how few honest decent people there are. Sometimes when I lie awake at night, I think: "Oh! Lord, thou hast given us immense forests, boundless plains, the widest horizons, and living here we ourselves ought really to be giants."

LYUBOV: You ask for giants! They are no good except in story-books; in real life they frighten us.

(EPIHODOV *advances in the background, playing on the guitar.*)

LYUBOV (*dreamily*): There goes Epihodov.
ANYA (*dreamily*): There goes Epihodov.
GAEV: The sun has set, my friends.
TROFIMOV: Yes.
GAEV (*not loudly, but, as it were, declaiming*): O nature, divine nature, thou art bright with eternal luster, beautiful and indifferent! Thou, whom we call mother, thou dost unite within thee life and death! Thou dost give life and dost destroy!
VARYA (*in a tone of supplication*): Uncle!
ANYA: Uncle, you are at it again!
TROFIMOV: You'd much better be cannoning off the red!
GAEV: I'll hold my tongue, I will.

(*All sit plunged in thought. Perfect stillness. The only thing audible is the muttering of* FIRS. *Suddenly there is a sound in the distance, as it were from the sky—the sound of a breaking harp-string, mournfully dying away.*)

LYUBOV: What is that?
LOPAHIN: I don't know. Somewhere far away a bucket fallen and broken in the pits. But somewhere very far away.
GAEV: It might be a bird of some sort—such as a heron.
TROFIMOV: Or an owl.
LYUBOV (*shudders*): I don't know why, but it's horrid.
   (*A pause.*)
FIRS: It was the same before the calamity.
GAEV: Before what calamity?
FIR:: Before the emancipation.
   (*A pause.*)
LYUBOV: Come, my friends, let us be going; evening is falling. (*To* ANYA.) There are tears in your eyes. What is it, darling? (*Embraces her.*)
ANYA: Nothing, mamma; it's nothing.
TROFIMOV: There is somebody coming.

(*The* WAYFARER *appears in a shabby white forage cap and an overcoat; he is slightly drunk.*)

WAYFARER: Allow me to inquire, can I get to the station this way?
GAEV: Yes. Go along that road.
WAYFARER: I thank you most feelingly. (*Coughing.*) The weather is superb. (*Declaims.*) My brother, my suffering brother! . . . Come out to the Volga! Whose groan do you hear? . . . (*To* VARYA.) Mademoiselle, vouchsafe a hungry Russian thirty kopecks.

(VARYA *utters a shriek of alarm.*)

LOPAHIN (*angrily*): There's a right and a wrong way of doing everything!
LYUBOV (*hurriedly*): Here, take this. (*Looks in her purse.*) I've no silver. No matter—here's gold for you.
WAYFARER: I thank you most feelingly! (*Goes off.*)

(*Laughter.*)

VARYA (*frightened*): I'm going home—I'm going. . . . Oh, mamma, the servants have nothing to eat, and you gave him gold!
LYUBOV: There's no doing anything with me. I'm so silly! When we get home, I'll give you all I possess, Yermolay Alexeyevitch, you will lend me some more! . . .
LOPAHIN: I will.
LYUBOV: Come, friends, it's time to be going. And Varya, we have made a match of it for you. I congratulate you.
VARYA (*through her tears*): Mamma, that's not a joking matter.
LOPAHIN: "Ophelia, get thee to a nunnery!"
GAEV: My hands are trembling; it's a long while since I had a game of billiards.
LOPAHIN: "Ophelia! Nymph, in thy orisons be all my sins remember'd."
LYUBOV: Come, it will soon be supper-time.
VARYA: How he frightened me! My heart's simply throbbing.
LOPAHIN: Let me remind you, ladies and gentlemen: on the 22nd of August the cherry orchard will be sold. Think about that! Think about it!

(*All go off, except* TROFIMOV *and* ANYA.)

ANYA (*laughing*): I'm grateful to the wayfarer! He frightened Varya and we are left alone.
TROFIMOV: Varya's afraid we shall fall in love with each other, and for days together she won't leave us. With her narrow brain she can't grasp that we are above love. To eliminate the petty and transitory which hinder us from being free and happy—that is the aim and meaning of our life. Forward! We go forward irresistibly toward the bright star that shines yonder in the distance. Forward! Do no lag behind, friends.
ANYA (*claps her hands*): How well you speak! (*A pause.*) It is divine here today.
TROFIMOV: Yes, it's glorious weather.

ANYA: Somehow, Petya, you've made me so that I don't love the cherry orchard as I used to. I used to love it so dearly. I used to think that there was no spot on earth like our garden.

TROFIMOV: All Russia is our garden. The earth is great and beautiful—there are many beautiful places in it. (*A pause.*) Think only, Anya, your grandfather, and great-grandfather, and all your ancestors were slave-owners—the owners of living souls—and from every cherry in the orchard, from every leaf, from every trunk there are human creatures looking at you. Cannot you hear their voices? Oh, it is awful! Your orchard is a fearful thing, and when in the evening or at night one walks about the orchard, the old bark on the trees glimmers dimly in the dusk, and the old cherry trees seem to be dreaming of centuries gone by and tortured by fearful visions. Yes! We are at least two hundred years behind, we have really gained nothing yet, we have no definite attitude to the past, we do nothing but theorize or complain of depression or drink vodka. It is clear that to begin to live in the present, we must first expiate our past; we must break with it; and we can expiate it only by suffering, by extraordinary unceasing labor. Understand that, Anya.

ANYA: The house we live in has long ceased to be our own, and I shall leave it, I give you my word.

TROFIMOV: If you have the house keys, fling them into the well and go away. Be free as the wind.

ANYA (*in ecstasy*): How beautifully you said that!

TROFIMOV: Believe me, Anya, believe me! I am not thirty yet. I am young. I am still a student, but I have gone through so much already! As soon as winter comes I am hungry, sick, careworn, poor as a beggar, and what up and downs of fortune have I not known! And my soul was always, every minute, day and night, full of inexplicable forebodings. I have a forebodings. I have a foreboding of happiness, Anya. I see glimpses of it already.

ANYA (*pensively*): The moon is rising.

(EPIHODOV *is heard playing still the same mournful song on the guitar. The moon rises. Somewhere near the poplars* VARYA *is looking for* ANYA *and calling* "Anya! where are you?")

TROFIMOV: Yes, the moon is rising. (*A pause.*) Here is happiness—here it comes! It is coming nearer and nearer; already I can hear its footsteps. And if we never see it—if we may never know it—what does it matter? Others will see it after us.

VARYA'S VOICE: Anya! Where are you?

TROFIMOV: That Varya again! (*Angrily.*) It's revolting!

ANYA: Well, let's go down to the river. It's lovely there.

TROFIMOV: Yes, let's go.

(They go.)

VARYA'S VOICE: Anya! Anya!

Curtain

ACT 3

(A drawing room divided by an arch from a larger drawing room. A chandelier burning. The Jewish orchestra, the same that was mentioned in Act 2, is heard playing in the anteroom. It is evening. In the larger drawing room they are dancing the grand chain. The voice of SEMYONOV-PISHTCHIK: *"Promenade à une paire!" Then enter the drawing room in couples, first* PISHTCHIK *and* CHARLOTTA IVANOVNA, *then* TROFIMOV *and* LYUBOV ANDREYEVNA, *thirdly* ANYA *with the* POST-OFFICE CLERK, *fourthly* VARYA *with the* STATION MASTER, *and other guests.* VARYA *is quietly weeping and wiping away her tears as she dances. In the last couple is* DUNYASHA. *They move across the drawing room.* PISHTCHIK *shouts: "Grand rond, balancez!" and "Les Cavaliers à genou et remerciez vos dames.")*

*(*FIRS *in a swallow-tail coat brings in seltzer water on a tray.* PISHTCHIK *and* TROFIMOV *enter the drawing room.)*

PISHTCHIK: I am a full-blooded man; I have already had two strokes. Dancing's hard work for me, but as they say, if you're in the pack, you must bark with the rest. I'm as strong, I may say, as a horse. My parent, who would have his joke—may the Kingdom of Heaven be his!—used to say about our origin that the ancient stock of the Semyonov-Pishtchiks was derived from the very horse that Caligula made a member of the senate. *(Sits down.)* But I've no money, that's where the mischief is. A hungry dog believes in nothing but meat. *(Snores, but at once wakes up.)* That's like me . . . I can think of nothing but money.

TROFIMOV: There really is something horsy about your appearance.

PISHTCHIK: Well . . . a horse is a fine beast . . . a horse can be sold.

(There is the sound of billiards being played in an adjoining room. VARYA *appears in the arch leading to the larger drawing room.)*

TROFIMOV *(teasing)*: Madame Lopahin! Madame Lopahin!

VARYA *(angrily)*: Mangy-looking gentleman!

TROFIMOV: Yes, I am a mangy-looking gentleman, and I'm proud of it!

VARYA *(pondering bitterly)*: Here we have hired musicians and nothing to pay them! *(Goes out.)*

TROFIMOV *(to* PISHTCHIK*)*: If the energy you have wasted during your lifetime in trying to find the money to pay your interest had gone to something else, you might in the end have turned the world upside down.

PISHTCHIK: Nietzsche, the philosopher, a very great and celebrated man . . . of enormous intellect . . . says in his works, that one can make forged banknotes.

TROFIMOV: Why, have you read Nietzsche?

PISHTCHIK: What next . . . Dashenka told me. . . . And now I am in such a position, I might just as well forge banknotes. The day after tomorrow I must pay 310 rubles—130 I have procured. *(Feels in his pockets, in alarm.)* The money's gone! I have lost my money! *(Through his tears.)* Where's the money? *(Gleefully.)* Why, here it is behind the lining. . . . It has made me hot all over.

(Enter LYUBOV ANDREYEVNA *and* CHARLOTTA IVANOVNA.*)*

LYUBOV *(hums the Lezginka)*: Why is Leonid so long? What can he be doing in town? *(To* DUNYASHA.*)* Offer the musicians some tea.

TROFIMOV: The sale hasn't taken place, most likely.

LYUBOV: It's the wrong time to have the orchestra, and the wrong time to give a dance. Well, never mind. *(Sits down and hums softly)*

CHARLOTTA *(gives* PISHTCHIK *a pack of cards)*: Here's a pack of cards. Think of any card you like.

PISHTCHIK: I've thought of one.

CHARLOTTA: Shuffle the pack now. That's right. Give it here, my dear Mr. Pishtchik. *Ein, zwei, drei*—now look, it's in your breast pocket.

PISHTCHIK *(taking a card out of his breast pocket)*: The eight of spades! Perfectly right! *(Wonderingly.)* Fancy that now!

CHARLOTTA *(holding pack of cards in her hands, to* TROFIMOV*)*: Tell me quickly which is the top card.

TROFIMOV: Well, the queen of spades.

CHARLOTTA: It is! *(To* PISHTCHIK.*)* Well, which card is uppermost?

PISHTCHIK: The ace of hearts.

CHARLOTTA: It is! *(Claps her hands, pack of cards disappears.)* Ah! what lovely weather it is today!

(A mysterious feminine voice which seems coming out of the floor answers her. "Oh, yes, it's magnificent weather, madam."*)*

CHARLOTTA: You are my perfect ideal.

VOICE: And I greatly admire you too, madam.

STATION MASTER *(applauding)*: The lady ventriloquist—bravo!

PISHTCHIK *(wonderingly)*: Fancy that now! Most enchanting, Charlotta Ivanovna. I'm simply in love with you.

CHARLOTTA: In love? *(Shrugging shoulders.)* What do you know of love, *guter Mensch, aber schlechter Musikant.*

TROFIMOV *(pats* PISHTCHIK *on the shoulder)*: You dear old horse. . . .

CHARLOTTA: Attention, please! Another trick! (*Takes a traveling rug from a chair.*) Here's a very good rug; I want to sell it. (*Shaking it out.*) Doesn't anyone want to buy it?

PISHTCHIK (*wonderingly*): Fancy that!

CHARLOTTA: *Ein, zwei, drei!*

(*Quickly picks up rig she has dropped; behind the rug stands* ANYA; *she makes a curtsey, runs to her mother, embraces her and runs back into the larger drawing room amidst general enthusiasm.*)

LYUBOV (*applauds*): Bravo! Bravo!

CHARLOTTA: Now again; *Ein, zwei, drei!*

(*Lifts up the rug; behind the rug stands* VARYA, *bowing.*)

PISHTCHIK (*wonderingly*): Fancy that now!

CHARLOTTA: That's the end. (*Throws the rug at* PISHTCKIK, *makes a curtsey, runs into the larger drawing room.*)

PISHTCHIK (*hurries after her*): Mischievous creature! Fancy! (*Goes out.*)

LYUBOV: And still Leonid doesn't come. I can't understand what he's doing in the town so long! Why, everything must be over by now. The estate is sold, or the sale has not taken place. Why keep us so long in suspense?

VARYA (*trying to console her*): Uncle's bought it. I feel sure of that.

TROFIMOV (*ironically*): Oh, yes!

VARYA: Great-aunt sent him an authorization to buy it in her name, and transfer the debt. She's doing it for Anya's sake, and I'm sure God will be merciful. Uncle will buy it.

LYUBOV: My aunt in Yaroslavl sent fifteen thousand to buy the estate in her name, she doesn't trust us—but that's not enough even to pay the arrears. (*Hides her face in her hands.*) My fate is being sealed today, my fate. . . .

TROFIMOV (*teasing* VARYA): Madame Lopahin.

VARYA (*angrily*): Perpetual student! Twice already you've been sent down from the University.

LYUBOV: Why are you angry, Varya? He's teasing you about Lopahin. Well, what of that? Marry Lopahin if you like, he's a good man, and interesting; if you don't want to, don't! Nobody compels, you, darling.

VARYA: I must tell you plainly, mamma, I look at the matter seriously; he's a good man, I like him.

LYUBOV: Well, marry him. I can't see what you're waiting for.

VARYA: Mamma. I can't make him an offer myself. For the last two years, everyone's been talking to me about him. Everyone talks; but he says nothing or else makes a joke. I see what it means. He's growing rich, he's absorbed in business, he has no thoughts for me. If I had money, were it ever so little, if I had only a hundred rubles, I'd throw everything up and go far away. I would go into a nunnery.

TROFIMOV: What bliss!

VARYA (*to* TROFIMOV): A student ought to have sense! (*In a soft tone with tears.*) How ugly you've grown, Petya! How old you look! (*To* LYUBOV ANDREYEVNA, *no longer crying.*) But I can't do without work, mamma; I must have something to do every minute.

(*Enter* YASHA.)

YASHA (*hardly restraining his laughter*): Epihodov has broken a billiard cue! (*Goes out.*)

VARYA: What is Epihodov doing here? Who gave him leave to play billiards? I can't make these people out. (*Goes out.*)

LYUBOV: Don't tease her, Petya. You see she has grief enough without that.

TROFIMOV: She is so very officious, meddling in what's not her business. All the summer she's given Anya and me no peace. She's afraid of a love affair between us. What's it to do with her? Besides, I have given no grounds for it. Such triviality is not in my line. We are above love!

LYUBOV: And I suppose I am beneath love. (*Very uneasily.*) Why is it Leonid's not here? If only I could know whether the estate is sold or not! It seems such an incredible calamity that I really don't know what to think. I am distracted. . . . I shall scream in a minute . . . I shall do something stupid. Save me, Petya, tell me something, talk to me!

TROFIMOV: What does it matter whether the estate is sold today or not? That's all done with long ago. There's no turning back, the path is overgrown. Don't worry yourself, dear Lyubov Andreyevna. You mustn't deceive yourself; for once in your life you must face the truth!

LYUBOV: What truth? You see where the truth lies, but I seem to have lost my sight, I see nothing. You settle every great problem so boldly, but tell me, my dear boy, isn't it because you're young—because you haven't yet understood one of your problems through suffering? You look forward boldly, and isn't it that you don't see and don't expect anything dreadful because life is still hidden from your young eyes? You're bolder, more honest, deeper than we are, but think, be just a little magnanimous, have pity on me. I was born here, you know, my father and mother lived here, my grandfather lived here, I love this house. I can't conceive of life without the cherry orchard, and if it really must be sold, then sell me with the orchard. (*Embraces* TROFIMOV, *kisses him on the forehead.*) My boy was drowned here. (*Weeps.*) Pity me, my dear kind fellow.

TROFIMOV: You know I feel for you with all my heart.

LYUBOV: But that should have been said differently, so differently. (*Takes out her handkerchief, telegram falls on the floor.*) My heart is so heavy today. It's so noisy here, my soul is quivering at every sound, I'm shuddering all over, but I can't go away; I'm afraid to be quiet and alone. Don't be hard on me, Petya . . . I love you as though you were one of ourselves. I would gladly let you marry Anya—I swear I would—only, my dear boy, you must take your degree, you do nothing—you're simply tossed by fate from place to place. That's so strange. It is, isn't it? And you must do something with your beard to make it grow somehow. (*Laughs.*) You look so funny!

TROFIMOV (*picks up the telegram*): I've no wish to be a beauty.

LYUBOV: That's a telegram from Paris. I get one every day. One yesterday and one today. That savage creature is ill again, he's in trouble again. He begs forgiveness, beseeches me to go, and really I ought to go to Paris to see him. You look shocked, Petya. What am I to do, my dear boy, what am I to do? He is ill, he is alone and unhappy, and who'll look after him, who'll keep him from doing the wrong thing, who'll give him his medicine at the right time? And why hide it or be silent? I love him, that's clear. I love him! I love him! He's a millstone about my neck, I'm going to the bottom with him, but I love that stone and can't live without it. (*Presses* TROFIMOV's *hand.*) Don't think ill of me, Petya, don't tell me anything, don't tell me. . . .

TROFIMOV (*through his tears*): For God's sake forgive my frankness: why, he robbed you!

LYUBOV: No! No! No! You mustn't speak like that. (*Covers her ears.*)

TROFIMOV: He is a wretch! You're the only person that doesn't know it! He's a worthless creature! A despicable wretch!

LYUBOV (*getting angry, but speaking with restraint*): You're twenty-six or twenty-seven years old, but you're still a schoolboy.

TROFIMOV: Possibly.

LYUBOV: You should be a man at your age! You should understand what love means! And you ought to be in love yourself. You ought to fall in love! (*Angrily.*) Yes, yes, and it's not purity in you, you're simply a prude, a comic fool, a freak.

TROFIMOV (*in horror*): The things she's saying!

LYUBOV: I am above love! You're not above love, but simply as our Firs here says, "You are a good-for-nothing." At your age not to have a mistress!

TROFIMOV (*in horror*): This is awful! The things she is saying! (*Goes rapidly into the larger drawing room clutching his head.*) This is awful! I can't stand it! I'm going. (*Goes off, but at once returns.*) All is over between us! (*Goes off into the anteroom.*)

LYUBOV (*shouts after him*): Petya! Wait a minute! You funny creature! I was joking! Petya!

(*There is a sound of somebody running quickly downstairs and suddenly falling with a crash.* ANYA *and* VARYA *scream, but there is a sound of laughter at once.*)

LYUBOV: What has happened?

(ANYA *runs in.*)

ANYA (*laughing*): Petya's fallen downstairs! (*Runs out.*)

LYUBOV: What a queer fellow that Petya is!

(*The* STATION MASTER *stands in the middle of the larger room and reads* The Magdalene, *by* Alexey Tolstoy. *They listen to him, but before he has recited many lines strains of a waltz are heard from the anteroom and the reading is broken off. All dance.* TROFIMOV, ANYA, VARYA *and* LYUBOV ANDREYEVNA *come in from the anteroom.*)

LYUBOV: Come, Petya—come, pure heart! I beg your pardon. Let's have a dance!

(*Dances with* PETYA. ANYA *and* VARYA *dance.* FIRS *comes in, puts his stick down near the side door.* YASHA *also comes into the drawing room and looks on at the dancing.*)

YASHA: What is it, old man?

FIRS: I don't feel well. In old days we used to have generals, barons and admirals dancing at our balls, and now we send for the post-office clerk and the station master and even they're not overanxious to come. I am getting feeble. The old master, the grandfather, used to give sealing-wax for twenty years or more. Perhaps that's what's kept me alive.

YASHA: You bore me, old man! (*Yawns.*) It's time you were done with.

FIRS: Ach, you're a good-for-nothing! (*Mutters.*)

(TROFIMOV *and* LYUBOV ANDREYEVNA *dance in larger room and then on to the stage.*)

LYUBOV: *Merci.* I'll sit down a little. (*Sits down.*) I'm tired.

(*Enter* ANYA.)

ANYA (*excitedly*): There's a man in the kitchen has been saying that the cherry orchard's been sold today.

LYUBOV: Sold to whom?

ANYA: He didn't say to whom. He's gone away.

(*She dances with* TROFIMOV, *and they go off into the larger room.*)

YASHA: There was an old man gossiping there, a stranger.

FIRS: Leonid Andreyevitch isn't here yet, he hasn't come back. He has his light overcoat on, *demi-saison,* he'll catch cold for sure. *Ach!* Foolish young things!

LYUBOV: I feel as though I should die. Go, Yasha, find out to whom it has been sold.

YASHA: But he went away long ago, the old chap. (*Laughs.*)

LYUBOV (*with slight vexation*): What are you laughing at? What are you at?

YASHA: Epihodov is so funny. He's a silly fellow, two and twenty misfortunes.

LYUBOV: Firs, if the estate is sold, where will you go?
FIRS: Where you bid me, there I'll go.
LYUBOV: Why do you look like that? Are you ill? You ought to be in bed.
FIRS: Yes. (*Ironically.*) Me go to bed and who's to wait here? Who's to see to things without me? I'm the only one in all the house.
YASHA (*to* LYUBOV ANDREYEVNA): Lyubov Andreyevna, permit me to make a request of you; if you go back to Paris again, be so kind as to take me with you. It's positively impossible for me to stay here. (*Looking about him; in an undertone.*) There's no need to say it, you see for yourself—an uncivilized country, the people have no morals, and then the dullness! The food in the kitchen's abominable, and then Firs runs after one muttering all sorts of unsuitable words. Take me with you, please do!

(*Enter* PISHTCHIK.)

PISHTCHIK: Allow me to ask you for a waltz, my dear lady. (LYUBOV ANDREYEVNA *goes with him.*) Enchanting lady, I really must borrow of you just 180 rubles, (*dances*) only 180 rubles.
(*They pass into the larger room. In the larger drawing room, a figure in a gray top hat and in checked trousers is gesticulating and jumping about. Shouts of* "Bravo, Charlotta Ivanovna.")
DUNYASHA (*she has stopped to powder herself*): My young lady tells me to dance. There are plenty of gentlemen, and too few ladies, but dancing makes me giddy and makes my heart beat. Firs, the post-office clerk said something to me just now that quite took my breath away.
(*Music becomes more subdued.*)
FIRS: What did he say to you?
DUNYASHA: He said I was like a flower.
YASHA (*yawns*): What ignorance! (*Goes out.*)
DUNYASHA: Like a flower. I am a girl of such delicate feelings, I am awfully fond of soft speeches.
FIRS: Your head's being turned.
(*Enter* EPIHODOV.)
EPIHODOV: You have no desire to see me, Dunyasha. I might be an insect. (*Sighs.*) Ah! life!
DUNYASHA: What is it you want?
EPIHODOV: Undoubtedly you may be right. (*Sighs.*) But, of course, if one looks at it from that point of view, if I may so express myself, you have, excuse my plain speaking, reduced me to a complete state of mind. I know my destiny. Every day some misfortune befalls me and I have long ago grown accustomed to it, so that I look upon my fate with a smile. You gave me your word, and though I—

DUNYASHA: Let us have a talk later, I entreat you, but now leave me in peace, for I am lost in reverie. (*Plays with her fan.*)
EPIHODOV: I have a misfortune every day, and if I may venture to express myself, I merely smile at it, I even laugh.

(VARYA *enters from the larger drawing room.*)

VARYA: You still have not gone, Epihodov. What a disrespectful creature you are, really! (*To* DUNYASHA.) Go along, Dunyasha! (*To* EPIHODOV.) First you play billiards and break the cue, then you go wandering about the drawing room like a visitor!
EPIHODOV: You really cannot, if I may so express myself, call me to account like this.
VARYA: I'm not calling you to account, I'm speaking to you. You do nothing but wander from place to place and don't do your work. We keep you as a counting-house clerk, but what use you are I can't say.
EPIHODOV (*offended*): Whether I work or whether I walk, whether I eat or whether I play billiards, is a matter to be judged by persons of understanding and my elders.
VARYA: You dare to tell me that! (*Firing up.*) You dare! You mean to say I've no understanding. Begone from here! This minute!
EPIHODOV (*intimidated*): I beg you to express yourself with delicacy.
VARYA (*beside herself with anger*): This moment! get out! away! (*He goes toward the door, she following him.*) Two and twenty misfortunes! Take yourself off! Don't let me set eyes on you! (EPIHODOV *has gone out, behind the door his voice,* "I shall lodge a complaint against you.") What! You're coming back? (*Snatches up the stick* FIRS *has put down near the door.*) Come! Come! Come! I'll show you! What! you're coming? Then take that! (*She swings the stick, at the very moment that* LOPAHIN *comes in.*)
LOPAHIN: Very much obliged to you!
VARYA (*angrily and ironically*): I beg your pardon!
LOPAHIN: Not at all! I humbly thank you for your kind reception!
VARYA: No need of thanks for it. (*Moves away, then looks round and asks softly.*) I haven't hurt you?
LOPAHIN: Oh, no! Not at all! There's an immense bump coming up, though!
VOICES FROM LARGER ROOM: Lopahin has come! Yermolay Alexeyevitch!
PISHTCHIK: What do I see and hear? (*Kisses* LOPAHIN.) There's a whiff of cognac about you, my dear soul, and we're making merry here too!

(*Enter* LYUBOV ANDREYEVNA.)

LYUBOV: Is it you, Yermolay Alexeyevitch? Why have you been so long? Where's Leonid?

LOPAHIN: Leonid Andreyevitch arrived with me. He is coming.
LYUBOV (*in agitation*): Well! Well! Was there a sale? Speak!
LOPAHIN (*embarrassed, afraid of betraying his joy*): The sale was over at four o'clock. We missed our train—had to wait till half-past nine. (*Sighing heavily.*) Ugh! I feel a little giddy.

(*Enter* GAEV. *In his right hand he has purchases, with his left hand he is wiping away his tears.*)

LYUBOV: Well, Leonid? What news? (*Impatiently, with tears.*) Make haste, for God's sake!
GAEV (*makes her no answer, simply waves his hand. To* FIRS, *weeping*): Here, take them; there's anchovies, Kertch herrings. I have eaten nothing all day. What I have been through! (*Door into the billiard room is open. There is heard a knocking of balls and the voice of* YASHA *saying* "Eighty-seven." GAEV's *expression changes, he leaves off weeping.*) I am fearfully tired. Firs, come and help me change my things. (*Goes to his own room across the larger drawing room.*)
PISHTCHIK: How about the sale? Tell us, do!
LYUBOV: Is the cherry orchard sold?
LOPAHIN: It is sold.
LYUBOV: Who has bought it?
LOPAHIN: I have bought it.

(*A pause.* LYUBOV *is crushed; she would fall down if she were not standing near a chair and table.* VARYA *takes keys from her waistband, flings them on the floor in middle of drawing room and goes out.*)

LOPAHIN: I have bought it! Wait a bit, ladies and gentlemen, pray. My head's a bit muddled, I can't speak. (*Laughs.*) We came to the auction. Deriganov was there already. Leonid Andreyevitch only had 15,000 and Deriganov bid 30,000, besides the arrears, straight off. I saw how the land lay. I bid against him. I bid 40,000, he bid 45,000, I said 55, and so he went on, adding 5 thousands and I adding 10. Well . . . So it ended. I bid 90, and it was knocked down to me. Now the cherry orchard's mine! Mine! (*Chuckles.*) My God, the cherry orchard's mine! Tell me that I'm drunk, that I'm out of my mind, that it's all a dream. (*Stamps with his feet.*) Don't laugh at me! If my father and my grandfather could rise from their graves and see all that has happened! How their Yermolay, ignorant, beaten Yermolay has bought the finest estate in the world! I have bought the estate where my father and grandfather were slaves, where they weren't even admitted into the kitchen. I am asleep, I am dreaming! It is all fancy, it is the work of your imagination plunged in the darkness of ignorance. (*Picks up keys, smiling fondly.*) She threw away the keys; she means to show she's not the housewife now. (*Jingles the keys.*) Well, no matter. (*The orchestra is heard tuning up.*) Hey, musicians! Play! I want to hear you. Come, all of you, and look how Yermolay Lopahin will take the ax to the cherry orchard, how the trees will fall to the ground! We will build houses on it and our grandsons and great-grandsons will see a new life springing up there. Music! Play up!

(*Music begins to play.* LYUBOV ANDREYEVNA *has sunk into a chair and is weeping bitterly.*)

LOPAHIN (*reproachfully*): Why, why didn't you listen to me? My poor friend! Dear lady, there's no turning back now. (*With tears.*) Oh, if all this could be over, oh, if our miserable disjointed life could somehow soon be changed!

PISHTCHIK (*take him by the arm, in an undertone*): She's weeping, let us go and leave her alone. Come. (*Takes him by the arm and leads him into the larger drawing room.*)

LOPAHIN: What's that? Musicians, play up! All must be as I wish it. (*With irony.*) Here comes the new master, the owner of the cherry orchard! (*Accidentally tips over a little table, almost upsetting the candelabra.*) I can pay for everything!

(*Goes out with* PISHTCHIK. *No one remains on the stage or in the larger drawing room except* LYUBOV, *who sits huddled up, weeping bitterly. The music plays softly.* ANYA *and* TROFIMOV *come in quickly.* ANYA *goes up to her mother and falls on her knees before her.* TROFIMOV *stands at the entrance to the larger drawing room.*)

ANYA: Mamma! Mamma, you're crying, dear, kind, good mamma! My precious! I love you! I gless you! The cherry orchard is sold, it is gone, that's true, that's true! But don't weep, mamma! Life is still before you, you have still your good, pure heart! Let us go, let us go, darling, away from here! We will make a new garden, more splendid than this one; you will see it, you will understand. And joy, quiet, deep joy, will sink into your soul like the sun at evening! And you will smile, mamma! Come, darling, let us go!

Curtain

ACT 4

(Scene: Same as in First Act. There are neither curtains on the windows nor pictures on the walls: only a little furniture remains piled up in a corner as if for sale. There is a sense of desolation; near the outer door and in the background of the scene are packed trunks, traveling bags, etc.

On the left the door is open, and from here the voices of VARYA and ANYA are audible. LOPAHIN is standing waiting. YASHA is holding a tray with glasses full of champagne. In front of the stage EPIHODOV is tying up a box. In the background behind the scene a hum of talk from the peasants who have come to say good-by. The voice of GAEV: Thanks, brothers, thanks!")

YASHA: The peasants have come to say good-by. In my opinion, Yermolay Alexeyevitch, the peasants are good-natured, but they don't know much about things.

(*The hum of talk dies away. Enter across front of stage.* LYUBOV ANDREYEVNA *and* GAEV. *She is not weeping, but is pale; her face is quivering—she cannot speak.*)

GAEV: You gave them your purse, Lyuba. That won't do—that won't do!
LYUBOV: I couldn't help it! I couldn't help it! (*Both go out*).
LOPAHIN (*in the doorway, calls after them*): You will take a glass at parting? Please do. I didn't think to bring any from the town, and at the station I could only get one bottle. Please take a glass (*A pause.*) What? You don't care for any? (*Comes away from the door.*) If I'd known, I wouldn't have bought it. Well, and I'm not going to drink it. (YASHA *carefully sets the tray down on a chair.*) You have a glass, Yasha, anyway.
YASHA: Good luck to the travelers, and luck to those that stay behind! (*Drinks.*) This champagne isn't the real thing, I can assure you.
LOPAHIN: It cost eight rubles the bottle. (*A pause.*) It's devilish cold here.
YASHA: They haven't heated the stove today—it's all the same since we're going. (*Laughs.*)
LOPAHIN: What are you laughing for?
YASHA: For pleasure.
LOPAHIN: Though it's October, it's as still and sunny as though it were summer. It's just right for building! (*Looks at his watch; says in doorway.*) Take note, ladies and gentlemen, the train goes in forty-seven minutes; so you ought to start for the station in twenty minutes. You must hurry up!

(TROFIMOV *comes in from out of doors wearing a greatcoat.*)

TROFIMOV: I think it must be time to start, the horses are ready. The devil only knows what's become of my goloshes; they're lost. (*In the doorway.*) Anya! My goloshes aren't here. I can't find them.
LOPAHIN: And I'm getting off to Harkov. I am going in the same train with you. I'm spending all the winter at Harkov. I've been wasting all

my time gossiping with you and fretting with no work to do. I can't get on without work. I don't know what to do with my hands, they flap about so queerly, as if they didn't belong to me.

TROFIMOV: Well, we're just going away, and you will take up your profitable labors again.

LOPAHIN: Do take a glass.

TROFIMOV: No, thanks.

LOPAHIN: Then you're going to Moscow now?

TROFIMOV: Yes. I shall see them as far as the town, and tomorrow I shall go on to Moscow.

LOPAHIN: Yes, I daresay, the professors aren't giving any lectures, they're waiting for your arrival.

TROFIMOV: That's not your business.

LOPAHIN: How many years have you been at the University?

TROFIMOV: Do think of something newer than that—that's stale and flat. (*Hunts for goloshes.*) You know we shall most likely never see each other again, so let me give you one piece of advice at parting: don't wave your arms about—get out of the habit. And another thing, building villas, reckoning up that the summer visitors will in time become independent farmers—reckoning like that, that's not the thing to do either. After all, I am fond of you: you have fine delicate fingers like an artist, you've a fine delicate soul.

LOPAHIN (*embraces him.*) Good-by, my dear fellow. Thanks for everything. Let me give you money for the journey, if you need it.

TROFIMOV: What for? I don't need it.

LOPAHIN: Why, you haven't got a half-penny.

TROFIMOV: Yes, I have, thank you. I got some money for a translation. Here it is in my pocket, (*anxiously*) but where can my goloshes be!

VARYA (*from the next room*): Take the nasty things! (*Flings a pair of goloshes on to the stage.*)

TROFIMOV: Why are you so cross, Varya? h'm . . . but those aren't my goloshes.

LOPAHIN: I sowed three thousand acres with poppies in the spring, and now I have cleared forty thousand profit. And when my poppies were in flower, wasn't it a picture! So here, as I say, I made forty thousand, and I'm offering you a loan because I can afford to. Why turn up your nose? I am a peasant—I speak bluntly.

TROFIMOV: Your father was a peasant, mine was a chemist—and that proves absolutely nothing whatever. (LOPAHIN *takes out his pocketbook.*) Stop that—stop that. If you were to offer me two hundred thousand I wouldn't take it. I am an independent man, and everything that all of you, rich and poor alike, prize so highly and sold so dear, hasn't the slightest power over me—it's like so much fluff fluttering in the air. I can get on without you. I can pass by you. I am strong and proud. Humanity is advancing toward the highest truth, the highest happiness which is possible on earth, and I am in the front ranks.

LOPAHIN: Will you get there?

TROFIMOV: I shall get there. (*A pause.*) I shall get there, or I shall show others the way to get there.

(*In the distance is heard the strike of an ax on a tree.*)

LOPAHIN: Good-by, my dear fellow; it's time to be off. We turn up our noses at one another, but life is passing all the while. When I am working hard without resting, then my mind is more at ease, and it seems to me as though I too know what I exist for; but how many people are in Russia, my dear boy, who exist, one doesn't know what for. Well, it doesn't matter. That's not what keeps things spinning. They tell me Leonid Andreyevitch has taken a situation. He is going to be a clerk at the bank—6,000 rubles a year. Only, of course, he won't stick to it—he's too lazy.

ANYA (*in the doorway*): Mamma begs you not to let them chop down the orchard until she's gone.

TROFIMOV: Yes, really, you might have the tact. (*Walks out across the front of the stage.*)

LOPAHIN: I'll see to it! I'll see to it! Stupid fellows! (*Goes out after him.*)

ANYA: Has Firs been taken to the hospital?

YASHA: I told them this morning. No doubt they have taken him.

ANYA (*to* EPIHODOV, *who passes across the drawing room*): Semyon Pantaleyevitch, inquire, please, if Firs has been taken to the hospital.

YASHA (*in a tone of offense*): I told Yegor this morning—why ask a dozen times?

EPIHODOV: Firs is advanced in years. It's my conclusive opinion no treatment would do him good; it's time he was gathered to his fathers. And I can only envy him. (*Puts a trunk down on a carboard hat-box and crushes it.*) There, now, of course—I knew it would be so.

YASHA (*jeeringly*): Two and twenty misfortunes!

VARYA (*through the door*): Has Firs been taken to the hospital?

ANYA: Yes.

VARYA: Why wasn't the note for the doctor taken too?

ANYA: Oh, then, we must send it after them. (*Goes out.*)

VARYA (*from the adjoining room*): Where's Yasha? Tell him his mother's come to say good-by to him.

YASHA (*waves his hand*): They put me out of all patience!

(DUNYASHA *has all this time been busy about the luggage. Now, when* YASHA *is left alone, she goes up to him.*)

DUNYASHA: You might just give me one look, Yasha. You're going away. You're leaving me. (*Weeps and throws herself on his neck.*)

YASHA: What are you crying for? (*Drinks the champagne.*) In six days I shall be in Paris again. Tomorrow we shall get into the express train and roll away in a flash. I can scarcely believe it! *Vive la France!* It doesn't suit me here—it's not the life for me; there's no doing anything. I have seen enough of the ignorance here. I have had enough of it. (*Drinks champagne.*) What are you crying for? Behave yourself properly, and then you won't cry.

DUNYASHA (*powders her face, looking in a pocket-mirror*): Do send me a letter from Paris. You know how I loved you, Yasha—how I loved you! I am a tender creature, Yasha.

YASHA: Here, they are coming!

(*Busies himself about the trunks, humming softly. Enter* LYUBOV ANDREYEVNA, GAEV, *and* CHARLOTTA IVANOVNA.)

GAEV: We ought to be off. There's not much time now. (*Looking at* YASHA.) What a smell of herrings!

LYUBOV: In ten minutes we must get into the carriage. (*Casts a look about the room.*) Farewell, dear house, dear old home of our fathers! Winter will pass and spring will come, and then you will be no more; they will tear you down! How much those walls have seen! (*Kisses her daughter passionately.*) My treasure, how bright you look! Your eyes are sparkling like diamonds! Are you glad? Very glad?

ANYA: Very glad! A new life is beginning, mamma.

GAEV: Yes, really, everything is all right now. Before the cherry orchard was sold, we were all worried and wretched, but afterward, when once the question was settled conclusively, irrevocably, we all felt calm and even cheerful. I am a bank clerk now—I am a financier—cannon off the red. And you, Lyuba, after all, you are looking better; there's no question of that.

LYUBOV: Yes. My nerves are better, that's true. (*Her hat and coat are handed to her.*) I'm sleeping well. Carry out my things, Yasha. It's time. (*To* ANYA.) My darling, we shall soon see each other again. I am going to Paris. I can live there on the money your Yaroslavl auntie sent us to buy the estate with—hurrah for auntie!—but that money won't last long.

ANYA: You'll come back soon, mamma, won't you? I'll be working up for my examination in the high school, and when I have passed that, I shall set to work and be a help to you. We will read all sorts of things together, mamma, won't we? (*Kisses her mother's hands.*) We will read in the autumn evenings. We'll read lots of books, and a new wonderful world will open out before us. (*Dreamily.*) Mamma, come soon.

LYUBOV: I shall come, my precious treasure.

(*Embraces her. Enter* LOPAHIN. CHARLOTTA *softly hums a song.*)

GAEV: Charlotta's happy; she's singing!

CHARLOTTA (*picks up a bundle like a swaddled baby*): By, by, my baby. (*A baby is heard crying:* "Ooah! ooah!") Hush, hush, my pretty boy! ("Ooah! ooah!") Poor little thing! (*Throws the bundle back.*) You must please find me a situation. I can't go on like this.

LOPAHIN: We'll find you one, Charlotta Ivanovna. Don't worry yourself

GAEV: Everyone's leaving us. Varya's going away. We have become of no use all at once.

CHARLOTTA: There's nowhere for me to be in the town. I must go away. (*Hums.*) What care I . . .

(*Enter* PISHTCHIK.)

LOPAHIN: The freak of nature.

PISHTCHIK (*gasping*): Oh . . . Let me get my breath. . . . I'm worn out . . . my most honored . . . Give me some water.

GAEV: Want some money, I suppose? Your humble servant! I'll go out of the way of temptation (*Goes out.*)

PISHTCHIK: It's a long while since I have been to see you . . . dearest lady. (*To* LOPAHIN.) You are here . . . glad to see you . . . a man of immense intellect . . . take . . . here. (*Gives to* LOPAHIN.) 400 rubles. That leaves me owing 840.

LOPAHIN (*shrugging his shoulders in amazement*): It's like a dream. Where did you get it?

PISHTCHIK: Wait a bit . . . I'm hot . . . a most extraordinary occurrence! Some Englishmen came along and found in my land some sort of white clay. (*To* LYUBOV ANDREYEVNA.) And 400 for you . . . most lovely . . . wonderful. (*Gives money.*) The rest later. (*Sips water.*) A young man in the train was telling me just now that a great philosopher advises jumping off a house-top. "Jump!" says he; "the whole gist of the problem lies in that." (*Wonderingly.*) Fancy that, now! Water, please!

LOPAHIN: What Englishmen?

PISHTCHIK: I have made over to them the rights to dig the clay for twenty-four years . . . and now, excuse me . . . I can't stay . . . I must be trotting on. I'm going to Znoikovo . . . to Kardamanovo . . . I'm in debt all round. (*Sips.*) . . . To your very good health! . . . I'll come in on Thursday.

LYUBOV: We are just off to the town, and tomorrow I start for abroad.

PISHTCHIK: What! (*In agitation.*) Why to the town? Oh, I see the furniture . . . the boxes. No matter . . . (*Through his tears.*) . . . no matter . . . men of enormous intellect . . . these Englishmen. . . . Never mind . . . be happy. God will succor you . . . no matter . . . everything in this world must have an end. (*Kisses* LYUBOV ANDREYEVNA'S *hand.*) If the rumor reaches you that my end has come, think of this . . . old horse, and say: "There once was such a man in the world . . . Semyonov-Pishtchik . . . the Kingdom of Heaven be his!" . . . most extraordinary weather . . . yes. (*Goes out in violent agitation, but at once returns and says in the doorway.*) Dashenka wishes to be remembered to you. (*Goes out.*)

LYUBOV: Now we can start. I leave with two cares in my heart. The first is leaving Firs ill. (*Looking at her watch.*) We have still five minutes.

ANYA: Mamma, Firs has been taken to the hospital, Yasha sent him off this morning.

LYUBOV: My other anviety is Varya. She is used to getting up early and working; and now, without work, she's like a fish out of water. She is thin and pale, and she's crying, poor dear! (*A pause.*) You are well aware, Yermolay Alexeyevitch, I dreamed of marrying her to you, and everything seemed to show that you would get married. (*Whispers to* ANYA *and motions to* CHARLOTTA *and both go out.*) She loves you—she suits you. And I don't know—I don't know why it is you seem, as it were, to avoid each other. I can't understand it!

LOPAHIN: I don't understand it myself, I confess. It's queer somehow, altogether. If there's still time, I'm ready now at once. Let's settle it straight off, and go ahead; but without you, I feel I shan't make her an offer.

LYUBOV: That's excellent. Why, a single moment's all that's necessary. I'll call her at once.

LOPAHIN: And there's champagne all ready too. (*Looking into the glasses.*) Empty! Someone's emptied them already. (YASHA *coughs.*) I call that greedy.

LYUBOV (*eagerly*): Capital! We will go out. Yasha, *allez!* I'll call her in. (*At the door.*) Varya, leave all that; come here. Come along! (*Goes out with* YASHA.)

LOPAHIN (*looking at his watch*): Yes.

(*A pause. Behind the door, smothered laughter and whispering, and, at last, enter* VARYA.)

VARYA (*looking a long while over the things*): It is strange, I can't find it anywhere.

LOPAHIN: What are you looking for?

VARYA: I packed it myself, and I can't remember.

(*A pause.*)

LOPAHIN: Where are you going now, Varvara Mihailova?

VARYA: I? To the Ragulins. I have arranged to go to them to look after the house—as a housekeeper.

LOPAHIN: That's in Yashnovo? It'll be seventy miles away. (*A pause.*) So this is the end of life in this house!

VARYA (*looking among the things*): Where is it? Perhaps I put it in the trunk. Yes, life in this house is over—there will be no more of it.

LOPAHIN: And I'm just off to Harkov—by this next train. I've a lot of business there. I'm leaving Epihodov here, and I've taken him on.

VARYA: Really!

LOPAHIN: This time last year we had snow already, if you remember; but now it's so fine and sunny. Though it's cold, to be sure—three degrees of frost.

VARYA: I haven't looked. (*A pause.*) And besides, our thermometer's broken.

(*A pause. Voice at the door from the yard:* "Yermolay Alexeyevitch!")

LOPAHIN (*as though he had long been expecting this summons*): This minute!

(LOPAHIN *goes out quickly.* VARYA *sitting on the floor and laying her head on a bag full of clothes, sobs quietly. The door opens,* LYUBOV ANDREYEVNA *comes in cautiously.*)

LYUBOV: Well? (*A pause.*) We must be going.

VARYA (*has wiped her eyes and is no longer crying*): Yes, mamma, it's time to start. I shall have time to get to the Ragulins today, if only you're not late for the train.

LYUBOV (*in the doorway*): Anya, put your things on.

(*Enter* ANYA, *then* GAEV *and* CHARLOTTA IVANOVNA. GAEV *has on a warm coat with a hood. Servants and cabmen come in.* EPIHODOV *bustles about the luggage.*)

LYUBOV: Now we can start on our travels.

ANYA (*joyfully*): On our travels!

GAEV: My friends—my dear, my precious friends! Leaving this house forever, can I be silent? Can I refrain from giving utterance at leave-taking to those emotions which now flood all my being?

ANYA (*supplicatingly*): Uncle!

VARYA: Uncle, you mustn't!

GAEV (*dejectedly*): Cannon and into the pocket . . . I'll be quiet . . .

(*Enter* TROFIMOV *and afterward* LOPAHIN.)

TROFIMOV: Well, ladies and gentlemen, we must start.

LOPAHIN: Epihodov, my coat!

LYUBOV: I'll stay just one minute. It seems as though I have never seen before what the walls, what the ceilings in this house were like, and now I look at them with greediness, with such tender love.

GAEV: I remember when I was six years old sitting in that window on, Trinity Day watching my father going to church.

LYUBOV: Have all the things been taken?

LOPAHIN: I think all. (*Putting on overcoat, to* EPIHODOV.) You, Epihodov, mind you see everything is right.

EPIHODOV (*in a husky voice*): Don't you trouble, Yermolay Alexeyevitch.

LOPAHIN: Why, what's wrong with your voice?

EPIHODOV: I've just had a drink of water, and I choked over something.

YASHA (*contemptuously*): The ignorance!

LYUBOV: We are going—and not a soul will be left here.

LOPAHIN: Not till the spring.

VARYA (*pulls a parasol out of a bundle, as though about to hit someone with it.* LOPAHIN *makes a gesture as though alarmed*): What is it? I didn't mean anything.

TROFIMOV: Ladies and gentlemen, let us get into the carriage. It's time. The train will be in directly.

VARYA: Petya, here they are, your goloshes, by that box. (*With tears.*) And what dirty old things they are!

TROFIMOV (*putting on his goloshes*): Let us go, friends!

GAEV (*greatly agitated, afraid of weeping*): The train—the station! Double balk, ah!

LYUBOV: Let us go!

LOPAHIN: Are we all here? (*Locks the side door on left.*) The things are all here. We must lock up. Let us go!

ANYA: Good-by, home! Good-by to the old life!

TROFIMOV: Welcome to the new life!

(TROFIMOV *goes out with* ANYA. VARYA *looks round the room and goes out slowly.* YASHA *and* CHARLOTTA IVANOVNA, *with her dog, go out.*)

LOPAHIN: Till the spring, then! Come, friends, till we meet! (*Goes out.*) (LYUBOV ANDREYEVNA *and* GAEV *remain alone. As though they had been waiting for this, they throw themselves on each other's necks, and break into subdued smothered sobbing, afraid of being overheard.*)

GAEV (*in despair*): Sister, my sister!

LYUBOV: Oh, my orchard!—my sweet, beautiful orchard! My life, my youth, my happiness, good-by! good-by!

VOICE OF ANYA (*calling gaily*): Mamma!

VOICE OF TROFIMOV (*gaily, excitedly*): Aa—oo!

LYUBOV: One last look at the walls, at the windows. My dear mother loved to walk about this room.
GAEV: Sister, sister!
VOICE OF ANYA: Mamma!
VOICE OF TROFIMOV: Aa—oo!
LYUBOV: We are coming.

(They go out. The stage is empty. There is the sound of the doors being locked up, then of the carriages driving away. There is silence. In the stillness there is the dull stroke of an ax in a tree, clanging with a mournful lonely sound. Footsteps are heard. FIRS *appears in the doorway on the right. H is dressed as always—in a pea-jacket and white waistcoat, with slippers on his feet. He is ill.)*

FIRS *(goes up to the doors, and tries the handles)*: Locked! They have gone . . . *(Sits down on sofa.)* They have forgotten me. . . . Never mind . . . I'll sit here a bit. . . . I'll be bound Leonid Andreyevitch' hasn't put his fur coat on and has gone off in his thin overcoat. *(Sighs anxiously.)* I didn't see after him. . . . These young people . . . *(Mutters something that can't be distinguished.)* Life has slipped by as though I hadn't lived. *(Lies down.)* I'll lie down a bit. . . . There's no strength in you, nothing left you—all gone! Ech! I'm good for nothing.

(Lies motionless. A sound is heard that seems to come from the sky, like a breaking harp-string, dying away mournfully. All is still again, and there is heard nothing but the strokes of the ax far away in the orchard.)

Curtain

Four
The Play's the Thing: Spectacle, Dance, and Ritual

Coleridge remarked that the audience at a play engaged in a willing suspension of disbelief in order to enjoy the theatrical spectacle. This does not mean that the audience becomes uncritical or childlike, but that it accepts the artificiality of the dramatic event so that the reality represented in the play can be better understood. The plays in this section deal with drama itself, with the complicated process of representing human experience in forms created by the human mind.

The Second Shepherd's Play is both a brilliantly funny and touching play and a remarkable document in the history of drama. The classical theater died with Rome and the emerging Church was a strong force in closing the theaters because the spectacles were considered lewd and sinful. Ironically, it was from the Church as an established and powerful social institution that the drama was born again. The two histories of the drama, in the classical world and in the countries of the western world, are indications of how much a part of the human mind is the impulse to play, to act, to represent, to watch the embodiment of those concerns most central to it.

The drama of the medieval world is an authentic communal art form. It grew from the religious rituals common to a country or community. (The mass itself is, of course, a dramatic ritual involving theme, dialogue, actor, and audience.) Beginning with the translation of a part of the Easter Mass to a dialogue concerning the risen Christ, the drama developed rapidly to include representations of events from Scripture and tradition. The drama moved from the church to the marketplace and soon became the focus for staged representations in which sacred mysteries and beliefs were enacted by the community for the edification of the community. This native drama, based in religious ritual and free to develop its own dramatic logic, merged in the Renaissance with the rediscovered and reinterpreted forms of classical drama to produce the masterpieces of Shakespeare and Molière.

The Second Shepherd's Play is an example of the strength of the drama of the medieval world. The play can and should be read as simply an effective theatrical piece. Yet it is also possible to understand from the text something of the evolution to secular concerns from a beginning in ritual, which marked the development of medieval and renaissance theatre. (It is interesting to note that the same kind of evolution apparently characterized drama in its first historical incarnation among the Greeks.) The core of *The Second Shepherd's Play* is the end. It is, after all, a Christmas play and the central event is the nativity and the visitation of the shepherds to the infant. But around that predetermined ritual scene, the anonymous author of the sequence of plays, of which this is the second on the theme, has fashioned a human comedy involving a trooping of the shepherds to another crib. The transformation of a sacred mystery into a secular metaphor in which real actions and motives of realistic characters are represented is a clear example of the tropism in the human mind for dramatic confirmation of its beliefs and expectations.

Drama, of course, continues to evolve. Not only do new forms of drama and new techniques of staging come into being, but in this century drama has been translated into new media: films and television. As it adapts itself to the new media, drama changes. But the principle remains; the play is an attempt to represent to the imagination some aspect of real experience in an absolutely artificial form.

The paradox that the "artificial" is not the opposite of the "real" is the core of drama and the central subject of the plays of Luigi Pirandello. Artificial contrasts with natural, but it is not unreal. Synthetic fabrics are real, but they do not appear in nature. Even cotton woven into cloth is an "artifact" and it is real. There is a sense, then, in which the artificial is real, and Pirandello exploits that sense to full dramatic effect. He is sometimes considered a difficult or puzzling playwright, but to do so is to ignore the clues to his plays embodied in everyday speech. "To play a role," "to preserve his image," and "to save face" are expressions of dramatic motives in ordinary experience. Pirandello simply reverses the emphasis by having ordinary events acted out in highly dramatic and theatrical settings. The point is not to perplex or baffle the audience, but to remind it that the real, the artificial, the ordinary, and the dramatic do not exist in isolation or opposition, but are, in fact, the characteristics of the theater and of human experience. The theater is, of course, a place in which to act out aspects of human experience.

All of these plays insist on their artificiality and their theatricality.

They demand that the audience suspend its disbelief. That suspension does not lead, however, to a brief escape from reality. It leads to a better understanding of how much a part of real experience is the impulse to act, the need to play, the desire to pretend.

Roger S. Loomis and Henry W. Wells

The Second Shepherds' Play
wakefield mystery cycle

Dramatis Personae

FIRST SHEPHERD (Coll)
SECOND SHEPHERD (Gib)
THIRD SHEPHERD (Daw), a youth
MAK
JILL
ANGEL
MARY

SCENE I

(Scene a moor. Enter FIRST SHEPHERD, stamping his feet and blowing on his nails.)

FIRST SHEPHERD: Lord, but it's cold and wretchedly I'm wrapped;
My wits are frozen, so long it is I've napped;
My legs are cramped, and every finger chapped.
All goes awry; in misery I'm trapped.
By storms and gales distressed,
Now in the east, now west,
Woe's him who gets no rest!
We simple shepherds walking on the moor,
We're like, in faith, to be put out of door,
And it's no wonder if we are so poor. 10
Our fields they lie as fallow as a floor;
We're driven till we're bowed;
We're taxed until we're cowed
By gentry, rich and proud.
They take our rest; them may our Lady blast!
For their own lords they make our plows stick fast.
Some say it's for the best, but at the last
We know that's false. We tenants are downcast,
And always we're kept under.
If we don't thrive, no wonder 20

When they so rob and plunder.
A man with broidered sleeve or brooch, these days,
Can ruin anyone who him gainsays.
There's not a soul believes one word he says,
Or dares rebuke him for his bumptious ways.
He makes his pride and boast,
He gets his very post
From those who have the most.
There comes a fellow, proud as a peacock, now, 30
He'd carry off my wagon and my plow.
Before he'd leave, I must seem glad and bow.
A wretched life we lead, you must allow.
Whatever he has willed
Must be at once fulfilled,
Or surely I'd be killed.
It does me good, when I walk round alone,
About this world to grumble and to groan.
Now to my sheep I'll slowly walk, and moan,
And rest awhile on some old balk or stone.
Some other men I'll see; 40
Before it's noon I'll be
In true men's company.

(*Enter* SECOND SHEPHERD, *not noticing* FIRST SHEPHERD.)

SECOND SHEPHERD: Good Lord, good Lord, what does this misery mean?
What ails the world? The like has seldom been.
The weather's spiteful cold and bitter keen;
My eyes they weep, such hideous frosts they've seen.
Now in the snow and sleet
My shoes freeze to my feet;
No easy life I meet.
So far as I can see, where'er I go, 50
The griefs of married men increase and grow.
We're always out of luck; I tell you so.
Capul, our hen, goes cackling to and fro,
But if she starts to croak,
Our cock suffers a stroke;
For him it is no joke.
These wedded men have never once their will;
When they're hard pressed, they sigh and just keep still,
Groan to themselves and take the bitter pill.
God knows they've got a nasty part to fill! 60
And as for me I've found—
I know the lesson's sound—
Woe to the man who's bound!

Late in my life it still amazes me,
And my heart stops such miracles to see;
But yet when destiny drives, such things can be:
Some men have two wives, some have even three!
But if his lot is sore
Who has one wife in store,
It's hell for him with more!
Young men who'd woo, before you're fairly caught,
Beware of wedding! Give the matter thought.
To moan, "Had I but known!" will help you nought.
Much misery has wedding often brought,
And many a stormy shower.
You catch in one short hour
A lifelong taste of sour.
I've one for mate, if ever I read the Epistle,
Who's rough as is a briar and sharp as thistle.
Her looks are sour; her eyebrows, like hog's bristle.
She'd sing "Our Father" if once she wet her whistle.
And like a whale she's fat,
Full of gall as a vat.
I don't know where I'm at.

FIRST SHEPHERD: Gib, look over the hedge! Are you deaf or no?
SECOND SHEPHERD: The devil take you! Was ever man so slow?
  Have you seen Daw?
FIRST SHEPHERD: Just now I heard him blow
  His horn. I see him on the lea below.
  Be quiet!
SECOND SHEPHERD: Tell me why.
FIRST SHEPHERD: I think he's coming by.
SECOND SHEPHERD: He'll trick us with some lie.

(FIRST *and* SECOND SHEPHERDS *hide. Enter* THIRD SHEPHERD.)

THIRD SHEPHERD: May Christ's cross help me, and St. Nicholas!
  I've need of it; life's harder than it was.
  Let men beware and let the false world pass.
  It slips and slides, more brittle far than glass.
  Never did it change so,
  For now it's weal, now woe.
  It's all a passing show.
  Since Noah's flood, such floods were never seen,
  Such dreadful winds and rains, and storms so keen.
  Folk stammer or stand dumb with fear, I ween.
  God turn it all to good! That's what I mean.
  Just think how these floods drown
  Us out in field and town;
  No wonder that we're down.

We that walk at night, our herds to keep,
We see queer sights when others are asleep.
(He spies the other shepherds.)
My heart jumps. There I see two fellows peep,
Tall rascals both. I'll turn back to my sheep. 110
It was a bad mistake
This lonely path to take;
My toes I'll stub and break.
(FIRST *and* SECOND SHEPHERDS *come forward.*)
May God save you, and you, O master sweet!
I want a drink and then a bite to eat.
FIRST SHEPHERD: Christ's curse, my boy, but you're a lazy cheat!
SECOND SHEPHERD: Does the boy rave? Let him wait for his meat!
Bad luck now on your pate!
The wretch, though he comes late,
Would eat, so starved his state. 120
THIRD SHEPHERD: Servants like me, who always sweat and swink,
We eat our bread too dry, that's what I think.
We're wet and weary while our masters blink.
It's late before we get to eat or drink.
Grand dame and noble sire
Delay and dock our hire,
Though we have run through mire.
But hear a truth, my master, for God's sake!
A fuss about my appetite you make!
But never supper gave me stomach-ache. 130
Henceforth I'll work as little as I take;
Or I can run away.
What one buys cheap, they say,
Won't in the long run pay.
FIRST SHEPHERD: A fool you'd be if you yourself should bring
To serve a man who'd not spend anything.
SECOND SHEPHERD: Peace, boy! I want no more rude chattering.
Or I will make you smart, by Heaven's King!
Our sheep are they left lorn?
THIRD SHEPHERD: This very day at morn 140
I left them in the corn.
They have good pasture, so they can't go wrong.
FIRST SHEPHERD: That's right. Oh, by the Rood, these nights are long!
Before we go, I wish we'd have a song.
SECOND SHEPHERD: I thought myself 'twould cheer us all along.
THIRD SHEPHERD: I'm set.
FIRST SHEPHERD: Tenor I'll try.
SECOND SHEPHERD: And I the treble high.
THIRD SHEPHERD: Then the middle am I. 150

(Then MAK *enters with a cloak drawn over his tunic.)*

MAK: Lord, of seven names, who made the moon that sails
And more stars than I know, Thy good will fails.
My brain is in a whirl; it's that which ails.
I wish I were in heaven where no child wails.
FIRST SHEPHERD: Who is it pipes so poor?
MAK: God knows what I endure,
A-walking on the moor!
SECOND SHEPHERD (*stepping forward*): Where do you come from,
Mak? What news d'you bring?
THIRD SHEPHERD: Is he come? Keep close watch on everything!

(He snatches the cloak from him.)

MAK (*with a southern accent*): I tell you I'm a yeoman of the King. 160
Make way for me! Lord's messages I bring.
Fie on you! Get ye hence!
This is no mere pretense.
I must have reverence!
FIRST SHEPHERD: Why put on airs, Mak? It's no good to try.
SECOND SHEPHERD: Or play the actor, for I know you lie.
THIRD SHEPHERD: The scamp talks well, the Devil hang him high!
MAK: I'll make complaint; I'll make you sizzle and fry!
I'll tell on you, in sooth.
FIRST SHEPHERD: O Mak, ere you speak truth, 170
Take out your Southron tooth!
SECOND SHEPHERD: The Devil's in your eye. You need a whack!
(*Strikes* MAK.)
THIRD SHEPHERD: So you don't know me? I'll teach you better, Mak!
MAK (*changing his tune*): God keep all three! What I said I take back.
You're all good fellows.
FIRST SHEPHERD: Now you've changed your tack.
SECOND SHEPHERD: Why out so late, pray tell?
Everyone knows right well
You love roast-mutton smell. 180
MAK: I'm true as steel, as anyone will say,
But I've a sickness takes my health away.
My belly's in a parlous state today.
THIRD SHEPHERD: "The Devil seldom lies dead by the way."
MAK: As still as stone I'll lie,
If this whole month have I
Eat even a needle's eye.
FIRST SHEPHERD: How is your wife? how is she? tell us true.
MAK: She's sprawling by the fire; that's nothing new.
The house is full of brats. She drinks ale, too. 190
Come good or ill, that she will always do.
She eats fast as she can,
And each year gives a man
A babe or two to scan.

Though I had much more money in my purse,
She'd eat and drink us to the Devil, sirs.
Just look at her near by, the ugly curse!
Will no one rid me of her?
I'd give all in my coffer
Mass for her soul to offer.   200
SECOND SHEPHERD: I swear there's no one so tired in this shire.
I must get sleep though I take less for hire.
THIRD SHEPHERD: I'm cold and nearly naked; I'd like a fire.
FIRST SHEPHERD: And I'm worn out with running in the mire.
Keep watch.

(Lies down.)

SECOND SHEPHERD: Not so, for I
Must sleep. I'll put me by.
(Lies down.)
THIRD SHEPHERD: Equal with you I'll lie.
(Lies down.)
Here, Mak, come here! Between us you must be.
MAK: You're sure you don't want to talk privately?

(Lies down, crosses himself and prays.)

And now from head to toe   210
Manus tuas commendo,
Pontio Pilato.
MAK, *while the* SHEPHERDS *sleep, rises and says:*
Now is the time for one who's short of gold
To enter stealthily into a fold
And nimbly work and yet be not too bold,
For he might rue the bargain if 'twere told.
He must be shrewd and wise
Who likes his victuals nice,
Yet hasn't got the price.
(Pretends to be a magician.)
A circle round the moon I here fulfill.   220
Until it's noon or I have done my will,
You must each one lie there and be stone still.
To make it sure some good strong words I'll spill.
Over you my hands I lift;
Your eyes go out and drift
Till I make better shift.
Lord, but they're sleeping sound! All men can hear!
I never was a shepherd, but now I'll learn their gear,
And though the flock be scared, I'll creep right near.
This fat sheep with its fleece improves my cheer. 230
And now goodbye to sorrow!
(Seizes sheep.)

Though I pay not tomorrow,
I'll in the meantime borrow.

(Exit MAK.)

SCENE II

(Interior of MAK's cottage. JILL sits spinning.)

MAK *(outside)*: Jill, are you in? Hello, get us some light!
JILL: Who makes this racket at this time of night?
    I'm busy spinning; I'll not stir a mite
    To get a day's pay. Curses on you light!
    It's thus a housewife fares.
    She's always rushed with cares,
    And all for nothing bears!
MAK *(outside)*: Open the latch, good wife! See what I bring!
JILL: I'll let you pull.

(Opens door. MAK *enters.)*

JILL: Come in, my own sweet thing!
MAK: Not much you care how long I stand and sing!
JILL: By your bare neck, for this you're like to swing!
MAK: I'm good for something yet;
    For at a pinch I get
    More than the fools who sweat.
    I had a lucky lot and God's own grace.
JILL: To hang for it would be a foul disgrace!
MAK: I've dodged before, my Jill, as hard a case.
JILL: Folk say that just so long a pot or vase
    To water it can come,
    Then broken it's brought home.
MAK: On that old saw me dumb!
    I wish that he were skinned; I want to eat.
    For twelve months I've not hankered so for meat.
JILL: Suppose they come here first and hear him bleat!
MAK: They'd catch me then. That puts me in a heat.
    Go bolt the door at back!
    I'd get from that whole pack
    The devil of a whack!
JILL: A good trick I have spied since you have none:
    We'll hide him in the crib till they have done.
    I'll lie and groan and say that he's my son.
    Let me alone to do what I've begun.
MAK: And I will say, tonight
    Of this boy you are light.

JILL: It's luck I was born bright.
   For cleverness this trick can't be surpassed.
   A woman's wit helps always at the last.
   Before they get suspicious, hurry fast.
MAK: If I don't get there soon, they'll blow a blast!

(*Exit* MAK.)

SCENE III

(The moor. SHEPHERDS *sleeping. Enter* MAK.)

MAK: These men are still asleep.
   Their company I'll keep
   As if I'd stolen no sheep.

(*Lies down between them.*)
(SHEPHERDS *wake one by one, and cross themselves.*)

FIRST SHEPHERD: *Resurrex a mortruis!* Here, take my hand!
   Judas carnas Dominus! I can't well stand.
   My foot's asleep and I'm as dry as sand.
   I dreamt we lay down near the English land!
SECOND SHEPHERD: I slept so well, I feel
   As fresh as any eel,
   And light upon my heel!   10
THIRD SHEPHERD: Lord bless us all! My body's all a-quake!
   My heart jumps from my skin, and that's no fake.
   Who's making all this din and my head ache?
   I'll teach him something! hear, you fellows, wake!
   Where's Mak?
FIRST SHEPHERD: I vow he's near.
   He went nowhere, that's clear.
THIRD SHEPHERD: I dreamt he was dressed up in a wolf's skin.
FIRST SHEPHERD: That's what too many rogues are wrapped up in!
THIRD SHEPHERD: While we were snoozing, seemed he did begin
   To catch a sheep, without the slightest din.   20
SECOND SHEPHERD: Your dream has made you brood
   On phantoms, by the Rood.
   May God turn all to good!

(*Shakes* MAK.)

   Rise, Mak, for shame! You're sleeping far too long.
MAK: Now may Christ's holy name keep us from wrong!
   What's this? St. James! I can hardly move along.
   I'm just the same, and yet my neck's all wrong.
   (SHEPHERDS *help him to his feet.*)
   Thank you! It's still uneven
   For I've been plagued since even

With nightmares, by St. Stephen! 30
I thought that Jill she groaned in travail bad;
At the first cockcrow she had borne a lad
To increase our flock. Guess whether I am glad!
That's more wool on my distaff than I had!
Woe's him who has no bread
For young ones to be fed.
The Devil crack each head!
I must go home to Jill; she's in my thought.
Just look into my sleeve that I steal nought.
I wouldn't grieve you or take from you aught. 40
THIRD SHEPHERD: Go on, bad luck to you!

(Exit MAK.*)*

    I think we ought
To count our sheep this morn.
FIRST SHEPHERD: I'll see if any's gone.
THIRD SHEPHERD: We'll meet at the Crooked Thorn.

(Exeunt SHEPHERDS.*)*

SCENE IV

(Interior of MAK's *cottage.* JILL *at work.)*
MAK *(outside):* Undo this door! How long shall I stand here?
JILL: Go walk in the waning moon! Who's shouting there?
MAK *(outside):* It's me, your husband, Mak. Hey, Jill, what cheer?
JILL: Now we shall see the Devil hanged, that's clear.
    I seem to hear a sound
    As if a rope were round
    His throat, and tightly bound.
MAK *(outside):* Just hear the fuss she makes for an excuse;
She doesn't do a stroke but to amuse.
JILL: Who sits up late? Who comes and goes? Who brews? 10
Who bakes? Whose hand knits stockings, tell me, whose?
(Opens the door. MAK *enters.)*
    It's a pity to behold,
    Whether in hot or cold,
    A womanless household!
But tell me how you left the herdsmen, Mak.
MAK: The last word that they said when I turned back
Was that they'd count the sheep, the cursed pack!
They'll not be pleased to find a sheep they lack!
    And so, however it goes,
    They surely will suppose 20
    From me the trouble rose.
    You'll keep your promise?

JILL:　　　　Why, of course, I will.
　　I'll put him in the cradle, and with skill
　　I'll swaddle him. Trust in a pinch to Jill!
　　　(She wraps sheep and puts it in cradle. Goes to bed.)
　　Come tuck me up. I'll lie here very still.
　　It may be a narrow squeak.
MAK:　Yes, if too close they peek,
　　Or if the sheep should speak!
JILL: Hark, when they call, for they'll be here anon.
　　Let everything be ready. Sing alone　　　　　　30
　　A lullaby, for I must lie and groan
　　And cry out by the wall on Mary and John.
　　You sing the lullaby,
　　And never doubt that I
　　Will pull wool over their eye.

SCENE V

(The moor. Enter three SHEPHERDS.)

THIRD SHEPHERD: Good morrow, Coll.
　　What's wrong? Why not asleep?
FIRST SHEPHERD: Alas that I was born! For this we'll keep
　　A villain's name. We've lost a good fat sheep!
SECOND SHEPHERD: God save us! Who on us such wrong would heap?
FIRST SHEPHERD: Some rascal. With my dogs
　　I've searched through Horbury Shrogs,
　　Found one ewe of fifteen hogs.[1]
THIRD SHEPHERD: Trust me, by Thomas, holy saint of Kent,
　　'Twas Mak or Jill who on that theft was bent.
FIRST SHEPHERD: Peace, man, be quiet. I saw when he went.　　10
　　You slander him unjustly and should repent.
SECOND SHEPHERD: Though I may never succeed,
　　I'd say it though I bleed,
　　'Twas he who did the deed.
THIRD SHEPHERD: Then let's go thither at a running trot.
　　I won't eat bread till at the truth I've got.
FIRST SHEPHERD: And I won't drink until I've solved the plot.
SECOND SHEPHERD: Until I find him, I won't rest one jot.
　　I make this vow aright:
　　Till I have him in sight　　　　　　　　　　　　　　20
　　I will not sleep one night
　　In the same spot.
　　　　　　　　　　　　　　　　　　　　(Exeunt.)

---

[1] Young sheep.

SCENE VI

(MAK's cottage. Within MAK sings, JILL groans. SHEPHERDS approach the door.)
THIRD SHEPHERD: D'you hear them sing? Mak thinks that he can croon!
FIRST SHEPHERD: I never heard a voice so out of tune!
SECOND SHEPHERD: Hey, Mak, open your door, and do it soon.
MAK: Who is it shouts as if it were high noon?
THIRD SHEPHERD: Good men, if it were day—
MAK (*opening door*):
   As much as ever you may,
   Speak very soft, I pray.
   Here is a woman sick and ill at ease;
   I'd rather die than she had more misease.
JILL: Go to some other place, I beg you, please,
   Each footfall knocks my nose and makes me sneeze.   10
FIRST SHEPHERD: How are you, Mak, I say?
MAK: And how are you today,
   And what brings you this way?
   You're wet all through; you've run so in the mire.
   If you'll sit down, I'll light you here a fire.
   I've got what's coming to me. I'm no liar;
   My dream's come true; a nurse I've got to hire.
   I've more babes than you knew.
   Surely the saying's true: 20
   "We must drink what we brew."
   Stay eat before you go; I see you sweat.
SECOND SHEPHERD: Nothing will cheer us, neither drink nor meat.
MAK: What ails you, sir?
THIRD SHEPHERD: We've had a loss that's great;
   We found a sheep was stolen, when we met.
MAK: Alas! Had I been there,
   Someone had paid full dear.
FIRST SHEPHERD: Marry, some think you were!
SECOND SHEPHERD: Yes, Mak, just tell us who else could it be?
THIRD SHEPHERD: 'Twas either you or else your wife, say we.   30
MAK: If you suspect us, either Jill or me,
   Come rip our house apart, and then you'll see
   That here within this spot
   No sheep or cow I've got;
   And Jill's not stirred a jot.
   As I am true and leal, to God I pray,
   This is the first meal that I've had today.
FIRST SHEPHERD: Upon my soul, Mak, have a care, I say;
   He's early learned to steal who can't say nay.

(SHEPHERDS *begin to search.*)

JILL: Out, thieves, get out from here! 40
MAK: When her great groans you hear,
   Your hearts should melt for fear.
JILL: Out, thieves; don't touch my child! Get out the door!
MAK: Knew you her pangs, your conscience would be sore.
   You're wrong, I warn you, thus to come before
   A woman in her pain. I say no more.
JILL: O God, who art so mild,
   If you I e'er beguiled,
   Let me eat up this child!
MAK: Peace, woman, for God's passion, speak more low! 50
   You spoil your brains and terrify me so.
SECOND SHEPHERD: I think our sheep is slain. Think you not so?
THIRD SHEPHERD: We search here all in vain. We may well go.
   There's nothing I can find,
   No bone or scrap or rind,
   But empty plates behind.
   Here's no tame cattle, and no wild there is
   That smells like our old ram, I'll swear to this.
JILL: You're right; and of this child God give me bliss!
FIRST SHEPHERD: I think we've failed and that we've done amiss. 60
SECOND SHEPHERD: Dame, is't a boy you have?
   Him may Our Lady save!
MAK: A son a lord might crave.
   He grabs so when he wakes, it's a joy to see
THIRD SHEPHERD: Luck on his buttocks! Happy may they be!
   But who god-fathered him so hurriedly?
MAK *(hesitating)*: Blest be their lips!
FIRST SHEPHERD: A lie it's going to be!
MAK: Gibbon Waller was one,
   And Perkin's mother's son;
   John Horn supplied the fun. 70
SECOND SHEPHERD: Mak, let us all be friends again, I say.
MAK *(haughtily)*: It's little friendship you've shown me today.
   Goodbye, I'm glad to see you go away.
THIRD SHEPHERD: Fair words, no warmth—that's just as plain as day.

   (SHEPHERDS *turn to go out.*)

FIRST SHEPHERD: Gave you the child a thing?
SECOND SHEPHERD: Not even one farthing!
THIRD SHEPHERD: Wait here; fast back I'll fling.
   (THIRD SHEPHERD *returns.* SECOND *and* FIRST SHEPHERDS *follow.*)
THIRD SHEPHERD: To see your baby, Mak, I ask your leave.
MAK: No. Only insults from you I receive.
THIRD SHEPHERD: Well, it won't make that little daystar grieve 80
   If you let me give sixpence, I believe.
   (Approaches cradle.)

MAK: Go way; I say he sleeps.
THIRD SHEPHERD: I think instead he peeps.
MAK: When he wakes up, he weeps.
THIRD SHEPHERD: Just let me kiss him once and lift the clout.
  What in the devil! What a monstrous snout!
FIRST SHEPHERD: He's birth-marked maybe. Let's not wait about!
  The ill-spun cloth in truth comes foully out.
  He looks like our own sheep!
THIRD SHEPHERD: What, Gib! give me a peep.   90
FIRST SHEPHERD: Where Truth can't walk 'twill creep.
SECOND SHEPHERD: That was a clever trick, a shabby fraud!
  The bare-faced swindle should be noised abroad.
THIRD SHEPHERD: Yes, sirs, let's bind her fast and burn the bawd.
  If she should hang, everyone would applaud.
  Tucked in a cradle so,
  I never saw, I vow,
  A boy with horns till now!
MAK: Peace, peace I ask! You'll give the child a scare.
  For I'm his father and that's his mother there.   100
FIRST SHEPHERD: What devil is he named for? Look, Mak's heir!
SECOND SHEPHERD: Let be all that! I say, God give him care!
JILL: A pretty child is he
  To sit on woman's knee,
  And make his father glee!
THIRD SHEPHERD: I know him by his earmark, a good token.
MAK: I tell you, sirs, his nose in truth was broken.
  He was bewitched; so has a wise clerk spoken.
FIRST SHEPHERD: Liar! you deserve to have your noddle broken!
JILL: An elf took him away;   110
  I saw him changed for aye
  At stroke of twelve today.
SECOND SHEPHERD: You two are fit to lie in the same bed!
THIRD SHEPHERD: Since they maintain their theft, let's leave them dead.
MAK: If I do wrong again, cut off my head!
  I'm at your will.
THIRD SHEPHERD: Men, take my plan instead.
  We'll neither curse nor fight,
  But here in canvas tight
  We'll toss him good and right.

(SHEPHERDS *exeunt, carrying* MAK *in a blanket.*)

SCENE VII

(Moor. Enter SHEPHERDS.)

FIRST SHEPHERD: Lord, I'm about to burst, I am so sore!
  Until I rest, in faith I can't do more.

SECOND SHEPHERD: He's heavy as a sheep of seven score.
 And now I'll lay me down to snooze and snore.
THIRD SHEPHERD: Let's lie down on this green.
FIRST SHEPHERD: These thieves are rascals mean!
THIRD SHEPHERD: We'd best forget what's been.

(SHEPHERDS *lie down. An* ANGEL *sings "Gloria in excelsis"; then let him say:*)

ANGEL: Rise, herdsmen, rise, for now the Child is born
 Who frees mankind, for Adam's sin forlorn.
 To thwart the wicked fiend this night He's born. 10
 High God is made your friend. This very morn,
 To Bethlehem go ye;
 The new-born Deity
 In manger laid ye'll see.

(The ANGEL *withdraws.)*

FIRST SHEPHERD: That was as queer a voice as ever I heard;
 Wonder enough to make a man be scared.
SECOND SHEPHERD: To speak of God's own Son of Heaven he dared,
 And all the wood I thought with lightning glared.
THIRD SHEPHERD: He said the Baby lay
 In Bethlehem today. 20
THIRD SHEPHERD: That star points out the way.
 (Points to star.)
 Let's seek Him there!
SECOND SHEPHERD: Did you hear how he cracked it?
 Three breves, one long.
THIRD SHEPHERD: Yes, and he surely smacked it.
 There was no crotchet wrong, and nothing lacked it.
FIRST SHEPHERD: I'd like us three to sing, just as he knacked it.
SECOND SHEPHERD: Let's harken how you croon.
 Can you bark at the moon?
THIRD SHEPHERD: Shut up and hark, you loon!

*(*SHEPHERDS *sing off tune.)*

SECOND SHEPHERD: To Bethlehem he ordered us to go.
 I'm much afraid that we have been too slow. 30
THIRD SHEPHERD: Be merry, fellow, and don't croak like a crow.
 This news means endless joy to men below.
FIRST SHEPHERD: Though we are tired and wet,
  We'll hurry now and get
  Where Mother and Child are set.
 (They start to walk.)
SECOND SHEPHERD: We find by ancient prophets—stop your din!—
 David, Isaiah, others of their kin,
 That God's own Son would someday light within
 A virgin's womb, to cleanse away our sin.

    Isaiah, don't forget,
    Foretold that one day yet
    "Virgo concipiet."
THIRD SHEPHERD: Right merry should we be that now's the day
    The lovely Lord is come who rules for aye.
    I'd be the happiest man if I could say
    That I had knelt before that Child to pray.
    But still the angel said
    The Babe was poorly arrayed
    And in a manger laid!
FIRST SHEPHERD: Prophets and patriarchs of old were torn
    With yearning to behold this Child now born.
    Without that sight they never ceased to mourn.
    But we shall see Him, now this very morn.
    When I see Him, I'll know
    The prophets' words were so.
    No liars were they, no!
    To men as poor as we He will appear.
    We'll find Him first, His messenger said clear.
SECOND SHEPHERD: Then let us hurry, for the place is near.
THIRD SHEPHERD: Ready am I and glad; let's go with cheer.
    Lord, if Thy will it be,
    Allow poor yokels three
    This happy sight to see.

SCENE VIII

(Bethlehem, a stable. The VIRGIN seated, the CHILD on her knee. The SHEPHERDS enter and kneel.)

FIRST SHEPHERD: Hail, pure and sweet one; hail, thou holy Child!
    Maker of all, born of a Maiden mild.
    Thou hast o'ercome the Devil, fierce and wild.
    That wily Trickster now has been beguiled.
    Look, how He laughs, sweet thing!
    As my poor offering
    A cherry bunch I bring.
SECOND SHEPHERD: Hail, Savior King, our ransom Thou hast bought!
    Hail, mighty Babe, Thou madest all of naught.
    Hail, God of mercy, Thou the Fiend hast fought.
    I kneel and bow before Thee. Look, I've brought
    A bird, my tiny one!
    Other faith we have none,
    Our day-star and God's Son.
THIRD SHEPHERD: Hail, pretty darling, Thou art God indeed.
    I pray to Thee, be near when I have need.

> Sweet is Thy look, although my heart does bleed
> To see Thee here, and dressed in such poor weed.
> Hail, Babe, on Thee I call.
> I bring a tennis ball.
> Take it and play withal.   20

MARY: The Lord of Heaven, God omnipotent,
> Who made all things aright, His Son has sent.
> My name He named and blessed me ere He went.
> Him I conceived through grace, as God had meant.
> And now I pray Him so
> To keep you from all woe!
> Tell this where'er you go.

FIRST SHEPHERD: Farewell, Lady, thou fairest to behold,
> With Christ-child on thy knee!

SECOND SHEPHERD: He lies full cold,   30
> But well it is for me that Him you hold.

THIRD SHEPHERD: Already this does seem a thing oft told.

FIRST SHEPHERD: Let's spread the tidings round!

SECOND SHEPHERD: Come; our salvation's found!

THIRD SHEPHERD: To sing it we are bound!

(Exeunt SHEPHERDS *singing.)*
Here ends the Pageant of the SHEPHERDS.

Luigi Pirandello

Henry IV
a tragedy in three acts

English version by Edward Storer

Characters

HENRY IV
THE MARCHIONESS MATILDA SPINA
FRIDA, *her daughter*
CHARLES DI NOLLI, *the young Marquis*
BARON TITO BELCREDI
DOCTOR DIONYSIUS GENONI
HAROLD (FRANCO)
LANDOLPH (LOLO)   *The four private counselors*
ORDULPH (MOMO)   *(The names in brackets are nicknames.)*
BERTHOLD (FINO)
JOHN, *the old waiter*
THE TWO VALETS IN COSTUME

A solitary villa in Italy in our own time.

ACT I

(Salon in the villa, furnished and decorated so as to look exactly like the throne room of HENRY IV in the royal residence at Goslar. Among the antique decorations there are two modern life-size portraits in oil painting. They are placed against the back wall, and mounted in a wooden stand that runs the whole length of the wall. (It is wide and protrudes, so that it is like a large bench.) One of the paintings is on the right; the other on the left of the throne, which is in the middle of the wall and divides the stand.

The Imperial chair and Baldachin.

The two portraits represent a lady and a gentleman, both young, dressed up in carnival costumes: one as "HENRY IV," the other as the "MARCHIONESS MATILDA OF TUSCANY." Exits to right and left.

When the curtain goes up, the TWO VALETS jump down, as if surprised, from the stand on which they have been lying, and go and take their positions, as rigid as statues, on either side below the throne with their halberds in their hands. Soon after, from the second exit, right, enter HAROLD, LANDOLPH, ORDULPH and BERTHOLD, young men employed by the MARQUIS CHARLES DI NOLLI to play the part of "Secret Counsellors" at the court of "HENRY IV." They are, therefore, dressed like German knights of the XIth century. BERTHOLD, nicknamed FINO, is just entering on his duties for the first time. His companions are telling him what he has to do and amusing themselves at his expense. The scene is to be played rapidly and vivaciously.)

LANDOLPH (*to* BERTHOLD *as if explaining*): And this is the throne room.
HAROLD: At Goslar.
ORDULPH: Or at the castle in the Hartz, if you prefer.
HAROLD: Or at Wurms.
LANDOLPH: According as to what's doing, it jumps about with us, now here, now there.
ORDULPH: In Saxony.
HAROLD: In Lombardy.
LANDOLPH: On the Rhine.
ONE OF THE VALETS (*without moving, just opening his lips*): I say . . .
HAROLD (*turning round*): What is it?
FIRST VALET (*like a statue*): Is he coming in or not? (*He alludes to* HENRY IV.)
ORDULPH: No, no, he's asleep. You needn't worry.
SECOND VALET (*releasing his pose, taking a long breath and going to lie down again on the stand*): You might have told us at once.
FIRST VALET (*going over to* HAROLD): Have you got a match, please?
LANDOLPH: What? You can't smoke a pipe here, you know.
FIRST VALET (*while* HAROLD *offers him a light*): No; a cigarette. (*Lights his cigarette and lies down again on the stand.*)
BERTHOLD (*who has been looking on in amazement, walking round in the room, regarding the costumes of the others*): I say . . . this room . . . these costumes . . . Which Henry IV is it? I don't quite get it. Is he Henry IV of France or not? (*At this* LANDOLPH, HAROLD, *and* ORDULPH, *burst out laughing.*)
LANDOLPH (*still laughing; and pointing to* BERTHOLD *as if inviting the others to make fun of him*): Henry of France he says: ha! ha!
ORDULPH: He thought it was the king of France!
HAROLD: Henry IV of Germany, my boy: the Salian dynasty!
ORDULPH: The great and tragic Emperor!
LANDOLPH: He of Canossa. Every day we carry on here the terrible war between Church and State, by Jove.

ORDULPH: The Empire against the Papacy!
HAROLD: Antipopes against the Pope!
LANDOLPH: Kings against anti-kings!
ORDULPH: War on the Saxons!
HAROLD: And all the rebels Princes!
LANDOLPH: Against the Emperor's own sons!
BERTHOLD (*covering his head with his hands to protect himself against this avalanche of information*): I understand! I understand! Naturally, I didn't get the idea at first. I'm right then: these aren't costumes of the XVIth century?
HAROLD: XVIth century be hanged!
ORDULPH: We're somewhere between a thousand and eleven hundred.
LANDOLPH: Work it out for yourself: if we are before Canossa on the 25th of January, 1071...
BERTHOLD (*more confused than ever*): Oh my God! What a mess I've made of it!
ORDULPH: Well, just slightly, if you supposed you were at the French court.
BERTHOLD: All that historical stuff I've swatted up!
LANDOLPH: My dear boy, it's four hundred years earlier.
BERTHOLD (*getting angry*): Good Heavens! You ought to have told me it was Germany and not France. I can't tell you how many books I've read in the last fifteen days.
HAROLD: But I say, surely you knew that poor Tito was Adalbert of Bremen, here?
BERTHOLD: Not a damned bit!
LANDOLPH: Well, don't you see how it is? When Tito died, the Marquis Di Nolli...
BERTHOLD: Oh, it was he, was it? He might have told me.
HAROLD: Perhaps he thought you knew.
LANDOLPH: He didn't want to engage anyone else in substitution. He thought the remaining three of us would do. But *he* began to cry out: "With Adalbert driven away...": because, you see, he didn't imagine poor Tito was dead; but that, as Bishop Adalbert, the rival bishops of Cologne and Mayence had driven him off...
BERTHOLD (*taking his head in his hand*): But I don't know a word of what you're talking about.
ORDULPH: So much the worse for you, my boy!
HAROLD: But the trouble is that not even we know who you are.
BERTHOLD: What? Not even you? You don't know who I'm supposed to be?
ORDULPH: Hum! "Berthold."
BERTHOLD: But which Berthold? And why Berthold?

LANDOLPH (*solemnly imitating* HENRY IV): "They've driven Adalbert away from me. Well then, I want Berthold! I want Berthold!" That's what he said.

HAROLD: We three looked one another in the eyes: who's got to be Berthold?

ORDULPH: And so here you are, "Berthold," my dear fellow!

LANDOLPH: I'm afraid you will make a bit of a mess of it.

BERTHOLD (*indignant, getting ready to go*): Ah, no! Thanks very much, but I'm off! I'm out of this!

HAROLD (*restraining him with the other two, amid laughter*): Steady now! Don't get excited!

LANDOLPH: Cheer up, my dear fellow! We don't any of us know who we are really. He's Harold; he's Ordulph; I'm Landolph! That's the way he calls us. We've got used to it. But who are we? Names of the period! Yours, too, is a name of the period: Berthold! Only one of us, poor Tito, had got a really decent part, as you can read in history: that of the Bishop of Bremen. He was just like a real bishop. Tito did it awfully well, poor chap!

HAROLD: Look at the study he put into it!

LANDOLPH: Why, he even ordered his Majesty about, opposed his views, guided and counselled him. We're "secret counsellors"—in a manner of speaking only; because it is written in history that Henry IV was hated by the upper aristocracy for surrounding himself at court with young men of the bourgeoise.

ORDULPH: Us, that is.

LANDOLPH: Yes, small devoted vassals, a bit dissolute and very gay . . .

BERTHOLD: So I've got to be gay as well?

HAROLD: I should say so! Same as we are!

ORDULPH: And it isn't too easy, you know.

LANDOLPH: It's a pity; because the way we're got up, we could do a fine historical reconstruction. There's any amount of material in the story of Henry IV. But, as a matter of fact, we do nothing. We have the form without the content. We're worse than the real secret counsellors of Henry IV; because certainly no one had given them a part to play—at any rate, they didn't feel they had a part to play. It was their life. They looked after their own interests at the expense of others, sold investitures and—what not! We stop here in this magnificent court—for what?—Just doing nothing. We're like so many puppets hung on the wall, waiting for some one to come and move us or make us talk.

HAROLD: Ah, no, old sport, not quite that! We've got to give the proper answer, you know. There's trouble if he asks you something and you don't chip in with the cue.

LANDOLPH: Yes, that's true.

BERTHOLD: Don't rub it in too hard! How the devil am I to give him the proper answer, if I've swatted up Henry IV of France, and now he turns out to be Henry IV of Germany? *(The other three laugh.)*

HAROLD: You'd better start and prepare yourself at once.

ORDULPH: We'll help you out.

HAROLD: We've got any amount of books on the subject. A brief run through the main points will do to begin with.

ORDULPH: At any rate, you must have got some sort of general idea.

HAROLD: Look here! *(Turns him around and shows him the portrait of the* MARCHIONESS MATILDA *on the wall.)* Who's that?

BERTHOLD *(looking at it)*: That? Well, the thing seems to me somewhat out of place, anyway: two modern paintings in the midst of all this respectable antiquity!

HAROLD: You're right! They weren't there in the beginning. There are two niches there behind the pictures. They were going to put up two statues in the style of the period. Then the places were covered with those canvases there.

LANDOLPH *(interrupting and continuing)*: They would certainly be out of place if they really were paintings!

BERTHOLD: What are they, if they aren't paintings?

LANDOLPH: Go and touch them! Pictures all right . . . but for him! *(Makes a mysterious gesture to the right, alluding to* HENRY IV.*)* . . . who never touches them! . . .

BERTHOLD: No? What are they for him?

LANDOLPH: Well, I'm only supposing, you know; but I imagine I'm about right. They're images such as . . . well—such as a mirror might throw back. Do you understand? That one there represents himself, as he is in this throne room, which is all in the style of the period. What's there to marvel at? If we put you before a mirror, won't you see yourself, alive, but dressed up in ancient costume? Well, it's as if there were two mirrors there, which cast back living images in the midst of a world which, as you well see, when you have lived with us, comes to life too.

BERTHOLD: I say, look here . . . I've no particular desire to go mad here.

HAROLD: Go mad, be hanged! You'll have a fine time!

BERTHOLD: Tell me this: how have you all managed to become so learned?

LANDOLPH: My dear fellow, you can't go back over 800 years of history without picking up a bit of experience.

HAROLD: Come on! Come on! You'll see how quickly you get into it!

ORDULPH: You'll learn wisdom, too, at this school.

BERTHOLD: Well, for Heaven's sake, help me a bit! Give me the main lines, anyway.

HAROLD: Leave it to us. We'll do it all between us.

LANDOLPH: We'll put your wires on you and fix you up like a first-class marionette. Come along! *(They take him by the arm to lead him away.)*

BERTHOLD *(stopping and looking at the portrait on the wall)*: Wait a minute! You haven't told me who that is. The Emperor's wife?

HAROLD: No! The Emperor's wife is Bertha of Susa, the sister of Amadeus II of Savoy.

ORDULPH: And the Emperor, who wants to be young with us, can't stand her, and wants to put her away.

LANDOLPH: That is his most ferocious enemy: Matilda, Marchioness of Tuscany.

BERTHOLD: Ah, I've got it: the one who gave hospitality to the Pope!

LANDOLPH: Exactly: at Canossa!

ORDULPH: Pope Gregory VII!

HAROLD: Our *bête noir!* Come on! come on! *(All four move toward the right to go out, when, from the left, the old servant* JOHN *enters in evening dress.)*

JOHN *(quickly, anxiously)*: Hss! Hss! Franco! Lolo!

HAROLD *(turning round)*: What is it?

BERTHOLD *(marvelling at seeing a man in modern clothes enter the throne room)*: Oh! I say, this is a bit too much, this chap here!

LANDOLPH: A man of the XXth century, here! Oh, go away! *(They run over to him, pretending to menace him and throw him out.)*

ORDULPH *(heroically)*: Messenger of Gregory VII, away!

HAROLD: Away! Away!

JOHN *(annoyed, defending himself)*: Oh, stop it! Stop it, I tell you!

ORDULPH: No, you can't set foot here!

HAROLD: Out with him!

LANDOLPH *(to* BERTHOLD*)*: Magic, you know! He's a demon conjured up by the Wizard of Rome! Out with your swords! *(Makes as if to draw a sword.)*

JOHN *(shouting)*: Stop it, will you? Don't play the fool with me! The Marquis has arrived with some friends . . .

LANDOLPH: Good! Good! Are there ladies too?

ORDULPH: Old or young?

JOHN: There are two gentlemen.

HAROLD: But the ladies, the ladies, who are they?

JOHN: The Marchioness and her daughter.

LANDOLPH *(surprised)*: What do you say?

ORDULPH: The Marchioness?

JOHN: The Marchioness! The Marchioness!

HAROLD: Who are the gentlemen?

JOHN: I don't know.

HAROLD (*to* BERTHOLD): They're coming to bring us a message from the Pope, do you see?
ORDULPH: All messengers of Gregory VII! What fun!
JOHN: Will you let me speak, or not?
HAROLD: Go on, then!
JOHN: One of the two gentlemen is a doctor, I fancy.
LANDOLPH: Oh, I see, one of the usual doctors.
HAROLD: Bravo Berthold, you'll bring us luck!
LANDOLPH: You wait and see how we'll manage this doctor!
BERTHOLD: It looks as if I were going to get into a nice mess right away.
JOHN: If the gentlemen would allow me to speak . . . they want to come here into the throne room.
LANDOLPH (*surprised*): What? She? The Marchioness here?
HAROLD: Then this is something quite different! No play-acting this time!
LANDOLPH: We'll have a real tragedy: that's what!
BERTHOLD (*curious*): Why? Why?
ORDULPH (*pointing to the portrait*): She is that person there, don't you understand?
LANDOLPH: The daughter is the fiancée of the Marquis. But what have they come for, I should like to know?
ORDULPH: If he sees her, there'll be trouble.
LANDOLPH: Perhaps he won't recognize her any more.
JOHN: You must keep him there, if he should wake up . . .
ORDULPH: Easier said than done, by Jove!
HAROLD: You know what he's like!
JOHN: —even by force, if necessary! Those are my orders. Go on! Go on!
HAROLD: Yes, because who knows if he hasn't already wakened up?
ORDULPH: Come on then!
LANDOLPH (*going towards* JOHN *with the others*). You'll tell us later what it all means.
JOHN (*shouting after them*): Close the door there, and hide the key! That other door too. (*Pointing to the other door on right.*)
JOHN (*to the* TWO VALETS): Be off, you two! There! (*Pointing to exit right.*) Close the door after you, and hide the key!

(*The* TWO VALETS *go out by the first door on right.* JOHN *moves over to the left to show in:* DONNA MATILDA SPINA, *the young* MARCHIONESS FRIDA, DR. DIONYSIUS GENONI, *the* BARON TITO BELCREDI *and the young* MARQUIS CHARLES DI NOLLI, *who, as master of the house, enters last.* DONNA MATILDA SPINA *is about 45, still handsome, although there are too patent signs of her attempts to remedy the ravages of time with make-up. Her head is thus rather like a Walkyrie. This facial make-up contrasts with her beautiful sad mouth. A widow for many years, she now has as her friends the* BARON TITO BELCREDI, *whom neither she nor anyone else takes seriously—at least so it would appear.*

What TITO BELCREDI *really is for her at bottom, he alone knows; and he is, therefore, entitled to laugh, if his friend feels the need of pretending not to know. He can always laugh at the jests which the beautiful* MARCHIONESS *makes with the others at his expense. He is slim, prematurely gray, and younger than she is. His head is birdlike in shape. He would be a very vivacious person, if his ductile agility (which among other things makes him a redoubtable swordsman) were not enclosed in a sheath of Arab-like laziness, which is revealed in his strange, nasal drawn-out voice.*

FRIDA, *the daughter of the* MARCHIONESS *is 19. She is sad; because her imperious and too beautiful mother puts her in the shade, and provokes facile gossip against her daughter as well as against herself. Fortunately for her, she is engaged to the* MARQUIS CHARLES DI NOLLI.

CHARLES DI NOLLI *is a stiff young man, very indulgent towards others, but sure of himself for what he amounts to in the world. He is worried about all the responsibilities which he believes weigh on him. He is dressed in deep mourning for the recent death of his mother.*

DR. DIONYSIUS GENONI *has a bold rubicund Satyr-like face, prominent eyes, a pointed beard (which is silvery and shiny) and elegant manners. He is nearly bald. All enter in a state of perturbation, almost as if afraid, and all (except* DI NOLLI) *looking curiously about the room. At first, they speak sotto voce.)*

DI NOLLI (*to* JOHN): Have you given the orders properly?

JOHN: Yes, my Lord; don't be anxious about that.

BELCREDI: Ah, magnificent! magnificent!

DOCTOR: How extremely interesting! Even in the surroundings his raving madness—is perfectly taken into account!

DONNA MATILDA (*glancing round for her portrait, discovers it, and goes up close to it*): Ah! Here it is! (*Going back to admire it, while mixed emotions stir within her.*) Yes . . . yes . . . (*Calls her daughter* FRIDA.)

FRIDA: Ah, your portrait!

DONNA MATILDA: No, no . . . look again; it's you, not I, there!

DI NOLLI: Yes, it's quite true. I told you so, I . . .

DONNA MATILDA: But I would never have believed it! (*Shaking as if with a chill.*) What a strange feeling it gives one! (*Then looking at her daughter.*) Frida, what's the matter? (*She pulls her to her side, and slips an arm round her waist.*) Come: don't you see yourself in me there?

FRIDA: Well, I really . . .

DONNA MATILDA: Don't you think so? Don't you, really? *(Turning to* BELCREDI.*)* Look at it, Tito! Speak up, man!
BELCREDI *(without looking)*: Ah, no! I shan't look at it. For me, *a priori,* certainly not!
DONNA MATILDA: Stupid! You think you are paying me a compliment! *(Turning to* DOCTOR GENONI.*)* What do you say, Doctor? Do say something, please!
DOCTOR *(makes a movement to go near to the picture)*.
BELCREDI *(with his back turned, pretending to attract his attenton secretly)*: —Hss! No, Doctor! For the love of Heaven, have nothing to do with it!
DOCTOR *(getting bewildered and smiling)*: And why shouldn't I?
DONNA MATILDA: Don't listen to him! Come here! He's insufferable!
FRIDA: He acts the fool by profession, didn't you know that?
BELCREDI *(to the* DOCTOR, *seeing him go over)*: Look at your feet, Doctor! Mind where you're going!
DOCTOR: Why?
BELCREDI: Be careful you don't put your foot in it!
DOCTOR *(laughing feebly)*: No, no. After all, it seems to me there's no reason to be astonished at the fact that a daughter should resemble her mother!
BELCREDI: Hullo! Hullo! He's done it now; he's said it.
DONNA MATILDA *(with exaggerated anger, advancing towards* BELCREDI*)*: What's the matter? What has he said? What has he done?
DOCTOR *(candidly)*: Well, isn't it so?
BELCREDI *(answering the* MARCHIONESS*)*: I said there was nothing to be astounded at—and you are astounded! And why so, then, if the thing is so simple and natural for you now?
DONNA MATILDA *(still more angry)*: Fool! fool! It's just because it is so natural! Just because it isn't my daughter who is there. *(Pointing to the canvas.)* That is my portrait; and to find my daughter there instead of me fills me with astonishment, an astonishment which, I beg you to believe, is sincere. I forbid you to cast doubts on it.
FRIDA *(slowly and wearily)*: My God! It's always like this . . . rows over nothing . . .
BELCREDI *(also slowly, looking dejected, in accents of apology)*: I cast no doubt on anything! I noticed from the beginning that you haven't shared your mother's astonishment; or, if something did astonish you, it was because the likeness between you and the portrait seemed so strong.
DONNA MATILDA: Naturally! She cannot recognize herself in me as I was at her age; while I, there, can very well recognize myself in her as she is now!

DOCTOR: Quite right! Because a portrait is always there fixed in the twinkling of an eye: for the young lady something far away and without memories, while, for the Marchioness, it can bring back everything: movements, gestures, looks, smiles, a whole heap of things . . .

DONNA MATILDA: Exactly!

DOCTOR (*continuing, turning towards her*): Naturally enough, you can live all these old sensations again in your daughter.

DONNA MATILDA: He always spoils every innocent pleasure for me, every touch I have of spontaneous sentiment! He does it merely to annoy me.

DOCTOR (*frightened at the disturbance he has caused, adopts a professional tone*): Likeness, dear Baron, is often the result of imponderable things. So one explains that . . .

BELCREDI (*interrupting the discourse*): Somebody will soon be finding a likeness between you and me, my dear Professor!

DI NOLLI: Oh! let's finish with this, please! (*Points to the two doors on the right, as a warning that there is someone there who may be listening.*) We've wasted too much time as it is!

FRIDA: As one might expect when *he's* present. (*Alludes to* BELCREDI.)

DI NOLLI: Enough! The Doctor is here; and we have come for a very serious purpose which you all know is important to me.

DOCTOR: Yes, that is so! But now, first of all, let's try to get some points down exactly. Excuse me, Marchioness, will you tell me why your portrait is here? Did you present it to him then?

DONNA MATILDA: No, not at all. How could I have given it to him? I was just like Frida then—and not even engaged. I gave it to him three or four years after the accident. I gave it to him because his mother wished it so much . . . (*Points to* DI NOLLI.)

DOCTOR: She was his sister? (*Alludes to* HENRY IV.)

DI NOLLI: Yes, Doctor; and our coming here is a debt we pay to my mother who has been dead for more than a month. Instead of being here, she and I (*indicating* FRIDA) ought to be traveling together . . .

DOCTOR: . . . taking a cure of quite a different kind!

DI NOLLI: —Hum Mother died in the firm conviction that her adored brother was just about to be cured.

DOCTOR: And can't you tell me, if you please, how she inferred this?

DI NOLLI: The conviction would appear to have derived from certain strange remarks which he made, a little before mother died.

DOCTOR: Oh, remarks! . . . Ah! . . . It would be extremely useful for me to have those remarks, word for word, if possible.

DI NOLLI: I can't remember them. I know that mother returned awfully upset from her last visit with him. On her death-bed, she made me promise that I would never neglect him, that I would have doctors see him, and examine him.

DOCTOR: Um! Um! Let me see! let me see! Sometimes very small reasons determine . . . and this portrait here then? . . .
DONNA MATILDA: For Heaven's sake, Doctor, don't attach excessive importance to this. It made an impression on me because I had not seen it for so many years!
DOCTOR: If you please, quietly, quietly . . .
DI NOLLI: —Well, yes, it must be about fifteen years ago.
DONNA MATILDA: More, more: eighteen!
DOCTOR: Forgive me, but you don't quite know what I'm trying to get at. I attach a very great importance to these two portraits . . . They were painted, naturally, prior to the famous—and most regrettable pageant, weren't they?
DONNA MATILDA: Of course!
DOCTOR: That is . . . when he was quite in his right mind—that's what I've been trying to say. Was it his suggestion that they should be painted?
DONNA MATILDA: Lots of the people who took part in the pageant had theirs done as a souvenir . . .
BELCREDI: I had mine done—as "Charles of Anjou!"
DONNA MATILDA: . . . as soon as the costumes were ready.
BELCREDI: As a matter of fact, it was proposed that the whole lot of us should be hung together in a gallery of the villa where the pageant took place. But in the end, everybody wanted to keeep his own portrait.
DONNA MATILDA: And I gave him this portrait of me without very much regret . . . since his mother . . . *(Indicates* DI NOLLI.*)*
DOCTOR: You don't remember if it was he who asked for it?
DONNA MATILDA: Ah, that I don't remember . . . Maybe it was his sister, wanting to help out . . .
DOCTOR: One other thing: was it his idea, this pageant?
BELCREDI (*at once*): No, no, it was mine!
DOCTOR: If you please . . .
DONNA MATILDA: Don't listen to him! It was poor Belassi's idea.
BELCREDI: Belassi! What had he got to do with it?
DONNA MATILDA: Count Belassi, who died, poor fellow, two or three months after . . .
BELCREDI: But if Belassi wasn't there when . . .
DI NOLLI: Excuse me, Doctor; but is it really necessary to establish whose the original idea was?
DOCTOR: It would help me, certainly!
BELCREDI: I tell you the idea was mine! There's nothing to be proud of in it, seeing what the result's been. Look here, Doctor, it was like this. One evening, in the first days of November, I was looking at an illustrated German review in the club. I was merely glancing at the

pictures, because I can't read German. There was a picture of the Kaiser, at some University town where he had been a student . . . I don't remember which.

DOCTOR: Bonn, Bonn!

BELCREDI: —You are right: Bonn! He was on horseback, dressed up in one of those ancient German student guild-costumes, followed by a procession of noble students, also in costume. The picture gave me the idea. Already someone at the club had spoken of a pageant for the forthcoming carnival. So I had the notion that each of us should choose for this Tower of Babel pageant to represent some character: a king, an emperor, a prince, with his queen, empress, or lady, alongside of him—and all on horseback. The suggestion was at once accepted.

DONNA MATILDA: I had my invitation from Belassi.

BELCREDI: Well, he wasn't speaking the truth! That's all I can say, if he told you the idea was his. He wasn't even at the club the evening I made the suggestion, just as he *(Meaning* HENRY IV.*)* wasn't there either.

DOCTOR: So he chose the character of Henry IV?

DONNA MATILDA: Because I . . . thinking of my name, and not giving the choice any importance, said I would be the Marchioness Matilda of Tuscany.

DOCTOR: I . . . don't understand the relation between the two.

DONNA MATILDA: —Neither did I, to begin with, when he said that in that case he would be at my feet like Henry IV at Canossa. I had heard of Canossa of course; but to tell the truth, I'd forgotten most of the story; and I remember I received a curious impression when I had to get up my part, and found that I was the faithful and zealous friend of Pope Gregory VII in deadly enmity with the Emperor of Germany. Then I understood why, since I had chosen to represent his implacable enemy, he wanted to be near me in the pageant as Henry IV.

DOCTOR: Ah, perhaps because . . .

BELCREDI: —Good Heavens, Doctor, because he was then paying furious court to her! *(Indicates the* MARCHIONESS.*)* And she, naturally . . .

DONNA MATILDA: Naturally? Not naturally at all . . .

BELCREDI *(pointing to her)*: She shouldn't stand him . . .

DONNA MATILDA: —No, that isn't true! I didn't dislike him. Not at all! But for me, when a man begins to want to be taken seriously, well . . .

BELCREDI *(continuing for her)*: He gives you the clearest proof of his stupidity.

DONNA MATILDA: No, dear; not in this case; because he was never a fool like you.

BELCREDI: Anyway, I've never asked you to take me seriously.

DONNA MATILDA: Yes, I know. But with him one couldn't joke. *(Chang-*

ing her tone and speaking to the DOCTOR.*)* One of the many misfortunes which happen to us women, Doctor, is to see before us every now and again a pair of eyes glaring at us with a contained intense promise of eternal devotion. *(Bursts out laughing.)* There is nothing quite so funny. If men could only see themselves with that eternal look of fidelity in their faces! I've always thought it comic; then more even than now. But I want to make a confession—I can do so after twenty years or more. When I laughed at him then, it was partly out of fear. One might have almost believed a promise from those eyes of his. But it would have been very daugerous.

DOCTOR *(with lively interest)*: Ah! ah! This is most interesting! Very dangerous, you say?

DONNA MATILDA: Yes, because he was very different from the others. And then, I am . . . well . . . what shall I say? . . . a little impatient of all that is pondered, or tedious. But I was too young then, and a woman. I had the bit between my teeth. It would have required more courage than I felt I possessed. So I laughed at him too—with remorse, to spite myself, indeed; since I saw that my own laugh mingled with those of all the others—the other fools—who made fun of him.

BELCREDI: My own case, more or less!

DONNA MATILDA: You make people laugh at you, my dear, with your trick of always humiliating yourself. It was quite a different affair with him. There's a vast difference. And you—you know—people laugh in your face!

BELCREDI: Well, that's better than behind one's back!

DOCTOR: Let's get to the facts. He was then already somewhat exalted, if I understand rightly.

BELCREDI: Yes, but in a curious fashion, Doctor.

DOCTOR: How?

BELCREDI: Well, cold-bloodedly so to speak.

DONNA MATILDA: Not at all! It was like this, Doctor! He was a bit strange, certainly; but only because he was fond of life: eccentric, there!

BELCREDI: I don't say he simulated exaltation. On the contrary, he was often genuinely exalted. But I could swear, Doctor, that he saw himself at once in his own exaltation. Moreover, I'm certain it made him suffer. Sometimes he had the most comical fits of rage against himself.

DOCTOR: Yes?

DONNA MATILDA: That is true.

BELCREDI *(to* DONNA MATILDA*)*: And why? *(To the* DOCTOR.*)* Evidently because that immediate lucidity that comes from acting, assuming a part, at once put him out of key with his own feelings, which seemed to him not exactly false, but like something he was obliged to give the value there and then of—what shall I say—of an act of intelligence, to make up for that sincere cordial warmth he felt lacking. So he improvised, exaggerated, let himself go, so as to distract and forget himself. He appeared inconstant, fatuous, and—yes—even ridiculous, sometimes.

DOCTOR: And may we say unsociable?

BELCREDI: No, not at all. He was famous for getting up things: *tableaux vivants*, dances, theatrical performances for charity: all for the fun of the thing, of course. He was a jolly good actor, you know!

DI NOLLI: Madness has made a superb actor of him.

BELCREDI: —Why, so he was even in the old days. When the accident happened, after the horse fell . . .

DOCTOR: Hit the back of his head, didn't he?

DONNA MATILDA: Oh, it was horrible! He was beside me! I saw him between the horse's hoofs! It was rearing!

BELCREDI: None of us thought it was anything serious at first. There was a stop in the pageant, a bit of disorder. People wanted to know what had happened. But they'd already taken him off to the villa.

DONNA MATILDA: There wasn't the least sign of a wound, not a drop of blood.

BELCREDI: We thought he had merely fainted.

DONNA MATILDA: But two hours afterwards . . .

BELCREDI: He reappeared in the drawing-room of the villa . . . that is what I wanted to say . . .

DONNA MATILDA: My God! What a face he had. I saw the whole thing at once!

BELCREDI: No, no! that isn't true. Nobody saw it, Doctor, believe me!

DONNA MATILDA: Doubtless, because you were all like mad folk.

BELCREDI: Everybody was pretending to act his part for a joke. It was a regular Babel.

DONNA MATILDA: And you can imagine, Doctor, what terror struck into us when we understood that he, on the contrary, was playing his part in deadly earnest . . .

DOCTOR: Oh, he was there too, was he?

BELCREDI: Of course! He came straight into the midst of us. We thought he'd quite recovered, and was pretending, fooling, like all the rest of us . . . only doing it rather better; because, as I say, he knew how to act.

DONNA MATILDA: Some of them began to hit him with their whips and fans and sticks.

BELCREDI: And then—as a king, he was armed, of course—he drew out his sword and menaced two or three of us . . . It was a terrible moment, I can assure you!

DONNA MATILDA: I shall never forget that scene—all our masked faces hideous and terrified gazing at him, at that terrible mask of his face, which was no longer a mask, but madness, madness personified.

BELCREDI: He was Henry IV, Henry IV in person, in a moment of fury.

DONNA MATILDA: He'd got into it all the detail and minute preparation of a month's careful study. And it all burned and blazed there in the terrible obsession which lit his face.

DOCTOR: Yes, that is quite natural, of course. The momentary obsession of a dilettante became fixed, owing to the fall and the damage to the brain.

BELCREDI (*to* FRIDA *and* DI NOLLI): You see the kind of jokes life can play on us. *(To* DI NOLLI.*)* You were four or five years old. *(To* FRIDA.*)* Your mother imagines you've taken her place there in that portrait; when, at the time, she had not the remotest idea that she would bring you into the world. My hair is already grey; and he—look at him—*(Points to portrait)*—ha! A smack on the head, and he never moves again: Henry IV for ever!

DOCTOR (*seeking to draw the attention of the others, looking learned and imposing*): Well, well, then it comes, we may say, to this . . .

(*Suddenly the first exit to right, the one nearest footlights, opens, and* BERTHOLD *enters all excited.*)

BERTHOLD (*rushing in*): I say! I say! *(Stops for a moment, arrested by the astonishment which his appearance has cause in the others.)*

FRIDA (*running away terrified*): Oh dear! oh dear! it's he, it's . . .

DONNA MATILDA (*covering her face with her hands so as not to see*): Is it, is it he?

DI NOLLI: No, no, what are you talking about? Be calm!

DOCTOR: Who is it then?

BELCREDI: One of our masqueraders.

DI NOLLI: He is one of the four youths we keep here to help him out in his madness . . .

BERTHOLD: I beg your pardon, Marquis . . .

DI NOLLI: Pardon be damned! I gave orders that the doors were to be closed, and that nobody should be allowed to enter.

BERTHOLD: Yes, sir, but I can't stand it any longer, and I ask you to let me go away this very minute.

DI NOLLI: Oh, you're the new valet, are you? You were supposed to begin this morning, weren't you?

BERTHOLD: Yes, sir, and I can't stand it, I can't bear it.

DONNA MATILDA (*to* DI NOLLI *excitedly*): What? Then he's not so calm as you said?

BERTHOLD (*quickly*): —No, no, my lady, it isn't he; it's my companions.

You say "help him out with his madness," Marquis; but they don't do anything of the kind. They're the real madmen. I come here for the first time, and instead of helping me . . .

(LANDOLPH *and* HAROLD *come in from the same door, but hesitate on the threshold.*)

LANDOLPH: Excuse me?
HAROLD: May I come in, my Lord?
DI NOLLI: Come in! What's the matter? What are you all doing?
FRIDA: Oh God! I'm frightened! I'm going to run away. *(Makes towards exit at left.)*
DI NOLLI *(restraining her at once)*: No, no Frida!
LANDOLPH: My Lord, this fool here . . . *(Indicates* BERTHOLD.*)*
BERTHOLD *(protesting)*: Ah, no thanks, my friends, no thanks! I'm not stopping here! I'm off!
LANDOLPH: What do you mean—you're not stopping here?
HAROLD: He's ruined everything, my Lord, running away in here!
LANDOLPH: He's made him quite mad. We can't keep him in there any longer. He's given orders that he's to be arrested; and he wants to "judge" him at once from the throne: What is to be done?
DI NOLLI: Shut the door, man! Shut the door! Go and close that door! (LANDOLPH *goes over to close it.)*
HAROLD: Ordulph, alone, won't be able to keep him there.
LANDOLPH: —My Lord, perhaps if we could announce the visitors at once, it would turn his thoughts. Have the gentlemen thought under what pretext they will present themselves to him?
DI NOLLI: —It's all been arranged! *(To the* DOCTOR.*)* If you Doctor, think it well to see him at once. . . .
FRIDA: I'm not coming! I'm not coming! I'll keep out of this. You too, mother, for Heaven's sake, come away with me!
DOCTOR: —I say . . . I suppose he's not armed, is he?
DI NOLLI: —Nonsense! Of course not. *(To* FRIDA.*)* Frida, ,you know this is childish of you. You wanted to come!
FRIDA: I didn't at all. It was mother's idea.
DONNA MATILDA: And I'm quite ready to see him. What are we going to do?
BELCREDI: Must we absolutely dress up in some fashion or other?
LANDOLPH: —Absolutely essential, indispensable, sir. Alas! as you see . . . *(Shows his costume)*, there'd be awful trouble if he saw you gentlemen in modern dress.
HAROLD: He would think it was some diabolical masquerade.
DI NOLLI: As these men seem to be in costume to you, so we appear to be in costume to him, in these modern clothes of ours.

LANDOLPH: It wouldn't matter so much if he wouldn't suppose it to be the work of his mortal enemy.
BELCREDI: Pope Gregory VII?
LANDOLPH: Precisely. He calls him "a pagan."
BELCREDI: The Pope a pagan? Not bad that!
LANDOLPH: —Yes, sir, —and a man who calls up the dead! He accuses him of all the diabolical arts. He's terribly afraid of him.
DOCTOR: Persecution mania!
HAROLD: He'd be simply furious.
DI NOLLI (*to* BELCREDI): But there's no need for you to be there, you know. It's sufficient for the Doctor to see him.
DOCTOR: —What do you mean? . . . I? Alone?
DI NOLLI: —But they are there. *(Indicates the three young men.)*
DOCTOR: I don't mean that . . . I mean if the Marchioness . . .
DONNA MATILDA: Of course. I mean to see him too, naturally. I want to see him again.
FRIDA: Oh, why mother, why? Do come away with me, I implore you!
DONNA MATILDA (*imperiously*): Let me do as I wish! I came here for this purpose! *(To* LANDOLPH.*)* I shall be "Adelaide," the mother.
LANDOLPH: Excellent! The mother of the Empress Bertha. Good! It will be enough if her Ladyship wears the ducal crown and puts on a mantle that will hide her other clothes entirely *(To* HAROLD.*)* Off you go, Harold!
HAROLD: Wait a moment! And this gentlemen here? . . . *(Alludes to the* DOCTOR.*)*
DOCTOR: —Ah yes . . . we decided I was to be . . . the Bishop of Cluny, Hugh of Cluny!
HAROLD: The gentleman means the Abbot. Very good! Hugh of Cluny.
LANDOLPH: —He's often been here before!
DOCTOR (*amazed*): —What? Been here before?
LANDOLPH: —Don't be alarmed! I mean that it's an easily prepared disguise . . .
HAROLD: We've made use of it on other occasions, you see!
DOCTOR: But . . .
LANDOLPH: Oh, no, there's no risk of his remembering. He pays more attention to the dress than to the person.
DONNA MATILDA: That's fortunate for me too then.
DI NOLLI: Frida, you and I'll get along. Come on, Tito!
BELCREDI: Ah, no. If she *(Indicates the* MARCHIONESS.*)* stops here, so do I!
DONNA MATILDA: But I don't need you at all.
BELCREDI: You may not need me, but I should like to see him again myself. Mayn't I?
LANDOLPH: Well, perhaps it would be better if there were three.

HAROLD: How is the gentleman to be dressed then?
BELCREDI: Oh, try and find some easy costume for me.
LANDOLPH (*to* HAROLD): Hum! Yes . . . he'd better be from Cluny too.
BELCREDI: What do you mean—from Cluny?
LANDOLPH: A Benedictine's habit of the Abbey of Cluny. He can be in attendance on Monsignor. (*To* HAROLD). Off you go! (*To* BERTHOLD.) And you too get away and keep out of sight all day. No, wait a bit! (*To* BERTHOLD.) You bring here the costumes he will give you (*To* HAROLD.) You go at once and announce the visit of the "Duchess Adelaide" and "Monsignor Hugh of Cluny." Do you understand? (HAROLD *and* BERTHOLD *go off by the first door on the right.*)
DI NOLLI: We'll retire now. (*Goes off with* FRIDA, *left.*)
DOCTOR: Shall I be a *persona grata* to him, as Hugh of Cluny?
LANDOLPH: Oh, rather! Don't worry about that! Monsignor has always been received here with great respect. You too, my Lady, he will be glad to see. He never forgets that it was owing to the intercession of you two that he was admitted to the Castle of Canossa and the presence of Gregory VII, who didn't want to receive him.
BELCREDI: And what do I do?
LANDOLPH: You stand a little apart, respectfully: that's all.
DONNA MATILDA (*irritated, nervous*): You would do well to go away, you know.
BELCREDI (*slowly, spitefully*): How upset you seem! . . .
DONNA MATILDA (*proudly*): I am as I am. Leave me alone!

(BERTHOLD *comes in with the costumes.*)

LANDOLPH (*seeing him enter*): Ah, the costumes: here they are. This mantle is for the Marchioness . . .
DONNA MATILDA: Wait a minute! I'll take off my hat.

(*Does so and gives it to* BERTHOLD.)

LANDOLPH: Put it down there! (*Then to the* MARCHIONESS, *while he offers to put the ducal crown on her head.*) Allow me!
DONNA MATILDA: Dear, dear! Isn't there a mirror here?
LANDOLPH: Yes, there's one there (*Points to the door on the left.*) If the Marchioness would rather put it on herself . . .
DONNA MATILDA: Yes, yes, that will be better. Give it to me! (*Takes up her hat and goes off with* BERTHOLD, *who carries the cloak and the crown.*)
BELCREDI: Well, I must say, I never thought I should be a Benedictine monk! By the way, this business must cost an awful lot of money.
THE DOCTOR: Like any other fantasy, naturally!
BELCREDI: Well, there's a fortune to go upon.

LANDOLPH: We have got there a whole wardrobe of costumes of the period, copied to perfection from old models. This is my special job. I get them from the best theatrical costumers. They cost lots of money. (DONNA MATILDA *re-enters, wearing mantle and crown.*)
BELCREDI (*at once, in admiration*): Oh magnificent! Oh, truly regal!
DONNA MATILDA (*looking at* BELCREDI *and bursting out into laughter*): Oh no, no! Take it off! You're impossible. You look like an ostrich dressed up as a monk.
BELCREDI: Well, how about the Doctor?
THE DOCTOR: I don't think I look so bad, do I?
DONNA MATILDA: No; the Doctor's all right... but you are too funny for words.
THE DOCTOR: Do you have many receptions here then?
LANDOLPH: It depends. He often gives orders that such and such a person appear before him. Then we have to find someone who will take the part. Women too...
DONNA MATILDA (*hurt, but trying to hide the fact*): Ah, women too?
LANDOLPH: Oh, yes; many at first.
BELCREDI (*laughing*): Oh, that's great! In costume, like the Marchioness?
LANDOLPH: Oh well, you know, women of the kind that lend themselves to...
BELCREDI: Ah, I see! (*Perfidiously to the* MARCHIONESS.) Look out, you know he's becoming dangerous for you.

(*The second door on the right opens, and* HAROLD *appears making first of all a discreet sign that all conversation should cease.*)

HAROLD: His Majesty, the Emperor!

(*The* TWO VALETS *enter first, and go and stand on either side of the throne. Then* HENRY IV *comes in between* ORDULPH *and* HAROLD, *who keep a little in the rear respectfully.*

HENRY IV *is about 50 and very pale. The hair on the back of his head is already grey; over the temples and forehead it appears blond, owing to its having been tinted in an evident and puerile fashion. On his cheek bones he has two small, doll-like dabs of color, that stand out prominently against the rest of his tragic pallor. He is wearing a penitent's sack over his regal habit, as at Canossa. His eyes have a fixed look which is dreadful to see, and this expression is in strained contrast with the sackcloth.* ORDULPH *carries the Imperial crown;* HAROLD, *the sceptre with eagle, and the globe with the cross.*)

HENRY IV (*bowing first to* DONNA MATILDA *and afterwards to the* DOCTOR): My lady... Monsignor... (*Then he looks at* BELCREDI *and seems about to greet him too; when, suddenly, he turns to* LANDOLPH, *who has approached him, and asks him sotto voce and with diffidence.*) Is that Peter Damiani?

LANDOLPH: No, Sire. He is a monk from Cluny who is accompanying the Abbot.

HENRY IV (*looks again at* BELCREDI *with increasing mistrust, and then noticing that he appears embarrassed and keeps glancing at* DONNA MATILDA *and the* DOCTOR, *stands upright and cries out*): No, it's Peter Damiani! It's no use, father, your looking at the Duchess. (*Then turning quickly to* DONNA MATILDA *and the* DOCTOR *as though to ward off a danger.*) I swear it! I swear that my heart is changed towards your daughter. I confess that if he (*Indicates* BELCREDI.) hadn't come to forbid it in the name of Pope Alexander, I'd have repudiated her. Yes, yes, there were people ready to favor the repudiation: the Bishop of Mayence would have done it for a matter of one hundred and twenty farms. (*Looks at* LANDOLPH *a little perplexed and adds.*) But I mustn't speak ill of the bishops at this moment! (*More humbly to* BELCREDI.) I am grateful to you, believe me, I am grateful to you for the hindrance you put in my way!—God knows, my life's been all made of humiliations: my mother, Adalbert, Tribur, Goslar! And now this sackcloth you see me wearing! (*Changes tone suddenly and speaks like one who goes over his part in a parenthesis of astuteness.*) It doesn't matter: clarity of ideas, perspicacity, firmness and patience under adversity that's the thing. (*Then turning to all and speaking solemnly.*) I know how to make amend for the mistakes I have made; and I can humiliate myself even before you, Peter Damiani. (*Bows profoundly to him and remains curved. Then a suspicion is born in him which he is obliged to utter in menacing tones, almost against his will.*) Was it not perhaps you who started that obscene rumor that my holy mother had illicit relations with the Bishop of Augusta?

BELCREDI (*since* HENRY IV *has his finger pointed at him*): No, no, it wasn't I . . .

HENRY IV (*straightening up*): Not true, not true? Infamy! (*Looks at him and then adds.*) I didn't think you capable of it! (*Goes to the* DOCTOR *and plucks his sleeve, while winking at him knowingly.*) Always the same, Monsignor, those bishops, always the same!

HAROLD (*softly, whispering as if to help out the* DOCTOR): Yes, yes, the rapacious bishops!

THE DOCTOR (*to* HAROLD, *trying to keep it up*): Ah, yes, those fellows . . . ah yes . . .

HENRY IV: Nothing satisfies them! I was a little boy, Monsignor . . . One passes the time, playing even, when, without knowing it, one is a king. —I was six years old; and they tore me away from my mother, and made use of me against her without my knowing anything about it . . .

always profaning, always stealing, stealing! . . . One greedier than the other . . . Hanno worse than Stephen! Stephen worse than Hanno!

LANDOLPH (*sotto voce, persuasively, to call his attention*): Majesty!

HENRY IV (*turning round quickly*): Ah yes . . . this isn't the moment to speak ill of the bishops. But this infamy against my mother, Monsignor, is too much. (*Looks at the* MARCHIONESS *and grows tender.*) And I can't even weep for her, Lady . . . I appeal to you who have a mother's heart! She came here to see me from her convent a month ago . . . They had told me she was dead! (*Sustained pause full of feeling. Then smiling sadly.*) I can't weep for her; because if you are here now, and I am like this (*Shows the sackcloth he is wearing.*) it means I am twenty-six years old!

HAROLD: And that she is therefore alive, Majesty! . . .

ORDULPH: Still in her convent!

HENRY IV (*looking at them*): Ah yes! And I can postpone my grief to another time. (*Shows the* MARCHIONESS *almost with coquetry the tint he has given to his hair.*) Look! I am still fair . . . (*Then slowly as if in confidence.*) For you . . . there's no need! But little exterior details do help! A matter of time, Monsignor, do you understand me? (*Turns to the* MARCHIONESS *and notices her hair.*) Ah, but I see that you, too, Duchess . . . Italian, eh? (*As much as to say "false"; but without any indignation, indeed rather with malicious admiration.*) Heaven forbid that I should show disgust or surprise(Nobody cares to recognize that obscure and fatal power which sets limits to our will. But I say, if one is born and one dies . . . Did you want to be born, Monsignor? I didn't! And in both cases, independently of our wills, so many things happen we would wish didn't happen, and to which we resign ourselves as best we can! . . .

DOCTOR (*merely to make a remark, while studying* HENRY IV *carefully*): Alas! Yes, alas!

HENRY IV: It's like this: When we are not resigned, out come our desires. A woman wants to be a man . . . an old man would be young again. Desires, ridiculous fixed ideas of course—But reflect! Monsignor, those other desires are not less ridiculous: I mean, those desires where the will is kept within the limits of the possible. Not one of us can lie or pretend. We're all fixed in good faith in a certain concept of ourselves. However, Monsignor, while you keep yourself in order, holding on with both your hands to your holy habit, there slips down from your sleeves, there peels off from you like . . . like a serpent . . . something you don't notice: life, Monsignor! (*Turns to the* MARCHIONESS.) Has it never happened to you, my Lady, to find a different self in yourself? Have you always been the same? My God! One day . . . How was it, how was it you were able to commit this or that action? (*Fixes her so intently in the eyes as almost to make her blanch.*) Yes, that particular action, that very one: we understand each other! But don't be afraid: I shall reveal it to none. And you, Peter Damiani, how could you be a friend of that man?...

LANDOLPH: Majesty!

HENRY IV (*at once*): No, I won't name him! (*Turning to* BELCREDI.) What did you think of him? But we all of us cling tight to our conceptions of ourselves, just as he who is growing old dyes his hair. What does it matter that this dyed hair of mine isn't a reality for you, if it *is*, to some extent, for me?—you, you, my Lady, certainly don't dye your hair to deceive the others, nor even yourself; but only to cheat your own image a little before the looking-glass. I do it for a joke! You do it seriously! But I assure you that you too, Madam, are in masquerade, though it be in all seriousness; and I am not speaking of the venerable crown on your brows or the ducal mantle. I am speaking only of the memory you wish to fix in yourself of your fair complexion one day when it pleased you—or of your dark complexion, if you were dark: the fading image of your youth! For you, Peter Damiani, on the contrary, the memory of what you have been, of what you have done, seems to you a recognition of past realities that remain within you like a dream. I'm in the same case too: with so many inexplicable memories—like dreams! Ah!... There's nothing to marvel at in it, Peter Damiani! Tomorrow it will be the same thing with our life of today! (*Suddenly getting excited and taking hold of his sackcloth.*) This sackcloth here... (*Beginning to take it off with a gesture of almost ferocious joy while the* THREE VALETS *run over to him, frightened, as if to prevent his doing so.*) Ah, my God! (*Draws back and throws off sackcloth.*) Tomorrow, at Bressanone, twenty-seven German and Lombard bishops will sign with me the act of deposition of Gregory VII! No Pope at all! Just a false monk!

ORDULPH (*with the other three*): Majesty! Majesty! In God's name!...

HAROLD (*inviting him to put on the sackcloth again*): Listen to what he says, Majesty!

LANDOLPH: Monsignor is here with the Duchess to intercede in your favor. (*Makes secret signs to the* DOCTOR *to say something at once.*)

DOCTOR (*foolishly*): Ah yes... yes... we are here to intercede...

HENRY IV (*repenting at once, almost terrified, allowing the three to put on the sackcloth again, and pulling it down over him with his own hands*): Pardon... yes... yes... pardon, Monsignor: forgive me, my Lady... I swear to you I feel the whole weight of the anathema. (*Bends himself, takes his face between his hands, as though waiting for something to crush him. Then changing tone, but without moving, says softly to* LANDOLPH, HAROLD *and* ORDULPH.) But I don't know why I cannot be humble before that man there! (*Indicates* BELCREDI.)

LANDOLPH (*sotto voce*): But why, Majesty, do you insist on believing he is Peter Damiani, when he isn't, at all?

HENRY IV (*looking at him timorously*): He isn't Peter Damiani?

HAROLD: No, no, he is a poor monk, Majesty.

HENRY IV (*sadly with a touch of exasperation*): Ah! None of us can estimate what we do when we do it from instinct... You perhaps, Madam, can understand me better than the others, since you are a woman and a Duchess. This is a solemn and decisive moment. I could, you know, accept the assistance of the Lombard bishops, arrest the Pope, lock him up here in the castle, run to Rome and elect an anti-Pope; offer alliance to Robert Guiscard—and Gregory VII would be lost! I resist the temptation; and, believe me, I am wise in doing so. I feel the atmosphere of our times and the majesty of one who knows how to be what he ought to be! a Pope! Do you feel inclined to laugh at me, seeing me like this? You would be foolish to do so; for you don't understand the political wisdom which makes this penitent's sack advisable. The parts may be changed tomorrow. What would you do then? Would you laugh to see the Pope a prisoner? No! It would come to the same thing: I dressed as a penitent, today; he, as prisoner tomorrow! But woe to him who doesn't know how to wear his mask, be he king or Pope!—'Perhaps he is a bit too cruel! No! Yes, yes, maybe!—You remember, my Lady, how your daughter Bertha, for whom, I repeat, my feelings have changed (*Turns to* BELCREDI *and shouts to his face as if he were being contradicted by him.*)—yes, changed on account of the affection and devotion she showed me in that terrible moment... (*Then once again to the* MARCHIONESS.)... you remember how she came with me, my Lady, followed me like a beggar and passed two nights out in the open, in the snow? You are her mother! Doesn't this touch your mother's heart? Doesn't this urge you to pity, so that you will beg His Holiness for pardon, beg him to receive us?

DONNA MATILDA (*trembling, with feeble voice*): Yes, yes, at once...

DOCTOR: It shall be done!

HENRY IV: And one thing more! (*Draws them in to listen to him.*) It isn't enough that he should receive me! You know he can do *everything*—*everything* I tell you! He can even call up the dead. (*Touches his chest.*) Behold me! Do you see me? There is no magic art unknown to him. Well, Monsignor, my Lady, my torment is really this: that whether here or there (*Pointing to his portrait almost in fear.*) I can't free myself from this magic. I am a penitent now, you see; and I swear to you I shall remain so until he receives me. But you two, when the excommunication is taken off, must ask the Pope to do this thing he can so easily do: to take me away from that; (*Indicating the portrait again.*) and let me live wholly and freely my miserable life. A man can't always be twenty-six, my Lady. I ask this of you for your daughter's sake too; that I may love her as she deserves to be loved, well disposed as I am now, all tender towards her for her pity. There: it's all there! I am in your hands! (*Bows.*) My Lady! Monsignor!

(*He goes off, bowing grandly, through the door by which he entered, leaving everyone stupefied, and the* MARCHIONESS *so profoundly touched, that no sooner has he gone than she breaks out into sobs and sits down almost fainting.*)

ACT II

(Another room of the villa, adjoining the throne room. Its furniture is antique and severe. Principal exit at rear in the background. To the left, two windows looking on the garden. To the right, a door opening into the throne room.

Late afternoon of the same day.

DONNA MATILDA, the DOCTOR and BELCREDI are on the stage engaged in conversation; but DONNA MATILDA stands to one side, evidently annoyed at what the other two are saying, although she cannot help listening, because, in her agitated state, everything interests her in spite of herself. The talk of the other two attracts her attention, because she instinctively feels the need for calm at the moment.)

BELCREDI: It may be as you say, Doctor, but that was my impression.

DOCTOR: I won't contradict you; but, believe me, it is only . . . an impression.

BELCREDI: Pardon me, but he even said so, and quite clearly (*Turning to the* MARCHIONESS.) Didn't he, Marchioness?

DONNA MATILDA (*turning round*): What did he say? . . . (*Then not agreeing.*) Oh yes . . . but not for the reason you think!

DOCTOR: He was alluding to the costumes we had slipped on . . . Your cloak (*Indicating the* MARCHIONESS.) our Benedictine habits . . . But all this is childish!

DONNA MATILDA (*turning quickly, indignant*): Childish? What do you mean, Doctor?

DOCTOR: From one point of view, it is—I beg you to let me say so, Marchioness! Yet, on the other hand, it is much more complicated than you can imagine.

DONNA MATILDA: To me, on the contrary, it is perfectly clear!

DOCTOR (*with a smile of pity of the competent person towards those who do not understand*): We must take into account the peculiar psychology of madmen; which, you must know, enables us to be certain that they observe things and can, for instance, easily detect people who are disguised; can in fact recognize the disguise and yet believe in it; just as children do, for whom disguise is both play and reality. That is why I used the word childish. But the thing is extremely complicated, inasmuch as he must be perfectly aware of being an image to himself and for himself—that image there, in fact! (*Alluding to the portrait in the throne room, and pointing to the left.*)

BELCREDI: That's what he said!

DOCTOR: Very well then—An image before which other images, ours, have appeared: understand? Now he, in his acute and perfectly lucid delirium, was able to detect at once a difference between his image and ours: that is, he saw that ours were make-believes. So he suspected us; because all madmen are armed with a special diffidence. But that's all there is to it! Our make-believe, built up all round his, did not seem pitiful to him. While his seemed all the more tragic to us, in that he, as if in defiance—understand?—and induced by his suspicion, wanted to show us up merely as a joke. That was also partly the case with him, in coming before us with painted cheeks and hair, and saying he had done it on purpose for a jest.

DONNA MATILDA (*impatiently*): No, it's not that, Doctor. It's not like that! It's not like that!

DOCTOR: Why isn't it, may I ask?

DONNA MATILDA (*with decision but trembling*): I am perfectly certain he recognized me!

DOCTOR: It's not possible . . . it's not possible!

BELCREDI (*at the same time*): Of course not!

DONNA MATILDA (*more than ever determined, almost convulsively*): I tell you, he recognized me! When he came close up to speak to me—looking in my eyes, right into my eyes—he recognized me!

BELCREDI: But he was talking of your daughter!

DONNA MATILDA: That's not true! He was talking of me! Of me!

BELCREDI: Yes, perhaps, when he said . . .

DONNA MATILDA (*letting herself go*): About my dyed hair! But didn't you notice that he added at once: "or the memory of your dark hair, if you were dark"? He remembered perfectly well that I was dark—then!

BELCREDI: Nonsense! nonsense!

DONNA MATILDA (*not listening to him, turning to the* DOCTOR): My hair, Doctor, is really dark—like my daughter's! That's why he spoke of her.

BELCREDI: But he doesn't even know your daughter! He's never seen her!

DONNA MATILDA: Exactly! Oh, you never understand anything! By my daughter, stupid, he meant me—as I was then!

BELCREDI: Oh, this is catching! This is catching, this madness!

DONNA MATILDA (*softly, with contempt*): Fool!

BELCREDI: Excuse me, were you ever his wife? Your daughter is his wife —in his delirium: Bertha of Susa.

DONNA MATILDA: Exactly! Because I, no longer dark—as he remembered me—but *fair*, introduced myself as "Adelaide," the mother. My daughter doesn't exist for him: he's never seen her—you said so yourself! So how can he know whether she's fair or dark?

BELCREDI: But he said dark, speaking generally, just as anyone who wants to recall, whether fair or dark, a memory of youth in the color of the hair! And you, as usual, begin to imagine things! Doctor, you said I ought not to have come! It's she who ought not to have come!

DONNA MATILDA (*upset for a moment by* BELCREDI'S *remark, recovers herself. Then with a touch of anger, because doubtful*). No, no . . . he spoke of me . . . He spoke all the time to me, with me, of me . . .

BELCREDI: That's not bad! He didn't leave me a moment's breathing space; and you say he was talking all the time to you? Unless you think he was alluding to you too, when he was talking to Peter Damiani!

DONNA MATILDA (*defiantly, almost exceeding the limits of courteous discussion*): Who knows? Can you tell me why, from the outset, he showed a strong dislike for you, for you alone? (*From the tone of the question, the expected answer must almost explicitly be: "because he understands you are my lover."* BELCREDI *feels this so well that he remains silent and can say nothing.*)

DOCTOR: The reason may also be found in the fact that only the visit of the Duchess Adelaide and the Abbot of Cluny was announced to him. Finding a third person present, who had not been announced, at once his suspicions . . .

BELCREDI: Yes, exactly! His suspicion made him see an enemy in me: Peter Damiani! But she's got it into her head, that he recognized her . . .

DONNA MATILDA: There's no doubt about it! I could see it from his eyes, doctor. You know, there's a way of looking that leaves no doubt whatever . . . Perhaps it was only for an instant, but I am sure!

DOCTOR: It is not impossible: a lucid moment . . .

DONNA MATILDA: Yes, perhaps . . . And then his speech seemed to me full of regret for his and my youth—for the horrible thing that happened to him, that has held him in that disguise from which he has never been able to free himself, and from which he longs to be free—he said so himself!

BELCREDI: Yes, so as to be able to make love to your daughter, or you, as you believe—having been touched by your pity.

DONNA MATILDA: Which is very great, I would ask you to believe.

BELCREDI: As one can see, Marchioness; so much so that a miracle-worker might expect a miracle from it!

DOCTOR: Will you let me speak? I don't work miracles, because I am a doctor and not a miracle-worker. I listened very intently to all he said; and I repeat that that certain analogical elasticity, common to all systematized delirium, is evidently with him much . . . what shall I say?—much relaxed! The elements, that is, of his delirium no longer hold together. It seems to me he has lost the equilibrium of his second personality and sudden recollections drag him—and this is very comforting—not from a state of incipient apathy, but rather from a morbid inclination to reflective melancholy, which shows a . . . a very considerable cerebral activity. Very comforting, I repeat! Now if, by this violent trick we've planned . . .

DONNA MATILDA (*turning to the window, in the tone of a sick person complaining*): But how is it that the motor has not returned? It's three hours and a half since . . .

DOCTOR: What do you say?

DONNA MATILDA: The motor, Doctor! It's more than three hours and a half . . .

DOCTOR (*taking out his watch and looking at it*): Yes, more than four hours, by this!

DONNA MATILDA: It could have reached here an hour ago at least! But, as usual . . .

BELCREDI: Perhaps they can't find the dress . . .

DONNA MATILDA: But I explained exactly where it was! (*Impatiently.*) And Frida . . . where is Frida?

BELCREDI (*looking out of the window*): Perhaps she is in the garden with Charles . . .

DOCTOR: He'll talk her out of her fright.

BELCREDI: She's not afraid, Doctor; don't you believe it: the thing bores her rather . . .

DONNA MATILDA: Just don't ask anything of her! I know what she's like.

DOCTOR: Let's wait patiently. Anyhow, it will soon be over, and it has to be in the evening . . . It will only be the matter of a moment! If we can succeed in rousing him, as I was saying, and in breaking at one go the threads—already slack—which still bind him to this fiction of his, giving him back what he himself asks for—you remember, he said: "one cannot always be twenty-six years old, madam!" if we can give him freedom from this torment, which even *he* feels is a torment, then if he is able to recover at one bound the sensation of the distance of time . . .

BELCREDI (*quickly*): He'll be cured! (*Then emphatically with irony.*) We'll pull him out of it all!

DOCTOR: Yes, we may hope to set him going again, like a watch which has stopped at a certain hour . . . just as if we had our watches in our hands and were waiting for that other watch to go again.—A shake—so—and let's hope it'll tell the time again after its long stop. (*At this point the* MARQUIS CHARLES DI NOLLI *enters from the principal entrance.*)

DONNA MATILDA: Oh, Charles! . . . And Frida? Where is she?

DI NOLLI: She'll be here in a moment.

DOCTOR: Has the motor arrived?

DI NOLLI: Yes.

DONNA MATILDA: Yes? Has the dress come?

DI NOLLI: It's been here some time.

DOCTOR: Good! Good!

DONNA MATILDA (*trembling*): Where is she? Where's Frida?

DI NOLLI (*shrugging his shoulders and smiling sadly, like one lending himself unwillingly to an untimely joke*): You'll see, you'll see! . . . (*Pointing towards the hall.*) Here she is! . . . (BERTHOLD *appears at the threshold of the hall, and announces with solemnity.*)

BERTHOLD: Her Highness the Countess Matilda of Canossa! (FRIDA *enters, magnificent and beautiful, arrayed in the robes of her mother as* "*Countess Matilda of Tuscany,*" *so that she is a living copy of the portrait in the throne room.*)

FRIDA (*passing* BERTHOLD, *who is bowing, says to him with disdain*): Of Tuscany, of Tuscany! Canossa is just one of my castles!

BELCREDI (*in admiration*): Look! Look! She seems another person . . .

DONNA MATILDA: One would say it were I! Look!—Why, Frida, look! She's exactly my portrait, alive!

DOCTOR: Yes, yes . . . Perfect! Perfect! The portrait, to the life.

BELCREDI: Yes, there's no question about it. She *is* the portrait! Magnificent!

FRIDA: Don't make me laugh, or I shall burst! I say, mother, what a tiny waist you had? I had to squeeze so to get into this!

DONNA MATILDA (*arranging her dress a little*): Wait! . . . Keep still! . . . These pleats . . . is it really so tight?

FRIDA: I'm suffocating! I implore you, to be quick! . . .

DOCTOR: But we must wait till it's evening!

FRIDA: No, no, I can't hold out till evening!

DONNA MATILDA: Why did you put it on so soon?

FRIDA: The moment I saw it, the temptation was irresistible . . .

DONNA MATILDA: At least you could have called me, or have had someone help you! It's still all crumpled.

FRIDA: So I saw, mother; but they are old creases; they won't come out.

DOCTOR: It doesn't matter, Marchioness! The illusion is perfect. (*Then coming nearer and asking her to come in front of her daughter, without*

Luigi Pirandello: *Henry IV*

hiding her.) If you please, stay there, there . . . at a certain distance . . . now a little more forward . . .

BELCREDI: For the feeling of the distance of time . . .

DONNA MATILDA (*slightly turning to him*): Twenty years after! A disaster! A tragedy!

BELCREDI: Now don't let's exaggerate!

DOCTOR (*embarrased, trying to save the situation*): No, no! I meant the dress . . . so as to see . . . You know . . .

BELCREDI (*laughing*): Oh, as for the dress, Doctor, it isn't a matter of twenty years! It's eight hundred! An abyss! Do you really want to shove him across it (*Pointing first to* FRIDA *and then to* MARCHIONESS.) from there to here? But you'll have to pick him up in pieces with a basket! Just think now: for us it is a matter of twenty years, a couple of dresses, and a masquerade. But, if, as you say, Doctor, time has stopped for and around him: if he lives there (*Pointing to* FRIDA.) with her, eight hundred years ago . . . I repeat: the giddiness of the jump will be such, that finding himself suddenly among us . . . (*The* DOCTOR *shakes his head in dissent.*) You don't think so?

DOCTOR: No, because life, my dear baron, can take up its rhythms. This —our life—will at once become real also to him; and will pull him up directly, wresting from him suddenly the illusion, ,and showing him that the eight hundred years, as you say, are only twenty! It will be like one of those tricks, such as the leap into space, for instance, of the Masonic rite, which appears to be heaven knows how far, and is only a step down the stairs.

BELCREDI: Ah! An idea! Yes! Look at Frida and the Marchioness, doctor! Which is more advanced in time? We old people, Doctor! The young ones think they are more ahead; but it isn't true: we are more ahead, because time belongs to us more than to them.

DOCTOR: If the past didn't alienate us . . .

BELCREDI: It doesn't matter at all! How does it alienate us? They (*Pointing to* FRIDA *and* DI NOLLI.) have still to do what we have accomplished, Doctor: to grow old, doing the same foolish things, more or less, as we did . . . This is the illusion: that one comes forward through a door to life. It isn't so! As soon as one is born, one starts dying; therefore, he who started first is the most advanced of all. The youngest of us is father Adam! Look there: (*Pointong to* FRIDA.) eight hundred years younger than all of us—the Countess Matilda of Tuscany. (*He makes her a deep bow.*)

DI NOLLI: I say, Tito, don't start joking.

BELCREDI: Oh, you think I am joking? . . .

DI NOLLI: Of course, of course . . . all the time.

BELCREDI: Impossible! I've even dressed up as a Benedictine . . .

DI NOLLI: Yes, but for a serious purpose.
BELCREDI: Well, exactly. If it has been serious for the others . . . for Frida, now, for instance. (*Then turning to the* DOCTOR.) I swear, Doctor, I don't yet understand what you want to do.
DOCTOR (*annoyed*): You'll see! Let me do as I wish . . . At present you see the Marchioness still dressed as . . .
BELCREDI: Oh, she also . . . has to masquerade?
DOCTOR: Of course! of course! In another dress that's in there ready to be used when it comes into his head he sees the Countess Matilda of Canossa before him.
FRIDA (*while talking quietly to* DI NOLLI *notices the doctor's mistake*): Of Tuscany, of Tuscany!
DOCTOR: It's all the same!
BELCREDI: Oh, I see! He'll be faced by two of them . . .
DOCTOR: Two, precisely! And then . . .
FRIDA (*calling him aside*): Come here, doctor! Listen!
DOCTOR: Here I am! (*Goes near the two young people and pretends to give some explanations to them.*)
BELCREDI (*softly to* DONNA MATILDA): I say, this is getting rather strong, you know!
DONNA MATILA (*looking him firmly in the face*): What?
BELCREDI: Does it really interest you as much as all that—to make you willing to take part in . . . ? For a woman this is simply enormous! . . .
DONNA MATILDA: Yes, for an ordinary woman.
BELCREDI: Oh, no, my dear, for all women,—in a question like this! It's an abnegation.
DONNA MATILDA: I owe it to him.
BELCREDI: Don't lie! You know well enough it's not hurting you!
DONNA MATILDA: Well, then, where does the abnegation come in?
BELCREDI: Just enough to prevent you losing caste in other people's eyes —and just enough to offend me!
DONNA MATILDA: But who is worrying about you now?
DI NOLLI (*coming forward*): It's all right. It's all right. That's what we'll do! (*Turning towards* BERTHOLD.) Here you, go and call one of those fellows!
BERTHOLD: At once! (*Exit.*)
DONNA MATILDA: But first of all we've go to pretend that we are going away.
DI NOLLI: Exactly! I'll see to that . . . (*To* BELCREDI.) you don't mind staying here?
BELCREDI (*ironically*): Oh, no, I don't mind, I don't mind! . . .
DI NOLLI: We must look out not to make him suspicious again, you know.
BELCREDI: Oh, Lord! *He* doesn't amount to anything!
DOCTOR: He must believe absolutely that we've gone away. (LANDOLPH

followed by BERTHOLD *enters from the right.*)

LANDOLPH: May I come in?

DI NOLLI: Come in! Come in; I say—your name's Lolo, isn't it?

LANDOLPH: Lolo, or Landolph, just as you like!

DI NOLLI: Well, look here: the Doctor and the Marchioness are leaving, at once.

LANDOLPH: Very well. All we've got to say is that they have been able to obtain the permission for the reception from His Holiness. He's in there in his own apartments repenting of all he said—and in an awful state to have the pardon! Would you mind coming a minute? . . . If you would, just for a minute . . . put on the dress again . . .

DOCTOR: Why, of course, with pleasure . . .

LANDOLPH: Might I be allowed to make a suggestion? Why not add that the Marchioness of Tuscany has interceded with the Pope that he should be received?

DONNA MATILDA: You see, he has recognized me!

LANDOLPH: Forgive me . . . I don't know my history very well. I am sure you gentlemen know it much better! But I thought it was believed that Henry IV had a secret passion for the Marchioness of Tuscany.

DONNA MATILDA (*at once*): Nothing of the kind! Nothing of the kind!

LANDOLPH: That's what I thought! But he says he's loved her . . . he's always saying it . . . And now he fears that her indignation for this secret love of his will work him harm with the Pope.

BELCREDI: We must let him understand that this aversion no longer exists.

LANDOLPH: Exactly! Of course!

DONNA MATILDA (*to* BELCREDI): History says—I don't know whether you know it or not—that the Pope gave way to the supplications of the Marchioness Matilda and the Abbot of Cluny. And I may say, my dear Belcredi, that I intended to take advantage of this fact—at the time of the pageant—to show him my feelings were not so hostile to him as he supposed.

BELCREDI: You are most faithful to history, Marchioness . . .

LANDOLPH: Well then, the Marchioness could spare herself a double disguise and present herself with Monsignor (*Indicating the* DOCTOR.) as the Marchioness of Tuscany.

DOCTOR (*quickly, energetically*): No, no! That won't do at all. It would ruin everything. The impression from the confrontation must be a sudden one, give a shock! No, no, Marchioness, you will appear again as the Duchess Adelaide, the mother of the Empress. And then we'll go away. This is most necessary: that he should know we've gone away. Come on! Don't let's waste any more time! There's a lot to prepare.

(*Exeunt the* DOCTOR, DONNA MATILDA, *and* LANDOLPH, *right.*)

FRIDA: I am beginning to feel afraid again.
DI NOLLI: Again, Frida?
FRIDA: It would have been better if I had seen him before.
DI NOLLI: There's nothing to be frightened of, really.
FRIDA: He isn't furious, is he?
DI NOLLI: Of course not! he's quite calm.
BELCREDI (*with ironic sentimental affectation*): Melancholy! Didn't you hear that he loves you?
FRIDA: Thanks! That's just why I am afraid.
BELCREDI: He won't do you any harm.
DI NOLLI: It'll only last a minute...
FRIDA: Yes, but there in the dark with him...
DI NOLLI: Only for a moment; and I will be near you, and all the others behind the door ready to run in. As soon as you see your mother, your part will be finished...
BELCREDI: I'm afraid of a different thing: that we're wasting our time...
DI NOLLI: Don't begin again! The remedy seems a sound one to me.
FRIDA: I think so too! I feel it! I'm all trembling!
BELCREDI: But, mad people, my dear friends—though they don't know it, alas—have this felicity which we don't take into account...
DI NOLLI (*interrupting, annoyed*): What felicity? Nonsense!
BELCREDI (*forcefully*): They don't reason!
DI NOLLI: What's reasoning got to do with it, anyway?
BELCREDI: Don't you call it reasoning that he will have to do—according to us—when he sees her (*Indicates* FRIDA.) and her mother? We've reasoned it all out, surely!
DI NOLLI: Nothing of the kind: no reasoning at all! We put before him a double image of his own fantasy, or fiction, as the doctor says.
BELCREDI (*suddenly*): I say, I've never understood why they take degrees in medicine.
DI NOLLI (*amazed*): Who?
BELCREDI: The alienists!
DI NOLLI: What ought they to take degrees in, then?
FRIDA: If they are alienists, in what else should they take degrees?
BELCREDI: In law, of course! All a matter of talk! The more they talk, the more highly they are considered. "Analogous elasticity," "the sensation of distance in time!" And the first thing they tell you is that they don't work miracles—when a miracle's just what is wanted! But they know that the more they say they are not miracleworkers, the more folk believe in their seriousness!
BERTHOLD (*who has been looking through the keyhole of the door on right*): There they are! There they are! They're coming in here.
DI NOLLI: Are they?

BERTHOLD: He wants to come with them... Yes!... He's coming too!
DI NOLLI: Let's get away, then! Let's get away, at once! (*To* BERTHOLD.) You stop here!
BERTHOLD: Must I?

(*Without answering him,* DI NOLLI, FRIDA, *and* BELCREDI *go out by the main exit, leaving* BERTHOLD *surprised. The door on the right opens, and* LANDOLPH *enters first, bowing. Then* DONNA MATILDA *comes in, with mantle and ducal crown as in the first act; also the* DOCTOR *as the Abbot of Cluny.* HENRY IV *is among them in royal dress.* ORDULPH *and* HAROLD *enter last of all.*)

HENRY IV (*following up what he has been saying in the other room*): And now I will ask you a question: how can I be astute, if you think me obstinate?
DOCTOR: No, no, not obstinate!
HENRY IV (*smiling, pleased*): Then you think me really astute?
DOCTOR: No, no, neither obstinate, nor astute.
HENRY IV (*with benevolent irony*): Monsignor, if obstinacy is not a vice which can go with astuteness, I hoped that in denying me the former, you would at least allow me a little of the latter. I can assure you I have great need of it. But if you want to keep it all for yourself...
DOCTOR: I? I? Do I seem astute to you?
HENRY IV: No. Monsignor! What do you say? Not in the least! Perhaps in this case, I may seem a little obstinate to you (*Cutting short to speak to* DONNA MATILDA.) With your permission: a word in confidence to the Duchess. (*Leads her aside and asks her very earnestly.*) Is your daughter really dear to you?
DONNA MATILDA (*dismayed*): Why, yes, certainly...
HENRY IV: Do you wish me to compensate her with all my love, with all my devotion, for the grave wrongs I have done her—though you must not believe all the stories my enemies tell about my dissoluteness!
DONNA MATILDA: No, no, I don't believe them. I never have believed such stories.
HENRY IV: Well, then are you willing?
DONNA MATILDA (*confused*): What?
HENRY IV: That I return to love your daughter again? (*Looks at her and adds, in a mysterious tone of warning.*) You mustn't be a friend of the Marchioness of Tuscany!
DONNA MATILDA: I tell you again that she has begged and tried not less than ourselves to obtain your pardon...
HENRY IV (*softly, but excitedly*): Don't tell me that! Don't say that to me! Don't you see the effect it has on me, my Lady?

DONNA MATILDA (*looks a him; then very softly as if in confidence*): You love her still?
HENRY IV (*puzzled*): Still? Still, you say? You know, then? But nobody knows! Nobody must know!
DONNA MATILDA: But perhaps she knows, if she has begged so hard for you!
HENRY IV (*looks at her and says*): And you love your daughter? (*Brief pause. He turns to the* DOCTOR *with laughing accents.*) Ah, Monsignor, it's strange how little I think of my wife! It may be a sin, but I swear to you that I hardly feel her at all in my heart. What is stranger is that her own mother scarcely feels her in her heart. Confess, my Lady, that she amounts to very little for you. (*Turning to* DOCTOR.) She talks to me of that other woman, insistently, insistently, I don't know why! ...
LANDOLPH (*humbly*): Maybe, Majesty, it is to disabuse you of some ideas you have had about the Marchioness of Tuscany. (*Then, dismayed at having allowed himself this observation, adds.*) I mean just now, of course ...
HENRY IV: You too maintain that she has been friendly to me?
LANDOLPH: Yes, at the moment, Majesty.
DONNA MATILDA: Exactly! Exactly! ...
HENRY IV: I understand. That is to say, you don't believe I love her. I see! I see! Nobody's ever believed it, nobody's ever thought it. Better so, then! But enough, enough! (*Turns to the* DOCTOR *with changed expression.*) Monsignor, you see? The reasons the Pope has had for revoking the excommunication have got nothing at all to do with the reasons for which he excommunicated me originally. Tell Pope Gregory we shall meet again at Brixen. And you, Madame, should you chance to meet your daughter in the courtyard of the castle of your friend the Marchioness, ask her to visit me. We shall see if I succeed in keeping her close beside me as wife and Empress. Many women have presented themselves here already assuring me that they were she. And I thought to have her—yes, tried sometimes—there's no shame in it, with one's wife!—But when they said they were Bertha, and they were from Susa, all of them—I can't think why—started laughing! (*Confidentially.*) Understand?—in bed—I undressed—so did she—yes, by God, undressed—a man and a woman—it's natural after all! Like that, we don't bother much about who we are. And one's dress is like a phantom that hovers always near one. Oh, Monsignor, phantoms in general are nothing more than trifling disorders of the spirit: images we cannot contain within the bounds of sleep. They reveal themselves even when we are awake, and they frighten us. I ... ah ... I am always afraid when, at night time, I see disordered images before me. Sometimes I am even afraid of my own blood pulsing loudly

in my arteries in the silence of night, like the sound of a distant step in a lonely corridor! . . . But, forgive me! I have kept you standing too long already. I thank you, my Lady, I thank you, Monsignor. (DONNA MATILDA *and the* DOCTOR *go off bowing. As soon as they have gone,* HENRY IV *suddenly changes his tone.*) Buffoons, buffoons! One can play any tune on them! And that other fellow . . . Pietro Damiani! . . . Caught him out perfectly! He's afraid to appear before me again. (*Moves up and down excitedly while saying this; then sees* BERTHOLD, *and points him out to the other three valets.*) Oh, look at this imbecile watching me with his mouth wide open! (*Shakes him.*) Don't you understand? Don't you see, idiot, how I treat them, how I play the fool with them, make them appear before me just as I wish? Miserable, frightened clowns that they are! And you (*Addressing the* VALETS.) are amazed that I tear off their ridiculous masks now, just as if it wasn't I who had made them mask themselves to satisfy this taste of mine for playing the madman!

LANDOLPH—HAROLD—ORDULPH (*bewildered, looking at one another*): What? What does he say? What?

HENRY IV (*answers them imperiously*): Enough! enough! Let's stop it. I'm tired of it. (*Then as if the thought left him no peace.*) By God! The impudence! To come here along with her lover! . . . And pretending to do it out of pity! So as not to infuriate a poor devil already out of the world, out of time, out of life! If it hadn't been supposed to be done out of pity, one can well imagine that fellow wouldn't have allowed it. Those people expect others to behave as they wish all the time. And, of course, there's nothing arrogant in that! Oh, no! Oh, no! It's merely their way of thinking, of feeling, of seeing. Everybody has his own way of thinking; you fellows, too. Yours is that of a flock of sheep—miserable, feeble, uncertain . . . But those others take advantage of this and make you accept their way of thinking; or, at least, they suppose they do; because, after all, what do they succeed in imposing on you? Words, words which anyone can interpret in his own manner! That's the way public opinion is formed! And it's a bad look out for a man who finds himself labelled one day with one of these words which everyone repeats; for example "madman," or "imbecile." Don't you think it is rather hard for a man to keep quiet, when he knows that there is a fellow going about trying to persuade everybody that he is as he sees him, trying to fix him in other people's opinion as a "madman"—according to him? Now I am talking seriously! Before I hurt my head, falling from my horse . . . (*Stops suddenly, noticing the dismay of the four young men.*) What's the matter with you? (*Imitates their amazed looks.*) What? Am I, or am I not, mad? Oh, yes! I'm mad all right! (*He becomes terrible.*) Well, then, by God, down on your knees, down on your knees! (*Makes them go down on their knees one by one.*) I order you to go down on your knees before me! And touch the ground three times with your foreheads! Down, down! That's the way you've got to be before madmen! (*Then annoyed with their facile humiliation.*) Get up, sheep! You obeyed me, didn't you? You might have put the strait jacket on me! . . . Crush a man with the weight of a word—it's nothing—a fly! all our life is crushed by the weight of words: the weight of the dead. Look at me here: can you really suppose that Henry IV is still alive? All the same, I speak, and order you live men about! Do you think it's a joke that the dead continue to live?—Yes, *here* it's a joke! But get out into the live world!—Ah, you say: what a beautiful sunrise—for us! All time is before us!—Dawn! We will do what we like with this day—. Ah, yes! To Hell with tradition, the old conventions! Well, go on! You will do nothing but repeat the old, old words, while you imagine you are living! (*Goes up to* BERTHOLD *who has now become quite stupid.*) You don't understand a word of this, do you? What's your name?

BERTHOLD: I? . . . What? . . . Berthold . . .

HENRY IV: Poor Berthold! What's your name here?

BERTHOLD: I . . . I . . . my name is Fino.

HENRY IV (*feeling the warning and critical glances of the others, turns to them to reduce them to silence*): Fino?

BERTHOLD: Fino Pagliuca, sire.

HENRY IV (*turning to* LANDOLPH): I've heard you call each other by your nick-names often enough! Your name is Lolo, isn't it?

LANDOLPH: Yes, sire . . . (*Then with a sense of immense joy.*) Oh Lord! Oh Lord! Then he is not mad . . .

HENRY IV (*brusquely*): What?

LANDOLPH (*hesitating*): No . . . I said . . .

HENRY IV: Not mad, any more. No. Don't you see? We're having a joke on those that think I am mad! (*To* HAROLD.) I say, boy, your name's Franco . . . (*To* ORDULPH) And yours . . .

ORDULPH: Momo.

HENRY IV: Momo, Momo . . . A nice name that!

LANDOLPH: So he isn't . . .

HENRY IV: What are you talking about? Of course not! Let's have a jolly, good laugh! . . . (*Laughs.*) Ah! . . . Ah! . . . Ah! . . .

LANDOLPH—HAROLD—ORDULPH (*looking at each other half happy and half dismayed*): Then he's cured! . . . he's all right! . . .

HENRY IV: Silence! Silence! . . . (*To* BERTHOLD.) Why don't you laugh? Are you offended? I didn't mean it especially for you. It's convenient for everybody to insist that certain people are mad, so they can shut up. Do you know why? Because it's impossible to hear them speak! What shall I say of these people who've just gone away? That one is a whore, another a libertine, another a swindler . . . don't you think so?

You can't believe a word he says . . . don't you think so?—By the way, they all listen to me terrified. And why are they terrified, if what I say isn't true? Of course, you can't believe what madmen say—yet, at the same time, they stand there with their eyes wide open with terror!—Why? Tell me, tell me, why?—You see I'm quite calm now!

BERTHOLD: But, perhaps, they think that . . .

HENRY IV: No, no, my dear fellow! Look me well in the eyes! . . . I don't say that it's true—nothing is true, Berthold! But . . . look me in the eyes!

BERTHOLD: Well . . .

HENRY IV: You see? You see? . . . You have terror in your own eyes now because I seem mad to you! There's the proof of it. (*Laughs.*)

LANDOLPH (*coming forward in the name of the others, exasperated*): What proof?

HENRY IV: Your being so dismayed because now I seem again mad to you. You have thought me mad up to now, haven't you? You feel that this dismay of yours can become terror too—something to dash away the ground from under your feet and deprive you of the air you breathe! Do you know what it means to find yourselves face to face with a madman—with one who shakes the foundations of all you have built up in yourselves, your logic, the logic of all your constructions? Madmen, lucky folk! construct without logic, or rather with a logic that flies like a feather. Voluble! Voluble! Today like this and tomorrow—who knows? You say: "This cannot be"; but for them everything can be. You say: "This isn't true!" And why? Because it doesn't seem true to you, or you, or you . . . (*Indicates the three of them in succession.*) . . . and to a hundred thousand others! One must see what seems true to these hundred thousand others who are not supposed to be mad! What a magnificent spectacle they afford, when they reason! What flowers of logic they scatter! I know that when I was a child, I thought the moon in the pond was real. How many things I thought real! I believed everything I was told—and I was happy! Because it's a terrible thing if you don't hold on to that which seems true to you today—to that which will seem true to you tomorrow, even if it is the opposite of that which seemed true to you yesterday. I would never wish you to think, as I have done, on this horrible thing which really drives one mad: that if you were beside another and looking into his eyes—as I one day looked into somebody's eyes—you might as well be a beggar before a door never to be opened to you; for he who does enter there will never be you, but someone unknown to you with his own different and impenetrable world . . . (*Long pause. Darkness gathers in the room, increasing the sense of strangeness and consternation in which the four young men are involved.* HENRY IV *remains aloof, pondering on the misery which is not only his, but everybody's. Then he pulls himself up, and says in an ordinary tone.*) It's getting dark here . . .

ORDULPH: Shall I go for a lamp?

HENRY IV (*ironically*): The lamp, yes the lamp! . . . Do you suppose I don't know that as soon as I turn my back with my oil lamp to go to bed, you turn on the electric light for yourselves, here, and even there, in the throne room? I pretend not to see it!

ORDULPH: Well, then, shall I turn it on now?

HENRY IV: No, it would blind me! I want my lamp!

ORDULPH: It's ready here behind the door. (*Goes to the main exit, opens the door, goes out for a moment, and returns with an ancient lamp which is held by a ring at the top.*)

HENRY IV: Ah, a little light! Sit there around the table, no, not like that; in an elegant, easy, manner! . . . (*To* HAROLD.) Yes, you, like that! (*Poses him.*) (*Then to* BERTHOLD.) You, so ! . . . and I, here! (*Sits opposite them.*) We could do with a little decorative moonlight. It's very useful for us, the moonlight. I feel a real necessity for it, and pass a lot of time looking up at the moon from my window. Who would think, to look at her that she knows that eight hundred years have passed, and that I, seated at the window, cannot really be Henry IV gazing at the moon like any poor devil? But, look, look! See what a magnificent night scene we have here: the emperor surrounded by his faithful counsellors! . . . How do you like it?

LANDOLPH (*softly to* HAROLD, *so as not to break the enchantment*): And to think it wasn't true! . . .

HENRY IV: True? What wasn't true?

LANDOLPH (*timidly as if to excuse himself*): No . . . I mean . . . I was saying this morning to him (*Indicates* BERTHOLD.)—he has just entered on service here—I was saying: what a pity that dressed like this and with so many beautiful costumes in the wardrobe . . . and with a room like that . . . (*Indicates the throne room.*)

HENRY IV: Well? what's the pity?

LANDOLPH: Well . . . that we didn't know . . .

HENRY IV: That it was all done in jest, this comedy?

LANDOLPH: Because we thought that . . .

HAROLD (*coming to his assistance*): Yes . . . that it was done seriously!

HENRY IV: What do you say? Doesn't it seem serious to you?

LANDOLPH: But if you say that . . .

HENRY IV: I say that—you are fools! You ought to have known how to create a fantasy for yourselves, not to act it for me, or anyone coming to see me; but naturally, simply, day by day, before nobody, feeling yourselves alive in the history of the eleventh century, here at the court of your emperor, Henry IV! You, Ordulph (*Taking him by the arm.*), alive in the castle of Goslar, waking up in the morning, getting out of bed, and entering straightway into the dream, clothing yourself in the dream that would be no more a dream, because you would have lived it, felt it all alive in you. You would have drunk it in with the air you breathed; yet knowing all the time that it was a dream, so you could better enjoy the privilege afforded you of having to do nothing else but live this dream, this far off and yet actual dream! And to think that at a distance of eight centuries from this remote age of ours, so colored and so sepulchral, the men of the twentieth century are torturing themselves in ceaseless anxiety to know how their fates and fortunes will work out! Whereas you are already in history with me . . .

LANDOLPH: Yes, yes, very good!

HENRY IV: . . . Everything determined, everything settled!

ORDULPH: Yes, yes!

HENRY IV: And sad as is my lot, hideous as some of the events are, bitter the struggles and troublous the time—still all history! All history that cannot change, understand? All fixed for ever! And you could have admired at your ease how every effect followed obediently its cause with perfect logic, how every event took place precisely and coherently in each minute particular! The pleasure, the pleasure of history, in fact, which is so great, was yours.

LANDOLPH: Beautiful, beautiful!

HENRY IV: Beautiful, but it's finished! Now that you know, I could not do it any more! (*Takes his lamp to go to bed.*) Neither could you, if up to now you haven't understood the reason of it! I am sick of it now. (*Almost to himself with violent contained rage.*) By God, I'll make her sorry she came here! Dressed herself up as a mother-in-law for me . . . ! And he as an abbot . . . ! And they bring a doctor with them to study me . . . ! Who knows if they don't hope to cure me? . . . Clowns . . . ! I'd like to smack one of them at least in the face: yes that one—a famous swordsman, they say! . . . He'll kill me . . . Well, we'll see, we'll see! . . . (*A knock at the door.*) Who is it?

THE VOICE OF JOHN: Deo Gratias!

HAROLD (*very pleased at the chance for another joke*): Oh, it's John, it's old John, who comes every night to play the monk.

ORDULPH (*rubbing his hands*): Yes, yes! Let's make him do it!

HENRY IV (*at once, severely*): Fool, why? Just to play a joke on a poor old man who does it for love of me?

LANDOLPH (*to* ORDULPH): It has to be as if it were true.

HENRY IV: Exactly,, as if true! Because, only so, truth is not a jest (*Opens the door and admits* JOHN *dressed as a humble friar with a roll of parchment under his arm.*) Come in, come in, father! (*Then assuming a tone of tragic gravity and deep resentment.*) All the documents of my life and reign favorable to me were destroyed deliberately by my enemies.

One only has escaped destruction, this, my life, written by a humble monk who is devoted to me. And you would laugh at him! (*Turns affectionately to* JOHN, *and invites him to sit down at the table.*) Sit down, father, sit down! Have the lamp near you! (*Puts the lamp near him.*) Write! Write!

JOHN (*opens the parchment and prepares to write from dictation*): I am ready, your Majesty!

HENRY IV (*dictating*): "The decree of peace proclaimed at Mayence helped the poor and the good, while it damaged the powerful and the bad. (*Curtain begins to fall.*) It brought wealth to the former, hunger and misery to the latter . . ."

Curtain

ACT III

(The throne room so dark that the wall at the bottom is hardly seen. The canvases of the two portraits have been taken away; and, within their frames, FRIDA, dressed as the "Marchioness of Tuscany" and CHARLES DI NOLLI, as "Henry IV," have taken the exact positions of the portraits.

For a moment, after the raising of curtain, the stage is empty. Then the door on the left opens; and HENRY IV, holding the lamp by the ring on top of it, enters. He looks back to speak to the four young men, who, with JOHN, are presumably in the adjoining hall, as at the end of the second act.)

HENRY IV: No, stay where you are, stay where you are. I shall manage all right by myself. Good night! (*Closes the door and walks, very sad and tired, across the hall towards the second door on the right, which leads into his apartments.*)

FRIDA (*as soon as she sees that he has just passed the throne, whispers from the niche like one who is on the point of fainting away with fright*): Henry . . .

HENRY IV: (*stopping at the voice as if someone had stabbed him traitorously in the back, turns a terror-stricken face towards the wall at the bottom of the room; raising an arm instinctively, as if to defend himself and ward off a blow*): Who is calling me? (*It is not a question, but an exclamation vibrating with terror, which does not expect a reply from the darkness and the terrible silence of the hall, which suddenly fills him with the suspicion that he is really mad.*)

FRIDA (*at his shudder of terror, is herself not less frightened at the part she is playing, and repeats a little more loudly*): Henry! . . . (*But, although*

Luigi Pirandello: *Henry IV*   *437*

she wishes to act the part as they have given it to her, she stretches her head a little out of the frame towards the other frame.)
HENRY IV (*gives a dreadful cry; lets the lamp fall from his hands to cover his head with his arms, and makes a movement as if to run away*).
FRIDA (*jumping from the frame on to the stand and shouting like a madwoman*): Henry! . . . Henry! . . . I'm afraid! . . . I'm terrified! . . .

(*And while* DI NOLLI *jumps in turn on to the stand and thence to the floor and runs to* FRIDA *who, on the verge of fainting, continues to cry out, the* DOCTOR, DONNA MATILDA, *also dressed as "Matilda of Tuscany,"* TITO BELCREDI, LANDOLPH, BERTHOLD *and* JOHN *enter the hall from the doors on the right and on the left. One of them turns on the light: a strange light coming from lamps hidden in the ceiling so that only the upper part of the stage is well lighted. The others without taking notice of* HENRY IV, *who looks on astonihed by the unexpected inrush, after the moment of terror which still causes him to tremble, run anxiously to support and comfort the still shaking* FRIDA, *who is moaning in the arms of her fiancé. All are speaking at the same time.*)

DI NOLLI: No, no, Frida . . . Here I am . . . I am beside you!
DOCTOR (*coming with the others*): Enough! Enough! Theres nothing more to be done! . . .
DONNA MATILDA: He is cured, Frida. Look! He is cured! Don't you see?
DI NOLLI (*astonished*): Cured?
BELCREDI: It was only for fun! Be calm!
FRIDA: No! I am afraid! I am afraid!
DONNA MATILDA: Afraid of what? Look at him! He was never mad at all! . . .
DI NOLLI: That isn't true! What are you saying? Cured?
DOCTOR: It appears so. I should say so . . .
BELCREDI: Yes, yes! They have told us so. (*Pointing to the four young men.*)
DONNA MATILDA: Yes, for a long time! He has confided in them, told them the truth!
DI NOLLI (*now more indignant than astonished*): But what does it mean? If, up to a short time ago . . . ?
BELCREDI: Hum! He was acting, to take you in and also us, who in good faith . . .
DI NOLLI: Is it possible? To deceive his sister, also, right up to the time of her death?
HENRY IV (*remains apart, peering at one and now at the other under the accusation and the mockery of what all believe to be a cruel joke of his, which is now revealed. He has shown by the flashing of his eyes that he is meditating a revenge, which his violent contempt prevents*

him from defining clearly, as yet. Stung to the quick and with a clear idea of accepting the fiction they have insidiously worked up as true, he bursts forth at this point): Go on, I say! Go on!

DI NOLLI (astonished at the cry): Go on! What do you mean?

HENRY IV: It isn't *your* sister only that is dead!

DI NOLLI: My sister? Yours, I say, whom you compelled up to the last moment, to present herself here as your mother Agnes!

HENRY IV: And was she not *your* mother?

DI NOLLI: My mother? Certainly my mother!

HENRY IV: But your mother is dead for me, *old and far away!* You have just got down now from there. (*Pointing to the frame from which he jumped down.*) And how do you know whether I have not wept her long in secret, dressed even as I am?

DONNA MATILDA (*dismayed, looking at the others*): What does he say? (*Much impressed, observing him.*) Quietly! quietly, for Heaven's sake!

HENRY IV: What do I say? I ask all of you if Agnes was not the mother of Henry IV? (*Turns to* FRIDA *as if she were really the "Marchioness of Tuscany."*) You, Marchioness, it seems to me, ought to know.

FRIDA (*still frightened, draws closer to* DI NOLLI): No, no, I don't know. Not I!

DOCTOR: It's the madness returning.... Quiet now, everybody!

BELCREDI (*indignant*): Madness indeed, Doctor! He's acting again! ...

HENRY IV (*suddenly*): I? You have emptied those two frames over there, and he stands before my eyes as Henry IV ...

BELCREDI: We've had enough of this joke now.

HENRY IV: Who said joke?

DOCTOR (*loudly to* BELCREDI): Don't excite him, for the love of God!

BELCREDI (*without lending an ear to him, but speaking louder*): But they have said so (*Pointing again to the four young men.*), they, they!

HENRY IV (*turning round and looking at them*): You? Did you say it was all a joke?

LANDOLPH (*timid and embarrassed*): No ... really we said that you were cured.

BELCREDI: Look here! Enough of this! (*To* DONNA MATILDA.) Doesn't it seem to you that the sight of him, (*Pointing to* DI NOLLI.) Marchioness, and that of your daughter dressed so, is becoming an intolerable puerility?

DONNA MATILDA: Oh, be quiet! What does the dress matter, if he is cured?

HENRY IV: Cured, yes! I am cured! (*To* BELCREDI.) ah, but not to let it end this way all at once, as you suppose! (*Attacks him.*) Do you know that for twenty years nobody has ever dared to appear before me here like you and that gentleman? (*Pointing to the* DOCTOR.)

BELCREDI: Of course I know it. As a matter of fact, I too appeared before you this morning dressed ...

HENRY IV: As a monk, yes!

BELCREDI: And you took me for Peter Damiani! And I didn't even laugh. believing, in fact, that . . .

HENRY IV: That I was mad! Does it make you laugh seeing her like that, now that I am cured? And yet you might have remembered that in my eyes her appearance now . . . (*Interrupts himself with a gesture of contempt.*) Ah (*Suddenly turns to the* DOCTOR.) You are a doctor, aren't you?

DOCTOR: Yes.

HENRY IV: And you also took part in dressing her up as the Marchioness of Tuscany? To prepare a counter-joke for me here, eh?

DONNA MATILDA (*impetuously*): No, no! What do you say? It was done for you! I did it for your sake.

DOCTOR (*quickly*): To attempt, to try, not knowing . . .

HENRY IV (*cutting him short*): I understand. I say counter-joke, in his case (*Indicates* BELCREDI.) because he believes that I have been carrying on a jest . . .

BELCREDI: But excuse me, what do you mean? You say yourself you are cured.

HENRY IV: Let me speak! (*To the* DOCTOR.) Do you know, Doctor, that for a moment you ran the risk of making me mad again? By God, to make the portraits speak; to make them jump alive out of their frames . . .

DOCTOR: But you saw that all of us ran in at once, as soon as they told us . . .

HENRY IV: Certainly! (*Contemplates* FRIDA *and* DI NOLLI, *and then looks at the* MARCHIONESS, *and finally at his own costume.*) The combination is very beautiful . . . Two couples . . . Very good, very good, Doctor! For a madman, not bad! . . . (*With a slight wave of his hand to* BELCREDI:) It seems to him now to be a carnival out of season eh? (*Turns to look at him.*) We'll get rid now of this masquerade costume of mine, so that I may come away with you. What do you say?

BELCREDI: With me? With us?

HENRY IV: Where shall we go? To the Club? In dress coats and with white ties? Or shall both of us go to the Marchioness' house?

BELCREDI: Wherever you like! Do you want to remain here still, to continue—alone—what was nothing but the unfortunate joke of a day of carnival? It is really incredible, incredible how you have been able to do all this, freed from the disaster that befell you!

HENRY IV: Yes, you see how it was! The fact is that falling from my horse and striking my head as I did, I was really mad for I know not how long . . .

DOCTOR: Ah! Did it last long?

HENRY IV (*very quickly to the* DOCTOR): Yes, Doctor, a long time! I think it must have been about twelve years. (*Then suddenly turning to speak to* BELCREDI.) Thus I saw nothing, my dear fellow, of all that, after that day of carnival, happened for you but not for me: how things changed, how my friends deceived me, how my place was taken by another, and all the rest of it! And suppose my place had been taken in the heart of the woman I loved? . . . And how should I know who was dead or who had disappeared? . . . All this, you know, wasn't exactly a jest for me, as it seems to you . . .

BELCREDI: No, no! I don't mean that if you please. I mean after . . .

HENRY IV: Ah, yes? After? One day (*Stops and addresses the* DOCTOR.)—A most interesting case, Doctor! Study me well! Study me carefully! (*Trembles while speaking.*) All by itself, who knows how, one day the trouble here (*Touches his forehead.*) mended. Little by little, I open my eyes, and at first I don't know whether I am asleep or awake. Then I know I am awake. I touch this thing and that; I see clearly again . . . Ah!—then, as *he* says (*Alludes to* BELCREDI.) away, away with this masquerade, this incubus! Let's open the windows, breathe life once again! Away! Away! Let's run out! (*Suddenly pulling himself up.*) But where? And to do what? To show myself to all, secretly, as Henry IV, not like this, but arm in arm with you, among my dear friends?

BELCREDI: What are you saying?

DONNA MATILDA: Who could think it? It's not to be imagined. It was an accident.

HENRY IV: They all said I was mad before. (*To* BELCREDI.) And you know it! You were more ferocious than any one against those who tried to defend me.

BELCREDI: Oh, that was only a joke!

HENRY IV: Look at my hair. (*Shows him the hair on the nape of his neck.*)

BELCREDI: But mine is grey too!

HENRY IV: Yes, with this difference: that mine went grey here, as Henry IV, do you understand? And I never knew it! I perceived it all of a sudden, one day, when I opened my eyes; and I was terrified because I understood at once that not only had my hair gone grey, but that I was all grey, inside; that everything had fallen to pieces, that everything was finished; and I was going to arrive, hungry as a wolf, at a banquet which had already been cleared away . . .

BELCREDI: Yes, but, what about the others? . . .

HENRY IV (*quickly*): Ah, yes, I know! They couldn't wait until I was cured, not even those, who, behind my back, pricked my saddled horse till it bled. . . .

DI NOLLI (*agitated*): What, what?

HENRY IV: Yes, treacherously, to make it rear and cause me to fall.

DONNA MATILDA (*quickly, in horror*): This is the first time I knew that.

HENRY IV: That was also a joke, probably!

DONNA MATILDA: But who did it? Who was behind us then?

HENRY IV: It doesn't matter who it was. All those that went on feasting and were ready to leave me their scrapings, Marchioness, of miserable pity, or some dirty remnant of remorse in the filthy plate! Thanks! (*Turning quickly to the* DOCTOR.) Now, Doctor, the case must be absolutely new in the history of madness; I preferred to remain mad—since I found everything ready and at my disposal for this new exquisite fantasy. I would live it—this madness of mine—with the most lucid consciousness; and thus revenge myself on the brutality of a stone which had dinted my head. The solitude—this solitude—squalid and empty as it appeared to me when I opened my eyes again—I determined to deck it out with all the colors and splendors of that far off day of carnival, when you (*Looks at* DONNA MATILDA *and points* FRIDA *out to her.*) —when you, Marchioness, triumphed. So I would oblige all those who were around me to follow, by God, at my orders that famous pageant which had been—for you and not for me—the jest of a day. I would make it become—for ever—no more a joke but a reality, the reality of a real madness: here, all in masquerade, with throne room, and these my four secret counsellors: secret and, of course, traitors. (*He turns quickly towards them.*) I should like to know what you have gained by revealing the fact that I was cured! If I am cured, there's no longer any need of you, and you will be discharged! To give anyone one's confidence . . . that is really the act of a madman. But now I accuse you in my turn. (*Turning to the others.*) Do you know? They thought (*Alludes to the* VALETS.) they could make fun of me too with you. (*Bursts out laughing. The others laugh, but shamefacedly, except* DONNA MATILDA.)

BELCREDI (*to* DI NOLLI): Well, imagine that . . . That's not bad . . .

DI NOLLI (*to the* FOUR YOUNG MEN): You?

HENRY IV: We must pardon them. This dress (*Plucking his dress.*) which is for me the evident, involuntary caricature of that other continuous, everlasting masquerade, of which we are the involuntary puppets (*Indicates* BELCREDI.), when, without knowing it, we mask ourselves with that which we appear to be . . . ah, that dress of theirs, this masquerade of theirs, of course, we must forgive it them, since they do not yet see it is identical with themselves . . . (*Turning again to* BELCREDI.) You know, it is quite easy to get accustomed to it. One walks about as a tragic character, just as if it were nothing . . . (*Imitates the tragic manner.*) in a room like this . . . Look here, doctor! I remember a priest, certainly Irish, a nice-looking priest, who was sleeping in the sun one November day, with his arm on the corner of the bench of a public garden. He was lost in the golden delight of the mild sunny air which must have seemed for him almost summery. One may be sure that in that moment he did not know any more that he was a priest, or even where he was. He was dreaming . . . A little boy passed with a flower in his hand. He touched the priest wtih it here on the neck. I saw him open his laughing eyes, while all his mouth smiled with the beauty of his dream. He was forgetful of everything . . . But all at once, he pulled himself together, and stretched out his priest's cassock; and there came back to his eyes the same seriousness which you have seen in mine; because the Irish priests defend the seriousness of their Catholic faith with the same zeal with which I defend the sacred rights of hereditary monarchy! I am cured, gentlemen: because I can act the madman to perfection, here; and I do it very quietly. I'm only sorry for you that have to live your madness so agitatedly, without knowing it or seeing it.

BELCREDI: It comes to this, then, that it is we who are mad. That's what it is!

HENRY IV *(containing his irritation)*: But if you weren't mad, both you and she *(Indicating the* MARCHIONESS.*)* would you have come here to see me?

BELCREDI: To tell the truth, I came here believing that you were the madman.

HENRY IV *(suddenly indicating the* MARCHIONESS*)*: And she?

BELCREDI: Ah, as for her . . . I can't say. I see she is all fascinated by your words, by this *conscious* madness of yours. *(Turns to her.)* Dressed as you are *(Speaking to her.)*, you could even remain here to live it out, Marchioness.

DONNA MATILDA: You are insolent!

HENRY IV *(conciliatingly)*: No, Marchioness, what he means to say is that the miracle would be complete, according to him, with you here, who —as the Marchioness of Tuscany, you well know,—could not be my friend, save, as at Canossa, to give me a little pity . . .

BELCREDI: Or even more than a little! She said so herself!

HENRY IV *(to the* MARCHIONESS, *continuing)*: And even, shall we say, a little remorse! . . .

BELCREDI: Yes, that too she has admitted.

DONNA MATILDA *(angry)*: Now look here . . .

HENRY IV *(quickly, to placate her)*: Don't bother about him! Don't mind him! Let him go on infuriating me—though the Doctor's told him not to. *(Turns to* BELCREDI.*)* But do you suppose I am going to trouble myself any more about what happened between us—the share you had in my misfortune with her *(Indicates the* MARCHIONESS *to him and pointing* BELCREDI *out to her.)* the part he has now in your life? This is my life! Quite a different thing from your life! Your life, the life in which you have grown old—I have not lived that life. *(To* DONNA MATILDA.*)* Was this what you wanted to show me with this sacrifice of yours, dressing yourself up like this, according to the Doctor's idea? Excellently done, Doctor! Oh, an excellent idea:—"As we were then, eh? and as we are now?" But I am not a madman according to your way of thinking, Doctor. I know very well that that man there *(Indi-*

cates DI NOLLI.) cannot be me; because I am Henry IV, and have been, these twenty years, cast in this eternal masquerade. She has lived these years! (*Indicates the* MARCHIONESS.) She has enjoyed them and has become—look at her!—a woman I can no longer recognize. It is so that I knew her! (*Points to* FRIDA *and draws near her.*) This is the Marchioness I know, always this one! . . . You seem a lot of children to be so easily frightened by me . . . (*To* FRIDA.) And you're frightened too, little girl, aren't you, by the jest that they made you take part in—though they didn't understand it wouldn't be the jest they meant it to be, for me? Oh miracle of miracles! Prodigy of prodigies! The dream alive in you! More than alive in you! It was an image that wavered there and they've made you come to life! Oh, mine! You're mine, mine, mine, in my own right! (*He holds her in his arms, laughing like a madman, while all stand still terrified. Then as they advance to tear* FRIDA *from his arms, he becomes furious, terrible and cries imperiously to his* VALETS.) Hold them! Hold them! I order you to hold them!

(*The* FOUR YOUNG MEN *amazed, yet fascinated, move to execute his orders, automatically, and seize* DI NOLLI, *the* DOCTOR, *and* BELCREDI.)

BELCREDI (*freeing himself*): Leave her alone! Leave her alone! You're no madman!

HENRY IV (*in a flash draws the sword from the side of* LANDOLPH, *who is close to him*): I'm not mad, eh! Take that, you! . . . (*Drives sword into him. A cry of horror goes up. All rush over to assist* BELCREDI, *crying out together.*)

DI NOLLI: Has he wounded you?

BERTHOLD: Yes, yes, seriously!

DOCTOR: I told you so!

FRIDA: Oh God, oh God!

DI NOLLI: Frida, come here!

DONNA MATILDA: He's mad, mad!

DI NOLLI: Hold him!

BELCREDI (*while They take him away by the left exit, He protests as he is borne out*): No, no, you're not mad! You're not mad. He's not mad!
(*They go out by the left amid cries and excitement. After a moment, one hears a still sharper, more piercing cry from* DONNA MATILDA, *and then, silence.*)

HENRY IV (*who has remained on the stage between* LANDOLPH, HAROLD *and* ORDULPH, *with his eyes almost starting out of his head, terrified by the life of his own masquerade which has driven him to crime.*): Now, yes . . . we'll have to (*Calls his* VALETS *around him as if to protect him.*) here we are . . . together . . . for ever!

Curtain

Five
Country and Conscience

The plays in this section offer a summary of drama itself. Drama, based on incongruity and conflict, involves a public, social world and a private sense of self and right. There are, then, in drama, public and private motives, public actions and private thoughts, social and personal consequences. The subject of the three plays that follow is, on one level, the conflict of conscience and duty, of law and right. On another level, the subject is drama itself: the motives, actions, and fate of an individual protagonist who must act out his or her sense of virtue on a public stage with other actors who cannot or will not understand.

Virtually all of the themes of drama are embodied in these plays. They involve parents and lovers, friends and enemies, alienation and citizenship, war and violence, the question of virtue and the danger of private morality. Drama is based on motivated action, and the protagonist in each of the following plays faces the question of loyalty and the doubts that follow. The audience acts out these dramas many times, because the question of the protagonist's life does not end when the play does. But drama is, after all, for our contemplation, not for our comfort.

Ibsen's *An Enemy of the People* is neither comedy nor tragedy. It is a modern problem play in which the choices of the protagonist are serious, but not fatal. Hard choices are involved, but there is not the sense of confrontation with an ultimate reality. The problem play is, instead, the tragedy for a secular, liberal world. In a world in which there are no absolute sanctions and no mysteries, the protagonist must, on his own, determine the most compelling moral action and perform it. His only justification is to perform absolutely what he sees as the most important of the relative possible actions.

Saint Joan and *Antigone* raise the question of obligation in a different sense. These two women both try to remain loyal to a religious dictate in a secular world. They demand justice, when their contemporaries want order. They want a state that conforms to a divine plan and authenticates itself in other than human, political terms, where country and conscience coexist. Their adversaries and their friends are troubled by their demands because they call into question the arrangements of power and the compromises with principle that are usually necessary if country and conscience are to coexist.

In one definition, drama is the public representation of private motives. That is, the protagonist is moved to action and the audience comes to understand the source of that action and its ultimate consequences for the protagonist and for all others in that world. The plays in this section focus on the conflict between a private vision and a collective concern. The dilemma of conscience for the citizen is the choice of action when the private motive is moral in itself, but not permissible in the world.

Sophocles
Antigone

Translated by Dudley Fitts and Robert Fitzgerald

Persons represented

ANTIGONE	TEIRESIAS
ISMENE	A SENTRY
EURYDICE	A MESSENGER
CREON	CHORUS
HAIMON	

SCENE: Before the palace of CREON, King of Thebes. A central double door, and two lateral doors. A platform extends the length of the façade, and from this platform three steps lead down into the *"orchestra,"* or chorus-ground. TIME: dawn of the day after the repulse of the Argive army from the assault on Thebes.

PROLOGUE

(ANTIGONE *and* ISMENE *enter from the central door of the Palace.*)

ANTIGONE: Ismenê, dear sister,
  You would think that we had already suffered enough
  For the curse on Oedipus:
  I cannot imagine any grief
  That you and I have not gone through. And now—
  Have they told you of the new decree of our King Creon?
ISMENE: I have heard nothing: I know
  That two sisters lost two brothers, a double death
  In a single hour; and I know that the Argive army
  Fled in the night; but beyond this, nothing.

ANTIGONE: I thought so. And that is why I wanted you
   To come out here with me. There is something we must do.
ISMENE: Why do you speak so strangely?
ANTIGONE: Listen, Ismenê:
   Creon buried our brother Eteoclês
   With military honors, gave him a soldier's funeral,
   And it was right that he should; but Polyneicês,
   Who fought as bravely and died as miserably,—
   They say that Creon has sworn
   No one shall bury him, no one mourn for him,
   But his body must lie in the fields, a sweet treasure
   For carrion birds to find as they search for food.
   That is what they say, and our good Creon is coming here
   To announce it publicly; and the penalty—
   Stoning to death in the public square!
                                          There it is,
   And now you can prove what you are:
   A true sister, or a traitor to your family.
ISMENE: Antigonê, you are mad! What could I possibly do?
ANTIGONE: You must decide whether you will help me or not.
ISMENE: I do not understand you. Help you in what?
ANTIGONE: Ismenê, I am going to bury him. Will you come?
ISMENE: Bury him! You have just said the new law forbids it.
ANTIGONE: He is my brother. And he is your brother, too.
ISMENE: But think of the danger! Think what Creon will do!
ANTIGONE: Creon is not strong enough to stand in my way.
ISMENE: Ah sister!
   Oedipus died, everyone hating him
   For what his own search brought to light, his eyes
   Ripped out by his own hand; and Iocastê died,
   His mother and wife at once: she twisted the cords
   That strangled her life; and our two brothers died,
   Each killed by the other's sword. And we are left:
   But oh, Antigonê,
   Think how much more terrible than these
   Our own death would be if we should go against Creon
   And do what he has forbidden! We are only women,
   We cannot fight with men, Antigonê!
   The law is strong, we must give in to the law
   In this thing, and in worse. I beg the Dead
   To forgive me, but I am helpless: I must yield
   To those in authority. And I think it is dangerous business
   To be always meddling.
ANTIGONE: If that is what you think,
   I should not want you, even if you asked to come.
   You have made your choice, you can be what you want to be.
   But I will bury him; and if I must die,

I say that this crime is holy: I shall lie down
With him in death, and I shall be as dear
To him as he to me.
                      It is the dead,
Not the living, who make the longest demands:
We die for ever . . .
                      You may do as you like,
Since apparently the laws of the gods mean nothing to you.
ISMENE: They mean a great deal to me; but I have no strength
    To break laws that were made for the public good.
ANTIGONE: That must be your excuse, I suppose. But as for me,
    I will bury the brother I love.
ISMENE: Antigonê,
    I am so afraid for you!
ANTIGONE: You need not be:
    You have yourself to consider, after all.
ISMENE: But no one must hear of this, you must tell no one!
    I will keep it a secret, I promise!
ANTIGONE: Oh tell it! Tell everyone!
    Think how they'll hate you when it all comes out
    If they learn that you knew about it all the time!
ISMENE: So fiery! You should be cold with fear.
ANTIGONE: Perhaps. But I am doing only what I must.
ISMENE: But can you do it? I say that you cannot.
ANTIGONE: Very well: when my strength gives out, I shall do no more.
ISMENE: Impossible things should not be tried at all.
ANTIGONE: Go away, Ismenê:
    I shall be hating you soon, and the dead will too,
    For your words are hateful. Leave me my foolish plan:
    I am not afraid of the danger; if it means death,
    It will not be the worst of deaths—death without honor.
ISMENE: Go then, if you feel that you must.
    You are unwise,
    But a loyal friend indeed to those who love you.

(Exit into the Palace. ANTIGONE *goes off, L.) (Enter the* CHORUS.*)*

PARODOS

CHORUS: Now the long blade of the sun, lying   (STROPHE 1)
    Level east to west, touches with glory
    Thebes of the Seven Gates. Open, unlidded
    Eye of golden day! O marching light
    Across the eddy and rush of Dircê's stream,
    Striking the white shields of the enemy
    Thrown headlong backward from the blaze of morning!

CHORAGOS: Polyneicês their commander
   Roused them with windy phrases,
   He the wild eagle screaming
   Insults above our land,
   His wings their shields of snow,
   His crest their marshalled helms.
CHORUS: Against our seven gates in a yawning ring   (ANTISTROPHE 1)
   The famished spears came onward in the night;
   But before his jaws were sated with our blood,
   Or pinefire took the garland of our towers,
   He was thrown back; and as he turned, great Thebes—
   No tender victim for his noisy power—
   Rose like a dragon behind him, shouting war.
CHORAGOS: For God hates utterly
   The bray of bragging tongues;
   And when he beheld their smiling,
   Their swagger of golden helms,
   The frown of his thunder blasted
   Their first man from our walls.
CHORUS: We heard his shout of triumph high in the air   (STROPHE 2)
   Turn to a scream; far out in a flaming arc
   He fell with his windy torch, and the earth struck him.
   And others storming in fury no less than his
   Found shock of death in the dusty joy of battle.
CHORAGOS: Seven captains at seven gates
   Yielded their clanging arms to the god
   That bends the battle-line and breaks it.
   These two only, brothers in blood,
   Face to face in matchless rage,
   Mirroring each the other's death,
   Clashed in long combat.
CHORUS: But now in the beautiful morning of victory   (ANTISTROPHE 2)
   Let Thebes of the many chariots sing for joy!
   With hearts for dancing we'll take leave of war:
   Our temples shall be sweet with hymns of praise,
   And the long night shall echo with our chorus.

SCENE I

CHORAGOS: But now at last our new King is coming:
   Creon of Thebes, Menoikeus' son.
   In this auspicious dawn of his reign
   What are the new complexities
   That shifting Fate has woven for him?
   What is his counsel? Why has he summoned
   The old men to hear him?

(Enter CREON from the Palace, C. He addresses the CHORUS from the top step.)

CREON: Gentlemen: I have the honor to inform you that our Ship of State, which recent storms have threatened to destroy, has come safely to harbor at last, guided by the merciful wisdom of Heaven. I have summoned you here this morning because I know that I can depend upon you: your devotion to King Laïos was absolute; you never hesitated in your duty to our late ruler Oedipus; and when Oedipus died, your loyalty was transferred to his children. Unfortunately, as you know, his two sons, the princes Eteoclês and Polyneicês, have killed each other in battle; and I, as the next in blood, have succeeded to the full power of the throne.

I am aware, of course, that no Ruler can expect complete loyalty from his subjects until he has been tested in office. Nevertheless, I say to you at the very outset that I have nothing but contempt for the kind of Governor who is afraid, for whatever reason, to follow the course that he knows is best for the State; and as for the man who sets private friendship above the public welfare,—I have no use for him, either. I call God to witness that if I saw my country headed for ruin, I should not be afraid to speak out plainly; and I need hardly remind you that I would never have any dealings with an enemy of the people. No one values friendship more highly than I; but we must remember that friends made at the risk of wrecking our Ship are not real friends at all.

These are my principles, at any rate, and that is why I have made the following decision concerning the sons of Oedipus: Eteoclês, who died as a man should die, fighting for his country, is to be buried with full military honors, with all the ceremony that is usual when the greatest heroes die; but his brother Polyneicês, who broke his exile to come back with fire and sword against his native city and the shrines of his fathers' gods, whose one idea was to spill the blood of his blood and sell his own people into slavery—Polyneicês, I say, is to have no burial: no man is to touch him or say the least prayer for him; he shall lie on the plain, unburied; and the birds and the scavenging dogs can do with him whatever they like.

This is my command, and you can see the wisdom behind it. As long as I am King, no traitor is going to be honored with the loyal man. But whoever shows by word and deed that he is on the side of the State,— he shall have my respect while he is living, and my reverence when he is dead.

CHORAGOS: If that is your will, Creon son of Menoikeus,
You have the right to enforce it: we are yours.

CREON: That is my will. Take care that you do your part.

CHORAGOS: We are old men: let the younger ones carry it out.

CREON: I do not mean that: the sentries have been appointed.

CHORAGOS: Then what is it that you would have us do?

CREON: You will give no support to whoever breaks this law.

CHORAGOS: Only a crazy man is in love with death!

CREON: And death it is; yet money talks, and the wisest
Have sometimes been known to count a few coins too many.

(*Enter* SENTRY *from L.*)

SENTRY: I'll not say that I'm out of breath from running, King, because every time I stopped to think about what I have to tell you, I felt like going back. And all the time a voice kept saying, "You fool, don't you know you're walking straight into trouble?"; and then another voice: "Yes, but if you let somebody else get the news to Creon first, it will be even worse than that for you!" But good sense won out, at least I hope it was good sense, and here I am with a story that makes no sense at all; but I'll tell it anyhow, because, as they say, what's going to happen's going to happen, and—
CREON: Come to the point. What have you to say?
SENTRY: I did not do it. I did not see who did it. You must
not punish me for what someone else has done.
CREON: A comprehensive defense! More effective, perhaps,
If I knew its purpose. Come: what is it?
SENTRY: A dreadful thing ... I don't know how to put it—
CREON: Out with it!
SENTRY: Well, then;
    The dead man—
          Polyneicês—

(*Pause. The* SENTRY *is overcome, fumbles for words,* CREON *waits impassively.*)

                     out there—
                              someone,—
New dust on the slimy flesh!
(*Pause. No sign from* CREON)
Someone has given it burial that way, and
Gone ...
(*Long pause.* CREON *finally speaks with deadly control:*)
CREON: And the man who dared do this?
SENTRY: I swear I
Do not know! You must believe me!
                      Listen:
The ground was dry, not a sign of digging, no,
Not a wheeltrack in the dust, no trace of anyone.
It was when they relieved us this morning: and one of them,
The corporal, pointed to it.
                  There it was,
The strangest—
        Look:
The body, just mounded over with light dust: you see?
Not buried really, but as if they'd covered it
Just enough for the ghost's peace. And no sign

Of dogs or any wild animal that had been there.
And then what a scene there was! Every man of us
Accusing the other: we all proved the other man did it,
We all had proof that we could not have done it.
We were ready to take hot iron in our hands,
Walk through fire, swear by all the gods,
It was not I!
I do not know who it was, but it was not I!

(CREON's *rage has been mounting steadily, but the* SENTRY *is too intent upon his story to notice it*)

And then, when this came to nothing, someone said
A thing that silenced us and made us stare
Down at the ground: you had to be told the news,
And one of us had to do it! We threw the dice,
And the bad luck fell to me. So here I am,
No happier to be here than you are to have me:
Nobody likes the man who brings bad news.

CHORAGOS: I have been wondering, King: can it be that the gods have done this?

CREON (*furiously*):
Stop!
Must you doddering wrecks
Go out of your heads entirely? "The gods!"
Intolerable!
The gods favor this corpse? Why? How had he served them?
Tried to loot their temples, burn thesir images,
Yes, and the whole State, and its laws with it!
Is it your senile opinion that the gods love to honor bad men?
A pious thought!—
                No, from the very beginning
There have been those who have whispered together,
Stiff-necked anarchists, putting their heads together,
Scheming against me in alleys. These are the men,
And they have bribed my own guard to do this thing.
(*Sententiously*)
Money!
There's nothing in the world so demoralizing as money.
Down go your cities,
Homes gone, men gone, honest hearts corrupted,
Crookedness of all kinds, and all for money!
(*To* SENTRY)
                                    But you—!
I swear by God and by the throne of God,
The man who has done this thing shall pay for it!
Find that man, bring him here to me, or your death
Will be the least of your problems: I'll string you up

Alive, and there will be certain ways to make you
Discover your employer before you die;
And the process may teach you a lesson you seem to have missed:
The dearest profit is sometimes all too dear:
That depends on the source. Do you understand me?
A fortune won is often misfortune.
SENTRY: King, may I speak?
CREON: Your very voice distresses me.
SENTRY: Are you sure that it is my voice, and not your conscience?
CREON: By God, he wants to analyze me now!
SENTRY: It is not what I say, but what has been done, that hurts you.
CREON: You talk too much.
SENTRY: Maybe; but I've done nothing.
CREON: Sold your soul for some silver: that's all you've done.
SENTRY: How dreadful it is when the right judge judges wrong!
CREON: Your figures of speech
   May entertain you now; but unless you bring me the man,
   You will get little profit from them in the end.

(Exit CREON *into the Palace.)*

SENTRY: "Bring me the man"—!
I'd like nothing better than bringing him the man!
But bring him or not, you have seen the last of me here.
At any rate, I am safe!

(Exit SENTRY*)*

ODE I

(STROPHE 1)

CHORUS: Numberless are the world's wonders, but none
   More wonderful than man; the storm gray sea
   Yields to his prows, the huge crests bear him high;
   Earth, holy and inexhaustible, is graven
   With shining furrows where his plows have gone
   Year after year, the timeless labor of stallions

(ANTISTROPHE 1)

   The lightboned birds and beasts that cling to cover,
   The lithe fish lighting their reaches of dim water,
   All are taken, tamed in the net of his mind;
   The lion on the hill, the wild horse windy-maned,
   Resign to him; and his blunt yoke has broken
   The sultry shoulders of the mountain bull.

(STROPHE 2)

   Words also, and thought as rapid as air,
   He fashions to his good use; statecraft is his,

And his the skill that deflects the arrows of snow,
The spears of winter rain: from every wind
He has made himself secure—from all but one:
In the late wind of death he cannot stand.

(ANTISTROPHE 2)

O clear intelligence, force beyond all measure!
O fate of man, working both good and evil!
When the laws are kept, how proudly his city stands!
When the laws are broken, what of his city then?
Never may the anárchic man find rest at my hearth,
Never be it said that my thoughts are his thoughts.

SCENE II

(Re-enter SENTRY *leading* ANTIGONE.*)*
CHORAGOS: What does this mean? Surely this captive woman
 Is the Princess, Antigonê. Why should she be taken?
SENTRY: Here is the one who did it! We caught her
 In the very act of burying him.—Where is Creon?
CHORAGOS: Just coming from the house.

(Enter CREON, C.*)*

CREON: What has happened?
 Why have you come back so soon?
SENTRY *(expansively)*: O King,
 A man should never be too sure of anything:
 I would have sworn
 That you'd not see me here again: your anger
 Frightened me so, and the things you threatened me with;
 But how could I tell then
 That I'd be able to solve the case so soon?
 No dice-throwing this time: I was only too glad to come!
 Here is this woman. She is the guilty one:
 We found her trying to bury him.
 Take her, then; question her; judge her as you will.
 I am through with the whole thing now, and glad of it.
CREON: But this is Antigonê! Why have you brought her here?
SENTRY: She was burying him, I tell you!
CREON *(severely)*: Is this the truth?
SENTRY: I saw her with my own eyes. Can I say more?
CREON: The details: come, tell me quickly!
SENTRY: It was like this:
 After those terrible threats of yours, King,
 We went back and brushed the dust away from the body.
 The flesh was soft by now, and stinking,

So we sat on a hill to windward and kept guard.
No napping this time! We kept each other awake.
But nothing happened until the white round sun
Whirled in the center of the round sky over us:
Then, suddenly,
A storm of dust roared up from the earth, and the sky
Went out, the plain vanished with all its trees
In the stinging dark. We closed our eyes and endured it.
The whirlwind lasted a long time, but it passed;
And then we looked, and there was Antigonê!
I have seen
A mother bird come back to a stripped nest, heard
Her crying bitterly a broken note or two
For the young ones stolen. Just so, when this girl
Found the bare corpse, and all her love's work wasted,
She wept, and cried on heaven to damn the hands
That had done this thing.
       And then she brought more dust
And sprinkled wine three times for her brother's ghost.
We ran and took her at once. She was not afraid,
Not even when we charged her with what she had done.
She denied nothing.
     And this was a comfort to me,
And some uneasiness: for it is a good thing
To escape from death, but it is no great pleasure
To bring death to a friend.
       Yet I always say
There is nothing so comfortable as your own safe skin!
CREON (*slowly, dangerously*): And you, Antigonê,
 You with your head hanging,—do you confess this thing?
ANTIGONE: I do. I deny nothing.
CREON (*to* SENTRY):   You may go.

                (*Exit* SENTRY)

(*To* ANTIGONE:)
Tell me, tell me briefly:
Had you heard my proclamation touching this matter?
ANTIGONE: It was public. Could I help hearing it?
CREON: And yet you dared defy the law.
ANTIGONE: I dared.
 It was not God's proclamation. That final Justice
 That rules the world below makes no such laws.
 Your edict, King, was strong,
 But all your strength is weakness itself against
 The immortal unrecorded laws of God.
 They are not merely now: they were, and shall be,
 Operative for ever, beyond man utterly.
 I knew I must die, even without your decree:

I am only mortal. And if I must die
Now, before it is my time to die,
Surely this is no hardship: can anyone
Living, as I live, with evil all about me,
Think Death less than a friend? This death of mine
Is of no importance; but if I had left my brother
Lying in death unburied, I should have suffered.
Now I do not.
               You smile at me. Ah Creon,
Think me a fool, if you like; but it may well be
That a fool convicts me of folly.
CHORAGOS: Like father, like daughter: both headstrong, deaf to reason!
She has never learned to yield.
CREON: She has much to learn.
The inflexible heart breaks first, the toughest iron
Cracks first, and the wildest horses bend their necks
At the pull of the smallest curb.
                           Pride? In a slave?
This girl is guilty of a double insolence,
Breaking the given laws and boasting of it.
Who is the man here,
She or I, if this crime goes unpunished?
Sister's child, or more than sister's child,
Or closer yet in blood—she and her sister
Win bitter death for this!
(To servants:)
                     Go, some of you,
Arrest Ismenê. I accuse her equally.
Bring her: you will find her sniffling in the house there.
Her mind's a traitor: crimes kept in the dark
Cry for light, and the guardian brain shudders;
But how much worse than this
Is brazen boasting of barefaced anarchy!
ANTIGONE: Creon, what more do you want than my death?
CREON: Nothing.
That gives me everything.
ANTIGONE: Then I beg you: kill me.
This talking is a great weariness: your words
Are distasteful to me, and I am sure that mine
Seem so to you. And yet they should not seem so:
I should have praise and honor for what I have done.
All these men here would praise me
Were their lips not frozen shut with fear of you.
(Bitterly)
Ah the good fortune of kings,
Licensed to say and do whatever they please!
CREON: You are alone here in that opinion.

ANTIGONE: No, they are with me. But they keep their tongues in leash.
CREON: Maybe. But you are guilty, and they are not.
ANTIGONE: There is no guilt in reverence for the dead.
CREON: But Eteoclês—was he not your brother too?
ANTIGONE: My brother too.
CREON: And you insult his memory?
ANTIGONE (*softly*): The dead man would not say that I insult it.
CREON: He would: for you honor a traitor as much as him.
ANTIGONE: His own brother, traitor or not, and equal in blood.
CREON: He made war on his country. Eteoclês defended it.
ANTIGONE: Nevertheless, there are honors due all the dead.
CREON: But not the same for the wicked as for the just.
ANTIGONE: Ah Creon, Creon,
   Which of us can say what the gods hold wicked?
CREON: An enemy is an enemy, even dead.
ANTIGONE: It is my nature to join in love, not hate.
CREON (*finally losing patience*): Go join them, then; if you must have your love,
   Find it in hell!
CHORAGOS: But see, Ismenê comes:

(*Enter* ISMENE, *guarded*)

   Those tears are sisterly, the cloud
   That shadows her eyes rains down gentle sorrow.
CREON: You too, Ismenê,
   Snake in my ordered house, sucking my blood
   Stealthily——and all the time I never knew
   That these two sisters were aiming at my throne!
                                        Ismenê,
   Do you confess your share in this crime, or deny it?
   Answer me.
ISMENE: Yes, if she will let me say so. I am guilty.
ANTIGONE (*coldly*): No, Ismenê. You have no right to say so.
   You would not help me, and I will not have you help me.
ISMENE: But now I know what you meant; and I am here
   To join you, to take my share of punishment.
ANTIGONE: The dead man and the gods who rule the dead
   Know whose act this was. Words are not friends.
ISMENE: Do you refuse me, Antigonê? I want to die with you:
   I too have a duty that I must discharge to the dead.
ANTIGONE: You shall not lessen my death by sharing it.
ISMENE: What do I care for life when you are dead?
ANTIGONE: Ask Creon. You're always hanging on his opinions.
ISMENE: You are laughing at me. Why, Antigonê?
ANTIGONE: It's a joyless laughter, Ismenê
ISMENE: But can I do nothing?
ANTIGONE: Yes. Save yourself. I shall not envy you.

There are those who will praise you; I shall have honor, too.
ISMENE: But we are equally guilty!
ANTIGONE: No more, Ismenê.
You are alive, but I belong to Death.
CREON (*to the* CHORUS): Gentlemen, I beg you to observe these girls:
One has just now lost her mind; the other,
It seems, has never had a mind at all.
ISMENE: Grief teaches the steadiest minds to waver, King.
CREON: Yours certainly did, when you assumed guilt with the guilty!
ISMENE: But how could I go on living without her?
CREON: You are.
She is already dead.
ISMENE: But your own son's bride!
CREON: There are places enough for him to push his plow.
I want no wicked women for my sons!
ISMENE: O dearest Haimon, how your father wrongs you!
CREON: I've had enough of your childish talk of marriage!
CHORAGOS: Do you really intend to steal this girl from your son?
CREON: No; Death will do that for me.
CHORAGOS: Then she must die?
CREON (*ironically*): You dazzle me.
—But enough of this talk!
You, there, take them away and guard them well:
For they are but women, and even brave men run
When they see Death coming.

(*Exeunt* ISMENE, ANTIGONE, *and* GUARDS)

ODE II

(STROPHE 1)

CHORUS: Fortunate is the man who has never tasted God's vengeance!
Where once the anger of heaven has struck, that house is shaken
For ever: damnation rises behind each child
Like a wave cresting out of the black northeast,
When the long darkness under sea roars up
And bursts drumming death upon the windwhipped sand.

(ANTISTROPHE 1)

I have seen this gathering sorrow from time long past
Loom upon Oedipus' children: generation from generation
Takes the compulsive rage of the enemy god.
So lately this last flower of Oedipus' line
Drank the sunlight! but now a passionate word
And a handful of dust have closed up all its beauty.

    What mortal arrogance (STROPHE 2)
    Transcends the wrath of Zeus?

Sleep cannot lull him, nor the effortless long months
Of the timeless gods: but he is young for ever,
And his house is the shining day of high Olympos.
    All that is and shall be,
    And all the past, is his.
No pride on earth is free of the curse of heaven.
    The straying dreams of men   (ANTISTROPHE 2)
    May bring them ghosts of joy:
But as they drowse, the waking embers burn them;
Or they walk with fixed eyes, as blind men walk.
But the ancient wisdom speaks for our own time:
    Fate works most for woe
    With Folly's fairest show.
Man's little pleasure is the spring of sorrow.

SCENE III

CHORAGOS: But here is Haimon, King, the last of all your sons.
  Is it grief for Antigonê that brings him here,
  And bitterness at being robbed of his bride?

(Enter HAIMON*)*

CREON: We shall soon see, and no need of diviners.
                                          —Son,
  You have heard my final judgment on that girl:
  Have you come here hating me, or have you come
  With deference and with love, whatever I do?
HAIMON: I am your son, father. You are my guide.
  You make things clear for me, and I obey you.
  No marriage means more to me than your continuing wisdom.
CREON: Good. That is the way to behave: subordinate
  Everything else, my son, to your father's will.
  This is what a man prays for, that he may get
  Sons attentive and dutiful in his house,
  Each one hating his father's enemies,
  Honoring his father's friends. But if his sons
  Fail him, if they turn out unprofitably,
  What has he fathered but trouble for himself
  And amusement for the malicious?
                                    So you are right
  Not to lose your head over this woman.
  Your pleasure with her would soon grow cold, Haimon,
  And then you'd have a hellcat in bed and elsewhere.
  Let her find her husband in Hell!
  Of all the people in this city, only she

Has had contempt for my law and broken it.
Do you want me to show myself weak before the people?
Or to break my sworn word? No, and I will not.
The woman dies.
I suppose she'll plead "family ties." Well, let her.
If I permit my own family to rebel,
How shall I earn the world's obedience?
Show me the man who keeps his house in hand,
He's fit for public authority.
                              I'll have no dealings
With law-breakers, critics of the government:
Whoever is chosen to govern should be obeyed—
Must be obeyed, in all things, great and small,
Just and unjust! O Haimon,
The man who knows how to obey, and that man only,
Knows how to given commands when the time comes.
You can depend on him, no matter how fast
The spears come: he's a good soldier, he'll stick it out.
Anarchy, anarchy! Show me a greater evil!
This is why cities tumble and the great houses rain down,
This is what scatters armies!
No, no: good lives are made so by discipline.
We keep the laws then, and the lawmakers,
And no woman shall seduce us. If we must lose,
Let's lose to a man, at least! Is a woman stronger than we?
CHORAGOS: Unless time has rusted my wits,
What you say, King, is said with point and dignity.
HAIMON (*boyishly earnest*): Father:
Reason is God's crowning gift to man, and you are right
To warn me against losing mine. I cannot say—
I hope that I shall never want to say!—that you
Have reasoned badly. Yet there are other men
Who can reason, too; and their opinions might be helpful.
You are not in a position to know everything
That people say or do, or what they feel:
Your temper terrifies them—everyone
Will tell you only what you like to hear.
But I, at any rate, can listen; and I have heard them
Muttering and whispering in the dark about this girl.
They say no woman has ever, so unreasonably,
Died so shameful a death for a generous act:
"She covered her brother's body. Is this indecent?
She kept him from dogs and vultures. Is this a crime?
Death?—She should have all the honor that we can give her!"
This is the way they talk out there in the city.
You must believe me:
Nothing is closer to me than your happiness.

What could be closer? Must not any son
Value his father's fortune as his father does his?
I beg you, do not be unchangeable:
Do not believe that you alone can be right.
The man who thinks that,
The man who maintains that only he has the power
To reason correctly, the gift to speak, the soul—
A man like that, when you know him, ,turns out empty.
It is not reason never to yield to reason!
In flood time you can see how some trees bend,
And because they bend, even their twigs are safe,
While stubborn trees are torn up, roots and all.
And the same thing happens in sailing:
Make your sheet fast, never slacken,—and over you go,
Head over heels and under: and there's your voyage.
Forget you are angry! Let yourself be moved!
I know I am young; but please let me say this:
The ideal condition
Would be, I admit, that men should be right by instinct;
But since we are all too likely to go astray,
The reasonable thing is to learn from those who can teach.

CHORAGOS: You will do well to listen to him, King,
If what he says is sensible. And you, Haimon,
Must listen to your father.—Both speak well.

CREON: You consider it right for a man of my years and experience
To go to school to a boy?

HAIMON: It is not right
If I am wrong. But if I am young, and right,
What does my age matter?

CREON: You think it right to stand up for an anarchist?

HAIMON: Not at all. I pay no respect to criminals.

CREON: Then she is not a criminal?

HAIMON: The City would deny it, to a man.

CREON: And the City proposes to teach me how to rule?

HAIMON: Ah. Who is it that's like a boy now?

CREON: My voice is the one voice giving orders in this City!

HAIMON: It is no City if it takes orders from one voice.

CREON: The State is the King!

HAIMON: Yes, if the State is a desert.

(Pause)

CREON: This boy, it seems, has sold out to a woman.

HAIMON: If you are a woman: my concern is only for you.

CREON: So? Your "concern"! In a public brawl with your father!

HAIMON: How about you, in a public brawl with justice?

CREON: With justice, when all that I do is within my rights?

HAIMON: You have no right to trample on God's right.

CREON (*completely out of control*): Fool, adolescent fool! Taken in by a
    woman!
HAIMON: You'll never see me taken in by anything vile.
CREON: Every word you say is for her!
HAIMON (*quietly, darkly*):   And for you.
    And for me. And for the gods under the earth.
CREON: You'll never marry her while she lives.
HAIMON: Then she must die.—But her death will cause another.
CREON: Another?
    Have you lost your senses? Is this an open threat?
HAIMON: There is no threat in speaking to emptiness.
CREON: I swear you'll regret this superior tone of yours!
    You are the empty one!
HAIMON: If you were not my father,
    I'd say you were perverse.
CREON: You girlstruck fool, don't play at words with me!
HAIMON: I am sorry. You prefer silence.
CREON: Now, by God—!
    I swear, by all the gods in heaven above us,
    You'll watch it, I swear you shall!

(*To the* SERVANTS:)

            Bring her out!
    Bring the woman out! Let her die before his eyes!
    Here, this instant, with her bridegroom beside her!
HAIMON: Not here, no; she will not die here, King.
    And you will never see my face again.
    Go on raving as long as you've a friend to endure you.

(*Exit* HAIMON)

CHORAGOS: Gone, gone.
    Creon, a young man in a rage is dangerous!
CREON: Let him do, or dream to do, more than a man can.
    He shall not save these girls from death.
CHORAGOS: These girls?
    You have sentenced them both?
CREON: No, you are right.
    I will not kill the one whose hands are clean.
CHORAGOS: But Antigonê?
CREON (*somberly*):   I will carry her far away
    Out there in the wilderness, and lock her
    Living in a vault of stone. She shall have food,
    As the custom is, to absolve the State of her death.
    And there let her pray to the gods of hell:
    They are her only gods:
    Perhaps they will show her an escape from death,
    Or she may learn,
            though late,

That piety shown the dead is pity in vain.
                                                    (Exit CREON*)*

ODE III

CHORUS: Love, unconquerable   (STROPHE)
  Waster of rich men, keeper
  Of warm lights and all-night vigil
  In the soft face of a girl:
  Sea-wanderer, forest-visitor!
  Even the pure Immortals cannot escape you,
  And mortal man, in his one day's dusk,
  Trembles before your glory.
  Surely you swerve upon ruin   (ANTISTROPHE)
  The just man's consenting heart,
  As here you have made bright anger
  Strike between father and son—
  And none has conquered but Love!
  A girl's glance working the will of heaven:
  Pleasure to her alone who mocks us,
  Merciless Aphroditê.

SCENE IV

CHORAGOS *(as* ANTIGONE *enters guarded)*: But I can no longer stand in awe
    of this,
  Nor, seeing what I see, keep back my tears.
  Here is Antigonê, passing to that chamber
  Where all find sleep at last.
ANTIGONE: Look upon me, friends, and pity me   (STROPHE 1)
  Turning back at the night's edge to say
  Good-by to the sun that shines for me no longer;
  Now sleepy Death
  Summons me down to Acheron, that cold shore:
  There is no bridesong there, nor any music.
CHORUS: Yet not unpraised, not without a kind of honor,
  You walk at last into the underworld;
  Untouched by sickness, broken by no sword.
  What woman has ever found your way to death?
ANTIGONE: How often I have heard the story of Niobê, (ANTISTROPHE 1)
  Tantalos' wretched daughter, how the stone
  Clung fast about her, ivy-close: and they say
  The rain falls endlessly
  And sifting soft snow; her tears are never done.
  I feel the loneliness of her death in mine.

Sophocles: *Antigone*

CHORUS: But she was born of heaven, and you
  Are woman, woman-born. If her death is yours,
  A mortal woman's, is this not for you
  Glory in our world and in the world beyond?
ANTIGONE: You laugh at me. Ah, friends, friends, (STROPHE 2)
  Can you not wait until I am dead? O Thebes,
  O men many-charioted, in love with Fortune,
  Dear springs of Dircê, sacred Theban grove,
  Be witnesses for me, denied all pity,
  Unjustly judged! and think a word of love
  For her whose path turns
  Under dark earth, where there are no more tears.
CHORUS: You have passed beyond human daring and come at last
  Into a place of stone where Justice sits.
  I cannot tell
  What shape of your father's guilt appears in this.
ANTIGONE: You have touched it at last: that bridal bed (ANTISTROPHE 2)
  Unspeakable, horror of son and mother mingling:
  Their crime, infection of all our family!
  O Oedipus, father and brother!
  Your marriage strikes from the grave to murder mine.
  I have been a stranger here in my own land:
  All my life
  The blasphemy of my birth has followed me.
CHORUS: Reverence is a virtue, but strength
  Lives in established law: that must prevail
  You have made your choice,
  Your death is the doing of your conscious hand.
ANTIGONE: Then let me go, since all your words are bitter, (EPODE)
  And the very light of the sun is cold to me.
  Lead me to my vigil, where I must have
  Neither love nor lamentation; no song, but silence.

  (CREON interrupts impatiently)

CREON: If dirges and planned lamentations could put off death,
  Men would be singing for ever.
  (To the SERVANTS:)
                      Take her, go!
  You know your orders: take her to the vault
  And leave her alone there. And if she lives or dies,
  That's her affair, not ours: our hands are clean.
ANTIGONE: O tomb, vaulted bride-bed in eternal rock,
  Soon I shall be with my own again
  Where Persephonê welcomes the thin ghosts underground:
  And I shall see my father again, and you, mother,
  And dearest Polyneicês—
              dearest indeed
  To me, since it was my hand

That washed him clean and poured the ritual wine:
   And my reward is death before my time!
   And yet, as men's hearts know, I have done no wrong,
   I have not sinned before God. Or if I have,
   I shall know the truth in death. But if the guilt
   Lies upon Creon who judged me, then, I pray,
   May his punishment equal my own.
CHORAGOS: O passionate heart,
   Unyielding, tormented still by the same winds!
CREON: Her guards shall have good cause to regret their delaying.
ANTIGONE: Ah! That voice is like the voice of death!
CREON: I can give you no reason to think you are mistaken.
ANTIGONE: Thebes, and you my fathers' gods,
   And rulers of Thebes, you see me now, the last
   Unhappy daughter of a line of kings,
   Your kings, led away to death. You will remember
   What things I suffer, and at what men's hands,
   Because I would not transgress the laws of heaven.
   (To the GUARDS simply:)
   Come: let us wait no longer.
                              (Exit ANTIGONE, L., guarded)

ODE IV

CHORUS: All Danaê's beauty was locked away   (STROPHE 1)
   In a brazen cell where the sunlight could not come:
   A small room, still as any grave, enclosed her.
   Yet she was a princess too,
   And Zeus in a rain of gold poured love upon her.
   O child, child,
   No power in wealth or war
   Or tough sea-blackened ships
   Can prevail against untiring Destiny!

                                                         (ANTISTROPHE 1)
   And Dryas' son also, that furious king,
   Bore the god's prisoning anger for his pride:
   Sealed up by Dionysos in deaf stone,
   His madness died among echoes.
   So at the last he learned what dreadful power
   His tongue had mocked:
   For he had profaned the revels,
   And fired the wrath of the nine
   Implacable Sisters that love the sound of the flute.

                                                         (STROPHE 2)
   And old men tell a half-remembered tale
   Of horror done where a dark ledge splits the sea
   And a double surf beats on the gráy shóres:

How a king's new woman, sick
With hatred for the queen he had imprisoned,
Ripped out his two sons' eyes with her bloody hands
While grinning Arês watched the shuttle plunge
Four times: four blind wounds crying for revenge,

(ANTISTROPHE 2)

Crying, tears and blood mingled.—Piteously born,
Those sons whose mother was of heavenly birth!
Her father was the god of the North Wind
And she was cradled by gales,
She raced with young colts on the glittering hills
And walked untrammeled in the open light:
But in her marriage deathless Fate found means
To build a tomb like yours for all her joy.

SCENE V

(Enter blind TEIRESIAS, *led by a boy. The opening speeches of* TEIRESIAS *should be in singsong contrast to the realistic lines of* CREON.*)*

TEIRESIAS: This is the way the blind man comes, Princes, Princes,
 Lock-step, two heads lit by the eyes of one.
CREON: What new thing have you to tell us, old Teiresias?
TEIRESIAS: I have much to tell you: listen to the prophet, Creon.
CREON: I am not aware that I have ever failed to listen.
TEIRESIAS: Then you have done wisely, King, and ruled well.
CREON: I admit my debt to you. But what have you to say?
TEIRESIAS: This, Creon: you stand once more on the edge of fate.
CREON: What do you mean? Your words are a kind of dread.
TEIRESIAS: Listen, Creon:
 I was sitting in my chair of augury, at the place
 Where the birds gather about me. They were all a-chatter,
 As in their habit, when suddenly I heard
 A strange note in their jangling, a scream, a
 Whirring fury; I knew that they were fighting,
 Tearing each other, dying
 In a whirlwind of wings clashing. And I was afraid.
 I began the rites of burnt-offering at the altar,
 But Hephaistos failed me: instead of bright flame,
 There was only the sputtering slime of the fat thighflesh
 Melting: the entrails dissolved in gray smoke,
 The bare bone burst from the welter. And no blaze!
 This was a sign from heaven. My boy described it,
 Seeing for me as I see for others.
 I tell you, Creon, you yourself have brought
 This new calamity upon us. Our hearths and altars
 Are stained with the corruption of dogs and carrion birds

That glut themselves on the corpse of Oedipus' son.
The gods are deaf when we pray to them, their fire
Recoils from our offering, their birds of omen
Have no cry of comfort, for they are gorged
With the thick blood of the dead.
        O my son,
These are no trifles! Think: all men make mistakes,
But a good man yields when he knows his course is wrong,
And repairs the evil. The only crime is pride.
Give in to the dead man, then: do not fight with a corpse—
What glory is it to kill a man who is dead?
Think, I beg you:
It is for your own good that I speak as I do.
You should be able to yield for your own good.
CREON: It seems that prophets have made me their especial province.
All my life long
I have been a kind of butt for the dull arrows
Of doddering fortune-tellers!
       No, Teiresias:
If your birds—if the great eagles of God himself
Should carry him stinking bit by bit to heaven,
I would not yield. I am not afraid of pollution:
No man can defile the gods.
       Do what you will,
Go into business, make money, speculate
In India gold or that synthetic gold from Sardis,
Get rich otherwise than by my consent to bury him.
Teiresias, it is a sorry thing when a wise man
Sells his wisdom, lets out his words for hire!
TEIRESIAS: Ah Creon! Is there no man left in the world—
CREON: To do what?— Come, let's have the aphorism!
TEIRESIAS: No man who knows that wisdom outweighs any wealth?
CREON: As surely as bribes are baser than any baseness.
TEIRESIAS: You are sick, Creon! You are deathly sick!
CREON: As you say: it is not my place to challenge a prophet.
TEIRESIAS: Yet you have said my prophecy is for sale.
CREON: The generation of prophets has always loved gold.
TEIRESIAS: The generation of kings has always loved brass.
CREON: You forget yourself! You are speaking to your King.
TEIRESIAS: I know it. You are a king because of me.
CREON: You have a certain skill; but you have sold out.
TEIRESIAS: King, you will drive me to words that—
CREON: Say them, say them!
Only remember: I will not pay you for them.
TEIRESIAS: No, you will find them too costly.
CREON: No doubt. Speak:
Whatever you say, you will not change my will.
TEIRESIAS: Then take this, and take it to heart!

The time is not far off when you shall pay back
Corpse for corpse, flesh of your own flesh.
You have thrust the child of this world into living night,
You have kept from the gods below the child that is theirs:
The one in a grave before her death, the other,
Dead, denied the grave. This is your crime:
And the Furies and the dark gods of Hell
Are swift with terrible punishment for you.

Do you want to buy me now, Creon?
                            Not many days,
And your house will be full of men and women weeping,
And curses will be hurled at you from far
Cities grieving for sons unburied, left to rot
Before the walls of Thebes.
These are my arrows, Creon: they are all for you.

(*To* BOY:)

But come, child: lead me home.
Let him waste his fine anger upon younger men.
Maybe he will learn at last
To control a wiser tongue in a better head.

(*Exit* TEIRESIAS)

CHORAGOS: The old man has gone, King, but his words
   Remain to plague us. I am old, too,
   But I cannot remember that he was ever false.
CREON: That is true. . . . It troubles me.
   Oh it is hard to give in! but it is worse
   To risk everything for stubborn pride.
CHORAGOS: Creon: take my advice.
CREON: What shall I do?
CHORAGOS: Go quickly: free Antigonê from her vault
   And build a tomb for the body of Polyneicê.
CREON: You would have me do this?
CHORAGOS: Creon, yes!
   And it must be done at once: God moves
   Swiftly to cancel the folly of stubborn men.
CREON: It is hard to deny the heart! But I
   Will do it: I will not fight with destiny.
CHORAGOS: You must go yourself, you cannot leave it to others.
CREON: I will go.
            —Bring axes, servants:
   Come with me to the tomb. I buried her, I
   Will set her free.
            Oh quickly!
   My mind misgives—
   The laws of the gods are mighty, and a man must serve them
   To the last day of his life!

(*Exit* CREON)

PÆAN

CHORAGOS: God of many names   (STROPHE 1)
                 O Iacchos
                        son
     of Kadmeian Sémelê
               O born of the Thunder!
     Guardian of the West
                 Regent
     of Eleusis' plain
                   O Prince of maenad Thebes
     and the Dragon Field by rippling Ismenos:
CHORAGOS: God of many names   (ANTISTROPHE 1)
CHORUS: the flame of torches
     flares on our hills
              the nymphs of Iacchos
     dance at the spring of Castalia:
     from the vine-close mountain
                      come ah come in ivy:
     Evohé evohé! sings through the streets of Thebes
CHORAGOS: God of many names   (STROPHE 2)
CHORUS: Iacchos of Thebes
     heavenly Child
               of Sémelê bride of the Thunderer!
     The shadow of plague is upon us:
                   come
     with clement feet
               oh come from Parnasos
     down the long slopes
                  across the lamenting water
CHORAGOS: Iô Fire! Chorister of the throbbing stairs!   (ANTISTROPHE 2)
     O purest among the voices of the night!
     Thou son of God, blaze for us!
CHORUS: Come with choric rapture of circling Maenads
     Who cry *Iô Iacche!*
            God of many names!

EXODOS

(Enter MESSENGER, L.*)*

MESSENGER: Men of the line of Kadmos, you who live
     Near Amphion's citadel:
               I cannot say
     Of any condition of human life "This is fixed,
     This is clearly good, or bad". Fate raises up,

And Fate casts down the happy and unhappy alike:
No man can foretell his Fate.
                    Take the case of Creon:
Creon was happy once, as I count happiness:
Victorious in battle, sole governor of the land,
Fortunate father of children nobly born.
And now it has all gone from him! Who can say
That a man is still alive when his life's joy fails?
He is a walking dead man. Grant him rich,
Let him live like a king in his great house:
If his pleasure is gone, I would not give
So much as the shadow of smoke for all he owns.
CHORAGOS: Your words hint at sorrow: what is your news for us?
MESSENGER: They are dead. The living are guilty of their death.
CHORAGOS: Who is guilty? Who is dead? Speak!
MESSENGER: Haimon.
Haimon is dead; and the hand that killed him
Is his own hand.
CHORAGOS: His father's? or his own?
MESSENGER: His own, driven mad by the murder his father had done.
CHORAGOS: Teiresias, Teiresias, how clearly you saw it all!
MESSENGER: This is my news: you must draw what conclusions you can
   from it.
CHORAGOS: But look: Eurydicê, our Queen:
   Has she overheard us?

   (Enter EURYDICE from the Palace, C.)

EURYDICE: I have heard something, friends:
   As I was unlocking the gate of Pallas' shrine,
   For I needed her help today, I heard a voice
   Telling of some new sorrow. And I fainted
   There at the temple with all my maidens about me.
   But speak again: whatever it is, I can bear it:
   Grief and I are no strangers.
MESSENGER: Dearest Lady,
   I will tell you plainly all that I have seen.
   I shall not try to comfort you: what is the use,
   Since comfort could lie only in what is not true?
   The truth is always best.
                      I went with Creon
   To the outer plain where Polyneicês was lying,
   No friend to pity him, his body shredded by dogs.
   We made our prayers in that place to Hecatê
   And Pluto, that they would be merciful. And we bathed
   The corpse with holy water, and we brought
   Fresh-broken branches to burn what was left of it,
   And upon the urn we heaped up a towering barrow

Of the earth of his own land.
                    When we were done, we ran
To the vault where Antigonê lay on her couch of stone.
One of the servants had gone ahead,
And while he was yet far off he heard a voice
Grieving within the chamber, and he came back
And told Creon. And as the King went closer,
The air was full of wailing, the words lost,
And he begged us to make all haste. "Am I a prophet?"
He said, weeping, "And must I walk this road,
The saddest of all that I have gone before?
My son's voice calls me on. Oh quickly, quickly!
Look through the crevice there, and tell me
If it is Haimon, or some deception of the gods!"
We obeyed; and in the cavern's farthest corner
We saw her lying:
She had made a noose of her fine linen veil
And hanged herself. Haimon lay beside her,
His arms about her waist, lamenting her,
His love lost under ground, crying out
That his father had stolen her away from him.
When Creon saw him the tears rushed to his eyes
And he called to him: "What have you done, child? Speak to me.
What are you thinking that makes your eyes so strange?
O my son, my son, I come to you on my knees!"
But Haimon spat in his face. He said not a word,
Staring—
            And suddenly drew his sword
And lunged. Creon shrank back, the blade missed; and the boy,
Desperate against himself, drove it half its length
Into his own side, and fell. And as he died
He gathered Antigonê close in his arms again,
Choking, his blood bright red on her white cheek.
And now he lies dead with the dead, and she is his
At last, his bride in the houses of the dead.
                    (*Exit* EURYDICE *into the Palace*)
CHORAGOS: She has left us without a word. What can this mean?
MESSENGER: It troubles me, too; yet she knows what is best,
   Her grief is too great for public lamentation,
   And doubtless she has gone to her chamber to weep
   For her dead son, leading her maidens in his dirge.
CHORAGOS: It may be so: but I fear this deep silence

   (*Pause*)

MESSENGER: I will see what she is doing. I will go in.
                    (*Exit* MESSENGER *into the Palace*)
   (*Enter* CREON *with attendants, bearing* HAIMON's *body*)

CHORAGOS: But here is the King himself: oh look at him,
   Bearing his own damnation in his arms.
CREON: Nothing you say can touch me any more.
   My own blind heart has brought me
   From darkness to final darkness. Here you see
   The father murdering, the murdered son—
   And all my civic wisdom!
   Haimon my son, so young, so young to die,
   I was the fool, not you; and you died for me.
CHORAGOS: That is the truth; but you were late in learning it.
CREON: This truth is hard to bear. Surely a god
   Has crushed me beneath the hugest weight of heaven,
   And driven me headlong a barbaric way
   To trample out the thing I held most dear.
   The pains that men will take to come to pain!

   (*Enter* MESSENGER *from the Palace*)

MESSENGER: The burden you carry in your hands is heavy,
   But it is not all: you will find more in your house.
CREON: What burden worse than this shall I find there?
MESSENGER: The Queen is dead.
CREON: O port of death, deaf world,
   Is there no pity for me? And you, Angel of evil,
   I was dead, and your words are death again.
   Is it true, boy? Can it be true?
   Is my wife dead? Has death bred death?
MESSENGER: You can see for yourself.
   (*The doors are opened, and the body of* EURYDICE *is disclosed within.*)
CREON: Oh pity!
   All true, all true, and more than I can bear!
   O my wife, my son!
MESSENGER: She stood before the altar, and her heart
   Welcomed the knife her own hand guided,
   And a great cry burst from her lips for Megareus dead,
   And for Haimon dead, her sons; and her last breath
   Was a curse for their father, the murderer of her sons.
   And she fell, and the dark flowed in through her closing eyes
CREON: O God, I am sick with fear.
   Are there no swords here? Has no one a blow for me?
MESSENGER: Her curse is upon you for the deaths of both.
CREON: It is right that it should be. I alone am guilty.
   I know it, and I say it. Lead me in,
   Quickly, friends.
   I have neither life nor substance. Lead me in.
CHORAGOS: You are right, if there can be right in so much wrong.
   The briefest way is best in a world of sorrow.
CREON: Let it come,

Let death come quickly, and be kind to me.
I would not ever see the sun again.
CHORAGOS: All that will come when it will; but we, meanwhile,
Have much to do. Leave the future to itself.
CREON: All my heart was in that prayer!
CHORAGOS: Then do not pray any more: the sky is deaf.
CREON: Lead me away. I have been rash and foolish.
I have killed my son and my wife.
I look for comfort; my comfort lies here dead.
Whatever my hands have touched has come to nothing.
Fate has brought all my pride to a thought of dust.

(As CREON *is being led into the house, the* CHORAGOS *advances and speaks directly to the audience)*

CHORAGOS: There is no happiness where there is no wisdom;
No wisdom but in submission to the gods.
Big words are always punished,
And proud men in old age learn to be wise.

Henrik Ibsen
An Enemy of the People
Translated by R. Farquharson Sharp

Dramatis Personae

DR. THOMAS STOCKMANN, *Medical Officer of the Municipal Baths*
MRS. STOCKMANN, *his wife*
PETRA, *their daughter, a teacher*
EJLIF ⎱ *their sons (aged 13 and 10 respectively)*
MORTEN ⎰
PETER STOCKMANN, *the Doctor's elder brother; Mayor of the Town and Chief Constable, Chairman of the Baths' Committee, etc., etc.*
MORTEN, KIIL, *a tanner (Mrs. Stockmann's adoptive father)*
HOVSTAD, *editor of the "People's Messenger"*
BILLING, *sub-editor*
CAPTAIN HORSTER
ASLAKSEN, *a printer*
Men of various conditions and occupations, some few women, and a troop of schoolboys—the audience at a public meeting.

The action takes place in a coast town in southern Norway.

ACT I

(*Scene*: DR. STOCKMANN's sitting-room. It is evening. The room is plainly but neatly appointed and furnished. In the right-hand wall are two doors; the farther leads out to the hall, the nearer to the doctor's study. In the left-hand wall, opposite the door leading to the hall, is a door leading to the other rooms occupied by the family. In the middle of the same wall stands the stove, and, further forward, a couch with a looking-glass hanging over it and an oval table in front of it. On the table, a lighted lamp, with a lampshade. At the back of the room, an open door leads to the dining-room. BILLING is seen sitting at the dining table, on which a lamp is burning. He has a napkin tucked under his chin, and MRS. STOCKMANN is standing by the table handing him a large plate-full of roast beef. The other places at the table are empty, and the table somewhat in disorder, a meal having evidently recently been finished.)

MRS. STOCKMANN: You see, if you come an hour late, Mr. Billing, you have to put up with cold meat.
BILLING (*as he eats*): It is uncommonly good, thank you—remarkably good.
MRS. STOCKMANN: My husband makes such a point of having his meals punctually, you know—
BILLING: That doesn't affect me a bit. Indeed, I almost think I enjoy a meal all the better when I can sit down and eat all by myself and undisturbed.
MRS. STOCKMANN: Oh well, as long as you are enjoying it—. (*Turns to the hall door, listening.*) I expect that is Mr. Hovstad coming too.
BILLING: Very likely.

(PETER STOCKMANN *comes in. He wears an overcoat and his official hat, and carries a stick.*)

PETER STOCKMANN: Good evening, Katherine.
MRS. STOCKMANN (*coming forward into the sitting-room*): Ah, good evening—is it you? How good of you to come up and see us!
PETER STOCKMANN: I happened to be passing, and so—(*looks into the dining-room*). But you have company with you, I see.
MRS. STOCKMANN (*to* HOVSTAD): But won't you—? (*Points to the dining-* he came in. (*Hurriedly.*) Won't you come in and have something, too?
PETER STOCKMANN: I! No, thank you. Good gracious—hot meat at night! Not with my digestion.
MRS. STOCKMANN: Oh, but just once in a way—
PETER STOCKMANN: No, no, my dear lady; I stick to my tea and bread and butter. It is much more wholesome in the long run—and a little economical, too.
MRS. STOCKMANN (*smiling*): Now you mustn't think that Thomas and I are spendthrifts.
PETER STOCKMANN: Not you, my dear; I would never think that of you. (*Points to the Doctor's study.*) Is he not at home?
MRS. STOCKMANN: No, he went for a little turn after supper—he and the boys.
PETER STOCKMANN: I doubt if that is a wise thing to do. (*Listens.*) I fancy I hear him coming now.
MRS. STOCKMANN: No, I don't think it is he. (*A knock is heard at the door.*) Come in! (HOVSTAD *comes in from the hall.*) Oh, it is you, Mr. Hovstad!
HOVSTAD: Yes, I hope you will forgive me, but I was delayed at the printers. Good evening, Mr. Mayor.

PETER STOCKMANN (*bowing a little distantly*): Good evening. You have come on business, no doubt.
HOVSTAD: Partly. It's about an article for the paper.
PETER STOCKMANN: So I imagined. I hear my brother has become a prolific contributor to the "People's Messenger."
HOVSTAD: Yes, he is good enough to write in the "People's Messenger" when he has any home truths to tell.
MRS. STOCKMANN (*to* HOVSTAD): But won't you—? (*Points to the dining-room.*)
PETER STOCKMANN: Quite so, quite so. I don't blame him in the least, as a writer, for addressing himself to the quarters where he will find the readiest sympathy. And, besides that, I personally have no reason to bear any ill will to your paper, Mr. Hovstad.
HOVSTAD: I quite agree with you.
PETER STOCKMANN: Taking one thing with another, there is an excellent spirit of toleration in the town—an admirable municipal spirit. And it all springs from the fact of our having a great common interest to unite us—an interest that is in an equally high degree the concern of every right-minded citizen—
HOVSTAD: The Baths, yes.
PETER STOCKMANN: Exactly—our fine, new, handsome Baths. Mark my words, Mr. Hovstad—the Baths will become the focus of our municipal life! Not a doubt of it!
MRS. STOCKMANN: That is just what Thomas says.
PETER STOCKMANN: Think how extraordinarily the place has developed within the last year or two! Money has been flowing in, and there is some life and some business doing in the town. Houses and landed property are rising in value every day.
HOVSTAD: And unemployment is diminishing.
PETER STOCKMANN: Yes, that is another thing. The burden of the poor rates has been lightened, to the great relief of the propertied classes; and that relief will be even greater if only we get a really good summer this year, and lots of visitors—plenty of invalids, who will make the Baths talked about.
HOVSTAD: And there is a good prospect of that, I hear.
PETER STOCKMANN: It looks very promising. Enquiries about apartments and that sort of thing is reaching us every day.
HOVSTAD: Well, the doctor's article will come in very suitably.
PETER STOCKMANN: Has he been writing something just lately?
HOVSTAD: This is something he wrote in the winter; a recommendation of the Baths—an account of the excellent sanitary conditions here. But I held the article over, temporarily.

PETER STOCKMANN: Ah,—some little difficulty about it, I suppose?

HOVSTAD: No, not at all; I thought it would be better to wait till the spring, because it is just at this time that people begin to think seriously about their summer quarters.

PETER STOCKMANN: Quite right; you were perfectly right, Mr. Hovstad.

HOVSTAD: Yes, Thomas is really indefatigable when it is a question of the Baths.

PETER STOCKMANN: Well—remember, he is the Medical Officer to the Baths.

HOVSTAD: Yes, and what is more, they owe their existence to him.

PETER STOCKMANN: To him? Indeed! It is true I have heard from time to time that some people are of that opinion. At the same time I must say I imagined that I took a modest part in the enterprise.

MRS. STOCKMANN: Yes, that is what Thomas is always saying.

HOVSTAD: But who denies it, Mr. Stockmann? You set the thing going and made a practical concern of it; we all know that. I only meant that the idea of it came first from the doctor.

PETER STOCKMANN: Oh, ideas—yes! My brother has had plenty of them in his time—unfortunately. But when it is a question of putting an idea into practical shape, you have to apply to a man of different mettle, Mr. Hovstad. And I certainly should have thought that in this house at least—

MRS. STOCKMANN: My dear Peter—

HOVSTAD: How can you think that—?

MRS. STOCKMANN: Won't you go in and have something, Mr. Hovstad? My husband is sure to be back directly.

HOVSTAD: Thank you, perhaps just a morsel. (*Goes into the dining-room.*)

PETER STOCKMANN (*lowering his voice a little*): It is a curious thing that these farmers' sons never seem to lose their want of tact.

MRS. STOCKMANN: Surely it is not worth bothering about! Cannot you and Thomas share the credit as brothers?

PETER STOCKMANN: I should have thought so; but apparently some people are not satisfied with a share.

MRS. STOCKMANN: What nonsense! You and Thomas get on so capitally together. (*Listens.*) There he is at last, I think. (*Goes out and opens the door leading to the hall.*)

DR. STOCKMANN (*laughing and talking outside*): Look here—here is another guest for you, Katherine. Isn't that jolly! Come in, Captain Horster; hang your coat upon this peg. Ah, you don't wear an overcoat. Just think, Katherine; I met him in the street and could hardly persuade him to come up! (CAPTAIN HORSTER *comes into the room and greets* MRS. STOCKMANN. *He is followed by* DR. STOCKMANN.) Come along in, boys. They are ravenously hungry again, you know. Come along, Captain Horster; you must have a slice of beef. (*Pushes* HORSTER *into the dining-room.* EJLIF *and* MORTEN *go in after them.*)

MRS. STOCKMANN: But, Thomas, don't you see—?

DR. STOCKMANN (*turning in the doorway*): Oh, is it you, Peter? (*Shakes hands with him.*) Now that is very delightful.

PETER STOCKMANN: Unfortunately I must go in a moment—

DR. STOCKMANN: Rubbish! There is some toddy just coming in. You haven't forgotten the toddy, Katherine?

MRS. STOCKMANN: Of course not; the water is boiling now. (*Goes into the dining-room.*)

PETER STOCKMANN: Toddy too!

DR. STOCKMANN: Yes, sit down and we will have it comfortably.

PETER STOCKMANN: Thanks, I never care about an evening's drinking.

DR. STOCKMANN: But this isn't an evening's drinking.

PETER STOCKMANN: It seems to me—. (*Looks towards the dining-room.*) It is extraordinary how they can put away all that food.

DR. STOCKMANN (*rubbing his hands*): Yes, isn't it splendid to see young people eat? They have always got an appetite, you know! That's as it should be. Lots of food—to build up their strength! They are the people who are going to stir up the fermenting forces of the future, Peter.

PETER STOCKMANN: May I ask what they will find here to "stir up," as you put it?

DR. STOCKMANN: Ah, you must ask the young people that—when the times comes. We shan't be able to see it, of course. That stands to reason—two old fogies, like us—

PETER STOCKMANN: Really, really! I must say that is an extremely odd expression to—

DR. STOCKMANN: Oh, you mustn't take me too literally, Peter. I am so heartily happy and contented, you know. I think it is such an extraordinary piece of good fortune to be in the middle of all this growing, germinating life. It is a splendid time to live in! It is as if a whole new world were being created around one.

PETER STOCKMANN: Do you really think so?

DR. STOCKMANN: Ah, naturally you can't appreciate it as keenly as I. You have lived all your life in these surroundings, and your impressions have got blunted. But I, who have been buried all these years in my little corner up north, almost without ever seeing a stranger who might bring new ideas with him—well, in my case it has just the same effect as if I had been transported into the middle of a crowded city.

PETER STOCKMANN: Oh, a city—!

DR. STOCKMANN: I know, I know; it is all cramped enough here, compared with many other places. But there is life here—there is promise—there are innumerable things to work for and fight for; and that is the main thing. (*Calls.*) Katherine, hasn't the postman been here?

MRS. STOCKMANN (*from the dining-room*): No.

DR. STOCKMANN: And then to be comfortably off, Peter! That is something one learns to value, when one has been on the brink of starvation, as we have.

PETER STOCKMANN: Oh, surely—

DR. STOCKMANN: Indeed I can assure you we have often been very hard put to it, up there. And now to be able to live like a lord! To-day, for instance, we had roast beef for dinner—and, what is more, for supper too. Won't you come and have a little bit? Or let me show it you, at any rate? Come here—

PETER STOCKMANN: No, no—not for worlds!

DR. STOCKMANN: Well, but just come here then. Do you see, we have got a table-cover?

PETER STOCKMANN: Yes, I noticed it.

DR. STOCKMANN: And we have got a lamp-shade too. Do you see? All out of Katherine's savings! It makes the room so cosy. Don't you think so? Just stand here for a moment—no, no, not there—just here, that's it! Look now, when you get the light on it altogether—I really think it looks very nice, doesn't it?

PETER STOCKMANN: Oh, if you can afford luxuries of this kind—

DR. STOCKMANN: Yes, I can afford it now. Katherine tells me I earn almost as much as we spend.

PETER STOCKMANN: Almost—yes!

DR. STOCKMAN: But a scientific man must live in a little bit of style. I am quite sure an ordinary civil servant spends more in a year than I do.

PETER STOCKMANN: I daresay. A civil servant—a man in a well-paid position—

DR. STOCKMANN: Well, any ordinary merchant, then! A man in that position spends two or three times as much as—

PETER STOCKMANN: It just depends on circumstances.

DR. STOCKMANN: At all events I assure you I don't waste money unprofitably. But I can't find it in my heart to deny myself the pleasure of entertaining my friends. I need that sort of thing, you know. I have lived for so long shut out of it all, that it is a necessity of life to me to mix with young, eager, ambitious men, men of liberal and active minds; and that describes every one of those fellows who are enjoying their supper in there. I wish you knew more of Hovstad—

PETER STOCKMANN: By the way, Hovstad was telling me he was going to print another article of yours.

DR. STOCKMANN: An article of mine?
PETER STOCKMANN: Yes, about the Baths. An article you wrote in the winter.
DR. STOCKMANN: Oh, that one! No, I don't intend that to appear just for the present.
PETER STOCKMANN: Why not? It seems to me that this would be the most opportune moment.
DR. STOCKMANN: Yes, very likely—under normal conditions. (*Crosses the room.*)
PETER STOCKMANN (*following him with his eyes*): Is there anything abnormal about the present conditions?
DR. STOCKMANN (*standing still*): To tell you the truth, Peter, I can't say just at this moment—at all events not tonight. There may be much that is very abnormal about the present conditions—and it is possible there may be nothing abnormal about them at all. It is quite possible it may be merely my imagination.
PETER STOCKMANN: I must say it all sounds most mysterious. Is there something going on that I am to be kept in ignorance of? I should have imagined that I, as Chairman of the governing body of the Baths—
DR. STOCKMANN: And I should have imagined that I—. Oh, come, don't let us fly out at one another, Peter.
PETER STOCKMANN: Heaven forbid! I am not in the habit of flying out at people, as you call it. But I am entitled to request most emphatically that all arrangements shall be made in a business-like manner, through the proper channels, and shall be dealt with by the legally constituted authorities. I can allow no going behind our backs by any roundabout means.
DR. STOCKMANN: Have I ever at any time tried to go behind your backs!
PETER STOCKMANN: You have an ingrained tendency to take your own way, at all events; and that is almost equally inadmissible in a well ordered community. The individual ought undoubtedly to acquiesce in subordinating himself to the community—or, to speak more accurately, to the authorities who have the care of the community's welfare.
DR. STOCKMANN: Very likely. But what the deuce has all this got to do with me?
PETER STOCKMANN: That is exactly what you never appear to be willing to learn, my dear Thomas. But, mark my words, some day you will have to suffer for it—sooner or later. Now I have told you. Good-bye.
DR. STOCKMANN: Have you taken leave of your senses? You are on the wrong scent altogether.

PETER STOCKMANN: I am not usually that. You must excuse me now if I—
(*calls into the dining-room*). Good night, Katherine. Good night, gentlemen. (*Goes out.*)

MRS. STOCKMANN (*coming from the dining-room*): Has he gone?

DR. STOCKMANN: Yes, and in such a bad temper.

MRS. STOCKMANN: But, dear Thomas, what have you been doing to him again?

DR. STOCKMANN: Nothing at all. And, anyhow, he can't oblige me to make my report before the proper time.

MRS. STOCKMANN: What have you got to make a report to him about?

DR. STOCKMANN: Hm! Leave that to me, Katherine.—It is an extraordinary thing that the postman doesn't come.

(HOVSTAD, BILLING and HORSTER *have got up from the table and come into the sitting-room.* EJLIF *and* MORTEN *come in after them.*)

BILLING (*stretching himself*): Ah!—one feels a new man after a meal like that.

HOVSTAD: The mayor wasn't in a very sweet temper tonight, then.

DR. STOCKMANN: It is his stomach; he has a wretched digestion.

HOVSTAD: I rather think it was us two of the "People's Messenger" that he couldn't digest.

MRS. STOCKMANN: I thought you came out of it pretty well with him.

HOVSTAD: Oh yes; but it isn't anything more than a sort of truce.

BILLING: That is just what it is! That word sums up the situation.

DR. STOCKMANN: We must remember that Peter is a lonely man, poor chap. He has no home comforts of any kind; nothing but everlasting business. And all that infernal weak tea wash that he pours into himself! Now then, my boys, bring chairs up to the table. Aren't we going to have that toddy, Katherine?

MRS. STOCKMANN (*going into the dining-room*). I am just getting it.

DR. STOCKMAN: Sit down here on the couch beside me, Captain Horster. We so seldom see you—. Please sit down, my friends. (*They sit down at the table.* MRS. STOCKMANN *brings a tray, with a spirit-lamp, glasses, bottles, etc., upon it.*)

MRS. STOCKMANN: There you are! This is arrack, and this is rum, and this one is the brandy. Now every one must help themselves.

DR. STOCKMANN (*taking a glass*): We will. (*They all mix themselves some toddy.*) And let us have the cigars. Ejlif, you know where the box is. And you, Morten, can fetch my pipe. (*The two boys go into the room on the right.*) I have a suspicion that Ejlif pockets a cigar now and then!—but I take no notice of it. (*Calls out.*) And my smoking-cap too, Morten. Katherine, you can tell him where I left it. Ah, he has got it. (*The boys bring the various things.*) Now, my friends. I stick to my pipe, you know. This one has seen plenty of bad weather with me up north. (*Touches glasses with them.*)Your good health! Ah, it is good to be sitting snug and warm here.

MRS. STOCKMANN (*who sits knitting*). Do you sail soon, Captain Horster?

HORSTER: I expect to be ready to sail next week.

MRS. STOCKMANN: I suppose you are going to America?

HORSTER: Yes, that is the plan.

MRS. STOCKMANN: Then you won't be able to take part in the coming election.

HORSTER: Is there going to be an election?

BILLING: Didn't you know?

HORSTER: No, I don't mix myself up with those things.

BILLING: But do you not take an interest in public affairs?

HORSTER: No, I don't know anything about politics.

BILLING: All the same, one ought to vote, at any rate.

HORSTER: Even if one doesn't know anything about what is going on?

BILLING: Doesn't know! What do you mean by that? A community is like a ship; every one ought to be prepared to take the helm.

HORSTER: May be that is all very well on shore; but on board ship it wouldn't work.

HOVSTAD: It is astonishing how little most sailors care about what goes on shore.

BILLING: Very extraordinary.

DR. STOCKMANN: Sailors are like birds of passage; they feel equally at home in any latitude. And that is only an additional reason for our being all the more keen, Hovstad. Is there to be anything of public interest in tomorrow's "Messenger"?

HOVSTAD: Nothing about municipal affairs. But the day after to-morrow I was thinking of printing your article—

DR. STOCKMANN: Ah, devil take it—my article! Look here, that must wait a bit.

HOVSTAD: Really? We had just got convenient space for it, and I thought it was just the opportune moment—

DR. STOCKMANN: Yes, yes, very likely you are right; but it must wait all the same. I will explain to you later. (PETRA *comes in from the hall, in hat and cloak and with a bundle of exercise books under her arm.*)

PETRA: Good evening.

DR. STOCKMANN: Good evening, Petra; come along.

(*Mutual greetings;* PETRA *takes off her things and puts them down on a chair by the door.*)

PETRA: And you have all been sitting here enjoying yourselves, while I have been out slaving!

DR. STOCKMAN: Well, come and enjoy yourself too!

BILLING: May I mix a glass for you?

PETRA (*coming to the table*): Thanks, I would rather do it; you always mix it too strong. But I forgot father—I have a letter for you. (*Goes to the chair where she has laid her things.*)

DR. STOCKMANN: A letter? From whom?

PETRA (*looking in her coat pocket*): The postman gave it to me just as I was going out—

DR. STOCKMANN (*getting up and going to her*): And you only give to me now!

PETRA: I really had not time to run up again. There it is!

DR. STOCKMANN (*seizing the letter*): Let's see, let's see, child! (*Looks at the address.*) Yes, that's all right!

MRS. STOCKMANN: Is it the one you have been expecting so anxiously, Thomas?

DR. STOCKMANN: Yes, it is. I must go to my room now and—. Where shall I get a light, Katherine? Is there no lamp in my room again?

MRS. STOCKMANN: Yes, your lamp is all ready lit on your desk.

DR. STOCKMANN: Good, good. Excuse me for a moment—. (*Goes into his study.*)

PETRA: What do you suppose it is, mother?

MRS. STOCKMANN: I don't know; for the last day or two he has always been asking if the postman has not been here.

BILLING: Probably some country patient.

PETRA: Poor old dad!—he will overwork himself soon. (*Mixes a glass for herself.*) There, that will taste good!

HOVSTAD: Have you been teaching in the evening school again to-day?

PETRA (*sipping from her glass*): Two hours.

BILLING: And four hours of school in the morning—

PETRA: Five hours.

MRS. STOCKMANN: And you have still got exercises to correct, I see.

PETRA: A whole heap, yes.

HORSTER: You are pretty full up with work too, it seems to me.

PETRA: Yes—but that is good. One is so delightfully tired after it.

BILLING: Do you like that?

PETRA: Yes, because one sleeps so well then.

MORTEN: You must be dreadfully wicked, Petra.

PETRA: Wicked?

MORTEN: Yes, because you work so much. Mr. Rörlund says work is a punishment for our sins.

EJLIF: Pooh, what a duffer you are, to believe a thing like that!

MRS. STOCKMANN: Come, come, Ejlif!

BILLING (*laughing*): That's capital!

HOVSTAD: Don't you want to work as hard as that, Morten?
MORTEN: No, indeed I don't.
HOVSTAD: What do you want to be, then?
MORTEN: I should like best to be a Viking.
EJLIF: You would have to be a pagan then.
MORTEN: Well, I could become a pagan, couldn't I?
BILLING: I agree with you, Morten! My sentiments, exactly.
MRS. STOCKMANN (*signalling to him*): I am sure that is not true, Mr. Billing.
BILLING: Yes, I swear it is! I am a pagan, and I am proud of it. Believe me, before long we shall all be pagans.
MORTEN: And then shall be allowed to do anything we like?
BILLING: Well, you see, Morten—.
MRS. STOCKMANN: You must go to your room now, boys; I am sure you have some lessons to learn for to-morrow.
EJLIF: I should like so much to stay a little longer—
MRS. STOCKMANN: No, no; away you go, both of you. (*The boys say good night and go into the rom on the left.*)
HOVSTAD: Do you really think it can do the boys any harm to hear such things?
MRS. STOCKMANN: I don't know; but I don't like it.
PETRA: But you know, mother, I think you really are wrong about it.
MRS. STOCKMANN: Maybe, but I don't like it—not in our own home.
PETRA: There is so much falsehood both at home and at school. At home one must not speak, and at school we have to stand and tell lies to the children.
HORSTER: Tell lies?
PETRA: Yes, don't you suppose we have to teach them all sorts of things that we don't believe?
BILLING: That is perfectly true.
PETRA: If only I had the means I would start a school of my own, and it would be conducted on very different lines.
BILLING: Oh, bother the means—!
HORSTER: Well if you are thinking of that, Miss Stockmann, I shall be delighted to provide you with a schoolroom. The great big old house my father left me is standing almost empty; there is an immense dining-room downstairs—
PETRA (*laughing*): Thank you very much; but I am afraid nothing will come of it.
HOVSTAD: No, Miss Petra is much more likely to take to journalism, I expect. By the way, have you had time to do anything with that English story you promised to translate for us?
PETRA: No, not yet; but you shall have it in good time.

(DR. STOCKMANN *comes in from his room with an open letter in his hand.*)

DR. STOCKMANN (*waving the letter*): Well, now the town will have something new to talk about, I can tell you!
BILLING: Something new?
MRS. STOCKMANN: What is this?
DR. STOCKMANN: A great discovery, Katherine.
HOVSTAD: Really?
DR. STOCKMANN: A discovery of mine. (*Walks up and down.*) Just let them come saying, as usual, that it is all fancy and a crazy man's imagination! But they will be careful what they say this time, I can tell you!
PETRA: But father, tell us what it is.
DR. STOCKMANN: Yes, yes—only give me time, and you shall know all about it. If only I had Peter here now! It just shows how we men can go about forming our judgments, when in reality we are as blind as any moles—
HOVSTAD: What are you driving at, Doctor?
DR. STOCKMANN (*standing still by the table*): Isn't it the universal opinion that our town is a healthy spot?
HOVSTAD: Certainly.
DR. STOCKMANN: Quite an unusually healthy spot, in fact—a place that deserves to be recommended in the warmest possible manner either for invalids or for people who are well—
MRS. STOCKMANN: Yes, but my dear Thomas—
DR. STOCKMANN: And we have been recommending it and praising it—I have written and written, both in the "Messenger" and in pamphlets—
HOVSTAD: Well, what then?
DR. STOCKMANN: And the Baths—we have called them the "main artery of the town's life-blood," the "nerve-centre of our town," and the devil knows what else—
BILLING: "The town's pulsating heart" was the expression I once used on an important occasion—
DR. STOCKMANN: Quite so. Well, do you know what they really are, these great, splendid, much praised Baths, that have cost so much money—do you know what they are?
HOVSTAD: No, what are they?
MRS. STOCKMANN: Yes, what are they?
DR. STOCKMANN: The whole place is a pesthouse!
PETRA: The Baths, father?
MRS. STOCKMANNS (*at the same time*): Our Baths!
HOVSTAD: But, Doctor—
BILLING: Absolutely incredible!
DR. STOCKMANN: The whole Bath establishment is a whited, poisoned

sepulchre, I tell you—the gravest possible danger to the public health! All the nastiness up at Mölledal, all that stinking filth, is infecting the water in the conduit-pipes leading to the reservoir; and the same cursed, filthy poison oozes out on the shore too—

HORSTER: Where the bathing-place is?

DR. STOCKMANN: Just there.

HOVSTAD: How do you come to be so certain of all this, Doctor?

DR. STOCKMANN: I have investigated the matter most conscientiously. For a long time past I have suspected something of the kind. Last year we had some very strange cases of illness among the visitors—typhoid cases, and cases of gastric fever—

MRS. STOCKMANN: Yes, that is quite true.

DR. STOCKMANN: At the time, we supposed the visitors had been infected before they came; but later on, in the winter, I began to have a different opinion; and so I set myself to examine the water, as well as I could.

MRS. STOCKMANN: Then that is what you have been so busy with?

DR. STOCKMANN: Indeed I have been busy, Katherine. But here I had none of the necessary scientific apparatus; so I sent samples, both of the drinking-water and of the sea-water, up to the University, to have an accurate analysis made by a chemist.

HOVSTAD: And have you got that?

DR. STOCKMANN (*showing him the letter*): Here it is! It proves the presence of decomposing organic matter in the water—it is full of infusoria. The water is absolutely dangerous to use, either internally or externally.

MRS. STOCKMANN: What a mercy you discovered it in time.

DR. STOCKMANN: You may well say so.

HOVSTAD: And what do you propose to do now, Doctor?

DR. STOCKMANN: To see the matter put right—naturally.

HOVSTAD: Can that be done?

DR. STOCKMANN: It must be done. Otherwise the Baths will be absolutely useless and wasted. But we need not anticipate that; I have a very clear idea what we shall have to do.

MRS. STOCKMANN: But why have you kept this all so secret, dear?

DR. STOCKMANN: Do you suppose I was going to run about the town gossiping about it, before I had absolute proof? No, thank you. I am not such a fool.

PETRA: Still, you might have told us—

DR. STOCKMANN: Not a living soul. But to-morrow you may run around to the old Badger—

MRS. STOCKMANN: Oh, Thomas! Thomas!

DR. STOCKMANN: Well, to your grandfather, then. The old boy will have something to be astonished at! I know he thinks I am cracked—and there are lots of other people think so too, I have noticed. But now these good folks shall see—they shall just see—! (*Walks about, rubbing his hands.*) There will be a nice upset in the town, Katherine; you can't imagine what it will be. All the conduit-pipes will have to be relaid.

HOVSTAD (*getting up*): All the conduit-pipes—?

DR. STOCKMANN: Yes, of course. The intake is too low down; it will have to be lifted to a position much higher up.

PETRA: Then you were right after all.

DR. STOCKMANN: Ah, you remember, Petra—I wrote opposing the plans before the work was begun. But at that time no one would listen to me. Well, I am going to let them have it, now! Of course I have prepared a report for the Baths Committee; I have had it ready for a week, and was only waiting for this to come. (*Shows the letter.*) Now it shall go off at once. (*Goes into his room and comes back with some papers.*) Look at that! Four closely written sheets!—and the letter shall go with them. Give me a bit of paper, Katherine—something to wrap them up in. That will do! Now give it to—to—(*stamps his foot*)—what the deuce is her name?—give it to the maid, and tell her to take it at once to the Mayor.

(MRS. STOCKMANN *takes the packet and goes out through the dining-room.*)

PETRA: What do you think uncle Peter will say, father?

DR. STOCKMANN: What is there for him to say? I should think he would be very glad that such an important truth has been brought to light.

HOVSTAD: Will you let me print a short note about your discovery in the "Messenger"?

DR. STOCKMANN: I shall be very much obliged if you will.

HOVSTAD: It is very desirable that the public should be informed of it without delay.

DR. STOCKMANN: Certainly.

MRS. STOCKMANN (*coming back*): She has just gone with it.

BILLING: Upon my soul, Doctor, you are going to be the foremost man in the town!

DR. STOCKMANN (*walking about happily*): Nonsense! As a matter of fact I have done nothing more than my duty. I have only made a lucky find—that's all. Still, all the same—

BILLING: Hovstad, don't you think the town ought to give Dr. Stockmann some sort of testimonial?

HOVSTAD: I will suggest it, anyway.

BILLING: And I will speak to Aslaksen about it.

DR. STOCKMANN: No, my good friends, don't let us have any of that nonsense. I won't hear of anything of the kind. And if the Baths Committee should think of voting me an increase of salary, I will not accept it. Do you hear, Katherine?—I won't accept it.

MRS. STOCKMANN: You are quite right, Thomas.

PETRA (*lifting her glass*): Your health, father!

HOVSTAD *and* BILLING: Your health, Doctor! Good health!

HORSTER (*touches glasses with* DR. STOCKMANN): I hope it will bring you nothing but good luck.

DR. STOCKMANN: Thank you, thank you, my dear fellows! I feel tremendously happy! It is a splendid thing for a man to be able to feel that he has done a service to his native town and to his fellow-citizens. Hurrah, Katherine! (*He puts his arms round her and whirls her round and round, while she protests with laughing cries. They all laugh, clap their hands, and cheer the* DOCTOR. *The boys put their heads in at the door to see what is going on.*)

ACT II

(*Scene:* The same. The door into the dining-room is shut. It is morning. MRS. STOCKMANN, with a sealed letter in her hand, comes in from the dining-room, goes to the door of the DOCTOR's study, and peeps in.)

MRS. STOCKMANN: Are you in, Thomas?

DR. STOCKMANN (*from within his room*): Yes, I have just come in. (*Comes into the room.*) What is it?

MRS. STOCKMANN: A letter from your brother.

DR. STOCKMANN: Aha, let us see! (*Opens the letter and reads:*) "I return herewith the manuscript you sent me"—(*reads on in a low murmur*) Hm!—

MRS. STOCKMANN: What does he say?

DR. STOCKMANN (*putting the papers in his pocket*): Oh, he only writes that he will come up here himself about midday.

MRS. STOCKMANN: Well, try and remember to be at home this time.

DR. STOCKMANN: That will be all right; I have got through all my morning visits.

MRS. STOCKMANN: I am extremely curious to know how he takes it.

DR. STOCKMANN: You will see he won't like it's having been I, and not he, that made the discovery.

MRS. STOCKMANN: Aren't you a little nervous about that?

DR. STOCKMANN: Oh, he really will be pleased enough, you know. But, at the same time, Peter is so confoundedly afraid of anyone's doing any service to the town except himself.

MRS. STOCKMANN: I will tell you what, Thomas—you should be good natured, and share the credit of this with him. Couldn't you make out that it was he who set you on the scent of this discovery?

DR. STOCKMANN: I am quite willing. If only I can get the thing set right. I—

(MORTEN KIIL *puts his head in through the door leading from the hall, looks round in an enquiring manner, and chuckles.*)

MORTEN KIIL (*slyly*): Is it—is it true?
MRS. STOCKMANN (*going to the door*): Father!—is it you?
DR. STOCKMANN: Ah, Mr. Kiil—good morning, good morning!
MRS. STOCKMANN: But come along in.
MORTEN KIIL: If it is true, I will; if not, I am off.
DR. STOCKMANN: If what is true?
MORTEN KIIL: This tale about the water supply. Is it true?
DR. STOCKMANN: Certainly it is true. But how did you come to hear it?
MORTEN KIIL (*coming in*): Petra ran in on her way to the school—
DR. STOCKMANN: Did she?
MORTEN KIIL: Yes; and she declares that—. I thought she was only making a fool of me, but it isn't like Petra to do that.
DR. STOCKMANN: Of course not. How could you imagine such a thing!
MORTEN KIIL: Oh well, it is better never to trust anybody; you may find you have been made a fool of before you know where you are. But it is really true, all the same?
DR. STOCKMANN: You can depend upon it that it is true. Won't you sit down? (*Settles him on the couch.*) Isn't it a real bit of luck for the town—
MORTEN KIIL (*suppressing his laughter*): A bit of luck for the town?
DR. STOCKMANN: Yes, that I made the discovery in good time.
MORTEN KIIL (*as before*): Yes, yes, yes!—But I should never have thought you the sort of man to pull your own brother's leg like this!
DR. STOCKMANN: Pull his leg!
MRS. STOCKMANN: Really, father dear—
MORTEN KIIL (*resting his hands and his chin on the handle of his stick and winking slyly at the* DOCTOR): Let me see, what was the story? Some kind of beast that had got into the water-pipes, wasn't it?
DR. STOCKMANN: Infusoria—yes.
MORTEN KIIL: And a lot of these beasts had got in, according to Petra—a tremendous lot.
DR. STOCKMANN: Certainly; hundreds of thousands of them, probably.
MORTEN KIIL: But no one can see them—isn't that so?
DR. STOCKMANN: Yes; you can't see them.
MORTEN KIIL (*with a quiet chuckle*): Damme—it's the finest story I have ever heard!
DR. STOCKMANN: What do you mean?
MORTEN KIIL: But you will never get the Mayor to believe a thing like that.

DR. STOCKMANN: We shall see.

MORTEN KIIL: Do you think he will be fool enough to—?

DR. STOCKMANN: I hope the whole town will be fools enough.

MORTEN KIIL: The whole town! Well, it wouldn't be a bad thing. It would just serve them right, and teach them a lesson. They think themselves so much cleverer than we old fellows. They hounded me out of the council; they did, I tell you—they hounded me out. Now they shall pay for it. You pull their legs too, Thomas!

DR. STOCKMANN: Really, I—

MORTEN KIIL: You pull their legs! (*Gets up.*) If you can work it so that the Mayor and his friends all swallow the same bait, I will give ten pounds to a charity—like a shot!

DR. STOCKMANN: That is very kind of you.

MORTEN KIIL: Yes, I haven't got much money to throw away, I can tell you; but if you can work this, I will give five pounds to a charity at Christmas.

(HOVSTAD *comes in by the hall door.*)

HOVSTAD: Good morning! (*Stops.*) Oh, I beg your pardon—

DR. STOCKMANN: Not at all; come in.

MORTEN KIIL (*with another chuckle*): Oho!—is he in this too?

HOVSTAD: What do you mean?

DR. STOCKMANN: Certainly he is.

MORTEN KIIL: I might have known it! It must get into the papers. You know how to do it, Thomas! Set your wits to work. Now I must go.

DR. STOCKMANN: Won't you stay a little while?

MORTEN KIIL: No, I must be off now. You keep up this game for all it is worth; you won't repent it, I'm damned if you will!

(*He goes out;* MRS. STOCKMANN *follows him into the hall.*)

DR. STOCKMANN (*laughing*): Just imagine—the old chap doesn't believe a word of all this about the water supply.

HOVSTAD: Oh that was it, then?

DR. STOCKMANN: Yes, that was what we were talking about. Perhaps it is the same thing that brings you here?

HOVSTAD: Yes, it is. Can you spare me a few minutes, Doctor?

DR. STOCKMANN: As long as you like, my dear fellow.

HOVSTAD: Have you heard from the Mayor yet?

DR. STOCKMANN: Not yet. He is coming here later.

HOVSTAD: I have given the matter a great deal of thought since last night.

DR. STOCKMANN: Well?

HOVSTAD: From your point of view, as a doctor and a man of science, this affair of the water-supply is an isolated matter. I mean, you do not realise that it involves a great many other things.

DR. STOCKMANN: How, do you mean?—Let us sit down, my dear fellow.

No, sit here on the couch. (HOVSTAD *sits down on the couch,* DR. STOCKMANN *on a chair on the other side of the table.*) Now then. You mean that—?

HOVSTAD: You said yesterday that the pollution of the water was due to impurities in the soil.

DR. STOCKMANN: Yes, unquestionably it is due to that poisonous morass up at Mölledal.

HOVSTAD: Begging your pardon, doctor, I fancy it is due to quite another morass altogether.

DR. STOCKMANN: What morass?

HOVSTAD: The morass that the whole life of our town is built on and is rotting in.

DR. STOCKMANN: What the deuce are you driving at, Hovstad?

HOVSTAD: The whole of the town's interests have, little by little, got into the hands of a pack of officials.

DR. STOCKMANN: Oh, come!—they are not all officials.

HOVSTAD: No, but those that are not officials are at any rate the officials' friends and adherents; it is the wealthy folk, the old families in the town, that have got us entirely in their hands.

DR. STOCKMANN: Yes, but after all they are men of ability and knowledge.

HOVSTAD: Did they show any ability or knowledge when they laid the conduit-pipes where they are now?

DR. STOCKMANN: No, of course that was a great piece of stupidity on their part. But that is going to be set right now.

HOVSTAD: Do you think that will be all such plain sailing?

DR. STOCKMANN: Plain sailing or no, it has got to be done, anyway.

HOVSTAD: Yes, provided the press takes up the question.

DR. STOCKMAN: I don't think that will be necessary, my dear fellow, I am certain my brother—

HOVSTAD: Excuse me, doctor; I feel bound to tell you I am inclined to take the matter up.

DR. STOCKMANN: In the paper?

HOVSTAD: Yes, When I took over the "People's Messenger" my idea was to break up this ring of self-opinionated old fossils who had got hold of all the influence.

DR. STOCKMANN: But you know you told me yourself what the result had been; you nearly ruined your paper.

HOVSTAD: Yes, at the time we were obliged to climb down a peg or two, it is quite true; because there was a danger of the whole project of the Baths coming to nothing if they failed us. But now the scheme has been carried through, and we can dispense with these grand gentlemen.

DR. STOCKMANN: Dispense with them, yes; but we owe them a great debt of gratitude.

HOVSTAD: That shall be recognised ungrudgingly. But a journalist of my

Henrik Ibsen: *An Enemy of the People*

democratic tendencies cannot let such an opportunity as this slip. The bubble of official infallibility must be pricked. This superstition must be destroyed, like any other.

DR. STOCKMANN: I am whole-heartedly with you in that, Mr. Hovstad; if it is a superstition, away with it!

HOVSTAD: I should be very reluctant to bring the Mayor into it, because he is your brother. But I am sure you will agree with me that truth should be the first consideration.

DR. STOCKMANN: That goes without saying. (*With sudden emphasis.*) Yes, but—but—

HOVSTAD: You must not misjudge me. I am neither more self-interested nor more ambitious than most men.

DR. STOCKMANN: My dear fellow—who suggests anything of that kind?

HOVSTAD: I am of humble origin, as you know; and that has given me opportunities of knowing what is the most crying need in the humbler ranks of life. It is that they should be allowed some part in the direction of public affairs, Doctor. That is what will develop their faculties and intelligence and self respect—

DR. STOCKMANN: I quite appreciate that.

HOVSTAD: Yes—and in my opinion a journalist incurs a heavy responsibility if he neglects a favourable opportuntiy of emancipating the masses—the humble and oppressed. I know well enough that in exalted circles I shall be called an agitator, and all that sort of thing; but they may call what they like. If only my conscience doesn't reproach me, then—

DR. STOCKMANN: Quite right! Quite right, Mr. Hovstad. But all the same —devil take it! (*A knock is heard at the door.*) Come in!

(ASLAKSEN *appears at the door. He is poorly but decently dressed, in black, with a slightly crumpled white neckcloth; he wears gloves and has a felt hat in his hand.*)

ASLAKSEN (*bowing*): Excuse my taking the liberty, Doctor—
DR. STOCKMANN (*getting up*): Ah, it is you, Aslaksen!
ASLAKSEN: Yes, Doctor.
HOVSTAD (*standing up*): Is it me you want, Aslaksen?
ASLAKSEN: No; I didn't know I should find you here. No, it was the Doctor I—
DR. STOCKMANN: I am quite at your service. What is it?
ASLAKSEN: Is what I heard from Mr. Billing true, sir—that you mean to improve our water-supply?
DR. STOCKMANN: Yes, for the Baths.
ASLAKSEN: Quite so, I understand. Well, I have come to say that I will back that up by every means in my power.

HOVSTAD (*to the* DOCTOR): You see!

DR. STOCKMANN: I shall be very grateful to you, but—

ASLAKSEN: Because it may be no bad thing to have us small tradesmen at your back. We form, as it were, a compact majority in the town—if we choose. And it is always a good thing to have the majority with you, Doctor.

DR. STOCKMANN: This is undeniably true; but I confess I don't see why such unusual precautions should be necessary in this case. It seems to me that such a plain, straightforward thing—

ASLAKSEN: Oh, it may be very desirable, all the same. I know our local authorities so well; officials are not generally very ready to act on proposals that come from other people. That is why I think it would not be at all amiss if we made a little demonstration.

HOVSTAD: That's right.

DR. STOCKMANN: Demonstration, did you say? What on earth are you going to make a demonstration about?

ASLAKSEN: We shall proceed with the greatest moderation, Doctor. Moderation is always my aim; it is the greatest virtue in a citizen—at least, I think so.

DR. STOCKMANN: It is well known to be a characteristic of yours, Mr. Aslaksen.

ASLAKSEN: Yes, I think I may pride myself on that. And this matter of the water-supply is of the greatest importance to us small tradesmen. The Baths promise to be a regular gold-mine for the town. We shall all make our living out of them, especially those of us who are householders. That is why we will back up the project as strongly as possible. And as I am at present Chairman of the Householders' Association—

DR. STOCKMANN: Yes—?

ASLAKSEN: And, what is more, local secretary of the Temperance Society —you know, sir, I suppose, that I am a worker in the temperance cause?

DR. STOCKMANN: Of course, of course.

ASLAKSEN: Well, you can understand that I come into contact with a great many people. And as I have the reputation of a temperate and law-abiding citizen—like yourself, Doctor—I have a certain influence in the town, a little bit of power, if I may be allowed to say so.

DR. STOCKMANN: I know that quite well, Mr. Aslaksen.

ASLAKSEN: So you see it would be an easy matter for me to set on foot some testimonial, if necessary.

DR. STOCKMANN: A testimonial?

ASLAKSEN: Yes, some kind of an address of thanks from the townsmen for your share in a matter of such importance to the community. I need scarcely say that it would have to be drawn up with the greatest regard to moderation, so as not to offend the authorities—who, after all, have the reins in their hands. If we pay strict attention to that, no one can take it amiss, I should think!

HOVSTAD: Well, and even supposing they didn't like it—

ASLAKSEN: No, no, no; there must be no discourtesy to the authorities, Mr. Hovstad. It is no use falling foul of those upon whom our welfare so closely depends. I have done that in my time, and no good ever comes of it. But no one can take exception to a reasonable and frank expression of a citizen's views.

DR. STOCKMANN (*shaking him by the hand*): I can't tell you, dear, Mr. Aslaksen, how extremely pleased I am to find such hearty support among my fellow-citizens. I am delighted—delighted! Now, you will take a small glass of sherry, eh?

ASLAKSEN: No, thank you; I never drink alcohol of that kind.

DR. STOCKMANN: Well, what do you say to a glass of beer, then?

ASLAKSEN: Nor that either, thank you, Doctor. I never drink anything as early as this. I am going into town now to talk this over with one or two householders, and prepare the ground.

DR. STOCKMANN: It is tremendously kind of you, Mr. Aslaksen; but I really cannot understand the necessity for all these precautions. It seems to me that the thing should go of itself.

ASLAKSEN: The authorities are somewhat slow to move, Doctor. Far be it from me to seem to blame them—

HOVSTAD: We are going to stir them up in the paper tomorrow, Aslaksen.

ASLAKSEN: But not violently, I trust, Mr. Hovstad. Proceed with moderation, or you will do nothing with them. You may take my advice; I have gathered my experience in the school of life. Well, I must say good-bye, Doctor. You know now that we small tradesmen are at your back at all events, like a solid wall. You have the compact majority on your side, Doctor.

DR. STOCKMANN: I am very much obliged, dear Mr. Aslaksen. (*Shakes hands with him.*) Good-bye, good-bye.

ASLAKSEN: Are you going my way, towards the printing-office, Mr. Hovstad?

HOVSTAD: I will come later; I have something to settle up first.

ASLAKSEN: Very well. (*Bows and goes out;* STOCKMANN *follows him into the hall.*)

HOVSTAD (*as* STOCKMANN *comes in again*): Well, what do you think of that, Doctor? Don't you think it is high time we stirred a little life into all this slackness and vacillation and cowardice?

DR. STOCKMANN: Are you referring to Aslaksen?

HOVSTAD: Yes, I am. He is one of those who are floundering in a bog—decent enough fellow though he may be, otherwise. And most of the people here are in just the same case—see-sawing and edging first to one side and then to the other, so overcome with caution and scruple that they never dare to take any decided step.

DR. STOCKMANN: Yes, but Aslaksen seemed to me so thoroughly well-intentioned.

HOVSTAD: There is one thing I esteem higher than that; and that is for a man to be self-reliant and sure of himself.

DR. STOCKMANN: I think you are perfectly right there.

HOVSTAD: That is why I want to seize this opportunity, and try if I cannot manage to put a little virility into these well-intentioned people for once. The idol of Authority must be shattered in this town. This gross and inexcusable blunder about the water-supply must be brought home to the mind of every municipal voter.

DR. STOCKMANN: Very well; if you are of opinion that it is for the good of the community, so be it. But not until I have had a talk with my brother.

HOVSTAD: Anyway, I will get a leading article ready; and if the Mayor refuses to take the matter up—

DR. STOCKMANN: How can you suppose such a thing possible?

HOVSTAD: It is conceivable. And in that case—

DR. STOCKMANN: In that case I promise you—. Look here, in that case you may print my report—every word of it.

HOVSTAD: May I? Have I your word for it?

DR. STOCKMANN (*giving him the MS.*): Here it is; take it with you. It can do no harm for you to read it through, and you can give it back to me later on.

HOVSTAD: Good, good! That is what I will do. And now good-bye, Doctor.

DR. STOCKMANN: Good-bye, good-bye. You will see everything will run quite smoothly, Mr. Hovstad—quite smoothly.

HOVSTAD: Hm!—we shall see. (*Bows and goes out.*)

DR. STOCKMANN (*opens the dining-room door and looks in*): Katherine! Oh, you are back, Petra?

PETRA (*coming in*): Yes, I have just come from the school.

MRS. STOCKMANN (*coming in*): Has he not been here yet?

DR. STOCKMANN: Peter? No. But I have had a long talk with Hovstad. He is quite excited about my discovery. I find it has a much wider bearing than I at first imagined. And he has put his paper at my disposal if necessity should arise.

MRS. STOCKMANN: Do you think it will?

DR. STOCKMANN: Not for a moment. But at all events it makes me feel proud to know that I have the liberal-minded independent press on my side. Yes, and—just imagine—I have had a visit from the Chairman of Householders' Association!

MRS. STOCKMANN: Oh! What did he want?

DR. STOCKMANN: To offer me his support too. They will support me in a body if it should be necessary. Katherine—do you know what I have got behind me?
MRS. STOCKMANN: Behind you? No, what have you got behind you?
DR. STOCKMANN: The compact majority.
MRS. STOCKMANN: Really? Is that a good thing for you, Thomas?
DR. STOCKMANN: I should think it was a good thing. (*Walks up and down rubbing his hands.*) By Jove, it's a fine thing to feel this bond of brotherhood between oneself and one's fellow citizens!
PETRA: And to be able to do so much that is good and useful, father!
DR. STOCKMANN: And for one's own native town into the bargain, my child!
MRS. STOCKMANN: That was a ring at the bell.
DR. STOCKMANN: It must be he, then. (*A knock is heard at the door.*) Come in!
PETER STOCKMANN (*comes in from the hall*): Good morning.
DR. STOCKMANN: Glad to see you, Peter!
MRS. STOCKMANN: Good morning, Peter. How are you?
PETER STOCKMANN: So so, thank you. (*To* DR. STOCKMANN.) I received from you yesterday, after office hours, a report dealing with the condition of the water at the Baths.
DR. STOCKMANN: Yes. Have you read it?
PETER STOCKMANN: Yes, I have.
DR. STOCKMANN: And what have you to say to it?
PETER STOCKMANN (*with a sidelong glance*): Hm!—
MRS. STOCKMANN: Come along, Petra. (*She and* PETRA *go into the room on the left.*)
PETER STOCKMANN (*after a pause*): Was it necessary to make all these investigations behind my back?
DR. STOCKMANN: Yes, because until I was absolutely certain about it—
PETER STOCKMANN: Then you mean that you are absolutely certain now?
DR. STOCKMANN: Surely you are convinced of that.
PETER STOCKMANN: Is it your intention to bring this document before the Baths Committee as a sort of official communication?
DR. STOCKMANN: Certainly. Something must be done in the matter—and that quickly.
PETER STOCKMANN: As usual, you employ violent expression in your report. You say, amongst other things, that what we offer visitors in our Baths is a permanent supply of poison.
DR. STOCKMANN: Well, can you describe it any other way, Peter? Just think—water that is poisonous, whether you drink it or bathe in it! And this we offer to the poor sick folk who come to us trustfully and pay us at an exorbitant rate to be made well again!

PETER STOCKMANN: And your reasoning leads you to this conclusion, that we must build a sewer to draw off the alleged impurities from Mölledal and must relay the water-conduits.

DR. STOCKMANN: Yes. Do you see any other way out of it? I don't.

PETER STOCKMANN: I made a pretext this morning to go and see the town engineer, and, as if only half seriously, broached the subject of these proposals as a thing we might perhaps have to take under consideration some time later on.

DR. STOCKMANN: Some time later on!

PETER STOCKMANN: He smiled at what he considered to be my extravagance, naturally. Have you taken the trouble to consider what your proposed alterations would cost? According to the information I obtained, the expenses would probably mount up to fifteen or twenty thousand pounds.

DR. STOCKMANN: Would it cost so much?

PETER STOCKMANN: Yes; and the worst part of it would be that the work would take at least two years.

DR. STOCKMANN: Two years? Two whole years?

PETER STOCKMANN: At least. And what are we to do with the Baths in the meantime? Close them? Indeed we should be obliged to. And do you suppose any one would come near the place after it had got about that the water was dangerous?

DR. STOCKMANN: Yes but, Peter, that is what it is.

PETER STOCKMANN: And all this at this juncture—just as the Baths are beginning to be known. There are other towns in the neighbourhood with qualifications to attract visitors for bathing purposes. Don't you suppose they would immediately strain every nerve to divert the entire stream of strangers to themselves? Unquestionably they would; and then where should we be? We should probably have to abandon the whole thing, which has cost us so much money—and then you would have ruined your native town.

DR. STOCKMANN: I—should have ruined—!

PETER STOCKMANN: It is simply and solely through the Baths that the town has before it any future worth mentioning. You know that just as well as I.

DR. STOCKMANN: But what do you think ought to be done, then?

PETER STOCKMANN: Your report has not convinced me that the condition of the water at the Baths is as bad as you represent it to be.

DR. STOCKMANN: I tell you it is even worse!—or at all events it will be in summer, when the warm weather comes.

PETER STOCKMANN: As I said, I believe you exaggerate the matter considerably. A capable physician ought to know what measures to take—

he ought to be capable of preventing injurious influences or of remedying them if they become obviously persistent.

DR. STOCKMANN: Well? What more?

PETER STOCKMANN: The water supply for the Baths is now an established fact and in consequence must be treated as such. But probably the Committee, at its discretion, will not be disinclined to consider the question of how far it might be possible to introduce certain improvements consistently with a reasonable expenditure.

DR. STOCKMANN: And do you suppose that I will have anything to do with such a piece of trickery as that?

PETER STOCKMANN: Trickery!!

DR. STOCKMANN: Yes, it would be a trick—a fraud, a lie, a downright crime towards the public, towards the whole community!

PETER STOCKMANN: I have not, as I remarked before, been able to convince myself that there is actually any imminent danger.

DR. STOCKMANN: You have! It is impossible that you should not be convinced. I know I have represented the facts absolutely truthfully and fairly. And you know it very well, Peter, only you won't acknowledge it. It was owing to your action that both the Baths and the water-conduits were built where they are; and that is what you won't acknowledge—that damnable blunder of yours. Pooh!—do you suppose I don't see through you?

PETER STOCKMANN: And even if that were true? If I perhaps guard my reputation somewhat anxiously, it is in the best interests of the town. Without moral authority I am powerless to direct public affairs as seems, to my judgment, to be best for the common good. And on that account—and for various other reasons too—it appears to me to be a matter of importance that your report should not be delivered to the Committee. In the interests of the public, you must withhold it. Then, later on, I will raise the question and we will do our best, privately; but nothing of this unfortunate affair—not a single word of it—must come to the ears of the public.

DR. STOCKMANN: I am afraid you will not be able to prevent that now, my dear Peter.

PETER STOCKMANN: It must and shall be prevented.

DR. STOCKMANN: It is no use, I tell you. There are too many people that know about it.

PETER STOCKMANN: That know about it? Who? Surely you don't mean those fellows on the "People's Messenger"?

DR. STOCKMANN: Yes, they know. The liberal-minded independent press is going to see that you do your duty.

PETER STOCKMANN (*after a short pause*): You are an extraordinarily independent man, Thomas. Have you given no thought to the consequences this may have for yourself?

DR. STOCKMANN: Consequences?—for me?

PETER STOCKMANN: For you and yours, yes.

DR. STOCKMANN: What the deuce do you mean?

PETER STOCKMANN: I believe I have always behaved in a brotherly way to you—have always been ready to oblige or to help you?

DR. STOCKMANN: Yes, you have, and I am grateful to you for it.

PETER STOCKMANN: There is no need. Indeed, to some extent I was forced to do so—for my own sake. I always hoped that, if I helped to improve your financial position, I should be able to keep some check on you.

DR. STOCKMANN: What! Then it was only for your own sake—!

PETER STOCKMANN: Up to a certain point, yes. It is painful for a man in an official position to have his nearest relative compromising himself time after time.

DR. STOCKMANN: And do you consider that I do that?

PETER STOCKMANN: Yes, unfortunately, you do, without even being aware of it. You have a restless, pugnacious, rebellious disposition. And then there is that disastrous propensity of yours to want to write about every sort of possible and impossible thing. The moment an idea comes into your head, you must needs go and write a newspaper article or a whole pamphlet about it.

DR. STOCKMANN: Well, but is it not the duty of a citizen to let the public share in any new ideas he may have?

PETER STOCKMANN: Oh, the public doesn't require any new ideas. The public is best served by the good, old-established ideas it already has.

DR. STOCKMANN: And that is your honest opinion?

PETER STOCKMANN: Yes, and for once I must talk frankly to you. Hitherto I have tried to avoid doing so, because I know how irritable you are; but now I must tell you the truth, Thomas. You have no conception what an amount of harm you do yourself by your impetuosity. You complain of the authorities, you even complain of the government— you are always pulling them to pieces; you insist that you have been neglected and persecuted. But what else can such a cantankerous man as you expect?

DR. STOCKMANN: What next! Cantankerous, am I?

PETER STOCKMANN: Yes, Thomas, you are an extremely cantankerous man to work with—I know that to my cost. You disregard everything that you ought to have consideration for. You seem completely to forget that it is me you have to thank for your appointment here as medical officer to the Baths—

DR. STOCKMANN: I was entitled to it as a matter of course!—I and nobody else! I was the first person to see that the town could be made into a flourishing watering-place, and I was the only one who saw it at that time. I had to fight single-handed in support of the idea for many years; and I wrote and wrote—

PETER STOCKMANN: Undoubtedly. But things were not ripe for the scheme then—though, of course, you could not judge of that in your out-of-the-way corner up north. But as soon as the opportune moment came I—and the others—took the matter into our hands—

DR. STOCKMANN: Yes, and made this mess of all my beautiful plan. It is pretty obvious now what clever fellows you were!

PETER STOCKMANN: To my mind the whole thing only seems to mean that you are seeking another outlet for your combativeness. You want to pick a quarrel with your superiors—an old habit of yours. You cannot put up with any authority over you. You look askance at anyone who occupies a superior official position; you regard him as a personal enemy, and then any stick is good enough to beat him with. But now I have called your attention to the fact that the town's interests are at stake—and, incidentally, my own too. And therefore I must tell you, Thomas, that you will find me inexorable with regard to what I am about to require you to do.

DR. STOCKMANN: And what is that?

PETER STOCKMANN: As you have been so indiscreet as to speak of this delicate matter to outsiders, despite the fact that you ought to have treated it as entirely official and confidential, it is obviously impossible to hush it up now. All sorts of rumours will get about directly, and everybody who has a grudge against us will take care to embellish these rumours. So it will be necessary for you to refute them publicly.

DR. STOCKMANN: I! How? I don't understand.

PETER STOCKMANN: What we shall expect is that, after making further investigations, you will come to the conclusion that the matter is not by any means as dangerous or as critical as you imagined in the first instance.

DR. STOCKMANN: Oho!—so that is what you expect!

PETER STOCKMANN: And, what is more, we shall expect you to make public profession of your confidence in the Committee and in their readiness to consider fully and conscientiously what steps may be necessary to remedy any possible defects.

DR. STOCKMANN: But you will never be able to do that by patching and tinkering at it—never! Take my word for it, Peter; I mean what I say, as deliberately and emphatically as possible.

PETER STOCKMANN: As an officer under the Committee, you have no right to any individual opinion.

DR. STOCKMANN (*amazed*): No right?

PETER STOCKMANN: In your official capacity, no. As a private person, it is quite another matter. But as a subordinate member of the staff of the Baths, you have no right to express any opinion which runs contrary to that of your superiors.

DR. STOCKMANN: This is too much! I, a doctor, a man of science, have no right to—!

PETER STOCKMANN: The matter in hand is not simply a scientific one. It is a complicated matter, and has its economic as well as its technical side.

DR. STOCKMANN: I don't care what it is! I intend to be free to express my opinion on any subject under the sun.

PETER STOCKMANN: As you please—but not on any subject concerning the Baths. That we forbid.

DR. STOCKMANN (*shouting*): You forbid—! You! A pack of—

PETER STOCKMANN: *I* forbid it—I, your chief; and if I forbid it, you have to obey.

DR. STOCKMANN (*controlling himself*): Peter—if you were not my brother—

PETRA (*throwing open the door*). Father, you shan't stand this!

MRS. STOCKMANN (*coming in after her*): Petra, Petra!

PETER STOCKMANN: Oh, so you have been eavesdropping.

MRS. STOCKMANN: You were talking so loud, we couldn't help—

PETRA: Yes, I was listening.

PETER STOCKMANN: Well, after all, I am very glad—

DR. STOCKMANN (*going up to him*): You were saying something about forbidding and obeying?

PETER STOCKMANN. You obliged me to take that tone with you.

DR. STOCKMANN: And so I am to give myself the lie, publicly?

PETER STOCKMANN: We consider it absolutely necessary that you should make some such public statement as I have asked for.

DR. STOCKMANN: And if I do not—obey?

PETER STOCKMANN: Then we shall publish a statement ourselves to reassure the public.

DR. STOCKMANN: Very well; but in that case I shall use my pen against you. I stick to what I have said; I will show that I am right and that you are wrong. And what will you do then?

PETER STOCKMANN: Then I shall not be able to prevent your being dismissed.

DR. STOCKMANN: What—?

PETRA: Father—dismissed!

MRS. STOCKMANN: Dismissed!

PETER STOCKMANN: Dismissed from the staff of the Baths. I shall be obliged to propose that you shall immediately be given notice, and shall not be allowed any further participation in the Baths' affairs.

DR. STOCKMANN: You would dare to do that!

PETER STOCKMANN: It is you that are playing the daring game.

PETRA: Uncle, that is a shameful way to treat a man like father!

MRS. STOCKMANN: Do hold your tongue, Petra!

PETER STOCKMANN (*looking at* PETRA): Oh, so we volunteer our opinions already, do we? Of course. (*To* MRS. STOCKMANN.) Katherine, I imagine you are the most sensible person in this house. Use any influence you may have over your husband, and make him see what this will entail for his family as well as—

DR. STOCKMANN: My family is my own concern and nobody else's!

PETER STOCKMANN: —for his own family, as I was saying, as well as for the town he lives in.

DR. STOCKMANN: It is I who have the real good of the town at heart! I want to lay bare the defects that sooner or later must come to the light of day. I will show whether I love my native town.

PETER STOCKMANN: You, who in your blind obstinacy want to cut off the most important source of the town's welfare?

DR. STOCKMANN: The source is poisoned, man! Are you mad? We are making our living by retailing filth and corruption! The whole of our flourishing municipal life derives its sustenance from a lie!

PETER STOCKMANN: All imagination—or something even worse. The man who can throw out such offensive insinuations about his native town must be an enemy to our community.

DR. STOCKMANN (*going up to him*). Do you dare to—!

MRS. STOCKMANN (*throwing herself between them*). Thomas!

PETRA (*catching her father by the arm*): Don't lose your temper, father!

PETER STOCKMANN: I will not expose myself to violence. Now you have had a warning; so reflect on what you owe to yourself and your family. Good-bye. (*Goes out.*)

DR. STOCKMANN (*walking up and down*): Am I to put up with such treatment as this? In my own house, Katherine! What do you think of that!

MRS. STOCKMANN: Indeed it is both shameful and absurd, Thomas—

PETRA: If only I could give uncle a piece of my mind—

DR. STOCKMANN: It is my own fault. I ought to have flown out at him long ago!—shown my teeth!—bitten! To hear him call me an enemy to our community! Me! I shall not take that lying down, upon my soul!

MRS. STOCKMANN: But, dear Thomas, your brother has power on his side—

DR. STOCKMANN: Yes, but I have right on mine, I tell you.

MRS. STOCKMANN: Oh, yes, right—right. What is the use of having right on your side if you have not got might?

PETRA: Oh, mother!—how can you say such a thing!

DR. STOCKMANN: Do you imagine that in a free country it is no use having right on your side? You are absurd, Katherine. Besides, haven't I got the liberal-minded independent press to lead the way, and the compact majority behind me? That is might enough, I should think!

MRS. STOCKMANN: But, good heavens, Thomas, you don't mean to—?

DR. STOCKMANN: Don't mean to what?

MRS. STOCKMANN: To set yourself up in opposition to your brother.

DR. STOCKMANN: In God's name, what else do you suppose I should do but take my stand on right and truth?

PETRA: Yes, I was just going to say that.

MRS. STOCKMANN: But it won't do you any earthly good. If they won't do it, they won't.

DR. STOCKMANN: Oho, Katherine! Just give me time, and you will see how I will carry the war into their camp.

MRS. STOCKMANN: Yes, you carry the war into their camp, and you get your dismissal—that is what you will do.

DR. STOCKMANN: In any case I shall have done my duty towards the public—towards the community. I, who am called its enemy!

MRS. STOCKMANN: But towards your family, Thomas? Towards your own home! Do you think that is doing your duty towards those you have to provide for?

PETRA: Ah, don't think always first of us, mother.

MRS. STOCKMANN: Oh it is easy for you to talk; you are able to shift for yourself, if need be. But remember the boys, Thomas; and think a little too of yourself, and of me—

DR. STOCKMANN: I think you are out of your senses, Katherine! If I were to be such a miserable coward as to go on my knees to Peter and his damned crew, do you suppose I should ever know an hour's peace of mind all my life afterwards?

MRS. STOCKMANN: I don't know anything about that; but God preserve us from the peace of mind we shall have, all the same, if you go on defying him! You will find yourself again without the means of subsistence, with no income to count upon. I should think we had had enough of that in the old days. Remember that, Thomas; think what that means.

DR. STOCKMANN (*collecting himself with a struggle and clenching his fists*): And this is what this slavery can bring upon a free, honourable man! Isn't it horrible, Katherine?

MRS. STOCKMANN: Yes, it is sinful to treat you so, it is perfectly true. But, good heavens, one has to put up with so much injustice in this world. —There are the boys, Thomas! Look at them! What is to become of them? Oh, no, you can never have the heart—. (EJLIF and MORTEN *have come in while she was speaking, with their school books in their hands.*)

DR. STOCKMANN: The boys—! (*Recovers himself suddenly.*) No, even if the whole world goes to pieces, I will never bow my neck to this yoke! (*Goes towards his room.*)

MRS. STOCKMANN (*following him*): Thomas—what are you going to do!

DR. STOCKMANN (*at his door*): I mean to have the right to look my sons in the face when they are grown men. (*Goes into his room.*)

MRS. STOCKMANN (*bursting into tears*): God help us all!

PETRA: Father is splendid! He will not give in.

(*The boys look on in amazement;* PETRA *signs to them not to speak.*)

ACT III

(SCENE: The editorial office of the "People's Messenger." The entrance door is on the left-hand side of the back wall; on the right-hand side is another door with glass panels through which the printing-room can be seen. Another door in the right-hand wall. In the middle of the room is a large table covered with papers, newspapers and books. In the foreground on the left a window, before which stands a desk and a high stool. There are a couple of easy chairs by the table, and other chairs standing along the wall. The room is dingy and uncomfortable; the furniture is old, the chairs stained and torn. In the printing-room the compositors are seen at work, and a printer is working a hand-press. HOVSTAD is sitting at the desk, writing. BILLING comes in from the right with DR. STOCKMANN's manuscript in his hand.)

BILLING: Well, I must say!

HOVSTAD (*still writing*): Have you read it through?

BILLING (*laying the MS. on the desk*): Yes, indeed I have.

HOVSTAD: Don't you think the Doctor hits them pretty hard?

BILLING: Hard? Bless my soul, he's crushing! Every word falls like—how shall I put it?—like the blow of a sledgehammer.

HOVSTAD: Yes, but they are not the people to throw up the sponge at the first blow.

BILLING: That is true; and for that reason we must strike blow upon blow until the whole of this aristocracy tumbles to pieces. As I sat there reading this, I almost seemed to see a revolution in being.

HOVSTAD (*turning round*): Hush!—Speak so that Aslaksen cannot hear you.

BILLING (*lowering his voice*): Aslaksen is a chicken-hearted chap, a coward; there is nothing of the man in him. But this time you will insist on your own way, won't you? You will put the Doctor's article in?

HOVSTAD: Yes, and if the Mayor doesn't like it—

BILLING: That will be the devil of a nuisance.

HOVSTAD: Well, fortunately we can turn the situation to good account, whatever happens. If the Mayor will not fall in with the Doctor's project, he will have all the small tradesmen down on him—the whole of the Householder's Association and the rest of them. And if he does fall in with it, he will fall out with the whole crowd of large shareholders in the Baths, who up to now have been his most valuable supporters—

BILLING: Yes, because they will certainly have to fork out a pretty penny—

HOVSTAD: Yes, you may be sure they will. And in this way the ring will be broken up, you see, and then in every issue of the paper we will enlighten the public on the Mayor's incapability on one point and another, and make it clear that all the positions of trust in the town, the whole control of municipal affairs, ought to be put in the hands of the Liberals.

BILLING: That is perfectly true! I see it coming—I see it coming; we are on the threshold of a revolution!

(A knock is heard at the door.)

HOVSTAD: Hush! *(Calls out.)* Come in! (DR. STOCKMANN *comes in by the street door.* HOVSTAD *goes to meet him.*) Ah, it is you, Doctor! Well?

DR. STOCKMANN: You may set to work and print it, Mr. Hovstad!

HOVSTAD: Has it come to that, then?

BILLING: Hurrah!

DR. STOCKMANN: Yes, print away. Undoubtedly it has come to that. Now they must take what they get. There is going to be a fight in the town, Mr. Billing!

BILLING: War to the knife, I hope! We will get our knives to their throats, Doctor!

DR. STOCKMANN: This article is only a beginning. I have already got four or five more sketched out in my head. Where is Aslaksen?

BILLING *(calls into the printing-room)*: Aslaksen, just come here for a minute!

HOVSTAD: Four or five more articles, did you say? On the same subject?

DR. STOCKMANN: No—far from it, my dear fellow. No, they are about quite another matter. But they all spring from the question of the water-supply and the drainage. One thing leads to another, you know. It is like beginning to pull down an old house, exactly.

BILLING: Upon my soul, it's true; you find you are not done till you have pulled all the old rubbish down.

ASLAKSEN *(coming in)*. Pulled down? You are not thinking of pulling down the Baths surely, Doctor?

HOVSTAD: Far from it, don't be afraid.

DR. STOCKMANN: No, we meant something quite different. Well, what do you think of my article, Mr. Hovstad?
HOVSTAD: I think it is simply a masterpiece—
DR. STOCKMANN: Do you really think so? Well, I am very pleased, very pleased.
HOVSTAD: It is so clear and intelligible. One need have no special knowledge to understand the bearing of it. You will have every enlightened man on your side.
ASLAKSEN: And every prudent man too, I hope?
BILLING: The prudent and the imprudent—almost the whole town.
ASLAKSEN: In that case we may venture to print it.
DR. STOCKMANN: I should think so!
HOVSTAD: We will put it in to-morrow morning.
DR. STOCKMANN: Of course—you must not lose a single day. What I wanted to ask you, Mr. Aslaksen, was if you would supervise the printing of it yourself.
ASLAKSEN: With pleasure.
DR. STOCKMANN: Take care of it as if it were a treasure! No misprints—every word is important. I will look in again a little later; perhaps you will be able to let me see a proof. I can't tell you how eager I am to see it in print, and see it burst upon the public—
BILLING: Burst upon them—yes, like a flash of lightning!
DR. STOCKMANN: —and to have it submitted to the judgment of my intelligent fellow-townsmen. You cannot imagine what I have gone through to-day. I have been threatened first with one thing and then with another; they have tried to rob me of my most elementary rights as a man—
BILLING: What! Your rights as a man!
DR. STOCKMANN: —they have tried to degrade me, to make a coward of me, to force me to put personal interests before my most sacred convictions—
BILLING: That is too much—I'm damned if it isn't.
HOVSTAD: Oh, you mustn't be surprised at anything from that quarter.
DR. STOCKMANN: Well, they will get the worst of it with me; they may assure themselves of that. I shall consider the "People's Messenger" my sheet-anchor now, and every single day I will bombard them with one article after another, like bomb-shells—
ASLAKSEN: Yes, but—
BILLING: Hurrah!—it is war, it is war!
DR. STOCKMANN: I shall smite them to the ground—I shall crush them—I shall break down all their defences, before the eyes of the honest public! That is what I shall do!
ASLAKSEN: Yes, but in moderation, Doctor—proceed with moderation—

BILLING: Not a bit of it, not a bit of it! Don't spare thee dynamite!

DR. STOCKMANN: Because it is not merely a question of water-supply and drains now, you know. No—it is the whole of our social life that we have got to purify and disinfect—

BILLING: Spoken like a deliverer!

DR. STOCKMANN: All the incapables must be turned out, you understand —and that in every walk of life! Endless vistas have opened themselves to my mind's eye to-day. I cannot see it all quite clearly yet, but I shall in time. Young and vigorous standard-bearers—those are what we need and must seek, my friends; we must have new men in command at all our outposts.

BILLING: Hear, hear!

DR. STOCKMANN: We only need to stand by one another, and it will all be perfectly easy. The revolution will be launched like a ship that runs smoothly off the stocks. Don't you think so?

HOVSTAD: For my part I think we have now a prospect of getting the municipal authority into the hands where it should lie.

ASLAKSEN: And if only we proceed with moderation, I cannot imagine that there will be any risk.

DR. STOCKMANN: Who the devil cares whether there is any risk or not! What I am doing, I am doing in the name of truth and for the sake of my conscience.

HOVSTAD: You are a man who deserves to be supported, Doctor.

ASLAKSEN: Yes, there is no denying that the Doctor is a true friend to the town—a real friend to the community, that he is.

BILLING: Take my word for it, Aslaksen, Dr. Stockmann is a friend of the people.

ASLAKSEN: I fancy the Householders' Association will make use of that expression before long.

DR. STOCKMANN (*affected, grasps their hands*): Thank you, thank you, my dear staunch friends. It is very refreshing to me to hear you say that; my brother called me something quite different. By Jove, he shall have it back, with interest! But now I must be off to see a poor devil—. I will come back, as I said. Keep a very careful eye on the manuscript, Aslaksen, and don't for worlds leave out any of my notes of exclamation! Rather put one or two more in! Capital, capital! Well, good-bye for the present—good-bye, good-bye!

(*They show him to the door, and bow him out.*)

HOVSTAD: He may prove an invaluably useful man to us.

ASLAKSEN: Yes, so long as he confines himself to this matter of the Baths. But if he goes farther afield, I don't think it would be advisable to follow him.

HOVSTAD: Hm!—that all depends—
BILLING: You are so infernally timid, Aslaksen!
ASLAKSEN: Timid? Yes, when it is a question of the local authorities, I am timid, Mr. Billing; it is a lesson I have learnt in the school of experience, let me tell you. But try me in higher politics, in matters that concern the government itself, and then see if I am timid.
BILLING: No, you aren't, I admit. But this is simply contradicting yourself.
ASLAKSEN: I am a man with a conscience, and that is the whole matter. If you attack the government, you don't do the community any harm, anyway; those fellows pay no attention to attacks, you see—they go on just as they are, in spite of them. But *local* authorities are different; they *can* be turned out, and then perhaps you may get an ignorant lot into office who may do irreparable harm to the householders and everybody else.
HOVSTAD: But what of the education of citizens by self government—don't you attach any importance to that?
ASLAKSEN: When a man has interests of his own to protect, he cannot think of everything, Mr. Hovstad.
HOVSTAD: Then I hope I shall never have interests of my own to protect!
BILLING: Hear, hear!
ASLAKSEN (*with a smile*): Hm! (*Points to the desk.*) Mr. Sheriff Stensgaard was your predecessor at that editorial desk.
BILLING (*spitting*): Bah! That turncoat.
HOVSTAD: I am not a weathercock—and never will be.
ASLAKSEN: A politician should never be too certain of anything, Mr. Hovstad. And as for you, Mr. Billing, I should think it is time for you to be taking in a reef or two in your sails, seeing that you are applying for the post of secretary to the Bench.
BILLING: I—!
HOVSTAD: Are you, Billing?
BILLING: Well, yes—but you must clearly understand I am only doing it to annoy the bigwigs.
ASLAKSEN: Anyhow, it is no business of mine. But if I am to be accused of timidity and of inconsistency in my principles, this is what I want to point out: my political past is an open book. I have never changed, except perhaps to become a little more moderate, you see. My heart is still with the people; but I don't deny that my reason has a certain bias towards the authorities—the local ones, I mean. (*Goes into the printing-room.*)
BILLING: Oughtn't we to try and get rid of him, Hovstad?
HOVSTAD: Do you know anyone else who will advance the money for our paper and printing bill?

BILLING: It is an infernal nuisance that we don't possess some capital to trade on.

HOVSTAD (*sitting down at his desk*): Yes, if we only had that, then—

BILLING: Suppose you were to apply to Dr. Stockmann?

HOVSTAD (*turning over some papers*): What is the use? He has got nothing.

BILLING: No, but he has got a warm man in the background, old Morten Kiil—"the Badger," as they call him.

HOVSTAD (*writing*): Are you so sure *he* has got anything?

BILLING: Good Lord, of course he has! And some of it must come to the Stockmanns. Most probably he will do something for the children, at all events.

HOVSTAD (*turning half round*): Are you counting on that?

BILLING: Counting on it? Of course I am not counting on anything.

HOVSTAD: That is right. And I should not count on the secretaryship to the Bench either, if I were you; for I can assure you—you won't get it.

BILLING: Do you think I am not quite aware of that? My object is precisely *not* to get it. A slight of that kind stimulates a man's fighting power—it is like getting a supply of fresh bile—and I am sure one needs that badly enough in a hole-and-corner place like this, where it is so seldom anything happens to stir one up.

HOVSTAD (*writing*): Quite so, quite so.

BILLING: Ah, I shall be heard of yet!—Now I shall go and write the appeal to the Householders' Association. (*Goes into the room on the right.*)

HOVSTAD (*sitting at his desk, biting his penholder, says slowly*): Hm!—that's it, is it. (*A knock is heard.*) Come in! (PETRA *comes in by the outer door.* HOVSTAD *get us.*) What, you!—here?

PETRA: Yes, you must forgive me—

HOVSTAD (*pulling a chair forward*): Won't you sit down?

PETRA: No, thank you; I must go again in a moment.

HOVSTAD: Have you come with a message from your father, by any chance?

PETRA: No, I have come on my own account. (*Takes a book out of her coat pocket.*) Here is the English story.

HOVSTAD: Why have you brought it back?

PETRA: Because I am not going to translate it.

HOVSTAD: But you promised me faithfully—

PETRA: Yes, but then I had not read it. I don't suppose you have read it either?

HOVSTAD: No, you know quite well I don't understand English; but—

PETRA: Quite so. That is why I wanted to tell you that you must find something else. (*Lays the book on the table.*) You can't use this for the "People's Messenger."

HOVSTAD: Why not?

PETRA: Because it conflicts with all your opinions.

HOVSTAD: Oh, for that matter—

PETRA: You don't understand me. The burden of this story is that there is a supernatural power that looks after the so-called good people in this world and makes everything happen for the best in their case—while all the so-called bad people are punished.

HOVSTAD: Well, but that is all right. That is just what our readers want.

PETRA: And are you going to be the one to give it to them? For myself, I do not believe a word of it. You know quite well that things do not happen so in reality.

HOVSTAD: You are perfectly right; but an editor cannot always act as he would prefer. He is often obliged to bow to the wishes of the public in unimportant matters. Politics are the most important thing in life—for a newspaper, anyway; and if I want to carry my public with me on the path that leads to liberty and progress, I must not frighten them away. If they find a moral tale of this sort in the serial at the bottom of the page, they will be all the more ready to read what is printed above it; they feel more secure, as it were.

PETRA: For shame! You would never go and set a snare like that for your readers; you are not a spider!

HOVSTAD (*smiling*): Thank you for having such a good opinion of me. No; as a matter of fact that is Billing's idea and not mine.

PETRA: Billing's!

HOVSTAD: Yes; anyway he propounded that theory here one day. And it is Billing who is so anxious to have that story in the paper; I don't know anything about the book.

PETRA: But how can Billing, with his emancipated views—

HOVSTAD: Oh, Billing is a many-sided man. He is applying for the post of secretary to the Bench, too, I hear.

PETRA: I don't believe it, Mr. Hovstad. How could he possibly bring himself to do such a thing?

HOVSTAD: Ah, you must ask him that.

PETRA: I should never have thought it of him.

HOVSTAD (*looking more closely at her*): No? Does it really surprise you so much?

PETRA: Yes. Or perhaps not altogether. Really, I don't quite know—

HOVSTAD: We journalists are not worth much, Miss Stockmann.

PETRA: Do you really mean that?

HOVSTAD: I think so sometimes.

PETRA: Yes, in the ordinary affairs of everyday life, perhaps; I can understand that. But now, when you have taken a weighty matter in hand—

HOVSTAD: This matter of your father's, you mean?

PETRA: Exactly. It seems to me that now you must feel you are a man worth more than most.

HOVSTAD: Yes, to-day I do feel something of that sort.

PETRA: Of course you do, don't you? It is a splendid vocation you have chosen—to smooth the way for the march of unappreciated truths, and new and courageous lines of thought. If it were nothing more than because you stand fearlessly in the open and take up the cause of an injured man—

HOVSTAD: Especially when that injured man is—ahem!—I don't rightly know how to—

PETRA: When that man is so upright and so honest, you mean?

HOVSTAD (*more gently*): Especially when he is your father, I meant.

PETRA (*suddenly checked*): That?

HOVSTAD: Yes, Petra—Miss Petra.

PETRA: Is it *that*, that is first and foremost with you? Not the matter itself? Not the truth?—not my father's big generous heart?

HOVSTAD: Certainly—of course—that too.

PETRA: No, thank you; you have betrayed yourself, Mr. Hovstad, and now I shall never trust you again in anything.

HOVSTAD: Can you really take it so amiss in me that it is mostly for your sake—?

PETRA: What I am angry with you for, is for not having been honest with my father. You talked to him as if the truth and the good of the community were what lay nearest to your heart. You have made fools of both my father and me. You are not the man you made yourself out to be. And that I shall never forgive you—never!

HOVSTAD: You ought not to speak so bitterly, Miss Petra—least of all now.

PETRA: Why not now, especially?

HOVSTAD: Because your father cannot do without my help.

PETRA (*looking him up and down*): Are you that sort of man too? For shame!

HOVSTAD: No, no, I am not. This came upon me so unexpectedly—you must believe that.

PETRA: I know what to believe. Good-bye.

ASLAKSEN (*coming from the printing-room, hurriedly and with an air of mystery*): Damnation, Hovstad!—(*Sees* PETRA.) Oh, this is awkward—

PETRA: There is the book; you must give it to some one else. (*Goes towards the door.*)

HOVSTAD (*following her*): But, Miss Stockmann—

PETRA: Good-bye. (*Goes out.*)

ASLAKSEN: I say—Mr. Hovstad—

HOVSTAD: Well, well!—what is it?

ASLAKSEN: The Mayor is outside in the printing-room.

HOVSTAD: The Mayor, did you say?

ASLAKSEN: Yes, he wants to speak to you. He came in by the back door—didn't want to be seen, you understand.

HOVSTAD: What can he want? Wait a bit—I will go myself. (*Goes to the door of the printing-room, opens it, bows and invites* PETER STOCKMANN *in.*) Just see, Aslaksen, that no one—

ASLAKSEN: Quite so. (*Goes into the printing-room.*)

PETER STOCKMANN: You did not expect to see me here, Mr. Hovstad.

HOVSTAD: No, I confess I did not.

PETER STOCKMANN (*looking round*): You are very snug in here—very nice indeed.

HOVSTAD: Oh—

PETER STOCKMANN: And here I come, without any notice, to take up your time!

HOVSTAD: By all means, Mr. Mayor. I am at your service. But let me relieve you of your— (*takes* STOCKMANN's *hat and stick and puts them on a chair*). Won't you sit down?

PETER STOCKMANN (*sitting down by the table*): Thank you. (HOVSTAD *sits down.*) I have had an extremely annoying experience to-day, Mr. Hovstad.

HOVSTAD: Really? Ah well, I expect with all the various business you have to attend to—

PETER STOCKMANN: The Medical Officer of the Baths is responsible for what happened to-day.

HOVSTAD: Indeed? The Doctor?

PETER STOCKMANN: He has addressed a kind of report to the Baths Committee on the subject of certain supposed defects in the Baths.

HOVSTAD: Has he indeed?

PETER STOCKMANN: Yes—has he not told you? I thought he said—

HOVSTAD: Ah, yes—it is true he did mention something about—

ASLAKSEN (*coming from the printing-room*): I ought to have that copy—

HOVSTAD (*angrily*): Ahem!—there it is on the desk.

ASLAKSEN (*taking it*): Right.

PETER STOCKMANN: But look there—that is the thing I was speaking of!

ASLAKSEN: Yes, that is the Doctor's article, Mr. Mayor.

HOVSTAD: Oh, is *that* what you were speaking about?

PETER STOCKMANN: Yes, that is it. What do you think of it?

HOVSTAD: Oh, I am only a layman—and I have only taken a very cursory glance at it.

PETER STOCKMANN: But you are going to print it?

HOVSTAD: I cannot very well refuse a distinguished man—

ASLAKSEN: I have nothing to do with editing the paper, Mr. Mayor—

PETER STOCKMANN: I understand.

ASLAKSEN: I merely print what is put into my hands.
PETER STOCKMANN: Quite so.
ASLAKSEN: And so I must—(*moves off towards the printing-room*).
PETER STOCKMANN: No, wait a moment, Mr. Aslaksen. You will allow me, Mr. Hovstad?
HOVSTAD: If you please, Mr. Mayor.
PETER STOCKMANN: You are a discreet and thoughtful man Mr. Aslaksen.
ASLAKSEN: I am delighted to hear you think so, sir.
PETER STOCKMANN: And a man of very considerable influence.
ASLAKSEN: Chiefly among the small tradesmen, sir.
PETER STOCKMANN: The small tax-payers are the majority—here as everywhere else.
ASLAKSEN: That is true.
PETER STOCKMANN: And I have no doubt you know the general trend of opinion among them, don't you?
ASLAKSEN: Yes I think I may say I do, Mr. Mayor.
PETER STOCKMANN: Yes. Well, since there is such a praiseworthy spirit of self-sacrifice among the less wealthy citizens of our town—
ASLAKSEN: What?
HOVSTAD: Self-sacrifice?
PETER STOCKMANN: It is pleasing evidence of a public-spirited feeling, extremely pleasing evidence. I might almost say I hardly expected it. But you have a closer knowledge of public opinion than I.
ASLAKSEN: But, Mr. Mayor—
PETER STOCKMANN: And indeed it is no small sacrifice that the town is going to make.
HOVSTAD: The town?
ASLAKSEN: But I don't understand. Is it the Baths—?
PETER STOCKMANN: At a provisional estimate, the alterations that the Medical Officer asserts to be desirable will cost somewhere about twenty thousand pounds.
ASLAKSEN: That is a lot of money, but—
PETER STOCKMANN: Of course it will be necessary to raise a municipal loan.
HOVSTAD (*getting up*): Surely you never mean that the town must pay—?
ASLAKSEN: Do you mean that it must come out of the municipal funds?—out of the ill-filled pockets of the small tradesmen?
PETER STOCKMANN: Well, my dear Mr. Aslaksen, where else is the money to come from?
ASLAKSEN: The gentlemen who own the Baths ought to provide that.
PETER STOCKMANN: The proprietors of the Baths are not in a position to incur any further expense.
ASLAKSEN: Is that absolutely certain, Mr. Mayor?

PETER STOCKMANN: I have satisfied myself that it is so. If the town wants these very extensive alterations, it will have to pay for them.
ASLAKSEN: But, damn it all—I beg your pardon—this is quite another matter, Mr. Hovstad!
HOVSTAD: It is, indeed.
PETER STOCKMANN: The most fatal part of it is that we shall be obliged to shut the Baths for a couple of years.
HOVSTAD: Shut them? Shut them altogether?
ASLAKSEN: For two years?
PETER STOCKMANN: Yes, the work will take as long as that—at least.
ASLAKSEN: I'm damned if we will stand that, Mr. Mayor! What are we householders to live upon in the meantime?
PETER STOCKMANN: Unfortunately that is an extremely difficult question to answer, Mr. Aslaksen. But what would you have us do? Do you suppose we shall have a single visitor in the town, if we go about proclaiming that our water is polluted, that we are living over a plague spot, that the entire town—
ASLAKSEN: And the whole thing is merely imagination?
PETER STOCKMANN: With the best will in the world, I have not been able to come to any other conclusion.
ASLAKSEN: Well then I must say it is absolutely unjustifiable of Dr. Stockmann—I beg your pardon, Mr. Mayor—
PETER STOCKMANN: What you say is lamentably true, Mr. Aslaksen. My brother has unfortunately always been a head-strong man.
ASLAKSEN: After his, do you mean to give him your support, Mr. Hovstad?
HOVSTAD: Can you suppose for a moment that I—?
PETER STOCKMANN: I have drawn up a short *résumé* of the situation as it appears from a reasonable man's point of view. In it I have indicated how certain possible defects might suitably be remedied without outrunning the resources of the Baths Committee.
HOVSTAD: Have you got it with you, Mr. Mayor.
PETER STOCKMANN (*fumbling in his pocket*): Yes, I brought it with me in case you should—
ASLAKSEN: Good Lord, there he is!
PETER STOCKMANN: Who? My brother?
HOVSTAD: Where? Where?
ASLAKSEN: He has just gone through the printing-room.
PETER STOCKMANN: How unlucky! I don't want to meet him here, and I had still several things to speak to you about.
HOVSTAD (*pointing to the door on the right*): Go in there for the present.
PETER STOCKMANN: But—?
HOVSTAD: You will only find Billing in there.
ASLAKSEN: Quick, quick, Mr. Mayor—he is just coming.

PETER STOCKMANN: Yes, very well; but see that you get rid of him quickly. (*Goes out through the door on the right, which* ASLAKSEN *opens for him and shuts after him.*)

HOVSTAD: Pretend to be doing something, Aslaksen. (*Sits down and writes.* ASLAKSEN *begins foraging among a heap of newspapers that are lying on a chair.*)

DR. STOCKMANN (*coming in from the printing-room*): Here I am again. (*Puts down his hat and stick.*)

HOVSTAD (*writing*): Already, Doctor? Hurry up with what we were speaking about, Aslaksen. We are very pressed for time to-day.

DR. STOCKMANN (*to* ASLAKSEN): No proof for me to see yet, I hear.

ASLAKSEN (*without turning round*): You couldn't expect it yet, Doctor.

DR. STOCKMANN: No no; but I am impatient, as you can understand. I shall not know a moment's peace of mind till I see it in print.

HOVSTAD: Hm!—It will take a good while yet, won't it, Aslaksen?

ASLAKSEN: Yes, I am almost afraid it will.

DR. STOCKMANN: All right, my dear friends; I will come back. I do not mind coming back twice if necessary. A matter of such great importance—the welfare of the town at stake—it is no time to shirk trouble. (*Is just going, but stops and comes back.*) Look here—there is one thing more I want to speak to you about.

HOVSTAD: Excuse me, but could it not wait till some other time?

DR. STOCKMANN: I can tell you in half a dozen words. It is only this. When my article is read to-morrow and it is realised that I have been quietly working the whole winter for the welfare of the town—

HOVSTAD: Yes but, Doctor—

DR. STOCKMANN: I know what you are going to say. You don't see how on earth it was any more than my duty—my obvious duty as a citizen. Of course it wasn't; I know that as well as you. But my fellow citizens, you know—! Good Lord, think of all the good souls who think so highly of me—!

ASLAKSEN: Yes, our townsfolk have had a very high opinion of you so far, Doctor.

DR. STOCKMANN: Yes, and that is just why I am afraid they—. Well, this is the point; when this reaches them, especially the poorer classes, and sounds in their ears like a summons to take the town's affairs into their own hands for the future—

HOVSTAD (*getting up*): Ahem! Doctor, I won't conceal from you the fact—

DR. STOCKMANN: Ah!—I knew there was something in the wind! But I won't hear a word of it. If anything of that sort is being set on foot—

HOVSTAD: Of what sort?

DR. STOCKMANN: Well, whatever it is—whether it is a demonstration in my honour, or a banquet, or a subscription list for some presentation to me—whatever it is, you must promise me solemnly and faithfully to put a stop to it. You too, Mr. Aslaksen; do you understand?

HOVSTAD: You must forgive me, Doctor, but sooner or later we must tell you the plain truth—

(*He is interrupted by the entrance of* MRS. STOCKMANN, *who comes in from the street door.*)

MRS. STOCKMANN (*seeing her husband*): Just as I thought!
HOVSTAD (*going towards her*): You too, Mrs. Stockmann?
DR. STOCKMANN: What on earth do *you* want here, Katherine?
MRS. STOCKMANN: I should think you know very well what I want.
HOVSTAD: Won't you sit down? Or perhaps—
MRS. STOCKMANN: No, thank you; don't trouble. And you must not be offended at my coming to fetch my husband; I am the mother of three children, you know.
DR. STOCKMANN: Nonsense!—we know all about that.
MRS. STOCKMANN: Well, one would not give you credit for much thought for your wife and children to-day; if you had had that, you would not have gone and dragged us all into misfortune.
DR. STOCKMANN: Are you out of your senses, Katherine! Because a man has a wife and children, is he not to be allowed to proclaim the truth—is he not to be allowed to be an actively useful citizen—is he not to be allowed to do a service to his native town!
MRS. STOCKMANN: Yes, Thomas—in reason.
ASLAKSEN: Just what I say. Moderation in everything.
MRS. STOCKMANN: And that is why you wrong us, Mr. Hovstad, in enticing my husband away from his home and making a dupe of him in all this.
HOVSTAD: I certainly am making a dupe of no one—
DR. STOCKMANN: Making a dupe of me! Do you suppose I should allow myself to be duped!
MRS. STOCKMANN: It is just what you do. I know quite well you have more brains than anyone in the town, but you are extremely easily duped, Thomas. (*To Hovstad.*) Please to realise that he loses his post at the Baths if you print what he has written—
ASLAKSEN: What!
HOVSTAD: Look here, Doctor—
DR. STOCKMANN (*laughing*): Ha—ha!—just let them try! No, no—they will take good care not to. I have got the compact majority behind me, let me tell you!
MRS. STOCKMANN: Yes, that is just the worst of it—your having any such horrid thing behind you.
DR. STOCKMANN: Rubbish, Katherine!—Go home and look after your house and leave me to look after the community. How can you be so

afraid, when I am so confident and happy? (*Walks up and down, rubbing his hands.*) Truth and the People will win the fight, you may be certain! I see the whole of the broad-minded middle class marching like a victorious army—! (*Stops beside a chair.*) What the deuce is that lying there?

ASLAKSEN: Good Lord!

HOVSTAD: Ahem!

DR. STOCKMANN: Here we have the topmost pinnacle of authority! (*Takes the Mayor's official hat carefully between his finger-tips and holds it up in the air.*)

MRS. STOCKMANN: The Mayor's hat!

DR. STOCKMANN: And here is the staff of office too. How in the name of all that's wonderful—?

HOVSTAD: Well, you see—

DR. STOCKMANN: Oh, I understand. He has been here trying to talk you over. Ha—ha!—he made rather a mistake there! And as soon as he caught sight of me in the printing-room—.(*Bursts out laughing.*) Did he run away, Mr. Aslaksen?

ASLAKSEN (*hurriedly*): Yes, he ran away, Doctor.

DR. STOCKMANN: Ran away without his stick or his—.Fiddlesticks! Peter doesn't run away and leave his belongings behind him. But what the deuce have you done with him? Ah!—in there, of course. Now you shall see, Katherine!

MRS. STOCKMANN: Thomas—please don't—!

ASLAKSEN: Don't be rash, Doctor.

(DR. STOCKMANN *has put on the Mayor's hat and taken his stick in his hand. He goes up to the door, opens it, and stands with his hand to his hat at the salute.* PETER STOCKMANN *comes in, red with anger.* BILLING *follows him.*)

PETER STOCKMANN: What does this tomfoolery mean?

DR. STOCKMANN: Be respectful, my good Peter. I am the chief authority in the town now. (*Walks up and down.*)

MRS. STOCKMANN (*almost in tears*): Really Thomas!

PETER STOCKMANN (*following him about*): Give me my hat and stick.

DR. STOCKMANN (*in the same tone as before*): If you are chief constable, let me tell you that I am the Mayor—I am the master of the whole town, please understand!

PETER STOCKMANN: Take off my hat, I tell you. Remember it is part of an official uniform.

DR. STOCKMANN: Pooh! Do you think the newly awakened lion-hearted people are going to be frightened by an official hat? There is going to be a revolution in the town to-morrow, let me tell you. You thought you could turn me out; but now I shall turn you out—turn you out of all your various offices. Do you think I cannot? Listen to me. I have triumphant social forces behind me. Hovstad and Billing will thunder in the "People's Messenger," and Aslaksen will take the field at the head of the whole Householders' Association—

ASLAKSEN: That I won't, Doctor.

DR. STOCKMANN: Of course you will—

PETER STOCKMANN: Ah!—may I ask then if Mr. Hovstad intends to join this agitation.

HOVSTAD: No, Mr. Mayor.

ASLAKSEN: No, Mr. Hovstad is not such a fool as to go and ruin his paper and himself for the sake of an imaginary grievance.

DR. STOCKMANN (*looking round him*): What does this mean?

HOVSTAD: You have represented your case in a false light, Doctor, and therefore I am unable to give you my support.

BILLING: And after what the Mayor was so kind as to tell me just now, I—

DR. STOCKMANN: A false light! Leave that part of it to me. Only print my article; I am quite capable of defending it.

HOVSTAD: I am not going to print it. I cannot and will not and dare not print it.

DR. STOCKMANN: You dare not? What nonsense!—you are the editor; and an editor controls his paper, I suppose!

ASLAKSEN: No, it is the subscribers, Doctor.

PETER STOCKMANN: Fortunately, yes.

ASLAKSEN: It is public opinion—the enlightened public—householders and people of that kind; they control the newspapers.

DR. STOCKMANN (*composedly*): And I have all these influences against me?

ASLAKSEN: Yes, you have. It would mean the absolute ruin of the community if your article were to appear.

DR. STOCKMANN: Indeed.

PETER STOCKMANN: My hat and stick, if you please. (DR. STOCKMANN *takes off the hat and lays it on the table with the stick.* PETER STOCKMANN *takes them up.*) Your authority as mayor has come to an untimely end.

DR. STOCKMANN: We have not got to the end yet. (*To* HOVSTAD.) Then it is quite impossible for you to print my article in the "People's Messenger"?

HOVSTAD: Quite impossible—out of regard for your family as well.

MRS. STOCKMANN: You need not concern yourself about his family, thank you, Mr. Hovstad.

PETER STOCKMANN (*taking a paper from his pocket*): It will be sufficient, for the guidance of the public, if this appears. It is an official statement. May I trouble you?

HOVSTAD (*taking the paper*): Certainly; I will see that it is printed.

DR. STOCKMANN: But not mine. Do you imagine that you can silence me and stifle the truth! You will not find it so easy as you suppose. Mr. Aslaksen, kindly take my manuscript at once and print it as a pamphlet at my expense. I will have four hundred copies—no, five—six hundred.

ASLAKSEN: If you offered me its weight in gold, I could not lend my press for any such purpose, Doctor. It would be flying in the face of public opinion. You will not get it printed anywhere in the town.

DR. STOCKMANN: Then give it back to me.

HOVSTAD (*giving him the MS*): Here it is.

DR. STOCKMANN (*taking his hat and stick*): It shall be made public all the same. I will read it out at a mass meeting of the townspeople. All my fellow-citizens shall hear the voice of truth!

PETER STOCKMANN: You will not find any public body in the town that will give you the use of their hall for such a purpose.

ASLAKSEN: Not a single one, I am certain.

BILLING: No, I'm damned if you will find one.

MRS. STOCKMANN: But this is too shameful! Why should every one turn against you like that?

DR. STOCKMANN (*angrily*): I will tell you why. It is because all the men in this town are old women—like you; they all think of nothing but their families, and never of the community.

MRS. STOCKMANN (*putting her arm into his*): Then I will show them that an—an old woman can be a man for once. I am going to stand by you, Thomas!

DR. STOCKMANN: Bravely said, Katherine! It shall be made public—as I am a living soul! If I can't hire a hall, I shall hire a drum, and parade the town with it and read it at every street-corner.

PETER STOCKMANN: You are surely not such an arrant fool as that!

DR. STOCKMANN: Yes, I am.

ASLAKSEN: You won't find a single man in the whole town to go with you.

BILLING: No, I'm damned if you will.

MRS. STOCKMANN: Don't give in, Thomas. I will tell the boys to go with you.

DR. STOCKMANN: That is a splendid idea!

MRS. STOCKMANN: Morten will be delighted; and Ejlif will do whatever he does.

DR. STOCKMANN: Yes, and Petra!—and you too, Katherine!

MRS. STOCKMANN: No, I won't do that; but I will stand at the window and watch you, that's what I will do.

DR. STOCKMANN (*puts his arms round her and kisses her*): Thank you, my dear! Now you and I are going to try a fall, my fine gentlemen! I am going to see whether a pack of cowards can succeed in gagging a patriot who wants to purify society! (*He and his wife go out by the street door.*)

PETER STOCKMANN (*shaking his head seriously*): Now he has sent *her* out of her senses, too.

ACT IV

(SCENE: A big old-fashioned room in CAPTAIN HORSTER's house. At the back folding-doors, which are standing open, lead to an ante-room. Three windows in the left-hand wall. In the middle of the opposite wall a platform has been erected. On this is a small table with two candles, a water-bottle and glass, and a bell. The room is lit by lamps placed between the windows. In the foreground on the left there is a table with candles and a chair. To the right is a door and some chairs standing near it. The room is nearly filled with a crowd of townspeople of all sorts, a few women and schoolboys being amongst them. People are still streaming in from the back, and the room is soon filled.)

1ST CITIZEN (*meeting another*): Hullo, Lamstad! You here too?
2ND CITIZEN: I go to every public meeting, I do.
3RD CITIZEN: Brought your whistle too, I expect!
2ND CITIZEN: I should think so. Haven't you?
3RD CITIZEN: Rather! And old Evensen said he was going to bring a cowhorn, he did.
2ND CITIZEN: Good old Evensen! (*Laughter among the crowd.*)
4TH CITIZEN (*coming up to them*): I say, tell me what is going on here to-night.
2ND CITIZEN: Dr. Stockmann is going to deliver an address attacking the Mayor.
4TH CITIZEN: But the Mayor is his brother.
1ST CITIZEN: That doesn't matter; Dr. Stockmann's not the chap to be afraid.
3RD CITIZEN: But he is in the wrong; it said so in the "People's Messenger."
2ND CITIZEN: Yes, I expect he must be in the wrong this time, because neither the Householders' Association nor the Citizens' Club would lend him their hall for his meeting.
1ST CITIZEN He couldn't even get the loan of the hall at the Baths.
2ND CITIZEN: No, I should think not.
A MAN IN ANOTHER PART OF THE CROWD: I say—who are we to back up in this?
ANOTHER MAN, BESIDE HIM: Watch Aslaksen, and do as he does.
BILLING (*pushing his way through the crowd, with a writing-case under his arm*): Excuse me, gentlemen—do you mind letting me through? I

am reporting for the "People's Messenger." Thank you very much! (*He sits down at the table on the left.*)

A WORKMAN: Who was that?

SECOND WORKMAN: Don't you know him? It's Billing, who writes for Aslaksen's paper.

(CAPTAIN HORSTER *brings in* MRS. STOCKMANN *and* PETRA *through the door on the right.* EJLIF *and* MORTEN *follow them in.*)

HORSTER: I thought you might all sit here; you can slip out easily from here, if things get too lively.

MRS. STOCKMANN: Do you think there will be a disturbance?

HORSTER: One can never tell—with such a crowd. But sit down and don't be uneasy.

MRS. STOCKMANN (*sitting down*): It was extremely kind of you to offer my husband the room.

HORSTER: Well, if nobody else would—

PETRA (*who has sat down beside her mother*): And it was a plucky thing to do, Captain Horster.

HORSTER: Oh, it is not such a great matter as all that.

(HOVSTAD *and* ASLAKSEN *make their way through the crowd.*)

ASLAKSEN (*going up to* HORSTER): Has the Doctor not come yet?

HORSTER: He is waiting in the next room. (*Movement in the crowd by the door at the back.*)

HOVSTAD: Look—here comes the Mayor!

BILLING: Yes, I'm damned if he hasn't come after all!

(PETER STOCKMANN *makes his way gradually through the crowd, bows courteously, and takes up a position by the wall on the left. Shortly afterwards* DR. STOCKMANN *comes in by the right-hand door. He is dressed in a black frock-coat, with a white tie. There is a little feeble applause, which is hushed down. Silence is obtained.*)

DR. STOCKMANN (*in an undertone*): How do you feel, Katherine?

MRS. STOCKMANN: All right, thank you. (*Lowering her voice.*) Be sure not to lose your temper, Thomas.

DR. STOCKMANN: Oh, I know how to control myself. (*Looks at his watch, steps on to the platform, and bows.*) It is a quarter past—so I will begin. (*Takes his MS. out of his pocket.*)

ASLAKSEN: I think we ought to elect a chairman first.

DR. STOCKMANN: No, it is quite unnecessary.

SOME OF THE CROWD: Yes—yes!

PETER STOCKMANN: I certainly think too that we ought to have a chairman.

DR. STOCKMANN: But I have called this meeting to deliver a lecture, Peter.

Henrik Ibsen: *An Enemy of the People*

PETER STOCKMANN: Dr. Stockmann's lecture may possibly lead to a considerable conflict of opinion.

VOICES IN THE CROWD: A chairman! A chairman!

HOVSTAD: The general wish of the meeting seems to be that a chairman should be elected.

DR. STOCKMANN (*restraining himself*): Very well—let the meeting have its way.

ASLAKSEN: Will the Mayor be good enough to undertake the task?

THREE MEN (*clapping their hands*): Bravo! Bravo!

PETER STOCKMANN: For various reasons, which you will easily understand, I must beg to be excused. But fortunately we have amongst us a man who I think will be acceptable to you all. I refer to the President of the Householders' Association, Mr. Aslaksen!

(DR. STOCKMANN *takes up his MS. and walks up and down the platform.*)

ASLAKSEN: Since my fellow-citizens choose to entrust me with this duty, I cannot refuse.

(*Loud applause.* ASLAKSEN *mounts the platform.*)

BILLING (*writing*): "Mr. Aslaksen was elected with enthusiasm."

ASLAKSEN: And now, as I am in this position, I should like to say a few brief words. I am a quiet and peaceable man, who believes in discreet moderation, and—and—in moderate discretion. All my friends can bear witness to that.

SEVERAL VOICES: That's right! That's right, Aslaksen!

ASLAKSEN: I have learnt in the school of life and experience that moderation is the most valuable virtue a citizen can possess—

PETER STOCKMANN: Hear, hear!

ASLAKSEN: —And moreover that discretion and moderation are what enable a man to be of most service to the community. I would therefore suggest to our esteemed fellow-citizen, who has called this meeting, that he should strive to keep strictly within the bounds of moderation.

A MAN BY THE DOOR: Three cheers for the Moderation Society!

A VOICE: Shame!

SEVERAL VOICES: Sh!—Sh!

ASLAKSEN: No interruptions, gentlemen, please! Does anyone wish to make any remarks?

PETER STOCKMANN: Mr. Chairman.

ASLAKSEN: The Mayor will address the meeting.

PETER STOCKMANN: In consideration of the close relationship in which, as you all know, I stand to the present Medical Officer of the Baths, I should have preferred not to speak this evening. But my official position with regard to the Baths and my solicitude for the vital interests of the town compel me to bring forward a motion. I venture to presume that there is not a single one of our citizens present who considers it desirable that unreliable and exaggerated accounts of the sanitary condition of the Baths and the town should be spread abroad.

SEVERAL VOICES: No, no! Certainly not! We protest against it!

PETER STOCKMANN: Therefore I should like to propose that the meeting should not permit the Medical Officer either to read or to comment on his proposed lecture.

DR. STOCKMANN (*impatiently*): Not permit—! What the devil—!

MRS. STOCKMANN (*coughing*): Ahem!—Ahem!

DR. STOCKMANN (*collecting himself*): Very well. Go ahead!

PETER STOCKMANN: In my communication to the "People's Messenger," I have put the essential facts before the public in such a way that every fair-minded citizen can easily form his own opinion. From it you will see that the main result of the Medical Officer's proposals—apart from their constituting a vote of censure on the leading men of the town—would be to saddle the ratepayers with an unnecessary expenditure of at least some thousands of pounds.

(*Sounds of disapproval among the audience, and some cat-calls.*)

ASLAKSEN (*ringing his bell*): Silence, please, gentlemen! I beg to support the Mayor's motion. I quite agree with him that there is something behind this agitation started by the Doctor. He talks about the Baths; but it is a revolution he is aiming at—he wants to get the administration of the town put into new hands. No one doubts the honesty of the Doctor's intentions—no one will suggest that there can be any two opinions as to that. I myself am a believer in self-government for the people, provided it does not fall too heavily on the ratepayers. But that would be the case here; and that is why I will see Dr. Stockmann damned—I beg your pardon—before I go with him in the matter. You can pay too dearly for a thing sometimes; that is my opinion.

(*Loud applause on all sides.*)

HOVSTAD: I, too, feel called upon to explain my position. Dr. Stockmann's agitation appeared to be gaining a certain amount of sympathy at first, so I supported it as impartially as I could. But presently we had reason to suspect that we had allowed ourselves to be misled by misrepresentation of the state of affairs—

DR. STOCKMANN: Misrepresentation—!

HOVSTAD: Well, let us say a not entirely trustworthy representation. The Mayor's statement has proved that. I hope no one here has any doubt as to my liberal principles; the attitude of the "People's Messenger" towards important political questions is well known to every one. But the advice of experienced and thoughtful men has convinced me that in purely local matters a newspaper ought to proceed with a certain caution.

ASLAKSEN: I entirely agree with the speaker.

HOVSTAD: And, in the matter before us, it is now an undoubted fact that Dr. Stockmann has public opinion against him. Now what is an editor's first and most obvious duty, gentlemen? Is it not to work in harmony with his readers? Has he not received a sort of tacit mandate to work persistently and assiduously for the welfare of those whose opinions he represents? Or is it possible I am mistaken in that?

VOICES FROM THE CROWD: No, no! You are quite right!

HOVSTAD: It has cost me a severe struggle to break with a man in whose house I have been lately a frequent guest—a man who till to-day has been able to pride himself on the undivided goodwill of his fellow-citizens—a man whose only, or at all events whose essential failing, is that he is swayed by his heart rather than his head.

A FEW SCATTERED VOICES: That is true! Bravo, Stockmann!

HOVSTAD: But my duty to the community obliged me to to break with him. And there is another consideration that impels me to oppose him, and, as far as possible, to arrest him on the perilous course he has adopted; that is, consideration for his family—

DR. STOCKMANN: Please stick to the water-supply and drainage!

HOVSTAD: —consideration, I repeat, for his wife and his children for whom he has made no provision.

MORTEN: Is that us, mother?

MRS. STOCKMANN: Hush!

ASLAKSEN: I will now put the Mayor's proposition to the vote.

DR. STOCKMANN: There is no necessity! To-night I have no intention of dealing with all that filth down at the Baths. No; I have something quite different to say to you.

PETER STOCKMANN (*aside*): What is coming now?

A DRUNKEN MAN (*by the entrance door*): I am a ratepayer! And therefore I have a right to speak too! And my entire—firm—inconceivable opinion is—

A NUMBER OF VOICES: Be quiet, at the back there!

OTHERS: He is drunk! Turn him out! (*They turn him out.*)

DR. STOCKMANN: Am I allowed to speak?

ASLAKSEN (*ringing his bell*): Dr. Stockmann will address the meeting.

DR. STOCKMANN: I should like to have seen anyone, a few days ago, dare to attempt to silence me as has been done to-night! I would have defended my sacred rights as a man, like a lion! But now it is all one to me; I have something of even weightier importance to say to you. (*The crowd presses nearer to him,* MORTEN KIIL *conspicuous among them.*)

DR. STOCKMANN (*continuing*): I have thought and pondered a great deal, these last few days—pondered over such a variety of things that in the end my head seemed too full to hold them—

PETER STOCKMANN (*with a cough*): Ahem!

DR. STOCKMANN: —but I got them clear in my mind at last, and then I saw the whole situation lucidly. And that is why I am standing here to-night. I have a great revelation to make to you, my fellow-citizens! I will impart to you a discovery of a far wider scope than the trifling matter that our water-supply is poisoned and our medicinal Baths are standing on pestiferous soil.

A NUMBER OF VOICES (*shouting*): Don't talk about the Baths! We won't hear you! None of that!

DR. STOCKMANN: I have already told you that what I want to speak about is the great discovery I have made lately—the discovery that all the sources of our *moral* life are poisoned and that the whole fabric of our civic community is founded on the pestiferous soil of falsehood.

VOICES OF DISCONCERTED CITIZENS: What is that he says?

PETER STOCKMANN: Such an insinuation—!

ASLAKSEN (*with his hand on his bell*): I call upon the speaker to moderate his language.

DR. STOCKMANN: I have always loved my native town as a man only can love the home of his youthful days. I was not old when I went away from here; and exile, longing and memories cast as it were an additional halo over both the town and its inhabitants. (*Some clapping and applouse.*) And there I stayed, for many years, in a horrible hole far away up north. When I came into contact with some of the people that lived scattered about among the rocks, I often thought it would of been more service to the poor half-starved creatures if a veterinary doctor had been sent up there, instead of a man like me. (*Murmurs among the crowd.*)

BILLING (*laying down his pen*): I'm damned if I have ever heard—!

HOVSTAD: It is an insult to a respectable population!

DR. STOCKMANN: Wait a bit! I do not think anyone will charge me with having forgotten my native town up there. I was like one of the eiderducks brooding on its nest, and what I hatched was—the plans for these Baths. (*Applause and protests.*) And then when fate at last decreed for me the great happiness of coming home again—I assure you, gentlemen, I thought I had nothing more in the world to wish for. Or, rather, there was one thing I wished for—eagerly, untiringly, ardently—and that was to be able to be of service to my native town and the good of the community.

PETER STOCKMANN (*looking at the ceiling*): You chose a strange way of doing it—ahem!

DR. STOCKMANN: And so, with my eyes blinded to the real facts, I revelled in happiness. But yesterday morning—no, to be precise, it was yesterday afternoon—the eyes of my mind were opened wide, and the first thing I realised was the colossal stupidity of the authorities—. (*Uproar, shouts and laughter.* MRS. STOCKMANN *coughs persistently.*)

PETER STOCKMANN: Mr. Chairman!

ASLAKSEN (*ringing his bell*): By virtue of my authority—!

DR. STOCKMANN: It is a pretty thing to catch me up on a word, Mr. Aslaksen. What I mean is only that I got scent of the unbelievable piggishness our leading men had been responsible for down at the Baths. I can't stand leading men at any price!—I have had enough of such people in my time. They are like billy-goats in a young plantation; they do mischief everywhere. They stand in a free man's way, whichever way he turns, and what I should like best would be to see them exterminated like any other vermin—. (*Uproar.*)

PETER STOCKMANN: Mr. Chairman, can we allow such expressions to pass?

ASLAKSEN (*with his hand on his bell*): Doctor—!

DR. STOCKMANN: I cannot understand how it is that I have only now acquired a clear conception of what these gentry are, when I had almost daily before my eyes in this town such an excellent specimen of them—my brother Peter—slow-witted and hide-bound in prejudice.— (*Laughter, uproar and hisses.* MRS. STOCKMANN *sits coughing assiduously.* ASLAKSEN *rings his bell violently.*)

THE DRUNKEN MAN (*who has got in again*): Is it me he is talking about? My name's Petersen, all right—but devil take me if I—

ANGRY VOICES: Turn out that drunken man! Turn him out. (*He is turned out again.*)

PETER STOCKMANN: Who was that person?

1ST CITIZEN: I don't know who he is, Mr. Mayor.

2ND CITIZEN: He doesn't belong here.

3RD CITIZEN: I expect he is a navvy from over at—(*the rest is inaudible*).

ASLAKSEN: He had obviously had too much beer.—Proceed, Doctor; but please strive to be moderate in your language.

DR. STOCKMANN: Very well, gentlemen, I will say no more about our leading men. And if anyone imagines, from what I have just said, that my object is to attack these people this evening, he is wrong—absolutely wide of the mark. For I cherish the comforting conviction that these parasites—all these venerable relics of a dying school of thought

—are most admirably paving the way for their own extinction; they need no doctor's help to hasten their end. Nor is it folk of that kind who constitute the most pressing danger to the community. It is not they who are most instrumental in poisoning the sources of our moral life and infecting the ground on which we stand. It is not they who are the most dangerous enemies of truth and freedom amongst us.

SHOUTS FROM ALL SIDES: Who then? Who is it? Name! Name!

DR. STOCKMANN: You may depend upon it I shall name them! That is precisely the great discovery I made yesterday. (*Raises his voice.*) The most dangerous enemy of truth and freedom amongst us is the compact majority—yes, the damned compact Liberty majority—that is it! Now you know!

(*Tremendous uproar. Most of the crowd are shouting, stamping and hissing. Some of the older men among them exchange stolen glances and seem to be enjoying themselves.* MRS. STOCKMANN *gets up, looking anxious.* EJLIF *and* MORTEN *advance threateningly upon some schoolboys who are playing pranks.* ASLAKSEN *rings his bell and begs for silence.* HOVSTAD *and* BILLING *both talk at once, but are inaudible. At last quiet is restored.*)

ASLAKSEN: As chairman, I call upon the speaker to withdraw the ill-considered expressions he has just used.

DR. STOCKMANN: Never, Mr. Aslaksen! It is the majority in our community that denies me my freedom and seeks to prevent my speaking the truth.

HOVSTAD: The majority always has right on its side.

BILLING: And truth too, by God!

DR. STOCKMANN: The majority *never* has right on its side. Never, I say! That is one of these social lies against which an independent, intelligent man must wage war. Who is it that constitute the majority of the population in a country? Is it the clever folk or the stupid? I don't imagine you will dispute the fact that at present the stupid people are in an absolutely overwhelming majority all the world over. But, good Lord!—you can never pretend that it is right that the stupid folk should govern the clever ones! (*Uproar and chies.*) Oh, yes—you can shout me down, I know! but you cannot answer me. The majority has *might* on its side—unfortunately; but *right* it has *not*. I am in the right—I and a few other scattered individuals. The minority is always in the right. (*Renewed uproar.*)

HOVSTAD: Aha!—so Dr. Stockmann has become an aristocrat since the day before yesterday!

DR. STOCKMANN: I have already said that I don't intend to waste a word on the puny, narrow-chested, short-winded crew whom we are leaving astern. Pulsating life no longer concerns itself with them. I am thinking of the few, the scattered few amongst us, who have absorbed new and vigorous truths. Such men stand, as it were, at the outposts, so far ahead that the compact majority has not yet been able to come up with them; and there they are fighting for truths that are too newly-born into the world of consciousness to have any considerable number of people on their side as yet.

HOVSTAD: So the Doctor is a revolutionary now!

DR. STOCKMANN: Good heavens—of course I am, Mr. Hovstad! I propose to raise a revolution against the lie that the majority has the monopoly on the truth. What sort of truths are they that the majority usually supports? They are truths that are of such advanced age that they are beginning to break up. And if a truth is as old as that, it is also in a fair way to become a lie, gentlemen. (*Laughter and mocking cries.*) Yes, believe me or not, as you like; but truths are by no means as long-lived at Methuselah—as some folks imagine. A normally constituted truth lives, let us say, as a rule seventeen or eighteen, or at most twenty years; seldom longer. But truths as aged as that are always worn frightfully thin, and nevertheless it is only then that the majority recognises them and recommends them to the community as wholesome moral nourishment. There is no great nutritive value in that sort of fare, I can assure you; and, as a doctor, I ought to know. These "majority truths" are like last year's cured meat—like rancid, tainted ham; and they are the origin of the moral scurvy that is rampant in our communities.

ASLAKSEN: It appears to me that the speaker is wandering a long way from his subject.

PETER STOCKMANN: I quite agree with the Chairman.

DR. STOCKMANN: Have you gone clean out of your senses, Peter? I am sticking as closely to my subject as I can; for my subject is precisely this, that it is the masses, the majority—this infernal compact majority—that poisons the sources of our moral life and infects the grounds we stand on.

HOVSTAD: And all this because the great, broad-minded majority of the people is prudent enough to show deference only to well-approved truths?

DR. STOCKMANN: Ah, my good Mr. Hovstad, don't talk nonsense about well-ascertained truths! The truths of which the masses now approve are the very truths that the fighters at the outposts held to in the days of our grandfathers. We fighters at the outposts nowadays no longer approve of them; and I do not believe there is any other well-ascertained truth except this, that no community can live a healthy life if it is nourished only on such old marrowless truths.

HOVSTAD: But instead of standing there using vague generalities, it would be interesting if you would tell us what these old marrowless truths are, that we are nourished on.

(Applause from many quarters.)

DR. STOCKMANN: Oh, I could give you a whole string of such abominations; but to begin with I will confine myself to one well-approved truth, which at bottom is a foul lie, but upon which nevertheless Mr. Hovstad and the "People's Messenger" and all the "Messenger's" supporters are nourished.

HOVSTAD: And that is—?

DR. STOCKMANN: That is, the doctrine you have inherited from your forefathers and proclaim thoughtlessly far and wide—the doctrine that the public, the crowd, the masses, are the essential part of the population—that they constitute the People—that the common folk, the ignorant and incomplete element in the community, have the same right to pronounce judgment and to approve, to direct and to govern, as the isolated, intellectually superior personalities in it.

BILLING: Well, damn me if ever I—

HOVSTAD (*at the same time, shouting out*): Fellow-citizens, take good note of that!

A NUMBER OF VOICES (*angrily*): Oho!—we are not the People! Only the superior folk are to govern, are they!

A WORKMAN: Turn the fellow out, for talking such rubbish!

ANOTHER: Out with him!

ANOTHER (*calling out*): Blow your horn, Evensen!

(*A horn is blown loudly, amidst hisses and an angry uproar.*)

DR. STOCKMANN (*when the noise has somewhat abated*): Be reasonable! Can't you stand hearing the voice of truth for once? I don't in the least expect you to agree with me all at once; but I must say I did expect Mr. Hovstad to admit I was right, when he had recovered his composure a little. He claims to be a freethinker—

VOICES (*in murmurs of astonishment*): Freethinker, did he say? Is Hovstad a freethinker?

HOVSTAD (*shouting*): Prove it, Dr. Stockmann! When have I said so in print?

DR. STOCKMANN (*reflecting*): No, confound it, you are right!—you have never had the courage to. Well, I won't put you in a hole, Mr. Hovstad. Let us say it is I that am the freethinker, then. I am going to prove to you, scientifically, that the "People's Messenger" leads you by the nose in a shameful manner when it tells you that you—that the common people, the crowd, the masses, are the real essence of the People. That is only a newspaper lie, I tell you! The common people are nothing more than the raw material of which a People is made. (*Groans, laugh-*

ter and uproar.) Well, isn't that the case. Isn't there an enormous difference between a well-bred and an ill-bred strain of animals? Take, for instance, a common barn-door hen. What sort of eating do you get from a shrivelled up old scrag of a fowl like that? Not much, do you! And what sort of eggs does it lay? A fairly good crow or a raven can lay pretty nearly as good an egg. But take a well-bred Spanish or Japanese hen, or a good pheasant or a turkey—then you will see the difference. Or take the case of dogs, with whom we humans are on such intimate terms. Think first of an ordinary common cur—I mean one of the horrible, coarse-haired, low-bred curs that do nothing but run about the streets and befoul the walls of the houses. Compare one of these curs with a poodle whose sires for many generations have been bred in a gentleman's house, where they have had the best of food and had the opportunity of hearing soft voices and music. Do you not think that the poodle's brain is developed to quite a different degree from that of the cur? Of course it is. It is puppies of well-bred poodles like that, that showmen train to do incredibly clever tricks—things that a common cur could never learn to do even if it stood on its head. (*Uproar and mocking cries.*)

A CITIZEN (*calls out*): Are you going to make out we are dogs, now?

ANOTHER CITIZEN: We are not animals, Doctor!

DR. STOCKMAN: Yes but, bless my soul, we *are*, my friend! It is true we are the finest animals anyone could wish for; but, even amongst us, exceptionally fine animals are rare. There is a tremendous difference between poodle-men and cur-men. And the amusing part of it is, that Mr. Hovstad quite agrees with me as long as it is a question of four-footed animals—

HOVSTAD: Yes, it is true enough as far as they are concerned.

DR. STOCKMANN: Very well. But as soon as I extend the principle and apply it to two-legged animals, Mr. Hovstad stops short. He no longer dares to think independently, or to pursue his ideas to their logical conclusion; so he turns the whole theory upside down and proclaims in the "People's Messenger" that it is the barn-door hens and street curs that are the finest specimens in the menagerie. But that is always the way, as long as a man retains the traces of common origin and has not worked his way up to intellectual distinction.

HOVSTAD: I lay no claim to any sort of distinction. I am the son of humble countryfolk, and I am proud that the stock I come from is rooted deep among the common people he insults.

VOICES: Bravo, Hovstad! Bravo! Bravo!

DR. STOCKMANN: The kind of common people I mean are not only to be found low down in the social scale; they crawl and swarm all around us—even in the highest social positions. You have only to look at your own fine, distinguished Mayor! My brother Peter is every bit as plebian as anyone that walks in two shoes— (*laughter and hisses*).

PETER STOCKMANN: I protest against personal allusions of this kind.

DR. STOCKMANN (*imperturbably*): —and that, not because he is, like myself, descended from some old rascal of a pirate from Pomerania or thereabouts—because that is who we are descended from—

PETER STOCKMANN: An absurd legend. I deny it!

DR. STOCKMANN: —but because he thinks what his superiors think and holds the same opinions as they. People who do that are, intellectually speaking, common people; and that is why my magnificent brother Peter is in reality so very far from any distinction—and consequently also so far from being liberal-minded.

PETER STOCKMANN: Mr. Chairman—!

HOVSTAD: So it is only the distinguished men that are liberal-minded in this country? We are learning something quite new! (*Laughter.*)

DR. STOCKMANN: Yes, that is part of my new discovery too. And another part of it is that broad-mindedness is almost precisely the same thing as morality. That is why I maintain that it is absolutely inexcusable in the "People's Messenger" to proclaim, day in and day out, the false doctrine that it is the masses, the crowd, the compact majority, that have the monopoly of broad-mindedness and morality—and that vice and corruption and every kind of intellectual depravity are the result of culture, just as all the filth that is draining into our Baths is the result of the tanneries up at Mölledal! (*Uproar and interruptions.* DR. STOCKMANN *is undisturbed, and goes on, carried away by his ardour, with a smile.*) And yet this same "People's Messenger" can go on preaching that the masses ought to be elevated to higher conditions of life! But, bless my soul, if the "Messenger's" teaching is to be depended upon, this very raising up the masses would mean nothing more or less than setting them straightway upon the paths of depravity! Happily the theory that culture demoralises is only an old falsehood that our forefathers believed in and we have inherited. No, it is ignorance, poverty, ugly conditions of life, that do the devil's work! In a house which does not get aired and swept every day—my wife Katherine maintains that the floor ought to be scrubbed as well, but that is a debatable question—in such a house, let me tell you, people will lose within two or three years the power of thinking or acting in a moral manner. Lack of oxygen weakens the conscience. And there must be a plentiful lack of oxygen in very many houses in this town, I should think, judging from the fact that the whole compact majority can be unconscientious enough to wish to build the town's prosperity on a quagmire of falsehood and deceit.

ASLAKSEN: We cannot allow such a grave accusation to be flung at a citizen community.

A CITIZEN: I move that the Chairman direct the speaker to sit down.

VOICES (*angrily*): Hear, hear! Quite right! Make him sit down!

DR. STOCKMANN (*losing his self-control*): Then I will go and shout the truth at every street corner! I will write it in other towns' newspapers! The whole country shall know what is going on here!

HOVSTAD: It almost seems as if Dr. Stockmann's intention were to ruin the town.

DR. STOCKMANN: Yes, my native town is so dear to me that I would rather ruin it than see it flourishing upon a lie.

ASLAKSEN: This is really serious. (*Uproar and cat-calls.* MRS. STOCKMANN *coughs, but to no purpose; her husband does not listen to her any longer.*)

HOVSTAD (*shouting above the din*): A man must be a public enemy to wish to ruin a whole community!

DR. STOCKMANN (*with growing fervour*): What does the destruction of a community matter, if it lives on lies! It ought to be razed to the ground, I tell you! All who live by lies ought to be exterminated like vermin! You will end by infecting the whole country; you will bring about such a state of things that the whole country will deserve to be ruined. And if things come to that pass, I shall say from the bottom of my heart: Let the whole country perish, let all these people be exterminated.

VOICES FROM THE CROWD: That is talking like an out-and-out enemy of the people!

BILLING: There sounded the voice of the people, by all that's holy!

THE WHOLE CROWD (*shouting*): Yes, yes! He is an enemy of the people! He hates his country! He hates his own people!

ASLAKSEN: Both as a citizen and as an individual, I am profoundly disturbed by what we have had to listen to. Dr. Stockmann has shown himself in a light I should never have dreamed of. I am unhappily obliged to subscribe to the opinion which I have just heard my estimable fellow-citizens utter; and I propose that we should give expression to that opinion in a resolution. I propose a resolution as follows: "This meeting declares that it considers Dr. Thomas Stockmann, Medical Officer of the Baths, to be an enemy of the people." (*A storm of cheers and applause. A number of men surround the* DOCTOR *and hiss him.* MRS. STOCKMANN *and* PETRA *have got up from their seats.* MORTEN *and* EJLIF *are fighting the other schoolboys for hissing; some of their elders separate them.*)

DR. STOCKMANN (*to the men who are hissing him*): Oh, you fools! I tell you that—

ASLAKSEN (*ringing his bell*): We cannot hear you now, Doctor. A formal vote is about to be taken; but, out of regard for personal feelings, it shall be by ballot and not verbal. Have you any clean paper, Mr. Billing?

BILLING: I have both blue and white here.

ASLAKSEN (*going to him*): That will do nicely; we shall get on more quickly that way. Cut it up into small strips—yes, that's it. (*To the meeting.*) Blue means no; white means yes. I will come round myself and collect votes. (PETER STOCKMANN *leaves the hall.* ASLAKSEN *and one or two others go round the room with the slips of paper in their hats.*)

1ST CITIZEN (*to* HOVSTAD): I say, what has come to the Doctor? What are we to think of it?

HOVSTAD: Oh, you know how headstrong he is.

2ND CITIZEN (*to* BILLING): Billing, you go to their house—have you ever noticed if the fellow drinks?

BILLING: Well I'm hanged if I know what to say. There are always spirits on the table when you go.

3RD CITIZEN: I rather think he goes quite off his head sometimes.

1ST CITIZEN: I wonder if there is any madness in his family?

BILLING: I shouldn't wonder if there were.

4TH CITIZEN: No, it is nothing more than sheer malice; he wants to get even with somebody for something or other.

BILLING: Well certainly he suggested a rise in his salary on one occasion lately, and did not get it.

THE CITIZENS (*together*): Ah!—then it is easy to understand how it is!

THE DRUNKEN MAN (*who has got amongst the audience again*): I want a blue one, I do! And I want a white one too!

VOICES: It's that drunken chap again! Turn him out!

MORTEN KIIL (*going up to* DR. STOCKMANN): Well, Stockmann, do you see what these monkey tricks of yours lead to?

DR. STOCKMANN: I have done my duty.

MORTEN KIIL: What was that you said about the tanneries at Mölledal?

DR. STOCKMANN: You heard well enough. I said they were the source of all the filth.

MORTEN KIIL: My tannery too?

DR. STOCKMANN: Unfortunately your tannery is by far the worst.

MORTEN KIIL: Are you going to put that in the papers?

DR. STOCKMANN: I shall conceal nothing.

MORTEN KIIL: That may cost you dear, Stockmann. (*Goes out.*)

A STOUT MAN (*going up to* CAPTAIN HORSTER, *without taking any notice of the ladies*): Well, Captain, so you lend your house to enemies of the people?

HORSTER: I imagine I can do what I like with my own possessions, Mr. Vik.

THE STOUT MAN: Then you can have no objection to my doing the same with mine.

HORSTER: What do you mean, sir?

THE STOUT MAN: You shall hear from me in the morning.

(*Turns his back on him and moves off.*)

PETRA: Was that not your owner, Captain Horster?

HORSTER: Yes, that was Mr. Vik the ship-owner.

ASLAKSEN (*with the voting-papers in his hands, gets up on to the platform and rings his bell*): Gentlemen, allow me to announce the result. By the votes of every one here except one person—

A YOUNG MAN: That is the drunk chap!

ASLAKSEN: By the votes of every one here except a tipsy man, this meeting of citizens declares Dr. Thomas Stockmann to be an enemy of the people. (*Shouts and applause.*) Three cheers for our ancient and honourable citizen community! (*Renewed applause.*) Three cheers for our able and energetic Mayor, who has so loyally suppressed the promptings of family feeling! (*Cheers.*) The meeting is dissolved. (*Gets down.*)

BILLING: Three cheers for the Chairman!

THE WHOLE CROWD: Three cheers for Aslaksen! Hurrah!

DR. STOCKMANN: My hat and coat, Petra! Captain, have you room on your ship for passengers to the New World?

HORSTER: For you and yours we will make room, Doctor.

DR. STOCKMANN (*as* PETRA *helps him into his coat*): Good. Come, Katherine! Come, boys!

MRS. STOCKMANN (*in an undertone*): Thomas, dear, let us go out by the back way.

DR. STOCKMANN: No back ways for me, Katherine. (*Raising his voice.*) You will hear more of this enemy of the people, before he shakes the dust off his shoes upon you! I am not so forgiving as a certain Person; I do not say: "I forgive you, for ye know not what ye do."

ASIAKSEN (*shouting*): That is a blasphemous comparison, Dr. Stockmann!

BILLING: It is, by God! It's dreadful for an earnest man to listen to.

A COARSE VOICE: Threatens us now, does he!

OTHER VOICES (*excitedly*): Let's go and break his windows! Duck him in the fjord!

ANOTHER VOICE: Blow your horn, Evensen! Pip, pip!

(*Horn-blowing, hisses, and wild cries.* DR. STOCKTON *goes out through the hall with his family,* HORSTER *elbowing a way for them.*)

THE WHOLE CROWD (*howling after them as they go*): Enemy of the People! Enemy of the People!

BILLING (*as he puts his papers together*): Well, I'm damned if I go and drink toddy with the Stockmanns to-night!

(*The crowd press towards the exit. The uproar continues outside; shouts of* "Enemy of the People!" *are heard from without.*)

ACT V

(SCENE: DR. STOCKMANN's study. Bookcases, and cabinets containing specimens, line the walls. At the back is a door leading to the hall; in the foreground on the left, a door leading to the sitting-room. In the right-hand wall are two windows, of which all the panes are broken. The DOCTOR's desk, littered with books and papers, stands in the middle of the room, which is in disorder. It is morning. DR. STOCKMANN in dressing-gown, slippers and a smoking-cap, is bending down and raking with an umbrella under one of the cabinets. After a little while he rakes out a stone.)

DR. STOCKMANN (*calling through the open sitting-room door*): Katherine, I have found another one.

MRS. STOCKMANN (*from the sitting-room*): Oh, you will find a lot more yet, I expect.

DR. STOCKMANN (*adding the stone to a heap of others on the table*): I shall treasure these stones as relics. Ejlif and Morton shall look at them every day, and when they are grown up they shall inherit them as heirlooms. (*Rakes about under a bookcase.*) Hasn't—what the deuce is her name?—the girl, you know—hasn't she been to fetch the glazier yet?

MRS. STOCKMANN (*coming in*): Yes, but he said he didn't know if he would be able to come to-day.

DR. STOCKMANN: You will see he won't dare to come.

MRS. STOCKMANN: Well, that is just what Randine thought—that he didn't dare to, on account of the neighbours. (*Calls into the sitting-room.*) What is it you want, Randine? Give it to me. (*Goes in, and comes out again directly.*) Here is a letter for you, Thomas.

DR. STOCKMANN: Let me see it. (*Opens and reads it.*) Ah!—of course.

MRS. STOCKMANN: Who is it from?

DR. STOCKMANN: From the landlord. Notice to quit.

MRS. STOCKMANN: Is it possible? Such a nice man—

DR. STOCKMANN (*looking at the letter*): Does not dare do otherwise, he says. Doesn't like doing it, but dare not do otherwise—on account of his fellow-citizens—out of regard for public opinion. Is in a dependent position—dare not offend certain influential men—

MRS. STOCKMANN: There, you see, Thomas!

DR. STOCKMANN: Yes, yes, I see well enough; the whole lot of them in the town are cowards; not a man among them dares do anything for fear of the others. (*Throws the letter on to the table.*) But it doesn't matter to us, Katherine. We are going to sail away to the New World, and—

MRS. STOCKMANN: But, Thomas, are you sure we are well advised to take this step?

DR. STOCKMANN: Are you suggesting that I should stay here, where they have pilloried me as an enemy of the people—branded me—broken

Henrik Ibsen: *An Enemy of the People*

my windows! And just look here, Katherine—they have torn a great rent in my black trousers too!

MRS. STOCKMANN: Oh, dear!—and they are the best pair you have got!

DR. STOCKMANN: You should never wear your best trousers when you go out to fight for freedom and truth. It is not that I care so much about the trousers, you know; you can always sew them up again for me. But that the common herd should dare to make this attack on me, as if they were my equals—that is what I cannot, for the life of me, swallow!

MRS. STOCKMANN: There is no doubt they have behaved very ill to you, Thomas; but is that sufficient reason for our leaving our native country for good and all?

DR. STOCKMANN: If we went to another town, do you suppose we should not find the common people just as insolent as they are here? Depend upon it, there is not much to choose between them. Oh, well, let the curs snap—that is not the worst part of it. The worst is that, from one end of this country to the other, every man is the slave of his Party. Although, as far as that goes, I daresay it is not much better in the free West either; the compact majority, and liberal public opinion, and all that infernel old bag of tricks are probably rampant there too. But there things are done on a larger scale, you see. They may kill you, but they won't put you to death by slow torture. They don't squeeze a free man's soul in a vice, as they do here. And, if need be, one can live in solitude. (*Walks up and down.*) If only I knew where there was a virgin forest or a small South Sea island for sale, cheap—

MRS. STOCKMANN: But think of the boys, Thomas!

DR. STOCKMANN (*standing still*): What a strange woman you are, Katherine! Would you prefer to have the boys grow up in a society like this? You saw for yourself last night that half the population are out of their minds; and if the other half have not lost their senses, it is because they are mere brutes, with no sense to lose.

MRS. STOCKMANN: But, Thomas dear, the imprudent things you said had something to do with it, you know.

DR. STOCKMANN: Well, isn't what I said perfectly true? Don't they turn every idea topsy-turvy? Don't they make a regular hotch-potch of right and wrong? Don't they say that the things I know are true, are lies? The craziest part of it all is the fact of these "liberals," men of full age, going about in crowds imagining that they are the broad-minded party? Did you ever hear anything like it, Katherine!

MRS. STOCKMANN: Yes, yes, it's mad enough of them, certainly; but— (PETRA *comes in from the sitting-room*). Back from school already?

PETRA: Yes. I have been given notice of dismissal.

MRS. STOCKMANN: Dismissal?

DR. STOCKMANN: You too?

PETRA: Mrs. Busk gave me my notice; so I thought it was best to go at once.

DR. STOCKMANN: You were perfectly right, too!

MRS. STOCKMANN: Who would have thought Mrs. Busk was a woman like that!

PETRA: Mrs. Busk isn't a bit like that, mother; I saw quite plainly how it hurt her to do it. But she didn't dare do otherwise, she said; and so I got my notice.

DR. STOCKMANN: *(laughing and rubbing his hands)*. She didn't dare do otherwise, either! It's delicious!

MRS. STOCKMANN: Well, after the dreadful scenes last night—

PETRA: It was not only that. Just listen to this, father!

DR. STOCKMANN: Well?

PETRA: Mrs. Busk showed me no less than three letters she received this morning—

DR. STOCKMANN: Anonymous, I suppose?

PETRA: Yes.

DR. STOCKMANN: Yes, because they didn't dare to risk signing their names, Katherine!

PETRA: And two of them were to the effect that a man, who has been our guest here, was declaring last night at the Club that my views on various subjects are extremely emancipated—

DR. STOCKMANN: You did not deny that, I hope?

PETRA: No, you know I wouldn't. Mrs. Busk's own views are tolerably emancipated, when we are alone together; but now that this report about me is being spread, she dare not keep me on any longer.

MRS. STOCKMANN: And some one who had been a guest of ours! That shows you the return you get for your hospitality, Thomas!

DR. STOCKMANN: We won't live in such a disgusting hole any longer. Pack up as quickly as you can, Katherine; the sooner we can get away, the better.

MRS. STOCKMANN: Be quiet—I think I hear some one in the hall. See who it is, Petra.

PETRA *(opening the door)*: Oh, it's you, Captain Horster! Do come in.

HORSTER *(coming in)*: Good morning. I thought I would just come in and see how you were.

DR. STOCKMANN *(shaking his hand)*: Thanks—that is really kind of you.

MRS. STOCKMANN: And thank you, too, for helping us through the crowd, Captain Horster.

PETRA: How did you manage to get home again?

HORSTER: Oh, somehow or other. I am fairly strong, and there is more sound than fury about these folk.

DR. STOCKMANN: Yes, isn't their swinish cowardice astonishing? Look here,

I will show you something! There are all the stones they have thrown through my windows. Just look at them! I'm hanged if there are more than two decently large bits of hardstone in the whole heap; the rest are nothing but gravel—wretched little things. And yet they stood out there bawling and swearing that they would do me some violence; but as far *doing* anything—you don't see much of that in this town.

HORSTER: Just as well for you this time, Doctor!

DR. STOCKMANN: True enough. But it makes one angry all the same; because if some day it should be a question of a national fight in real earnest, you will see that public opinion will be in favor of taking to one's heels, and the compact majority will turn tail like a flock of sheep, Captain Horster. This is what is so mournful to think of; it gives me so much concern, that—. No, devil take it, it is ridiculous to care about it! They have called me an enemy of the people, so an enemy of the people let me be!

MRS. STOCKMANN: You will never be that, Thomas.

DR. STOCKMANN: Don't swear to that, Katherine. To be called an ugly name may have the same effect as a pin-scratch in the lung. And that hateful name—I can't get quit of it. It is sticking here in the pit of my stomach, eating into me like a corrosive acid. And no magnesia will remove it.

PETRA: Bah—you should only laugh at them, father.

HORSTER: They will change their minds some day, Doctor.

MRS. STOCKMANN: Yes, Thomas, as sure as you are standing here.

DR. STOCKMANN: Perhaps, when it is too late. Much good may it do them! They may wallow in their filth then and rue the day when they drove a patriot into exile. When do you sail, Captain Horster?

HORSTER: Hm!—that was just what I had come to speak about—

DR. STOCKMANN: Why, has anything gone wrong with the ship?

HORSTER: No; but what has happened is that I am not to sail in it.

PETRA: Do you mean that you have been dismissed from your command?

HORSTER (*smiling*): Yes, that's just it.

PETRA: You too.

MRS. STOCKMANN: There, you see, Thomas!

DR. STOCKMANN: And that for the truth's sake! Oh, if I had thought such a thing possible—

HORSTER: You mustn't take it to heart; I shall be sure to find a job with some ship-owner or other, elsewhere.

DR. STOCKMANN: And that is this man Vik—a wealthy man, independent of every one and everything—! Shame on him!

HORSTER: He is quite an excellent fellow otherwise; he told me himself he would willingly have kept me on, if only he had dared—

DR. STOCKMANN: But he didn't dare? No, of course not.

HORSTER: It is not such an easy matter, he said, for a party man—

DR. STOCKMANN: The worthy man spoke the truth. A party is like a sausage machine; it mashes up all sorts of heads together into the same mincement—fatheads and blockheads, all in one mash!

MRS. STOCKMANN: Come, come, Thomas dear!

PETRA (*to* HORSTER): If only you had not come home with us, things might not have come to this pass.

HORSTER: I do not regret it.

PETRA (*holding out her hand to him*): Thank you for that!

HORSTER (*to* DR. STOCKMANN): And so what I came to say was that if you are determined to go away, I have thought of another plan—

DR. STOCKMANN: That's splendid!—if only we can get away at once.

MRS. STOCKMANN: Hush!—wasn't that some one knocking?

PETRA: That is uncle, surely.

DR. STOCKMANN: Aha! (*Calls out.*) Come in!

MRS. STOCKMANN: Dear Thomas, promise me definitely—.

(PETER STOCKMANN *comes in from the hall.*)

PETER STOCKMANN: Oh, you are engaged. In that case, I will—

DR. STOCKMANN: No, no, come in.

PETER STOCKMANN: But I wanted to speak to you alone.

MRS. STOCKMANN: We will go into the sitting-room in the meanwhile.

HORSTER: And I will look in again later.

DR. STOCKMANN: No, go in there with them, Captain Horster; I want to hear more about—.

HORSTER: Very well, I will wait, then. (*He follows* MRS. STOCKMANN *and* PETRA *into the sitting-room.*)

DR. STOCKMANN: I daresay you find it rather draughty here to-day. Put your hat on.

PETER STOCKMANN: Thank you, if I may. (*Does so.*) I think I caught cold last night; I stood and shivered—

DR. STOCKMANN: Really? I found it warm enough.

PETER STOCKMANN: I regret that it was not in my power to prevent those excesses last night.

DR. STOCKMANN: Have you anything particular to say to me besides that?

PETER STOCKMANN (*taking a big letter from his pocket*): I have this document for you, from the Baths Committee.

DR. STOCKMANN: My dismissal?

PETER STOCKMANN: Yes, dating from to-day. (*Lays the letter on the table.*) It gives us pain to do it; but, to speak frankly, we dared not do otherwise on account of public opinion.

DR. STOCKMANN (*smiling*): Dared not? I seem to have heard that word before, to-day.

PETER STOCKMANN: I must beg you to understand your position clearly. For the future you must not count on any practice whatever in the town.

DR. STOCKMANN: Devil take the practice! But why are you so sure of that?

PETER STOCKMANN: The Householders' Association is circulating a list from house to house. All right-minded citizens are being called upon to give up employing you; and I can assure you that not a single head of a family will risk refusing his signature. They simply dare not.

DR. STOCKMANN: No, no; I don't doubt it. But what then?

PETER STOCKMANN: If I might advise you, it would be best to leave the place for a little while—

DR. STOCKMANN: Yes, the propriety of leaving the place *has* occured to me.

PETER STOCKMANN: Good. And then, when you have had six months to think things over, if, after mature consideration, you can persuade yourself to write a few words of regret, acknowledging your error—

DR. STOCKMANN: I might have my appointment restored to me, do you mean?

PETER STOCKMANN: Perhaps. It is not at all impossible.

DR. STOCKMANN: But what about public opinion, then? Surely you would not dare to do it on account of public feeling.

PETER STOCKMANN: Public opinion is an extremely mutable thing. And, to be quite candid with you, it is a matter of great importance to us to have some admission of that sort from you in writing.

DR. STOCKMAN: Oh, that's what you are after, is it! I will just trouble you to remember what I said to you lately about foxy tricks of that sort!

PETER STOCKMANN: Your position was quite different then. At that time you had reason to suppose you had the whole town at your back—

DR. STOCKMANN: Yes, and now I feel I have the whole town *on* my back— *(flaring up)*. I would not do it if I had the devil and his dam on my back—! Never—never, I tell you!

PETER STOCKMANN: A man with a family has no right to behave as you do. You have no right to do it, Thomas.

DR. STOCKMAN: I have no right! There is only one single thing in the world a free man has no right do do. Do you know what that is?

PETER STOCKMANN: No.

DR. STOCKMANN: Of course you don't, but I will tell you. A free man has no right to soil himself with filth; he has no right to behave in a way that would justify his spitting in his own face.

PETER STOCKMANN: This sort of thing sounds extremely plausible, of course; and if there were no other explanation for your obstinacy—. But as it happens that there is.

DR. STOCKMANN: What do you mean?

PETER STOCKMANN: You understand very well what I mean. But, as your brother and as a man of discretion, I advise you not to build too much upon expectations and prospects that may so very easily fail you.

DR. STOCKMANN: What in the world is all this about?

PETER STOCKMANN: Do you really ask me to believe that you are ignorant of terms of Mr. Kiil's will?

DR. STOCKMANN: I know that the small amount he possesses is to go to an institution for indigent old workpeople. How does that concern me?

PETER STOCKMANN: In the first place, it is by no means a small amount that is in question. Mr. Kiil is a fairly wealthy man.

DR. STOCKMANN: I had no notion of that!

PETER STOCKMANN: Hm!—hadn't you really? Then I suppose you had no notion, either, that a considerable portion of his wealth will come to your children, you and your wife having a life-rent of the capital. Has he never told you so?

DR. STOCKMANN: Never, on my honour! Quite the reverse; he has consistently done nothing but fume at being so unconscionably heavily taxed. But are you perfectly certain of this, Peter?

PETER STOCKMANN: I have it from an absolutely reliable source.

DR. STOCKMANN: Then, thank God, Katherine is provided for—and the children too! I must tell her this at once—(*calls out*) Katherine, Katherine!

PETER STOCKMANN (*restraining him*): Hush, don't say a word yet!

MRS. STOCKMANN (*opening the door*): What is the matter?

DR. STOCKMANN: Oh, nothing, nothing; you can go back. (*She shuts the door.* DR. STOCKMANN *walks up and down in his excitement*). Provided for!—Just think of it, we are all provided for! And for life! What a blessed feeling it is to know one is provided for!

PETER STOCKMANN: Yes, but that is just exactly what you are not. Mr. Kiil can alter his will any day he likes.

DR. STOCKMANN: But he won't do that, my dear Peter. The "Badger" is much too delighted at my attack on you and your wise friends.

PETER STOCKMANN (*starts and looks intently at him*): Ah, that throws a light on various things.

DR. STOCKMANN: What things?

PETER STOCKMANN: I see that the whole thing was a combined manœuvre on your part and his. These violent, reckless attacks that you have made against the leading men of the town, under the pretence that it was in the name of truth—

DR. STOCKMANN: What about them?

PETER SCOCKMANN: I see that they were nothing else than the stipulated price for that vindictive old man's will.

DR. STOCKMANN (*almost speechless*): Peter—you are the most disgusting plebeian I have ever met in all my life.

PETER STOCKMANN: All is over between us. Your dismissal is irrevocable—we have a weapon against you now. (*Goes out.*)

DR. STOCKMANN: For shame! For shame! (*Calls out.*) Katherine, you must have the floor scrubbed after him! Let—what's her name—devil take it, the girl who has always got soot on her nose—

MRS. STOCKMANN (*in the sitting-room*): Hush, Thomas, be quiet!

PETRA (*coming to the door*): Father, grandfather is here, asking if he may speak to you alone.

DR. STOCKMANN: Certainly he may. (*Going to the door.*) Come in, Mr. Kiil. (MORTEN KIIL *comes in.* DR. STOCKMANN *shuts the door after him*). What can I do for you? Won't you sit down?

MORTEN KIIL: I won't sit. (*Looks around*). You look very comfortable here to-day, Thomas.

DR. STOCKMANN: Yes, don't we!

MORTEN KIIL: Very comfortable—plenty of fresh air. I should think you have got enough to-day of that oxygen you were talking about yesterday. Your conscience must be in splendid order to-day, I should think.

DR. STOCKMANN: It is.

MORTEN KIIL: So I should think. (*Taps his chest.*) Do you know what I have got here?

DR. STOCKMANN: A good conscience, too, I hope.

MORTEN KIIL: Bah!—No, it is something better than that.

(*He takes a thick pocket-book from his breast-pocket, opens it, and displays a packet of papers*).

DR. STOCKMANN (*looking at him in astonishment*): Shares in the Baths?

MORTEN KIIL: They were not difficult to get to-day.

DR. STOCKMANN: And you have been buying—?

MORTEN KIIL: As many as I could pay for.

DR. STOCKMANN: But, my dear Mr. Kiil—consider the state of the Baths' affairs!

MORTEN KIIL: If you believe like a reasonable man, you can soon set the Baths on their feet again.

DR. STOCKMANN: Well, you can see for yourself that I have done all I can, but—. They are all mad in this town!

MORTEN KIIL: You said yesterday that the worst of this pollution came from my tannery. If that is true, then my grandfather and my father before me, and I myself, for many years past, have been poisoning the town like three destroying angels. Do you think I am going to sit quiet under that reproach?

DR. STOCKMANN: Unfortunately I am afraid you will have to.

MORTEN KIIL: No, thank you. I am jealous of my name and reputation. They call me "the Badger," I am told. A badger is a kind of pig,

I believe; but I am not going to give them the right to call me that. I mean to live and die a clean man.

DR. STOCKMANN: And how are you going to set about it?

MORTEN KIIL: You shall cleanse me, Thomas.

DR. STOCKMANN: I!

MORTEN KIIL: Do you know what money I have bought these shares with? No, of course you can't know—but I will tell you. It is the money that Katherine and Petra and the boys will have when I am gone. Because I have been able to save a little bit after all, you know.

DR. STOCKMANN (*flaring up*): And you have gone and taken Katherine's money for *this*!

MORTEN KIIL: Yes, the whole of the money is invested in the Baths now. And now I just want to see whether you are quite stark, staring mad, Thomas! If you still make out that these animals and other nasty things of that sort come from my tannery, it will be exactly as if you were to flay broad strips of skin from Katherine's body, and Petra's, and the boys'; and no decent man would do that—unless he were mad.

DR. STOCKMANN (*walking up and down*): Yes, but I *am* mad; I *am* mad!

MORTEN KIIL: You cannot be so absurdly mad as all that, when it is a question of your wife and children.

DR. STOCKMANN (*standing still in front of him*): Why couldn't you consult me about it, before you went and bought all that trash?

MORTEN KIIL: What is done cannot be undone.

DR. STOCKMANN (*walks about uneasily*): If only I were not so certain about it—! But I am absolutely convinced that I am right.

MORTEN KIIL (*weighing the pocket-book in his hand*): If you stick to your mad idea, this won't be worth much, you know. (*Puts the pocket-book in his pocket.*)

DR. STOCKMANN: But, hang it all! it might be possible for science to discover some prophylactic, I should think—or some antidote of some kind—

MORTEN KIIL: To kill these animals, do you mean?

DR. STOCKMANN: Yes, or to make them innocuous.

MORTEN KIIL: Couldn't you try some rat's-bane?

DR. STOCKMANN: Don't talk nonsense! They all say it is only imagination, you now. Well, let it go at that! Let them have their own way about it! Haven't the ignorant, narrowminded curs reviled me as an enemy of the people?—and haven't they been ready to tear the clothes off my back too?

MORTEN KIIL: And broken all your windows to pieces!

DR. STOCKMANN: And then there is my duty to my family. I must talk it over with Katherine; she is great on those things.

MORTEN KIIL: That is right; be guided by a reasonable woman's advice.

DR. STOCKMANN (*advancing towards him*): To think you could do such a preposterous thing! Risking Katherine's money in this way, and putting me in such a horribly painful dilemma! When I look at you, I think I see the devil himself—.

MORTEN KIIL: Then I had better go. But I must have an answer from you before two o'clock—yes or no. If it is no, the shares go to a charity, and that this very day.

DR. STOCKMANN: And what does Katherine get?

MORTON KIIL: Not a halfpenny. (*The door leading to the hall opens, and* HOVSTAL *and* ASLAKSEN *make their appearance.*) Look at those two!

DR. STOCKMANN (*staring at them*). What the devil!—have *you* actually the face to come into my house?

HOVSTAD: Certainly.

ASLAKSEN: We have something to say to you, you see.

MORTEN KILL (*in a whisper*). Yes or no—before two o'clock.

ASLAKSEN (*glancing at* HOVSTAD): Aha! (MORTEN KIIL *goes out.*)

DR. STOCKMANN: Well, what do you want with me? Be brief.

HOVSTAD: I can quite understand that you are annoyed with us for our attitude at the meeting yesterday—

DR. STOCKMANN: Attitude, do you call it? Yes, it was a charming attitude! I call it weak, womanish—damnably shameful!

HOVSTAD: Call it what you like, we could not do otherwise.

DR. STOCKMANN: You *dared* not do otherwise—isn't that it?

HOVSTAD: Well, if you like to put it that way.

ASLAKSEN: But why did you not let us have word of it beforehand?—just a hint to Mr. Hovstad or to me?

DR. STOCKMANN: A hint? Of what?

ASLAKSEN: Of what was behind it all.

DR. STOCKMANN: I don't understand you in the least.

ASLAKSEN (*with a confidential nod*): Oh yes, you do. Dr. Stockmann.

HOVSTAD: It is no good making a mystery of it any longer.

DR. STOCKMANN (*looking first at one of them and then at the other*): What the devil do you both mean?

ASLAKSEN: May I ask if your father-in-law is not going round the town buying up all the shares in the Baths?

DR. STOCKMANN: Yes, he has been buying Baths shares to-day; but—

ASLAKSEN: It would have been more prudent to get some one else to do it—some one less nearly related to you.

HOVSTAD: And you should not have let your name appear in the affair. There was no need for anyone to know that the attack on the Baths came from you. You ought to have consulted me, Dr. Stockmann.

DR. STOCKMANN (*looks in front of him; then a light seems to dawn on him and he says in amazement*): Are such things conceivable? Are such things possible?

ASLAKSEN (*with a smile*): Evidently they are. But it is better to use a little *finesse*, you know.

HOVSTAD: And it is much better to have several persons in a thing of that sort; because the responsibility of each individual is lessened, when there are others with him.

DR. STOCKMANN (*composedly*): Come to the point, gentlemen. What do you want?

ASLAKSEN: Perhaps Mr. Hovstad had better—

HOVSTAL: No, you tell him, Aslaksen.

ASLAKSEN: Well, the fact is that, now we know the bearings of the whole affair, we think we might venture to put the "People's Messenger" at your disposal.

DR. STOCKMANN: Do you dare do that now? What about public opinion? Are you not afraid of a storm breaking upon our heads?

HOVSTAD: We will try to weather it.

ASLAKSEN: And you must be ready to go off quickly on a new tack, Doctor. As soon as your invective has done its work—

DR. STOCKMANN: Do you mean, as soon as my father-in-law and I have got hold of the shares at a low figure?

HOVSTAD: Your reasons for wishing to get the control of the Baths are mainly scientific, I take it.

DR. STOCKMANN: Of course; it was for scientific reasons that I persuaded the old "Badger" to stand in with me in the matter. So we will tinker at the conduit-pipes a little, and dig up a little bit of the shore, and it shan't cost the town a sixpence. That will be all right—eh?

HOVSTAD: I think so—if you have the "People's Messenger" behind you.

ASLAKSEN: The Press is a power in a free community, Doctor.

DR. STOCKMANN: Quite so. And so is public opinion. And you, Mr. Aslaksen—I suppose you will be answerable for the Householders' Association?

ASLAKSEN: Yes, and for the Temperance Society. You may rely on that.

DR. STOCKMANN: But, gentlemen—I really am ashamed to ask the question—but, what return do you—?

HOVSTAD: We should prefer to help you without any return whatever, believe me. But the "People's Messenger" is in rather a shaky condition; it doesn't go really well; and I should be very unwilling to suspend the paper now, when there is so much work to do here in the political way.

DR. STOCKMANN: Quite so; that would be a great trial to such a friend of the people as you are. (*Flares up*). But I am an enemy of the people, remember! (*Walks about the room.*) Where have I put my stick? Where the devil is my stick?

HOVSTAD: What's that?

ASLAKSEN: Surely you never mean—?

DR. STOCKMANN (*standing still*): And suppose I don't give you a single penny of all I get out of it? Money is not very easy to get out of us rich folk, please to remember!

HOVSTAD: And you please to remember that this affair of the shares can be represented in two ways!

DR. STOCKMANN: Yes, and you are just the man to do it. If I don't come to the rescue of the "People's Messenger," you will certainly take an evil view of the affair; you will hunt me down, I can well imagine—pursue me—try to throttle me as a dog does a hare.

HOVSTAD: It is a natural law; every animal must fight for its own livelihood.

ASLAKSEN: And get its food where it can, you know.

DR. STOCKMANN (*walking about the room*): Then you go and look for yours in the gutter; because I am going to show you which is the strongest animal of us three! (*Finds an umbrella and brandishes it above his head.*) Ah, now—!

HOVSTAD: You are surely not going to use violence!

ASLAKSEN: Take care what you are doing with that umbrella.

DR. STOCKMANN: Out of the window with you, Mr. Hovstad!

HOVSTAD (*edging to the door*): Are you quite mad!

DR. STOCKMANN: Out of the window, Mr. Aslaksen! Jump, I tell you! You will have to do it, sooner or later.

ASLAKSEN (*running round the writing-table*): Moderation, Doctor—I am a delicate man—I can stand so little—(*calls out*) help, help!

(MRS. STOCKMANN, PETRA *and* HORSTER *come in from the sitting-room.*)

MRS. STOCKMANN: Good gracious, Thomas! What is happening?

DR. STOCKMANN (*brandishing the umbrella*): Jump out, I tell you! Out into the gutter!

HOVSTAD: An assault on an unoffending man! I call you to witness, Captain Horster. (*Hurries out through the hall.*)

ASLAKSEN (*irresolutely*): If only I knew the way about here—. (*Steals out through the sitting-room*).

MRS. STOCKMANN (*holding her husband back*): Control yourself, Thomas!

DR. STOCKMANN (*throwing down the umbrella*): Upon my soul, they have escaped after all.

MRS. STOCKMANN: What did they want you to do?

DR. STOCKMANN: I will tell you later on; I have something else to think about now. (*Goes to the table and writes something on a calling-card.*) Look there, Katherine; what is written there?

MRS. STOCKMANN: Three big *Notes*; what does that mean.

DR. STOCKMANN: I will tell you that too, later on. (*Holds out the card to* PETRA.) There, Petra; tell sooty-face to run over to the "Badger's" with that, as quick as she can. Hurry up! (PETRA *takes the card and goes out to the hall.*)

DR. STOCKMANN: Well, I think I have had a visit from every one of the devil's messengers to-day! But now I am going to sharpen my pen till they can feel its point; I shall dip it in venom and gall; I shall hurl my ink-pot at their heads!

MRS. STOCKMANN: Yes, but we are going away, you know, Thomas.

(PETRA *comes back.*)

DR. STOCKMANN: Well?

PETRA: She has gone with it.

DR. STOCKMANN: Good.—Going away, did you say? No, I'll be hanged if we are going away! We are going to stay where we are, Katherine!

PETRA: Stay here?

MRS. STOCKMAN: Here, in the town?

DR. STOCKMANN: Yes, here. This is the field of battle—this is where the fight will be. This is where I shall triumph! As soon as I have had my trousers sewn up I shall go out and look for another house. We must have a roof over our heads for the winter.

HORSTER: That you shall have in my house.

DR. STOCKMANN: Can I?

HORSTER: Yes, quite well. I have plenty of room, and I am almost never at home.

MRS. STOCKMANN: How good of you, Captain Horster!

PETRA: Thank you!

DR. STOCKMANN (*grasping his hand*): Thank you, thank you! That is one trouble over! Now I can set to work in earnest at once. There is an endless amount of things to look through here, Katherine! Luckily I shall have all my time at my disposal; because I have been dismissed from the Baths, you know.

MRS. STOCKMANN (*with a sigh*): Oh yes, I expected that.

DR. STOCKMANN: And they want to take my practice away from me too. Let them! I have got the poor people to fall back upon, anyway—those that don't pay anything! and, after all, they need me most, too. But, by Jove, they will have to listen to me; I shall preach to them in season and out of season, as it says somewhere.

MRS. STOCKMANN: But, dear Thomas, I should have thought events had showed you what use it is to preach.

DR. STOCKMANN: You are really ridiculous, Katherine. Do you want me to let myself be beaten off the field by public opinion and the compact majority and all that deviltry? No, thank you! And what I want to do is so simple and clear and straightforward. I only want to drum into the heads of these curs the fact that the liberals are the most insidious enemies of freedom—that party programmes strangle every young and vigorous truth—that considerations of expediency turn morality and injustice upside down—and that they will end by making life here unbearable. Don't you think, Captain Horster, that I ought to be able to make people understand that?

HORSTER: Very likely; I don't know much about such things myself.

DR. STOCKMANN: Well, look here—I will explain! It is the party leaders that must be exterminated. A party leader is like a wolf, you see—like a voracious wolf. He requires a certain number of smaller victims to prey upon every year, if he is to live. Just look at Hovstad and Aslaksen! How many smaller victims have they not put an end to—or at any rate maimed and mangled until they are fit for nothing except to be householders or subscribers to the "People's Messenger"! (*Sits down on the edge of the table.*) Come here, Katherine—look how beautifully the sun shines to-day! And this lovely spring air I am drinking in!

MRS. STOCKMANN: Yes, if only we could live on sunshine and spring air, Thomas.

DR. STOCKMANN: Oh, you will have to pinch and save a bit—then we shall get along. That gives me very little concern. What is much worse is, that I know of no one who is liberal-minded and high-minded enough to venture to take up my work after me.

PETRA: Don't think about that, father; you have plenty of time before you.—Hullo, here are the boys already!

(EJLIF *and* MORTEN *come in from the sitting-room.*)

MRS. STOCKMANN: Have you got a holiday?

MORTEN: No; but we were fighting with the other boys between lessons—

EJLIF: That isn't true; it was the other boys were fighting with us.

MORTEN: Well, and then Mr. Rörlund said we had better stay at home for a day or two.

DR. STOCKMANN (*snapping his fingers and getting up from the table*): I have it! I have it, by Jove! You shall never set foot in the school again!

THE BOYS: No more school!

MRS. STOCKMANN: But, Thomas—

DR. STOCKMANN: Never, I say. I will educate you myself; that is to say, you shan't learn a blessed thing—

MORTEN: Hooray!

DR. STOCKMANN: —but I will make liberal-minded and high-minded men of you. You must help me with that, Petra.

PETRA: Yes, father, you may be sure I will.

DR. STOCKMANN: And my school shall be in the room where they insulted me and called me an enemy of the people. But we are too few as we are; I must have at least twelve boys to begin with.

MRS. STOCKMANN: You will certainly never get them in this town.

DR. STOCKMANN: We shall. (*To the boys.*) Don't you know any street urchins—regular ragamuffins—?

MORTEN: Yes, father, I know lots!

DR. STOCKMANN: That's capital! Bring me some specimens of them. I am going to experiment with curs, just for once; there may be some exceptional heads amongst them.

MORTEN: And what are we going to do, when you have made liberal-minded and high-minded men of us?

DR. STOCKMANN: Then you shall drive all the wolves out of the country, my boys!

(EJLIF *looks rather doubtful about it;* MORTEN *jumps about crying* "Hurrah!")

MRS. STOCKMANN: Let us hope it won't be the wolves that will drive you out of the country, Thomas.

DR. STOCKMANN: Are you out of your mind, Katherine? Drive me out! Now—when I am the strongest man in the town!

MRS. STOCKMANN: The strongest—now?

DR. STOCKMANN: Yes, and I will go so far as to say that now I am the strongest man in the whole world.

MORTEN: I say!

DR. STOCKMANN (*lowering his voice*): Hush! You mustn't say anything about it yet; but I have made a great discovery.

MRS. STOCKMANN: Another one?

DR. STOCKMANN: Yes, (*Gathers them round him, and says confidentially:*) It is this, let me tell you—that the strongest man in the world is he who stands most alone.

MRS. STOCKMANN (*smiling and shaking her head*): Oh, Thomas, Thomas!

PETRA (*encouragingly, as she grasps her father's hands*): Father!

George Bernard Shaw

Saint Joan

Characters

BERTRAND DE POULENGY
STEWARD
JOAN
ROBERT DE BAUDRICOURT
THE ARCHBISHOP OF RHEIMS
MGR DE LA TREMOUILLE
COURT PAGE
GILLES DE RAIS
CAPTAIN LA HIRE
THE DAUPHIN (*later* CHARLES VII)
DUCHESS DE LA TREMOUILLE
DUNOIS, BASTARD OF ORLEANS
DUNOIS' PAGE
RICHARD DE BEAUCHAMP, EARL OF WARWICK
CHAPLAIN DE STOGUMBER
PETER CAUCHON, BISHOP OF BEAUVAIS
WARWICK'S PAGE
THE INQUISITOR
D'ESTIVET
DE COURCELLES
BROTHER MARTIN LADVENU
THE EXECUTIONER
AN ENGLISH SOLDIER
A GENTLEMAN OF 1920

SCENE I

(A fine spring morning on the river Meuse, between Lorraine and Champagne, in the year 1429 A.D., in the castle of Vaucouleurs.

CAPTAIN ROBERT DE BAUDRICOURT, a military squire, handsome and physically energetic, but with no will of his own, is disguising that defect in his usual fashion by storming terribly at his steward, a trodden worm, scanty of flesh, scanty of hair, who might be any age from 18 to 55, being the sort of man whom age cannot wither because he has never bloomed.

The two are in a sunny stone chamber on the first floor of the castle. At a plain strong oak table, seated in chair to match, the captain presents his left profile. The STEWARD stands facing him at the other side of the table, if so deprecatory a stance as his can be called standing. The mullioned thirteenth-century window is open behind him. Near it in the corner is a turret with a narrow arched doorway leading to a winding stair which descends to the courtyard. There is a stout fourlegged stool under the table, and a wooden chest under the window.)

ROBERT: No eggs! No eggs!! Thousand thunders, man, what do you mean by no eggs?

STEWARD: Sir: it is not my fault. It is the act of God.

ROBERT: Blasphemy. You tell me there are no eggs; and you blame your Maker for it.

STEWARD: Sir: what can I do? I cannot lay eggs.

ROBERT (*sarcastic*): Ha! You jest about it.

STEWARD: No, sir, God knows. We all have to go without eggs just as you have, sir. The hens will not lay.

ROBERT: Indeed! (*Rising*) Now listen to me, you.

STEWARD (*humbly*): Yes, sir.

ROBERT: What am I?

STEWARD: What are you, sir?

ROBERT (*coming at him*): Yes: what am I? Am I Robert, squire of Baudricourt and captain of this castle of Vaucouleurs; or am I a cowboy?

STEWARD: Oh, sir, you know you are a greater man here than the king himself.

ROBERT: Precisely. And now, do you know what you are?

STEWARD: I am nobody, sir, except that I have the honor to be your steward.

ROBERT (*driving him to the wall, adjective by adjective*): You have not only the honor of being my steward, but the privilege of being the worst, most incompetent, drivelling snivelling jibbering jabbering idiot of a steward in France. (*He strides back to the table.*)

STEWARD (*cowering on the chest*): Yes, sir: to a great man like you I must seem like that.

ROBERT (*turning*): My fault, I suppose. Eh?

STEWARD (*coming to him deprecatingly*): Oh, sir: you always give my most innnocent words such a turn!

ROBERT: I will give your neck a turn if you dare tell me when I ask you how many eggs there are that you cannot lay any.

STEWARD (*protesting*): Oh sir, oh sir—

ROBERT: No: not oh sir, oh sir, but no sir, no sir. My three Barbary hens and the black are the best layers in Champagne. And you come and tell me that there are no eggs! Who stole them? Tell me that, before I kick you out through the castle gate for a liar and a seller of my goods to thieves. The milk was short yesterday, too: do not forget that.

STEWARD (*desperate*): I know, sir. I know only too well. There is no milk: there are no eggs: tomorrow there will be nothing.

ROBERT: Nothing! You will steal the lot: eh?

STEWARD: No, sir: nobody will steal anything. But there is a spell on us: we are bewitched.

ROBERT: That story is not good enough for me. Robert de Baudricourt burns witches and hangs thieves. Go. Bring me four dozen eggs and two gallons of milk here in this room before noon, or Heaven have mercy on your bones! I will teach you to make a fool of me. (*He resumes his seat with an air of finality.*)

STEWARD: Sir: I tell you there are no eggs. There will be none—not if you were to kill me for it—as long as The Maid is at the door.

ROBERT: The Maid! What maid? What are you talking about?

STEWARD: The girl from Lorraine, sir. From Domrémy.

ROBERT (*rising in fearful wrath*): Thirty thousand thunders! Fifty thousand devils! Do you mean to say that that girl, who had the impudence to ask to see me two days ago, and whom I told you to send back to her father with my orders that he was to give her a good hiding, is here still?

STEWARD: I have told her to go, sir. She won't.

ROBERT: I did not tell you to tell her to go: I told you to throw her out. You have fifty men-at-arms and a dozen lumps of able-bodied servants to carry out my orders. Are they afraid of her?

STEWARD: She is so positive, sir.

ROBERT (*seizing him by the scruff of the neck*): Positive! Now see here. I am going to throw you downstairs.

STEWARD: No, sir. Please.

ROBERT: Well, stop me by being positive. It's quite easy: any slut of a girl can do it.

STEWARD (*hanging limp in his hands*): Sir, sir: you cannot get rid of her by throwing me out. (ROBERT *has to let him drop. He squats on his knees on the floor, contemplating his master resignedly.*) You see, sir, you are much more positive than I am. But so is she.

ROBERT: I am stronger than you are, you fool.

STEWARD: No, sir: it isnt that: its your strong character, sir. She is weaker than we are: she is only a slip of a girl; but we cannot make her go.

ROBERT: You parcel of curs: you are afraid of her.

STEWARD (*rising cautiously*): No sir: we are afraid of you; but she puts courage into us. She really doesnt seem to be afraid of anything. Perhaps you could frighten her, sir.

ROBERT (*grimly*): Perhaps. Where is she now?

STEWARD: Down in the courtyard, sir, talking to the soldiers as usual. She is always talking to the soldiers except when she is praying.

ROBERT: Praying! Ha! You believe she prays, you idiot. I know the sort of girl that is always talking to soldiers. She shall talk to me a bit. (*He goes to the window and shouts fiercely through it.*) Hallo, you there!

A GIRL'S VOICE (*bright, strong and rough*): Is it me, sir?

ROBERT: Yes, you.

THE VOICE: Be you captain?

ROBERT: Yes, damn your impudence, I be captain. Come up here. (*To the soldiers in the yard*) Shew her the way, you. And shove her along quick. (*He leaves the window, and returns to his place at the table, where he sits magisterially.*)

STEWARD (*whispering*): She wants to go and be a soldier herself. She wants you to give her soldier's clothes. Armor, sir! And a sword! Actually! (*He steals behind Robert.*)

(JOAN *appears in the turret doorway. She is an ablebodied country girl of 17 or 18, respectably dressed in red, with an uncommon face; eyes very wide apart and bulging as they often do in very imaginative people, a long well-shaped nose with wide nostrils, a short upper lip, resolute but full-lipped mouth, and handsome fighting chin. She comes eagerly to the table, delighted at having penetrated to* BAUDRICOURT'S *presence at last, and full of hope as to the results. His scowl does not check or frighten her in the least. Her voice is normally a hearty coaxing voice, very confident, very appealing, very hard to resist.*)

JOAN (*bobbing a curtsey*): Good morning, captain squire. Captain: you are to give me a horse and armor and some soldiers, and send me to the Dauphin. Those are your orders from my Lord.

ROBERT (*outraged*): Orders from your lord! And who the devil may your lord be? Go back to him, and tell him that I am neither duke nor peer at his orders: I am squire of Baudricourt; and I take no orders except from the king.

JOAN (*reassuringly*): Yes, squire: that is all right. My Lord is the King of Heaven.

ROBERT: Why, the girl's mad. (*To the steward*) Why didn't you tell me so, you blockhead?

STEWARD: Sir: do not anger her: give her what she wants.

JOAN (*impatient, but friendly*): They all say I am mad until I talk to them, squire. But you see that it is the will of God that you are to do what He has put into my mind.

ROBERT: It is the will of God that I shall send you back to your father with orders to put you under lock and key and thrash the madness out of you. What have you to say to that?

JOAN: You think you will, squire; but you will find it all coming quite different. You said you would not see me; but here I am.

STEWARD (*appealing*): Yes, sir. You see, sir.

ROBERT: Hold your tongue, you.

STEWARD (*abjectly*): Yes, sir.

ROBERT (*to Joan, with a sour loss of confidence*): So you are presuming on my seeing you, are you?

JOAN (*sweetly*): Yes, squire.

ROBERT (*feeling that he has lost ground, brings down his two fists squarely on the table, and inflates his chest imposingly to cure the unwelcome and only too familiar sensation*): Now listen to me. I am going to assert myself.

JOAN (*busily*): Please do, squire. The horse will cost sixteen francs. It is a good deal of money: but I can save it on the armor. I can find a soldier's armor that will fit me well enough: I am very hardy; and I do not need beautiful armor made to my measure like you wear. I shall not want many soldiers: the Dauphin will give me all I need to raise the siege of Orleans.

ROBERT (*flabbergasted*): To raise the siege of Orleans!

JOAN (*simply*): Yes, squire: that is what God is sending me to do. Three men will be enough for you to send with me if they are good men and gentle to me. They have promised to come with me. Polly and Jack and—

ROBERT: Polly!! You impudent baggage, do you dare call squire Bertrand de Poulengey Polly to my face?

JOAN: His friends call him so, squire: I did not know he had any other name. Jack—

ROBERT: That is Monsieur John of Metz, I suppose?

JOAN: Yes, squire. Jack will come willingly: he is a very kind gentleman, and gives me money to give to the poor. I think John Godsave will come, and Dick the Archer, and their servants John of Honecourt and Julian. There will be no trouble for you, squire: I have arranged it all: you have only to give the order.

ROBERT (*contemplating her in a stupor of amazement*): Well, I am damned!

JOAN (*with unruffled sweetness*): No, squire: God is very merciful; and the blessed saints Catherine and Margaret, who speak to me every day (*he gapes*), will intercede for you. You will go to paradise; and your name will be remembered for ever as my first helper.

ROBERT (*to the* STEWARD, *still much bothered, but changing his tone as he pursues a new clue*): Is this true about Monsieur de Poulengey?

STEWARD (*eagerly*): Yes, sir, and about Monsier de Metz too. They both want to go with her.

ROBERT (*thoughtful*): Mf! (*He goes to the window, and shouts into the courtyard*) Hallo! You there: send Monsieur de Poulengey to me, will you? (*He turns to* JOAN) Get out; and wait in the yard.

JOAN (*smiling brightly at him*): Right, squire. (*She goes out.*)

ROBERT (*to the* STEWARD): Go with her, you, you dithering imbecile. Stay within call; and keep your eye on her. I shall have her up here again.

STEWARD: Do so in God's name, sir. Think of those hens, the best layers in Champagne; and—

ROBERT: Think of my boot; and take your backside out of reach of it.

(*The steward retreats hastily and finds himself confronted in the doorway by* BERTRAND DE POULENGEY, *a lymphatic French gentleman-at-arms, aged 36 or thereabout, employed in the department of the provost-marshal, dreamily absent-minded, seldom speaking unless spoken to, and then slow and obstinate in reply; altogether in contrast to the self-assertive, loud-mouthed, superficially energetic, fundamentally will-less* ROBERT. *The* STEWARD *makes way for him, and vanishes.*)

(POULENGEY *salutes, and stands awaiting orders.*)

ROBERT (*genially*): It isn't service, Polly. A friendly talk. Sit down. (*He hooks the stool from under the table with his instep.*)

(POULENGEY, *relaxing, comes into the room: places the stool between the table and the window: and sits down ruminatively.* ROBERT, *half sitting on the end of the table, begins the friendly talk.*)

ROBERT: Now listen to me, Polly. I must talk to you like a father.

(POULENGEY *looks up at him gravely for a moment, but says nothing.*)

ROBERT: It's about this girl you are interested in. Now, I have seen her. I have talked to her. First, she's mad. That doesn't matter. Second, she's not a farm wench. She's a bourgeoise. That matters a good deal. I know her class exactly. Her father came here last year to represent his village in a lawsuit: he is one of their notables. A farmer. Not a gentleman farmer: he makes money by it, and lives by it. Still, not a laborer. Not a mechanic. He might have a cousin a lawyer, or in the Church. People of this sort may be of no account socially; but they can give a lot of bother to the authorities. That is to say, to me. Now no doubt it seems to you a very simple thing to take this girl away, humbugging her into the belief that you are taking her to the Dauphin. But if you get her into trouble, you may get me into no end of a mess, as I am her father's lord, and responsible for her protection. So friends or no friends, Polly, hands off her.

POULENGEY (*with deliberate impressiveness*): I should as soon think of the Blessed Virgin herself in that way, as of this girl.

ROBERT (*coming off the table*): But she says you and Jack and Dick have offered to go with her. What for? You are not going to tell me that you take her crazy notion of going to the Dauphin seriously, are you?

POULENGEY (*slowly*): There is something about her. They are pretty foul-mouthed and foulminded down there in the guardroom, some of them. But there hasnt been a word that has anything to do with her being a woman. They have stopped swearing before her. There is something. Something. It may be worth trying.

ROBERT: Oh, come, Polly! pull yourself together. Common sense was never your strong point; but this is a little too much. (*He retreats disgustedly.*)

POULENGEY (*unmoved*): What is the good of commonsense? If we had any commonsense we should join the Duke of Burgundy and the English king. They hold half the country, right down to the Loire. They have Paris. They have this castle: you know very well that we had to surrender it to the Duke of Bedford, and that you are only holding it on parole. The Dauphin is in Chinon, like a rat in a corner, except that he wont fight. We dont even know that he is the Dauphin: his mother says he isnt; and she ought to know. Think of that! Think of that! the queen denying the legitimacy of her own son!

ROBERT: Well, she married her daughter to the English king. Can you blame the woman?

POULENGEY: I blame nobody. But thanks to her, the Dauphin is down and out; and we may as well face it. The English will take Orleans: the Bastard will not be able to stop them.

ROBERT: He beat the English the year before last at Montargis. I was with him.

POULENGEY: No matter: his men are cowed now; and he cant work miracles. And I tell you that nothing can save our side now but a miracle.

ROBERT: Miracles are all right, Polly. The only difficulty about them is that they dont happen nowadays.

POULENGEY: I used to think so. I am not so sure now. (*Rising, and moving ruminatively towards the window*) At all events this is not a time to leave any stone unturned. There is something about the girl.

ROBERT: Oh! You think the girl can work miracles, do you?

POULENGEY: I think the girl herself is a bit of a miracle. Anyhow, she is the last card left in our hand. Better play her than throw up the game.

(*He wanders to the turret.*)

ROBERT (*wavering*). You really think that?

POULENGEY (*turning*): Is there anything else left for us to think?

ROBERT (*going to him*): Look here, Polly. If you were in my place would you let a girl like that do you out of sixteen francs for a horse?

POULENGEY: I will pay for the horse.

ROBERT: You will!

POULENGEY: Yes: I will back my opinion.

ROBERT: You will really gamble on a forlorn hope to the tune of sixteen francs?

POULENGEY: It is not a gamble.

ROBERT: What else is it?

POULENGEY: It is a certainty. Her words and her ardent faith in God have put fire into me.

ROBERT (*giving him up*): Whew! You are as mad as she is.

POULENGEY (*ostinately*): We want a few mad people now. See where the sane ones have landed us!

ROBERT (*his irresoluteness now openly swamping his affected decisiveness*): I shall feel like a precious fool. Still, if you feel sure—?

POULENGEY: I feel sure enough to take her to Chinon—unless you stop me.

ROBERT: This is not fair. You are putting the responsibility on me.

POULENGEY: It is on you whichever way you decide.

ROBERT: Yes: thats just it. Which way am I to decide? You dont see how awkward this is for me. (*Snatching at a dilatory step with an unconscious hope that* JOAN *will make up his mind for him*). Do you think I ought to have another talk with her?

POULENGEY (*rising*): Yes. (*He goes to the window and calls*) Joan!

JOAN'S VOICE: Will he let us go, Polly?

POULENGEY: Come up. Come in. (*Turning to* ROBERT) Shall I leave you with her?

ROBERT: No: stay here; and back me up.

(POULENGEY *sits down on the chest.* ROBERT *goes back to his magisterial chair, but remains standing to inflate himself more imposingly.* JOAN *comes in, full of good news.*)

JOAN: Jack will go halves for the horse.

ROBERT: Well!! (*He sits, deflated*).

POULENGEY (*gravely*): Sit down, Joan.

JOAN (*checked a little, and looking to* ROBERT): May I?

ROBERT: Do what you are told.

(JOAN *curtsies and sits down on the stool between them.* ROBERT *outfaces his perplexity with his most peremptory air.*)

ROBERT: What is your name?

JOAN (*chattily*): They always call me Jenny in Lorraine. Here in France I am Joan. The soldiers call me The Maid.

ROBERT: What is your surname?

JOAN: Surname? What is that? My father sometimes calls himself d'Arc; but I know nothing about it. You met my father. He—

ROBERT: Yes, yes; I remember. You come from Domrémy in Lorraine, I think.

JOAN: Yes; but what does it matter? we all speak French.

ROBERT: Dont ask questions: answer them. How old are you?

JOAN: Seventeen: so they tell me. It might be nineteen. I dont remember.

ROBERT: What did you mean when you said that St Catherine and St Margaret talked to you every day?

JOAN: They do.

ROBERT: What are they like?

JOAN (*suddenly obstinate*): I will tell you nothing about that: they have not given me leave.

ROBERT: But you actually see them; and they talk to you just as I am talking to you?

JOAN: No: it is quite different. I cannot tell you: you must not talk to me about my voices.

ROBERT: How do you mean? voices?

JOAN: I hear voices telling me what to do. They come from God.

ROBERT: They come from your imagination.

JOAN: Of course. That is how the messages of God come to us.

POULENGEY: Checkmate.

ROBERT: No fear! (*To* JOAN) So God says you are to raise the siege of Orleans?

JOAN: And to crown the Dauphin in Rheims Cathedral.

ROBERT (*gasping*): Crown the D—! Gosh!

JOAN: And to make the English leave France.

ROBERTS (*sarcastic*): Anything else?

JOAN (*charming*): Not just at present, thank you, squire.

ROBERT: I suppose you think raising a siege is as easy as chasing a cow out of a meadow. You think soldiering is anybody's job?

JOAN: I do not think it can be very difficult if God is on your side, and you are willing to put your life in His hand. But many soldiers are very simple.

ROBERT (*grimly*): Simple! Did you ever see English soldiers fighting?

JOAN: They are only men. God made them just like us; but He gave them their own country and their own language; and it is not His will that they should come into our country and try to speak our language.

ROBERT: Who has been putting such nonsense into your head? Dont you know that soldiers are subject to their feudal lord, and that it is nothing to them to to you whether he is the duke of Burgundy or the king of England or the king of France? What has their language to do with it?

JOAN: I do not understand that a bit. We are all subject to the King of Heaven; and He gave us our countries and our languages, and meant us to keep to them. If it were not so it would be murder to kill an Englishman in battle; and you, squire, would be in great danger of hell fire. You must not think about your duty to your feudal lord, but about your duty to God.

POULENGEY: It's no use, Robert: she can choke you like that every time.

ROBERT: Can she, by Saint Dennis! We shall see. (*To* JOAN) We are not talking about God: we are talking about practical affairs. I ask you again, girl, have you ever seen English soldiers fighting? Have you ever seen them plundering, burning, turning the countryside into a desert? Have you heard no tales of their Black Prince who was blacker than the devil himself, or of the English king's father?

JOAN: You must not be afraid, Robert—

ROBERT: Damn you, I am not afraid. And who gave you leave to call me Robert?

JOAN: You were called so in church in the name of our Lord. All the other names are your father's or your brother's or anybody's.

ROBERT: Tcha!

JOAN: Listen to me, squire. At Domrémy we had to fly to the next village to escape from the English soldiers. Three of them were left behind, wounded. I came to know these three poor goddams quite well. They had not half my strength.

ROBERT: Do you know why they are called goddams?

JOAN: No. Everyone calls them goddams.

ROBERT: It is because they are always calling on their God to condemn their souls to perdition. That is what goddam means in their language. How do you like it?

JOAN: God will be merciful to them; and they will act like His good children when they go back to the country He made for them, and made them for. I have heard the tales of the Black Prince. The moment he touched the soil of our country the devil entered into him, and made him a black fiend. But at home, in the place made for him by God, he was good. It is always so. If I went into England against the will of God to conquer England, and tried to live there and speak its language, the devil would enter into me; and when I was old I should shudder to remember the wickedness I did.

ROBERT: Perhaps. But the more devil you were the better you might fight. That is why the goddams will take Orleans. And you cannot stop them, nor ten thousand like you.

JOAN: One thousand like me can stop them. Ten like me can stop them with God on our side. (*She rises impetuously, and goes at him, unable to sit quiet any longer.*) You do not understand, squire. Our soldiers are always beaten because they are fighting only to save their skins; and the shortest way to save your skin is to run away. Our knights are thinking only of the money they will make in ransoms: it is not kill or be killed with them, but pay or be paid. But I will teach them all to fight that the will of God may be done in France; and they will drive the poor goddams before them like sheep. You and Polly will live to see the day when there will not be an English soldier on the soil of France; and there will be but one king there: not the feudal English king, but God's French one.

ROBERT (*to* POULENGEY): This may be all rot, Polly; but the troops might swallow it, though nothing that we can say seems able to put any fight into them. Even the Dauphin might swallow it. And if she can put fight into him, she can put it into anybody.

POULENGEY: I can see no harm in trying. Can you? And there is something about the girl—

ROBERT (*turning to* JOAN): Now listen you to me; and (*desperately*) dont cut in before I have time to think.

JOAN (*plumping down on the stool again, like an obedient schoolgirl*): Yes, squire.

ROBERT: Your orders are, that you are to go to Chinon under the escort of this gentleman and three of his friends.

JOAN (*radiant, clasping her hands*): Oh, squire! Your head is all circled with light, like a saint's.

POULENGEY: How is she to get into the royal presence?

ROBERT (*who has looked up for his halo rather apprehensively*): I dont know: how did she get into my presence? If the Dauphin can keep her out he is a better man than I take him for. (*Rising*) I will send her to Chinon; and she can say I sent her. Then let come what may: I can do no more.

JOAN: And the dress? I may have a soldier's dress, maynt I, squire?

ROBERT: Have what you please. I wash my hands of it.

JOAN (*wildly excited by her success*): Come, Polly. (*She dashes out.*)

ROBERT (*shaking* POULENGEY'S *hand*): Goodbye, old man, I am taking a big chance. Few other men would have done it. But as you say, there is something about her.

POULENGEY: Yes: there is something about her. Goodbye. (*He goes out.*)

(ROBERT, *still very doubtful whether he has not been made a fool of by a crazy female, and a social inferior to boot, scratches his head and slowly comes back from the door.*)

(*The* STEWARD *runs in with a basket.*)

STEWARD: Sir, sir—
ROBERT: What now?
STEWARD: The hens are laying like mad, sir. Five dozen eggs!

ROBERT (*stiffens convulsively: crosses himself: and forms with his pale lips the words*): Christ in heaven! (*Aloud but breathless*) She did come from God.

SCENE II

(Chinon, in Touraine. An end of the throne room in the castle, curtained off to make an antechamber. The ARCHBISHOP OF RHEIMS, close on 50, a full-fed prelate with nothing of the ecclesiastic about him except his imposing bearing, and the LORD CHAMBERLAIN, MONSIEGNEUR DE LA TREMOUILLE, a monstrous arrogant wineskin of a man, are waiting for the DAUPHIN. There is a door in the wall to the right of the two men. It is late in the afternoon on the 8th of March, 1429. The ARCHBISHOP stands with dignity whilst the CHAMBERLAIN, on his left, fumes about in the worst of tempers.)

LA TREMOUILLE: What the devil does the Dauphin mean by keeping us waiting like this? I dont know how you have the patience to stand there like a stone idol.

THE ARCHBISHOP: You see, I am an archbishop; and an archbishop is a sort of idol. At any rate he has to learn to keep still and suffer fools patiently. Besides, my dear Lord Chamberlain, it is the Dauphin's royal privilege to keep you waiting, is it not?

LA TREMOUILLE: Dauphin be damned! saving your reverence. Do you know how much money he owes me?

THE ARCHBISHOP: Much more than he owes me, I have no doubt, because you are a much richer man. But I take it he owes you all you could afford to lend him. That is what he owes me.

LA TREMOUILLE: Twenty-seven thousand: that was his last haul. A cool twenty-seven thousand!

THE ARCHBISHOP: What becomes of it all? He never has a suit of clothes that I would throw to a curate.

LA TREMOUILLE: He dines on a chicken or a scrap of mutton. He borrows my last penny; and there is nothing to shew for it. (*A* PAGE *appears in the doorway.*) At last!

THE PAGE: No, my lord: it is not His Majesty. Monsieur de Rais is approaching.

LA TREMOUILLE: Young Bluebeard! Why announce him?

THE PAGE: Captain La Hire is with him. Something has happened, I think.

(GILLES DE RAIS, *a young man of 25, very smart and self-possessed, and sporting the extravagance of a little curled beard dyed blue at a clean-*

shaven court, comes in. He is determined to make himself agreeable, but lacks natural joyousness, and is not really pleasant. In fact when he defies the Church some eleven years later he is accused of trying to extract pleasure from horrible cruelties, and hanged. So far, however, there is no shadow of the gallows on him. He advances gaily to the ARCHBISHOP. *The* PAGE *withdraws.)*

BLUEBEARD: Your faithful lamb, Archbishop. Good day, my lord. Do you know what has happened to La Hire?

LA TREMOUILLE: He has sworn himself into a fit, perhaps.

BLUEBEARD: No: just the opposite. Foul Mouthed Frank, the only man in Touraine who could beat him at swearing, was told by a soldier that he shouldnt use such language when he was at the point of death.

THE ARCHBISHOP: Nor at any other point. But was Foul Mouthed Frank on the point of death?

BLUEBEARD: Yes: he has just fallen into a well and been drowned. La Hire is frightened out of his wits.

*(*CAPTAIN LA HIRE *comes in: a war dog with no court manners and pronounced camp ones.)*

BLUEBEARD: I have just been telling the Chamberlain and the Archbishop. The Archbishop says you are a lost man.

LA HIRE *(striding past* BLUEBEARD, *and planting himself between the* ARCHBISHOP *and* LA TREMOUILLE*)*: This is nothing to joke about. It is worse than we thought. It was not a soldier, but an angel dressed as a soldier.

THE ARCHBISHOP
THE CHAMBERLAIN *(exclaiming all together)*: An angel!
BLUEBEARD

LA HIRE: Yes, an angel. She has made her way from Champagne with half a dozen men through the thick of everything: Burgundians, Goddams, deserters, robbers, and Lord knows who; and they never met a soul except the country folk. I know one of them: de Poulengey. He says she's an angel. If ever I utter an oath again may my soul be blasted to eternal damnation!

THE ARCHBISHOP: A very pious beginning, Captain.

*(*BLUEBEARD *and* LA TREMOUILLE *laugh at him. The page returns.)*

THE PAGE: His Majesty.

(They stand perfunctorily at court attention. The DAUPHIN, *aged 26, really* KING CHARLES THE SEVENTH *since the death of his father, but as yet uncrowned, comes in through the curtains with a paper in his hands. He is a poor creature physically; and the current fashion of shaving closely, and hiding every scrap of hair under the headcovering or headdress, both by women and men, makes the worst of his appear-*

ance. *He has little narrow eyes, near together, a long pendulous nose that droops over his thick short upper lip, and the expression of a young dog accustomed to be kicked, yet incorrigible and irrepressible. But he is neither vulgar nor stupid; and he has a cheeky humor which enables him to hold his own in conversation. Just at present he is excited, like a child with a new toy. He comes to the* ARCHBISHOP'S *left hand.* BLUEBEARD *and* LA HIRE *retire towards the curtains.)*

CHARLES: Oh, Archbishop, do you know what Robert de Baudricourt is sending me from Vaucouleurs?

THE ARCHBISHOP *(contemptuously)*: I am not interested in the newest toys.

CHARLES *(indignantly)*: It isnt a toy. *(Sulkily)* However, I can get on very well without your interest.

THE ARCHBISHOP: Your Highness is taking offense very unnecessarily.

CHARLES: Thank you. You are always ready with a lecture, arnt you?

LA TREMOUILLE *(roughly)*: Enough grumbling. What have you got there?

CHARLES:: What is that to you?

LA TREMOUILLE: It is my business to know what is passing between you and the garrison at Vaucouleurs. *(He snatches the paper from the* DAUPHIN'S *hand, and begins reading it with some difficulty, following the words with his finger and spelling them out syllable by syllable.)*

CHARLES *(mortified)*: You all think you can treat me as you please because I owe you money, and because I am no good at fighting. But I have the blood royal in my veins.

THE ARCHBISHOP: Even that has been questioned, your Highness. One hardly recognizes in you the grandson of Charles the Wise.

CHARLES: I want to hear no more of my grandfather. He was so wise that he used up the whole family stock of wisdom for five generations, and left me the poor fool I am, bullied and insulted by all of you.

THE ARCHBISHOP: Control yourself, sir. These outbursts of petulance are not seemly.

CHARLES: Another lecture! Thank you. What a pity it is that though you are an archbishop saints and angels dont come to see you!

THE ARCHBISHOP: What do you mean?

CHARLES: Aha! Ask that bully there *(pointing to* LA TREMOUILLE*)*.

LA TREMOUILLE *(furious)*: Hold your tongue. Do you hear?

CHARLES: Oh, I hear. You neednt shout. The whole castle can hear. Why dont you go and shout at the English, and beat them for me?

LA TREMOULLE *(raising his fist)*: You young—

CHARLES *(running behind the* ARCHBISHOP*)*: Dont you raise your hand to me. It's high treason.

LA HIRE: Steady, Duke! Steady!

THE ARCHBISHOP (*resolutely*): Come, come! this will not do. My Lord Chamberlain: please! please! we must keep some sort of order. (*To the* DAUPHIN): And you, sir: if you cannot rule your kingdom, at least try to rule yourself.

CHARLES: Another lecture! Thank you.

LA TREMOUILLE (*handing over the paper to the* ARCHBISHOP): Here: read the accursed thing for me. He has sent the blood boiling into my head: I cant distinguish the letters.

CHARLES (*coming back and peering round* LA TREMOUILLE's *left shoulder*): I will read it for you if you like. I can read, you know.

LA TREMOUILLE (*with intense contempt, not at all stung by the taunt*): Yes: reading is about all you are fit for. Can you make it out, Archbishop?

THE ARCHBISHOP: I should have expected more commonsense from De Baudricourt. He is sending some cracked country lass here—

CHARLES (*interrupting*): No: he is sending a saint: an angel. And she is coming to me: to me, the king, and not to you, Archbishop, holy as you are. She know the blood royal if you dont. (*He struts up to the curtains between* BLUEBEARD *and* LA HIRE.)

THE ARCHBISHOP: You cannot be allowed to see this crazy wench.

CHARLES (*turning*): But I am the king; and I will.

LA TREMOUILLE (*brutally*): Then she cannot be allowed to see you. Now!

CHARLES: I tell you I will. I am going to put my foot down—

BLUEBEARD (*laughing at him*): Naughty! What would your wise grandfather say?

CHARLES: That just shews your ignorance, Bluebeard. My grandfather had a saint who used to float in the air when she was praying, and told him everything he wanted to know. My poor father had two saints, Marie de Maillé and the Gasque of Avignon. It is in our family; and I dont care what you say: I will have my saint too.

THE ARCHBISHOP: This creature is not a saint. She is not even a respectable woman. She does not wear women's clothes. She is dressed like a soldier, and rides round the country with soldiers. Do you suppose such a person can be admitted to your Highness's court?

LA HIRE: Stop. (*Going to the* ARCHBISHOP) Did you say a girl in armor, like a soldier?

THE ARCHBISHOP: So De Baudricourt describes her.

LA HIRE: But by all the devils in hell—Oh, God forgive me, what am I saying?—by Our Lady and all the saints, this must be the angel that struck Foul Mouthed Frank dead for swearing.

CHARLES (*triumphant*): You see! A miracle!

LA HIRE: She may strike the lot of us dead if we cross her. For Heaven's sake, Archbishop, be careful what you are doing.

THE ARCHBISHOP (*severely*): Rubbish! Nobody has been struck dead. A drunken blackguard who has been rebuked a hundred times for swearing has fallen into a well, and been drowned. A mere coincidence.

LA HIRE: I do not know what a coincidence is. I do know that the man is dead, and that she told him he was going to die.

THE ARCHBISHOP: We are all going to die, Captain.

LA HIRE (*crossing himself*): I hope not. (*He backs out of the conversation.*)

BLUEBEARD: We can easily find out whether she is an angel or not. Let us arrange when she comes that I shall be the Dauphin, and see whether she will find me out.

CHARLES: Yes: I agree to that. If she cannot find the blood royal I will have nothing to do with her.

THE ARCHBISHOP: It is for the Church to make saints: let De Baudricourt mind his own business, and not dare usurp the function of his priest. I say the girl shall not be admitted.

BLUEBEARD: But, Archbishop—

THE ARCHBISHOP (*sternly*): I speak in the Church's name. (*To the* DAUPHIN) Do you dare say she shall?

CHARLES (*intimidated but sulky*): Oh, if you make it an excommunication matter, I have nothing more to say, of course. But you havnt read the end of the letter. De Baudricourt says she will raise the siege of Orleans, and beat the English for us.

LA TREMOUILLE: Rot!

CHARLES: Well, will you save Orleans for us, with all your bullying?

LA TREMOUILLE (*savagely*): Do not throw that in my face again: do you hear? I have done more fighting than you ever did or ever will. But I cannot be everywhere.

THE DAUPHIN: Well, thats something.

BLUEBEARD (*coming between the* ARCHBISHOP *and* CHARLES): You have Jack Dunois at the head of your troops in Orleans: the brave Dunois, the handsome Dunois, the wonderful invincible Dunois, the darling of all the ladies, the beautiful bastard. Is it likely that the country lass can do what he cannot do?

CHARLES: Why doesnt he raise the siege, then?

LA HIRE: The wind is against him.

BLUEBEARD: How can the wind hurt him at Orleans? It is not on the Channel.

LA HIRE: It is on the river Loire; and the English hold the bridgehead. He must ship his men across the river and upstream, if he is to take them in the rear. Well, he cannot, because there is a devil of a wind blowing the other way. He is tired of paying the priests to pray for a west wind. What he needs is a miracle. You tell me what the girl did to Foul Mouthed Frank was no miracle. No matter: it finished Frank. If she changes the wind for Dunois, that may not be a miracle either; but it may finish the English. What harm is there in trying?

THE ARCHBISHOP (*who has read the end of the letter and become more thoughtful*): It is true that De Baudricourt seems extraordinarily impressed.

LA HIRE: De Baudricourt is a blazing ass; but he is a soldier; and if he thinks she can beat the English, all the rest of the army will think so too.

LA TREMOUILLE (*to the* ARCHBISHOP, *who is hesitating*): Oh, let them have their way. Dunois' men will give up the town in spite of him if somebody does not put some fresh spunk into them.

THE ARCHBISHOP: The Church must examine the girl before anything decisive is done about her. However, since his Highness desires it, let her attend the Court.

LA HIRE: I will find her and tell her. (*He goes out.*)

CHARLES: Come with me, Bluebeard; and let us arrange so that she will not know who I am. You will pretend to be me. (*He goes out through the curtains.*)

BLUEBEARD: Pretend to be that thing! Holy Michael! (*He follows the* DAUPHIN.)

LA TREMOUILLE: I wonder will she pick him out!

THE ARCHBISHOP: Of course she will.

LA TREMOUILLE: Why? How is she to know?

THE ARCHBISHOP: She will know what everybody in Chinon knows: that the Dauphin is the meanest-looking and worst-dressed figure in the Court, and that the man with the blue beard is Gilles de Rais.

LA TREMOUILLE: I never thought of that.

THE ARCHBISHOP: You are not so accustomed to miracles as I am. It is part of my profession.

LA TREMOUILLE (*puzzled and a little scandalized*): But that would not be a miracle at all.

THE ARCHBISHOP (*calmly*): Why not?

LA TREMOUILLE: Well, come! what is a miracle?

THE ARCHBISHOP: A miracle, my friend, is an event which creates faith. That is the purpose and nature of miracles. They may seem very wonderful to the people who witness them, and very simple to those who perform them. That does not matter: if they confirm or create faith they are true miracles.

LA TREMOUILLE: Even when they are frauds, do you mean?

THE ARCHBISHOP: Frauds deceive. An event which creates faith does not deceive: therefore it is not fraud, but a miracle.

LA TREMOUILLE (*scratching his neck in his perplexity*): Well, I suppose as you are an archbishop you must be right. It seems a bit fishy to me. But I am no churchman, and dont understand these matters.

THE ARCHBISHOP: You are not a churchman; but you are a diplomatist and a soldier. Could you make our citizens pay war taxes, or our soldiers sacrifice their lives, if they knew what is really happening instead of what seems to them to be happening?

LA TREMOUILLE: No, by Saint Dennis: the fat would be in the fire before sundown.

THE ARCHBISHOP: Would it not be quite easy to tell them the truth?

LA TREMOUILLE: Man alive, they wouldnt believe it.

THE ARCHBISHOP: Just so. Well, the Church has to rule men for the good of their souls as you have to rule them for the good of their bodies. To do that, the Church must do as you do: nourish their faith by poetry.

LA TREMOUILLE: Poetry! I should call it humbug.

THE ARCHBISHOP: You would be wrong, my friend. Parables are not lies because they describe events that have never happened. Miracles are not frauds because they are often—I do not say always—very simple and innocent contrivances by which the priest fortifies the faith of his flock. When this girl picks out the Dauphin among his courtiers, it will not be a miracle for me, because I shall know how it has been done, and my faith will not be increased. But as for the others, if they feel the thrill of the supernatural, and forget their sinful clay in a sudden sense of the glory of God, it will be a miracle and a blessed one. And you will find that the girl herself will be more affected than anyone else. She will forget how she really picked him out. So, perhaps, will you.

LA TREMOUILLE: Well, I wish I were clever enough to know how much of you is God's archbishop and how much the most artful fox in Touraine. Come on, or we shall be late for the fun; and I want to see it, miracle or no miracle.

THE ARCHBISHOP (*detaining him a moment*): Do not think that I am a lover of crooked ways. There is a new spirit rising in men: we are at the dawning of a wider epoch. If I were a simple monk, and had not to rule men, I should seek peace for my spirit with Aristotle and Pythagoras rather than with the saints and their miracles.

LA TREMOUILLE: And who the deuce was Pythagoras?

THE ARCHBISHOP: A sage who held that the earth is round, and that it moves round the sun.

LA TREMOUILLE: What an utter fool! Couldnt he use his eyes?

(*They go out together through the curtains, which are presently withdrawn, revealing the full depth of the throne room with the Court*

assembled. On the right are two Chairs of State on a dais. BLUEBEARD *is standing theatrically on the dais, playing the king, and, like the courtiers, enjoying the joke rather obviously. There is a curtained arch in the wall behind the dais; but the main door, guarded by men-at-arms, is at the other side of the room; and a clear path across is kept and lined by the courtiers.* CHARLES *is in this path in the middle of the room.* LA HIRE *is on his right. The* ARCHBISHOP, *on his left, has taken his place by the dais:* LA TREMOUILLE *at the other side of it. The* DUCHESS DE LA TREMOUILLE, *pretending to be the* QUEEN, *sits in the Consort's chair, with a group of ladies in waiting close by, behind the Archbishop.)*
(The chatter of the courtiers makes such a noise that nobody notices the appearance of the page at the door.)

THE PAGE: The Duke of—*(Nobody listens.)* The Duke of—*(The chatter continues. Indignant at his failure to command a hearing, he snatches the halberd of the nearest man-at-arms, and thumps the floor with it. The chatter ceases; and everybody looks at him in silence.)* Attention! *(He restores the halberd to the man-at-arms.)* The Duke of Vendôme presents Joan the Maid to his Majesty.

CHARLES *(putting his finger on his lip)*: Ssh! *(He hides behind the nearest courtier, peering out to see what happens.)*

BLUEBEARD *(majestically)*: Let her approach the throne.

*(*JOAN, *dressed as a soldier, with her hair bobbed and hanging thickly around her face, is led in by a bashful and speechless nobleman, from whom she detaches herself to stop and look around eagerly for the* DAUPHIN.*)*

THE DUCHESS *(to the nearest lady in waiting)*: My dear! Her hair!

(All the ladies explode in uncontrollable laughter.)

BLUEBEARD *(trying not to laugh, and waving his hand in deprecation of their merriment)*: Ssh—ssh! Ladies! Ladies!

JOAN *(not at all embarrassed)*: I wear it like this because I am a soldier. Where be Dauphin?

(A titter runs through the Court as she walks to the dais.)

BLUEBEARD *(condescendingly)*: You are in the presence of the Dauphin.

*(*JOAN *looks at him sceptically for a moment, scanning him hard up and down to make sure. Dead silence, all watching her. Fun dawns in her face.)*

JOAN: Coom, Bluebeard! Thou canst not fool me. Where be Dauphin?

(A roar of laughter breaks out as GILLES, *with a gesture of surrender, joins in the laugh, and jumps down from the dais beside* LA TRE-

MOUILLE. JOAN, *also on the broad grin, turns back, searching along the row of courtiers, and presently makes a dive, and drags out* CHARLES *by the arm.*)

JOAN (*releasing him and bobbing him a little curtsey*): Gentle little Dauphin, I am sent to you to drive the English away from Orleans and from France, and to crown you king in the cathedral at Rheims, where all true kings of France are crowned.

CHARLES (*triumphant, to the Court*): You see, all of you: she knew the blood royal. Who dare say now that I am not my father's son? (*To* JOAN) But if you want me to be crowned at Rheims you must talk to the Archbishop, not to me. There he is (*he is standing behind her*)!

JOAN (*turning quickly, overwhelmed with emotion*): Oh, my lord! (*She falls on both knees before him, with bowed head, not daring to look up*) My lord: I am only a poor country girl; and you are filled with the the blessedness and glory of God Himself; but you will touch me with your hands, and give me your blessing, wont you?

BLUEBEARD (*whispering to* LA TREMOUILLE): The old fox blushes.

LA TREMOUILLE: Another miracle!

THE ARCHBISHOP (*touched, putting his hand on her head*): Child: you are in love with religion.

JOAN (*startled: looking up at him*): Am I? I never thought of that. Is there any harm in it?

THE ARCHBISHOP: There is no harm in it, my child. But there is danger.

JOAN (*rising, with a sunflush of reckless happiness irradiating her face*): There is always danger, except in heaven. Oh, my lord, you have given me such strength, such courage. It must be a most wonderful thing to be Archbishop.

(*The* COURT *smiles broadly: even titters a little.*)

THE ARCHBISHOP (*drawing himself up sensitively*): Gentlemen: your levity is rebuked by this maid's faith. I am, God help me, all unworthy; but your mirth is a deadly sin.

(*Their faces fall. Dead silence.*)

BLUEBEARD: My lord: we were laughing at her, not at you.

THE ARCHBISHOP: What? Not at my unworthiness but at her faith! Gilles de Rais: this maid prophesied that the blasphemer should be drowned in his sin—

JOAN (*distressed*): No!

THE ARCHBISHOP (*silencing her by a gesture*): I prophesy now that you will be hanged in yours if you do not learn when to laugh and when to pray.

BLUEBEARD: My lord: I stand rebuked. I am sorry: I can say no more. But if you prophesy that I shall be hanged, I shall never be able to

resist temptation, because I shall always be telling myself that I may as well be hanged for a sheep as a lamb.
(The courtiers take heart at this. There is more tittering.)

JOAN *(scandalized)*: You are an idle fellow, Bluebeard; and you have great impudence to answer the Archbishop.

LA HIRE *(with a huge chuckle)*: Well said, lass! Well said!

JOAN *(impatiently to the* ARCHBISHOP*)*: Oh, my lord, will you send all these silly folks away so that I may speak to the Dauphin alone?

LA HIRE *(goodhumoredly)*: I can take a hint. *(He salutes; turns on his heel; and goes out.)*

THE ARCHBISHOP: Come, gentlemen. The Maid comes with God's blessing, and must be obeyed.

(The courtiers withdraw, some through the arch, others at the opposite side. The ARCHBISHOP *marches across to the door, followed by the* DUCHESS *and* LA TREMOUILLE. *As the* ARCHBISHOP *passes* JOAN, *she falls on her knees, and kisses the hem of his robe fervently. He shakes his head in instinctive remonstrance; gathers the robe from her; and goes out. She is left kneeling directly in the* DUCHESS'S *way.)*

THE DUCHESS *(coldly)*: Will you allow me to pass, please?

JOAN *(hastily rising, and standing back)*: Beg pardon, maam, I am sure.
(The DUCHESS *passes on.* JOAN *stares after her; then whispers to the* DAUPHIN.*)*

JOAN: Be that Queen?

CHARLES: No. She thinks she is.

JOAN *(again staring after the* DUCHESS*)*: Oo-oo-ooh! *(Her awe-struck amazement at the figure cut by the magnificently dressed lady is not wholly complimentary.)*

LA TREMOUILLE *(very surly)*: I'll trouble your Highness not to gibe at my wife *(He goes out. The others have already gone.)*

JOAN *(to the* DAUPHIN*)*: Who be old Gruff-and-Grum?

CHARLES: He is the Duke de la Trémouille.

JOAN: What be his job?

CHARLES: He pretends to command the army. And whenever I find a friend I can care for, he kills him.

JOAN: Why dost let him?

CHARLES *(petulantly moving to the throne side of the room to escape from her magnetic field)*: How can I prevent him? He bullies me. They all bully me.

JOAN: Art afraid?

CHARLES: Yes: I am afraid. It's no use preaching to me about it. It's all very well for these big men with their armor that is too heavy for me, and their swords that I can hardly lift, and their muscle and their shouting and their bad tempers. They like fighting: most of them are making fools of themselves all the time they are not fighting; but I am quiet and sensible; and I dont want to kill people: I only want to be left alone to enjoy myself in my own way. I never asked to be a king: it was pushed on me. So if you are going to say 'Son of St Louis: gird on the sword of your ancestors, and lead us to victory' you may spare your breath to cool your porridge; for I cannot do it. I am not built that way; and there is an end of it.

JOAN (*trenchant and masterful*): Blethers! We are all like that to begin with. I shall put courage into thee.

CHARLES: But I dont want to have courage put into me. I want to sleep in a comfortable bed, and not live in continual terror of being killed or wounded. Put courage into the others, and let them have their bellyful of fighting; but let me alone.

JOAN: It's no use, Charlie: thou must face what God puts on thee. If thou fail to make thyself king, thoult be a beggar: what else art fit for? Come! Let me see thee sitting on the throne. I have looked forward to that.

CHARLES: What is the good of sitting on the throne when the other fellows give all the orders? However! (*he sits enthroned, a piteous figure*) here is the king for you! Look your fill at the poor devil.

JOAN: Thourt not king yet, lad: thourt but Dauphin. Be not led away by them around thee. Dressing up dont fill empty noddle. I know the people: the real people that make thy bread for thee; and I tell thee they count no man king of France until the holy oil has been poured on his hair, and himself consecrated and crowned in Rheims Cathedral. And thou needs new clothes, Charlie. Why does not Queen look after thee properly?

CHARLES: We're too poor. She wants all the money we can spare to put on her own back. Besides, I like to see her beautifully dressed; and I dont care what I wear myself: I should look ugly anyhow.

JOAN: There is some good in thee, Charlie; but it is not yet a king's good.

CHARLES: We shall see. I am not such a fool as I look. I have my eyes open; and I can tell you that one good treaty is worth ten good fights. These fighting fellows lose all on the treaties that they gain on the fights. If we can only have a treaty, the English are sure to have the worst of it, because they are better at fighting than at thinking.

JOAN: If the English win, it is they that will make the treaty: and then God help poor France! Thou must fight, Charlie, whether thou will or no. I will go first to hearten thee. We must take our courage in both hands: aye, and pray for it with both hands too.

CHARLES (*descending from his throne and again crossing the room to escape from her dominating urgency*): Oh do stop talking about God and praying. I cant bear people who are always praying. Isnt it bad enough to have to do it at the proper times?

JOAN (*pitying him*): Thou poor child, thou hast never prayed in thy life. I must teach thee from the beginning.

CHARLES: I am not a child: I am a grown man and a father; and I will not be taught any more.

JOAN: Aye, you have a little son. He that will be Louis the Eleventh when you die. Would you not fight for him?

CHARLES: No: a horrid boy. He hates me. He hates everybody, selfish little beast! I dont want to be bothered with children. I dont want to be a father; and I dont want to be a son: especially a son of St Louis. I dont want to be any of these fine things you all have your heads full of: I want to be just what I am. Why cant you mind your own business, and let me mind mine?

JOAN (*again contemptuous*): Minding your own business is like minding your own body: it's the shortest way to make yourself sick. What is my business? Helping mother at home. What is thine? Petting lapdogs and sucking sugarsticks. I call that muck. I tell thee it is God's business we are here to do: not our own. I have a message to thee from God; and thou must listen to it, though thy heart break with the terror of it.

CHARLES: I dont want a message; but can you tell me any secrets? Can you do any cures? Can you turn lead into gold, or anything of that sort?

JOAN: I can turn thee into a king, in Rheims Cathedral; and that is a miracle that will take some doing, it seems.

CHARLES: If we go to Rheims, and have a coronation, Anne will want new dresses. We cant afford them. I am all right as I am.

JOAN: As you are! And what is that? Less than my father's poorest shepherd. Thourt not lawful owner of thy own land of France till thou be consecrated.

CHARLES: But I shall not be lawful owner of my own land anyhow. Will the consecration pay off my mortgages? I have pledged my last acre to the Archbishop and that fat bully. I owe money even to Bluebeard.

JOAN (*earnestly*): Charlie: I come from the land, and have gotten my strength working on the land; and I tell thee that the land is thine to rule righteously and keep God's peace in, and not to pledge at the pawnshop as a drunken woman pledges her children's clothes. And I come from God to tell thee to kneel in the cathedral and solemnly give thy kingdom to Him for ever and ever, and become the greatest king in the world as His steward and His bailiff, His soldier and His servant. The very clay of France will become holy: her soldiers will be the soldiers of God: the rebel dukes will be rebels against God: the

English will fall on their knees and beg thee let them return to their lawful homes in peace. Wilt be a poor little Judas, and betray me and Him that sent me?

CHARLES (*tempted at last*): Oh, if I only dare!

JOAN: I shall dare, dare, and dare again, in God's name! Art for or against me?

CHARLES (*excited*): I'll risk it, I warn you I shant be able to keep it up; but I'll risk it. You shall see. (*Running to the main door and shouting*) Hallo! Come back, everybody. (*To* JOAN, *as he runs back to the arch opposite*) Mind you stand by and dont let me be bullied. (*Through the arch*) Come along, will you: the whole Court. (*He sits down in the royal chair as they all hurry in to their former places, chattering and wondering.*) Now I'm in for it; but no matter: here goes! (*To the* PAGE) Call for silence, you little beast, will you?

THE PAGE (*snatching a halberd as before and thumping with it repeatedly*): Silence for His Majesty the King. The King speaks. (*Peremptorily*) Will you be silent there? (*Silence*).

CHARLES (*rising*): I have given the command of the army to The Maid. The Maid is to do as she likes with it. (*He descends from the dais.*)

(*General amazement.* LA HIRE, *delighted, slaps his steel thigh-piece with his gauntlet.*)

LA TREMOUILLE (*turning threateningly towards* CHARLES): What is this? *I* command the army.

(JOAN *quickly puts her hand on* CHARLES's *shoulder as he instinctively recoils.* CHARLES, *with a grotesque effort culminating in an extravagant gesture, snaps his fingers in the* CHAMBERLAIN's *face.*)

JOAN: Thourt answered, old Gruff-and-Grum. (*Suddenly flashing out her sword as she divines that her moment has come*) Who is for God and His Maid? Who is for Orleans with me?

LA HIRE (*carried away, drawing also*): For God and His Maid! To Orleans!

ALL THE KNIGHTS (*following his lead with enthusiasm*): To Orleans!

(JOAN, *radiant, falls on her knees in thanksgiving to God. They all kneel, except the* ARCHBISHOP, *who gives his benediction with a sigh, and* LA TREMOUILLE, *who collapses, cursing.*)

SCENE III

(Orleans, April 29th, 1429. DUNOIS, aged 26, is pacing up and down a patch of ground on the south bank of the silver Loire, commanding a long view of the river in both directions. He has had his lance stuck up with a pennon, which streams in a strong east wind. His shield with its bend sinister lies beside it. He has his commander's baton in his hand. He is well built, carrying his armor easily. His broad brow and pointed chin give him an equilaterally triangular face, already marked by active service and responsibility, with the expression of a good-natured and capable man who has no affectations and no foolish illusions. His PAGE is sitting on the ground, elbows on knees, cheeks on fists, idly watching the water. It is evening; and both man and boy are affected by the loveliness of the Loire.)

DUNOIS (*halting for a moment to glance up at the streaming pennon and shake his head wearily before he resumes his pacing*): West wind, west wind, west wind. Strumpet: steadfast when you should be wanton, wanton when you should be steadfast. West wind on the silver Loire: what rhymes to Loire? (*He looks again at the pennon, and shakes his fist at it*) Change, curse you, change, English harlot of a wind, change. West, west, I tell you. (*With a growl he resumes his march in silence, but soon begins again*) West wind, wanton wind, wilful wind, womanish wind, false wind from over the water, will you never blow again?

THE PAGE (*bounding to his feet*): See! There! There she goes!

DUNOIS (*startled from his reverie: eagerly*): Where? Who? The Maid?

THE PAGE: No: the kingfisher. Like blue lightning. She went into that bush.

DUNOIS (*furiously disappointed*): Is that all? You infernal young idiot: I have a mind to pitch you into the river.

THE PAGE (*not afraid, knowing his man*): It looked frightfully jolly, that flash of blue. Look! There goes the other!

DUNOIS (*running eagerly to the river brim*): Where? Where?

THE PAGE (*pointing*): Passing the reeds.

DUNOIS (*delighted*): I see.

(*They follow the flight till the bird takes cover.*)

THE PAGE: You blew me up because you were not in time to see them yesterday.

DUNOIS: You knew I was expecting The Maid when you set up your yelping. I will give you something to yelp for next time.

THE PAGE: Arnt they lovely? I wish I could catch them.

DUNOIS: Let me catch you trying to trap them, and I will put you in the iron cage for a month to teach you what a cage feels like. You are an abominable boy.

THE PAGE (*laughs, and squats down as before*)!

DUNOIS (*pacing*): Blue bird, blue bird, since I am friend to thee, change thou the wind for me. No: it does not rhyme. He who has sinned for thee: thats better. No sense in it, though. (*He finds himself close to the*

PAGE) You abominable boy! (*He turns away from him*) Mary in the blue snood, kingfisher color: will you grudge me a west wind?

A SENTRY'S VOICE WESTWARD: Halt! Who goes there?

JOAN'S VOICE: The Maid.

DUNOIS: Let her pass. Hither, Maid! To me!

(JOAN, *in splendid armor, rushes in in a blazing rage. The wind drops; and the pennon flaps idly down the lance but* DUNOIS *is too much occupied with* JOAN *to notice it.*)

JOAN (*bluntly*): Be you Bastard of Orleans?

DUNOIS (*cool and stern, pointing to his shield*): You see the bend sinister. Are you Joan the Maid?

JOAN: Sure.

DUNOIS: Where are your troops?

JOAN: Miles behind. They have cheated me. They have brought me to the wrong side of the river.

DUNOIS: I told them to.

JOAN: Why did you? The English are on the other side!

DUNOIS: The English are on both sides.

JOAN: But Orleans is on the other side. We must fight the English there. How can we cross the river?

DUNOIS (*grimly*): There is a bridge.

JOAN: In God's name, then, let us cross the bridge, and fall on them.

DUNOIS: It seems simple; but it cannot be done.

JOAN: Who says so?

DUNOIS: I say so; and older and wiser heads than mine are of the same opinion.

JOAN (*roundly*): Then your older and wiser heads are fatheads: they have made a fool of you; and now they want to make a fool of me too, bringing me to the wrong side of the river. Do you not know that I bring you better help than ever came to any general or any town?

DUNOIS (*smiling patiently*): Your own?

JOAN: No: the help and counsel of the King of Heaven. Which is the way to the bridge?

DUNOIS: You are impatient, Maid.

JOAN: Is this a time for patience? Our enemy is at our gates; and here we stand doing nothing. Oh, why are you not fighting? Listen to me: I will deliver you from fear. I—

DUNOIS (*laughing heartily, and waving her off*): No, no, my girl: if you delivered me from fear I should be a good knight for a story book, but a very bad commander of the army. Come! let me begin to make a soldier of you. (*He takes her to the water's edge.*) Do you see those two forts at this end of the bridge? the big ones?

JOAN: Yes. Are they ours or the goddams'?

DUNOIS: Be quiet, and listen to me. If I were in either of those forts with only ten men I could hold it against an army. The English have more than ten times ten goddams in those forts to hold them against us.

JOAN: They cannot hold them against God. God did not give them the land under those forts; they stole it from Him. He gave it to us. I will take those forts.

DUNOIS: Single-handed?

JOAN: Our men will take them. I will lead them.

DUNOIS: Not a man will follow you.

JOAN: I will not look back to see whether anyone is following me.

DUNOIS (*recognizing her mettle, and clapping her heartily on the shoulder*): Good. You have the makings of a soldier in you. You are in love with war.

JOAN (*startled*): Oh! And the Archbishop said I was in love with religion.

DUNOIS: I, God forgive me, am a little in love with war myself, the ugly devil! I am like a man with two wives. Do you want to be like a woman with two husbands?

JOAN (*matter-of-fact*): I will never take a husband. A man in Toul took an action against me for breach of promise; but I never promised him. I am a soldier: I do not want to be thought of as a woman. I will not dress as a woman. I do not care for the things women care for. They dream of lovers, and of money. I dream of leading a charge, and of placing the big guns. You soldiers do not know how to use the big guns: you think you can win battles with a great noise and smoke.

DUNOIS (*with a shrug*): True. Half the time the artillery is more trouble than it is worth.

JOAN: Aye, lad; but you cannot fight stone walls with horses: you must have guns, and much bigger guns too.

DUNOIS (*grinning at her familiarity, and echoing it*): Aye, lass; but a good heart and a stout ladder will get over the stoniest wall.

JOAN: I will be first up the ladder when we reach the fort, Bastard. I dare you to follow me.

DUNOI: You must not dare a staff officer, Joan: only company officers are allowed to indulge in displays of personal courage. Besides, you must know that I welcome you as a saint, not a soldier. I have daredevils enough at my call, if they could help me.

JOAN: I am not a daredevil: I am a servant of God. My sword is sacred: I found it behind the altar in the church of St Catherine, where God hid it for me; and I may not strike a blow with it. My heart is full of courage, not of anger. I will lead; and your men will follow: that is all I can do. But I must do it: you shall not stop me.

DUNOIS: All in good time. Our men cannot take those forts by a sally across the bridge. They must come by water, and take the English in the rear on this side.

JOAN (*her military sense asserting itself*): Then make rats and put big guns on them; and let your men cross to us.

DUNOIS: The rafts are ready; and the men are embarked. But they must wait for God.

JOAN: What do you mean? God is waiting for them.

DUNOIS: Let Him send us a wind then. My boats are downstream: they cannot come up against both wind and current. We must wait until God changes the wind. Come: let me take you to the church.

JOAN: No. I love church; but the English will not yield to prayers: they understand nothing but hard knocks and slashes. I will not go to church until we have beaten them.

DUNOIS: You must: I have business for you there.

JOAN: What business?

DUNOIS: To pray for a west wind. I have prayed; and I have given two silver candlesticks; but my prayers are not answered. Yours may be: you are young and innocent.

JOAN: Oh yes: you are right. I will pray: I will tell St Catherine: she will make God give me a west wind. Quick: shew me the way to the church.

THE PAGE (*sneezes violently*): At-cha!!!

JOAN: God bless you, child! Coom, Bastard.

(*They go out. The* PAGE *rises to follow. He picks up the shield, and is taking the spear as well when he notices the pennon, which is now streaming eastward.*)

THE PAGE (*dropping the shield and calling excitedly after them*): Seigneur! Seigneur! Mademoiselle!

DUNOIS (*running back*): What is it? The kingfisher? (*He looks eagerly for it up the river.*)

JOAN (*joining them*): Oh, a kingfisher! Where?

THE PAGE: No: the wind, the wind, the wind (*pointing to the pennon*): that is what made me sneeze.

DUNOIS (*looking at the pennon*): The wind has changed. (*He crosses himself*) God has spoken. (*Kneeling and handing his baton to* JOAN) You command the king's army. I am your soldier.

THE PAGE (*looking down the river*): The boats have put off. They are ripping upstream like anything.

DUNOIS (*rising*): Now for the forts. You dared me to follow. Dare you lead?

JOAN (*bursting into tears and flinging her arms round* DUNOIS, *kissing him on both cheeks*): Dunois, dear comrade in arms, help me. My eyes are blinded with tears. Set my foot on the ladder, and say 'Up, Joan.'

DUNOIS (*dragging her out*): Never mind the tears: make for the flash of the guns.
JOAN (*in a blaze of courage*): Ah!
DUNOIS (*dragging her along with him*): For God and Saint Dennis!
THE PAGE (*shrilly*): The Maid! The Maid! God and The Maid! Hurray-ay-ay! (*He snatches up the shield and lance, and capers out after them, mad with excitement.*)

SCENE IV

(A tent in the English camp. A bullnecked English CHAPLAIN of 50 is sitting on a stool at a table, hard at work writing. At the other side of the table an imposing NOBLEMAN, aged 46, is seated in a handsome chair turning over the leaves of an illuminated Book of Hours. The NOBLEMAN is enjoying himself: the CHAPLAIN is struggling with suppressed wrath. There is an unoccupied leather stool on the NOBLEMAN's left. The table is on his right.)

THE NOBLEMAN: Now this is what I call workmanship. There is nothing on earth more exquisite than a bonny book, with well-placed columns of rich black writing in beautiful borders, and illuminated pictures cunningly inset. But nowadays, instead of looking at books, people read them. A book might as well be one of those orders for bacon and bran that you are scribbling.
THE CHAPLAIN: I must say, my lord, you take our situation very coolly. Very coolly indeed.
THE NOBLEMAN (*supercilious*): What is the matter?
THE CHAPLAIN: The matter, my lord, is that we English have been defeated.
THE NOBLEMAN: That happens, you know. It is only in history books and ballads that the enemy is always defeated.
THE CHAPLAIN: But we are being defeated over and over again. First, Orleans—
THE NOBLEMAN (*poohpoohing*): Oh, Orleans!
THE CHAPLAIN: I know what you are going to say, my lord: that was a clear case of witchcraft and sorcery. But we are still being defeated. Jargeau, Meung, Beaugency, just like Orleans. And now we have been butchered at Patay, and Sir John Talbot taken prisoner. (*He throws down his pen, almost in tears*) I feel it, my lord: I feel it very deeply. I cannot bear to see my countrymen defeated by a parcel of foreigners.
THE NOBLEMAN: Oh! you are an Englishman, are you?
THE CHAPLAIN: Certainly not, my lord: I am a gentleman. Still, like your lordship, I was born in England; and it makes a difference.

THE NOBLEMAN: You are attached to the soil, eh?

THE CHAPLAIN: It pleases your lordship to be satirical at my expense: your greatness privileges you to be so with impunity. But your lordship knows very well that I am not attached to the soil in a vulgar manner, like a serf. Still, I have a feeling about it; *(with growing agitation)* and I am not ashamed of it; and *(rising wildly)* by God, if this goes on any longer I will fling my cassock to the devil, and take arms myself, and strangle the accursed witch with my own hands.

THE NOBLEMAN *(laughing at him goodnaturedly)*: So you shall, chaplain: so you shall, if we can do nothing better. But not yet, not quite yet. *(The* CHAPLAIN *resumes his seat very sulkily.)*

THE NOBLEMAN *(airily)*: I should not care very much about the witch—you see, I have made my pilgrimage to the Holy Land; and the Heavenly Powers, for their own credit, can hardly allow me to be worsted by a village sorceress—but the Bastard of Orleans is a harder nut to crack; and as he has been to the Holy Land too, honors are easy between us as far as that goes.

THE CHAPLAIN: He is only a Frenchman, my lord.

THE NOBLEMAN: A Frenchman! Where did you pick up that expression? Are these Burgundians and Bretons and Picards and Gascons beginning to call themselves Frenchmen, just as our fellows are beginning to call themselves Englishmen? They actually talk of France and England as their countries. Theirs, if you please! What is to become of me and you if that way of thinking comes into fashion?

THE CHAPLAIN: Why, my lord? Can it hurt us?

THE NOBLEMAN: Men cannot serve two masters. If this cant of serving their country once takes hold of them, goodbye to the authority of their feudal lords, and goodbye to the authority of the Church. That is, goodbye to you and me.

THE CHAPLAIN: I hope I am a faithful servant of the Church; and there are only six cousins between me and the barony of Stogumber, which was created by the Conqueror. But is that any reason why I should stand by and see Englishmen beaten by a French bastard and a witch from Lousy Champagne?

THE NOBLEMAN: Easy, man, easy: we shall burn the witch and beat the bastard all in good time. Indeed I am waiting at present for the Bishop of Beauvais, to arrange the burning with him. He has been turned out of his diocese by her faction.

THE CHAPLAIN: You have first to catch her, my lord.

THE NOBLEMAN: Or buy her. I will offer a king's ransom.

THE CHAPLAIN: A king's ransom! For that slut!

THE NOBLEMAN: One has to leave a margin. Some of Charles's people will sell her to the Burgundians; the Burgundians will sell her to us; and there will probably be three or four middlemen who will expect their little commissions.

THE CHAPLAIN: Monstrous. It is all those scoundrels of Jews: they get in every time money changes hands. I would not leave a Jew alive in Christendom if I had my way.

THE NOBLEMAN: Why not? The Jews generally give value. They make you pay; but they deliver the goods. In my experience the men who want something for nothing are invariably Christians.

(A PAGE appears.)

THE PAGE: The Right Reverend the Bishop of Beauvais: Monseigneur Cauchon.
(CAUCHON, *aged about 60, comes in. The* PAGE *withdraws. The two Englishmen rise.*)

THE NOBLEMAN *(with effusive courtesy)*: My dear Bishop, how good of you to come! Allow me to introduce myself: Richard de Beauchamp, Earl of Warwick, at your service.

CAUCHON: Your lordship's fame is well known to me.

WARWICK: This reverend cleric is Master John de Stogumber.

THE CHAPLAIN *(glibly)*: John Bowyer Spenser Neville de Stogumber, at your service, my lord: Bachelor of Theology, and Keeper of the Private Seal to His Eminence the Cardinal of Winchester.

WARWICK *(to* CAUCHON*)*: You call him the Cardinal of England, I believe. Our king's uncle.

CAUCHON: Messire John de Stogumber: I am always the very good friend of His Eminence. (*He extends his hand to the* CHAPLAIN, *who kisses his ring.*)

WARWICK: Do me the honor to be seated. (*He gives* CAUCHON *his chair, placing it at the head of the table.*)

(CAUCHON *accepts the place of honor with a grave inclination.* WARWICK *fetches the leather stool carelessly, and sits in his former place. The* CHAPLAIN *goes back to his chair.*)

(*Though* WARWICK *has taken second place in calculated deference to the* BISHOP, *he assumes the lead in opening the proceedings as a matter of course. He is still cordial and expansive; but there is a new note in his voice which means that he is coming to business.*)

WARWICK: Well, my Lord Bishop, you find us in one of our unlucky moments. Charles is to be crowned at Rheims, practically by the young woman from Lorraine; and—I must not deceive you, nor flatter your hopes—we cannot prevent it. I suppose it will make a great difference to Charles's position.

CAUCHON: Undoubtedly. It is a masterstroke of The Maid's.

THE CHAPLAIN (*again agitated*): We were not fairly beaten, my lord. No Englishman is ever fairly beaten.

(CAUCHON *raises his eyebrow slightly, then quickly composes his face.*)

WARWICK: Our friend here takes the view that the young woman is a sorceress. It would, I presume, be the duty of your reverend lordship to denounce her to the Inquisition, and have her burnt for that offence.

CAUCHON: If she were captured in my diocese: yes.

WARWICK (*feeling that they are getting on capitally*): Just so. Now I suppose there can be no reasonable doubt that she is a sorceress.

THE CHAPLAIN: Not the least. An arrant witch.

WARWICK (*gently reproving the interruption*): We are asking for the Bishop's opinion, Messire John.

CAUCHON: We shall have to consider not merely our own opinions here, but the opinions—the prejudices, if you like—of a French court.

WARWICK (*correcting*): A Catholic court, my lord.

CAUCHON: Catholic courts are composed of mortal men, like other courts, however sacred their function and inspiration may be. And if the men are Frenchmen, as the modern fashion calls them, I am afraid the bare fact that an English army has been defeated by a French one will not convince them that there is any sorcery in the matter.

THE CHAPLAIN: What! Not when the famous Sir Talbot himself has been defeated and actually taken prisoner by a drab from the ditches of Lorraine!

CAUCHON: Sir John Talbot, we all know, is a fierce and formidable soldier, Messire; but I have yet to learn that he is an able general. And though it pleases you to say that he has been defeated by this girl, some of us may be disposed to give a little of the credit to Dunois.

THE CHAPLAIN (*contemptuously*): The Bastard of Orleans!

CAUCHON: Let me remind—

WARWICK (*interposing*): I know what you are going to say, my lord. Dunois defeated me at Montargis.

CAUCHON (*bowing*): I take that as evidence that the Seigneur Dunois is a very able commander indeed.

WARWICK: Your lordship is the flower of courtesy. I admit, on our side, that Talbot is a mere fighting animal, and that it probably served him right to be taken at Patay.

THE CHAPLAIN (*chafing*): My lord: at Orleans this woman had her throat pierced by an English arrow, and was seen to cry like a child from the pain of it. It was a death wound; yet she fought all day; and when our men had repulsed all her attacks like true Englishmen, she walked alone to the wall of our fort with a white banner in her hand; and our men were paralyzed, and could neither shoot nor strike whilst the French fell on them and drove them on to the bridge, which immediately burst into flames and crumbled under them, letting them down into the river, where they were drowned in heaps. Was this your bastard's generalship? or were those flames of hell, conjured up by witchcraft?

WARWICK: You will forgive Messire John's vehemence, my lord; but he has put our case. Dunois is a great captain, we admit; but why could he do nothing until the witch came?

CAUCHON: I do not say that there were no supernatural powers on her side. But the names on that white banner were not the names of Satan and Beelzebub, but the blessed names of our Lord and His holy mother. And your commander who was drowned—Clahz-da I think you call him—

WARWICK: Glasdale, Sir William Glasdale.

CAUCHON: Glass-dell, thank you. He was no saint; and many of our people think that he was drowned for his blasphemies against The Maid.

WARWICK (*beginning to look very dubious*): Well, what are we to infer from all this, my lord? Has The Maid converted you?

CAUCHON: If she had, my lord, I should have known better than to have trusted myself here within your grasp.

WARWICK (*blandly deprecating*): Oh! oh! My lord!

CAUCHON: If the devil is making use of this girl—and I believe he is—

WARWICK (*reassured*): Ah! You hear, Messire John? I knew your lordship would not fail us. Pardon my interruption. Proceed.

CAUCHON: If it be so, the devil has longer views than you give him credit for.

WARWICK: Indeed? In what way? Listen to this, Messire John.

CAUCHON: If the devil wanted to damn a country girl, do you think so easy a task would cost him the winning of half a dozen battles? No, my lord: any trumpery imp could do that much if the girl could be damned at all. The Prince of Darkness does not condescend to such cheap drudgery. When he strikes, he strikes at the Catholic Church, whose realm is the whole spiritual world. When he damns, he damns the souls of the entire human race. Against that dreadful design the Church stands ever on guard. And it is as one of the instruments of that design that I see this girl. She is inspired, but diabolically inspired.

THE CHAPLAIN: I told you she was a witch.

CAUCHON (*fiercely*): She is not a witch. She is a heretic.

THE CHAPLAIN: What difference does that make?

CAUCHON: You, a priest, ask me that! You English are strangely blunt in the mind. All these things that you call witchcraft are capable of a natural explanation. The woman's miracles would not impose on a rabbit: she does not claim them as miracles herself. What do her victories prove but that she has a better head on her shoulders than your swearing Glass-dells and mad bull Talbots, and that the courage of faith, even though it be a false faith, will always outstay the courage of wrath?

THE CHAPLAIN (*hardly able to believe his ears*): Does your lordship compare Sir John Talbot, three times Governor of Ireland, to a mad bull?!!!

WARWICK: It would not be seemly for you to do so, Messire John, as you are still six removes from a barony. But as I am an earl, and Talbot is only a knight, I may make bold to accept the comparison. (*To the* BISHOP) My lord: I wipe the slate as far as the witchcraft goes. None the less, we must burn the woman.

CAUCHON: I cannot burn her. The Church cannot take life. And my first duty is to seek this girl's salvation.

WARWICK: No doubt. But you do burn people occasionally.

CAUCHON: No. When The Church cuts off an obstinate heretic as a dead branch from the tree of life, the heretic is handed over to the secular arm. The Church has no part in what the secular arm may see fit to do.

WARWICK: Precisely. And I shall be the secular arm in this case. Well, my lord, hand over your dead branch; and I will see that the fire is ready for it. If you will answer for The Church's part, I will answer for the secular part.

CAUCHON (*with smouldering anger*): I can answer for nothing. You great lords are too prone to treat The Church as a mere political convenience.

WARWICK (*smiling and propiliatory*): Not in England, I assure you.

CAUCHON: In England more than anywhere else. No, my lord: the soul of this village girl is of equal value with yours or your king's before the throne of God; and my first duty is to save it. I will not suffer your lordship to smile at me as if I were repeating a meaningless form of words, and it were well understood between us that I should betray the girl to you. I am no mere political bishop: my faith is to me what your honor is to you; and if there be a loophole through which this baptized child of God can creep to her salvation, I shall guide her to it.

THE CHAPLAIN (*rising in a fury*): You are a traitor.

CAUCHON (*springing up*): You lie, priest. (*Trembling with rage*) If you dare do what this woman has done—set your country above the holy Catholic Church—you shall go to the fire with her.

THE CHAPLAIN: My lord: I—I went too far.—(*he sits down with a submissive gesture*).

WARWICK (*who has risen apprehensively*): My lord: I apologize to you for the word used by Messire John de Stogumber. It does not mean in England what it does in France. In your language traitor means betrayer: one who is perfidious, treacherous, unfaithful, disloyal. In our country it means simply one who is not wholly devoted to our English interests.

CAUCHON: I am sorry: I did not understand. (*He subsides into his chair with dignity.*)

WARWICK (*resuming his seat, much relieved*): I must apologize on my own account if I have seemed to take the burning of this poor girl too lightly. When one has seen whole countrysides burnt over and over again as mere items in military routine, one has to grow a very thick skin. Otherwise one might go mad: at all events, I should. May I venture to assume that your lordship also, having to see so many heretics burned from time to time, is compelled to take—shall I say a professional view of what would otherwise be a very horrible incident?

CAUCHON: Yes: it is a painful duty: even, as you say, a horrible one. But in comparison with the horror of heresy it is less than nothing. I am not thinking of this girl's body, which will suffer for a few moments only, and which must in any event die in some more or less painful manner, but of her soul, which may suffer to all eternity.

WARWICK: Just so; and God grant that her soul may be saved! But the practical problem would seem to be how to save her soul without saving her body. For we must face it, my lord: if this cult of The Maid goes on, our cause is lost.

THE CHAPLAIN (*his voice broken like that of a man who has been crying*): May I speak, my lord?

WARWICK: Really, Messire John, I had rather you did not, unless you can keep your temper.

THE CHAPLAIN: It is only this. I speak under correction; but The Maid is full of deceit: she pretends to be devout. Her prayers and confessions are endless. How can she be accused of heresy when she neglects no observance of a faithful daughter of The Church?

CAUCHON (*flaming up*): A faithful daughter of The Church! The Pope himself at his proudest dare not presume as this woman presumes. She acts as if she herself were The Church. She brings the message of God to Charles; and The Church must stand aside. She will crown him in the cathedral of Rheims: she, not The Church! She sends letters to the king of England giving him God's command through her to return to his island on pain of God's vengeance, which she will execute. Let me tell you that the writing of such letters was the practice of the accursed Mahomet, the anti-Christ. Has she ever in all her utterances said one word of The Church? Never. It is always God and herself.

WARWICK: What can you expect? A beggar on horseback! Her head is turned.

CAUCHON: Who has turned it? The devil. And for a mighty purpose. He is spreading this heresy eveerywhere. The man Hus, burnt only thirteen years ago at Constance, infected all Bohemia with it. A man named WcLeef, himself an anointed priest, spread the pestilence in England; and to your shame you let him die in his bed. We have such people here in France too: I know the breed. It is cancerous: if it be not cut out, stamped out, burnt out, it will not stop until it has brought the whole body of human society into sin and corruption, into waste and ruin. By it an Arab camel driver drove Christ and His Church out of Jerusalem, and ravaged his way west like a wild beast until at last there stood only the Pyrenees and God's mercy between France and damnation. Yet what did the camel driver do at the beginning more than this shepherd girl is doing? He had his voices from the angel Gabriel: she has her voices from St Catherine and St Margaret and the Blessed Michael. He declared himself the messenger of God, and wrote in God's name to the kings of the earth. Her letters to them are going forth daily. It is not the Mother of God now to whom we must look for intercession, but to Joan the Maid. What will the world be like when The Church's accumulated wisdom and knowledge and experience, its councils of learned, venerable pious men, are thrust into the kennel by every ignorant laborer or dairymaid whom the devil can puff up with the monstrous self-conceit of being directly inspired from heaven? It will be a world of blood, of fury, of devastation, of each man striving for his own hand: in the end a world wrecked back into barbarism. For now you have only Mahomet and his dupes, and the Maid and her dupes; but what will it be when every girl thinks herself a Joan and every man a Mahomet? I shudder to the very marrow of my bones when I think of it. I have fought it all my life; and I will fight it to the end. Let all this woman's sins be forgiven her except only this sin; for it is the sin against the Holy Ghost; and if she does not recant in the dust before the world, and submit herself to the last inch of her soul to her Church, to the fire she shall go if she once falls into my hand.

WARWICK (*unimpressed*): You feel strongly about it, naturally.

CAUCHON: Do not you?

WARWICK: I am a soldier, not a churchman. As a pilgrim I saw something of the Mahometans. They were not so illbred as I had been led to believe. In some respects their conduct compared favorably with ours.

CAUCHON (*displeased*): I have noticed this before. Men go to the East to convert the infidels. And the infidels pervert them. The Crusader comes back more than half a Saracen. Not to mention that all Englishmen are born heretics.

THE CHAPLAIN: Englishmen heretics!!! (*Appealing to* WARWICK) My lord: must we endure this? His lordship is beside himself. How can what an Englishman believes be heresy? It is a contradiction in terms.

CAUCHON: I absolve you, Messire de Stogumber, on the ground of invincible ignorance. The thick air of your country does not breed theologians.

WARWICK: You would not say so if you heard us quarrelling about religion, my lord! I am sorry you think I must be either a heretic or a blockhead because, as a travelled man, I know that the followers of Mahomet profess great respect for our Lord, and are more ready to forgive St Peter for being a fisherman than your lordship is to forgive Mahomet for being a camel driver. But at least we can proceed in this matter without bigotry.

CAUCHON: When men call the zeal of the Christian Church bigotry I know what to think.

WARWICK: They are only east and west views of the same thing.

CAUCHON (*bitterly ironical*): Only east and west! Only!!

WARWICK: Oh, my Lord Bishop, I am not gainsaying you. You will carry The Church with you; but you have to carry the nobles also. To my mind there is a stronger case against The Maid than the one you have so forcibly put. Frankly, I am not afraid of this girl becoming another Mahomet, and superseding The Church by a great heresy. I think you exaggerate that risk. But have you noticed that in these letters of hers, she proposes to all the kings of Europe, as she has already pressed on Charles, a transaction which would wreck the whole social structure of Christendom?

CAUCHON: Wreck The Church. I tell you so.

WARWICK (*whose patience is wearing out*): My lord: pray get The Church out of your head for a moment; and remember that there are temporal institutions in the world as well as spiritual ones. I and my peers represent the feudal aristocracy as you represent The Church. We are the temporal power. Well, do you not see how this girl's idea strikes at us?

CAUCHON: How does her idea strike at you, except as it strikes at all of us, through The Church?

WARWICK: Her idea is that the kings should give their realms to God, and then reign as God's bailiffs.

CAUCHON (*not interested*): Quite sound theologically, my lord. But the king will hardly care, provided he reign. It is an abstract idea: a mere form of words.

WARWICK: By no means. It is a cunning device to supersede the aristocracy, and make the king sole and absolute autocrat. Instead of the king being merely the first among his peers, he becomes their master. That we cannot suffer: we call no man master. Nominally we hold our lands and dignities from the king, because there must be a keystone to the arch of human society; but we hold our lands in our own hands, and defend them with our own swords and those of our own tenants.

Now by The Maid's doctrine the king will take our lands—our lands! —and make them a present to God; and God will then vest them wholly in the king.

CAUCHON: Need you fear that? You are the makers of kings after all. York or Lancaster in England, Lancaster or Valois in France: they reign according to your pleasure.

WARWICK: Yes; but only as long as the people follow their feudal lords, and know the king only as a travelling show, owning nothing but the highway that belongs to everybody. If the people's thoughts and hearts were turned to the king, and their lords became only the king's servants in their eyes, the king could break us across his knee one by one; and then what should we be but liveried courtiers in his halls?

CAUCHON: Still you need not fear, my lord. Some men are born kings; and some are born statesmen. The two are seldom the same. Where would the king find counsellors to plan and carry out such a policy for him?

WARWICK (*with a not too friendly smile*): Perhaps in the Church, my lord.

(*Cauchon, with an equally sour smile, shrugs his shoulders, and does not contradict him.*)

CAUCHON (*conciliatory, dropping his polemical tone*): My lord: we shall not defeat The Maid if we strive against one another. I know well that there is a Will to Power in the world. I know that while it lasts there will be a struggle between the Emperor and the Pope, between the dukes and the political cardinals, between the barons and the kings. The devil divides us and governs. I see you are no friend to The Church: you are an earl first and last, as I am a churchman first and last. But can we not sink our differences in the face of a common enemy? I see now that what is in your mind is not that this girl has never once mentioned The Church, and thinks only of God and herself, but that she has never once mentioned the peerage, and thinks only of the king and herself.

WARWICK: Quite so. These two ideas of hers are the same idea at bottom. It goes deep, my lord. It is the protest of the individual soul against the interference of priest or peer between the private man and his God. I should call it Protestantism if I had to find a name for it.

CAUCHON (*looking hard at him*): You understand it wonderfully well, my lord. Scratch an Englishman, and find a Protestant.

WARWICK (*playing the pink of courtesy*): I think you are not entirely void of sympathy with The Maid's secular heresy, my lord. I leave you to find a name for it.

CAUCHON: You mistake me, my lord. I have no sympathy with her political presumptions. But as a priest I have gained a knowledge of the minds of the common people; and there you will find yet another most dangerous idea. I can express it only by such phrases as France for the French, England for the English, Italy for the Italians, Spain for the Spanish, and so forth. It is sometimes so narrow and bitter in country folk that it surprises me that this country girl can rise above the idea of her village for its villagers. But she can. She does. When she threatens to drive the English from the soil of France she is undoubtedly thinking of the whole extent of country in which French is spoken. To her the French-speaking people are what the Holy Scriptures describe as a nation. Call this side of her heresy Nationalism if you will: I can find you no better name for it. I can only tell you that it is essentially anti-Catholic and anti-Christian; for the Catholic Church knows only one realm, and that is the realm of Christ's kingdom. Divide that kingdom into nations, and you dethrone Christ. Dethrone Christ, and who will stand between our throats and the sword? The world will perish in a welter of war.

WARWICK: Well, if you will burn the Protestant, I will burn the Nationalist, though perhaps I shall not carry Messire John with me there. England for the English will appeal to him.

THE CHAPLAIN: Certainly England for the English goes without saying: it is the simple law of nature. But this woman denies to England her legitimate conquests, given her by God because of her peculiar fitness to rule over less civilized races for their own good. I do not understand what your lordships mean by Protestant and Nationalist: you are too learned and subtle for a poor clerk like myself. But I know as a matter of plain commonsense that the woman is a rebel; and that is enough for me. She rebels against Nature by wearing man's clothes, and fighting. She rebels against The Church by usurping the divine authority of the Pope. She rebels against God by her damnable league with Satan and his evil spirits against our army. And all these rebellions are only excuses for her great rebellion against England. That is not to be endured. Let her perish. Let her burn. Let her not infect the whole flock. It is expedient that one woman die for the people.

WARWICK (*rising*): My lord: we seem to be agreed.

CAUCHON (*rising also, but in protest*): I will not imperil my soul. I will uphold the justice of the Church. I will strive to the utmost for this woman's salvation.

WARWICK: I am sorry for the poor girl. I hate these severities. I will spare her if I can.

THE CHAPLAIN (*implacably*): I would burn her with my own hands.

CAUCHON (*blessing him*): Sancta simplicitas!

SCENE V

(The ambulatory in the cathedral of Rheims, near the door of the vestry. A pillar bears one of the stations of the cross. The organ is playing the people out of the nave after the coronation. JOAN is kneeling in prayer before the station. She is beautifully dressed, but still in male attire. The organ ceases as DUNOIS, also splendidly arrayed, comes into the ambulatory from the vestry.)

DUNOIS: Come, Joan! you have had enough praying. After that fit of crying you will catch a chill if you stay here any longer. It is all over: the cathedral is empty; and the streets are full. They are calling for The Maid. We have told them you are staying here alone to pray; but they want to see you again.

JOAN: No: let the king have all the glory.

DUNOIS: He only spoils the show, poor devil. No, Joan: you have crowned him; and you must go through with it.

JOAN (shakes her head reluctantly).

DUNOIS (raising her): Come come! it will be over in a couple of hours. It's better than the bridge at Orleans: eh?

JOAN: Oh, dear Dunois, how I wish it were the bridge at Orleans again! We lived at that bridge.

DUNOIS: Yes, faith, and died too: some of us.

JOAN: Isnt it strange, Jack? I am such a coward: I am frightened beyond words before a battle; but it is so dull afterwards when there is no danger: oh, so dull! dull! dull!

DUNOIS: You must learn to be abstemious in war, just as you are in your food and drink, my little saint.

JOAN: Dear Jack: I think you like me as a soldier likes his comrade.

DUNOIS: You need it, poor innocent child of God. You have not many friends at court.

JOAN: Why do all these courtiers and knights and churchmen hate me? What have I done to them? I have asked nothing for myself except that my village shall not be taxed; for we cannot afford war taxes. I have brought them luck and victory: I have set them right when they were doing all sorts of stupid things: I have crowned Charles and made him a real king; and all the honors he is handing out have gone to them. Then why do they not love me?

DUNOIS (rallying her): Sim-ple-ton! Do you expect stupid people to love you for shewing them up? Do blundering old military dug-outs love the successful young captains who supersede them? Do ambitious politicians love the climbers who take the front seats from them? Do archbishops enjoy being played off their own altars, even by saints? Why, I should be jealous of you myself if I were ambitious enough.

JOAN: You are the pick of the basket here, Jack: the only friend I have among all these nobles. I'll wager your mother was from the country. I will go back to the farm when I have taken Paris.

DUNOIS: I am not so sure that they will let you take Paris.

JOAN (*startled*): What!

DUNOIS: I should have taken it myself before this if they had all been sound about it. Some of them would rather Paris took you, I think. So take care.

JOAN: Jack: the world is too wicked for me. If the goddams and the Burgundians do not make an end of me, the French will. Only for my voices I should lose all heart. That is why I had to steal away to pray here alone after the coronation. I'll tell you something, Jack. It is in the bells I hear my voices. Not to-day, when they all rang: that was nothing but jangling. But here in this corner, where the bells come down from heaven, and the echoes linger, or in the fields, where they come from a distance through the quiet of the countryside, my voices are in them. (*The cathedral clock chimes the quarter*) Hark! (*She becomes rapt*) Do you hear? 'Dear-child-of-God': just what you said. At the half-hour they will say 'Be-brave-go-on'. At the three-quarters they will say 'I-am-thy-Help'. But it is at the hour, when the great bell goes after 'God-will-save-France': it is then that St Margaret and St Catherine and sometimes even the blessed Michael will say things that I cannot tell beforehand. Then, oh then—

DUNOIS (*interrupting her kindly but not sympathetically*): Then, Joan, we shall hear whatever we fancy in the booming of the bell. You make me uneasy when you talk about your voices: I should think you were a bit cracked if I hadnt noticed that you give me very sensible reasons for what you do, though I hear you telling others you are only obeying Madame Saint Catherine.

JOAN (*crossly*): Well, I have to find reasons for you, because you do not believe in my voices. But the voices come first; and I find the reasons after: whatever you may choose to believe.

DUNOIS: Are you angry, Joan?

JOAN: Yes. (*Smiling*) No: not with you. I wish you were one of the village babies.

DUNOIS: Why?

JOAN: I could nurse you for awhile.

DUNOIS: You are a bit of woman after all.

JOAN: No: not a bit: I am a soldier and nothing else. Soldiers always nurse children when they get a chance.

DUNOIS: That is true. (*He laughs.*)

(KING CHARLES, *with* BLUEBEARD *on his left and* LA HIRE *on his right, comes from the vestry, where he has been disrobing.* JOAN *shrinks away behind the pillar.* DUNOIS *is left between* CHARLES *and* LA HIRE.)

DUNOIS: Well, your Majesty is an anointed king at last. How do you like it?

CHARLES: I would not go through it again to be emperor of the sun and moon. The weight of those robes! I thought I should have dropped when they loaded that crown on to me. And the famous holy oil they talked so much about was rancid: phew! The Archbishop must be nearly dead: his robes must have weighed a ton: they are stripping him still in the vestry.

DUNOIS (*drily*): Your majesty should wear armor oftener. That would accustom you to heavy dressing.

CHARLES: Yes: the old jibe! Well, I am not going to wear armor: fighting is not my job. Where is The Maid?

JOAN (*coming forward between* CHARLES *and* BLUEBEARD, *and falling on her knee*): Sire: I have made you king: my work is done. I am going back to my father's farm.

CHARLES (*surprised, but relieved*): Oh, are you? Well, that will be very nice.

(JOAN *rises, deeply discouraged.*)

CHARLES (*continuing heedlessly*): A healthy life, you know.

DUNOIS: But a dull one.

BLUEBEARD: You will find the petticoats tripping you up after leaving them off for so long.

LA HIRE: You will miss the fighting. It's a bad habit, but a grand one, and the hardest of all to break yourself of.

CHARLES (*anxiously*): Still, we dont want you to stay if you would really rather go home.

JOAN (*bitterly*): I know well that none of you will be sorry to see me go. (*She turns her shoulder to* CHARLES *and walks past him to the more congenial neighborhood of* DUNOIS *and* LA HIRE.)

LA HIRE: Well, I shall be able to swear when I want to. But I shall miss you at times.

JOAN: La Hire: in spite of all your sins and swears we shall meet in heaven; for I love you as I love Pitou, my old sheep dog. Pitou could kill a wolf. You will kill the English wolves until they go back to their country and become good dogs of God, will you not?

LA HIRE: You and I together: yes.

JOAN: No: I shall last only a year from the beginning.

ALL THE OTHERS: What!

JOAN: I know it somehow.

DUNOIS: Nonsense!

JOAN: Jack: do you think you will be able to drive them out?

DUNOIS (*with quiet conviction*): Yes: I shall drive them out. They beat us because we thought battles were tournaments and ransom markets.

We played the fool while the goddams took war seriously. But I have learnt my lesson, and taken their measure. They have no roots here. I have beaten them before; and I shall beat them again.

JOAN: You will not be cruel to them, Jack?

DUNOIS: The goddams will not yield to tender handling. We did not begin it.

JOAN (*suddenly*): Jack: before I go home, let us take Paris.

CHARLES (*terrified*): Oh no no. We shall lose everything we have gained. Oh dont let us have any more fighitng. We can make a very good treaty with the Duke of Burgundy.

JOAN: Treaty! (*She stamps with impatience.*)

CHARLES: Well, why not, now that I am crowned and anointed? Oh, that oil!

(*The* ARCHBISHOP *comes from the vestry, and joins the group between* CHARLES *and* BLUEBEARD.)

CHARLES:* Archbishop: The Maid wants to start fighting again.

THE ARCHBISHOP: Have we ceased fighting, then? Are we at peace?

CHARLES: No: I suppose not; but let us be content with what we have done. Let us make a treaty. Our luck is too good to last; and now is our chance to stop before it turns.

JOAN: Luck! God has fought for us; and you call it luck! And you would stop while there are still Englishmen on this holy earth of dear France!

THE ARCHBISHOP (*sternly*): Maid: the king addressed himself to me, not to you. You forget yourself. You very often forget yourself.

JOAN (*unabashed, and rather roughly*): Then speak, you; and tell him that it is not God's will that he should take his hand from the plough.

THE ARCHBISHOP: If I am not so glib with the name of God as you are, it is because I interpret His will with the authority of the Church and of my sacred office. When you first came you respected it, and would not have dared to speak as you are now speaking. You came clothed with the virtue of humility; and because God blessed your enterprises accordingly, you have stained yourself with the sin of pride. The old Greek tragedy is rising among us. It is the chastisement of hubris.

CHARLES: Yes: she thinks she knows better than everyone else.

JOAN (*distressed, but naïvely incapable of seeing the effect she is producing*): But I do know better than any of you seem to. And I am not proud: I never speak unless I know I am right.

BLUEBEARD } (*exclaiming* { Ha ha!
CHARLES } *together*) { Just so.

THE ARCHBISHOP: How do you know you are right?

JOAN: I always know. My voices—

CHARLES: Oh, your voices, your voices. Why dont the voices come to me? I am king, not you.

JOAN: They do come to you; but you do not hear them. You have not sat in the field in the evening listening for them. When the angelus rings you cross yourself and have done with it; but if you prayed from your heart, and listened to the thrilling of the bells in the air after they stop ringing, you would hear the voices as well as I do. (*Turning brusquely from him*) But what voices do you need to tell you what the blacksmith can tell you: that you must strike while the iron is hot? I tell you we must make a dash at Compiègne and relieve it as we relieved Orleans. Then Paris will open its gates; or if not, we will break through them. What is your crown worth without your capital?

LA HIRE: That is what I say too. We shall go through them like a red hot shot through a pound of butter. What do you say, Bastard?

DUNOIS: If our cannon balls were all as hot as your head, and we had enough of them, we should conquer the earth, no doubt. Pluck and impetuosity are good servants in war, but bad masters: they have delivered us into the hands of the English every time we have trusted to them. We never know when we are beaten: that is our great fault.

JOAN: You never know when you are victorious: that is a worse fault. I shall have to make you carry looking-glasses in battle to convince you that the English have not cut off all your noses. You would have been besieged in Orleans still, you and your councils of war, if I had not made you attack. You should always attack; and if you only hold on long enough the enemy will stop first. You dont know how to begin a battle; and you dont know how to use your cannons. And I do.

(*She squats down on the flags with crossed ankles, pouting.*)

DUNOIS: I know what you think of us, General Joan.

JOAN: Never mind that, Jack. Tell them what you think of me.

DUNOIS: I think that God was on your side; for I have not forgotten how the wind changed, and how our hearts changed when you came; and by my faith I shall never deny that it was in your sign that we conquered. But I tell you as a soldier that God is no man's daily drudge, and no maid's either. If you are worthy of it He will sometimes snatch you out of the jaws of death and set you on your feet again; but that is all: once on your feet you must fight with all your might and all your craft. For He has to be fair to your enemy too: dont forget that. Well, He set us on our feet through you at Orleans; and the glory of it has carried us through a few good battles here to the coronation. But if we presume on it further, and trust to God to do the work we should do ourselves, we shall be defeated; and serve us right!

JOAN: But—

DUNOIS: Sh! I have not finished. Do not think, any of you, that these victories of ours were won without generalship. King Charles: you have said no word in your proclamations of my part in this campaign; and

George Bernard Shaw: *Saint Joan*

I make no complaint of that; for the people will run after The Maid and her miracles and not after the Bastard's hard work finding troops for her and feeding them. But I know exactly how much God did for us through The Maid, and how much He left me to do by my own wits; and I tell you that your little hour of miracles is over, and that from this time on he who plays the war game best will win—if the luck is on his side.

JOAN: Ah! if, if, if, if! If ifs and ans were pots and pans there'd be no need of tinkers. (*Rising impetuously*) I tell you, Bastard, your art of war is no use, because your knights are no good for real fighting. War is only a game to them, like tennis and all their other games: they make rules as to what is fair and what is not fair, and heap armor on themselves and on their poor horses to keep out the arrows; and when they fall they cant get up, and have to wait for their squires to come and lift them to arrange about the ransom with the man that has poked them off their horse. Cant you see that all the like of that is gone by and done with? What use is armor against gunpowder? And if it was, do you think men that are fighting for France and for God will stop to bargain about ransoms, as half your knights live by doing? No: they will fight to win; and they will give up their lives out of their own hand into the hand of God when they go into battle, as I do. Common folks understand this. They cannot afford armor and cannot pay ransoms; but they followed me half naked into the moat and up the ladder and over the wall. With them it is my life or thine, and God defend the right! You may shake your head, Jack; and Bluebeard may twirl his billygoat's beard and cock his nose at me; but remember the day your knights and captains refused to follow me to attack the English at Orleans! You locked the gates to keep me in; and it was the townsfolk and the common people that followed me, and forced the gate, and shewed you the way to fight in earnest.

BLUEBEARD (*offended*): Not content with being Pope Joan, you must be Caesar and Alexander as well.

THE ARCHBISHOP: Pride will have a fall, Joan.

JOAN: Oh, never mind whether it is pride or not: is it true? is it commonsense?

LA HIRE: It is true. Half of us are afraid of having our handsome noses broken; and the other half are out for paying off their mortgages. Let her have her way, Dunois: she does not know everything; but she has got hold of the right end of the stick. Fighting is not what it was; and those who know least about it often make the best job of it.

DUNOIS: I know all that. I do not fight in the old way: I have learnt the lesson of Agincourt, of Poitiers and Crecy. I know how many lives any move of mine will cost; and if the move is worth the cost I make it and pay the cost. But Joan never counts the cost at all: she goes ahead and trusts to God: she thinks she has God in her pocket. Up to now she has had the numbers on her side; and she has won. But I know Joan; and I see that some day she will go ahead when she has only ten men to do the work of a hundred. And then she will find that God is on the side of the big battalions. She will be taken by the enemy. And the lucky man that makes the capture will receive sixteen thousand pounds from the Earl of Warwick.

JOAN (*flattered*): Sixteen thousand pounds! Eh, laddie, have they offered that for me? There cannot be so much money in the world.

DUNOIS: There is, in England. And now tell me, all of you, which of you will lift a finger to save Joan once the English have got her? I speak first, for the army. The day after she has been dragged from her horse by a goddam or a Burgundian, and he is not struck dead: the day after she is locked in a dungeon, and the bars and bolts do not fly open at the touch of St Peter's angel: the day when the enemy finds out that she is as vulnerable as I am and not a bit more invincible, she will not be worth the life of a single soldier to us; and I will not risk that life, much as I cherish her as a companion-in-arms.

JOAN: I dont blame you, Jack: you are right. I am not worth one soldier's life if God lets me be beaten; but France may think me worth my ransom after what God has done for her through me.

CHARLES: I tell you I have no money; and this coronation, which is all your fault, has cost me the last farthing I can borrow.

JOAN: The Church is richer than you. I put my trust in the Church.

THE ARCHBISHOP: Woman: they will drag you through the streets, and burn you as a witch.

JOAN (*running to him*): Oh, my lord, do not say that. It is impossible. I a witch!

THE ARCHBISHOP: Peter Cauchon knows his business. The University of Paris has burnt a woman for saying that what you have done was well done, and according to God.

JOAN (*bewildered*): But why? What sense is there in it? What I have done is according to God. They could not burn a woman for speaking the truth.

THE ARCHBISHOP: They did.

JOAN: But you know that she was speaking the truth. You would not let them burn me.

THE ARCHBISHOP: How could I prevent them?

JOAN: You would speak in the name of the Church. You are a great prince of the Church. I would go anywhere with your blessing to protect me.

THE ARCHBISHOP: I have no blessing for you while you are proud and disobedient.

JOAN: Oh, why will you go on saying things like that? I am not proud and disobedient. I am a poor girl, and so ignorant that I do not know A from B. How could I be proud? And how can you say that I am disobedient when I always obey my voices, because they come from God.

THE ARCHBISHOP: The voice of God on earth is the voice of the Church Militant; and all the voices that come to you are the echoes of your own wilfulness.

JOAN: It is not true.

THE ARCHBISHOP (*flushing angrily*): You tell the Archbishop in his cathedral that he lies; and yet you say you are not proud and disobedient.

JOAN: I never said you lied. It was you that as good as said my voices lied. When have they ever lied? If you will not believe in them: even if they are only the echoes of my own commonsense, are they not always right? and are not your earthly counsels always wrong?

THE ARCHBISHOP (*indignantly*): It is waste of time admonishing you.

CHARLES: It always comes back to the same thing. She is right; and everyone else is wrong.

THE ARCHBISHOP: Take this as your last warning. If you perish through setting your private judgment above the instructions of your spiritual directors, the Church disowns you, and leaves you to whatever fate your presumption may bring upon you. The Bastard has told you that if you persist in setting up your military conceit above the counsels of your commanders—

DUNOIS (*interposing*): To put it quite exactly, if you attempt to relieve the garrison in Compiègne without the same superiority in numbers you had at Orleans—

THE ARCHBISHOP: The army will disown you, and will not rescue you. And His Majesty the King has told you that the throne has not the means of ransoming you.

CHARLES: Not a penny.

THE ARCHBISHOP: You stand alone: absolutely alone, trusting to your own conceit, your own ignorance, your own headstrong presumption, your own impiety in hiding all these sins under the cloak of a trust in God. When you pass through these doors into the sunlight, the crowd will cheer you. They will bring you their little children and their invalids to heal: they will kiss your hands and feet, and do what they can, poor simple souls, to turn your head, and madden you with the self-confidence that is leading you to your destruction. But you will be none the less alone: they cannot save you. We and we only can stand between you and the stake at which our enemies have burnt that wretched woman in Paris.

JOAN (*her eyes skyward*): I have better friends and better counsel than yours.

THE ARCHBISHOP: I see that I am speaking in vain to a hardened heart.

You reject our protection, and are determined to turn us all against you. In future, then, fend for yourself; and if you fail, God have mercy on your soul.

DUNOIS: That is the truth, Joan. Heed it.

JOAN: Where would you all have been now if I had heeded that sort of truth? There is no help, no counsel, in any of you. Yes: I am alone on earth: I have always been alone. My father told my brothers to drown me if I would not stay to mind his sheep while France was bleeding to death: France might perish if only our lambs were safe. I thought France would have friends at the court of the king of France; and I find only wolves fighting for pieces of her poor torn body. I thought God would have friends everywhere, because He is the friend of everyone; and in my innocence I believed that you who now cast me out would be like strong towers to keep harm from me. But I am wiser now; and nobody is any the worse for being wiser. Do not think you can frighten me by telling me that I am alone. France is alone; and God is alone; and what is my loneliness before the loneliness of my country and my God? I see now that the loneliness of God is His strength: what would He be if He listened to your jealous little counsels? Well, my loneliness shall be my strength too; it is better to be alone with God; His friendship will not fail me, nor His counsel, nor His love. In His strength I will dare, and dare, and dare, until I die. I will go out now to the common people, and let the love in their eyes comfort me for the hate in yours. You will all be glad to see me burnt; but if I go through the fire I shall go through it to their hearts for ever and ever. And so, God be with me!

(She goes from them. They stare after her in glum silence for a moment. Then GILLES DE RAIS *twirls his beard.)*

BLUEBEARD: You know, the woman is quite impossible. I dont dislike her, really; but what are you to do with such a character?

DUNOIS: As God is my judge, if she fell into the Loire I would jump in in full armor to fish her out. But if she plays the fool at Compiègne, and gets caught: I must leave her to her doom.

LA HIRE: Then you had better chain me up; for I could follow her to hell when the spirit rises in her like that.

THE ARCHBISHOP: She disturbs my judgment too: there is a dangerous power in her outbursts. But the pit is open at her feet; and for good or evil we cannot turn her from it.

CHARLES: If only she would keep quiet, or go home!

(They follow her dispiritedly.)

George Bernard Shaw: *Saint Joan*

SCENE VI

(Rouen, 30th May 1431. A great stone hall in the castle, arranged for a trial-at-law, but not a trial-by-jury, the court being the BISHOP's court with the inquisition participating: hence there are two raised chairs side by side for the BISHOP and the INQUISITOR as judges. Rows of chairs radiating from them at an obtuse angle are for the CANONS, the DOCTORS OF LAW AND THEOLOGY, and the DOMINICAN MONKS, who act as assessors. In the angle is a table for the scribes, with stools. There is also a heavy rough wooden stool for the prisoner. All these are at the inner end of the hall. The further end is open to the courtyard through a row of arches. The court is shielded from the weather by screens and curtains.

Looking down the great hall from the middle of the inner end, the judicial chairs and scribes' table are to the right. The prisoner's stool is to the left. There are arched doors right and left. It is a fine sunshiny May morning.

WARWICK comes in through the arched doorway on the judges' side, followed by his PAGE.)

THE PAGE (*pertly*): I suppose your lordship is aware that we have no business here. This is an ecclesiastical court; and we are only the secular arm.
WARWICK: I am aware of that fact. Will it please your impudence to find the Bishop of Beauvais for me, and give him a hint that he can have a word with me here before the trial, if he wishes?
THE PAGE (*going*): Yes, my lord.
WARWICK: And mind you behave yourself. Do not address him as Pious Peter.
THE PAGE: No, my lord. I shall be kind to him, because, when The Maid is brought in, Pious Peter will have to pick a peck of pickled pepper.

(CAUCHON *enters through the same door with a* DOMINICAN MONK *and a* CANON, *the latter carrying a brief.*)

THE PAGE: The Right Reverend his lordship the Bishop of Beauvais. And two other reverend gentlemen.
WARWICK: Get out; and see that we are not interrupted.
THE PAGE: Right, my lord (*he vanishes airily*).
CAUCHON: I wish your lordship good-morrow.
WARWICK: Good-morrow to your lordship. Have I had the pleasure of meeting your friends before? I think not.
CAUCHON (*introducing the* MONK, *who is on his right*): This, my lord, is Brother John Lemaître, of the order of St Dominic. He is acting as

deputy for the Chief Inquisitor into the evil of heresy in France. Brother John: the Earl of Warwick.

WARWICK: Your Reverence is most welcome. We have no Inquisitor in England, unfortunately; though we miss him greatly, especially on occasions like the present.

(*The* INQUISITOR *smiles patiently, and bows. He is a mild elderly gentleman, but has evident reserves of authority and firmness.*)

CAUCHON (*introducing the* CANON, *who is on his left*): This gentleman is Canon John D'Estivet, of the Chapter of Bayeux. He is acting as Promoter.

WARWICK: Promoter?

CAUCHON: Prosecutor, you would call him in civil law.

WARWICK: Ah! prosecutor. Quite, quite. I am very glad to make your acquaintance, Canon D'Estivet.

(D'ESTIVET *bows.* [*He is on the young side of middle age, well mannered, but vulpine beneath his veneer.*])

WARWICK: May I ask what stage the proceedings have reached? It is now more than nine months since The Maid was captured at Compiègne by the Burgundians. It is fully four months since I bought her from the Burgundians for a very handsome sum, solely that she might be brought to justice. It is very nearly three months since I delivered her up to you, my Lord Bishop, as a person suspected of heresy. May I suggest that you are taking a rather unconscionable time to make up your minds about a very plain case? Is this trial never going to end?

THE INQUISITOR (*smiling*): It has not yet begun, my lord.

WARWICK: Not yet begun! Why, you have been at it eleven weeks!

CAUCHON: We have not been idle, my lord. We have held fifteen examinations of The Maid: six public and nine private.

THE INQUISITOR (*always patiently smiling*): You see, my lord, I have been present at only two of these examinations. They were proceedings of the Bishop's court solely, and not of the Holy Office. I have only just decided to associate myself—that is, to associate the Holy Inquisition—with the Bishop's court. I did not at first think that this was a case of heresy at all. I regarded it as a political case, and The Maid as a prisoner of war. But having now been present at two of the examinations, I must admit that this seems to be one of the gravest cases of heresy within my experience. Therefore everything is now in order, and we proceed to trial this morning. (*He moves towards the judicial chairs.*)

CAUCHON: This moment, if your lordship's convenience allows.

WARWICK (*graciously*): Well, that is good news, gentlemen. I will not attempt to conceal from you that our patience was becoming strained.

CAUCHON: So I gathered from the threats of your soldiers to drown those of our people who favor The Maid.

WARWICK: Dear me! At all events their intentions were friendly to you, my lord.

CAUCHON (*sternly*): I hope not. I am determined that the woman shall have a fair hearing. The justice of the Church is not a mockery, my lord.

THE INQUISITOR (*returning*): Never has there been a fairer examination within my experience, my lord. The Maid needs no lawyers to take her part: she will be tried by her most faithful friends, all ardently desirous to save her soul from perdition.

D'ESTIVET: Sir: I am the Promoter; and it has been my painful duty to present the case against the girl; but believe me, I would throw up my case today and hasten to her defence if I did not know that men far my superiors in learning and piety, in eloquence and persuasiveness, have been sent to reason with her, to explain to her the danger she is running, and the ease with which she may avoid it. (*Suddenly bursting into forensic eloquence, to the disgust of* CAUCHON *and the* INQUISITOR, *who have listened to him so far with patronizing approval*) Men have dared to say that we are acting from hate; but God is our witness that they lie. Have we tortured her? No. Have we ceased to exhort her; to implore her to have pity on herself; to come to the bosom of her Church as an erring but beloved child? Have we—

CAUCHON (*interrupting drily*): Take care, Canon. All that you say is true; but if you make his lordship believe it I will not answer for your life, and hardly for my own.

WARWICK (*deprecating, but by no means denying*): Oh, my lord, you are very hard on us poor English. But we certainly do not share your pious desire to save The Maid: in fact I tell you now plainly that her death is a political necessity which I regret but cannot help. If the Church lets her go—

CAUCHON (*with fierce and menacing pride*): If the Church lets her go, woe to the man, were he the Emperor himself, who dares lay a finger on her! The Church is not subject to political necessity, my lord.

THE INQUISITOR (*interposing smoothly*): You need have no anxiety about the result, my lord. You have an invincible ally in the matter: one who is far more determined than you that she shall burn.

WARWICK: And who is this very convenient partisan, may I ask?

THE INQUISITOR: The Maid herself. Unless you put a gag in her mouth you cannot prevent her from convicting herself ten times over every time she opens it.

D'ESTIVET: That is perfectly true, my lord. My hair bristles on my head when I hear so young a creature utter such blasphemies.

WARWICK: Well, by all means do your best for her if you are quite sure it will be of no avail. (*Looking hard at* CAUCHON) I should be sorry to have to act without the blessing of the Church.

CAUCHON (*with a mixture of cynical admiration and contempt*): And yet they say Englishmen are hypocrites! You play for your side, my lord, even at the peril of your soul. I cannot but admire such devotion; but I dare not go so far myself. I fear damnation.

WARWICK: If we feared anything we could never govern England, my lord. Shall I send your people in to you?

CAUCHON: Yes: it will be very good of your lordship to withdraw and allow the court to assemble.

(WARWICK *turns on his heel, and goes out through the courtyard.* CAUCHON *takes one of the judicial seats; and* D'ESTIVET *sits at the scribes' table, studying his brief.*)

CAUCHON (*casually, as he makes himself comfortable*): What scoundrels these English nobles are!

THE INQUISITOR (*taking the other judicial chair on* CAUCHON's *left*): All secular power makes men scoundrels. They are not trained for the work; and they have not the Apostolic Succession. Our own nobles are just as bad.

(*The Bishop's* ASSESSORS *hurry into the hall, headed by* CHAPLAIN DE STOGUMBER *and* CANON DE COURCELLES, *a young priest of 30. The scribes sit at the table, leaving a chair vacant opposite* D'ESTIVET. *Some of the* ASSESSORS *take their seats: others stand chatting, waiting for the proceedings to begin formally.* DE STOGUMBER, *aggrieved and obstinate, will not take his seat: neither will the* CANON, *who stands on his right.*)

CAUCHON: Good morning, Master de Stogumber. (*To the* INQUISITOR): Chaplain to the Cardinal of England.

THE CHAPLAIN (*correcting him*): Of Winchester, my lord. I have to make a protest, my lord.

CAUCHON: You make a great many.

THE CHAPLAIN: I am not without support, my lord. Here is Master de Courcelles, Canon of Paris, who associates himself with me in my protest.

CAUCHON: Well, what is the matter?

THE CHAPLAIN (*sulkily*): Speak you, Master de Courcelles, since I do not seem to enjoy his lordship's confidence. (*He sits down in dudgeon next to* CAUCHON, *on his right.*)

COURCELLES: My lord: we have been at great pains to draw up an indictment of The Maid on sixty-four counts. We are now told that they have been reduced, without consulting us.

THE INQUISITOR: Master de Courcelles: I am the culprit. I am overwhelmed with admiration for the zeal displayed in your sixty-four counts; but in accusing a heretic, as in other things, enough is enough. Also you must remember that all the members of the court are not so subtle and profound as you, and that some of your very great learning might appear to them to be very great nonsense. Therefore I have thought it well to have your sixty-four articles cut down to twelve—

COURCELLES (*thunderstruck*): Twelve!!!

THE INQUISITOR: Twelve will, believe me, be quite enough for your purpose.

THE CHAPLAIN: But some of the most important points have been reduced almost to nothing. For instance, The Maid has actually declared that the blessed saints Margaret and Catherine, and the holy Archangel Michael, spoke to her in French. That is a vital point.

THE INQUISITOR: You think, doubtless, that they should have spoken in Latin?

CAUCHON: No: he thinks they should have spoken in English.

THE CHAPLAIN: Naturally, my lord.

THE INQUISITOR: Well, as we are all here agreed, I think, that these voices of The Maid are the voices of evil spirits tempting her to her damnation, it would not be very courteous to you, Master de Stogumber, or to the King of England, to assume that English is the devil's native language. So let it pass. The matter is not wholly omitted from the twelve articles. Pray take your places, gentlemen; and let us proceed to business.

(*All who have not taken their seats, do so.*)

THE CHAPLAIN: Well, I protest. That is all.

COURCELLES: I think it hard that all our work should go for nothing. It is only another example of the diabolical influence which this woman exercises over the court. (*He takes his chair, which is on the* CHAPLAIN's *right.*)

CAUCHON: Do you suggest that I am under diabolical influence?

COURCELLES: I suggest nothing, my lord. But it seems to me that there is a conspiracy here to hush up the fact that The Maid stole the Bishop of Senlis's horse.

CAUCHON (*keeping his temper with difficulty*): This is not a police court. Are we to waste our time on such rubbish?

COURCELLES (*rising, shocked*): My lord: do you call the Bishop's horse rubbish?

THE INQUISITOR (*blandly*): Master de Courcelles: The Maid alleges that she paid handsomely for the Bishop's horse, and that if he did not get the money the fault was not hers. As that may be true, the point is one on which The Maid may well be acquitted.

COURCELLES: Yes, if it were an ordinary horse. But the Bishop's horse! how can she be acquitted for that? (*He sits down again, bewildered and discouraged.*)

THE INQUISITOR: I submit to you, with great respect, that if we persist in trying The Maid on trumpery issues on which we may have to declare her innocent, she may escape us on the great main issue of heresy, on which she seems so far to insist on her own guilt. I will ask you, therefore, to say nothing, when The Maid is brought before us, of these stealings of horses, and dancings round fairy trees with the village children, and prayings at haunted wells, and a dozen other things which you were diligently inquiring into until my arrival. There is not a village girl in France against whom you could not prove such things: they all dance round haunted trees, and pray at magic wells. Some of them would steal the Pope's horse if they got the chance. Heresy, gentlemen, heresy is the charge we have to try. The detection and suppression of heresy is my peculiar business; I am here as an inquisitor, not as an ordinary magistrate. Stick to the heresy, gentlemen; and leave the other matters alone.

CAUCHON: I may say that we have sent to the girl's village to make inquiries about her, and there is practically nothing serious against her.

THE CHAPLAIN (*rising and clamoring together*) Nothing serious, my lord—
COURCELLES What! The fairy tree not—

CAUCHON (*out of patience*): Be silent, gentlemen; or speak one at a time.

(COURCELLES *collapses into his chair, intimidated.*)

THE CHAPLAIN (*sulkily resuming his seat*): That is what The Maid said to us last Friday.

CAUCHON: I wish you had followed her counsel, sir. When I say nothing serious, I mean nothing that men of sufficiently large mind to conduct an inquiry like this would consider serious. I agree with my colleague the Inquisitor that it is on the count of heresy that we must proceed.

LADVENU (*a young but ascetically fine-drawn Dominican who is sitting next* COURCELLES, *on his right*): But is there any great harm in the girl's heresy? Is it not merely her simplicity? Many saints have said as much as Joan.

THE INQUISITOR (*dropping his blandness and speaking very gravely*): Brother Martin: if you had seen what I have seen of heresy, you would not think it a light thing even in its most apparently harmless and even lovable and pious origins. Heresy begins with people who are to all appearance better than their neighbors. A gentle and pious girl, or a young man who has obeyed the command of our Lord by giving all his riches to the poor, and putting on the garb of poverty, the life of austerity, and the rule of humility and charity, may be the founder of a heresy that will wreck both Church and Empire if not ruthlessly stamped out in time. The records of the Holy Inquisition are full of histories we dare not give to the world, because they are beyond the belief of honest men and innocent women; yet they all began with saintly simpletons. I have seen this again and again. Mark what I say: the woman who quarrels with her clothes, and puts on the dress of a man, is like the man who throws off his fur gown and dresses like John the Baptist: they are followed, as surely as the night follows the day, by bands of wild women and men who refuse to wear any clothes at all. When maids will neither marry nor take regular vows, and men reject marriage and exalt their lusts into divine inspirations, then, as surely as the summer follows the spring, they begin with polygamy, and end by incest. Heresy at first seems innocent and even laudable; but it ends in such a monstrous horror of unnatural wickedness that the most tender-hearted among you, if you saw it at work as I have seen it, would clamor against the mercy of the Church in dealing with it. For two hundred years the Holy Office has striven with these diabolical madnesses; and it knows that they begin always by vain and ignorant persons setting up their own judgment against the Church, and taking it upon themselves to be the interpreters of God's will. You must not fall into the common error of mistaking these simpletons for liars and hypocrites. They believe honestly and sincerely that their diabolical inspiration is divine. Therefore you must be on your guard against your natural compassion. You are all, I hope, merciful men: how else could you have devoted your lives to the service of our gentle Savior? You are going to see before you a young girl, pious and chaste; for I must tell you, gentlemen, that the things said of her by our English friends are supported by no evidence, whilst there is abundant testimony that her excesses have been excesses of religion and charity and not of worldliness and wantonness. This girl is not one of those whose hard features are the sign of hard hearts, and whose brazen looks and lewd demeanor condemn them before they are accused. The devilish pride that has led her into her present peril has left no mark on her countenance. Strange as it may seem to you, it has even left no mark on her character outside those special matters in which she is proud; so that you will see a diabolical pride and a natural humility seated side by side in the selfsame soul. Therefore be on your guard. God forbid that I should tell you to harden your hearts; for her punishment if we condemn her will be so cruel that we should forfeit our own hope of divine mercy were there one grain of malice against her in our hearts. But if you hate cruelty—and if any man here does not hate it I command him on his soul's salvation to quit this holy court—I say, if you hate cruelty, remember that nothing is so cruel in its consequences as the toleration of heresy. Remember also that no court of law can be so cruel as the common people are to those whom they suspect of heresy. The heretic in the hands of the Holy Office is safe from violence, is assured of a fair trial, and cannot suffer death, even when guilty, if repentance follows sin. Innumerable lives of heretics have been saved because the Holy Office has taken them out of the hands of the people, and because the people have yielded them up, knowing that the Holy Office would deal with them. Before the Holy Inquisition existed, and even now when its officers are not within reach, the unfortunate wretch suspected of heresy, perhaps quite ignorantly and unjustly, is stoned, torn in pieces, drowned, burned in his house with all his innocent children, without a trial, unshriven, unburied save as a dog is buried: all of them deeds hateful to God and most cruel to man. Gentlemen: I am compassionate by nature as well as by my profession; and though the work I have to do may seem cruel to those who do not know how much more cruel it would be to leave it undone, I would go to the stake myself sooner than do it if I did not know its righteousness, its necessity, its essential mercy. I ask you to address yourself to this trial in that conviction. Anger is a bad counsellor: cast out anger. Pity is sometimes worse: cast out pity. But do not cast out mercy. Remember only that justice comes first. Have you anything to say, my lord, before we proceed to trial?

CAUCHON: You have spoken for me, and spoken better than I could. I do not see how any sane man could disagree with word that has fallen from you. But this I will add. The crude heresies of which you have told us are horrible; but their horror is like that of the black death: they rage for a while and then die out, because sound and sensible men will not under any incitement be reconciled to nakedness and incest and polygamy and the like. But we are confronted today throughout Europe with a heresy that is spreading among men not weak in mind nor diseased in brain: nay, the stronger the mind, the more obstinate the heretic. It is neither discredited by fantastic extremes nor corrupted by the common lust of the flesh; but it, too, sets up the private judgment of the single erring mortal against the considered wisdom and experience of the Church. The mighty structure of Catholic Christendom will never be shaken by naked madmen or by the sins of Moab and Ammon. But it may be betrayed from within, and brought to barbarous ruin and desolation, by this arch heresy which the English Commander calls Protestantism.

THE ASSESSORS (*whispering*): Protestantism! What was that? What does the

Bishop mean? Is it a new heresy? The English Commander, he said. Did you ever hear of Protestantism? etc., etc.

CAUCHON (*continuing*): And that reminds me. What provision has the Earl of Warwick made for the defence of the secular arm should The Maid prove obdurate, and the people be moved to pity her?

THE CHAPLAIN: Have no fear on that score, my lord. The noble earl has eight hundred men-at-arms at the gates. She will not slip through our English fingers even if the whole city be on her side.

CAUCHON (*revolted*): Will you not add, God grant that she repent and purge her sin?

THE CHAPLAIN: That does not seem to me to be consistent; but of course I agree with your lordship.

CAUCHON (*giving him up with a shrug of contempt*): The court sits.

THE INQUISITOR: Let the accused be brought in.

LADVENU (*calling*): The accused. Let her be brought in.

(JOAN, *chained by the ankles, is brought in through the arched door behind the prisoner's stool by a guard of English soldiers. With them is the* EXECUTIONER *and his assistants. They lead her to the prisoner's stool, and place themselves behind it after taking off her chain. She wears a page's black suit. Her long imprisonment and the strain of the examinations which have preceded the trial have left their mark on her; but her vitality still holds; she confronts the court unabashed, without a trace of the awe which their formal solemnity seems to require for the complete success of its impressiveness.*)

THE INQUISITOR (*kindly*): Sit down, Joan. (*She sits on the prisoner's stool.*) You look very pale today. Are you not well?

JOAN: Thank you kindly: I am well enough. But the Bishop sent me some carp; and it made me ill.

CAUCHON: I am sorry. I told them to see that it was fresh.

JOAN: You meant to be good to me, I know; but it is a fish that does not agree with me. The English thought you were trying to poison me—

CAUCHON (*together*) What!
THE CHAPLAIN No, my lord.

JOAN (*continuing*): They are determined that I shall be burnt as a witch; and they sent their doctor to cure me; but he was forbidden to bleed me because the silly people believe that a witch's witchery leaves her if she is bled; so he only called me filthy names. Why do you leave me in the hands of the English? I should be in the hands of the Church. And why must I be chained by the feet to a log of wood? Are you afraid I will fly away?

D'ESTIVET (*harshly*): Woman: it is not for you to question the court: it is for us to question you.

COURCELLES: When you were left unchained, did you not try to escape by jumping from a tower sixty feet high? If you cannot fly like a witch, how is it that you are still alive?

JOAN: I suppose because the tower was not so high then. It has grown higher every day since you began asking me questions about it.

D'ESTIVET: Why did you jump from the tower?

JOAN: How do you know that I jumped?

D'ESTIVET: You were found lying in the moat. Why did you leave the tower?

JOAN: Why would anybody leave a prison if they could get out?

D'ESTIVET: You tried to escape?

JOAN: Of course I did; and not for the first time either. If you leave the door of the cage open the bird will fly out.

D'ESTIVET (*rising*): That is a confession of heresy. I call the attention of the court to it.

JOAN: Heresy, he calls it! Am I a heretic because I try to escape from prison?

D'ESTIVET: Assuredly, if you are in the hands of the Church, and you wilfully take yourself out of its hands, you are deserting the Church; and that is heresy.

JOAN: It is great nonsense. Nobody could be such a fool as to think that.

D'ESTIVET: You hear, my lord, how I am reviled in the execution of my duty by this woman. (*He sits down indignantly.*)

CAUCHON: I have warned you before, Joan, that you are doing yourself no good by these pert answers.

JOAN: But you will not talk sense to me. I am reasonable if you will be reasonable.

THE INQUISITOR (*interposing*): This is not yet in order. You forget, Master Promoter, that the proceedings have not been formally opened. The time for questions is after she has sworn on the Gospels to tell us the whole truth.

JOAN: You say this to me every time. I have said again and again that I will tell you all that concerns this trial. But I cannot tell you the whole truth: God does not allow the whole truth to be told. You do not understand it when I tell it. It is an old saying that he who tells too much truth is sure to be hanged. I am weary of this argument: we have been over it nine times already. I have sworn as much as I will swear; and I will swear no more.

COURCELLES: My lord: she should be put to the torture.

THE INQUISITOR: You hear, Joan? That is what happens to the obdurate. Think before you answer. Has she been shewn the instruments?

THE EXECUTIONERS They are ready, my lord. She has seen them.

JOAN: If you tear me limb from limb until you separate my soul from my body you will get nothing out of me beyond what I have told you. What more is there to tell you could understand? Besides, I cannot bear to be hurt; and if you hurt me I will say anything you like to stop the pain. But I will take it all back afterwards; so what is the use of it?

LADVENU: There is much in that. We should proceed mercifully.

COURCELLES: But the torture is customary.

THE INQUISITOR: It must not be applied wantonly. If the accused will confess voluntarily, then its use cannot be justified.

COURCELLES: But this is unusual and irregular. She refuses to take the oath.

LADVENU (*disgusted*): Do you want to torture the girl for the mere pleasure of it?

COURCELLES (*bewildered*): But it is not a pleasure. It is the law. It is customary. It is always done.

THE INQUISITOR: That is not so, Master, except when the inquiries are carried on by people who do not know their legal business.

COURCELLES: But the woman is a heretic. I assure you it is always done.

CAUCHON (*decisively*): It will not be done today if it is not necessary. Let there be an end of this. I will not have it said that we proceeded on forced confessions. We have sent our best preachers and doctors to this woman to exhort and implore her to save her soul and body from the fire: we shall not now send the executioner to thrust her into it.

COURCELLES: Your lordship is merciful, of course. But it is a great responsibility to depart from the usual practice.

JOAN: Thou art a rare noodle, Master. Do what was done last time is thy rule, eh?

COURCELLES (*rising*): Thou wanton: dost thou dare call me noodle?

THE INQUISITOR: Patience, Master, patience: I fear you will soon be only too terribly avenged.

COURCELLES (*mutters*): Noodle indeed! (*He sits down, much discontented.*)

THE INQUISITOR: Meanwhile, let us not be moved by the rough side of a shepherd lass's tongue.

JOAN: Nay: I am no shepherd lass, though I have helped with the sheep like anyone else. I will do a lady's work in the house—spin or weave—against any woman in Rouen.

THE INQUISITOR: This is not a time for vanity, Joan. You stand in great peril.

JOAN: I know it: have I not been punished for my vanity? If I had not worn my cloth of gold surcoat in battle like a fool, that Burgundian soldier would never have pulled me backwards off my horse; and I should not have been here.

THE CHAPLAIN: If you are so clever at woman's work why do you not stay at home and do it?

JOAN: There are plenty of other women to do it; but there is nobody to do my work.

CAUCHON: Come! we are wasting time on trifles. Joan: I am going to put a most solemn question to you. Take care how you answer; for your life and salvation are at stake on it. Will you for all you have said and done, be it good or bad, accept the judgment of God's Church on earth? More especially as to the acts and words that are imputed to you in this trial by the Promoter here, will you submit your case to the inspired interpretation of the Church Militant?

JOAN: I am a faithful child of the Church. I will obey the Church—

CAUCHON (*hopefully leaning forward*): You will?

JOAN: —provided it does not command anything impossible.

(CAUCHON *sinks back in his chair with a heavy sigh. The* INQUISITOR *purses his lips and frowns.* LADVENU *shakes his head pitifully.*)

D'ESTIVET: She imputes to the Church the error and folly of commanding the impossible.

JOAN: If you command me to declare that all that I have done and said, and all the visions and revelations I have had, were not from God, then that is impossible: I will not declare it for anything in the world. What God made me do I will never go back on; and what He has commanded or shall command I will not fail to do in spite of any man alive. That is what I mean by impossible. And in case the Church should bid me do anything contrary to the command I have from God, I will not consent to it, no matter what it may be.

THE ASSESSORS (*shocked and indignant*): Oh! The Church contrary to God! What do you say now? Flat heresy. This is beyond everything, etc., etc.

D'ESTIVET (*throwing down his brief*): My lord: do you need anything more than this?

CAUCHON: Woman: you have said enough to burn ten heretics. Will you not be warned? Will you not understand?

THE INQUISITOR: If the Church Militant tells you that your revelations and visions are sent by the devil to tempt you to your damnation, will you not believe that the Church is wiser than you?

JOAN: I believe that God is wiser than I; and it is His commands that I will do. All the things that you call my crimes have come to me by the command of God. I say that I have done them by the order of God: it is impossible for me to say anything else. If any Churchman says the contrary I shall not mind him: I shall mind God alone, whose command I always follow.

LADVENU (*pleading with her urgently*): You do not know what you are saying, child. Do you want to kill yourself? Listen. Do you not believe that you are subject to the Church of God on earth?

JOAN: Yes. When have I ever denied it?

LADVENU: Good. That means, does it not, that you are subject to our Lord the Pope, to the cardinals, the archbishops, and the bishops for whom his lordship stands here today?

JOAN: God must be served first.

D'ESTIVET: Then your voices command you not to submit yourself to the Church Militant?

JOAN: My voices do not tell me to disobey the Church; but God must be served first.

CAUCHON: And you, and not the Church, are to be the judge?

JOAN: What other judgment can I judge by but my own?

THE ASSESSORS (*scandalized*): Oh! (*They cannot find words*).

CAUCHON: Out of your own mouth you have condemned yourself. We have striven for your salvation to the verge of sinning ourselves: we have opened the door to you again and again; and you have shut it in our faces and in the face of God. Dare you pretend, after what you have said, that you are in a state of grace?

JOAN: If I am not, may God bring me to it: if I am, may God keep me in it!

LADVENU: That is a very good reply, my lord.

COURCELLES: Were you in a state of grace when you stole the Bishop's horse?

CAUCHON (*rising in a fury*): Oh, devil take the Bishop's horse and you too! We are here to try a case of heresy; and no sooner do we come to the root of the matter than we are thrown back by idiots who understand nothing but horses.

(*Trembling with rage, he forces himself to sit down.*)

THE INQUISITOR: Gentlemen, gentlemen: in clinging to these small issues you are The Maid's best advocates. I am not surprised that his lordship has lost patience with you. What does the Promoter say? Does he press these trumpery matters?

D'ESTIVET: I am bound by my office to press everything; but when the woman confesses a heresy that must bring upon her the doom of excommunication, of what consequence is it that she has been guilty also of offences which expose her to minor penances? I share the impatience of his lordship as to these minor charges. Only, with great respect, I must emphasize the gravity of two very horrible and blasphemous crimes which she does not deny. First, she has intercourse with evil spirits, and is therefore a sorceress. Second, she wears men's clothes, which is indecent, unnatural, and abominable; and in spite of our most earnest remonstrances and entreaties, she will not change them even to receive the sacrament.

JOAN: Is the blessed St Catherine an evil spirit? Is St Margaret? Is Michael the Archangel?

COURCELLES: How do you know that the spirit which appears to you is an archangel? Does he not appear to you as a naked man?

JOAN: Do you think God cannot afford clothes for him?

(The ASSESSORS *cannot help smiling, especially as the joke is against* COURCELLES.*)*

LADVENU: Well answered, Joan.

THE INQUISITOR: It is, in effect, well answered. But no evil spirit would be so simple as to appear to a young girl in a guise that would scandalize her when he meant her to take him for a messenger from the Most High. Joan: the Church instructs you that these apparitions are demons seeking your soul's perdition. Do you accept the instruction of the Church?

JOAN: I accept the messenger of God. How could any faithful believer in the Church refuse him?

CAUCHON: Wretched woman: again I ask you, do you know what you are saying?

THE INQUISITOR: You wrestle in vain with the devil for her soul, my lord: she will not be saved. Now as to this matter of the man's dress. For the last time, will you put off that impudent attire, and dress as becomes your sex?

JOAN: I will not.

D'ESTIVET *(pouncing)*: The sin of disobedience, my lord.

JOAN *(distressed)*: But my voices tell me I must dress as a soldier.

LADVENU: Joan, Joan: does not that prove to you that the voices are the voices of evil spirits? Can you suggest to us one good reason why an angel of God should give you such shameless advice?

JOAN: Why, yes: what can be plainer commonsense? I was a soldier living among soldiers. I am a prisoner guarded by soldiers. If I were to dress as a woman they would think of me as a woman; and then what would become of me? If I dress as a soldier they think of me as a soldier, and I can live with them as I do at home with my brothers. That is why St Catherine tells me I must not dress as a woman until she gives me leave.

COURCELLES: When will she give you leave?

JOAN: When you take me out of the hands of the English soldiers. I have told you that I should be in the hands of the Church, and not left night and day with four soldiers of the Earl of Warwick. Do you want me to live with them in petticoats?

LADVENU: My lord: what she says is, God knows, very wrong and shocking; but there is a grain of worldly sense in it such as might impose on a simple village maiden.

JOAN: If we were as simple in the village as you are in your courts and palaces, there would soon be no wheat to make bread for you.

CAUCHON: That is the thanks you get for trying to save her, Brother Martin.

LADVENU: Joan: we are all trying to save you. His lordship is trying to save you. The Inquisitor could not be more just to you if you were his own daughter. But you are blinded by a terrible pride and self-sufficiency.

JOAN: Why do you say that? I have said nothing wrong. I cannot understand.

THE INQUISITOR: The blessed St Athanasius has laid it down in his creed that those who cannot understand are damned. It is not enough to be simple. It is not enough even to be what simple people call good. The simplicity of a darkened mind is no better than the simplicity of a beast.

JOAN: There is great wisdom in the simplicity of a beast, let me tell you; and sometimes great foolishness in the wisdom of scholars.

LADVENU: We know that, Joan: we are not so foolish as you think us. Try to resist the temptation to make pert replies to us. Do you see that man who stands behind you (*he indicates the* EXECUTIONER)?

JOAN (*turning and looking at the man*): Your torturer? But the Bishop said I was not to be tortured.

LADVENU: You are not to be tortured because you have confessed everything that is necessary to your condemnation. That man is not only the torturer: he is also the Executioner. Executioner: let The Maid hear your answers to my questions. Are you prepared for the burning of a heretic this day?

THE EXECUTIONER: Yes, Master.

LADVENU: Is the stake ready?

THE EXECUTIONER: It is. In the market-place. The English have built it too high for me to get near her and make the death easier. It will be a cruel death.

JOAN (*horrified*): But you are not going to burn me now?

THE INQUISITOR: You realize it at last.

LADVENU: There are eight hundred English soldiers waiting to take you to the market-place the moment the sentence of excommunication has passed the lips of your judges. You are within a few short moments of that doom.

JOAN (*looking round desperately for rescue*): Oh God!

LADVENU: Do not despair, Joan. The Church is merciful. You can save yourself.

JOAN (*hopefully*): Yes: my voices promised me I should not be burnt. St Catherine bade me be bold.

CAUCHON: Woman: are you quite mad? Do you not yet see that your voices have deceived you?

JOAN: Oh no: that is impossible.

CAUCHON: Impossible! They have led you straight to your excommunication, and to the stake which is there waiting for you.

LADVENU (*pressing the point hard*): Have they kept a single promise to you since you were taken at Compiègne? The devil has betrayed you. The Church holds out its arms to you.

JOAN (*despairing*): Oh, it is true: it is true: my voices have deceived me. I have been mocked by devils: my faith is broken. I have dared and dared; but only a fool will walk into a fire: God, who gave me my commonsense, cannot will me to do that.

LADVENU: Now God be praised that He has saved you at the eleventh hour! (*He hurries to the vacant seat at the scribes' table, and snatches a sheet of paper, on which he sets to work writing eagerly.*)

CAUCHON: Amen!

JOAN: What must I do?

CAUCHON: You must sign a solemn recantation of your heresy.

JOAN: Sign? That means to write my name. I cannot write.

CAUCHON: You have signed many letters before.

JOAN: Yes; but someone held my hand and guided the pen. I can make my mark.

THE CHAPLAIN (*who has been listening with growing alarm and indignation*): My lord: do you mean that you are going to allow this woman to escape us?

THE INQUISITOR: The law must take its course, Master de Stogumber. And you know the law.

THE CHAPLAIN (*rising, purple with fury*): I know that there is no faith in a Frenchman. (*Tumult, which he shouts down.*) I know what my lord the Cardinal of Winchester will say when he hears of this. I know what the Earl of Warwick will do when he learns that you intend to betray him. There are eight hundred men at the gate who will see that this abominable witch is burnt in spite of your teeth.

THE ASSESSORS (*meanwhile*): What is this? What did he say? He accuses us of treachery! This is past bearing. No faith in a Frenchman! Did you hear that? This is an intolerable fellow. Who is he? Is this what English Churchmen are like? He must be mad or drunk, etc., etc.

THE INQUISITOR (*rising*): Silence, pray! Gentlemen: pray silence! Master

Chaplain: bethink you a moment of your holy office: of what you are, and where you are. I direct you to sit down.

THE CHAPLAIN (*folding his arms doggedly, his face working convulsively*): I will NOT sit down.

CAUCHON: Master Inquisitor: this man has called me a traitor to my face before now.

THE CHAPLAIN: So you are a traitor. You are all traitors. You have been doing nothing but begging this damnable witch on your knees to recant all through this trial.

THE INQUISITOR (*placidly resuming his seat*): If you will not sit, you must stand: that is all.

THE CHAPLAIN: I will NOT stand (*he flings himself back into his chair*).

LADVENU (*rising with the paper in his hand*): My lord: here is the form of recantation for The Maid to sign.

CAUCHON: Read it to her.

JOAN: Do not trouble. I will sign it.

THE INQUISITOR: Woman: you must know what you are putting your hand to. Read it to her, Brother Martin. And let all be silent.

LADVENU (*reading quietly*): 'I, Joan, commonly called The Maid, a miserable sinner, do confess that I have most grievously sinned in the following articles. I have pretended to have revelations from God and the angels and the blessed saints, and perversely rejected the Church's warnings that these were temptations by demons. I have blasphemed abominably by wearing an immodest dress, contrary to the Holy Scripture and the canons of the Church. Also I have clipped my hair in the style of a man, and, against all the duties which have made my sex specially acceptable in heaven, have taken up the sword, even to the shedding of human blood, inciting men to slay each other, invoking evil spirits to delude them, and stubbornly and most blasphemously imputing these sins to Almighty God. I confess to the sin of sedition, to the sin of idolatry, to the sin of disobedience, to the sin of pride, and to the sin of heresy. All of which sins I now renounce and abjure and depart from, humbly thanking you Doctors and Masters who have brought me back to the truth and into the grace of our Lord. And I will never return to my errors, but will remain in communion with our Holy Church and in obedience to our Holy Father the Pope of Rome. All this I swear by God Almighty and the Holy Gospels, in witness whereto I sign my name to this recantation.'

THE INQUISITOR: You understand this, Joan?

JOAN (*listless*): It is plain enough, sir.

THE INQUISITOR: And it is true?

JOAN: It may be true. If it were not true, the fire would not be ready for me in the market-place.

LADVENU (*taking up his pen and a book, and going to her quickly lest she should compromise herself again*). Come, child: let me guide your hand. Take the pen. (*She does so; and they begin to write, using the book as a desk*) J.E.H.A.N.E. So. Now make your mark by yourself.

JOAN (*makes her mark, and gives him back the pen, tormented by the rebellion of her soul against her mind and body*): There!

LADVENU (*replacing the pen on the table, and handing the recantation to* CAUCHON *with a reverence*): Praise be to God, my brothers, the lamb has returned to the flock; and the shepherd rejoices in her more than in ninety and nine just persons. (*He returns to his seat.*)

THE INQUISITOR (*taking the paper from* CAUCHON): We declare thee by this act set free from the danger of excommunication in which thou stoodest. (*He throws the paper down to the table.*)

JOAN: I thank you.

THE INQUISITOR: But because thou has sinned most presumptuously against God and the Holy Church, and that thou mayst repent thy errors in solitary contemplation, and be shielded from all temptation to return to them, we, for the good of thy soul, and for a penance that may wipe out thy sins and bring thee finally unspotted to the throne of grace, do condemn thee to eat the bread of sorrow and drink the water of affliction to the end of thy earthly days in perpetual imprisonment.

JOAN (*rising in consternation and terrible anger*): Perpetual imprisonment! Am I not then to be set free?

LADVENU (*mildly shocked*): Set free, child, after such wickedness as yours! What are you dreaming of?

JOAN: Give me that writing. (*She rushes to the table; snatches up the paper; and tears it into fragments*): Light your fire: do you think I dread it as much as the life of a rat in a hole? My voices were right.

LADVENU: Joan! Joan!

JOAN: Yes: they told me you were fools (*the word gives great offence*), and that I was not to listen to your fine words nor trust to your charity. You promised me my life; but you lied (*indignant exclamations*). You think that life is nothing but not being stone dead. It is not the bread and water I fear: I can live on bread: when have I asked for more? It is no hardship to drink water if the water be clean. Bread has no sorrow for me, and water no affliction. But to shut me from the light of the sky and the sight of the fields and flowers; to chain my feet so that I can never again ride with the soldiers nor climb the hills; to make me breathe foul damp darkness, and keep from me everything that brings me back to the love of God when your wickedness and foolishness tempt me to hate Him: all this is worse than the furnace in the Bible that was heated seven times. I could do without my war-horse; I could drag about in a skirt; I could let the banners and the trumpets and the knights and soldiers pass me and leave me behind as they leave the other women, if only I could still hear the wind in the trees, the larks in the sunshine, the young lambs crying through the healthy frost, and the blessed blessed church bells that send my angel voices floating to me on the wind. But without these things I cannot live; and by your wanting to take them away from me, or from any human creature, I know that your counsel is of the devil, and that mine is of God.

THE ASSESSORS (*in great commotion*): Blasphemy! blasphemy! She is possessed. She said our counsel was of the devil. And hers of God. Monstrous! The devil is in our midst, etc., etc.

D'ESTIVET (*shouting above the din*): She is a relapsed heretic, obstinate, incorrigible, and altogether unworthy of the mercy we have shewn her I call for her excommunication.

THE CHAPLAIN (*to the* EXECUTIONER): Light your fire, man. To the stake with her.

(*The* EXECUTIONER *and his* ASSISTANTS *hurry out through the courtyard.*)

LADVENU: You wicked girl: if your counsel were of God would He not deliver you?

JOAN: His ways are not your ways. He wills that I go through the fire to his bosom; for I am His child, and you are not fit that I should live among you. That is my last word to you.

(*The* SOLDIERS *seize her.*)

CAUCHON (*rising*): Not yet.

(*They wait. There is a dead silence.* CAUCHON *turns to the* INQUISITOR *with an inquiring look. The* INQUISITOR *nods affirmatively. They rise solemnly, and intone the sentence antiphonally.*)

CAUCHON: We decree that thou art a relapsed heretic.
THE INQUISITOR: Cast out from the unity of the Church.
CAUCHON: Sundered from her body.
THE INQUISITOR: Infected with the leprosy of heresy.
CAUCHON: A member of Satan.
THE INQUISITOR: We declare that thou must be excommunicate.
CAUCHON: And now we do cast thee out, segregate thee, and abandon thee to the secular power.
THE INQUISITOR: Admonishing the same secular power that it moderate its judgment of thee in respect of death and division of the limbs. (*He resumes his seat.*)
CAUCHON: And if any true sign of penitence appear in thee, to permit

our Brother Martin to administer to thee the sacrament of penance.

THE CHAPLAIN: Into the fire with the witch (*he rushes at her, and helps the* SOLDIERS *to push her out*).

(JOAN *is taken away through the courtyard. The* ASSESSORS *rise in disorder, and follow the* SOLDIERS, *except* LADVENU, *who has hidden his face in his hands.*)

CAUCHON (*rising again in the act of sitting down*): No, no: this is irregular. The representative of the secular arm should be here to receive her from us.

THE INQUISITOR (*also on his feet again*): That man is an incorrigible fool.

CAUCHON: Brother Martin: see that everything is done in order.

LADVENU: My place is at her side, my Lord. You must exercise your own authority. (*He hurries out.*)

CAUCHON: These English are impossible: they will thrust her straight into the fire. Look!

(*He points to the courtyard, in which the glow and flicker of fire can now be seen reddening the May daylight. Only the* BISHOP *and the* INQUISITOR *are left in the court.*)

CAUCHON (*turning to go*): We must stop that.

THE INQUISITOR (*calmly*): Yes; but not too fast, my lord.

CAUCHON (*halting*): But there is not a moment to lose.

THE INQUISITOR: We have proceeded in perfect order. If the English choose to put themselves in the wrong, it is not our business to put them in the right. A flaw in the procedure may be useful later on: one never knows. And the sooner it is over, the better for that poor girl.

CAUCHON (*relaxing*): That is true. But I suppose we must see this dreadful thing through.

THE INQUISITOR: One gets used to it. Habit is everything. I am accustomed to the fire: it is soon over. But it is a terrible thing to see a young and innocent creature crushed between these mighty forces, the Church and the Law.

CAUCHON: You call her innocent!

THE INQUISITOR: Oh, quite innocent. What does she know of the Church and the Law? She did not understand a word we were saying. It is the ignorant who suffer. Come, or we shall be late for the end.

CAUCHON (*going with him*): I shall not be sorry if we are: I am not so accustomed as you.

(*They are going out when* WARWICK *comes in, meeting them.*)

WARWICK: Oh, I am intruding. I thought it was all over. (*He makes a feint of retiring.*)

CAUCHON: Do not go, my lord. It is all over.

THE INQUISITOR: The execution is not in our hands, my lord; but it is desirable that we should witness the end. So by your leave—(*He bows, and goes out through the courtyard.*)
CAUCHON: There is some doubt whether your people have observed the forms of law, my lord.
WARWICK: I am told that there is some doubt whether your authority runs in this city, my lord. It is not in your diocese. However, if you will answer for that I will answer for the rest.
CAUCHON: It is to God that we both must answer. Good morning, my lord.
WARWICK: My lord: good morning.

(*They look at one another for a moment with unconcealed hostility. Then* CAUCHON *follows the* INQUISITOR *out.* WARWICK *looks round. Finding himself alone, he calls for attendance.*)

WARWICK: Hallo: some attendance here! (*Silence.*) Hallo, there! (*Silence.*) Hallo! Brian, you young blackguard, where are you? (*Silence.*) Guard! (*Silence*). They have all gone to see the burning: even that child.

(*The silence is broken by someone frantically howling and sobbing.*)

WARWICK: What in the devil's name—?

(*The* CHAPLAIN *staggers in from the courtyard like a demented creature, his face streaming with tears, making the piteous sounds that* WARWICK *has heard. He stumbles to the prisoner's stool, and throws himself upon it with heartrending sobs.*)

WARWICK (*going to him and patting him on the shoulder*): What is it, Master John? What is the matter?
THE CHAPLAIN (*clutching at his hand*): My lord, my lord: for Christ's sake pray for my wretched guilty soul.
WARWICK (*soothing him*): Yes, yes: of course I will. Calmly, gently—
THE CHAPLAIN (*blubbering miserably*): I am not a bad man, my lord.
WARWICK: No, no: not at all.
THE CHAPLAIN: I meant no harm. I did not know what it would be like.
WARWICK (*hardening*): Oh! You saw it, then?
THE CHAPLAIN: I did not know what I was doing. I am a hotheaded fool; and I shall be damned to all eternity for it.
WARWICK: Nonsense! Very distressing, no doubt; but it was not your doing.
THE CHAPLAIN (*lamentably*): I let them do it. If I had known, I would have torn her from their hands. You dont know: you havnt seen: it is so easy to talk when you dont know. You madden yourself with words: you damn yourself because it feels grand to throw oil on the

flaming hell of your own temper. But when it is brought home to you; when you see the thing you have done; when it is blinding your eyes, stifling your nostrils, tearing your heart, then—then—(*Falling on his knees*) O God, take away this sight from me! O Christ, deliver me from this fire that is consuming me! She cried to Thee in the midst of it: Jesus! Jesus! Jesus! She is in Thy bosom; and I am in hell for evermore.

WARWICK (*summarily hauling him to his feet*): Come come, man! you must pull yourself together. We shall have the whole town talking of this. (*He throws him not too gently into a chair at the table.*) If you have not the nerve to see these things, why do you not do as I do, and stay away?

THE CHAPLAIN (*bewildered and submissive*): She asked for a cross. A soldier gave her two sticks tied together. Thank God he was an Englishman! I might have done it; but I did not: I am a coward, a mad dog, a fool. But he was an Englishman too.

WARWICK: The fool! they will burn him too if the priests get hold of him.

THE CHAPLAIN (*shaken with a convulsion*): Some of the people laughed at her. They would have laughed at Christ. They were French people, my lord: I know they were French.

WARWICK: Hush! someone is coming. Control yourself.

(LADVENU *comes back through the courtyard to* WARWICK'S *right hand, carrying a bishop's cross which he has taken from a church. He is very grave and composed.*)

WARWICK: I am informed that it is all over, Brother Martin.

LADVENU (*enigmatically*): We do not know, my lord. It may have only just begun.

WARWICK: What does that mean, exactly?

LADVENU: I took this cross from the church for her that she might see it to the last: she had only two sticks that she put into her bosom. When the fire crept round us, and she saw that if I held the cross before her I should be burnt myself, she warned me to get down and save myself. My lord: a girl who could think of another's danger in such a moment was not inspired by the devil. When I had to snatch the cross from her sight, she looked up to heaven. And I do not believe that the heavens were empty. I firmly believe that her Savior appeared to her then in His tenderest glory. She called to Him and died. This is not the end for her, but the beginning.

WARWICK: I am afraid it will have a bad effect on the people.

LADVENU: It had, my lord, on some of them. I heard laughter. Forgive me for saying that I hope and believe it was English laughter.

THE CHAPLAIN (*rising frantically*): No: it was not. There was only one

Englishman there that disgraced his country; and that was the mad dog, de Stogumber. (*He rushes wildly out, shrieking.*) Let them torture him. Let them burn him. I will go pray among her ashes. I am no better than Judas: I will hang myself.

WARWICK: Quick, Brother Martin: follow him: he will do himself some mischief. After him, quick.

(LADVENU *hurries out,* WARWICK *urging him. The* EXECUTIONER *comes in by the door behind the judges' chairs; and* WARWICK, *returning, finds himself face to face with him.*)

WARWICK: Well, fellow: who are you?

THE EXECUTIONER (*with dignity*): I am not addressed as fellow, my lord. I am the Master Executioner of Rouen: it is a highly skilled mystery. I am come to tell your lordship that your orders have been obeyed.

WARWICK: I crave your pardon, Master Executioner; and I will see that you lose nothing by having no relics to sell. I have your word, have I, that nothing remains, not a bone, not a nail, not a hair?

THE EXECUTIONER: Her heart would not burn, my lord; but everything that was left is at the bottom of the river. You have heard the last of her.

WARWICK (*with a wry smile, thinking of what* LADVENU *said*): The last of her? Hm! I wonder!

EPILOGUE

(A restless fitfully windy night in June 1456, full of summer lightning after many days of heat. KING CHARLES THE SEVENTH OF FRANCE, formerly Joan's DAUPHIN, now CHARLES THE VICTORIOUS, aged 51, is in bed in one of his royal chateaux. The bed, raised on a dais of two steps, is towards the side of the room so as to avoid blocking a tall lancet window in the middle. Its canopy bears the royal arms in embroidery. Except for the canopy and the huge down pillows there is nothing to distinguish it from a broad settee with bed-clothes and a valance. Thus its occupant is in full view from the foot.

CHARLES is not asleep: he is reading in bed, or rather looking at the pictures in Fouquet's Boccaccio with his knees doubled up to make a reading-desk. Beside the bed on his left is a little table with a picture of the Virgin, lighted by candles of painted wax. The walls are hung from ceiling to floor with painted curtains which stir at times in the draughts. At first glance the prevailing yellow and red in these hanging pictures is somewhat flamelike when the folds breathe in the wind.

The door is on CHARLES's left, but in front of him close to the corner farthest from him. A large watchman's rattle, handsomely designed and gaily painted, is in the bed under his hand.

CHARLES turns a leaf. A distant clock strikes the half-hour softly. CHARLES shuts the book with a clap; throws it aside; snatches up the rattle; and whirls it energetically, making a deafening clatter. LADVENU enters, 25 years older, strange and stark in bearing, and still carrying the cross from Rouen. CHARLES evidently does not expect him; for he springs out of bed on the farther side from the door.)

CHARLES: Who are you? Where is my gentleman of the bedchamber? What do you want?

LADVENU (*solemnly*): I bring you glad tidings of great joy. Rejoice, O king; for the taint is removed from your blood, and the stain from your crown. Justice, long delayed, is at last triumphant.

CHARLES: What are you talking about? Who are you?

LADVENU: I am Brother Martin.

CHARLES: And who, saving your reverence, may Brother Martin be?

LADVENU: I held this cross when The Maid perished in the fire. Twenty-five years have passed since then: nearly ten thousand days. And on every one of those days I have prayed to God to justify His daughter on earth as she is justified in heaven.

CHARLES (*reassured, sitting down on the foot of the bed*): Oh, I remember now. I have heard of you. You have a bee in your bonnet about The Maid. Have you been at the inquiry?

LADVENU: I have given my testimony.

CHARLES: Is it over?

LADVENU: It is over.

CHARLES: Satisfactorily?

LADVENU: The ways of God are very strange.

CHARLES: How so?

LADVENU: At the trial which sent a saint to the stake as a heretic and a sorceress, the truth was told; the law was upheld; mercy was shewn beyond all custom; no wrong was done but the final and dreadful wrong of the lying sentence and the pitiless fire. At this inquiry from which I have just come, there was shameless perjury, courtly corruption, calumny of the dead who did their duty according to their lights, cowardly evasion of the issue, testimony made of idle tales that could not impose on a ploughboy. Yet out of this insult to justice, this defamation of the Church, this orgy of lying and foolishness, the truth is set in the noonday sun on the hilltop; the white robe of innocence is cleansed from the smirch of the burning faggots; the holy life is sanctified; the true heart that lived through the flame is consecrated; a great lie is silenced for ever; and a great wrong is set right before all men.

CHARLES: My friend: provided they can no longer say that I was crowned by a witch and a heretic, I shall not fuss about how the trick has been done. Joan would not have fussed about it if it came all right in the end: she was not that sort: I knew her. Is her rehabilitation complete? I made it pretty clear that there was to be no nonsense about it.

LADVENU: It is solemnly declared that her judges were full of corruption, cozenage, fraud, and malice. Four falsehoods.

CHARLES: Never mind the falsehoods: her judges are dead.

LADVENU: The sentence on her is broken, annulled, annihilated, set aside as non-existent, without value or effect.

CHARLES: Good. Nobody can challenge my consecration now, can they?

LADVENU: Not Charlemagne nor King David himself was more sacredly crowned.

CHARLES (*rising*): Excellent. Think of what that means to me!

LADVENU: I think of what it means to her!

CHARLES: You cannot. None of us ever knew what anything meant to her. She was like nobody else; and she must take care of herself wherever she is; for *I* cannot take care of her; and neither can you, whatever you may think: you are not big enough. But I will tell you this about her. If you could bring her back to life, they would burn her again within six months, for all their present adoration of her. And you would hold up the cross, too, just the same. So (*crossing himself*) let her rest; and let you and I mind our own business, and not meddle with hers.

LADVENU: God forbid that I should have no share in her, nor she in me! (*He turns and strides out as he came, saying*) Henceforth my path will not lie through palaces, nor my conversation be with kings.

CHARLES (*following him towards the door, and shouting after him*): Much good may it do you, holy man! (*He returns to the middle of the chamber, where he halts, and says quizzically to himself*) That was a funny chap. How did he get in? Where are my people? (*He goes impatiently to the bed, and swings the rattle. A rush of wind through the open door sets the walls swaying agitatedly. The candles go out. He calls in the darkness*) Hallo! Someone come and shut the windows: everything is being blown all over the place. (*A flash of summer lightning shews up the lancet window. A figure is seen in silhouette against it*) Who is there? Who is that? Help! Murder! (*Thunder. He jumps into bed, and hides under the clothes.*)

JOAN'S VOICE: Easy, Charlie, easy. What art making all that noise for? No one can hear thee. Thourt asleep. (*She is dimly seen in a pallid greenish light by the bedside.*)

CHARLES (*peeping out*): Joan! Are you a ghost, Joan?

JOAN: Hardly even that, lad. Can a poor burnt-up lass have a ghost? I am but a dream that thourt dreaming. (*The light increases: they become plainly visible as he sits up*) Thou looks older, lad.

CHARLES: I am older. Am I really asleep?

JOAN: Fallen asleep over thy silly book.

CHARLES: That's funny.

JOAN: Not so funny as that I am dead, is it?

CHARLES: Are you really dead?

JOAN: As dead as anybody ever is, laddie. I am out of the body.

CHARLES: Just fancy! Did it hurt much?

JOAN: Did what hurt much?

CHARLES: Being burnt.

JOAN: Oh, that! I cannot remember very well. I think it did at first; but then it all got mixed up; and I was not in my right mind until I was free of the body. But do not thou go handling fire and thinking it will not hurt thee. How hast been ever since?

CHARLES: Oh, not so bad. Do you know, I actually lead my army out and win battles? Down into the moat up to my waist in mud and blood. Up the ladders with the stones and hot pitch raining down. Like you.

JOAN: No! Did I make a man of thee after all, Charlie?

CHARLES: I am Charles the Victorious now. I had to be brave because you were. Agnes put a little pluck into me too.

JOAN: Agnes! Who was Agnes?

CHARLES: Agnes Sorel. A woman I fell in love with. I dream of her often. I never dreamed of you before.

JOAN: Is she dead, like me?

CHARLES: Yes. But she was not like you. She was very beautiful.

JOAN (*laughing heartily*): Ha ha! I was no beauty: I was always a rough one: a regular soldier. I might almost as well have been a man. Pity I wasnt: but I should not have bothered you all so much then. But my head was in the skies; and the glory of God was upon me; and, man or woman, I should have bothered you as long as your noses were in the mud. Now tell me what has happened since you wise men knew no better than to make a heap of cinders of me?

CHARLES: Your mother and brothers have sued the courts to have your case tried over again. And the courts have declared that your judges were full of corruption and cozenage, fraud and malice.

JOAN: Not they. They were as honest a lot of poor fools as ever burned their betters.

CHARLES: The sentence on you is broken, annihilated, annulled: null, non-existent, without value or effect.

JOAN: I was burned, all the same. Can they unburn me?

CHARLES: If they could, they would think twice before they did it. But they have decreed that a beautiful cross be placed where the stake stood, for your perpetual memory and for your salvation.

JOAN: It is the memory and the salvation that sanctify the cross, not the cross that sanctifies the memory and the salvation. *(She turns away, forgetting him)* I shall outlast that cross. I shall be remembered when men will have forgotten where Rouen stood.

CHARLES: There you go with your self-conceit, the same as ever! I think you might say a word of thanks to me for having had justice done at last.

CAUCHON *(appearing at the window between them)*: Liar!

CHARLES: Thank you.

JOAN: Why, if it isnt Peter Cauchon! How are you, Peter? What luck have you had since you burned me?

CAUCHON: None. I arraign the justice of Man. It is not the justice of God.

JOAN: Still dreaming of justice, Peter? See what justice came to with me! But what has happened to thee? Art dead or alive?

CAUCHON: Dead. Dishonored. They pursued me beyond the grave. They excommunicated my dead body: they dug it up and flung it into the common sewer.

JOAN: Your dead body did not feel the spade and the sewer as my live body felt the fire.

CAUCHON: But this thing that they have done against me hurts justice: destroys faith; saps the foundation of the Church. The solid earth sways like the treacherous sea beneath the feet of men and spirits alike when the innocent are slain in the name of law, and their wrongs are undone by slandering the pure of heart.

JOAN: Well, well, Peter, I hope men will be the better for remembering me; and they would not remember me so well if you had not burned me.

CAUCHON: They will be the worse for remembering me: they will see in me evil triumphing over good, falsehood over truth, cruelty over mercy, hell over heaven. Their courage will rise as they think of you, only to faint as they think of me. Yet God is my witness I was just: I was merciful: I was faithful to my light: I could do no other than I did.

CHARLES *(scrambling out of the sheets and enthroning himself on the side of the bed)*: Yes: it is always you good men that do the big mischiefs. Look at me! I am not Charles the Good, nor Charles the Wise, nor Charles the Bold. Joan's worshippers may even call me Charles the Coward because I did not pull her out of the fire. But I have done less harm than any of you. You people with your heads in the sky spend all your time trying to turn the world upside down; but I take the world as it is, and say that top-side-up is right-side-up; and I keep my nose pretty close to the ground. And I ask you, what king of France has done better, or been a better fellow in his little way?

JOAN: Art really king of France, Charlie? Be the English gone?

DUNOIS (*coming through the tapestry on* JOAN's *left, the candles relighting themselves at the same moment, and illuminating his armor and surcoat cheerfully*): I have kept my word: the English are gone.

JOAN: Praised be God! now is fair France a province in heaven. Tell me all about the fighting, Jack. Was it thou that led them? Wert thou God's captain to thy death?

DUNOIS: I am not dead. My body is very comfortably asleep in my bed at Chateaudun; but my spirit is called here by yours.

JOAN: And you fought them my way, Jack: eh? Not the old way, chaffering for ransoms; but The Maid's way: staking life against death, with the heart high and humble and void of malice, and nothing counting under God but France free and French. Was it my way, Jack?

DUNOIS: Faith, it was any way that would win. But the way that won was always your way. I give you best, lassie. I wrote a fine letter to set you right at the new trial. Perhaps I should never have let the priests burn you; but I was busy fighting; and it was the Church's business, not mine. There was no use in both of us being burned, was there?

CAUCHON: Ay! put the blame on the priests. But I, who am beyond praise and blame, tell you that the world is saved neither by its priests nor its soldiers, but by God and His Saints. The Church Militant sent this woman to the fire; but even as she burned, the flames whitened into the radiance of the Church Triumphant.

(*The clock strikes the third quarter. A rough male voice is heard trolling an improvised tune.*)

    Rum tum trumpledum,
    Bacon fat and rumpledum,
    Old Saint mumpledum,
    Pull his tail and stumpledum
     O my Ma—ry Ann!

(*A ruffianly English soldier comes through the curtains and marches between* DUNOIS *and* JOAN.)

DUNOIS: What villainous troubadour taught you that doggrel?

THE SOLDIER: No troubadour. We made it up ourselves as we marched. We were not gentlefolks and troubadours. Music straight out of the heart of the people, as you might say. Rum tum trumpledum, Bacon fat and rumpledum, Old Saint mumpledum, Pull his tail and stumpledum: that dont mean anything, you know; but it keeps you marching. Your servant, ladies and gentlemen. Who asked for a saint?

JOAN: Be you a saint?

THE SOLDIER: Yes, lady, straight from hell.

DUNOIS: A saint, and from hell!

THE SOLDIER: Yes, noble captain: I have a day off. Every year, you know. Thats my allowance for my one good action.

CAUCHON: Wretch! In all the years of your life did you do only one good action?

THE SOLDIER: I never thought about it: it came natural like. But they scored it up for me.

CHARLES: What was it?

THE SOLDIER: Why, the silliest thing you ever heard of. I—

JOAN (*interrupting him by strolling across to the bed, where she sits beside* CHARLES): He tied two sticks together, and gave them to a poor lass that was going to be burned.

THE SOLDIER: Right. Who told you that?

JOAN: Never mind. Would you know her if you saw her again?

THE SOLDIER: Not I. There are so many girls! and they all expect you to remember them as if there was only one in the world. This one must have been a prime sort; for I have a day off every year for her; and so, until twelve o'clock punctually, I am a saint, at your service, noble lords and lovely ladies.

CHARLES: And after twelve?

THE SOLDIER: After twelve, back to the only place fit for the likes of me.

JOAN (*rising*): Back there! You! that gave the lass the cross!

THE SOLDIER (*excusing his unsoldierly conduct*): Well, she asked for it; and they were going to burn her. She had as good a right to a cross as they had; and they had dozens of them. It was her funeral, not theirs. Where was the harm in it?

JOAN: Man: I am not reproaching you. But I cannot bear to think of you in torment.

THE SOLDIER (*cheerfully*): No great torment, lady. You see I was used to worse.

CHARLES: What! worse than hell?

THE SOLDIER: Fifteen years' service in the French wars. Hell was a treat after that.

(JOAN *throws up her arms, and takes refuge from despair of humanity before the picture of the Virgin.*)

THE SOLDIER (*continuing*): Suits me somehow. The day off was dull at first, like a wet Sunday. I dont mind it so much now. They tell me I can have as many as I like as soon as I want them.

CHARLES: What is hell like?

THE SOLDIER: You wont find it so bad, sir. Jolly. Like as if you were always drunk without the trouble and expense of drinking. Tip top company too: emperors and popes and kings and all sorts. They chip me about giving that young judy the cross; but I dont care: I stand up to them proper, and tell them that if she hadnt a better right to it than they, she'd be where they are. That dumbfounds them, that does. All they can do is gnash their teeth, hell fashion; and I just laugh, and go off singing the old chanty: Rum tum trumple—Hullo! Who's that knocking at the door?

(They listen. A long gentle knocking is heard.)

CHARLES: Come in.

(The door opens; and an old PRIEST, white-haired, bent, with a silly but benevolent smile, comes in and trots over to JOAN.)

THE NEWCOMER: Excuse me, gentle lords and ladies. Do not let me disturb you. Only a poor old harmless English rector. Formerly chaplain to the cardinal: to my lord of Winchester. John de Stogumber, at your service. *(He looks at them inquiringly)* Did you say anything? I am a little deaf, unfortunately. Also a little—well, not always in my right mind, perhaps; but still, it is a small village with a few simple people. I suffice: I suffice: they love me there; and I am able to do a little good. I am well connected, you see; and they indulge me.

JOAN: Poor old John! What, brought thee to this state?

DE STOGUMBER: I tell my folks they must be very careful. I say to them, 'If you only saw what you think about you would think quite differently about it. It would give you a great shock. Oh, a great shock.' And they all say 'Yes, parson: we all know you are a kind man, and would not harm a fly.' That is a great comfort to me. For I am not cruel by nature, you know.

THE SOLDIER: Who said you were?

DE STOGUMBER: Well, you see, I did a very cruel thing once because I did not know what cruelty was like. I had not seen it, you know. That is the great thing: you must see it. And then you are redeemed and saved.

CAUCHON: Were not the sufferings of our Lord Christ enough for you?

DE STOGUMBER: No. Oh no: not at all. I had seen them in pictures, and read of them in books, and been greatly moved by them, as I thought. But it was no use: it was not our Lord that redeemed me, but a young woman whom I saw actually burned to death. It was dreadful: oh, most dreadful. But it saved me. I have been a different man ever since, though a little astray in my wits sometimes.

CAUCHON: Must then a Christ perish in torment in every age to save those that have no imagination?

George Bernard Shaw: *Saint Joan*

JOAN: Well, if I saved all those he would have been cruel to if he had not been cruel to me, I was not burnt for nothing, was I?

DE STOGUMBER: Oh no; it was not you. My sight is bad: I cannot distinguish your features: but you are not she: oh no: she was burned to a cinder: dead and gone, dead and gone.

THE EXECUTIONER (*stepping from behind the bed curtains on* CHARLES's *right, the bed being between them*): She is more alive than you, old man. Her heart would not burn; and it would not drown. I was a master at my craft: better than the master of Paris, better than the master of Toulouse; but I could not kill The Maid. She is up and alive everywhere.

THE EARL OF WARWICK (*sallying from the bed curtains on the other side, and coming to* JOAN's *left hand*): Madani, my congratulations on your rehabilitation. I feel that I owe you an apology.

JOAN: Oh, please don't mention it.

WARWICK (*pleasantly*): The burning was purely political. There was no personal feeling against you, I assure you.

JOAN: I bear no malice, my lord.

WARWICK: Just so. Very kind of you to meet me in that way: a touch of true breeding. But I must insist on apologizing very amply. The truth is, these political necessities sometimes turn out to be political mistakes; and this one was a veritable howler; for your spirit conquered us, madam, in spite of our faggots. History will remember me for your sake, though the incidents of the connection were perhaps a little unfortunate.

JOAN: Ay, perhaps just a little, you funny man.

WARWICK: Still, when they make you a saint, you will owe your halo to me, just as this lucky monarch owes his crown to you.

JOAN (*turning from him*): I shall owe nothing to any man: I owe everything to the spirit of God that was within me. But fancy me a saint! What would St Catherine and St Margaret say if the farm girl was cocked up beside them!

(*A clerical-looking* GENTLEMAN *in black frockcoat and trousers, and tall hat, in the fashion of the year 1920, suddenly appears before them in the corner on their right. They all stare at him. Then they burst into uncontrollable laughter.*)

THE GENTLEMAN: Why this mirth, gentlemen?

WARWICK: I congratulate you on having invented a most extraordinarily comic dress.

THE GENTLEMAN: I do not understand. You are all in fancy dress: I am properly dressed.

DUNOIS: All dress is fancy dress, is it not, except our natural skins?

THE GENTLEMAN: Pardon me: I am here on serious business, and cannot engage in frivolous discussions. (*He takes out a paper, and assumes a dry official manner.*) I am sent to announce to you that Joan of Arc, formerly known as The Maid, having been the subject of an inquiry instituted by the Bishop of Orleans—

JOAN (*interrupting*): Ah! They remember me still in Orleans.

THE GENTLEMAN (*emphatically, to mark his indignation at the interruption*): — by the Bishop of Orleans into the claim of the said Joan of Arc to be canonized as a saint—

JOAN (*again interrupting*): But I never made any such claim.

THE GENTLEMAN (*as before*): —the Church has examined the claim exhaustively in the usual course, and having admitted the said Joan successively to the ranks of Venerable and Blessed, —

JOAN (*chuckling*): Me venerable!

THE GENTLEMAN: — has finally declared her to have been endowed with heroic virtues and favored with private revelations, and calls the said Venerable and Blessed Joan to the communion of the Church Triumphant as Saint Joan.

JOAN (*rapt*): Saint Joan!

THE GENTLEMAN: On every thirtieth day of May, being the anniversary of the death of the said most blessed daughter of God, there shall in every Catholic church to the end of time be celebrated a special office in commemoration of her; and it shall be lawful to dedicate a special chapel to her, and to place her image on its altar in every such church. And it shall be lawful and laudable for the faithful to kneel and address their prayers through her to the Mercy Seat.

JOAN: Oh no. It is for the saint to kneel. (*She falls on her knees, still rapt*).

THE GENTLEMAN (*putting up his paper, and retiring beside the* EXECUTIONER): In Basilica Vaticana, the sixteenth day of May, nineteen hundred and twenty.

DUNOIS (*raising* JOAN): Half an hour to burn you, dear Saint, and four centuries to find out the truth about you!

DE STOGUMBER: Sir, I was chaplain to the Cardinal of Winchester once. They always would call him the Cardinal of England. It would be a great comfort to me and to my master to see a fair statue to The Maid in Winchester Cathedral. Will they put one there, do you think?

THE GENTLEMAN: As the building is temporarily in the hands of the Anglican heresy, I cannot answer for that.

(*A vision of the statue in Winchester Cathedral is seen through the window.*)

DE STOGUMBER: Oh look! look! that is Winchester.

JOAN: Is that meant to be me? I was stiffer on my feet.

(*The vision fades.*)

THE GENTLEMAN: I have been requested by the temporal authorities of France to mention that the multiplication of public statues to The Maid threatens to become an obstruction to traffic. I do so as a matter of courtesy to the said authorities, but must point out on behalf of the Church that The Maid's horse is no greater obstruction to traffic than any other horse.
JOAN: Eh! I am glad they have not forgotten my horse.
(A vision of the statue before Rheims Cathedral appears.)
JOAN: Is that funny little thing me too?
CHARLES: That is Rheims Cathedral where you had me crowned. It must be you.
JOAN: Who has broken my sword? My sword was never broken. It is the sword of France.
DUNOIS: Never mind. Swords can be mended. Your soul is unbroken; and you are the soul of France.

(The vision fades. The ARCHBISHOP *and the* INQUISITOR *are now seen on the right and left of* CAUCHON.*)*

JOAN: My sword shall conquer yet: the sword that never struck a blow. Though men destroyed my body, yet in my soul I have seen God.
CAUCHON *(kneeling to her)*: The girls in the field praise thee; for thou hast raised their eyes; and they see that there is nothing between them and heaven.
DUNOIS *(kneeling to her)*: The dying soldiers praise thee, because thou art a shield of glory between them and the judgment.
THE ARCHBISHOP *(kneeling to her)*: The princes of the Church praise thee, because thou hast redeemed the faith their worldlinesses have dragged through the mire.
WARWICK *(kneeling to her)*: The cunning counsellors praise thee, because thou hast cut the knots in which they have tied their own souls.
DE STOGUMBER *(kneeling to her)*: The foolish old men on their deathbeds praise thee, because their sins against thee are turned into blessings.
THE INQUISITOR *(kneeling to her)*: The judges in the blindness and bondage of the law praise thee, because thou hast vindicated the vision and the freedom of the living soul.
THE SOLDIER *(kneeling to her)*: The wicked out of hell praise thee, because thou has shewn them that the fire that is not quenched is a holy fire.
THE EXECUTIONER *(kneeling to her)*: The tormentors and executioners praise thee, because thou hast shewn that their hands are guiltless of death of the soul.
CHARLES *(kneeling to her)*: The unpretending praise thee, because thou hast taken upon thyself the heroic burdens that are too heavy for them.

JOAN: Woe unto me when all men praise me! I bid you remember that I am a saint, and that saints can work miracles. And now tell me: shall I rise from the dead, and come back to you a living woman?

(A sudden darkness blots out the walls of the room as they all spring to their feet in consternation. Only the figures and the bed remain visible.)

JOAN: What! Must I burn again? Are none of you ready to receive me?

CAUCHON: The heretic is always better dead. And mortal eyes cannot distinguish the saint from the heretic. Spare them. *(He goes out as he came.)*

DUNOIS: Forgive us, Joan: we are not yet good enough for you. I shall go back to my bed. *(He also goes.)*

WARWICK: We sincerely regret our little mistake; but political necessities, though occasionally erroneous, are still imperative; so if you will be good enough to excuse me— *(He steals discretely away.)*

THE ARCHBISHOP: Your return would not make me the man you once thought me. The utmost I can say is that though I dare not bless you, I hope I may one day enter into your blessedness. Meanwhile, however— *(He goes.)*

THE INQUISITOR: I who am of the dead, testified that day that you were innocent. But I do not see how The Inquisition could possibly be dispensed with under existing circumstances. Therefore— *(He goes.)*

DE STOGUMBER: Oh, do not come back: you must not come back! I must die in peace. Give us peace in our time, O Lord! *(He goes.)*

THE GENTLEMAN: The possibility of your resurrection was not contemplated in the recent proceedings for your canonization. I must return to Rome for fresh instructions. *(He bows formally, and withdraws.)*

THE EXECUTIONER: As a master in my profession I have to consider its interests. And, after all, my first duty is to my wife and children. I must have time to think over this. *(He goes.)*

CHARLES: Poor old Joan! They have all run away from you except this blackguard who has to go back to hell at twelve o'clock. And what can I do but follow Jack Dunois' example, and go back to bed too? *(He does so.)*

JOAN *(sadly)*: Goodnight, Charlie.

CHARLES *(mumbling in his pillows)*: Goo ni. *(He sleeps. The darkness envelops the bed.)*

JOAN *(to the SOLDIER)*: And you, my one faithful? What comfort have you for Saint Joan?

THE SOLDIER: Well, what do they all amount to, these kings and captains and bishops and lawyers and such like? They just leave you in the ditch to bleed to death; and the next thing is, you meet them down there, for all the airs they give themselves. What I say is, you have as good a right to your notions as they have to theirs, and perhaps better. *(Settling himself for a lecture on the subject)* You see, it's like this. If— *(the first stroke of midnight is heard softly from a distant bell).* Excuse me: a pressing appointment— *(He goes on tiptoe.)*

(The last remaining rays of light gather into a white radiance descending on JOAN. *The hour continues to strike.)*

JOAN: O God that madest this beautiful earth, when will it be ready to receive Thy saints? How long, O Lord, how long?

Glossary

acts: curtain closings denoting the end of important action, giving the audience time to reflect. *An Enemy of People; Cherry Orchard.*

agon: verbal struggle or debate between two characters in Greek drama. *Oedipus.*

antagonist: character or force opposed to hero, protagonist. Creon in *Antigone*; Jean in *Miss Julie.*

anticlimax: action that follows the climax and reduces the tension. *Saint Joan; Dutchman; Benito Cereno.*

antihero: a chief character with no heroic appeal. Cusins in *Major Barbara*; Delano in *Benito Cereno*; Jean in *Miss Julie.*

apron: part of the stage in front of the curtain.

apron stage: stage jutting out into auditorium.

arena stage: stage surrounded by spectators.

aside: a dramatic convention where actor's words are not heard by other actors on the stage.

atmosphere: general mood of play or special effects of setting frequently produced by scenery and lighting. *Henry IV.*

ballet: play set to music without words; danced in a stylized manner to convey conflict, resolution, and character. *Miss Julie.*

backdrop: flat used to mask off rear wall, painted with some scene.

burlesque: speech or action mocking other drama.

business: a bit of action, a gesture, or a grimace used to illuminate a character or set of lines. Iago in *Othello.*

catharsis: tragedy effecting the purgation of emotions through pity and fear. *Oedipus; Othello.*

character development: change in character through self-knowledge revelation or outside force. Lopahin in *The Cherry Orchard.*

characterization: shows inner growth and change based on heredity, environment, and the times in which he lives. *Miss Julie.*

chorus: group of actors who danced and sang choral odes in unison. Function varied from direct participation in action (*Trojan Women*); commenting on action (*Antigone*); or small group participating in action (choragos in *Oedipus*).

climax: turning point of play; peak of emotional tension; crisis itself.

comedy: an infinitely complex drama with as many varied forms as there are types of laughter, ranging in this book from *The Second Shepherd's Play* to *An Enemy of the People*.

comedy of humors: built on dominant traits such as jealousy, greed. *Volpone*.

commedia dell'arte: form popular in Italy from sixteenth to eighteenth centuries. Professional actors cast to type and went on stage with only a sketchy scenario prepared. They improvised dialogue.

conflict: protagonist or collective hero is opposed by a person or persons, force or forces. Phaedre and her love for Hippolytus; Oedipus and fate; Antigone and Creon.

confidante: secondary character to whom main character confides for purpose of exposition. Phaedre and Oenone; Aricia and Ismene.

convention: any practice or rule that operates by consent of audience even though it may be unrealistic or arbitrary. Asides, soliloquies, prologues, three act structure.

cue: last few words or business by one actor that signals another actor's entrance, speech, or business.

cyclorama: semicircular, taut back curtain that gives illusion of depth.

denouement: final disentangling of the intricacies of the plot. Act V in *Othello*; Theseus at end of *Phaedre*.

depth stage: picture box stage with action deep behind proscenium arch.

deus ex machina: introduction of a god, usually lowered on a crane was an easy means of resolving plot. Phrase now refers to denouement achieved by surprising turn of events that does not grow naturally out of plot or character. *Benito Cereno*.

decorum: manner appropriate to a style or period. *Phaedre*.

dialogue: words spoken by actors that reveal character and move the action.

downstage: nearest audience.

dramatic irony: irony growing out of situation where audience is aware of information of which one or more characters on stage is ignorant. *Oedipus; Othello; Saint Joan*.

dramatis personae: list of characters according to entrance.

episodic plot: incidents not linked by character in unified plot but by loose chronological treatment of a central figure.

exodus: final scene in Greek tragedy following the last choral ode. *Antigone*.

exposition: presentation of relevant background information necessary to understand the action that follows.

expressionism: drama with dreamlike symbolic action. *Purgatory*.

farce: comedy characterized by improbable situations, horseplay, and broad humor. *The Second Shepherd's Play.*

foil: a character who sets off or enhances another as Creon does for Oedipus in *Oedipus Rex.*

foreshadowing: exposition that hints of trouble to come. *Othello; Saint Joan; An Enemy of the People.*

fourth wall: invisible wall between actors and audience, convention.

hamartia: is the fault of character or error of judgment that brings misfortune to the tragic hero. *Phaedre.*

heroic tragedy: tragedy of seventeenth and eighteenth centuries dealing with romantic love and honor. *Phaedre.*

hubris: overweening pride that makes protagonist forget or ignore his proper relationship to the gods. *Oedipus.*

immediacy: sense of the action happening now. *Dutchman.*

messenger: character in a play who brings news of events represented as having occurred off stage. Guard in *Antigone.*

method acting: actor endeavors to understand psychological motivation of a character in order to become that character. Stanislavsky method. *The Cherry Orchard.*

mise en scene: stage director's plan showing grouping of actors related to sets.

motivation: the reason or reasons for character's behavior. Dauphin in *Saint Joan*; Lula in *Dutchman.*

monologue: relatively long speech delivered by one person, addressed to audience.

myth: (1) ancient, traditional, fictitious story expressing an allegorical truth about life. *Oedipus; Antigone.* (2) when the patterns of communal thought and feeling are made concrete in drama, poetry, or fiction. *Dutchman; Benito Cereno.*

mystery play: medieval drama based on Biblical story. *The Second Shepherd's Play.*

naturalism: deterministic in attitude, characters conditioned by social, psychological, and physiological elements. *Miss Julie.*

neoclassicism: rigid adherence to the "rules" of unity and decorum as set forth by Aristotle and Horace. *Phaedre*, takes place in 24 hours with only two actors on stage at one time, and in one locale.

Noh: lyrical drama, Japanese in origin, which drew its forms from the ritual dances of the temple and the folk dances of the countryside. *Purgatory.*

opera: a play entirely sung and orchestrated. *Othello.*

pageant: medieval stage on wagon. *Second Shepherd's Play* performed on such a wagon.

paradox: contradictory but true statement or idea. *Misanthrope*.

parados: first ode chorus sings in a Greek play.

peripeteia: reversal, where action produces opposite effect than intended. Messenger from Corinth in *Oedipus; Saint Joan*.

platform stage: Elizabethan stage with action in front of proscenium arch and spectators on three sides.

play within a play: present one play during the action of another. *Benito Cereno*.

plot: actions that characters perform to solve conflict and prove premise.

polemical: argumentative; controversial. *Dutchman*.

premise: dramatists point of view about some aspect of life. *Henry IV*.

prologue: introductory expository speech in Greek drama used most frequently by Euripides. *Trojan Women*.

proscenium (arch): architectural frame around the stage that separates the actors from the audience; the architectural opening through which a play is seen by the audience.

protagonist: originally first actor in Greek drama, now applied to central figure in a play. *Henry IV*; Old Man in *Purgatory*.

raisonneur: character who acts as guide for audience. Philinthe in *Misanthrope*.

realism: in theater emphasis of realism is on language, gesture, situation, and scene as found in world. *The Second Shepherd's Play*.

recognition scene: character recognizes some crucial fact about his identity or that of another character. Dance scene in *Dutchman*.

satire: drama that corrects manners and morals by ridicule. *Volpone*.

scenes: curtain closings to show the passage of time or change of locale. *Saint Joan; The Cherry Orchard*.

scrim: transparent curtain when lighted from rear; solid when lighted from front.

Senecan drama: violent in plot, stoic in attitude, rhetorical in style. Theater of violence cruelty. *Spurt of Blood*.

spectacle: ritual in which individuals perform predetermined actions or speak established dialogue and whose total impression is extraordinary. Religious ceremonies, bullfights, and courtroom procedures come under this heading. *Second Shepherd's Play; Henry IV*.

suspension of disbelief: willingness on part of audience to accept make believe. *Henry IV*.

stage directions: notes added to text explaining details of movement, gesture, setting, and properties. Compare those of Shakespeare in *Othello* with Shaw's in *Saint Joan*.

stasimon: any choral ode after the first one, parados. Oedipus has four.

subplot: a plot developed in addition to main plot. *Volpone*.

symbolism: character, situation, or setting standing for more than itself. *Purgatory*.

theater of cruelty: drama designed to shock audience. *Dutchman; Benito Cereno*.

theatricality: artificiality, striking effects, or sensationalism introduced for their own sake rather than for their function in the whole.

tragedy: an infinitely complex drama with as many forms as there are shades of human emotion. *Oedipus; Dutchman*.

unity of action: one plot. *Purgatory*.

unity of place: one location. *Dutchman*.

unity of time: action takes place in one day. *Benito Cereno*.

INDEX

Acaste, 301
Alcestes, 286
Angel, 394
Antigone, 445, 446
Anya, 335
Arande, Don, 282
Archbishop, 562
Aricia, 52
Arsinoe, 309
Aslaksen, 493
Atufal, 268

Babu, 253
Badger, the, 490
Basque, 300
Baudricourt de, Robert, 532
Belcredi, Tito Baron, 403, 443
Benito Cereno, 120, 121, 122, 123, 248, 253
Berthold, 398
Billing, 476
Bluebeard, 563
Brabantio, 128

Cassio, 133
Cauchon, 581
Celimene, 298
Chaplain, 579
Character, Comic, 286
Character, Tragic, 1, 2, 3, 286
Charles, 564
Charlotta, 342
Chekhov, 285
Cherry Orchard, 286, 333
Citandre, 301
Citizens and Strangers, 121
Clay, 233
Coleridge, 377
Comedy, 285
Country and Conscience, 445
Courcelles, 602
Creon, 7, 451

Dauphin, 564
Delano, Amasa, 248
Desdemona, 142
D'Estinet, 601
Di Nolli, Charles, 403
Don Aranda, 282
Donna Matilda Spina, 403
Duke of Venice, 136
Dunois, 575
Dunyasha, 333
Dutchman, 120, 121, 122, 232

Eliante, 301, 316
Emelia, 153
Enemy of the People, The, 445, 475
Epihodov, 334
Epilogue, 621
Eteocles, 448
Eurydice, 471
Executioner, 621
Exodos, 470

Firs, 338, 354, 375
Fitts, Dudley, 5, 446
Francesco, 273
Fitzgerald, Robert, 5, 446
Frida, 403

Gaev, 336
Garnet, Constance, 333
Genoni, Dionysius, Dr., 403
Glossary, 635, 636, 637

Haimon, 461
Handkerchief scene, 183, 190
Harold, 398, 402
Henry IV, 397
Hippolytus, 43
Horstad, 476
Horster, Captain, 478

Iago, 126

Ibsen, Henrik, 475
Inquisitor, 599
Iocaste, 21
Ismene, 52, 446

Jean, 84
Jill, 387
Joan, St., 554
Jocasta, 21
John, 402
Jones, Le Roi, 232
Julie, Miss, 2, 84, 86

Keil, Martin, 490
Kristin, 84

Ladvenu, 604
La Hire, 563
Landolph, 398
Lemaitre, John, 599
Loomis, Roger S., 381
Lopahin, 333, 365
Lowell, Robert, 248
Lula, 233
Lyubov, 335

Mak, 385
Mary, 396
Matilda, Donna, 403
Medieval Drama, 377
Messenger, 27
Misanthrope, The, 286, 287
Miss Julie, 84
Montano, 149

Oedipus, 1, 5
Oenone, 47
Ode, 454, 459, 466
Old Man, 114
Ordulph, 398
Oronte, 293
Othello, 120, 121, 122, 132

Parados, 449
Parents, Lovers and other enemies, 1
People's Messenger, 505
Perkins, 249
Petra, 483
Phaedre, 2, 43, 47
Phoedre, 47
Philinte, 286

Pirandello, Luigi, 378, 397
Pishtchik, 336
Plays the Thing, The, 377
Polyneices, 448
Poulengey, 556
Promoter, 601
Purgatory, 3, 114

Racine, 2, 43
Rewards of Virtue, 285
Roderigo, 126

San Domingo, 252
Second Shepherds' Play, The, 377, 378
Sentry, 452
Sharp, R. Farguharson, 475
Shaw, George, 551
Shepherd, 32
Shepherd, First, 381
Shepherd, Second, 382
Shepherd, Third, 383
Sophocles, 5, 446
Spectacle, Dance, Ritual, 377
St. Joan, 445, 531
Stockmann, Catherine, 476
Stockmann, Ejlif, 484
Stockmann, Morten, 484
Stockmann, Peter, 476
Stockmann, Petra, 483
Stockmann, Thomas, 478
Stogumber, John, 581
Storer, Edward, 397
Strindberg, August, 84

Teiresias, 12, 467
Theramenes, 43
Theseus, 65
Tremouille, 562
Trofinov, 344, 353

Varya, 335

Wakefield Mystery Cycle, 381
Warwick, 581
Wayfarer, 354

Wells, Henry W., 381
Wilbur, Richard, 43

Yasha, 338
Yeats, 114